D0086806

DOUGLAS J. SOCCIO
Shasta College

Archetypes

of Wisdom

SECOND EDITION

WADSWORTH PUBLISHING COMPANY
I(T)P™ An International Thomson Publishing Company

Belmont • Albany • Bonn • Boston • Cincinnati • Detroit •
London • Madrid • Melbourne • Mexico City • New York • Paris •
San Francisco • Singapore • Tokyo • Toronto • Washington

Philosophy Editor: Tammy Goldfeld
Editorial Assistant: Kelly Zavislak
Production Editor: Carol Carreon Lombardi
Designer: Andrew H. Ogus
Art Editor: Roberta Broyer
Print Buyer: Diana Spence
Copy Editor: Jacqueline Tasch
Cover Design: Andrew H. Ogus
Photo Research: Photosearch
Compositor: Thompson Type
Printer: Quebecor Printing/Hawkins
Cover: *Portrait of Paquio Proculo and his Wife.* Museo Archeologico
 Nazionale, Naples. Scala/Art Resource, NY.

Printed in the United States of America
1 2 3 4 5 6 7 8 9 10—01 00 99 98 97 96 95

For more information, contact Wadsworth Publishing Company:

Wadsworth Publishing Company
10 Davis Drive
Belmont, California 94002, USA

International Thomson Editores
Campos Eliseos 385, Piso 7
Col. Polanco
11560 México D.F. México

International Thomson Publishing Europe
Berkshire House 168-173
High Holborn
London, WC1V 7AA, England

International Thomson Publishing
GmbH Königswinterer Strasse 418
53227 Bonn, Germany

Thomas Nelson Australia
102 Dodds Street
South Melbourne 3205
Victoria, Australia

International Thomson Publishing Asia
221 Henderson Road
#05-10 Henderson Building
Singapore 0315

Nelson Canada
1120 Birchmount Road
Scarborough, Ontario
Canada M1K 5G4

International Thomson Publishing Japan
Hirakawacho Kyowa Building, 3F
2-2-1 Hirakawacho
Chiyoda-ku, Tokyo 102, Japan

Library of Congress Cataloging-in-Publication Data
Soccio, Douglas J.
          Archetypes of wisdom : introduction to philosophy / Douglas J.
Soccio. — 2nd ed.
                       p.   cm.
          Includes bibliographical references and index.
          ISBN: 0-534-21690-0
          1. Philosophy—Introductions.   I. Title
BD21.S616   1994   94-22217
100—dc20   CIP

For my sisters, Gina and Lucianna,
and their sons, Jake and James,
who know that the first word in
philosophy is love

CONTENTS

CHAPTER 10

THE SCHOLAR:

THOMAS AQUINAS 270

CHAPTER 11

THE RATIONALIST:

RENÉ DESCARTES 298

CHAPTER 12

THE SKEPTIC:

DAVID HUME 334

To the

Instructor

*A*rchetypes of Wisdom is the only current introductory philosophy text to use wisdom as a key concept throughout. The qualities of the *sophos* (wise person) are addressed throughout the text in reference to contemporary issues whenever possible. And because wisdom concerns both what is true and what is important, the subject matter of *Archetypes of Wisdom* is inherently topical, accessible, and relevant.

This second edition of *Archetypes of Wisdom* is a major revision that combines the strengths of the first edition with significant improvements suggested by professors and students. These improvements were based on two principles: (1) The best teaching begins where students are, not where they "should be"; and (2) If a book is worth writing, it should be a book worth keeping.

Archetypes of Wisdom is a unique blend of philosophy, history, social science, and anecdote. It stands on its own as a good read. I am especially pleased about reviewers' positive comments concerning the seamless integration of the form and content.

I am gratified to have heard from so many students and professors, expressing not only their satisfaction with the text, but also offering wise advice for improvements—all of which were taken seriously, and many of which appear in this edition. Though sometimes one person's advice contradicted someone else's suggestions, there were many points of agreement. I have tried to incorporate most of the major convergent suggestions in this revision.

No longer can philosophy instructors assume that most members of a class will share a common fund of knowledge or even a relatively similar range of language skills. Many introductory students are unfamiliar with critical philosophical analysis and argument. Consequently, lengthy primary sources may seem forbidding.

Students from divergent backgrounds enjoy reading *Archetypes of Wisdom* because it shows respect for them by presenting difficult material in a manageable form. It talks to and with them, not over their heads or down to them in a trendy, pandering way. They can and will read it. Philosophical material varies in degree of difficulty, and sophisticated philosophical arguments are presented as part of a cultural context. Philosophical passages are explained in a manner that unobtrusively teaches students how to read critically and carefully by asking them pointed questions and connecting philosophical issues to students' current interests in a natural, unforced, and nontrivializing way.

About the Second Edition

- *New streamlined Chapter 1* gets students off to a fast start; new, brief section "Are Philosophers Always Men?" addresses current concerns about the content of philosophical surveys in a straightforward, moderate fashion early in the text.

- *New Chapter 2: The Sage* combines material about Buddha and Lao-tzu with a fuller discussion of the Asian sage as a philosophical archetype.

- *New Chapter 3: The Sophos* presents a survey of the Presocratic philosophers with emphasis on Heraclitus and Parmenides; provides more material to set the stage for Plato's Theory of Forms; Zeno's paradoxes are presented in box form; a brief discussion of the atomists completes the chapter.

- *Chapter 4: The Sophist,* one of the most highly praised chapters in the first edition, now includes a box on The Ring of Gyges.

- *Chapter 5: The Wise Man* adds more philosophical passages to the treatment of Socrates, including new sections on Socratic egotism, Virtue is Wisdom, All Evil is Ignorance, and the problem of weakness of will.

- *Chapter 6: The Philosopher-King* boasts a more thorough treatment of Plato's Theory of Forms, including the full Allegory of the Cave plus expanded sections about the Divided Line and Simile of the Sun.

- *Chapter 7: The Naturalist* has been edited for concision and clarity.

- *Chapter 8: The Epicurean* has been streamlined, and the Alan Watts material is set off in a box.

- *Chapter 9: The Stoic*—one of the chapters most highly praised by student correspondents—contains new material from Admiral James Stockdale.

- *Chapter 10: The Scholar* has been polished with an eye toward improved readability.

- *Chapter 11: The Rationalist* now concludes with discussion of the "epistemological turn;" a boxed passage from the Persian philosopher al-Ghazali contrasts mysticism with rationalism.

- *Chapter 12: The Skeptic* includes a new section called The Limits of Rationalistic Ethics, which discusses Hume's ethical ideas and offers a model of analytic reasoning.

- *Chapter 13: The Formalist* has been refined to enhance reader interest.

- *Chapter 14: The Utilitarian* benefits from streamlined treatment of Bentham and careful tightening throughout.

- *Chapter 15: The Materialist* contains additional material on Hegel and a more streamlined treatment of Marx.

- *New Chapter 16: The Individualist* is a completely new chapter that combines first edition material about Kierkegaard and Nietzsche. It includes a new introduction, new Nietzsche material about *Ressentiment* and Master Morality, and a new, provocative box "Was Nietzsche A Nazi?"

- *Chapter 17: The Pragmatist* has been reorganized for clarity and concision.

- *Chapter 18: The Existentialist* adds new sections by Albert Camus concerning The Absurd and The Myth of Sisyphus to first edition material about Sartre; a new Miguel de Unamuno box has been added.

- *New Chapter 19: The Prophet* is an expansion of the first edition interlude about Martin Luther King, Jr. This new chapter discusses the prophet as a philosophical archetype and adds new, timely material from Malcolm X and Cornel West; boxes about Henry David Thoreau and Mahatma Gandhi enrich the discussion of civil disobedience.

- *New Chapter 20: The Feminist* introduces the feminist as a philosophical archetype. The feminist analysis of justice reasoning is presented in a larger context with the addition of selections from John Rawls and Susan Moller Okin. In addition to first edition material by Carol Gilligan and Alison Jaggar, there are new selections from Marilyn Friedman and boxed passages from Annie Leclerc and Simone de Beauvoir.

About Pedagogy

This edition also includes the following pedagogical elements:

- *Commentaries* Clearly identified brief commentaries at the end of each chapter include general evaluations of the philosophical ideas covered in the chapter and connect those ideas to contemporary issues.

- *Summary of Main Points* Highlights of key ideas, providing a handy chapter review and discussion aid for each chapter.

- *Study Questions* Questions range from specific to general and can function as review questions, as test or essay questions, or as paper topics.

- *Two Glossaries* In addition to the handy Margin Glossary, which defines key terms in the margins to highlight their importance and facilitate text reviews, a new alphabetical Glossary makes it easy to find key terms and chapter references.

- *Bibliography of Interesting Sources* This collection of texts contains some real gems, as well as the usual philosophy texts. A Notes section documents the major philosophical sources.

- *Index to Margin Quotes* helps students locate authors of interesting Margin Quotes featured throughout the text.

Ancillary materials available to accompany this text include

- *Unique Instructor's Manual* In addition to the usual sections containing Test Questions and Essay Questions, this manual includes a section on the Philosophy of Testing (how to prepare tests), Lecture and Discussion Tips for all chapters, Tips for New Philosophy Teachers (which are useful for all teachers), and a discussion of the Special Pedagogical Features of *Archetypes of Wisdom*. Few if any other manuals are as practical or complete; this is not a cursory job, but a true *instructor's* manual of useful tips and time-saving test questions and lecture guides.

- *Student Study Guide* This optional supplement consists of an overview of key concepts, selected study questions and philosophical queries, sample test questions, and an analytic exercise for each chapter in tear-sheet format, making it convenient for students and for instructors to use as a source of written assignments both in and out of class.

- *How To Get The Most Out Of Philosophy, Second Edition* This unique handbook for philosophy students proved to be the surprise success of the first edition. So many instructors and students asked to order extra stand-alone copies that I have expanded the text, enhancing the critical thinking and writing sections, adding samples of student writing, and elaborating on various study strategies. *How To Get The Most Out Of Philosophy, Second Edition* is now available as an optional supplement at a significantly reduced cost for purchasers of *Archetypes of Wisdom*, or as an independent text.

What Has Been Retained from the First Edition

- *Inviting, visually appealing format.* A large format allows for illustrations, margin quotes, a margin glossary, and boxed quotes. Responses from readers indicate that many students enjoy browsing through the text and reading margin and boxed material for pleasure. Most margin quotes are from the central figures in the chapters and were chosen to add spice and information to the body of the text. Margin quotes and boxed passages make excellent discussion material, and browsing through them is a painless introduction to a philosopher's ideas.

- *The call of stories.* Even the most uninterested students respond to personal anecdotes about philosophers. Each chapter contains a brief but engaging philosophical biography of one or two main figures, which provide cultural and historical context for the philosophical ideas covered in the chapter and show how philosophers respond to important concerns of their times. A story-telling approach avoids depersonalization and the distancing effect of texts that treat issues and arguments as somehow independent of time, place, and person.

- *Accessible depth.* Archetypes of Wisdom solves the problem of choosing between accessibility and depth by covering fewer philosophers and philosophical ideas on a more fundamental level. Primary sources are integrated with secondary explanations in passages of varying length. Secondary commentary teaches students how to read philosophical literature.

- *Cultural breadth.* Archetypes of Wisdom blends traditional Western philosophy, nonwestern and nontraditional philosophy, and contemporary issues.

- *Ongoing student involvement.* The Philosophical Queries, a unique feature of *Archetypes of Wisdom,* are topical questions that directly address the reader, prompting her or him to react critically to specific passages of text. They range from the personal to the controversial and can be readily modified to use as essay questions or to focus class discussion.

- *A wide range of contemporary sources.* Archetypes of Wisdom contains a variety of contemporary sources that address philosophical issues from beyond academic philosophy. These show—rather than merely tell—students that philosophy occurs outside of philosophy class and under other guises.

- *Flexible structure.* Each chapter is a self-contained unit. It is not necessary to cover chapters in chronological order or to cover every chapter in order to have an effective class. Chapters not covered by the instructor can be used for outside writing assignments.

Acknowledgments

The generous and positive response to the first edition of *Archetypes of Wisdom* puts me at loss for words (a rare condition, indeed). Most gratifying, perhaps, were the many students who wrote to say they plan to keep *Archetypes of Wisdom* in their personal libraries.

Among the people at the Wadsworth Publishing Company who worked on the first edition, I remain grateful to Ken King for his enthusiasm for my original proposal and his willingness to produce a complicated, unique text; and Mary Arbogast, whose insight, intelligence, and sensitivity improved the initial text beyond measure.

For the second edition, I thank Tammy Goldfeld for the generous support, solid advice, and hard work that helped make this a serious, worthwhile revision. Carol Carreon's editorial skill caught many an oversight and helped shape an unwieldy manuscript into a coherent text, and copyeditor Jackie Tasch's eagle eye saved the day on numerous occasions. Joy Westberg, Laury Olson, David Leach, and Susan Shook deserve public thanks. Permissions editor Bob Kauser deserves special recognition and undying gratitude for cheerfully helping me when I completely forgot about one entire set of permissions. Lastly, but significantly, I feel very fortunate to have had Andrew Ogus in charge of design for both editions. Andrew's love of this book and intuitive aesthetic sensibility have added beauty to the text and an impressive new cover that captures my sense of the archetypal quality of philosophy.

I thank the many reviewers who worked on both editions of the text for their thoughtful, timely, and helpful advice, which often went well beyond the call of duty. I hope these revisions live up to their high standards. The second edition reviewers are Waldo Asp, Normandale Community College; Gregory Bassham, King's College; Mary Ann Cutter, University of Colorado, Colorado Springs; Thomas Franks, Eastern Michigan University; Galina Iachkina, Hillsborough Community College; John Longeway, University of Wisconsin, Parkside; Richard Loofbourrow, Antelope Valley College; Jan Milligan, Belleville Area College; Judith Netzer, Rockland Community College; and Jorge L. Nobo, Washburn University of Topeka.

The reviewers of the first edition are Joanne Bielick, Sacramento City College; Julia E. Brooks, Brevard Community College; Job B. Clement, Daytona Beach Community College; Ronald H. Epp, University of Hartford; Thomas H. Franks, Eastern Michigan University; Jack Furlong, Transylvania University; Gary Kessler, California State University, Bakersfield; Maire K. Liberace, Rockland Community College; Edward McCamy, State University of New York College of Technology; Hal McMullen, Lord Fairfax Community College; Richard L. Oliver, San Antonio College; John R. Scudder, Jr., Lynchburg College; Douglas Shrader, State University of New York at Oneonta; Eugene C. Sorensen, Rochester Community College; and Dennis T. Wimbish, Coastal Carolina Community College.

The publication of the first edition brought an unexpected honor and privilege to my life in the form of a "long-distance friendship" with Admiral James Stockdale who, in spite of his busy schedule and national stature, has been very generous and courteous to an obscure teacher of philosophy and fellow admirer of Epictetus. I cannot adequately convey my gratitude for this unexpected gift.

Among my many kind and supportive friends, the following continue to provide special support and encouragement: I thank Ross Fetters for being a living library of trivia and profundity and recycler of my best jokes. I grow ever more grateful to Joe Vargas for his encouragement, compelling honesty, and special insight as a *paisan* and master of Socratic teaching, and for introducing me to Amy. Wallace Phillips and John "Little Bobby" Johnson teach me that it is possible not to grow up. And George Linville, "the Nietzsche of Shasta County," reminds me that the sophos is still among us.

My family continues to keep me grounded and in touch with what matters most. My brother and sisters, Mike, Gina, and Lucianna, teach me about love and good humor and character. My parents, Helon and Eddie, teach me about generosity, willingness, faith, and, most of all, unconditional love. From the first edition to the second, the deaths of my grandmother Lucy Varano and my uncle Eugene Soccio form a continuum with the birth of my nephews, James Pesavento and Jake Hickerson, that confirms what Marcus Aurelius described as "the perpetual renewing of the world's youthfulness." Ray Borst has provided countless examples of graciousness under pressure, stoic resolve at its best, and the kind of love that enables the spirit and strengthens the heart. In his magnificent fight for life, Bob Stoltzfus showed that, even in dying, there can be wisdom, courage, love, and renewal. My young disciples, Patricia Borst, Mike Vargas, Greg Fetters, and Deanna Soccio, assure me that good humor and solid character are alive and well into another generation.

Lastly, Margaret L. Malone, my wife and assistant, deserves more than I can repay for loving and supporting me through yet another edition of this book, of which she remains so much a part.

The virtuous [person] cultivates above all wisdom and friendship; and of these the one is a mortal good, the other is immortal.

Epicurus

A STUDENT'S

VISUAL GUIDE

TO THIS BOOK

As you begin reading this book, I hope you will put aside the thought that philosophy is something inscrutable and complex and think of it simply as the love of wisdom. The book tells the great story of wise men and women through the ages who have devoted their lives to discovering and expressing wisdom that is both timeless and timely, because it concerns what is true and what is important. As you read, I hope you will consider how the questions that inspire philosophical inquiry have meaning in your life today.

On the pages that follow, you will find examples of some of the features that appear in the text that can make your introduction to philosophy an enjoyable quest in pursuit of wisdom.

I also encourage you to read the small handbook—*How to Get the Most Out of Philosophy*—that accompanies the text before starting your study of philosophy. It contains valuable tips you can apply to your own pursuit of wisdom, in philosophy and other courses as well.

Douglas J. Soccio

Everything that happens is as normal and expected as the spring rose or the summer fruit; this is true of sickness, death, slander, intrigue, and all the other things that delight or trouble foolish men.
Marcus Aurelius

STOICISM
Philosophy that counsels self-control, detachment, and acceptance of one's fate as identified by the objective use of reason.

STOIC
Individual who attempts to live according to Stoic doctrine.

238

It's the Friday before a three-day weekend and you are looking forward to a romantic vacation on the beach with your special friend. You get off work a bit late and head for the bank to get some cash. Pulling onto the freeway, you're immediately locked into a bumper-to-bumper mass of vehicles, lurching along at fifteen miles per hour. Forty-five minutes later, still a couple of miles from the bank, you notice that you're low on fuel. You begin to steam. Someone tries to cut in front of you and you explode in a rage, shaking your fist and shouting obscenities. When you finally get to the bank, there's no place to park.

After circling the parking lot for twenty minutes, you manage to park. The line in the bank looks endless and there are only three tellers. The man in front of you has a bag of checks and cash from his business. You continue to steam. It seems like every customer chats with the tellers. And the tellers! It takes them forever to do anything. As you inch along in line you glare at various bank officers in order to let them know how angry you are at the inefficient way they run their bank.

By the time you get out of the bank, you're behind schedule and it's rush hour—pre-holiday, Friday-afternoon rush hour. You race out of the parking lot, squealing your tires as you cut into traffic. Rushing through an intersection at high speed, you catch the attention of a police officer. It's not enough that you get a ticket for reckless driving, the officer takes forever checking out your license and writing the ticket. When you finally get going again, you feel like a bomb about to go off.

If you have ever had an experience anything close to the one just described, you've shared the nearly universal sense of frustration, anger, and anxiety caused by "stupid people" and "events beyond our control." This kind of reaction to external events is so common that a school of philosophy sprang up to deal with just such experiences, among other things. Yet its basic tenets go against the grain for most people, at least initially. It is called **Stoicism**, and those who practice it are called **Stoics**.

Stoicism initially emerged as a reaction against hedonism. Whereas the hedonist seeks pleasure or avoids pain, the Stoic seeks serenity (peace of mind) through self-discipline. Stoicism asserts that seeking anything but self-control results in *avoidable* unhappiness. Happiness comes only through detachment from all "externals." Put another way: Everything is a matter of attitude. The disciplined, reasonable person can be happy under any and all conditions.

Stoics believe that *nothing can make you happy or unhappy without your consent*. All unhappiness is the result of bad thinking, poor character, and confusing what we can control with what we cannot control. Regarding the opening story, a Stoic would diagnose your frustration and anger as self-induced. Traffic jams, lines and crowds, little brothers, dumb sweethearts, and cars

Read the introduction that opens each chapter carefully. Each one sets the stage for the material that follows, relating topics and quoted passages in the chapter to fundamental human concerns. This one, for instance, talks about stoicism and how it developed as a reaction to hedonism. Using the contemporary example of someone trying to get out of town for a romantic weekend, it demonstrates very vividly how the philosophy of stoicism developed as a response to the frustrations we face in our daily lives.

Biographical stories show you the human side of major philosophers. This background information provides "a good read" and, by examining philosophers' lives in terms of their own time and place, you will begin to understand the cultural context of ideas.

You will find quoted passages from original sources throughout the book. This example, by Epicurus, is juxtaposed with Nietzsche's tongue-in-cheek reaction.

Interesting boxed material—like this passage by the great Taoist sage Chuang-tzu—extends the ideas presented in the chapter, often demonstrating the influence of time and culture on individual answers to universal issues.

THE EPICUREAN: EPICURUS   221

EPICURUS

Though **Epicurus (341–270 B.C.)** was born in the Asia Minor city of Samos, he was an Athenian citizen because his father had moved to Samos as an Athenian colonist. When he was eighteen years old, Epicurus went to Athens in order to complete the two years of military service required of Athenian males. The Macedonian king of Greece, Alexander the Great, had just died, and the Athenians, who had resented his rule, revolted against the regent Alexander had imposed on them. It took less than a year for this revolt to be crushed, but Epicurus drew an important lesson from it: Political activities and ambitions are pointless.

Epicurus remained in Athens for a time, and studied with major followers of both Plato and Aristotle. He never accepted Plato's philosophy and came to reject Aristotle's as well. He referred to himself as self-taught and never acknowledged any philosophical teacher or master. He saw himself as a moral reformer who had discovered a brand-new message, one that could save others from unhappiness:

> Vain is the word of a philosopher which does not heal any suffering of man. For just as there is no profit in medicine if it does not expel the diseases of the body, so there is no profit in philosophy either if it does not expel the suffering of the mind.[7]

Epicurus left Athens and for some years taught in outlying cities. But Athens remained the cultural and intellectual center of the Greek-influenced world. The two most important schools of the era were there: Plato's Academy and Aristotle's Lyceum. They attracted the finest minds of the time. It is not surprising, then, that Epicurus returned to Athens to establish his own school.[8]

Epicurus

And so we speak of pleasure as the starting point and the goal of the happy life because we realize that it is our primary native good, because every act of choice and aversion originates with it, and because we come back to it when we judge every good by using the pleasure feeling as our criterion.
Epicurus

*es, I am proud
. . I experience
f Epicurus
y from per-
e else. . . . Such
d be invented
who was suf-
lly.*
ietzsche

---

48   CHAPTER TWO

THREE IN THE MORNING

Chuang-tzu (c. 399–295 B.C.) is the second great Taoist sage. Very little is known about his life, but the book bearing his name contains some of the richest stories in Taoist literature. Chuang-tzu sometimes referred to himself as "the Great Clod." The stories attributed to him reflect a generous soul, capable of great humor and great sadness. Here's an excellent example:

On Knowing and Not Knowing the Oneness of Things. Only the truly intelligent understand this principle of the levelling of all things into One. . . . But to wear out one's intellect in an obstinate adherence to the individuality of things, not recognizing the fact that all things are One—this is called "Three in the Morning." What is "Three in the Morning"? A keeper of monkeys said that with regard to their rations of nuts each monkey was to have three in the morning and four at night. At this the monkeys were very angry. Then the keeper said they might have four in the morning and three at night, with which arrangement they were well pleased. The actual number of nuts remained the same, but there was a difference owing to (subjective evaluations of) likes and dislikes. It also derives from this (principle of subjectivity). Wherefore the true Sage brings all the contraries together and rests in the natural Balance of Heaven. This is called (the principle of following) two courses (at once).

Chuang-tzu
In *The Wisdom of Laotse*, trans. and ed. Lin Yutang (New York: Modern Library, 1976), p. 244.

THE DOCTRINE OF INACTION

"He abused me, he beat me, he defeated me, he robbed me"—in those who harbor such thoughts hatred will never cease. For hatred does not cease by hatred at any time; hatred ceases by love— this is an eternal law.
The Buddha

Lao-tzu compiled his book during a time of great political and social turmoil. This was a period of fierce struggle for power, waged among a succession of warring princes. As these civil wars progressed, they became increasingly violent. Armies increasingly ignored the *li* or rites that prevented pillage and wanton destruction. To cite just one instance, at the height of this instability and terror, soldiers from one army were not paid until they showed the paymaster severed heads of their enemies. Each atrocity was answered with an equal or greater atrocity. This period was known as the "Period of the Fighting States."

Lao-tzu's response to terror, chaos, and betrayal was the doctrine of inaction. According to this doctrine, the best way to deal with social turmoil is "not to do anything about it." If this sounds crazy to you, you are not alone. Such an idea goes against everything our society stands for: we exert great efforts to "solve problems," "fix things," "save the environment," "win the war on drugs," "end racism," and so on. Are such goals feasible? Does social and political effort really work—or does it result in contest after contest, with factions struggling against each other for control?

All through the book, you will find margin quotes—including comments from poets and writers, scientists and psychologists, as well as philosophers—that reinforce themes from the text. In addition to providing interesting reading, they show you that philosophy occurs outside philosophy class, in our everyday concerns with personal, religious, social, and ethical beliefs.

To introduce you to the specialized language of philosophy, key terms appear in boldface type in the text and are defined in an adjoining margin glossary the first time they appear. You can use these highlighted features as a resource for study and review. (All key terms are also defined in an end-of-text glossary for convenient reference.)

Several philosophical queries appear in each chapter. They can help you relate the material you have just read to current issues and think about the personal meaning philosophical perspectives have in your own life. These queries invite you to make connections with philosophical ideas presented in earlier chapters.

Commentaries present brief personal reflections on material covered in the chapter you have just finished. They help you understand the value and importance of philosophical ideas and encourage you to think critically about those you may disagree with.

THE SAGE: BUDDHA AND LAO-TZU

31

Siddhārtha saw himself and *all life* as part of an unending process of change, a great chain of being through which things come into and leave one form of existence for another. Everything is one. The whole universe is a system of interconnected, inseparable parts, rich and complex, composed of all varieties of life forever moving from one form to another.

The Buddha did not arrive at this perception intellectually. He *saw* it all at once, in what we in the West might call a mystical vision. The now-Buddha realized instantly how difficult it would be to teach a doctrine that could not be grasped by mere reasoning and that could not be realized by blind faith, but only by unswerving personal effort. Only by the greatest effort could an individual achieve release from suffering. The price of wisdom is love of the whole rather than love of any one part—including, especially, ourselves.[8]

The intellect can understand any part of a thing as a part, but not as a whole.
R. H. Blyth

The Bodhisattva

Siddhārtha had reached a state of bliss and utter detachment called nirvana. **Nirvana** is annihilation of the ego, a state of emptiness or "no-thing-ness." It is described as a state of bliss because there is only "pure consciousness" with no sense of individuality, separateness, discrimination, or intellectualizing. It cannot be explained in words, since words are limiting and exist to identify similarities and differences. Nirvana is beyond even similarity. It can only be talked around or expressed in contradictions. It transcends all ordinary experience. Nirvana is release from suffering while conscious. (If you do not "understand" what nirvana is, don't feel inadequate. Nirvana can be experienced; it cannot be described or understood.) The experience of nirvana transforms us because it shifts our attention from timely concerns to timeless issues.

NIRVANA
Annihilation of the ego; a state of emptiness or "no-thing-ness"; "pure consciousness" that leads to release from suffering while remaining conscious.

106

CHAPTER FOUR

house where you'll be the only visitor! You must emulate, not those whose very refutations are paltry, but men of substance and high repute and everything else that is good.[12]

PHILOSOPHICAL QUERY

Is some part of you stirred by all this talk of power and superiority? The Sophists would say that if you can be honest, you'll answer in the affirmative. What might prevent you (in the Sophists' view) from admitting that you agree with them? Are they correct? Even if you personally reject Callicles' position, how common do you think it is? What's your evidence?

COMMENTARY

If ethical relativism is correct, it is clearly impossible for the moral beliefs of a society to be mistaken because the certainty of the majority that its beliefs were right would prove that those beliefs were right for that society at that time. The minority view would therefore be mistaken, no matter what it was. Needless to say, most people who state that "in morals everything is relative" and who proceed to call themselves ethical relativists are unaware of these implications of their theory.
John Hospers

The questions raised by the Sophists are important, not just in the dusty archives of scholarly concerns but also for the continuing influence sophistic ideas exert on our lives and beliefs. Sophists helped free the Greeks to think on new, less restricted levels. From this beginning emerged a nonreligious (amoral) scientific method as well as a philosophic method of questioning, both of which are free to pursue knowledge for its own sake and wherever it leads. In other words, the Sophists helped break the shackles of dogma and superstition. For that we remain in their debt. They laid the cornerstone for the scientific study of human behavior—what would become the social, psychological, political, and anthropological sciences.

The Sophists' emphasis on the individual as determiner of value and the challenges they posed to the possibility of a moral absolute were contributing factors to increasing democracy in Athens. Thus, the Sophists were perceived as a direct threat by the "establishment" of privileged aristocrats.

The youth of Athens responded with gusto to these ideas as a call to unrestrained self-assertion and personal freedom. It was stimulating to challenge the stuffy, square, straight, uptight values of the establishment. The glorification of the "superior individual" or "natural man" has always appealed to adolescent cravings for power, fame, freedom, and identity. Logic and the rhetorical devices refined by the Sophists were liberally applied to legal maneuvering, politics, techniques of manipulation, and control of the marketplace. By the third generation, Sophists no longer claimed to be sophistai, teachers of wisdom, but advertised shortcuts to guaranteed social, political, financial, and personal success. These were the forerunners of today's how-to-succeed, you-can-have-it-all books, courses, and techniques. Freed of any moral anchor, the Sophists were often deadly and effective. They took no responsibility for the ways people might use their ideas, as the great Sophist Gorgias reminds us:

And if a man learns rhetoric, and then does injustice through the power of his art, we shall not be right, in my opinion, in

The drawings and photographs that appear throughout the text show you that, because philosophy is a human enterprise, created by flesh-and-blood men and women of diverse races, cultures, and eras, it applies to every aspect of our lives.

Eudaimonia results when pleasure is the natural companion of a fully functioning life, rather than the goal of life. Artisans working at their true calling—such as this glassblower—combine hard work and happiness in a vital, rich way.

son does not avoid life: he or she engages in it fully. A rich and full life is a social life. "No one," Aristotle says in the *Ethics*, "would choose to live with

Continued observations of this basic dynamic nature of [...] *especially in clini-* [...] *al practice,* [...] *evitably to the* [...] *deeper and* [...] *ntal than sex-* [...] *han the crav-* [...] *ower, deeper* [...] *desire for pos-* [...] *a still more* [...] *d more univer-* [...] *he human* [...] *te craving for* [...] *he right direc-* [...] *tation.* [...] *heldon, M.D.*

. . . We who are in hierarchies—be they academic, business, military, or otherwise—are always in positions in which people are trying to manipulate us, to get moral leverage on us. The only defense is to keep yourself clean—never to do or say anything of which you can be made to feel ashamed. . . .

Am I personally still hooked on Epictetus's Principle of Life? Yes, but not in the sense of following a memorized doctrine. I sometimes become amused at how I have applied it and continue to apply it unconsciously. An example is the following story about myself.

As the months and years wear on in solitary confinement, it turns out each man goes crazy if he doesn't get some ritual into his life. I mean by that a self-imposed obligation to do certain things in a certain order each day. Like most prisoners, I prayed each day, month after month, continually altering and refining a long memorized monologue that probably ran to ten or fifteen minutes. At some point, my frame of mind became so pure that I started deleting any begging of God and any requests that would work specifically for my benefit. This didn't come out of any new Principle of Life that I had developed; it just suddenly started to seem unbecoming to beg. I knew the lesson of the book of Job: life is not fair. What claim had I for special consideration? And anyway, by then I had seen enough misery to know that He had enough to worry about without trying to appease a crybaby like me. And so it has been ever since.[34]

What is the result at which all virtue aims? Serenity.
Epictetus

In this day and age, the greatest devotion, greater than learning and praying, consists in accepting the world exactly as it happens to be.
Rabbi Moshe of Kobryn

SUMMARY OF MAIN POINTS

Antisthenes was the founder of a philosophical school known as Cynicism and Diogenes was its most famous advocate. The Cynics believed that the very essence of civilization is corrupt, that manners are hypocritical, that material wealth weakens people, and that civilization destroys the individual and makes him or her vulnerable to the whims of fortune.

According to the Cynics, the death of Socrates showed that not even the wisest person can control other people or external events. They concluded that the less an individual needs to be happy, the less vulnerable he or she will be. Cynics live austere, unconventional lives.

Founded in Greece by Zeno, Stoicism grew out of Cynicism and achieved widespread influence in first-century Rome, ultimately spreading throughout Christianized Europe. The Roman slave Epictetus, the Emperor Marcus Aurelius, and the senator Seneca are the most influential Stoic writers.

Stoics advised learning to want whatever we get by willing ourselves to accept whatever circumstances we are in without resentment. They believed that the cosmos is wisely governed by the Logos (World Reason) and that everything happens as part of a divine plan. The wise person anticipates and goes along with fate, the foolish one wishes things were otherwise.

A Summary of Main Points at the end of each chapter reinforces your reading and helps you organize your study and focus on important material. These condensed summaries provide a good starting point for review as you study for examinations.

268   CHAPTER NINE

According to the Stoics, human beings are bits of the Logos because we have rational souls. Happiness comes from the effective use of reason to alter the will. Based on their concept of a disinterested World Reason, the Stoics taught that it is wise to minimize personal attachments and motives. One way to do this is to evaluate things in terms of the goal of a universal harmony rather than from an individualistic view.

The Stoics rejected emotion to the extent it was humanly possible, favoring detached, rational acceptance over personal, emotional involvement.

Central to Stoicism is the distinction between control and influence. Though the Stoics believed that life is fated, they understood this in a loose sense. Because we cannot know precisely what our fate is, we must take reasonable action without pinning our happiness on a particular result.

According to the Stoics, we can control our ideas and attitudes but we cannot control "externals" such as reputation, social status, relationships, health, and wealth. A great deal of Stoic literature concerns learning how to identify what we cannot control and exercising control over our will.

Stoic virtues include strength of will, courage, dignity, and maturity.

According to Stoic doctrine, everything has a price that reason can reveal. The ultimate price of happiness is personal detachment from external conditions; peace of mind comes from indifference to everything except accepting the will of the Logos.

The Stoics looked upon suffering as a test of character and praised the ability to accept unavoidable suffering without bitterness or complaint. They taught that only great struggle could produce greatness of character.

Stoicism remains influential today in the form of various schools of cognitive psychotherapy. Three of the most important are William Glasser's reality therapy, Albert Ellis's rational-emotive therapy, and Viktor Frankl's logotherapy. The philosopher-warrior James Bond Stockdale continues to define Epictetus's Principle of Life and communicate it to a growing audience.

STUDY QUESTIONS

1. What is Cynicism?

2. Explain how Cynicism influenced Stoicism. Be specific.

3. What is the relationship of Socrates to Cynicism and Stoicism?

4. Compare and contrast Hedonism, Cynicism, and Stoicism.

5. Discuss how the social climate of ancient Rome encouraged the emergence of Stoicism.

6. Discuss the relationship of the lives of Marcus Aurelius and Epictetus to their philosophies.

7. What is the Logos?

8. How are the Logos and fate related in Stoicism?

9. Identify and discuss possible problems with the Stoic notion of fate.

10. Stoicism was quickly absorbed into Christianity. Identify and comment on any similarities you are aware of.

11. What is the disinterested rational will, and why is it important to Stoic doctrine?

12. Explain and defend the Stoic view of emotions. Then analyze it.

13. What do the Stoics think falls under our control? What do the Stoics think does not fall under our control? Do you agree? Why or why not?

14. Analyze the relationship between influence and control.

15. Discuss the difference between avoidable and unavoidable suffering. How can we tell which is which? Why does it matter?

You can use the end-of-chapter Study Questions as self-tests. They give you an opportunity to check on how well you have understood what you have read and on your ability to state philosophical concepts in your own words and provide ideas for papers or essay topics.

CHAPTER ONE

Philosophy

and Wisdom

I do not know how
to teach philosophy
without becoming a
disturber of the peace.

BARUCH SPINOZA

ou are about to embark on the study of a subject that is unlike any other. Historically, most academic subjects began as some aspect of philosophy and branched off as knowledge became specialized. Philosophy resembles history and social science when it studies the development of ideas in terms of the social climate from which they emerged. It resembles art criticism when it analyzes the meaning and function of poetry, painting, or music, the nature of beauty, or the moral qualities of art. It resembles physics and chemistry in its efforts to describe ultimate reality. It resembles linguistics and semantics in its analyses of language, communication, and meaning. It resembles geometry and algebra in the theorems and proofs of symbolic logic. Informal logic may remind you of English or communications classes in its identification of fallacies and of persuasive maneuvers.

The word **philosophy** comes from Greek roots meaning "the love of wisdom." The earliest philosophers were considered wise men and women or sages because they devoted themselves to asking "big questions": What is the meaning of life? Where did everything come from? What is the nature of reality? For a long time, most philosophers were wisdom-seeking amateurs. Philosophy was a way of living for them, not a way of making a living.

We often use the term philosophy in just that sense, when we think of a person's basic philosophy as the code of values and beliefs by which he or she lives. Sometimes we talk about Nicky's philosophy of cooking or Mike's philosophy of betting on the horses. In such instances, we are thinking of philosophy as involving general principles or guidelines. Technically, that's known as *having a philosophy*; it is not the same thing as *being a philosopher*. Philosophy is all around us, even if we don't recognize it or agree on what it is.

PHILOSOPHY AND THE CONTEMPORARY SCENE

Do philosophers (lovers of wisdom) have anything important and valuable to say to us today? Does the study of philosophy and wisdom have any practical value in a world where more and more people cannot even afford to own homes or feed their children? Doesn't it seem to make more sense for schools to turn out more doctors and scientists who can provide the knowledge and technology necessary for a better world, rather than to turn out philosophers?

Indeed, contemporary education is becoming more and more technical. You have no doubt recognized the increasingly specialized nature of your courses as you progress through the educational maze. A *technique* is nothing more than a way of doing something. There is a technique for solving a

SURELY, LIFE IS NOT MERELY A JOB

Why do we go through the struggle to be educated? Is it merely in order to pass some examinations and get a job? Or is it the function of education to prepare us while we are young to understand the whole process of life? Having a job and earning one's livelihood is necessary—but is that all? Are we being educated only for that? Surely, life is not merely a job, an occupation; life is wide and profound, it is a great mystery, a vast realm in which we function as human beings. If we merely prepare our-selves to earn a livelihood, we shall miss the whole point of life; and to understand life is much more important than merely to prepare for examinations and become very proficient in mathematics, physics, or what you will.

Jiddu Krishnamurti
"The Function of Education," in Daniel Kolak and Raymond Martin, *The Experience of Philosophy* (Belmont, Calif.: Wadsworth, 1990), pp. 20–21.

certain kind of math problem; there is one technique for writing English 1A papers and another for writing Psychology 1A papers. There are techniques for getting dates or painting cars or casting statues. Many Americans express contradictory fears concerning technology: that we are falling behind other countries technologically, and that we are being destroyed by an over-reliance on technology.

One of the things philosophers do is point out such contradictions. Then we analyze them to see if they are resolvable. Technical specialists, by contrast, understandably concentrate on a clearly defined area of study and can usually identify inconsistencies and contradictions within that area. But specializing makes it hard to see more general contradictions and implications among the values and needs of different specialties. All sorts of common human complications make it difficult for us to see inconsistencies and contradictions in our own lives. Enter the philosopher.

Of course, there's a difference between sitting around saying philosophical-sounding things and actually philosophizing. One vital difference involves the degree of rigor and discipline applied to our reflections. A simple way to make the point is by an analogy with swimming: Compare someone who swims a few laps in the backyard pool fairly regularly to an Olympic swimmer. They are both swimmers, but there's being a swimmer and being a *swimmer*.

I think we are probably all philosophers once in a while, and some of us are even *philosophers*. When we face a difficult change, we reflect on life, death, loss, and growth. But when things are going well, we tend to just enjoy. Perhaps we articulately express our beliefs about affirmative action,

I see many people die because they judge that life is not worth living. I see others paradoxically getting killed for the ideas and illusions that give them a reason for living (what is called a reason for living is also an excellent reason for dying). I therefore conclude that the meaning of life is the most urgent of questions.

Albert Camus

Is it possible to justify the study of philosophy considering the urgent needs of such overwhelming contemporary problems as world hunger? "Philosophy bakes no bread," and people need bread to live.

human nature, justice, or suicide. But do we study and restudy these issues, consulting a wide array of opinions and doing our best to suspend final judgment until we are clear about all key terms and facts? Do we always remain willing to modify our strongest beliefs should new evidence warrant that? *Philosophers* do.

Timely Questions

Technical thinking is concerned chiefly with the means to achieve particular ends: curing AIDS, stopping automobile exhaust pollution, teaching people to read. These are different from what philosophers sometimes call **ultimate ends**.

ULTIMATE ENDS
Goals that are valued for their own sake, not as means to something else.

Having a job at a fast-food restaurant, for example, is probably not your idea of an ultimate end. You have the job to make money. But money is probably not your ultimate goal either. You want it to pay for clothes, food, or a car. These in turn are supposed to make you happy. Happiness is an example of an ultimate end. It makes sense to ask, "Why do you want that money?" because for most people money is important only as a means to other things. But we do not ask, "Why do you want to be happy?" because

THE PREJUDICES OF PRACTICAL MEN

If we are not to fail in our endeavour to determine the value of philosophy, we must first free our minds from the prejudices of what are wrongly called "practical" men. The "practical" man, as this word is often used, is one who recognizes only material needs, who realizes that men must have food for the body, but is oblivious of the necessity of providing food for the mind. If all men were well off, if poverty and disease had been reduced to their lowest possible point, there would still remain much to be done to produce a valuable society; and even in the existing world the goods of the mind are at least as important as the goods of the body. It is exclusively among the goods of the mind that the value of philosophy is to be found; and only those who are not indifferent to these goods can be persuaded that the study of philosophy is not a waste of time.

. . . Philosophy is to be studied, not for the sake of any definite answers to its questions, since no definite answers can, as a rule, be known to be true, but rather for the sake of the questions themselves; because these questions enlarge our conception of what is possible, enrich our intellectual imagination and diminish the dogmatic assurance which closes the mind against speculation; but above all because, through the greatness of the universe which philosophy contemplates, the mind also is rendered great, and becomes capable of that union with the universe which constitutes its highest good.

Bertrand Russell
The Problems of Philosophy (Oxford: Oxford University Press, 1912), selections from Chapters 1, 14, and 15.

we see happiness as an ultimate end, an end in itself, and not merely a means to something else.

Technology is chiefly concerned with means to specific ends, not with ultimate ends. As important as this kind of knowledge is, it cannot make us happy. For instance, many people see the global problems of oil spills, destruction of the atmosphere and the rain forests, terrorism, the breakdown of family values, high crime rates, drug abuse, and so on as evidence of a world crisis. A growing number of social commentators attribute this crisis in part to the fact that we concentrate too much on technical solutions, too much on factual information and statistics, and too little on basic thinking skills, moral reasoning, and sensitivity to ultimate ends.

It may be that we expend too much of our energy and intelligence addressing **timely questions**. Timely questions involve current issues, issues that are important to a particular time or place. They focus on strategies for solving technical or specific problems: Can we find a substitute for fossil fuel? How can we improve the quality of education? Where's the best place to invest my lottery winnings? Timely questions can be very important, but

TIMELY QUESTIONS
Questions involving issues that are important to a particular time or place.

Reprinted by permission of NEA, Inc.

they address only part of the human condition. How and in what order we answer today's timely questions should depend on our ultimate goals and most basic values. We can discover what they are only by asking another kind of question.

Timeless Questions

TIMELESS QUESTIONS
Questions concerning ultimate values, general principles, and the very nature of reality, knowledge, justice, happiness, truth, God, beauty, and morality; asked in virtually every culture.

A **timeless question** is one that has been asked in virtually every culture for which we have historical records. Timeless questions concern ultimate values, general principles, and the very nature of reality, knowledge, justice, happiness, truth, God, beauty, and morality. Philosophy addresses the timeless questions that other kinds of thinking cannot.

Timeless philosophical questions include: Does life have any purpose? Does my life have a purpose? Is there a God? If so, how should I live? If not, how should I live? Is it possible to escape suffering? Why not commit suicide? Is it really better to be good than evil? Are people basically good or bad? Does might make right? Is pleasure the same thing as good? Is the happiness of the greatest number always to be pursued? Are we free or the products of fate? Is it possible to turn the other cheek? Is it desirable? Are we part of nature or overlords of it? Is truth relative?

First learn, then form opinions.
The Talmud

Such questions cannot be answered in the sense that a mathematical or factual question can be answered with "4" or "1066 A.D." Timeless questions must be asked and answered anew by each culture and by any person who awakens to what Plato and Aristotle called the philosophical sense of wonder. Indeed, individuals must wrestle with these most basic questions throughout their lives.

In my own case, many of the answers to timeless questions I found as a freshman have long since ceased to satisfy me. In fact, today I have more questions and fewer answers than I did twenty-plus years ago when I was bitten by a philosophical gadfly named Socrates (Chapter 5). And yet my questions of today are more satisfying than my answers of yesterday. If this pattern keeps up, I'll have fewer and fewer answers, but more and better questions for the rest of my life. Of course, this pattern unsettles lots of folks. There's an enormous industry based on providing them with "the answer." It has a religion branch, a psychology branch, a biology department. And let's not forget the astrologers and psychics or all those friends and acquaintances who know exactly how things are—and answer us before we even realize we have any questions.

A closed mind is a dying mind.
Edna Ferber

PHILOSOPHICAL QUERY

Do you agree that timeless questions are important in a practical way? That is, do you think that a person needs to address timeless issues in order to be happy? Is being happy the same thing as living a good life? Is it the same as living a full life? If you had the choice of being happy and unaware or aware but not always happy, which would you choose? Discuss and explain your answers to these questions. Are any of them timeless questions? Why or why not?

Wisdom outweighs any wealth.
Sophocles

Areas of Philosophy

What, exactly, is philosophy? There is no single, conclusive answer. In general, philosophy consists of the systematic, comprehensive study of certain questions. For the most part, philosophical questions involve meaning, interpretation, evaluation, and logical or rational consistency. The primary areas of philosophy are delineated below.

Metaphysics addresses the problem of what is real. Metaphysical questions concern whether or not we have free will; how the mind and body are related to each other; whether there can be a supernatural, immaterial level of existence; whether personal immortality is possible; and what the nature of reality is.

Epistemology, the study of knowledge, poses questions about the relationship of faith to reason; the difference between knowing that we know and believing that we know; whether all knowledge comes from the senses; the roles of reason and experience in determining the truth; the characteristics of artificial intelligence; and the nature of truth.

Axiology, the study of values, questions whether or not value judgments are more than matters of opinion, the relation between facts and values, and to what extent, if any, values can be objective.

Ethics includes the careful analysis of moral problems such as capital punishment, suicide, lying, sexual conduct, and unfair discrimination; the possibility of a universal moral code; and the characteristics of the good life.

METAPHYSICS
Branch of philosophy that addresses the problem of what is real.

EPISTEMOLOGY
Branch of philosophy that studies the nature and possibility of knowledge.

AXIOLOGY
Branch of philosophy that studies values in general.

ETHICS
Branch of philosophy concerned with the good life and with moral value and moral reasoning.

AESTHETICS
Branch of philosophy that
studies all forms of art.

POLITICAL PHILOSOPHY
Branch of philosophy con-
cerned with the state and
issues of sovereignty.

SOCIAL PHILOSOPHY
Branch of philosophy con-
cerned with social institutions and relations.

LOGIC
Branch of philosophy that
studies the rules of correct
reasoning.

Aesthetics is the study of art and raises questions about the nature of beauty, the proper uses of art, and whether or not the artist's opinion of her artwork is always correct.

Political philosophy includes the study of the state and the nature of sovereignty. It addresses the right to exercise power and the limits of the state or government.

Social philosophy is concerned with the effects of social institutions on individuals, race and gender relations, and comparisons of various types of societies.

Logic, the study of the rules of correct reasoning, includes the analysis of different kinds of evidence; the study of analogies and comparisons; precise standards of proof; the relationship between what we say and what we mean; the adequacy of feelings of certainty; and the identification of misleading arguments and reasoning errors.

Philosophers sometimes concentrate on one primary area or another. Today some philosophers go so far as to reject whole areas of philosophy as unfit for study. For example, a logician might view metaphysics as overly abstract and confused; a moral philosopher might see the study of symbolic logic as belonging to mathematics, not philosophy. Whenever philosophers concern themselves with the meaning of life or the general search for wisdom, however, all of these primary areas are involved, even if some are not dealt with explicitly.

Contemporary academic philosophers tend to specialize within these primary areas, concentrating on historical periods, certain philosophers, the philosophy of music, religion, or law, for example, or on particular philosophical issues. More than two hundred areas of specialization are currently listed by the Philosophical Documentation Center.

PHILOSOPHICAL ARCHETYPES

In cartoons a sage or guru is often depicted wearing a robe of some sort, maybe carrying a staff, and sporting a long white beard. Why do you suppose that is? One possibility is that cartoonists have tapped into a basic image shared by many cultures.

In China and Japan, the sage is a "wise guide"; in some other parts of Asia, a yogi or guru; in parts of Africa, a witch doctor; among Native Americans and the nomadic tribes of Asia, a shaman. In the Bible, the prophets were people of wisdom. In many cultures, the "grandmother" or "grandfather" or some other elder also represents this basic image. In the West, the wise person is often depicted as a male, but not always.

What I have referred to as a basic image is also known as an **archetype**. According to psychologist C. G. Jung, an archetype is an image that has been shared by the whole human race from the earliest times. In its more traditional sense, an archetype represents our conception of the

ARCHETYPE
Basic image that represents
our conception of the es-
sence of a certain type of
person; according to psy-
chologist C. G. Jung, some
of the images have been
shared by the whole human
race from the earliest times.

NO AGE IS FORBIDDEN US

The only people who are really at leisure are those who take time for philosophy. They alone really live. It is not their lifetime alone of which they are careful stewards: they annex every age to their own and exploit all the years that have gone before. Unless we prove ingrate, it was for us that the illustrious founders of divine schools of thought came into being, for they prepared a way of life. . . . No age is forbidden us, we have admittance to all, and if we choose to transcend the narrow bounds of human frailty by loftiness of mind, there is a vast stretch of time for us to roam. We may dispute with Socrates, doubt with Carneades, repose with Epicurus, transcend human nature with the Stoics, defy it with the Cynics. Since nature allows us to participate in any age, why should we not betake ourselves in mind from this petty and ephemeral span to the boundless and timeless region we can share with our betters? . . . The philosopher's life is therefore spacious; he is not hemmed in and constricted like others. . . . all ages are at his service.

Seneca
The Stoic Philosophy of Seneca, trans. Moses Hadas (New York: W. W. Norton, 1958), pp. 65–67.

essence of a certain kind of person. An archetype is a fundamental, original model of some type: cynic, saint, pessimist, optimist, atheist, rationalist, idealist, and so on. A **philosophical archetype** is a philosopher who expresses an original or influential point of view in a way that significantly affects subsequent philosophers and nonphilosophers.

The difference between an archetype and an ideal is that the archetype need not be good or perfect. The difference between an archetype and a stereotype is one of depth. A stereotype is a simplistic distortion of a type of person. An archetype, by contrast, is a powerful representation of a fundamental response to universal experiences. Archetypes exemplify essential ways of coping with the universal aspects of life (suffering, death, loss, society, wealth, knowledge, love, purpose) in uncommonly pure ways. There are archetypes of evil as well as good, and of foolish as well as wise responses to life.

This book is an introduction to philosophy in its original sense—the search for wisdom—organized around philosophical archetypes. Philosophy in the original sense is philosophy that confronts life by offering consolation or criticism, ways to succeed in the world or ways to withdraw from it. Even those people who have not studied philosophy recognize the basic qualities of many philosophical archetypes. Most likely you have already encountered individuals who resemble some of them. Two brief examples will show you what I mean.

PHILOSOPHICAL ARCHETYPE
A philosopher who represents an original or influential point of view in a way that significantly affects philosophers and nonphilosophers: cynic, saint, pessimist, optimist, atheist, rationalist, idealist, and such.

Archetypes of wisdom appear in many forms, from the rational Greek *sophos* (above) to the whirling Sufi *dervish* (right).

One philosophical archetype is the skeptic (Chapter 12). Skeptics believe that any claim to knowledge must be personally verified by their own sense experience. They want to see, touch, taste, or measure everything. The New Testament contains an excellent example of this archetype in the person of Doubting Thomas, the disciple who would not believe that Jesus had risen from the grave until he carefully examined Jesus' wounds for himself. Another philosophical archetype is the unreflective hedonist (Chapter 8). Unreflective hedonists live only for intense, immediate pleasure. They seek instant gratification and don't worry about the long-range consequences of what they do. They are pretty easy to identify.

The philosophers we will meet include archetypes of these and other significant philosophical schools and orientations. These archetypes are often the founders of the schools they represent; if not, they are important exponents of them. In addition to their significance in the history of philosophy, the archetypes confront timeless questions in ways that remain uniquely interesting and engaging in light of today's timely concerns.

A special virtue of archetypes is their intensity and purity in relation to their philosophies. They are strict advocates of a philosophical worldview or philosophical method. The intensity with which they hold to their views, combined with philosophical depth and rigor, almost always challenges our own, often unclarified beliefs—whether we want it to or not. Never fear. You alone always remain responsible for what you choose, reject, or modify. If you give them a chance, the archetypes can give you a clear picture of both a philosophy and the kind of philosopher who tries to live it. They may

To be a philosopher is not merely to have subtle thoughts, nor even to found a school, but to so love wisdom as to live, according to its dictates, a life of simplicity, independence, magnanimity, and trust.

Henry David Thoreau

also give you a better sense of your own present philosophy of life, or at least some aspects of it.

The heart of philosophy in the original sense always includes the search for wisdom. That's the common theme in this book. Philosophers may do battle over what is and is not wisdom, but all philosophers remain lovers: lovers of truth, lovers of clarity, lovers of wisdom and the pursuit of it.

Are Philosophers Always Men?

The history of Western philosophy contains mostly male representatives, most of them of European ancestry. This has led to the sarcastic, but important, charge that Western philosophy is nothing but the study of "dead white males." Even though there are increasing numbers of women and other non-European minorities entering the ranks of professional philosophy today, men still outnumber women among professional philosophers.

Although throughout history individual women were recognized for their insight and brilliance, most of them remained—or were kept—outside of the formal history of philosophy. In our own time things are a little better. Although Susanne Langer, L. Susan Stebbing, Simone de Beauvoir, Simone Weil, Ayn Rand, Christina Hoff Sommers, Alison Jaggar, and Susan Moller Okin, among many others, have achieved renown as philosophers, philosophy has lagged behind the social sciences in providing opportunities for women. Ruth Benedict, Margaret Mead, Marie Louise von Franz, Karen Horney, and Carol Gilligan are well-known examples of more widely influential women in such fields as anthropology and psychology. (In Chapter 20, we'll take a look at the work of Okin, Jaggar, and Gilligan.) We can expect to see more and more women philosophers, until at last philosophy becomes a truly *human* pursuit of wisdom.

Because the history of Western philosophy has been increasingly dominated by an emphasis on logical reasoning and written argument, other expressions of wisdom have been given less attention. Also, until the eighteenth century, most Western philosophers represented a small class of highly educated men, able to support themselves independently or associated with the church or some other source of income. Only with the increasing influence of great public universities were higher education and philosophy open to people from ever-widening backgrounds. And even then, philosophers tended to remain members of an educated male elite.

Consequently, wisdom found among other cultures or expressed in other ways has been overlooked by many philosophers. Only relatively recently have professional philosophers begun to recognize other rich expressions of philosophical ideas: the shamanic traditions of Native American, South American, African, and Asian cultures; the oral traditions of Eastern European Hasidic Judaism, Sufism, and so forth. There has also always been a powerful tradition of applied philosophy, which challenges the status quo

There is a principle which is a bar against all information, which is proof against all arguments and which cannot fail to keep a man in everlasting ignorance—that principle is contempt prior to investigation.
Herbert Spencer

Since ignorance is no guarantee of security, and in fact only makes our insecurity still worse, it is probably better despite our fear to know where the danger lies. To ask the right question is already half the solution of a problem. . . . Discerning persons have realized for some time that external . . . conditions, of whatever kind, are only . . . jumping-off grounds, for the real dangers that threaten our lives.
C. G. Jung

Let no one be slow to seek
wisdom when he is young,
nor weary in the search
thereof when he is grown old.
For no age is too early or too
late for the health of the soul.
And to say that the season for
studying philosophy has not
yet come, or that it is past
and gone, is like saying that
the season for happiness is
not yet or that it is now no
more.

Epicurus

and confronts social institutions. In recent times it has found especially effective and powerful expression among philosophers concerned with the environment, animal rights, family structure, racism, and sexism.

But there is no escaping the fact that the history of Western philosophy is predominantly male-influenced, shaped by a strong preference for rational and objective evidence as opposed to more holistic and intuitive approaches to problems. The pervasiveness of this orientation makes it imperative that we at least acknowledge this problem.

Mary Ellen Waithe of the University of Minnesota is the head of a team of scholars compiling a valuable four-volume series called *A History of Women Philosophers*. In the following passage she notes firsthand the difficulty of filling in gaps in the history of philosophy:

> On a sweltering October afternoon in 1980 . . . I sought comfort in the basement library of City University of New York's Graduate Center. I came upon a reference to a work by Aegidius Menagius [on the history of women philosophers] published in 1690 and 1692. I had never heard of any women philosophers prior to the 20th century with the exceptions of Queen Christina of Sweden, known as Descartes' student, and Hildegard von Bingen, who lived in the 12th century. . . .
>
> It took sixteen months to obtain a copy of Menagius' book. . . . As it turns out, many of the women he listed as philosophers were astronomers, astrologers, gynecologists, or simply relatives of male philosophers. Nevertheless, the list of women alleged to have been philosophers was impressive.
>
> . . . By the end of 1981 I had concluded that the accomplishments of some one hundred or more women philosophers had been omitted from the standard philosophic reference works and histories of philosophy. Just check sources such as *The Encyclopedia of Philosophy*, Copleston, Zeller, Bury, Grote and others. If the women are mentioned at all, it is in passing, in a footnote.[1]

One may view the history
of philosophy as a history
of heresy.

Walter Kaufmann

Most of our sources will reflect the historical limits of Western philosophy, but that will not prevent us from looking at such interesting and important non-Western philosophers as Buddha, Chuang-tzu, and Lao-tzu in Chapter 2. In Chapter 19 we will encounter Martin Luther King's compelling ethic of love and courage and, in Chapter 20, we will examine a lively contemporary philosophical interchange concerning the influence of gender on our fundamental conceptions of justice and knowledge.

There is no such crime as
a crime of thought; there are
only crimes of action.

Clarence Darrow

The history of philosophy is a living thing. It is still being written. Perhaps you will contribute to it. Eventually all facets of wisdom may be equally welcome—and future textbooks will not have sections like this one. And as you will quickly see, the ultimate issue is not who said something first, but whether it is true and worthwhile. Wisdom knows no color or gender.

THE PURSUIT OF WISDOM

Where can we go to study wisdom? We don't find "Wise People" listed in the Yellow Pages. We don't even find "Philosophers" listed, though things may be changing—at least in Amsterdam, where "practicing philosophers" charge more than fifty dollars an hour. One of them is Ad Hoogendijk, who says, "There's a new generation of philosophers who want to take part in society, not just work in ivory towers . . . [who help people] answer very basic questions like: 'Who are you, and what do you want out of life?' "[2]

But even if we did find "practicing philosophers," we would still face the problem of deciding whether to consult them. What criteria could we use? After all, if I am not yet wise, how can I recognize a genuine wise person?

Sometimes people cannot recognize wisdom, and then they get taken in by a cult leader or other guru type claiming to show them "the" way to happiness. And let's not forget that many of those who get taken are highly educated, successful people. Clearly, then, there is a difference between knowledge and wisdom, just as there is between success and happiness. An underlying theme of this book involves distinguishing between knowledge and wisdom.

Let's begin by seeing how knowledge differs from belief.

It is said that when Empedocles told Xenophanes that it was impossible to find a wise man, Xenophanes replied: "Naturally, for it takes a wise man to recognize a wise man."

philophaster: a pretender or dabbler in philosophy.

KNOWLEDGE, BELIEF, AND IGNORANCE

Trusting X to be true and knowing for ourselves that X is true are two very different things. Intellectual honesty demands that I distinguish between what I know and what I think I know. Sadly, some people do not make this distinction. They confuse the quality of their beliefs with the intensity of their beliefs. In other words, they equate knowledge with belief.

Philosophers generally define **knowledge** as justified true belief. Thus, to know X means, first, that X actually is true; second, that I believe X to be true; and third, that I can justify my belief in X by providing "adequate evidence." Of course, these requirements raise some interesting questions. Is a strong personal feeling adequate evidence? How much proof is enough? According to whose criteria? The philosopher demands that we be able to articulate reasons to justify claims to knowledge.

Belief refers to the subjective mental acceptance that a claim is true. Beliefs—as distinct from knowledge—need not be true or adequately justified. Since beliefs are subjective mental states, it is possible to be firmly convinced that a belief is correct when it is not. Sometimes we are correct in our beliefs but cannot offer adequate evidence for them. We can have true and false beliefs, but technically speaking we cannot have false knowledge.

KNOWLEDGE
Justified true belief.

BELIEF
Conviction or trust that a claim is true; an individual's subjective mental state; distinct from knowledge.

PHILOSOPHY IS AN AXE

There is a frozen sea within us. Philosophy is an axe.

Everything you believe is questionable. How deeply have you questioned it? The uncritical acceptance of beliefs handed down by parents, teachers, politicians, and religious leaders is dangerous. Many of these beliefs are simply false. Some of them are lies designed to control you. Even when what has been handed down is true, it is not your truth. To merely accept anything without questioning it is to be somebody else's puppet, a second-hand person.

Beliefs can be handed down. Knowledge can perhaps be handed down. Wisdom can never be handed down. The goal of philosophy is wisdom. Trying to hand down philosophy is unphilosophical. Wisdom requires questioning what is questionable. Since everything is questionable, wisdom requires questioning everything. That is what philosophy is: the art of questioning everything.

Daniel Kolak and Raymond Martin
The Experience of Philosophy (Belmont, Calif.: Wadsworth, 1990), p. 2.

MERE BELIEF
A conviction that something is true for which the only evidence is the sincerity of the believer.

Rather, what we thought we knew turns out to be mistaken. **Mere belief** is a conviction that something is true for which the only evidence is the sincere conviction of the believer.

If any position is sound and worth holding, there will be ample reasons for believing it. Questioning our beliefs is frightening only if we don't think they will survive serious study. If a position cannot survive reasonable questioning and cannot hold up against counterevidence, then the rational thing to do is to reject it. Yet it is quite common to encounter a wall of resistance to the spirit of wonder and inquiry: "I don't care what anybody says, nobody can convince me of X." "No, I haven't read the book. I know it's obscene without having to read it." "Nothing you can say will make me change my mind." "Once a Z always a Z, as far as I'm concerned." Even more subtly, we can shut off challenging questions by prejudging them, by being inattentive and bored when they come up, or by mocking other points of view without investigating them. When we do this, we hold on to a position regardless of the facts; we are indifferent to the possibility of error or enlightenment. Such an attitude is called **willed ignorance**, and it is as opposite from the love of wisdom as any attitude I can think of.

WILLED IGNORANCE
An attitude of indifference to the possibility of error or enlightenment that holds on to beliefs regardless of the facts.

PHILOSOPHICAL QUERY

Have you ever been guilty of willed ignorance? If so, why do you think you were? Are you still? Why? What do you suppose the relationships between willed ignorance and arrogance and between willed ignorance and bored disinterest might be? What's the difference between willed ignorance and simply having made up your mind about something?

WISDOM AND KNOWLEDGE

Wisdom is general knowledge of what does and does not produce human happiness. Wisdom requires knowing the difference between right and wrong combined with the desire and ability to act in basic accord with that knowledge. Unlike forms of knowledge based primarily on education and intelligence, wisdom involves an accumulation of experiences beyond the intellectual or theoretical variety. **Theoretical knowledge**, by contrast, is the accurate compilation and assessment of factual and systematic information and relationships. **Practical knowledge** consists of skills needed to do things, such as play the piano, use a band saw, remove a tumor, or bake a cake. All knowledge involves identification and justification in the form of logical arguments, scientific predictions, or the demonstration of skillful performance, depending on the kind of knowledge.

Philosophers generally separate knowledge from personality traits and moral character. This seems correct, for it is possible to be knowledgeable in one or many areas and foolish in others. It is also possible to be wise without being knowledgeable in many areas. A person may be wise without knowing the periodic table of elements or how to spell, balance a checkbook, remove a tumor, or bake a cake.

Traditionally, wisdom has been associated with maturity and experience in a way that knowledge has not. That is probably why wisdom is so often associated with the elders of a tribe or clan. Yet, clearly, age alone does not guarantee wisdom. Wisdom is also a function of personal, moral, intellectual, and spiritual growth. It is associated with personal virtue in a way that knowledge is not.

PHILOSOPHICAL QUERY

What is the relationship of increased awareness to wisdom? Is wisdom merely a matter of being more aware? What are some of the factors that may encourage or inhibit the development of wisdom? Some young people seem to be "wise beyond their years." What do you think might account for wisdom at an early age? On the other side of life, some older people seem exceptionally foolish for their age. What factors might account for this?

LEARNING WISDOM

Wisdom is not neat and orderly; it addresses the whole range of life, slopping over the boundaries of academic specialties. Further complicating the academic study of wisdom is the fact that wisdom is always concerned with the practical conduct of life; everything else is viewed in terms of its helpfulness to this purpose, including collecting facts and creating theories to explain them. Wisdom is not scientific or technical knowledge, though it may borrow from them. It involves

WISDOM
General knowledge of what does and does not produce human happiness, including the difference between right and wrong combined with the desire and ability to act in basic accord with that knowledge.

THEORETICAL KNOWLEDGE
The accurate compilation and assessment of factual and systematic relationships.

PRACTICAL KNOWLEDGE
Consists of skills needed to do things like play the piano, use a band saw, remove a tumor, or bake a cake.

Specialization is the price we pay for the advancement of knowledge. A price, because the path of specialization leads away from the ordinary and concrete acts of understanding in terms of which man actually lives his day-to-day life.
William Barrett

THE SKILLS WE NEED MOST

I cannot accept the idea that our proper schooling lies in the urbane skills of making conversation and making a living, each in its preferred style and time. Rather, the skills we need most are the skills of mortality—the soul and the spittle to accept and to share, decently, even nobly, even more graciously, a common human calling and a common human fate. The proper aim of education is then, above all else, not competence but wisdom, which has always been seen to be at one with holiness. It is fitting that education should undertake the discipline demanded for the full and decent living of one's life and dying of one's death. This wisdom and holiness and their attending discipline are not the preserve or the preoccupation of a single generation or time of life or period of history. They are the concern of the young when one is young and the concern of the old when one is old.

Robert E. Meagher
Cave Notes: First Reflections on Sense and Spirit (Philadelphia: Fortress Press, 1975), p. 3.

The only important problem of philosophy, the only problem which concerns us and our fellow men, is the problem of the wisdom of living. Wisdom is not wisdom unless it knows its own subject and scope.
Lin Yutang

There is only one wisdom: to recognize the intelligence who steers all things through all things.
Heraclitus

insight and the capacity to learn from experience, but wisdom is not the same thing as educated intelligence. Albert Hakim puts it this way:

> Wisdom stands for more than the kind of knowledge a pilot has who knows how to set a compass for direction or the sociologist who knows the right sampling device for making a survey. We do not call the pilot or the sociologist "wise" because each knows how to use the compass or the sampling device. Wisdom looks for more; it touches a level where separate things can be seen in unity, or disparate things in interrelatedness.[3]

The sense of unity and interrelatedness that Hakim attributes to wisdom must be acquired through living as well as through thinking. Wisdom looks past accidental differences to the essences of things. Thus the pain of discrimination felt by a woman of color can give her a feeling of relatedness with the man who wasn't hired because he is too fat or the teenagers who are always unwelcome at the corner store, in a way that merely intellectual knowledge cannot provide. Passing on knowledge is the primary aim of education. When we go beyond education, beyond learning what others have known, and try to apply their insights to life, we enter the realm of wisdom. The popular historian of ideas, Will Durant, knew this:

> Our culture is superficial today, and our knowledge dangerous, because we are rich in mechanisms and poor in purposes. The balance of mind which once came of a warm religious faith is gone; science has taken from us the supernatural

bases of our morality, and all the world seems consumed
in a disorderly individualism that reflects the chaotic fragmentation of our character. . . . We move about the earth
with unprecedented speed, but we do not know, and have
not thought, where we are going, or whether we shall find
any happiness there for our harassed souls. We are being destroyed by our knowledge, which has made us drunk with
our power. And we shall not be saved without wisdom.[4]

Can we not understand that all the outward tinkerings and improvements do not touch man's inner nature, and that everything ulti- mately depends upon whether the man who wields the sci- ence and the techniques is ca- pable of responsibility or not?
C. G. Jung

The Pursuit of Wisdom Can Be Dangerous

Serious thinking will inevitably challenge some of our present beliefs. The
serious pursuit of wisdom demands that we question and perhaps reject
some of the values we currently hold dear. This often makes other people
uncomfortable, for it can reveal the weaknesses of their own ideas or their
own complacency.

Over the years, students have told me about friends, advisers, or family
members who warned them not to take philosophy classes, for reasons as
old as the history of philosophy: "Philosophy will destroy your faith." "All
philosophers do is criticize and tear down." "Philosophers are elitist; they
make fun of democracy and America." "You'll only get stirred up. Philosophy questions everything, and then leaves you without any answers."

Such criticisms, though overly general and vague, are based on a sense
of another, more personal kind of danger that is also part of thinking deeply.
It is the danger of tearing down inadequate ideas and then finding nothing
to replace them. This is a form of fear of the unknown. I know that sounds
like a cliché, but fear of the unknown is a real, severely limiting fear. The
pursuit of wisdom makes a direct assault on the unknown. No area is off-
limits, no important question unasked.

Of what use is a philosopher who doesn't hurt anybody's feelings?
Diogenes

PHILOSOPHICAL QUERY

Have you encountered any criticism of the dangers of philosophy?
Was it informed or uninformed criticism? How did/would you respond to it?

Suppose that after taking a philosophy class, you lose your
religious faith or change your attitude toward America or democracy. Would that mean philosophy had destroyed your beliefs? Is
there another way to interpret what happened?

We ultimately suffer when we fail to address the fundamental issues of
our lives: purpose, unity, and value. In a world of limited choices, given a
life span of uncertain and finite scope, one of the most tragic wastes of a life
is to settle for simply passing time from one event to another: drifting into
a college major or a job or a marriage—in other words, living without a

IT IS A SHAMEFUL QUESTION

The busy reader will ask, is all this philosophy useful? It is a shameful question: we do not ask it of poetry, which is also an imaginative construction of a world incompletely known. If poetry reveals to us the beauty our untaught eyes have missed, and philosophy gives us the wisdom to understand and forgive, it is enough, and more than the world's wealth. Philosophy will not fatten our purses, nor lift us to dizzy dignities in a democratic state; it may even make us a little careless of these things. For what if we should fatten our purses, or rise to high office, and yet all the while remain ignorantly naive, coarsely unfurnished in the mind, brutal in behavior, unstable in character, chaotic in desire, and blindly miserable?

. . . Perhaps philosophy will give us, if we are faithful to it, a healing unity of soul. We are so slovenly and self-contradictory in our thinking; it may be that we shall clarify ourselves, and pull ourselves together into consistency, and be ashamed to harbor contradictory desires or beliefs. And through unity of mind may come that unity of purpose and character which makes a personality, and lends some order and dignity to our existence.

Will Durant
The Mansions of Philosophy (New York: Simon & Schuster, 1929), p. x.

---

coherent vision. Without philosophizing at least a little bit, we do not live our lives, circumstances live us.

Once wisdom becomes our goal, we are dangerous to a social order that encourages conformity; to an educational system that exists primarily to train specialists; to a church that regards certain questions as blasphemous and heretical; to a society that pays an actor millions of dollars to appear in a film or an athlete millions of dollars to throw a ball a few months a year, yet pays its grade school teachers a comparably negligible amount; to a society that esteems as its highest bastions of learning universities whose most important professors sometimes resent having to do undergraduate teaching, and whose faculties cannot even agree on what the educated person must know.

Philosophy is dangerous whenever it is taken seriously. But so is life. *Safety is not an option.* Our choices, then, are not between risk and security, but between a life lived consciously, fully, humanly in the most complete sense and a life that just happens. In the end, as the poet says, the grave claims each of us. The issue, then, is how to live. No longer just what *can* I do, but what *should* I do? No longer just what is true, but what is *valuable* and *worthwhile*? Because of its fragility and finiteness, life is too important not to wonder about.

The effect of life in society is to complicate our existence, making us forget who we really are by causing us to become obsessed with what we are not.
Chuang-tzu

The recipe for perpetual ignorance is: be satisfied with your opinions and content with your knowledge.
Elbert Hubbard

When you no longer just look but also notice, when you are no longer content to settle for never-questioned beliefs, when you are at last troubled by the inconsistencies among your own beliefs and actions, when the wind of wonder raises the hair on the back of your neck, then the spirit of the ancient wise ones catches fire one more time.

SUMMARY OF MAIN POINTS

The word philosophy comes from Greek roots meaning "the love of wisdom." The difference between expressing philosophical opinions and actually philosophizing involves the degree of rigor and discipline applied to our reflections. Philosophy in the original sense always includes the search for wisdom.

Ultimate ends are valued for their own sake, not as means to something else. Happiness is an example of an ultimate end.

Timely questions are concerned with means to specific ends and involve current issues that are important to a particular time or place.

Timeless questions have been asked in virtually every culture and concern ultimate values, general principles, and the very nature of reality, knowledge, justice, happiness, truth, God, beauty, and morality. Philosophy addresses timeless questions.

Philosophy in the original sense is an activity as well as a fixed body of knowledge. A philosopher is a lover of wisdom, someone who has a compelling need to pursue wisdom.

Bertrand Russell said that philosophy is valuable because its emphasis on questions reveals unsuspected possibilities and because the greatness of the objects it contemplates frees us from narrow, personally limited perspectives.

The primary areas of philosophy are metaphysics (which addresses the problem of what is real), epistemology (the study of knowledge), axiology (the study of values in general), ethics (which is concerned with the good life and moral reasoning), aesthetics (the study of art in all its forms), political philosophy (the study of the state), social philosophy (the study of social institutions and relations), and logic (the study of the rules of correct reasoning).

Philosophical archetypes are philosophers who express an original or influential point of view in a way that significantly affects subsequent philosophers and nonphilosophers. They are powerful representations of fundamental responses to universal experiences of suffering, death, loss, society, wealth, knowledge, love, and purpose.

The history of Western philosophy has been dominated by males of European ancestry, but increasing interest in women and non-European philosophers is expanding the scope and nature of philosophy.

Philosophers distinguish between knowledge (justified true belief), belief (an individual's subjective mental state), and mere belief (a conviction that something is true for which the only evidence is the sincerity of the believer).

Willed ignorance is an attitude of indifference to the possibility of error or enlightenment that holds onto beliefs regardless of the facts.

Wisdom is general knowledge of what does and does not produce human happiness, including the difference between right and wrong, combined with the desire and ability to act in basic accord with that knowledge. Traditionally, wisdom has been associated with maturity (experience) and moral character.

Theoretical knowledge is the accurate compilation and assessment of factual and systematic relationships. Practical knowledge consists of skills needed to do things. Knowledge requires demonstration in the form of arguments, predictions, or performance, depending on the kind of knowledge.

Because wisdom involves insight and the capacity to learn from experience, it differs from educated intelligence. Wisdom is associated with a sense of unity that comes from living. Formal education is chiefly concerned with the transmission of knowledge and social skills. Wisdom goes beyond learning what others have known and applies their insights to life.

The pursuit of wisdom always changes us because serious thinking will inevitably challenge some of our present beliefs. No questions are off-limits to philosophy in the original sense, and this makes philosophical inquiry threatening to those whose allegiance is to their current beliefs. Philosophy is dangerous because it threatens to change our lives.

STUDY QUESTIONS

1. Distinguish between timely and timeless questions. Define each, and give examples.

2. How would you explain what philosophy is to someone who did not know?

3. Identify the primary areas of philosophy and give an example of the kinds of questions covered in each.

4. What does Bertrand Russell mean by "practical men"?

5. What is the value of philosophy, according to Russell?

6. What is an archetype? How does it differ from a stereotype? Give examples of each.

7. What are the advantages of studying philosophical archetypes?

8. Make the case that our culture is suffering from a kind of philosophical illiteracy. Don't be overly general. Cite examples and identify patterns. Why study philosophy?

9. Do you think that there should be "practicing philosophers"? Would they be more like priests or psychologists? Explain. Would you ever consult one? Why or why not?

10. What is wisdom? Explain how it is related to knowledge.

11. What do people mean when they say that philosophy is dangerous? Are they correct? Explain.

12. Do you think a universal hunger for meaning really exists? How good are we at satisfying it? Support your position.

13. Analyze your own education up to this point. In what ways has it hindered and in what ways has it supported your love of wisdom?

14. If you could make only one improvement in the American educational system, what would it be and why?

15. To what extent do you think gender and ethnic background should be considered in evaluating an individual's beliefs? Do gender, ethnic background, and other factors (age, income, and so on) control what we think?

The Sage: Buddha and Lao-tzu

As to the Sage, no one will know whether he existed or not.

LAO-TZU

SHAMAN
A specialist in techniques for making contact with the sacred forces that govern the world by going "outside of" him- or herself; in tribal cultures the shaman usually receives wisdom through a public initiation ceremony that involves "ritualized suffering" and ecstatic trance, though in some cultures the gods come to the shaman.

PROPHET
From the Greek roots *pro* (before) and *phanai* (to speak), originally a prophet was a person who spoke with divine guidance and who was said to be able to predict the course of events; prophets functioned as religious leaders and teachers, as advisers to rulers, and cried out for justice and mercy in the face of tyranny.

SAGE
Derived from the Latin *sapiens*, meaning "wise"; in Asian traditions, an archetypal figure who combines religious inspiration with a love of wisdom; gurus, *yogis*, and Zen *roshis* are examples of sages; in Western traditions, the *sophos* and Hasidic *rebbe* fulfill the role of sage.

he prophet and shaman are the two direct ancestors of the sage, the oldest philosophical archetype. According to anthropologist Mircea Eliade, the **shaman** specializes in techniques for making contact with the sacred forces that govern the world by going "outside of" him- or herself.[1] In most tribal cultures, the shaman receives wisdom through a public initiation ceremony that involves ritualized suffering and ecstatic trance. Depending on the culture, a shaman may fly to heaven, walk on a rainbow, climb a sacred pole symbolizing the *axis mundi* that connects the earth to heaven, soar as a bird, become a fish, and so forth. In Asian cultures especially, the gods come to the shaman. Among Native Americans, the "vision quest" is a regular part of moving from adolescence to adulthood.[2]

Though primarily a healer and link between the living and dead for his or her tribe, the shaman's reports of visionary experiences reaffirm, clarify, and shape the tribe's fundamental beliefs about the nature of the universe and the people's relationship to it. The shaman expresses the sacred wisdom of nonliterate cultures.

The term **prophet** comes from the Greek roots *pro* (before) and *phanai* (to speak). Originally, a prophet was a person who spoke with divine guidance and who was said to be able to predict the course of events. Prophets functioned as religious leaders, teachers, or advisers to rulers, and often cried out for justice and mercy in the face of tyranny.

Shamans and prophets appear in both Western and Eastern cultures. In ancient Egypt, the priest filled the role of shaman-prophet, and in Persia (now Iran), Zoroastrian prophets known as *magi* were highly respected for their wisdom. Prophets such as Elijah, Jeremiah, and Hosea were the conduits of God's will (wisdom) in Old Testament Judaism. Muhammad was known as the *rasul* of early Islam, the prophet of God, the messenger commanded to recite Allah's sacred *Qur'an*. In early Christianity, Jesus fulfilled the role of a prophet communicating the divine will to nonliterate people. In prephilosophical ancient Greece, priests and oracles performed the shamanistic-prophetic role when the Olympian religion dominated Greek culture.[3] The prephilosophical shaman-prophet developed into the wise person known as the *sophos*, the subject of Chapter 3.

In Asian cultures, echoes of the shaman are found in the sage. The **sage** is an archetypal figure who combines religious inspiration with a love of wisdom. The word *sage* is derived from the Latin *sapiens*, meaning "wise." Today, the term sage is often used to refer to masters associated with religious traditions or to the wise elders of a group or tribe. Sages understand and teach the requirements of the good life, when the good life is understood to include peace of mind, compassion, social harmony, and respect for nature.

The sage has no exact equivalent in our society today. Sages perform a complex function: part therapist, part prophet, part philosopher, part friend. They appeal to our hearts and minds in their efforts to dissolve fragmentation and to heal alienation from our true selves, from each other, and from nature.

In northwest Siberia's Khanty-Mansai National District, hunter and shaman Pyotor Yukhlymov unites his village in celebration of the sacred connection of all spirits by performing an ancient shamanic rite honoring a just-killed bear, reverently thought of as the Old Clawed One.

In Hinduism and Buddhism, the Indian sage is usually a *yogi*, chiefly concerned with enlightenment and liberation from illusion, ignorance, greed, lust, and all "attaching" emotions. In East Asia, the sage tended to play a more social role, addressing political and ethical issues.

Religious studies Professors Denise L. Carmody and John T. Carmody suggest that "whereas the nonliterate traditions have tended to pivot on the shaman and the Western traditions have tended to pivot on the prophet, the Asian traditions have tended to pivot on the sage. . . . Buddha, Confucius, and Lao-tzu—the three most influential Asian personalities—have all been more sagacious than prophetic."[4]

Let's take a close look at two kinds of Eastern sage whose influence in contemporary America continues to grow: the Buddhist bodhisattva and the Taoist sage.

THE BUDDHA

So powerful was the person and vision of **Siddhārtha Gautama (c. 560–480 B.C.)** that he was recognized during his

All humanity is sick. I come therefore to you as a physician who has diagnosed this universal disease and is prepared to cure it.
The Buddha

lifetime as an archetype unto himself. Today the archetype of the Buddha is a major source of meaning and purpose for over two billion people. The Buddha was a sage, yet more than a sage. He was fully human, yet more than human. Among his many names, perhaps the most enduring are the Awakened or Enlightened One (the original meaning of "the Buddha" in Sanskrit) and the Compassionate Buddha. Yet for all his influence, we have very little factual information about him; most of what we know comes from oral tradition and myth.[5]

Siddhārtha Gautama was born into wealth and power as the son of a prince (rajah) in what is today Nepal. Siddhārtha was intelligent and alert, a talented student and athlete. Legend says that he was a first-rate hunter and archer, and enjoyed a rich and active life. An only son, Siddhārtha was spoiled and indulged by his family; he became a hedonist and a womanizer. At sixteen he married his cousin, but this does not seem to have slowed his pleasure seeking.

The young prince lived in protected isolation, surrounded by servants who catered to his slightest whim. One version of his life claims that Siddhārtha's parents took great pains to shield him from the ugliness of life, even surrounding him with young, attractive servants to spare him the sight of the ravages of age. His parents protected him from the knowledge of poverty and suffering by seducing him with every imaginable delight—within their palatial grounds. Hunger, sickness, and death were too crude for their precious son. He knew only luxury and pleasure; the outside world remained a mystery to him.

But Siddhārtha was not content. As with many young people, curiosity and rebelliousness led him away from home. During secret trips outside the palace to a nearby city he saw three of the now-famous Four Signs that altered his life forever. He saw a destitute and homeless beggar. He saw a dead man being prepared for cremation by weeping mourners. He saw a diseased and handicapped person. The seeds of the Buddha were planted when Siddhārtha encountered suffering.

Siddhārtha the Seeker

Before his forbidden excursions outside the family compound, Siddhārtha had no real idea of what sickness or old age could do to the body and spirit. He had no sense of the depths that poverty could reach. He was unaware of the power of grief. The price he had paid for living in a cocoon of soft pleasures and blindness to the suffering of others was a feeling of bored disease. Even ignorance failed to protect him, however. Driven by the restless boredom that almost always accompanies an unproductive, self-indulgent life, Siddhārtha felt compelled to stray outside. All the pleasures of his wealthy family could not quell his nagging sense of discomfort. He had to know more.

Indeed, the saving truth has never been preached by the Buddha, seeing that one has to realize it within oneself.
Sutralamkara

Cut out the love of self, like an autumn lotus with your hand! Cherish the road to peace. Nirvana has been shown by the Blessed One.
The Buddha

If a fool is associated with a wise man even all his life, he will perceive the truth as little as a spoon perceives the taste of soup.
The Buddha

The young prince had no one to talk with about his troubling questions but his servant Channa, who was his hired companion and charioteer, his guardian and bodyguard. To every question Siddhārtha raised, Channa could only reply with great sadness and resignation, "Yes, master, there is no escape. Old age, sickness, death—such is the lot of all men."[6]

In today's language, we might say that Siddhārtha "had his eyes opened." His naive unawareness was spoiled forever. No longer were his pleasures as sweet. Try as he might, Siddhārtha could not shake the haunting images of old age, sickness, and death. His anxiety grew. How, he asked himself again and again, could anyone be happy, since—ultimately—there is absolutely no escape from suffering, disappointment, sadness, and loss? If no one escapes, why be born at all? How could any woman want to give birth knowing what awaited her child? None of his family or servants could answer him.

Walking outside the palace grounds one day, deep in despair, he saw a wandering monk, an ascetic. **Ascetics** turn away from pleasure and severely limit all sensual appetites in order to achieve salvation or peace of mind. Asceticism involves long hours of prayer and fasting, living on plain food, wearing simple clothes. Monks in many cultures live ascetic lives. In Western traditions Old Testament prophets were often ascetics. When John the Baptist and Jesus went into the desert and lived on locusts, honey, and water and fasted, they were going through ascetic trials.

When Siddhārtha looked closely into the face of the wandering monk he was astonished to see serenity, purpose, and detachment. Here was the last of the Four Signs. Here, finally, was an answer. Siddhārtha knew that he must leave the security of his home and live as a monk, homeless, with only a simple robe and beggar's bowl. He would go to the wisest sages, no matter how far and difficult the journey. He would find someone to tell him the answers to life's most basic questions: Why live if suffering is inescapable? Is it possible to be happy in the face of inevitable sickness, old age, and death? What is the real meaning of life?

ASCETIC
Individual who turns away from pleasure and severely limits all sensual appetites in order to achieve salvation or peace of mind.

The adult has to break his attachment to persons and things.
Walter Lippmann

The Long Search

For years Siddhārtha wandered with his beggar's bowl, seeking one master or guru after another. Even though many of them were wise and deeply interested in helping Siddhārtha, he did not find his answer. He found only more teachers, and though he learned many clever philosophical notions, as well as techniques for meditating and disciplining the body, he found no satisfying answers to his basic, timeless questions.

Finally tiring of gurus and ordinary sages, he settled in a grove of trees on the outskirts of the village of Uruvela, India. There he formed a little community with a few other seekers. For six years he meditated, fasted, and concentrated daily on his original questions. During this time, he is said to

I once went a day without food and all night without sleep to enable me to think. I found no advantage in it; it's best to study.
Confucius

have conquered most physical appetites and weaknesses and learned how to control "the mad monkey of the mind."[7] But still he found no answers.

In his efforts to subdue his body, he nearly destroyed it. He is supposed to have said, "When I touched my stomach I felt my backbone." His extreme asceticism left him a wasted shell. In Buddhist art portraying him during this period, every bone and muscle pushes through his skin. Ultimately, Siddhārtha realized that his body was an important instrument in his search, and he realized that he must honor the spirit by honoring the body that houses it. This lesson was clear: The Way cannot be found by either indulgence or denial. We must walk a Middle Path.

Siddhārtha's fellow monks were disgusted when he began to take proper nourishment. They had been impressed with his ascetic ways as signs of strength and willpower. From this Siddhārtha learned another lesson: We must stop worrying about what others think of us and quit trying to impress people if we are ever to find wisdom. He realized that ascetic self-denial can be of value as a temporary corrective for indulgences or as a momentary cleansing, but it is not an adequate way of life. To subdue the appetites in order to show strength and willpower is a way of showing off, which prevents one from growing wise.

So Siddhārtha returned to his lonely wandering. One day when he was thirty, as he sat in meditation under a fig tree, he was given a special bowl of rice milk by a young woman because he reminded her of a figure she had seen in a vision. In her vision, she had presented rice milk in a golden bowl to a single figure seated under a tree. She took this figure to be a god because of a special glow she saw around him. He was, of course, the Buddha.

Siddhārtha accepted the rice milk and, according to one legend, did not eat again for forty-nine days. Another legend says that he divided the milk into numerous portions, and these sustained him during his deepening meditation. After Siddhārtha had finished the rice milk, he threw the golden bowl into a nearby river, where it miraculously floated *upstream*. (This symbolizes the fact that the Buddha's teachings go against the currents of our ordinary, unenlightened thinking.) Siddhārtha then ceremoniously bathed in the river, and, taking the lotus position, once more sat under the fig tree and said: "Here I shall remain until I am answered or dead." The tree under which the Buddha sat became known as the Bodhi Tree—the Tree of Wisdom.

Finally, the awakening came. What Buddhist tradition refers to as the "greatest event in human history" occurred during the full moon of May, c. 524 B.C. Refusing to be swayed from his goal, heeding some inner call despite all costs, Siddhārtha Gautama had transformed himself from a spoiled, pampered young man into "the one who had awakened": the Buddha.

The Enlightened Vision

According to Buddhist teachings, it is impossible to "explain" the awakening. Nonetheless, we can get a rough idea of what the Buddha "saw."

What ought to be done is neglected, what ought not to be done is done; the desires of unruly, thoughtless people are always increasing.
The Buddha

Though my skin, my nerves, and my bones should waste away and my lifeblood dry, I will not leave this seat until I have attained Supreme Enlightenment.
The Buddha

Siddhārtha saw himself and *all life* as part of an unending process of change, a great chain of being through which things come into and leave one form of existence for another. Everything is one. The whole universe is a system of interconnected, inseparable parts, rich and complex, composed of all varieties of life forever moving from one form to another.

The Buddha did not arrive at this perception intellectually. He *saw* it all at once, in what we in the West might call a mystical vision. The now-Buddha realized instantly how difficult it would be to teach a doctrine that could not be grasped by mere reasoning and that could not be realized by blind faith, but only by unswerving personal effort. Only by the greatest effort could an individual achieve release from suffering. The price of wisdom is love of the whole rather than love of any one part—including, especially, ourselves.[8]

The intellect can understand any part of a thing as a part, but not as a whole.
R. H. Blyth

The Bodhisattva

Siddhārtha had reached a state of bliss and utter detachment called nirvana. **Nirvana** is annihilation of the ego, a state of emptiness or "no-thing-ness." It is described as a state of bliss because there is only "pure consciousness" with no sense of individuality, separateness, discrimination, or intellectualizing. It cannot be explained in words, since words are limiting and exist to identify similarities and differences. Nirvana is beyond even similarity. It can only be talked around or expressed in contradictions. It transcends all ordinary experience. Nirvana is release from suffering while conscious. (If you do not "understand" what nirvana is, don't feel inadequate. Nirvana can be experienced; it cannot be described or understood.) The experience of nirvana transforms us because it shifts our attention from timely concerns to timeless issues.

Siddhārtha now had to make another important choice: He could stay in nirvana, meditating and remaining uninvolved with the commotion and suffering of life. Or he could share his vision. Legend says that "the very earth trembled" while waiting for his decision. At last, the "Great Buddha Heart of Infinite Compassion prevailed."[9] Siddhārtha refused ultimate release and, because he chose to stay and help others, became the Buddha, "He Who Awoke," or "He Who Became Aware." This helpful part of him is sometimes referred to as "The Walking Buddha," the man who wandered about once more, only now as a teacher rather than as a seeker.

This Buddha who chose to remain among people giving help to other lost souls is known as the Bodhisattva in some branches of Buddhism. A **bodhisattva** is an enlightened being who voluntarily postpones his own nirvana in order to help all other conscious life-forms find "supreme release." A bodhisattva is *not* a savior. The Buddha did not intercede for others; he showed them a path. A bodhisattva is a wise and compassionate being who has gone beyond discrimination: there is no more "I," "mine," "yours." He no longer perceives separateness on any level. The bodhisattva

NIRVANA
Annihilation of the ego; a state of emptiness or "no-thing-ness"; "pure consciousness" that leads to release from suffering while remaining conscious.

BODHISATTVA
An enlightened being who voluntarily postpones his own nirvana in order to help all other conscious life-forms find "supreme release"; not a savior.

no longer even perceives *a* self, *a* being, *a* person. His consciousness is forever altered. Siddhārtha, the Buddha, the great bodhisattva, was at last ready to teach personal transformation through compassion.

Do you know where to stop? Can you let unimportant things go? Can you learn not to depend on others but to seek it in yourself?
Chuang-tzu

PHILOSOPHICAL QUERY

Compare the Buddha's decision to become a bodhisattva with Plato's characterization of the enlightened figure who escapes from the Cave and then returns to help others ascend to the Realm of the Good in Chapter 6.

It did not take long for the Buddha to acquire many followers. As with other great sages, who the Buddha was became as significant as what he taught. In addition to his wife and son, Siddhārtha's disappointed ascetic companions became disciples of the Buddha. In order to "beat the drum of [truth] in the darkness of the world" and share his message with everyone, the Buddha sent groups of his earliest disciples out as teachers. The Buddha did not seek converts, and his monks were not missionaries. Their goal was to spread information that people could use to reduce suffering.

The Death of the Buddha

A man who talks much of his teaching but does not practice it himself is like a cattleman counting another man's cattle. . . . Like beautiful flowers full of color, but without scent, are the well-chosen words of the man who does not act accordingly.
The Buddha

Legend teaches that the Buddha died from either poisonous mushrooms or tainted pork. His last meal was at the humble home of a blacksmith (significantly, a person of low status in ancient Asian culture). Soon after eating, the Buddha took sick. He asked his host to bury the rest of the food so that no one else would eat it. Calling upon the discipline learned through years of meditation, he was able to control his pain well enough to travel to a certain river. He bathed in the river and then lay down in a mango grove "on his right side in the attitude of a lion with one foot on the other."[10]

As he lay dying, the Buddha made a special point to tell his closest disciple, Ananda, that the blacksmith was not to blame. The Buddha also sent special word to the blacksmith thanking him for his "alms." By this the Buddha meant that the blacksmith was blessed for having been the vehicle by which the Buddha would escape "the wheel of suffering" and attain nirvana. After sending this message, the Buddha crossed the river and resumed the lion's pose in a different grove.

The Buddha said, "Do not weep, do not mourn, oh ye monks." Like Socrates speaking to his disciples while the hemlock was being prepared (see Chapter 5), before his death the Buddha reassured his followers that change—including death and decay—is universal, natural, and inescapable.

> As a mother, even at the risk of her own life, protects and
> loves her child, her only child, so let a man cultivate love
> without measure toward the whole world, above, below, and
> around, unstinted, unmixed with any feeling of differing or

Surrounded on his deathbed, as in life, by sadness, wailing, and torment, Buddha remained serene, detached, and accepting.

opposing interests. Let a man remain steadfastly in this state of mind, walking, sitting or lying down. This state of mind is the best in the world.[11]

WHAT THE BUDDHA TAUGHT

The Buddha's basic teachings rest on what are called the **Four Noble Truths**:

1. No one can deny that suffering is the condition of all existence.

2. Suffering and general dissatisfaction come to human beings because they are possessive, greedy, and, above all, self-centered.

3. Egocentrism, possessiveness, and greed can, however, be understood, overcome, rooted out.

4. This rooting out, this vanquishing, can be brought about by following a simple, reasonable Eightfold Path of behavior in thought, word, and deed. Change of viewpoint will manifest itself in a new outlook and new patterns of behavior.[12]

FOUR NOBLE TRUTHS
Foundation of Buddha's teachings: (1) to exist is to suffer; (2) self-centeredness is the chief cause of human suffering; (3) the cause of suffering can be understood and rooted out; (4) suffering can be alleviated by following the Eightfold Path.

The Buddha taught that we suffer because we are partial to ourselves. For example, I cannot be bored listening to you complain about your philosophy class for the umpteenth time unless I am judging you or wishing you were talking about something interesting to *me*. It's the *me* that gets bored. I cannot be envious of the attention my parents give my brother without being greedy for more attention for *me*. If I were not greedy for *my* share, I would be delighted by his delight. The more self-conscious I am, the more selfish ego I have to place at the center of things.

Spiritual philosophies like Buddhism, Hinduism, and Sufism use the term *ego* differently from psychologists, to mean self-centered, immature, and selfish tendencies. A person with too much ego thinks of himself or herself as unique and special in ways that emphasize differences. The loss or annihilation of this false ego results in the emergence of the soul or true self. The awakened or reborn soul/self sees similarities rather than differences, acts from love rather than fear, helps rather than judges. The bliss of nirvana comes from the annihilation of the self-consciousness, judgmentalism, greed, and fear that characterize ego.

The Buddha taught that the way to transcend the ego and see the interconnected whole of life is through *loving-kindness*. At the moment we feel love for others we cannot be bored or hostile with them. In moments of love, we take joy in a three-year-old's scribbles or Grandpa's poems. We listen to sister's problems with concern; we cannot be hostile or bored or defensive at the same time we feel compassion for her. As the Buddha promised, a change of viewpoint results in a new outlook and new patterns of behavior. But it is difficult to maintain our compassion even with those we already love. How can we alter our viewpoint to love every living thing? The Buddha says with the Eightfold Path.

Your self-partiality is the root of all your illusions. There aren't any illusions when you don't have this preference for yourself.
Bankei

PHILOSOPHICAL QUERY

Think back to circumstances in which you were bored or hostile. Did ego play a role in your discomfort? Do you believe that all suffering comes from self-partiality? Discuss.

THE EIGHTFOLD PATH

First, let's look at the **Eightfold Path** as the Buddha characterized it:

EIGHTFOLD PATH
Buddha's prescription for rooting out suffering: (1) right understanding; (2) right purpose; (3) right speech; (4) right conduct; (5) right livelihood; (6) right effort; (7) right mindfulness; (8) right meditation.

1. Right understanding (or views).

2. Right purpose.

3. Right speech.

4. Right conduct.

5. Right livelihood.

6. Right effort.

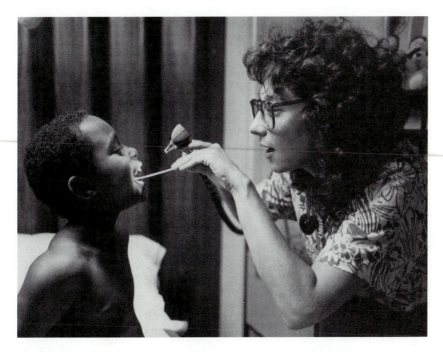

The first step in Buddha's Eightfold Path echoes the teachings of other great sages and prophets: "First you must see clearly what is wrong." Buddha, like Jesus and Socrates, used the rhetoric of sickness and healing to underscore both the diagnostic and therapeutic power of wisdom. Sages are "physicians of the soul."

7. Right mindfulness (or awareness).

8. Right meditation.[13]

Now let's look at a modified version. Gerald Heard, an Anglo-Irish historian and philosopher, phrased the Eightfold Path in an especially contemporary and insightful form:

1. First you must see clearly what is wrong.

2. Next you must decide that you want to be cured.

3. You must act and

4. speak so as to aim at being cured.

5. Your livelihood must not conflict with your therapy.

6. That therapy must go forward at the "staying speed," that is, the critical velocity that can be sustained.

7. You must think about it incessantly and

8. learn how to contemplate with the *deep mind*.[14]

These teachings are simple truth, and their power is that they can be applied immediately to our everyday life and the world we live in.
Jösel Tendzin

It is probably quite an understatement to note that the wisdom expressed in the Eightfold Path sounds so obvious, almost trivially simple. But simple is not always easy, and we often overlook the obvious. Consider: In many schools of psychology, the most important therapeutic event is the moment of insight in which the client *sees for the first time* some important factor in his or her unhappiness. Something similar occurs in many religions, either at the moment of "rebirth" or during periods of atonement: The fallen soul *sees by the grace of God* his or her fallen nature and the way of salvation.

One of the most effective treatment programs for alcoholism is Alcoholics Anonymous (AA), which is based on a list of guidelines for living called the Twelve Steps. The very first step begins, "We admitted we were powerless over alcohol and that our lives were unmanageable." The key to the first step is to *see* fully *our own* actual condition, whatever it involves. This, of course, is the first step on the Eightfold Path.

As you reflect on the rest of the Eightfold Path, keep in mind that it was presented as a guideline for a way of life. Following this deceptively simple program takes years of dedication. It helps to remind ourselves that the Eightfold Path is designed to change *us* by changing our way of seeing things (consciousness), our behavior, and our emotions. It is designed to subdue our egocentric sense of identity, replacing the self-centered *me* with a compassionate heart. If I can change the way I view things, I have in effect changed the world.

The difficulty of the Eightfold Path is underscored by one poignant version of the Buddha's deathbed statement to his monks which ends, "Perhaps someone, somewhere will not misunderstand me." Buddha said:

> By one's self evil is done, by one's self one is purified. The pure and the impure stand and fall by themselves. No one can purify another. . . . Work with diligence. Be lamps unto yourselves. Betake yourselves to no external refuge. Look not for refuge to anyone beside yourself. Hold fast to the Truth as to a lamp.[15]

PHILOSOPHICAL QUERY

Discuss some of the difficulties you might encounter by trying to follow the Eightfold Path. What, for example, might consist of "wrong livelihoods"? Are there some jobs that no truly wise and healthy person could perform? What determines whether an occupation is right? Explain.

THE BUDDHA'S LEGACY

Contemporary Buddhists sometimes refer to the Buddha's teachings as "scientific." Their purpose might be compared to a physical trainer who imparts knowledge of training techniques and nutrition based on firsthand experience with what works. You need not "believe in" the benefits of aerobic training; you need only to work out reg-

It should not be thought that the eight categories or divisions of the Path should be followed and practised one after the other in the numerical order given in the usual list . . . But they are to be developed more or less simultaneously, as far as possible according to the capacity of each individual. They are all linked together and each helps the cultivation of the others.

Wapola Rahula

ONE DAY . . .

Some of the richest Buddhist literature consists of stories, which reveal the process of enlightenment indirectly. Though highly refined, these gemlike little tales leave the heart of the story unspoken. Thus they function like spiritual inkblots, drawing new insights from each listener's response. Here's a sampler of four.

One day a potential suicide was talking to a Buddhist monk, asking whether he had the right to commit suicide if he wanted to. The monk replied, "Anyone has the right to do anything. Everyone else has the right to resist it."

The student said, "Do you see suicide as a moral act?"

The monk answered, "Where there is no victim, every act is morally right, but I personally think suicide is a symptom of taking oneself too seriously."

One day the Buddhist monk Joshu fell down in the snow. He began wailing and crying for help. Seeing his distress, another monk lay down beside him and began thrashing about, crying and wailing as well. Joshu got up and left.

One day Chinso was up in a tower with some important people, and one of them saw a group of monks approaching. "Look," he said, "holy men." "No they aren't," Chinso said, "and I'll prove it." When the monks were directly below, Chinso leaned out of the tower window and yelled, "Hey! Holy men!" When they all looked up in response to his call, he said to his companions, "See?"

One day a rich man asked Sengai to write something ensuring the continued prosperity of his family. Sengai wrote: "Father dies, son dies, grandson dies." This angered the rich man, who said, "I asked you to write something for the happiness of my family! Why do you make such a joke as this?" "This is no joke," Sengai explained. "If your son dies before you do, you would grieve greatly. If your grandson dies before your son, both of you would be brokenhearted. If your family, generation after generation, passes away in the order I have named, it will be the natural course of life. I call this real prosperity."

The first story is from Camden Benares, *Zen without Zen Masters* (Berkeley: And/Or Press, 1977), p. 37. The next three are paraphrased from Paul Reps, *Zen Flesh, Zen Bones: A Collection of Zen and Pre-Zen Writings* (Garden City, N.Y.: Anchor Books, 1973), p. 67.

ularly and wisely. The Buddha's early disciples were taught to repeat a simple formula:

> I take my refuge in the Buddha.
> I take my refuge in the *Dharma* [the teachings].
> I take my refuge in the *Sangha* [the community of believers].[16]

This three-part formula is still repeated daily by millions of Buddhists.

" IN TODAY'S VIOLENT WORLD,
FIGURING OUT THE SOUND
OF ONE HAND CLAPPING
SEEMS BESIDE THE POINT —
WHAT, O WISE ONE, IS YOUR
THOUGHT ON THE MATTER? "

© 1986, reprinted by permission of Richard Stine

We are all chained to Fortune. Some chains are golden and loose, some tight and of base metal; but what difference does it make? All of us are in custody, the binders as well as the bound—unless you suppose the left of the chain is lighter. Some of us are chained by office, some by wealth; some are weighed down by high birth, some by low; some are subject to another's tyranny, some to their own; some are confined to one spot by banishment, some by a priesthood. All life is bondage.

Seneca

The Buddha stands between the traditional Western models of a philosopher and a saint or prophet. Saints and prophets of the Judeo-Christian-Muslim religious traditions differ from the Buddha's conception of the sage in important ways. The most significant is in their relationship to "the one, true God," the Creator who is distinct from his creatures. For the Buddha, "all is one," and there is no equivalent to the God of the Bible.

For the Buddha, only those who actively work to achieve awareness deserve the title "sage"—and then only if they act on and live by what they have discovered to be true *for themselves*. No teachings, no scriptures, no theories take the place of experience. When we see clearly, we do not need teachers, scriptures, or theories. When we do not see clearly, nothing else matters.

Like all sages, the Buddha was a perceptive psychological observer. He realized that even though we all must actively work for our own enlightenment, most of us benefit from the support and guidance of regular, intimate association with others working toward a common goal.[17] What he envisioned was the free association of seekers on all levels of the path. What occurred was something else.

The Buddha himself never prescribed certain dress, such as shaved heads and saffron (yellow/orange) robes.

If the mere wearing of a robe could banish greed, malice and other weaknesses, then as soon as a child was born his friends

and kinfolk would make him wear the robe and would press
him to wear it saying, "Come thou favored of fortune! Come
wear the robe; for by the mere wearing of it the greedy will
put from them their greed, the malicious their malice, and
so on!"[18]

He did not think it mattered where one lived, what one ate, and so on. Any
serious seeker following the Eightfold Path would avoid extremes and remain in the *Middle Way*. Awareness, compassion, and helpfulness were more
important than the particular clothes we wear or food we eat or place we
live: "Let those who wish to dwell in the forest, dwell in the forest, and let
those who wish to live in the village, live in the village."[19]

   Ironically, but probably unavoidably, in the centuries since the Buddha
lived, his basic message has been transformed into "schools of Buddhism,"
as if there could be "schools of truth."

   As happened among the followers of Socrates, Moses, Jesus, and
Muhammad, sects and divisions arose. "Experts" in theory and ritual
emerged, quarreling and competing for the title of true successor. The two
main branches of Buddhism are Theravada, the Way of the Elders, and Mahayana, after its founder Mahayana, "The Greater Vehicle of Salvation."
Other Buddhist sects such as Tibetan Buddhism and Japanese Zen Buddhism are usually seen as branches of the many-sided Mahayana branch.

   The quarrels among Buddhists are less hostile and more tolerant than
those among other philosophies and religions. The power of the Buddha's
original vision is perhaps nowhere more clearly felt than in this restraint.
Buddhists of one school tend to accept Buddhists of another, for in all cases,
"the individual disciple is seen as directly, personally involved in his own
salvation, a point of view which allows exceptional latitude in matters of instruction and practice."[20]

WHAT THE BUDDHA
DID NOT EXPLAIN

No amount of interpretation or study can explain awakening or enlightenment. The Buddha said:

We merely talk about "studying the Way" using the phrase
simply as a term to arouse people's interest. In fact, the Way
cannot be studied. If concepts based on [factual] study are retained, they only result in the Way being misunderstood. . . .

   If you will at all times, whether walking, standing, sitting,
or lying, only concentrate on eliminating analytic thinking, at
long last you will inevitably discover the truth.[21]

*Whether you believe in God
or not does not matter so
much, whether you believe in
Buddha or not does not matter so much; as a Buddhist,
whether you believe in reincarnation or not does not
matter so much. You must
lead a good life.*
The Dalai Lama

*The follower of the law, even
if he can recite only a small
portion of it but, having for-
saken passion and hatred
and foolishness, possesses
true knowledge and serenity
of mind; he is attached to
nothing in this world or that
to come, has indeed a share
in the religious life.*
The Buddha

*Would a sick person
be helped
Merely by reading a
medical text?*
Shantiveda

Even if we cannot *study* the Way, we can sense some of the power of the Buddha's transforming experience by considering one of his most famous and intriguing sermons, called "On Questions Not Tending Toward Edification." Another title might be, "What You Don't Need to Know to Live Wisely and Compassionately." This sermon touches on one of the most difficult things for most of us to accept: We need to find a way of living a meaningful life in the absence of absolute answers.

Western philosophers and theologians seem to find it especially difficult to accept the Buddha's refusal to present a theology or system of metaphysics. The Buddha was a pragmatic and insightful spiritual teacher who believed that questions of theology and complex philosophy only confuse and distract us from our search for wisdom. This underscores the irony in the existence of "schools" of Buddhism. The Buddha believed that we are better served by dealing with the here and now in helpful, honest ways than in fretting and quibbling over unanswerable metaphysical claims and theological doctrines. The insistence on absolute, ultimate explanations, answers, and proofs gets in the way of living fully in the moment. Here's a brief excerpt from one of the richest passages in Buddhist literature:

It is as if . . . a man had been wounded by an arrow thickly smeared with poison, and his friends and companions, his relatives and kinsfolk, were to procure for him a physician or surgeon; and the sick man were to say, "I will not have this arrow taken out until I have learnt . . . the name of the man who wounded me or whether the man who wounded me was . . . tall, or short, or of the middle height . . . whether the man who wounded me was black, or dusky, or of a yellow skin . . . whether the man who wounded me was from this or that village, or town, or city. . . .

That man would die without ever having learnt this. . . .

In exactly the same way . . . anyone who should say, "I will not lead the religious life under the Blessed One until the Blessed One shall explain to me that the world is eternal or that the world is not eternal . . . or that the saint either exists or does not exist after death";—that person would die . . . before [it was] ever explained to him.

The religious life . . . does not depend on the dogma. . . .

Accordingly, . . . bear always in mind what it is that I have not explained. . . .

And what . . . have I explained? Misery . . . have I explained; the origin of misery have I explained; the cessation of misery have I explained. And why . . . have I explained this? Because . . . this does profit, has to do with the fundamentals of religion, and tends to . . . [tranquillity], knowledge, supreme wisdom, and Nirvana; therefore, I have explained it.[22]

THE OLD BOY AND THE WORLD

The people of the world are merry-making,
As if partaking of the sacrificial feasts,
As if mounting the terrace in spring;
I alone am mild, like one unemployed,
Like a new-born babe that cannot yet smile,
Unattached, like one without a home.

The people of the world have enough
  and to spare,
But I am like one left out,
My heart must be that of a fool,
Being muddled and nebulous!

The vulgar are knowing, luminous;
I alone am dull, confused.

The vulgar are clever, self-assured;
I alone, depressed.
Patient as the sea,
Adrift, seemingly aimless.

The people of the world all have a purpose;
I alone appear stubborn and uncouth.
I alone differ from other people,
And value drawing sustenance from the
  Mother.

Lao-tzu
The Wisdom of Laotse, trans. and ed. Lin
Yutang (New York: Modern Library, 1976),
pp. 128–29.

THE SAGE: LAO-TZU

Legend says that **Lao-tzu (c. 575 B.C.)** was a bureaucrat in ancient China, known only by his nickname, Lao-tzu, variously translated as the Old Master, the Old Man, the Old Boy, or the Old Philosopher. According to legend, when Lao-tzu was 160 years old he grew so disgusted with the hypocrisy and decay of his time that he decided to resign from his bureaucratic position in order to pursue virtue in a more natural environment. Heading west, he reached the Han-ku Pass, where the keeper of the pass recognized the old sage, saying, "You are about to withdraw yourself from sight. I pray you compose a book for me." Lao-tzu honored the keeper's request by producing a little (5,000-word) book known today as the *Tao Te Ching*.[23]

Next to the *Analects* of Confucius, the *Tao Te Ching* is the most influential book in Chinese history. Nearly a thousand commentaries on it have been written in China and Japan. The *Tao Te Ching*, or *The Classic of the Way and the Power*, is second only to the Bible in the number of translations available in English. Today, interpretations of Taoism are continuously emerging in popular philosophical and psychological literature.

What accounts for the power of this slim volume, usually divided into eighty-one "chapters" of a page or less in length? Some scholars claim that the *Tao Te Ching* is so cloudy and obscure, so romantic and "poetic," that the reader is free to make it mean anything. In other words, the popularity of the *Tao Te Ching* derives from its lack of clarity, its ability to mean all things to all people. Part of its popularity also may be attributable to its brevity.

Lao-tzu

If thou knewest all the Bible without book and the sayings of all the philosophers, what should it avail thee without charity and grace?
Thomas à Kempis

A more intriguing possibility is that the book credited to Lao-tzu, the modest, self-effacing bureaucrat of ancient China, expresses genuine, timeless wisdom. Let's see what the Old Boy has to say to us as we face the twenty-first century.

THE WAY

Literally, **Tao** means "way" or "path" in the sense of "the way to go." Rather than present a *philosophic system*, Lao-tzu struggled to express a *sense of* the ultimate, underlying great principle, rule, or cause of "the way all things are." His vision is holistic: it encompasses the totality of the cosmos. When viewed holistically, the Old Boy suggests, the universe expresses harmony, purpose, order, majesty, and "calm power." Error, suffering, and unhappiness accompany all attempts to separate things, to understand the part without the whole.

Yin-Yang

The whole of nature consists of the continual interaction of two opposing forces: **yin** (passive element) and **yang** (active element). Yin is weak, negative, dark, and destructive; yang is strong, positive, light, and constructive. These two concepts go so far back in Chinese history that we cannot be sure of their original meanings. By Lao-tzu's time, yin and yang were thought of together: each is an expression of the other. Yin and yang operate together in a never-ending cycle of coming together and falling apart, birth and death, wet and dry, day and night, good and evil, male and female, full and empty. Their ceaseless interplay is manifest in the natural order of things. Parts and whole cannot be understood—cannot even exist—without the other.

Things cannot be understood alone, as fragments. Everything is part of a seamless cycle; a wise person recognizes this and realizes that not only is nothing permanent, conditions call up opposite conditions. The bad produces the good (and the good is but the other side of the bad). Thus a wise person is patient, knowing that today's unfortunate circumstance will change into something good. Thus a wise person is appreciative, knowing that today's blessing is only on loan.

Who knows why Heaven dislikes what it dislikes? Even the sage considers it a difficult question.
Lao-tzu

The Flow of Being

Given his holistic, cyclic vision, Lao-tzu does not concern himself with rational consistency or systematic thoroughness. Ever-flowing being cannot be captured in systems or even in words. In Chapter 6 we will see the diffi-

Yin and yang are distinguishable yet inseparable.

culty Plato faced in expressing his *hierarchy* of being, which culminated in eternal archetypes or forms. By being even that specific, Plato generated a series of logical problems: Are there forms of forms? Forms of forms of forms?

Rather than make distinctions of the sort Plato was to make with his forms, Lao-tzu simply refers to *the Way* in poetic, suggestive terms. He appeals to our "natural instincts" and intuitions. In so doing, he hopes to render as little injustice as possible to the throbbing, rich, ever-flowing stream of being. The Tao is, he *senses*, too rich, too big *and* too small, simply "too much" to be trapped in any definition, description, or system. Thus the sage often speaks in apparent contradictions, in pairs of opposites. He points out "the rest of the story" by calling our attention to overlooked, but essential, aspects of the Way.

How can one person, even a very wise one, express the whole? The Old Boy says by a kind of holy stammering. Consider the subtle differences among the following three versions of the famous opening lines of Chapter 1 of the *Tao Te Ching*:

> The Tao that can be told of
> Is not the absolute Tao;
> The Names that can be given
> Are not the Absolute Names.

The commotion of our human life, which lets in everything, all the light and all the music, all the mad pranks of thought and all the variations of pain, the fullness of memory and the fullness of expectation, is closed only to one thing: unity.
Martin Buber

The Logos is eternal but men have not heard it and men have heard it and not understood.
Heraclitus

The Nameless is the origin of Heaven and Earth;
The Named is the Mother of All Things.[24]

or

God is day night winter sum-
mer war peace enough too
little, but disguised in each
and known in each by a sep-
arate flavor.
Heraclitus

The tao that can be told
is not the eternal Tao.
The name that can be named
is not the eternal Name.
The unnameable is the eternally real.
Naming is the origin
of all particular things.[25]

or

As for the Way, the Way that can be spoken of is not the con-
stant Way;
As for names, the name that can be named is not the constant
name.
The nameless is the beginning of the ten thousand things;
The named is the mother of the ten thousand things.[26]

Each version *approximates* a "sense of something," circles but cannot explicitly define the Tao. In Lao-tzu's phrase, words cannot "trap" the Tao. A sage
must "speak without speaking" and "discuss what cannot be discussed."
That is, a sage must attempt to communicate *the experience of a cosmic or spiritual pattern.* This is quite different from expressing a *concept, idea, or principle.*

Although the Tao, the Whole, the One cannot be reduced to words or
principles, something important and useful can still be said. Lao-tzu
poignantly remarks that although we cannot talk about the Tao, "people
cannot cease discussing It." The only way to glimpse this point is indirectly.

The greatest eloquence seems
to stutter.
Lao-tzu

All experience defies complete verbalization; no matter what we say
about life, *life itself* is always *something more.* Thus all attempts to define or
explain "the meaning of life" fail. Yet the attempts themselves, the very failures themselves, are part of the Tao, part of the One, part of life. Further,
words, though ultimately inadequate, are among our most important channels of communication and learning. The difficult task of a sage is to know
when to stop talking.

He who knows does not speak.
He who speaks does not
know.
Close the mouth.
Lao-tzu

When we consider all the philosophical, religious, and scientific talk
about life, virtue, ultimate meaning, Lao-tzu's puzzling opening lines attain
the power of profound insight: Talk in the form of systems, dogmas, theories, and the like pales beside the richness of life itself. Talk can help, but it
can also hurt. Talk helps when it points us to the Tao, when it awakens us
to something more, something beyond ordinary understanding; talk hurts
when labels substitute for perception, when abstract ideas and rigid, exclusive notions of good *or* bad, right *or* wrong, true *or* false block feeling and
intuition.

The Mystery Which Is Darker Than Any Mystery

With his announcement that the Tao "cannot be told of," Lao-tzu indirectly informs us that he is a mystic. **Mysticism** is a term derived from the Greek root *mystes*, meaning "initiate of the secret mysteries of life and the higher realities."

In broad terms, mystics believe that ordinary levels of understanding and ordinary language cannot grasp the "ultimate something." This "ultimate something" has been referred to as the One, the Logos, Nature, God, the Tao, the Way, the Great Spirit, Reality, Truth, the Good, and so forth. Mystics claim that special insights—mystical experiences—are necessary to get beyond the world of differences, individuality, particulars, and limits. Mystics believe that analytic rationality and synthetic system building distort reality by fragmenting it into disjointed "facts" and "truths," which obscure awareness of the flow and meaning of the whole.

Such claims present difficulties for nonmystical philosophers. How can we evaluate a "philosophy" that does not attempt to be systematic, rational, even organized in any ordinary sense? Indeed, what are we to make of a philosophy that insists that systems, logical reasoning, and linguistic precision—usually thought of as the basic tools of philosophy—are not only inadequate, but may actually obscure the truth? It is not surprising that some philosophers reject mysticism as meaningless babble. Even mystics themselves warn that it can be difficult to distinguish mystical insight from delusion and false mystics from the truly enlightened.

And certainly, a case can be made that the more fixed, less paradoxical, less contradictory systems of philosophy and science pay a price for their systematic knowledge: They seem, somehow, always to miss something. No matter how profound, how careful, how tightly reasoned, traditional philosophies and logically oriented *systems* seem somehow fundamentally inadequate.

We must, Lao-tzu suggests, sometimes violate our rules and systems if we wish to be decent human beings *responsive* to the ebb and flow of life teeming around us. Life is not a problem to be solved; it cannot be contained in any "system." We must do more than understand; more than provide rules; more than explain with tightly reasoned precision: we must respond and resonate to the "ultimate something" that throbs with life just beyond the edge of understanding.

This is what it means to say "The Old Sage preaches the doctrine without words." Lao-tzu *reminds us* of the Tao, but cannot tell us what it is. If we are fortunate and can quiet the chatter of reason, we might "hear what is not said"; we might respond with our whole being rather than remain confined to the limits of reason:

> We look at it and do not see it;
>   Its name is The Invisible.
> We listen to it and do not hear it;
>   Its name is The Inaudible.

MYSTICISM
From the Greek root *mystes*, meaning "initiate of the secret mysteries of life and the higher realities," belief that ordinary levels of understanding and ordinary language cannot grasp the "ultimate something" variously referred to as the One, Logos, Nature, God, Tao, the Way, the Great Spirit, and so forth.

To live is to die, to be awake is to sleep, to be young is to be old, for the one flows into the other, and the process is capable of being reversed.
Heraclitus

Great Man is always at ease; Petty Man is always on edge.
Confucius

We touch it and do not find it;
  Its name is The Subtle (formless).
These three cannot be further inquired into,
And hence merge into one.
Going up high, it is not bright, and coming down low, it is not dark.
Infinite and boundless, it cannot be given any name;
It reverts to nothingness. . . .
It is The Vague and Elusive.[27]

THE UNION OF
RELATIVE OPPOSITES

Taoism teaches that if there is one ultimate reality, one way things really are, then neat distinctions are in some sense arbitrary and misleading. Nothing is purely matter or spirit (energy). Nothing is completely male or female, wet or dry. As the *sophos* Heraclitus said, "All things are becoming." (See Chapter 3.)

The good and the bad both exist in an everlasting exchange. For instance, rain is good in a time of drought, bad in a time of flood. Great size is good on the football field; great size is bad when trying to squeeze out of a tiny window during a fire. The good and the bad are relative opposites. As the Stoics (see Chapter 9) and the Buddha saw, things become good or bad according to our reactions.

Yet even in this flux, we can glimpse the great Tao, the Way. The Way can be studied in nature and through calm contemplation. Chaos and disorder are only apparent. They are interpretations and judgments made from too small a perspective. Things seem out of control when we look at isolated particulars instead of looking for patterns. The wise person is the person who recognizes himself or herself as a child of the Tao and embraces the opposites—the yin and the yang.

So it is that Lao-tzu advises getting beyond judgments of good and bad, since good requires the bad for its very existence.

When you find something that is bad or that turns out bad, drop it and leave it alone.
Sitting Bull

Great Man, being universal in his outlook, is impartial; Petty Man, being partial, is not universal in outlook.
Confucius

When the people of the world all know beauty as beauty
  There arises the recognition of ugliness.
When they all know the good as good,
  There arises the recognition of evil.
Therefore:
  Being and non-being produce each other;
  Difficult and easy complete each other;
  Long and short contrast each other;
  High and low distinguish each other;
  Sound and voice harmonize with each other;
  Front and back follow each other.[28]

**The Buddhist priest Chüjan's paint-
ing** *Seeking the Tao in the Autumn
Mountains* **(c. 940–1000) reflects his
vision of Tao as the fundamental natural harmony of all things.**

Mystery (yin) and clarity (yang), or mysticism and rationalism, complete
each other in such a view. The sage speaks to the soul and the philosopher
speaks to reason. The tension between philosophy and mysticism may result from a fundamental tension between our head and heart. Religions
sometimes describe this tension as the soul's struggle with the world. We
experience it in the dilemma of free will as William James (Chapter 17) expressed it: From science we learn that we are determined (yin); from our
own experience, we feel that we are free (yang). Rather than force us to
choose, however, Lao-tzu acknowledges the fundamental union between
pairs of related opposites. This insight leads to some of the most intriguing
aspects of Taoism.

*Great knowledge is leisurely
and at ease (or all-embracing
and extensive), whereas
small knowledge is inquisi-
tive (or partial and discrimi-
native). Great speech is
simple (as in simple taste),
whereas small speech is full
of details.*
Chuang-tzu

PHILOSOPHICAL QUERY

Compare the sage's position concerning arguing about ultimate
reality with the sophos in Chapter 3. Identify some of the chief
differences between ancient Asian expressions of wisdom and
early expressions of ancient Greek philosophy.

THREE IN THE MORNING

Chuang-tzu (c. 399–295 B.C.) is the second great Taoist sage. Very little is known about his life, but the book bearing his name contains some of the richest stories in Taoist literature. Chuang-tzu sometimes referred to himself as "the Great Clod." The stories attributed to him reflect a generous soul, capable of great humor and great sadness. Here's an excellent example:

On Knowing and Not Knowing the Oneness of Things. Only the truly intelligent understand this principle of the levelling of all things into One. . . . But to wear out one's intellect in an obstinate adherence to the individuality of things, not recognizing the fact that all things are One—this is called "Three in the Morning." What is "Three in the Morning"? A keeper of monkeys said that with regard to their rations of nuts each monkey was to have three in the morning and four at night. At this the monkeys were very angry. Then the keeper said they might have four in the morning and three at night, with which arrangement they were well pleased. The actual number of nuts remained the same, but there was a difference owing to (subjective evaluations of) likes and dislikes. It also derives from this (principle of subjectivity). Wherefore the true Sage brings all the contraries together and rests in the natural Balance of Heaven. This is called (the principle of following) two courses (at once).

Chuang-tzu
In *The Wisdom of Laotse,* trans. and ed. Lin Yutang (New York: Modern Library, 1976), p. 244.

THE DOCTRINE OF INACTION

> *"He abused me, he beat me, he defeated me, he robbed me"—in those who harbor such thoughts hatred will never cease. For hatred does not cease by hatred at any time; hatred ceases by love—this is an eternal law.*
> The Buddha

Lao-tzu compiled his book during a time of great political and social turmoil. This was a period of fierce struggle for power, waged among a succession of warring princes. As these civil wars progressed, they became increasingly violent. Armies increasingly ignored the *li* or rites that prevented pillage and wanton destruction. To cite just one instance, at the height of this instability and terror, soldiers from one army were not paid until they showed the paymaster severed heads of their enemies. Each atrocity was answered with an equal or greater atrocity. This period was known as the "Period of the Fighting States."

Lao-tzu's response to terror, chaos, and betrayal was the doctrine of inaction. According to this doctrine, the best way to deal with social turmoil is "not to do anything about it." If this sounds crazy to you, you are not alone. Such an idea goes against everything our society stands for: we exert great efforts to "solve problems," "fix things," "save the environment," "win the war on drugs," "end racism," and so on. Are such goals feasible? Does social and political effort really work—or does it result in contest after contest, with factions struggling against each other for control?

Do you think social actions, such as this needle exchange to halt the spread of AIDS among IV-drug users, are what Lao-tzu meant by "action"? Is there a way to work for social good that does not count as "action"?

For most of us, certainly, circumstances are not quite as bad as those Lao-tzu lived through. Yet in one way or another, we all live without complete guarantees of physical safety, financial security, and social harmony. It seems as if each step to legislate or enforce social order and harmony backfires. For instance, although it is illegal to utter "hate words," racism, sexism, and violence continue at alarming—and some say increasing—rates. We have thick books containing countless thousands of laws protecting the environment, but accidents, widespread laziness, and deliberate deception continue to pollute it. Each new political administration jumps into "action" with a grand plan to fix things. Yet struggle and turmoil never really go away. More laws do not make better people. Since more "action" may not be the answer, we might do well to take a closer look at Lao-tzu's paradoxical "do nothing" strategy.

Even though Lao-tzu's doctrine of inaction originated as a response to social and political turmoil, it applies to personal concerns as well. Consequently, we'll take a look at ways in which we can test it in our daily affairs.

It is my contention that in the field of morals . . . the insight of the sages into the value of disinterestedness has become the clue to otherwise insoluble perplexities.
Walter Lippman

The Sage in Inaction

According to Lao-tzu, the sage preaches "without words" and "manages affairs without action." By "doing little, he accomplishes great deeds." Let's see how.

Let the other man do his job without your interference.
Confucius

In *A Source Book in Chinese Philosophy*, Wing-Tsit Chan points out that Tao does not refer to a system or moral truth but to a *way of life*. The Tao is

> the One which is natural, eternal, spontaneous, nameless, and indescribable. . . . As a way of life, it denotes simplicity, spontaneity, tranquility, weakness, and most important of all, non-action (wu wei). By the latter is not meant literally "inactivity" but rather "taking no action that is contrary to Nature"—in other words, letting Nature take its own course.[29]

Wu Wei

WU WEI
Taoist principle of "inaction," a warning against "unnatural" or "demanding" action, which runs counter to Tao and so produces disharmony or violence.

The doctrine of **wu wei** is a most intriguing aspect of Taoism. Its literal translation is "not to act," but it is probably more accurate to think of wu wei as a warning against unnatural or demanding action. In this case, natural action does not mean common or widespread, but natural in the sense of healthy and in harmony with the Tao. Concentrating on being a cheerful, helpful, tolerant "friend of Tao," the sage is consistently nonjudgmental. He acts, to be sure, but through his very nature or essence, through his *being*, not through his specific efforts, words, or attachment to results.

> I treat those who are good with goodness,
> And I also treat those who are not good with goodness.
> Thus goodness is attained.
> I am honest with those who are honest,
> And I am also honest with those who are not honest.
> Thus honesty is attained.[30]

No matter what others may do, a sage remains virtuous. A sage is strong without being pushy or demanding.

Having recognized the union of relative opposites, the sage ceases quibbling over semantics (since things are not their names) or fretting about what is not in his control. He or she does not resist the dry spell, knowing that rain will come in its own time. He or she accepts the inevitability of death without psychological resistance in the form of bitterness.

How can it be known that what I call knowing is not really not knowing and that what I call not knowing is not really knowing? . . . From my point of view, the principle of humanity and righteousness and the doctrine of right and wrong are mixed and confused. How do I know the difference among them?

Chuang-tzu

Suppose you try so hard to make good grades that tension, fear, and exhaustion interfere. You freeze on tests or overstudy. Backing off just a bit, worrying less about grades, and just trying to learn for your own sake and for the joy of learning may free you from errors caused by your own anxiety, which is a type of "action." Not trying so desperately to "force" good grades, your grades go up. This is Tao.

> Therefore the sage manages affairs without action (wu wei)
> And spreads doctrines without words.
> All things arise, and he does not turn away from them.

He acts, but does not rely on his own ability.
He accomplishes his task, but does not claim credit for it.
It is precisely because he does not claim credit that his accomplishment remains with him.[31]

PHILOSOPHICAL QUERY

Compare and contrast Buddha's teaching that all suffering comes from the ego with Taoist teachings about inaction and the Stoic doctrine of detachment discussed in Chapter 9. It might be especially interesting to consider how the application of these ideas might affect a friendship or relationship.

When there is a motive to be virtuous, there is no virtue.
Lie Zi

Action That Rebounds

What counts as action in the bad sense to Lao-tzu? Manipulation is action; possessiveness is action; self-righteousness is action; harboring hostile feelings is action; trying to control or reform others is action. The problem with action is that our own desires and beliefs interfere with our intuition of the Tao. Thus, in my jealousy, I do not notice how much I am smothering and abusing you. The more I try to manage our friendship, the more I spy on you and try to control your life, the more reasons I give you to get away from me. This is another paradox of the Tao. The more I do to force you to love me, the less I accomplish.

Let me say to you now that to do nothing at all is the most difficult thing in the world.
Oscar Wilde

Yet if I can manage to do less, to impose fewer of my limiting desires and fears, I will see more clearly. I will relax and understand a universal truth: People cannot make others love them (or hate them); people lack the power to determine how long relationships last. This is a universal mystery. Sages from all times and places glimpse it. Yet how hard it is to manage affairs without action.

*Unawareness of one's feet is
the mark of shoes that fit;
unawareness of the waist is
the sign of a belt that fits;
unawareness of right and
wrong is the mark of a mind
that is at ease. It does not
change inside and is not affected by external events, and
one feels at ease in all circumstances and situations.
That is to be at ease through
unawareness of being at ease.*
Chuang-tzu

*He who would wait on me,
let him wait on the sick.*
The Buddha

Deal with things before they appear.
Put things in order before disorder arises.
A tree as big as a man's embrace grows from a tiny shoot.
A tower of nine storeys begins with a heap of earth.
He who takes an action fails.
He who grasps things loses them.
For this reason the Sage takes no action and therefore does
not fail.
He grasps nothing and therefore he does not lose anything.
People in their handling of affairs often fail when they are
about to succeed.
If one remains as careful at the end as he was at the
beginning, there will be no failure.
Therefore, the Sage desires to have no desire.
He does not value rare treasures.
He learns to be unlearned, and returns to what the multitude
has missed (Tao).
Thus he supports all things in their natural state but does not
take any action.[32]

We see that Taoism merely shifts the direction of our efforts from controlling, managing, fixing, and interfering to helping, getting out of the
way, going along, and accepting. Lao-tzu "spreads doctrines without words"
because his very nature is the doctrine. His serenity and calm strength, his
lack of anxiety and fear are more eloquent than words.

In a remarkably insightful and timeless passage, the sage Chuang-tzu
speaks across generations and cultures:

There is often chaos in the world, and the love of knowledge
is ever at the bottom of it. For all men strive to grasp what
they do not know, while none strive to grasp what they
already know. . . . Thus, above, the spendor of the heavenly
bodies is dimmed; below, the power of land and water is
burned up, while in between the influence of the four seasons
is upset. There is not one tiny worm that moves on earth or
an insect that flies in the air but has lost its original nature.
Such indeed is the world chaos caused by the desire for
knowledge![33]

The sage does not impose himself on nature by trying to explain things
once and for all. The sage offers tentative suggestions, always deferring to
wholesome instincts and learning from nature:

From the point of view of Tao, what is noble and what is
humble? They all merge into one. Never stick to one's own
intention and thus handicap the operation of Tao. What is
much and what is little? They replace and apply to each

THE FUTILITY OF ARGUMENT

Suppose you and I argue. If you beat me instead of my beating you, are you really right and am I really wrong? If I beat you instead of your beating me, am I really right and are you really wrong? Or are we both partly right and partly wrong? Or are we both wholly right and wholly wrong? Since between us neither you nor I know which is right, others are naturally in the dark. Whom shall we ask to arbitrate? If we ask someone who agrees with you, since he has already agreed with you, how can he arbitrate? If we ask someone who has already agreed with me, how can he arbitrate? If we ask someone who disagrees with both you and me to arbitrate, since he has already disagreed with you and me, how can he arbitrate? If we ask someone who agrees with both you and me to arbitrate, since he has already agreed with you and me, how can he arbitrate? Thus, among you, me, and others, none knows which is right. Shall we wait for still others?

Chuang-tzu
In Wing-Tsit Chan, trans. and comp., *A Source Book in Chinese Philosophy*. (Princeton, N.J.: Princeton University Press, 1963), pp. 189–90.

other. . . . Time cannot be arrested. The succession of decline, growth, fullness, and emptiness go in a cycle, each end becoming a new beginning. This is the way to talk about the workings of the great principle and to discuss the principle of all things. The life of things passes by like a galloping horse. With no activity it is not changing, and at no time is it not moving. What shall we do? What shall we not do? The thing to do is to leave it to self-transformation.[34]

To be born when you will be born, that's good fortune. To die when you will die, that's good fortune. To be born and yet not to cherish life, that's opposing heaven. Not to want to die when it's time to die, that's opposing heaven.
Lie Zi

COMMENTARY

It is tempting for contemporary Americans to dismiss the ancient Asian sages as paradox-spouting, head-in-the-clouds primitives—or to romanticize them as founts of all wisdom who possess the cure for all the ills of our confused, technological, crowded society. Both views miss the true splendor and power of the sages' varying expressions of one important aspect of wisdom. This is the therapeutic, unifying function of wisdom, a kind of "spiritual psychology" that combines a sense of the sacred with respect for the here and now.

As we will discover beginning with the next chapter, Western philosophy (and science) developed in the direction of objective, rational knowledge rather than intuitive, holistic wisdom. One result is a technologically sophisticated culture that provides us with material comforts beyond our

[Sophisticated] knowledge is more poisonous than a scorpion's tail. . . . Henceforth the people are not able to fulfill peacefully the natural instincts of their lives.
Chuang-tzu

ancestors' wildest imaginings. But—as the unity of opposites reminds us—the price for concentrating on this objective, rational paradigm has been alienation from nature and other rich sources of knowledge and wisdom.

Rooted in the shamanistic tradition, the sage did not separate the human from the divine, or daily life from a sacred Way. The sage saw himself as a part of nature and the cosmos, not apart from it. In our rediscovery of the environment, we move a little more in the direction of the sage. In our growing awareness of what Carol Gilligan called the "different voice" of compassion and care expressed by women and nontraditional philosophers, we move a little more in the direction of the sage (see Chapters 19 and 20).

The sages teach that a wise person is "nature's companion." The wise person does not interfere with nature, but follows nature's way. In this way, the wise individual's life will remain simple no matter how complex society becomes. For example, a wise person's diet will be basic, wholesome, and mostly unrefined. A wise person will avoid the toxic clamor of society, aware that fame is a cage, that possessions are also burdens, and that artificial manners—in contrast to heartfelt courtesy and respect—are lies.

In our haste to acquire sophisticated knowledge and its fruits—prestige, gadgets, the satisfaction of being "experts"—we can easily become unbalanced. Aggressive efforts (yang) to manage, analyze, and possess nature overlook the inevitability of flux (yin must follow). For example, using complex engineering principles, people build elaborate houses in the floodplains of the Mississippi River or crowd together in California coastal canyons (yang), only to see storms and fires bring them down (yin). In order to pursue sophisticated pleasures, we crowd into cities, which run short of water; we dirty the air; we pile up on freeways. Perhaps it would be wiser to follow Tao and live where we work and build simpler homes where nature welcomes us.

In the last decade, philosophers, psychologists, ministers, environmentalists, and others have increasingly turned toward the East to complement—as in "complete"—Western knowledge of technique and mastery. Social criticisms of elitist divisions have reawakened us to the need to see beyond differences to some kind of commonality. Perhaps these trends reflect greater sensitivity to the sacred essence the sages "stammer" about.

Yet we must not make the mistake of elevating Eastern philosophy above Western science and philosophy—or vice versa. To do that is merely to perpetuate the chief problem the sages attack: alienation and division, argumentation and "action." In the following passage, Denise L. Carmody and John T. Carmody capture the problem of resurrecting respect for wisdom in today's world, and suggest a direction:

> . . . You do not like these quirky phrases? Paradoxes put you
> off? Ah well, no Eastern sage ever promised you a garden
> of platitudes. . . . It is not cruelty that makes good gurus de-
> manding. It is unusual kindness. In the spiritual life you be-

It is like the woman in a story, to whom a chest was bequeathed. Not knowing that the chest contained gold, she continued to live in poverty until another person opened it and showed her the gold. Buddha opens the minds of the people and shows them the purity of their Buddha—nature.
The Buddha

A bait is used to catch fish. When you have gotten the fish, you can forget about the bait. A rabbit trap is used to catch rabbits. When the rabbits are caught, you can forget about the trap. Words are used to express meaning. When you understand the meaning, you can forget about the words. Where can I find a man who forgets about words to talk with him?
Chuang-tzu

come what you do . . . outer persona and inner self must come closer and closer together.

What doth it profit a person if she can assemble any stereo and never hears the music of the spheres? What doth it profit a person to place all his energies in the stock market? Stereos and the stock market have their place—all the Eastern sages allow them. What the Eastern sages do not allow them is primacy of place. . . . To hear the *Tao* in the morning or in the evening, to die content, one must vacate assembling and selling. The business of life is not business. The business of life is being. . . . It does not matter that many of our schools know nothing of such Eastern wisdom. The college catalogue is seldom a great book. Real learning occurs in dark nights and painful passages. Wisdom to live goes far below figures and facts.

. . . If today you would possess your soul, you must empty it of what is tawdry. If today you would hear the *Tao*, you must attune your inner ear.[35]

SUMMARY OF MAIN POINTS

The prophet and shaman are the two direct ancestors of the sage, the oldest philosophical archetype. The shaman specializes in techniques for making contact with the sacred forces that govern the world by going "outside of" him- or herself.

Originally, a prophet was a person who spoke with divine guidance and who was said to be able to predict the course of events. Prophets functioned as religious leaders, teachers, or advisers to rulers and often cried out for justice and mercy in the face of tyranny.

The sage is an archetypal figure who combines religious inspiration with a love of wisdom. Sages understand and teach the requirements of the good life, when the good life is understood to include peace of mind, compassion, social harmony, and respect for nature.

Siddhārtha Gautama was born into wealth and power as the son of a prince (rajah) in what is today Nepal. He was so disturbed by his first encounters with old age, sickness, and death that

Siddhārtha began the search for enlightenment that resulted in his transformation into the Buddha (the One Who Awakened).

Siddhārtha rejected asceticism when he finally realized that his body was an important instrument in his search and that to honor the spirit we must honor the body that houses it. Rejecting the extremes of indulgence or denial, Siddhārtha proposed a Middle Path.

Nirvana is annihilation of the ego, a state of emptiness or "no-thing-ness." Described as a state of bliss because there is only "pure consciousness" with no sense of individuality, separateness, discrimination, or intellectualizing, nirvana is beyond even similarity. Nirvana is release from suffering while conscious.

By choosing to remain among people in order to help other lost souls, the Buddha became a bodhisattva—an enlightened being who voluntarily postpones his own nirvana in order to help all other conscious life-forms find "supreme release."

A bodhisattva is not a savior, but a wise and compassionate being who has gone beyond discrimination: there is no more "I," "mine," "yours."

The Buddha's basic teachings rest on what are called the Four Noble Truths: 1. No one can deny that suffering is the condition of all existence. 2. Suffering and general dissatisfaction come to human beings because they are possessive, greedy, and, above all, self-centered. 3. Egocentrism, possessiveness, and greed can, however, be understood, overcome, rooted out. 4. This rooting out, this vanquishing, can be brought about by following a simple, reasonable Eightfold Path.

The Eightfold Path is a practical cure for the suffering caused by being partial to ourselves: 1. Right understanding (or views). 2. Right purpose. 3. Right speech. 4. Right conduct. 5. Right livelihood. 6. Right effort. 7. Right mindfulness (or awareness). 8. Right meditation.

Lao-tzu (c. 575 B.C.) was a bureaucrat in ancient China, known only by his nickname, Lao-tzu, variously translated as the Old Master, the Old Man, the Old Boy, or the Old Philosopher. According to legend, he is the author of the *Tao Te Ching*.

Literally, Tao means "way" or "path" in the sense of "the way to go." Rather than a philosophic system, the *Tao Te Ching* expresses a sense of the ultimate, underlying great principle, rule, or cause of "the way all things are." Its vision is holistic, encompassing the totality of the cosmos, which expresses harmony, purpose, order, majesty, and "calm power." According to the *Tao Te Ching*, error, suffering, and unhappiness accompanying all attempts to separate things, to understand the part without the whole.

According to the Taoists, the whole of nature consists of the continual interaction of two opposing forces: yin (passive element) and yang (active element). Yin is weak, negative, dark, and destructive; yang is strong, positive, light, and constructive; each is an expression of the other, operating together in a never-ending cycle of coming together and falling apart, birth and death, wet and dry, day and night, good and evil, male and female, full and empty.

Lao-tzu indirectly informs us that he is a mystic. Mysticism is a term derived from the Greek root *mystes*, meaning "initiate of the secret mysteries of life and the higher realities." In broad terms, mystics believe that ordinary levels of understanding and ordinary language cannot grasp the "ultimate something." This ultimate something has been referred to as the One, the Logos, Nature, God, the Tao, the Way, the Great Spirit, Reality, Truth, the Good, and so forth.

The Taoists taught that if there is one ultimate reality, one way things really are, then neat distinctions are in some sense arbitrary and misleading. Nothing is purely matter or spirit (energy). Nothing is completely male or female, wet or dry. The good and the bad both exist in an everlasting exchange; they are "relative opposites."

Lao-tzu compiled his book during a time of great political and social turmoil during which atrocity was answered with atrocity. Lao-tzu's response to terror, chaos, and betrayal was the doctrine of inaction. In other words, the best way to deal with social turmoil is not to do anything about it. Even though the doctrine of inaction originated as a response to social and political turmoil, it applies to personal concerns as well.

In its literal translation wu wei means "not to act," but it is probably more accurate to think of wu wei as a warning against unnatural or demanding action. Natural action is "natural" in the sense of healthy and in harmony with the Tao. Wu wei is also known as the Doctrine of Inaction.

STUDY QUESTIONS

1. How did the Buddha's protected early life contribute to his enlightenment?

2. What is asceticism? What role did it play in Buddha's search for wisdom? What did Buddha teach concerning asceticism?

3. Identify key elements in Buddha's long search for enlightenment and explain their significance.

4. What is nirvana?

5. What is a bodhisattva?

6. What is the relationship between nirvana and becoming a bodhisattva?

7. Did the Buddha establish a religion? Explain.

8. What is the Middle Way?

9. What are the Four Noble Truths and what is their place in Buddha's teaching?

10. What is the Eightfold Path? What is its relationship to the Four Noble Truths?

11. What is significant about "what the Buddha did not explain"?

12. What is the Tao?

13. What is the doctrine of yin and yang? How does it figure into Taoist teachings?

14. What is mysticism? What are its two basic forms?

15. What is the teaching known as "Three in the Morning"? What is its lesson?

16. What is the "union of relative opposites"? What can it teach us about living?

17. What is meant by wu wei?

18. What is the doctrine of inaction? Explain how it works.

19. Give an example of "action which rebounds."

20. In your own words, summarize the Carmodys' evaluation of the Eastern sage.

CHAPTER THREE

The Sophos:

Heraclitus

and Parmenides

All things which have
life, both the greater
and the less, are ruled
by mind.

ANAXAGORAS

estern philosophy began in ancient Greece about eight hundred years before the time of Christ. At that time, the chief component of Greek culture was a powerful religious mythology. These early myths offered primitive explanations of natural phenomena, human history, and the gods. They provided standards of conduct, morality, social obligations, education, art, religious practices, and so on. The most important mythical view of life was expressed in the *Iliad* and the *Odyssey*, two epic poems attributed to the ancient Greek poet **Homer (c. 8th century B.C.).**

For the Greeks of Homer's era, everything happened through some kind of divine agency. They believed, for example, that the sun was carried around the heavens by Apollo's golden chariot, that thunder and lightning were hurled down from the top of Mount Olympus by Zeus, and that the motion of Poseidon's trident created waves. Other natural phenomena were thought to have similar divine origins. The nature of the community, victory or defeat in war, the course of love, and other human affairs were also directly tied to the gods.

The ancient Greek gods were exaggerated human beings: bigger, stronger, faster, and so forth. Like human beings, they were also jealous, sneaky, biased, lazy, promiscuous, and violent. They were not, however, morally or spiritually superior to humans. In fact, the gods were often indifferent to human affairs, including human suffering, because they were involved in complicated soap operas of their own. Occasionally the gods took an interest in an individual human being or involved themselves in wars or politics, often treating people as pieces in an elaborate chesslike game.

Although the ancient Greeks' mythological accounting of events ultimately failed, it established two crucial principles:

1. There is a difference between the way the things *appear* and the way *they really are*.

2. There are unseen causes of events; things happen as they do for some reason.

These insights marked a major advance beyond earlier, less critical characterizations of nature and society.

Greek mythology was not sheer fantasy; it was the product of a desire to find explanations. Science grew out of this search for explanations, and philosophy grew out of attempts to provide rational justification for these early prescientific explanations.[1]

THE PRESOCRATICS

As ancient Greece developed, its social structure became less restrictive (though by no means democratic in the

Homer's *Iliad* had a major impact on ancient Greek culture. This powerful tale of the Trojan war intertwined the lives of humans with the whims of Olympian gods and provided a mythical ideal of the hero.

modern sense). Colonization of outlying cities and communities contributed to the rise of philosophy, as increased social and political freedom combined with an established culture to permit increasingly free inquiry and exchange of ideas.

Explaining events with "the gods willed it" may have been good enough when people had very little understanding of and control over their environment, but as Greek civilization grew, and as colonization led to increasing interaction with sophisticated nearby Eastern cultures, the mythological worldview became less effective.

The first Western philosophers challenged the mythological worldview by asking for rational explanations of questions that mythology could not adequately answer: "Why doesn't the earth fall out of the sky like an apple from a tree?" "What holds it up? And what holds that up?" "Why don't the stars fall out of the sky?" Or, more subtly yet, "How come if I eat fish and grain, I don't look like a fish or stalk of wheat? How does 'fish stuff' become fingernail 'stuff'? Where does the stone go that is worn away by the waterfall? I cannot see it being chipped away. What is this invisible 'stuff' that 'goes away'?" And, again: "Where did 'stuff' come from? Where does it go?"

These first philosophers were called **sophos**, or sage, from the Greek word for wise. What we know of them is fragmentary and intriguing. They were initially concerned with questions about the nature of nature. Today, we would classify many of their concerns as scientific. These earliest Western philosophers are usually referred to as the *Presocratics* because they appeared prior to Socrates, the first major figure in the Western tradition

The gods help them that help themselves.
Aesop

SOPHOS
Sage or wise man; term applied to the first philosophers; from the Greek word for "wise."

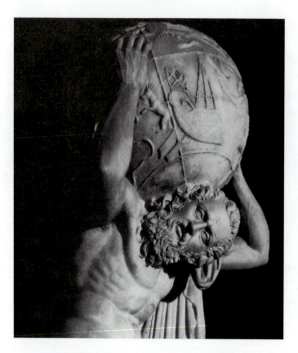

The Olympian god Atlas was said to support the world on his shoulders. Growing dissatisfied with such mythological accounts of natural phenomena, Presocratic philosophers sought rational explanations.

(Chapter 5). The Presocratics are also known as *proto-scientists* because they took steps to transform mythology into rational inquiry about the cosmos. Originally, the difference between a *sophos* who became a philosopher and one who became a proto-scientist was one of subject matter; later it became one of method.

The Search for a Common Principle

Traditionally, the first Western philosopher is said to have been **Thales (c. 624–545 B.C.).** Thales lived in the city of Miletus, part of a Greek colony on the Asian coast in an area known as Ionia. His parents are thought to have been Phoenician.

For the most part, it seems that Thales was absorbed in his speculative studies, devoting only the minimum effort necessary to his financial affairs. In one of the earliest "absent-minded professor" stories, Plato records that Thales fell into a well "when he was looking up to study the stars . . . being so eager to know what was happening in the sky that he could not see what lay at his feet."[2] Thales is credited with introducing astronomy and mathematics into Greece. He studied geometry and deduced several theorems later

There are in fact two things, science and opinion: the former begets knowledge, the latter ignorance.
Hippocrates

collected by Euclid. Thales startled the Ionians by predicting an eclipse of the sun on May 28, 585 B.C. He is even supposed to have traveled to Egypt, where he measured the heights of the pyramids by measuring their shadows at the precise moment when a man's shadow equaled his height.[3]

Philosophically, Thales is significant for his attempt to find a common source, a single substance underlying all things. For him, this basic "stuff" was water. Aristotle says that Thales "observed" that "the nutriment of everything is moist, and that . . . the seeds of everything have a moist nature; . . . and that from which everything is generated is always its first principle."[4]

The great power of Thales' insight was not his specific conclusion that all things are water, but his reduction of all things to one substance. The name for such single-substance philosophies is **monism**, the belief that reality is essentially one—either one reality, one process, one substance, one structure, or one "ground."

Thales believed that water is the cause of all things, and that every particle of the world is alive. He believed that "soul" imbues all things, and that "the world is full of gods."[5] According to Thales, the "vital power" in a plant or stone or human being changes form at death, but soul itself does not die.[6]

Thales' belief that everything is composed of water was a major move beyond mythological accounts of nature because it rested on systematic, rational evidence and careful observation, rather than mythical stories and poetic images. Thales tried to "figure out" or reason his way to a theoretical explanation of the changes he saw throughout nature. His ideas inspired others to refine or reject them—based on carefully *reasoned* arguments. The resulting interplay of carefully argued ideas became known as **rational discourse**: the use of reason to order, clarify, and identify reality and truth according to agreed-upon standards of verification. In his last years, Thales was accorded the title *sophos* by common opinion.

Thales' pupil **Anaximander (611–546 B.C.)**, who was also from Miletus, thought that the first principle was a vast "Indefinite–Infinite," which he called the **apeiron**. Although the apeiron had no specific qualities, being an infinite mass of forces, Anaximander thought that it developed into the variety of particular things which exist in the universe.

Anaximander furthered Thales' recognition of the need for a unifying principle to explain natural occurrences by providing a systematic explanation of the origin of life. He thought that in the beginning the earth was fluid, and that an external source of heat dried some of it. The dried sections became land. Variations in temperature caused winds, and living organisms arose at varying stages of this drying-out process.[7]

Anaximander thought that particular "stuffs" emerged from the apeiron in pairs of opposites: hot–cold, dry–wet, hard–soft, and so on. He believed that a continuous exchange can be seen throughout nature as cold winter becomes warm spring which becomes hot summer which becomes cool fall

Thales so surpassed those who preceded him that everyone has forgotten them.
Simplicius

MONISM
General name for the belief that everything consists of only one, ultimate, unique substance such as matter or spirit.

RATIONAL DISCOURSE
The interplay of carefully argued ideas; the use of reason to order, clarify, and identify reality and truth according to agreed-upon standards of verification.

APEIRON
According to Anaximander, the first principle from which all existing things develop, a vast "Indefinite–Infinite"; the apeiron is an infinite mass of forces with no specific qualities.

which becomes cold winter, and on and on. When, for example, hot comes into existence, cold returns to the apeiron, and vice versa.

Thales' direct legacy culminated in Anaximander's pupil, **Anaximenes (died c. 500 B.C.)**, the third of the Presocratic Milesian philosophers. Anaximenes' notion that the first, universal, underlying element is air or *pneuma* was yet a further refinement of early philosophical reasoning. **Pneuma** is the ultimate, pervasive spirit that holds the world together.

Just as Anaximander identified problems in Thales' thinking, Anaximenes recognized an important question raised by Anaximander's doctrine: On one hand, Anaximander characterized the apeiron as indefinite or "boundless"; on the other hand, he insisted that the apeiron is one thing. How can one thing contain many particular things? In what sense is it "one" thing then? If it is indefinite, limitless, how can it be a "single thing"?

Anaximenes advanced the search for a common principle with the introduction of the argument that *qualitative* differences can result from *quantitative* changes. If correct, Anaximenes' argument could account for the problem of generating many things from a single stuff. But what stuff?

PNEUMA
According to Anaximenes, the ultimate, pervasive spirit that holds the world together; all things are produced by either "rarefaction" of the *pneuma*, which creates fire, or condensation of the *pneuma*, which creates (in order of density) wind, cloud, water, earth, and stone.

HERACLITUS OF EPHESUS

According to **Heraclitus (fl. 500 B.C., d. 510–480 B.C.)**, the basic stuff is fire: "Everything becomes fire, and from fire everything is born."[8] A native of Ephesus, a city on the Ionian coast north of Miletus, Heraclitus is one of the most intriguing of the Presocratics. Although virtually nothing is known of his life, the fragments of Heraclitus reveal a powerful intellect, a profound artist, and a withering social critic.[9] Greatly admired by the Cynics and Stoics (Chapter 9), Heraclitus was claimed by Nietzsche (Chapter 16) as a philosophical ancestor. The Sophists, Plato, and Aristotle (Chapters 4, 6, and 7) were also influenced by Heraclitus's ideas.

Heraclitus

You would not by your going discover the limits of soul though you traveled over every path, so deep has it a logos.
Heraclitus

Wisdom is learning what to overlook.
William James

Fire and Change

Heraclitus used the idea of fire to solve the problem of "the one and the many": How is it possible that many different things can come from one basic stuff? Heraclitus thought that fire could represent change because a burning fire is an ongoing process, an exchange. According to Heraclitus, fire is the energy of change rather than a static thing. During a fire, fuel is continuously consumed, producing heat, movement of air, various flame patterns, smoke, and ashes. "Fire," Heraclitus claimed, "catches up with everything, in time."[10]

According to Heraclitus, the fiery "one" is some kind of orderly cycle or process of change: "Change alone is unchanging."[11] Heraclitus went so far as to claim that *everything is always changing all the time*. The following fragments deal with Heraclitean change:

> Everything flows; nothing remains.
>
> One cannot step twice into the same river, for the water into which you first step has flowed on.
>
> This world, which is always the same for all men, neither god nor man made; it has always been, it is, and always shall be: an everlasting fire rhythmically dying and flaring up again.
>
> There is a new sun every day.
>
> The river we stepped into is not river in which we stand.
>
> To live is to die, to be awake is to sleep, to be young is to be old, for the one flows into the other, and the process is capable of being reversed.[12]

PHILOSOPHICAL QUERY

Compare Heraclitus's language (in translation, of course) with Lao-tzu's in Chapter 2. How are they alike and different? Could they be talking about the same thing? Discuss.

Appearance and Reality

Heraclitus's concept of change is not what you and I usually mean by change. Remember, he implied that *everything is always changing*. Our common experience suggests that, on the contrary, many things stay the same for very long periods of time; most things do not change all the time. In order to reconcile the common perception of permanence with his belief that everything is always changing, Heraclitus distinguished between *appearance* and *reality* in a way that contrasted apparent permanence with the hidden reality of continuous change.[13] The following fragments refer to this philosophically important distinction between appearance and reality.

> Men have talked about the world without paying attention to the world of their own minds, as if they were asleep or absent-minded.
>
> Nature loves to hide.
>
> Many people learn nothing from what they see and experience, nor do they understand what they hear explained, but imagine that they have.
>
> The unseen design of things is more harmonious than the seen.[14]

I make no claim to be a sage or to be Manhood-at-its-best; but it can be said of me that I act unstintingly with them in view, and that I never weary of teaching others.

Confucius

Many people learn nothing from what they see and experience, nor do they understand what they hear explained, but imagine that they have.

Heraclitus

War and Strife

Heraclitus suggested that the world is in a constant struggle between op-posing forces. He compared stability (permanence) to the kind of tension a bent bow or stringed instrument is under: "We do not notice how opposing forces agree. Look at the bow and lyre."[15] A bow appears to be "at rest" only because the bowstring and bow pull equally against each other. According to Heraclitus, throughout nature and the social world, stability (perma-nence) is actually a state of tension between equal and opposite forces.[16]

For example, peace and stability exist only when equal opposing forces or pressures hold each other in check. Social struggle is the maneuvering of various forces for domination. Social stability is thus analogous to two equally powerful wrestlers pushing in opposite directions. So long as their strength, angle of attack, and so forth are identical, they will appear to be immobile—even though they are locked in a mighty struggle—a war.

PHILOSOPHICAL QUERY

In September 1993, a momentous event took place in the Middle East when the Palestinian, Yasser Arafat, and the Israeli, Yitzhak Rabin, reached a peace accord on behalf of their respective peo-ples. Review the history of relations between these two groups and subsequent events. Do you think that war or peace is the re-sult of tension in such cases? Explain.

Some of Heraclitus's most famous fragments deal with strife and con-tention. His powerful language and use of the rhetoric of war and opposition make him controversial and difficult to interpret. Consider the following.

War is father of us all and our king. War discloses who is god-like and who but a man, who is a slave and who is freeman.

It must be seen clearly that war is the natural state of man. Justice is contention. Through contention all things come to be.

When Homer said that he wished war might disappear from the lives of gods and men, he forgot that without opposition all things would cease to exist.

Opposites cooperate. The beautifullest harmonies come from opposition. All things repel each other.

We know health by illness, good by evil, satisfaction by hunger, leisure by failure.[17]

PHILOSOPHICAL QUERY

Substitute the words *struggle* or *effort* for *war* in the preceding passages and reconsider what Heraclitus might be saying. Is

---

It is not possible with mortal mind to search out the pur-poses of the gods.
Pindar

Concepts of gain and loss, joy and sorrow, good and bad, are all man-made. If one wants to live a life of freedom, then one must not be caught in such states of duality.
Lie Zi

There are those who sense the ultimate question in mo-ments of wonder, in moments of joy; there are those who sense the ultimate question in moments of horror, in mo-ments of despair. It is both the grandeur and the misery of living that makes [us] sensi-tive to the ultimate question.
Abraham Joshua Heschel

there, perhaps, a need for struggle or effort in our lives? Can you think of a circumstance in which struggle and opposition have done you good? Harm? Consider their effects on society also. What do you think is the difference between good and bad struggle?

The Logos

Heraclitus thought that he had identified "the unity of opposites" and the even deeper unity of all things. He believed that knowledge of the unity of all things provides the best framework for understanding human life and death.[18] Ignorance occurs when people do not comprehend the basic structure of the human *psyche* (soul) and its relationship to the universal principle through which all things come to exist. Heraclitus called this universal principle *logos*.

The Greek word *logos* is rich and complex, meaning all of the following: intelligence, speech, discourse, thought, reason, word, meaning, study of, the record of, the science of, the fundamental principles of, the basic principles and procedures of a particular discipline, those features of a thing that make it intelligible to us, the rationale for a thing.

Although logos retains these associated meanings for Heraclitus, in its most important sense the **Logos** was *the rule according to which all things are accomplished and the law which is found in all things.*[19]

The Heraclitean capital-L Logos lacks the anthropomorphizing (humanizing) characteristics that the earlier philosophers and poets attributed to the gods. According to Heraclitus's impersonal view, the Logos is a process, not an entity. As such, the Logos is unconcerned with individuals and human affairs, in much the same way that gravity affects us but is unconcerned with us.

Heraclitus's rich use of language reflects his attempts to express the "universal law" of the Logos. His use of the imagery of fire, thunderbolt (lightning), war, perpetual change, and so forth adds a mystical quality to the fragments about the Logos that probably accounts for some of Heraclitus's persistent appeal. Another likely source of this persistent appeal may be rooted in a widespread, transcultural affinity with Heraclitus's conviction that the world order must be intelligent, that a nonintelligent world order is impossible.

As you read the following fragments, note how Heraclitus distinguishes *comprehension* and *understanding* from *knowledge*, and how he distinguishes being asleep or dreaming (ignorance and foolishness) from being awake (wisdom that comes only from recognizing the Logos):

> The Logos is eternal
> but men have not heard it
> and men have heard it and not understood.

The struggle against desire is difficult, because it must be purchased at the soul's expense.
Heraclitus

LOGOS
One of the richest and most complex terms in ancient philosophy; associated meanings include: "intelligence," "speech," "discourse," "thought," "reason," "word," "meaning"; the root of "log" (record), "logo," "logic," and the "ology" suffix found in terms like sociology and physiology; according to Heraclitus, the rule according to which all things are accomplished and the law which is found in all things; according to the Stoics, World Reason, also referred to as Cosmic Mind, God, Zeus, Nature, Fate: the force that governs the world.

WOMAN AS SOPHOS

Aesara of Lucania (c. 3rd century B.C.–1st century A.D.) was a Pythagorean philosopher who has only recently attracted any attention. In the single existing fragment of her book, *On Human Nature*, she says that through the introspection and contemplation of our own souls we can discover the "natural" foundation of all law and the structure of morality. In the following passage, Aesara wisely acknowledges the importance of reason as a guide, without overlooking the importance of emotions. Reading it, we cannot help but wonder what philosophy may have lost by overlooking the contributions of women philosophers for so long.

By following the tracks within himself whoever seeks will make a discovery: Law is in him and justice, which is the orderly arrangement of the soul. Being threefold, it is organized in accordance with triple functions: That which effects judgment and thoughtfulness is [the mind] . . . that which effects strength and ability is [high spirit] . . . and that which effects love and kindness is desire. These are all so disposed relatively to one another that the best part is in command, the most inferior part is governed, and the one in between holds a middle place; it both governs and is governed.

. . . And indeed, a certain unanimity and agreement in sentiment accompanies

The unnameable is the eternally real.
Lao-tzu

Through the Logos all things are understood yet men do not understand as you shall see when you put acts and words to the test I am going to propose.

One must talk about everything according to its nature, how it comes to be and how it grows. Men have talked about the world without paying attention to the world or to their own minds, as if they were asleep or absent-minded.

Man, who is an organic continuation of the Logos, thinks he can sever that continuity and exist apart from it.

How can you hide from what never goes away?

To God all is beautiful, good, and as it should be. Man must see things as either good or bad.

Not I but the world says it: All is one.

God is day night winter summer war peace enough too little, but disguised in each and known in each by a separate flavor.[20]

Knowledge is not intelligence.
Heraclitus

Heraclitus thought that fire was aware and intelligent, and that because we are fire, the Logos is very close to us. For Heraclitus, the love and pursuit of wisdom is the love and pursuit of the Logos. He rejected all other conceptions of wisdom because they were not based on comprehension of the Logos as it operates in all things:

such an arrangement. This sort would justly be called good order, whichever, due to the better part's ruling and the inferior part's being ruled, should add the strength of virtue to itself. Friendship and love and kindliness, cognate and kindred, will sprout from these parts. For closely-inspecting mind persuades, desire loves, and high spirit is filled with strength; once seething with hatred, it becomes friendly to desire.

Mind having fitted the pleasant together with the painful, mingling also the tense and robust with the slight and relaxed portion of the soul, each part is distributed in accordance with its kindred and suitable concern for each thing: mind closely inspecting and tracking out things, high spirit adding impetuosity and strength to what is closely inspected, and desire, being kin to affection, adapts to the mind, preserving the pleasant as its own and giving up [reasoning] to the thoughtful part of the soul. By virtue of these things the best life for man seems to me to be whenever the pleasant should be mixed with the earnest, and pleasure with virtue. Mind is able to fit these things to itself, becoming lovely through systematic education and virtue.

Holger Thesleff, "Pythagorean Texts of the Hellenistic Period," in Mary Ellen Waithe, ed., *Introduction to the Series, A History of Women Philosophers*, vol. 1, 600 B.C.–A.D. 500, trans. Vicki Lynn Harper (Dordrecht: Martinus Nijhoff Publishers, 1987), pp. 20–21.

There is only one wisdom: to recognize the intelligence who steers all things through all things.[21]

PHILOSOPHICAL QUERY

Compare and contrast Heraclitus's attempts to unify opposites with the Taoist concept yin-yang, referred to in Chapter 2. Also compare and contrast the *Logos* with Tao.

THE PYTHAGOREANS

In 546 B.C., the Persians conquered Ionia, and the geographic center of Greek intellectual life shifted toward great city-states like Athens on the Greek coast, and cities in southern Italy and Sicily. About 530 B.C., **Pythagoras of Samos (6th century B.C.)** left the Greek mainland for the Greek colony of Crotona in southern Italy, where he established a religious community that existed in one form or another for hundreds of years. The Pythagorean community eventually developed important mathematical and philosophical ideas which grew out of efforts to purify the psyche.

Although we know that Pythagoras was a historical figure, it is difficult to determine exactly what Pythagoras himself taught. He wrote nothing, and the ideas of other members of the community were attributed to him as a sign of respect and as a way of lending weight to the ideas. Plato and

All things which can be known have a number; without this nothing could possibly be known. . . . The nature of number and harmony admits of no falsehood; for this is unrelated to them. Falsehood and envy belong to the nature of the unlimited and unintelligent and the irrational . . . whereas truth is related to and in close natural union with the race of number.

Philolaus the Pythagorean

The "celestial music of the spheres" is the hauntingly beautiful phrase the Pythagoreans coined to describe the sound of heavenly bodies as they rotate according to cosmic number and harmony. One point of view held that, because we have been exposed to the music of the spheres from birth, we do not hear it.

Aristotle rarely assign ideas to Pythagoras himself, although Pythagorean ideas were especially influential to the development of Plato's philosophy.[22]

The Pythagoreans asserted that number is the first principle of all things. In the West, the Pythagoreans were the first systematic developers of mathematics. They discovered that natural events could be described in mathematical terms, especially as ratios.[23]

Rejecting the apeiron, pneuma, fire, and water, the early Pythagoreans focused attention on *form*—instead of *matter*—as a reality. Later Pythagoreans argued that "all things must be number" because otherwise they would not be understood.

To the Pythagoreans, the principle of number accounted for everything; number was a real thing. Numbers existed in space, so to speak, not just as mental constructs. One, for instance, was a point, two a line, three a surface, four a solid, and so forth. The earth, being a solid, was associated with the cube; fire was associated with the pyramid, air the octahedron, and water the icosahedron. In such a view, all things "follow rules," are "ordered."[24]

According to Pythagorean doctrine, the entire universe is an ordered whole consisting of harmonies of contrasting elements. The Greek for "ordered whole" is **cosmos**. The Pythagoreans were the first philosophers to

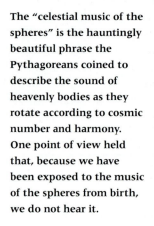

COSMOS
Greek term for "ordered whole"; first used by the Pythagoreans to characterize the universe as an ordered whole consisting of harmonies of contrasting elements.

use the term cosmos to refer to the universe in this way. In contrast to the nearly mystical quality of the Heraclitean logos, the Pythagorean cosmos is accessible to arithmetic, geometry, and rationality on a far greater scale. Rationality itself and even truth are functions of number.

PARMENIDES

Parmenides of Elea (fl. 5th century B.C.) radically transformed the early philosophers' interest in **cosmology**, the study of the universe as a rationally ordered system (cosmos), into **ontology**, the study of "being." Parmenides was probably born around 515 B.C. in Elea, a Greek colony in southern Italy. His work was criticized by Heraclitus and was a major influence on Plato, who suggests that Parmenides and his pupil Zeno (see box page 74) came to Athens, where they met young Socrates.[25]

According to Parmenides, none of his predecessors adequately accounted for the process by which the one basic stuff of the cosmos changes into the many individual things we experience everyday. In his search for a solution to the problem of "the one and the many," Parmenides turned to an analysis of the process of change itself.

What Is Not, Is Not

Parmenides presented his philosophy in the form of a poem called *On Nature*, which recounts how a goddess revealed "the whole truth" to Parmenides. In this poem, the goddess identifies three possible "paths" of study and understanding and indicates that only one is true.

Parmenides' reasoning is based on two key premises: "What is, is," and "What is not, is not." "What is not" equals "not being"—nothing, or not anything at all. In other words, the term *nothing* does not name anything. It is impossible to even imagine nothing. According to Parmenides, strictly speaking, *nothing* can never refer to any thing or object. Thus, strictly speaking, the sentence "Nothing exists" is self-contradictory.

The Parmenidean nothing paralyzes reason: Lacking any content whatsoever, it cannot be comprehended at all. Since it cannot be comprehended, it cannot be described—there is nothing to refer to. The goddess says:

> [The path] that *it is not . . . is bound not to be*: this I tell you is a path that cannot be explored; for you could neither recognize that which is not, nor express it.[26]

What Is, Is

Parmenides was a monist who characterized the one real thing as being. "What is" equals *being*. According to Parmenides, being is purely positive, simple, and unconditioned. That is, being is one, eternal, and indivisible; it

Parmenides

COSMOLOGY
In philosophy, the study of the universe as a rationally ordered system or cosmos; sometimes used to refer to metaphysics in general; in science, the study of the nature and physical origins of the universe itself, astronomy.

ONTOLOGY
From the Greek root *onta* meaning "the really existing things" or "true reality"; the study of "being" itself as opposed to the study of particular existing things; branch of philosophy that deals with the order and structure of reality in the broadest possible sense.

*It is both necessary to say and think that **being** is; for to be is possible, and nothingness is not possible.*
Parmenides

is the "unchanging one." *Not-being*, in contrast, is negative, complex, and impure. Being ("what is") can be conceived of and expressed. Not-being ("what is not"), as we have seen, is unintelligible; it "paralyzes" thought and is inexpressible.

According to Parmenides, change and variety (the many) are only appearances; they are not real. Parmenides placed all sensations in the realm of appearance. In other words, reality cannot be apprehended by the senses. If this is true, then our most commonly held opinions are "mere opinions" and most of us are unaware of reality, which is one being.

Parmenides associated being with correct thinking and not-being with illusion. Correct thinking is always about being, according to Parmenides, because we can only think about subjects that exist, that *are:* "In fact it is the same thing to think and to be."[27]

PHILOSOPHICAL QUERY

Compare Parmenides' assertions about "what is not" with Thomas Aquinas's argument from necessity in Chapter 10. Is the concept of nothing clear to you? Do you agree that talk about "what is not" paralyzes reason? Can something that cannot be described clearly exist anyway? Can you describe "God" or "soul" clearly? Discuss.

Being and Change

Most of Parmenides' poem consists of logical inferences about the qualities of being based on its fundamental nature, its purity. For example, being must be eternal because to come from something other than being would be to come from not-being—which would be to come from nothing, and nothing can come from nothing. Being cannot change into something else because to do so would require being to be not-being—a clear impossibility.

Being is not a "principle" or fundamental "stuff" like the basic principles of the earlier Presocratic philosophers. Parmenides thought that being is perfect and complete, or "whole." Thus, it cannot move or change. Philosophical historian Giovanni Reale characterizes Parmenidean being as "the being of the visible cosmos, immobilized, and to a great extent purified, but still clearly recognizable."[28] Fragment 8 says:

> To [the path of truth or *being*] there are many sign-posts: that being has no coming-into-being and no destruction, for it is whole of limb, without motion, and without end. And it never *was*, nor *will be*, because it is now, a whole all together, one, continuous; for what creation of it will you look for? How, whence sprung? Nor shall I allow you to speak or think of it as springing from not being; for it is neither expressible nor thinkable that what is not is. . . . The decision on these mat-

ters depends on the following: *it is*, or *it is not*. It is therefore decided—as is inevitable—(that one must) ignore the one way as unthinkable and inexpressible (for it is not a true way) and take the other as the way of being and truth. How could being perish? How could it come into being? If it came into being, it is not; and so too if it is about to be at some future time.[29]

Being is recognized by reason (logos) as a perfect whole, as One. Yet our senses only experience becoming: living and dying, moving, changing. The senses cannot recognize being, much less can they discover that being is One. In other words, you cannot see, touch, taste, hear, or smell being.

In his poem, the goddess advises Parmenides to follow logos rather than the senses because being can only be recognized by correct thinking in the form of reason (logos) as One. In other words, Parmenides' poem views the world of the senses as corrupted by appearances and by "mere belief" in the reality of not-being.

Most startling of all, Parmenides "solved" the problem of the appearance of change by concluding that the very concept of change is self-contradictory. What we think of as change is really an illusion. The reasoning runs as follows:

"Change" equals transformation into something else.

When a thing becomes "something else" it becomes what it was not. But since it is impossible for "nothing" to exist, there is no "nothing" into which the old thing can disappear. (There is no "no place" for the thing to go into.)

Therefore, change cannot occur.[30]

Whatever the power of Parmenides' vision of being as One, change and motion remain basic facts of experience for most of us. The unpopularity of an opinion is not a measure of its merit, however. And Parmenides' position was the product of careful reasoning in a way that "common sense" rarely is. Further, Parmenides' contemporaries took his arguments seriously, and Parmenides' notion of being played an important part in the development of Plato's theory of forms (Chapter 6).

THE PLURALISTS

The next major shift in Presocratic philosophy was the emergence of **pluralism**, the belief that there exist many realities or substances. Building on Parmenides' belief that motion is impossible because there is no empty space (no "what is not"), **Empedocles (c. 5th century B.C.)** concluded that reality must be "completely full." According to Empedocles, reality is a *plenum* without any gaps.

Because he agreed with Parmenides that nothing comes into existence or goes out of existence, Empedocles decided that all motion and change take place *within* existing reality. Things do not move into empty space but exchange places with each other.

The more comprehensive the meaning, the less comprehensible it is. Infinite meaning is necessarily beyond the comprehension of a finite being. Here is the point at which science gives up and wisdom takes over. . . . Wisdom is knowledge plus: knowledge—and the knowledge of its own limits.
Viktor Frankl

In Greece wise men speak and fools decide.
Anacharsis

PLURALISM
The belief that there exist many realities or substances.

ZENO'S PARADOXES

Zeno of Elea (c. 490–430 B.C.) forcefully defended the idea that change in the form of motion is impossible. These intriguing paradoxes present one of the earliest examples of a particular method of proof known as a **reductio ad absurdum** (reduce to absurdity). In a *reductio*, an opponent's position is refuted by showing that accepting it leads to absurd, unacceptable, or contradictory conclusions. Zeno is credited with perfecting a way of revealing an idea's absurdity by: (1) showing that accepting it leads to a logical contradiction, or (2) showing that it leads to a logical conclusion that is somehow obviously ridiculous because it offends either our reason or common sense.

Using a form of the *reductio*, Zeno tried to show that the Heraclitean claim that everything is always changing is absurd because the very idea of change or motion is absurd. The paradoxes also reveal the ultimate inadequacy of the Presocratic notion of the continuum.

Zeno's paradoxes were admired by ancient philosophers and continue to generate lively discussions among contemporary philosophers. See what you make of the three most famous.

The Dichotomy

The first argument is this: if movement exists, it is necessary that the mobile [moving thing] traverse an infinite number of points in a finite time; but this is impossible, hence movement does not exist. Zeno demonstrated his position affirming that whatever is moved must traverse a certain distance: but any distance is divisible to infinity, what is moved must first traverse half of the distance and then the whole of it. But first he must traverse the entire half of the distance, and the half of that and the new half of the previous half. But if the halves are infinite in number, since for every whole taken it is possible to take half, then it is impossible to traverse in a finite time an infinite number of points. . . . Then, given that every magnitude admits of infinite divisions, it is impossible to traverse any magnitude in a finite time.

Simplicius
In Aristotle's Physics, 1013.4ff.; quoted in Giovanni Reale, *A History of Ancient*

REDUCTIO AD ABSURDUM
From the Latin for "reduce to absurdity"; form of argument that refutes an opponent's position by showing that accepting it leads to absurd, unacceptable, or contradictory conclusions because: (1) accepting it leads to a logical contradiction, or (2) it leads to a logical conclusion that is somehow obviously ridiculous because it offends either our reason or common sense.

Rather than a One (being) that does not move, reality consists of six basic components, according to Empedocles: Four basic "roots" and two basic "motions." The roots are: earth, air, fire, and water. Each root is eternal—uncreated, indestructible, and unchanging. The two basic motions are Love, which unites different things, and Strife, which breaks things up into their basic elements. Wisdom falls under the domain of Love, being "of like by like," and ignorance falls under the domain of Strife, being of "unlike by unlike."[31]

According to Empedocles, at the beginning of the "world cycle," the four roots were all mixed together, under the motion of Love. Eventually, Strife took over and the four roots separated into their own individual domains. Once Strife dominates and the separation is complete, Love emerges again and the process repeats itself. During the rule of Love, the four roots are so evenly mixed that nothing is distinguishable, no individual thing can

Philosophy, vol. 1, *From the Origins to Socrates*, trans. John R. Catan (Albany: State University of New York Press, 1987), p. 91.

Achilles and the Tortoise

The second [paradox] is the so-called "Achilles," and it amounts to this, that in a race the quickest runner can never overtake the slowest, since the pursuer must first reach the point whence the pursued started, so that the slower must always hold a lead. This argument is the same in principle as that which depends on bisection [cutting the distance in half], though it differs from it in that the spaces with which we successively have to deal are not divided into halves. The result of the argument is that the slower is not overtaken: but it proceeds along the same lines as the dichotomy argument (for in both, a division of the space in a certain way leads to the result that the goal is not reached, though the Achilles goes further in that it affirms that even the quickest runner in legendary tradition must fail in his pursuit of the slowest). . . .

Aristotle, *Physics*, Hardie and Gaye translation, 239B.14ff.

The Flying Arrow

The argument of Zeno, beginning from the premise that everything which occupies a space equal to itself either is in motion or is at rest, that nothing is moved in an instant, and that the mobile always occupies in each instant a space equal to itself, seems to adjust itself in this way: the flying arrow in every instant occupies a place equal to itself, and thus, for the whole time of its motion. But what occupies in an instant a place equal to itself does not move because nothing is moved in an instant. Hence the flying arrow, as long as it is in motion, does not move for the whole time of its flight.

Simplicius, *In Aristotle's Physics*, 1015.19ff.; in Reale, *A History of Ancient Philosophy vol. 1, From the Origins to Socrates*, trans. John R. Catan (Albany: State University of New York Press, 1987), p. 93.

have any perceptible qualities, whereas during the rule of Strife, the four basic elements are completely separated from each other.[32]

In Empedocles' view, Love's domination creates some bizarre mixtures:

> Here sprang up many faces without necks, arms wandered without shoulders, unattached, and eyes strayed alone, in need of foreheads.

> . . . Many creatures were born with faces and breasts on both sides, man-faced ox-progeny, while others again sprang forth as ox-headed offspring of man, creatures compounded partly of male, partly of the nature of female, and fitted with shadow [sterile] parts.[33]

Things perish into those from which they have been born.
Anaximander

According to Empedocles, certain "mixtures" of elements could not survive. But in the course of the great random "mixing together" of different

*Many a head came to birth
without a neck.*
Empedocles

combinations, survivable ones would eventually result. It is chance, in the form of "random combinations," then, that accounts for human beings and all other things that are part of this particular world cycle.

Empedocles was not consistent in his attitude toward the evolutionary cycle he describes. Although he sometimes talks about "accidental" combinations, his whole tone shifts when he talks about the world cycle or process itself. He uses the term *god* for the process—which he worships. The god of Empedocles lacks a body and is "only a sacred and unutterable mind flashing through the whole world with rapid thoughts."[34]

Anaxagoras

*From what source things
arise, to that they return
of necessity when they are
destroyed; for they suffer
punishment and make repa-
ration to one another for
their injustice according to
the order of time.*
Anaximander

Anaxagoras (c. 500–428 B.C.) realized that Empedocles' four basic roots were no more helpful in explaining change and transformation than water, fire, apeiron, pneuma, or number were. "How," he wondered, "could hair come from what is not hair or flesh from what is not flesh?"[35]

For Anaxagoras, change was not the transformation of one kind of stuff into another kind. He believed that "in everything there is a portion of everything."[36] A fingernail, for example, contains bits of whale and plum. Any given sensible stuff contains bits of an infinite variety of ultimate stuffs or "seeds." What we see when we look at a fingernail—or at anything—is the dominant stuff in the mixture. Our eyes and other senses are too gross (unrefined) to see everything: "From the weakness of our sense we are not able to judge the truth. What appears is a vision of the unseen."[37]

If there are seeds of every kind of stuff in every sensible thing, clearly, they must be very, very small. Indeed, in order for a very small thing like a speck of dust or diamond chip to contain seeds of every other kind of thing, seeds must be infinitely small. Thus, things as we perceive them are in fact composed of tiny bits or seeds that we cannot see individually. We can see things only when seeds are combined in sufficient quantity.

Nous

NOUS
From the Greek for "mind"; according to Anaxagoras, "the all-pervading Mind which imposes (brings about) an intelligible pattern in an otherwise unintelligible universe"; a material being that affects all things without being in them.

What triggers the combinations of seeds that make up the world process? Anaxagoras rejected Empedocles' two fundamental motions, Love and Strife. In their place he posited *Nous* (Greek for "mind"). **Nous** is the "all-pervading Mind which imposes (brings about) an intelligible pattern in an otherwise unintelligible universe." Nous affects all things without being in them, but it is not a process or force in the contemporary scientific sense. The fragments of Anaxagoras reveal difficulty in clearly articulating the nature of Nous. Some passages stress that Nous "sets all things in order," but others treat it as purely mechanical.[38]

According to Anaxagoras, in the beginning everything was so evenly distributed that it would have been impossible to recognize things as we now know them. Then Nous produced a kind of "shuffling" in which individual things were separated out, much like separating out the suits of a deck of cards that have been randomly put together. Anaxagoras says:

> Mind began to revolve first from a small beginning; but the revolution now extends over a larger space, and will extend over a larger still. [In] this revolution . . . now revolve the stars and the sun and the moon, and the air and aether that are separated off. And this revolution caused the separating off, and the rare is separated off from the dense, the warm from the cold, the light from the dark, and the dry from the moist.[39]

Anaxagoras's concept of Nous also provided "one of the most powerful intuitions . . . in the whole course of Presocratic philosophy . . . that the [basic] principle is an infinite reality, separate from everything else."[40] The beautiful and haunting Fragment 12 is worth reading carefully:

> All things which have life, both the greater and the less, are ruled by mind. Mind took command of the universal revolution, so as to make (things) revolve at the outset. At first things began to revolve from some small point, but now the revolution extends over a greater area, and will spread even further. And the things which were mixed together, and separated off, and divided, were all understood by mind. And whatever they were going to be, and whatever things were then in existence that are not now, and all things that now exist and whatever shall exist—all were arranged by mind, as also the revolution now followed by the stars, the sun and moon, and the air and aither [ether] which were separated off. It was this revolution which caused the separation off. And dense separates from rare, and hot from cold, and bright from dark, and dry from wet. There are many portions of many things. And nothing is absolutely separated off or divided the one from the other except mind. Mind is all alike, both the greater and the less. But nothing else is like anything else . . .[41]

Reason is immortal, all else is mortal.
Pythagoras

For already have I once been a boy and a girl, a bush and a bird and a dumb sea fish.
Empedocles

THE ATOMISTS

Anaxagoras did not solve the problem of "the one and the many," but he and Empedocles helped further clarify it: How does the world of things as we ordinarily perceive them "emerge from" some kind of basic stuff that is quite different in its characteristics from the things of our experience? How can the variety of colors, textures, odors, densities, and so on that we see all around us "come from" a single, completely different something else?

The Parmenidean assault on the senses (aided by Zeno's paradoxes, see box on page 74) was not adequately "resolved" until the middle of the fifth century B.C., when **Leucippus of Miletus (c. 5th century B.C.)** and **Democritus of Abdera (c. 460–370 B.C.)** argued that there are many Parmenidean ones. Leucippus is credited with being the originator of atomism, and Democritus further developed his ideas. **Atomism** is the materialistic view that the universe consists entirely of empty space and ultimately simple entities that combine to form objects. The most thorough expression of early atomism occurs in the Roman poet **Lucretius's (c. 99–55 B.C.)** great poem, *De Rerum Natura*. Lucretius's poem helped popularize the ideas of both Democritus and Epicurus (Chapter 8).

Rather than reject Parmenidean being by denying the obvious—the existence of motion, variety, and change—Leucippus argued that there are many "ones" or beings. According to Leucippus, being is infinite. Democritus termed these "ones" *atoms*.

The Void

Democritus accepted Parmenides' dichotomy between being and not-being. From this fundamental division, he reasoned that not-being cannot exist since it "is not." Further, Democritus argued, the absence of not-being is not the same thing as the absence of empty space. Space is empty, Democritus stated, when it does not contain "things" or "bodies." Space can be empty of bodies without being empty of being.

Democritus argued that it is possible to separate "ones" from each other by empty space devoid of any bodies. The **void** is Democritus's term for no-thing (no-bodies), or empty space. *No-thing* is not the same as *nothing*. Parmenides failed to make this important distinction, according to Democritus. The significance of Democritus's argument can be grasped if we compare a Parmenidean picture of reality with a Democritean picture, shown in Figure 3.1.

Atoms

The word *atom* comes from the Greek *atomos*, meaning "indivisible," "having no parts," or "uncuttable." **Atoms** are minute material particles, the ultimate material constituents of all things. Atoms have properties such as size, shape, position, arrangement (combination), and motion, but they do not possess sensible qualities like color, taste, temperature, or smell. However, combinations (compounds and composites) of atoms can grow large enough for us to perceive.

According to Democritus, atoms are so small that they are invisible to the naked eye. Being so small, they are uncuttable, and thus they cannot be destroyed. In other words, atoms are eternal. Because motion is an inherent property of atoms, they are constantly moving, bumping into each other and bouncing away or quivering in one spot.

ATOMISM
Early Greek philosophy developed by Leucippus and Democritus and later refined by Epicurus and Lucretius; materialistic view that the universe consists entirely of empty space and ultimately simple entities that combine to form objects.

VOID
Democritus' term for no-thing (no-bodies); empty space in Atomist theory.

ATOMS
From the Greek *atomos*, meaning "indivisible," "having no parts," or "uncuttable"; minute material particles; the ultimate material constituents of all things. Atoms have such properties as size, shape, position, arrangement (combination), and motion, but lack qualities like color, taste, temperature, or smell.

PARMENIDES

Being	Not-Being
(What Is)	(What Is Not)

DEMOCRITUS

Being	Not-Being
(What Is)	(What Is Not)

Atoms	Void
(Things)	(No-Things)

FIGURE 3.1 Comparison of two conceptions of reality.

Reason and Necessity

According to Democritus, things come into existence when atoms combine in certain ways, and they go out of existence when their parts or atoms separate. Stable substances and things are composed of highly compatible atoms, and less stable ones are composed of less compatible atoms. Marble, for instance, contains more stable atoms than nitroglycerin.

If we ask why certain things exist, Democritus's answer is that given the eternal swirling of atoms, some collisions are bound to stick due to the nature of the atoms involved. There is no divine order, no nous or Heraclitean Logos guiding or combining these atoms. All that exists in this view are atoms and the void—nothing else. There is no intentional order to the universe, though there is predictability. That is, "nothing occurs at random." Mechanical laws of motion explain everything; there is no deeper or higher explanation. What appears to be chance is simply a lack of information and knowledge. If we could observe a long sequence of atomistic behavior the way we might observe a game of billiards, we could—in theory—predict the positions and combinations of various atoms.

Not even the gods fight against necessity.
Diogenes Laertius

The sage probes, not the fact of survival, but the reasons.
Guan Yin

Nature and Convention

We never experience atoms directly, according to Democritus. Shape, taste, and other sensible properties are the result of "effluences" and "images" as we sense atoms striking the eye, ear, skin, tongue, and so on. Thus, we are "cut off from the real" because our sensations are products of our own particular condition: our sensory acuity, whether we are sick, and so forth.

Not only do we never experience atoms directly, even perceptual qualities like sweet and sour, hot and cold, smooth and rough, hard and soft are matters of convention, not nature: "Sweet exists by convention, bitter by convention, color by convention; but in reality atoms and the void alone exist," according to Democritus.

Although Democritus rejected the skeptical implications of this insight, subsequent philosophers have elaborated on them with stunning effect. In

According to Democritus, we never experience reality directly, and perceptual qualities are all matters of convention. This raises the question of whether any two people can ever actually observe "the same thing"—and, if they can, how they can know it. (See also "Subjectivity," page 217.)

Whenever this essential nature is analyzed by the intellect, it will seem absurd and paradoxical.
Fritjof Capra

subsequent chapters we shall look at some of the far-reaching consequences engendered by the issue of what is true by nature and what is true by convention. (See especially Chapters 4–6, which cover some of the most exciting aspects of this struggle, and Chapters 11–13, which concern the modern search for an answer to the skepticism.)

COMMENTARY

Zeno's difficulty demands an explanation: for if everything that exists has a place, place too will have a place, and so on ad infinitum.
Aristotle

When the sophos first emerged from the mists of prehistory, knowledge and wisdom were not neatly divided. As early Greek civilization became more refined and sophisticated, mythology and religion developed into philosophy (and later branched off into science). Social historian Amaury de Riencourt traces the early history of philosophy as a series of increasingly abstract steps, until a "fanatical concern" with logical consistency and rules of thinking (Parmenides and Zeno are examples) led to theories which, though logically consistent, did not match observed facts.[42] The result, de Riencourt says, was "The absolute predominance of the *dissociating*, analytical . . . principle in Greek thought . . . its strength and its weakness."[43]

Philosophical speculation became increasingly alienated from common experience, and unemotional, implacable reason (modeled after the logos) threatened to dominate other sources of wisdom. Seemingly bizarre theories and countertheories struggled for dominance as the first principle of existence: water, apeiron, pneuma, fire, being, Nous, atoms, and the void. Everyday experiences and the evidence of the senses were rejected as illusory, products of ignorance.

To many people, the philosophers were the ones utterly out of touch with reality. Philosophical speculation was sometimes viewed as an indulgence suitable only for those not fit for "real life"—individuals supported by a wealthy elite or absorbed in pointless "intellectual squabbles." Philosophy became a subject of confusion and ridicule, as well as awe and respect.

Words are the physicians of a mind diseased.
Aeschylus

A clouded reputation haunts philosophy to this day, as we saw in Chapter 1. "What," we are asked, "is philosophy good for, if philosophers can hold contradictory and absurd ideas that bear no resemblance to common sense? How can we take seriously charges that we can never experience reality, that our most cherished and widely held beliefs are merely illusions?" If careful thinkers end up in such tangles, maybe it's better to think less and live more.

This suspicious attitude toward philosophy contributed to a kind of philosophical revolution that occurred when the first "professional" thinkers, known as Sophists, turned from the study of the cosmos to the study of human beings. The Sophists' demands for practical philosophy blew through the early history of philosophy like a bracing wind. Their work is the subject of the next chapter.

SUMMARY OF MAIN POINTS

Although the ancient Greeks' mythological accounting of events ultimately failed, it established two crucial principles: (1) There is a difference between the way the things *appear* and the way *they really are*. (2) There are unseen causes of events; things happen as they do for some reason.

The first Western philosophers challenged the mythological worldview by asking for *rational* explanations of questions that mythology could not adequately answer.

Traditionally, the first Western philosopher is said to have been Thales. Thales is significant for his attempt to find a common source, a single substance underlying all things. For him, this basic "stuff" was water. Thales' insight was not his specific conclusion that all things are water, but his

reduction of all things to one substance. The name for such single-substance philosophies is monism, the belief that reality is essentially one reality or one "ground."

Thales tried to "figure out" or reason his way to a theoretical explanation of the changes he saw throughout nature. His ideas inspired others to refine or reject them—based on carefully *reasoned* arguments. The resulting interplay of carefully argued ideas became known as rational discourse, the use of reason to order, clarify, and identify reality and truth according to agreed-upon standards of verification.

Thales' pupil, Anaximander, thought that the first principle was a vast "Indefinite-Infinite," which he called the *apeiron*. Although the apeiron had no specific qualities, Anaximander thought that it developed into the variety of particular things which exist in the universe. Particular "stuffs" were said to have emerged from the apeiron in pairs of opposites: hot–cold, dry–wet, hard–soft, and so on.

Anaximander's pupil, Anaximenes, argued that the first, universal, underlying element is air or *pneuma*, the ultimate, pervasive spirit that holds the world together. Anaximenes introduced the idea that *qualitative* differences result from *quantitative* changes to account for the problem of generating many things from a single stuff.

Heraclitus used the idea that the basic stuff is fire to solve the problem of "the one and the many": How is it possible that many different things can come from one basic stuff? He thought that fire could represent change because a burning fire is an ongoing process, an exchange, rather than a static "thing."

Heraclitus distinguished between *appearance* and *reality* in a way that contrasted *apparent permanence* with the *hidden reality* of continuous change. He suggested that the world is in a constant struggle between opposing forces, and that throughout nature and the social world, stability (permanence) is actually a state of tension between equal and opposite forces. Heraclitus believed in "the unity of opposites" and a deeper unity of all things.

Heraclitus called this universal principle *logos*. The Greek word logos is rich and complex, meaning intelligence, speech, reason, word, and the fundamental principles of. Although logos retains these associated meanings for Heraclitus, in its most important sense the Logos was the rule according to which all things are accomplished and the law which is found in all things.

Pythagoras of Samos established a religious community that existed in one form or another for hundreds of years. The Pythagoreans asserted that number is the first principle of all things.

Parmenides of Elea radically transformed the early philosophers' interest in *cosmology*, the study of the universe as a rationally ordered system (cosmos), into *ontology*, the study of "being."

According to Parmenides, strictly speaking, *nothing* can never refer to any thing or object. Thus, the sentence "Nothing exists" is self-contradictory. When we talk about nothing we always refer to something—just not the particular thing we are using the word *nothing* to refer to. The Parmenidean nothing paralyzes reason: Lacking any content whatsoever, it cannot be comprehended at all.

Parmenides was a monist who characterized the one real thing as being. "What is" equals *being*. According to Parmenides, being is purely positive, simple, and unconditioned. Thinking is always about being, according to Parmenides. It is perfect and complete, or "whole"; thus, it cannot move or change, though it is material.

Parmenides' pupil, Zeno of Elea, forcefully defended the idea that motion is "impossible," using a method of proof known as a *reductio ad absurdum* (reduce to absurdity). In a *reductio*, an opponent's position is refuted by showing that accepting it leads to absurd, unacceptable, or contradictory conclusions because: (1) it leads to a logical contradiction, or (2) it leads to a logical conclusion that is somehow obviously ridiculous because it offends either our reason or common sense. Zeno's three paradoxes are the dichotomy (there's always still halfway to go), the Achilles (in a foot race, fleet-footed Achilles will never catch a tortoise with a head start), and the flying arrow (an arrow in flight cannot move).

The next major shift in Presocratic philosophy was the emergence of pluralism, the belief that there exist many realities or substances. Empedocles concluded that reality must be "completely full." Reality is a *plenum* without any gaps. Empedocles claimed that all motion and change take place *within* existing reality. Things do not move into empty space, but exchange places with each other.

Anaxagoras believed that "in everything there is a portion of everything." Anaxagoras rejected Empedocles' two fundamental motions of Love and Strife. In their place he posited *Nous*, the "all-pervading Mind which brings about an intelligible pattern in an otherwise unintelligible universe."

Nous is a material being that affects all things without being in them. It is not a process or force in the contemporary scientific sense.

The Atomists Leucippus of Miletus and Democritus of Abdera argued that there are really many Parmenidean "ones." Democritus termed these ones *atoms*. Democritus argued that the absence of not-being is not the same thing as the absence of empty space. Space is empty when it does not contain "things" or "bodies." Space is not empty of being. The *void* is Democritus's term for no-thing (no-bodies). No-thing is not the same as *nothing*. According to Democritus, Parmenides failed to make this important distinction.

Atoms are minute material particles, the ultimate material constituents of all things. They have such properties as size, shape, position, arrangement (combination), and motion, but they do not possess sensible qualities like color, taste, temperature, or smell. Since motion is an inherent property of atoms, they are constantly moving around, bumping into each other and bouncing away or quivering in one spot.

According to Democritus, there is no intentional order to the universe, though there is predictability because mechanical laws of motion explain everything.

According to Democritus, we are "cut off from the real" because we never experience atoms directly. Our sensations are products of our sensory acuity. Although Democritus rejected the skeptical implications of this insight, subsequent philosophers have elaborated on them with stunning effect.

STUDY QUESTIONS

1. Distinguish between mythological and philosophical thinking.

2. What role did the need for explanations play in the development of Presocratic philosophy?

3. What is a *sophos*?

4. Who was Thales? Summarize his fundamental insight.

5. What is the *apeiron*? How is it related to Thales' philosophy?

6. How does Anaximander explain the origin of particular things?

7. What is the *pneuma*? What significant distinction does it involve?

8. What does Heraclitus mean by fire? By war?

9. What question was fire supposed to solve for Heraclitus?

10. What is the Logos? How does it differ from God?

11. What is the fundamental principle, according to the Pythagoreans?

12. What is cosmology?

13. What is ontology?

14. What is the cosmos?

15. What is being? What is not-being?

16. Reconstruct Parmenides' argument rejecting not-being.

17. What is monism? Pluralism?

18. What is the plenum?

19. Name and explain each of Zeno's paradoxes.

20. What is *reductio ad absurdum*? Construct one.

21. Show how Zeno uses the *reductio* to generate his paradoxes.

22. Identify the four roots and two motions of Empedocles.

23. What is meant by the claim that Empedocles' theory was evolutionary?

24. What is nous?

25. How did Democritus deal with Parmenides' problem of reconciling being with motion?

26. What are atoms?

27. What is the void?

28. What does Democritus mean when he says that we are "cut off from reality"? What is the significance of this assertion?

29. How does Democritus account for sensations of color, taste, and so forth?

The Sophist:
Protagoras

Man is the measure of all things, of the things that are, [how] they are, and the things that are not, [how] they are not.

PROTAGORAS OF ABDERA

Ancients of our culture sought clarity: Plato portrays Socrates tirelessly splitting hairs to extract essential truth from the ambiguities of language and thought. Two thousand years later we are reversing that, for now we pay intellectual talent a high price to amplify ambiguities, distort thought, and bury reality. . . . One of the discoveries of the twentieth century is the enormous variety of ways of compelling language to lie.

Jules Henry

he scene: A society showing signs of tension and strain, yet still exciting and important. The privileges of the establishment are being challenged by more liberal democratic groups. Wealthy parents pay outrageous tuitions to have their children taught by prestigious educators, only to have these very same children then reject their parents' ideals and beliefs. People complain that atheistic, relativistic trends are permeating the schools and that basic values are breaking down. Traditional religions and beliefs are challenged by intellectuals, by occult practices, and by competing Eastern religions. Scientific, mathematical, and intellectual advances compete for social control and influence with conservative, fundamentalist religious and moral tenets. Political corruption is pervasive and public. People take one another to court for a variety of real and inflated slights and transgressions. Success, prestige, and power become the overriding goals of many. Consider one commentator's description:

> It seems as if the dominant drive of more and more citizens is the objective of getting as rich as possible. . . . Meanwhile the money-makers, bent on their business, . . . continue to inject their poisoned loans wherever they can, and to demand high rates of interest, with the result that drones and beggars multiply. . . . Yet even when the evil becomes flagrant [the rulers] will do nothing to quench it. . . . This being so, won't everyone arrange his life as pleases him best? It's a wonderfully pleasant way of carrying on in the short-run, isn't it? It's an agreeable, anarchic form of society, with plenty of variety, which treats all men as equal, whether they are or not.
>
> It is a picture easy to recognize.[1]

America today? No. You have just read Plato's characterization of the "democratic" state. Because of their sophisticated, successful civilization, the Athenian people had long viewed themselves as unique, special, superior to all others. But the Athens of around 500–400 B.C. attracted aspiring entrepreneurs from all over Greece and parts of Asia. Those who considered themselves to be "original, true Athenians" grew uncomfortable and defensive. Social scientists call this attitude **ethnocentrism** (from Greek roots meaning "the race or group is the center"). Ethnocentric individuals see their ways as inherently superior to all others: Their religion is the one true religion. Their science, music, tastes in all areas of life are unsurpassed. The ethnocentric person thinks: "The gods speak *our* language, look like *us*, are *our* color. *Our* family practices are *natural*, others are *deviant*."

For instance, in some Hindu cultures, eating the flesh of a cow is forbidden. In other cultures, it is not. Some people get sick at the mere idea of eating a dog or monkey; to others, such culinary practices are normal. Ethnocentrism is what makes us laugh at the way other people dress or talk. We

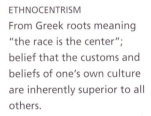

ETHNOCENTRISM
From Greek roots meaning "the race is the center"; belief that the customs and beliefs of one's own culture are inherently superior to all others.

Drawing by S. Harris; © 1992 *The New Yorker Magazine*, Inc.

can even do this to other citizens of our own country. Some Southerners make fun of people with a "New York accent," and New Yorkers in their turn may mock those with "Southern accents." The ethnocentric person thinks that he or she doesn't even have an accent!

The Greeks were so ethnocentric they invented the term **barbarian** to mock people who spoke in other languages. They mimicked the way foreigners talked by making a sound something like "bar, bar, bar." Today we would probably say, "blah, blah, blah." So the outsiders were bar-bar-ians (or blah-blah-ians), people whose language sounded like noise or nonsense to the Greeks. To these Greeks, other cultures were simply "uncivilized," "less human." But what happens when a closed-off culture begins to interact with other highly civilized cultures on a regular basis?

BARBARIAN
From a rude "bar-bar" noise used to mock dialects considered crude by the ancient Athenians; originally referred to other cultures considered "less than human" or uncivilized.

PHILOSOPHICAL QUERY

Can you think of any ways you are ethnocentric? What are some close parallels between Athens of the fifth century B.C. and America today? Discuss.

THE ADVENT OF PROFESSIONAL EDUCATORS

If a man were really able to instruct mankind, to receive money for giving instruction would, in my opinion, be an honour to him.
Socrates

The art of the Sophist is the semblance of wisdom without the reality, and the Sophist is one who makes money from an apparent but unreal wisdom.
Aristotle

Reality has nothing to do with reputation, reputation has nothing to do with reality. Reputation is nothing but pretence.
Lie Zi

Ancient Athens was chauvinistic in many respects. For example, full citizenship was originally confined to males from certain aristocratic families. The ambitious, talented young immigrants from throughout the Mediterranean area who were attracted by Athens's vitality as a trading center had fewer rights and opportunities than Athenian citizens. Regardless of their ability, it was difficult, if not impossible, for them to achieve the same levels of success as those lucky enough to have been born into the right families.

As the number of capable immigrants settling in and around Athens grew, tension and conflict became inevitable. The Athenians' snobbery was challenged. Some Persians and Spartans and Milesians were smarter, quicker, stronger, more attractive; some of their goods were of higher quality; their traders sometimes outfoxed Athenians. Thus the Athenians' image of themselves as unique and superior people became increasingly difficult to maintain as interaction with people from other cultures increased (as is always ultimately the case). Indeed, great deliberate effort was required to maintain a view of unquestioned superiority.

As the lively trade center flourished, the privileges of birth were challenged by the emergence of a wealthy new business class. Good business sense, personal charm and persuasiveness, willingness to work hard, and individual ability began to compete with merely having been born in the right place to the right kind of family.[2]

In this changing climate, more and more individuals were allowed both to speak before the Athenian Assembly and to sue one another over business and personal matters. The ability to think clearly and speak persuasively was a means for members of the new middle class to enter political life and to improve their social status. These conditions combined to create a demand for something unknown in the Mediterranean world before this time: formal, specialized higher education in such subjects as letters, rhetoric (persuasive speaking), science, statesmanship, and philosophy.[3]

While these social changes were taking place, philosophy was also affected by growth. As we have seen in Chapter 3, Presocratic philosophers had asserted that everything was fundamentally composed of water, or air, or earth, or fire, or flux, or number, or one, or many, or some combination of these. Thales, for example, said, "the [basic] principle is water." Anaximander disagreed, claiming, "It is neither water nor any other of those things that are called elements." Anaximenes thought it was air: "The other things are then derived from air." Heraclitus said, "Lightning is lord over all." And Pythagoras saw ultimate reality as being mathematical in nature: "All things which can be known have a number; without this nothing could possibly be thought or known." And that's only a partial list.

Each theory was flawed. Each philosopher's position was criticized logically by a newer point of view, which was in turn criticized. Even good logic and sound reasoning seemed ultimately unhelpful in sorting things out. One problem was with the characteristics of arguments themselves. All arguments consist of two aspects, their logical structure and the truth or falsity of their content. Sound arguments consist of good reasoning based on true premises. If one or more premises of an argument are false, the conclusion will be unreliable. Thus, *if its starting point is flawed, even the most tightly reasoned argument or theory will be flawed*.

Overwhelmed by so many conflicting theories, the "new *sophos*" of the fifth century B.C., now called a **Sophist**, concluded that it was impossible to discover "The Truth." If good reasoning could lead to inconsistent results, then the difference between a "good" argument and a "bad" argument was just a matter of the starting point. And the only difference between one starting point and another, according to the Sophists, was custom and individual preference.

THE SOPHISTS

The Sophists were a group of wandering teachers who gravitated toward Athens during this fertile period. They were the first professional teachers, charging a fee to teach any who wished to study with them. They made Athenian education democratic at least in the sense that all who could pay were equal. It was no longer necessary to belong to a certain family—as long as you had enough money to pay high tuitions. The *sophos*, in contrast, had followers and disciples, not paying students.

The Sophists also differed from the *sophos* in that the Sophists turned increasingly from the study of nature to the formal study of human life and conduct. Many of them had traveled rather widely and thus were "*sophisticated*," or worldly-wise. We get that word from them. The Sophists knew firsthand about various cultures; they had witnessed a variety of religious practices, and had experienced a variety of tastes in clothing, food, family patterns, legal values, and morals. They might be thought of as the first social scientists, combining, as it were, anthropology, psychology, and sociology to produce a particular view of social life and human nature. Their sophistication was a direct threat to the chauvinistic elite that ruled Athens. The idea that anyone with the fee could be educated was offensive to those who saw themselves as inherently superior.

SOPHISTS
Fifth-century B.C. paid teachers of rhetoric; relativists who taught that might makes right, truth is a matter of appearance and convention, and power is the ultimate value.

The Sophists speak in order to deceive, and they write for their own gain, and in no way to be of use to anyone.
Xenophon

Power and Education

The Sophists looked closely at what worked in various cultures and concluded that virtually nothing was good or bad by nature, but that good and bad were matters of custom and preference. Further, they noticed that although different individuals desire different things, everyone seeks some form of power. Indeed, every living thing seeks to be happy and to survive as long as possible, and so the only "natural" good is power, because power increases control over the conditions of happiness and survival. For instance, getting a new car won't make you happy if you cannot keep it. Being right about something at work won't help if you lack the ability (power) to get your boss to recognize it. Based on such observations, the Sophists concluded: So-called truth is subservient to power.[4]

The Sophists remained professionals, in the sense of always demanding payment, eventually becoming infamous for their insistence on being well paid. It was widely believed that the worst of them would teach anything they could get someone to pay for. The Sophists' reputation also suffered because of their emphasis on winning debates in and out of court. Since they believed that power was the ultimate value, the key issue became not right or wrong, but getting your own way. The Sophists became expert debaters and advertisers; they learned to use emotional appeals, physical appearance, and clever language to "sell" their particular point of view. These characteristics have led to the modern meaning of **sophistry** as subtle, plausible, but fallacious reasoning. Plato characterizes the Sophist this way:

> First, I believe he was found to be a paid hunter after the
> young and wealthy . . . secondly a kind of merchant in articles
> of knowledge for the soul . . . third did he not turn up as a
> retailer of these same articles of knowledge? . . . and in the
> fourth place we found he was a seller of his own products of
> knowledge . . . and in the fifth he was an athlete in contests of
> words, who had taken for his own the art of disputation . . .
> the sixth case was doubtful, but nevertheless we agreed to
> consider him a purger of souls, who removes opinions that
> obstruct learning.[5]

Socrates, the first great Western philosopher, lived at the same time as the Sophists and was also a famous educator. He often had what he claimed were discussions with Sophists; the Sophists, however, thought they were contests. Many Athenians weren't sure whether or not Socrates was a Sophist or a *sophos*. Socrates himself, though, was clear on one thing: It is wrong to charge money for teaching philosophy. He said:

> [I believe] that it is possible to dispose of beauty or of wisdom
> alike honorably or dishonorably; for if a person sells his
> beauty for money to anyone who wishes to purchase it, men
> call him a male prostitute; but if anyone makes a friend of a

There is no definite right or wrong human principle. To be able to adapt to the changing times is true wisdom.
Lie Zi

SOPHISTRY
The teachings and practices of the original Sophists; modern usage refers to subtle, plausible, but fallacious reasoning used to persuade rather than discover truth.

person whom he knows to be an honorable and worthy admirer, we regard him as prudent. In like manner those who sell their wisdom for money to any that will buy, men call sophists, or, as it were, prostitutes of wisdom; but whoever makes a friend of a person whom he knows to be deserving, and teaches him all the good that he knows, we consider him to act the part which becomes a good and honorable citizen.[6]

PHILOSOPHICAL QUERY

Discuss some of the pros and cons of personal education versus professional education. Try to consider a variety of factors: efficiency; effects of money on pupils, teachers, and institutions; mediocrity; conformity. Do you agree that it is wrong to "sell wisdom"? Is it realistic to expect teachers (or philosophers) to teach for free, for love only? Can't any source of financial support lead to bias? Must it?

For all their shameless accusations, my accusers have not been able in all their impudence to bring forward a single witness to say I have ever received a fee or asked for one. I, on the other hand, have a convincing witness that I speak the truth, my poverty.

Socrates

RELATIVISM

The Sophists were among the first systematic thinkers to conclude that the truth is relative. **Relativism** is the belief that knowledge is determined by specific qualities of the observer. The Sophists, for example, claimed that place of birth, family habits, personal abilities and preferences, religious training, age, and so forth control an individual's beliefs, values, and even perceptions. (Don't confuse relativism with subjectivism. See page 217 for a discussion of subjectivism—the belief that we can only know our own sensations.)

Based on this tenet, they argued that we need only accept what *seems* true at the moment, according to our culture. The most extreme Sophists claimed that even within the same culture, individuals have their own truths. The consequences of this position can be unsettling, to say the least. If no ultimate truth exists, no moral code is universally correct or absolutely superior to any other. The Sophists taught that each culture (or individual!) only *believes* that its ways are best, but the person who has studied many cultures knows better: One is as good as another if you believe in it.

There are two basic variants of what is known as *moral relativism*: cultural and individual. Cultural relativism is the belief that all values are culturally determined. Values do not reflect a divine order or a natural pattern, but merely the customs and preferences that develop in a given culture. Thus what is right in 1990s America is not necessarily right in South Africa or Brazil. Your grandmother's sexual morality was right for a particular person at a particular time and place, but not for all people all the time and in every place. What is right for a twenty-year-old African-American woman will be different from what is right for a ninety-year-old Chinese-American

RELATIVISM
Belief that knowledge is determined by specific qualities of the observer, including age, race, gender, cultural conditioning.

Traditions and customs are set by people. Therefore what people regard as "truth" tends to be a subjective matter.

Lie Zi

man, and so on. Consequently, what's right for you may very well be different from what's right for people of different ages and backgrounds.

The narrower, more radical view of moral relativism, called individual relativism, simply carries the logic of cultural relativism to a more refined conclusion. It goes like this: Even in the same place and time, right and wrong are relative to the unique experiences and preferences of the individual. There is no unbiased way to say that one standard is better than another, for the standard used to make *that* claim is itself the reflection of a preference, ad infinitum. No matter how far back we push "ultimate" reasons, they always reduce to someone's preference. Hence, moral values are matters of individual taste and opinion.

PHILOSOPHICAL QUERY

Some English teachers hesitate to impose standards of English grammar. They see all grammar as "preferences." Do you agree? Ask your English teacher about this.

PROTAGORAS THE PRAGMATIST

Protagoras

We recognize that morality differs in every society, and is a convenient term for socially approved habits. Mankind has always preferred to say, "It is morally good," rather than "It is habitual," and the fact of this preference is matter enough for a critical science of ethics. But historically the two phrases are synonymous.

Ruth Benedict

Perhaps the greatest of the Sophists was **Protagoras of Abdera (481–411 B.C.).** Attracted to Athens around the middle of the fifth century, he became a famous teacher there. He was befriended by wealthy and powerful Athenians, and as a consequence became rich and powerful himself. Plato even named a dialogue after him.

Protagoras was an archetypal Sophist: an active traveler and first-rate observer of other cultures who noted that although there are a variety of customs and beliefs, each culture believes unquestioningly that its own ways are right—and roundly condemns (or at least criticizes) views that differ from its own. So he asked himself: What really makes something right or wrong? Is anything *really* right or wrong? What is truth? Can we know it? Can we *know that we know it*, or are we limited to mere beliefs? His answers may strike you as surprisingly contemporary. And they are—as the term *Sophist* suggests—quite sophisticated.

Based on his observations and travels, Protagoras concluded that morals were nothing more than the social traditions, or mores, of a society or group. What makes the Athenian way right for someone living in Athens is the fact that following the mores of one's place is the best way to live successfully and well—in that place. The task of the truly wise observer is to record accurately and describe without bias what works and what does not work. Hence the famous remark quoted at the beginning of this chapter: *Man is the measure of all things.* Here is how Plato reported Socrates' characterization of what Protagoras meant:

> Well, is not this what [Protagoras] means, that individual things are for me such as they appear to me, and for you in turn such as they appear to you—you and I being "man"? . . .

Comparing the lifestyles and beliefs of these contemporary Islamic women to those of contemporary American women shows how difficult it is to dispute the sophists' claim that all values are culturally determined.

Is it not true that sometimes, when the same wind blows, one of us feels cold and the other does not? or one feels slightly and the other exceedingly cold? . . . Then in that case, shall we say that the wind is in itself cold or not cold; or shall we accept Protagoras' saying that it is cold for him who feels cold, not for him who does not?[7]

Since we do not have complete texts of Protagoras's actual essays available, we must rely on fragments and commentaries. One of the clearest presentations of Protagoras's relativism is a partial reconstruction of his philosophy by Gregory Vlastos, a contemporary scholar who specializes in ancient philosophy. Using the form of a dialogue between himself and Protagoras, Vlastos begins with a reference to the famous opening sentence of Protagoras's essay "Truth." In Vlastos's translation the opening sentence reads: "Of all things man is the measure: both of things that are (man is the measure) that they are, and of things that are not (man is the measure) that they are not."

> Protagoras: Appearance *is* reality. Even what you philosophers call "reality" is just what appears true to them.
> Vlastos: But appearances are not consistent. The same wind often feels warm to me, cold to you.
> Protagoras: Then it *is* warm for you, cold for me.
> Vlastos: But what is it in itself?

"Pick the right time and flourish, miss the right time and perish." Nowhere is there a principle which is right in all circumstances, or an action that is wrong in all circumstances. The method we used yesterday we may discard today and use again in the future. There is no fixed right and wrong to decide whether we use it or not.
Lie Zi

The Ethiopians say that their gods are snub-nosed and black, the Thracians that theirs have light blue eyes and red hair.
Xenophanes

The religion of one seems madness unto another.
Sir Thomas Browne

When Aesop's lion was shown a painting in which a man was depicted killing a lion, he commented contemptuously, "The artist was obviously a man."
B. F. Skinner

Protagoras: "Wind-in-itself"? I know of no such thing. Do you? The only wind you can know is the one you can feel: this is the wind for you, and you are its measure.

Vlastos: If that is the way you reason, you might as well hold that all beliefs are true.

Protagoras: I do. All beliefs *are* true for those who believe them.

Vlastos: I suppose you have no scruples about applying your appearance-is-reality doctrine to morals.

Protagoras: Are you insinuating there is something unscrupulous about that? . . . anything held right and just in a given state is right and just for it.

Vlastos: But there is often disagreement *within* a state. Is the minority view wrong when it conflicts with the official doctrine?

Protagoras: Not wrong for the minority.

Vlastos: So you would require the minority to act in ways that seem unjust to them, and are unjust for them?

Protagoras: I see no logical inconsistency in that, but if you mean that it would be very awkward, I quite agree. When people differ in their moral judgments, it is very hard for them to avoid acting out their disagreements, and then the very purpose for which morality was invented—to facilitate friendly and harmonious social relations—would be defeated. This is a practical problem, and it calls for a practical answer. On my view, moral disagreement is like a disease. You don't argue about it. You cure it.

Vlastos: How do you propose to do that?

Protagoras: The way it is done in every civilized community. Just think how many of the things you do are concerned with the *prevention* of disagreement in the first place, and then if this fails, with its *cure*. You start with the child telling him, "This is just, that is unjust . . . ; do this, don't do that," and if he goes along with you the problem has been forestalled. If not, then, "like a bent and warped wood," you "straighten it out by blows."

Vlastos: By "straightening" it out, you mean you bring it into line with the mores of its elders?

Protagoras: What else? Or are you hankering after straight-in-itself?

Vlastos: But isn't what the little rebel thinks straight, straight for him?

Protagoras: Certainly. But you are missing the point. The point is not, who is right—the child or his parents? There is no sense to that question: there never is, in any case of moral disagreement. The only question that makes sense is how to get rid of the disagreement. And the answer to this is obvious. The parents can straighten the child according to their views, while the child is in no position to impose his on them.[8]

Protagoras predicted a crucial tenet of modern social science: Our values are determined by our culture, our conditioning, our experience, and our particular biopsychology. It is, according to Protagoras, utterly impossible to form a culture-free or context-free belief. For instance, philosophy students born, raised, and educated in Moscow, Russia, cannot help but "see" a different world than those born, raised, and educated in Moscow, Idaho.

Thus the real issue is not what is true, since true always means "true for the believer," and if Student A believes something, that alone makes it true from her perspective. The worthwhile issue is what works for Student A, not what is universally true or what works for Student B. The point of view that beliefs are to be interpreted in terms of "whether they work" (their usefulness) is called **pragmatism**, from the Greek *pragma*, "deed." Ideas have meaning or truth value to the extent that they produce practical results and are effective in furthering our aims.

Plato criticized Protagoras for—in Plato's view—reducing the concept of what is "useful" to whatever people think is useful. Of course Protagoras could respond to Plato this way: "What is useful if not useful to some particular individual, at some particular place and time? What sense is there in talking about 'useful in general'? Useful always means useful for the specific purposes and desires of an individual. And even for individuals, what is useful changes." (For a fuller account of modern pragmatism, see Chapter 17.)

In a speech Plato attributes to Protagoras, the Sophist makes the case that *wisdom is what works*:

> For I maintain that the truth is as I have written; each one of us is the measure of the things that are and those that are not; but each person differs immeasurably from every other in just this, that to one person some things appear and are, and to another person other things . . . do not lay too much stress upon the words of my argument, but get a clearer understanding of my meaning from what I am going to say. Recall to your mind what was said before, that his food appears and is bitter to the sick man, but appears and is the opposite of bitter to the man in health. Now neither of these two is to be made wiser than he is—that is not possible—nor should the claim be made that the sick man is ignorant because his opinions are ignorant, or the healthy man wise because his opinions are different; but a change must be made from the one condition to the other, for the other is better. So, too, in education a change has to be made from a worse condition to a better condition; but the physician causes the change by means of drugs, and the teacher of wisdom by means of words. . . . And

Of what value is smartness of speech? Opposing a man with the mouth excites anger.
Confucius

PRAGMATISM
From the Greek for "deed"; ideas have meaning or truth value to the extent that they produce practical results and effectively further our aims; empirically based philosophy that defines knowledge and truth in terms of practical consequences.

But if a man arises endowed with a nature sufficiently strong he will, I believe, shake off these controls, burst his fetters, and break loose. And trampling upon our scraps of paper, our spells and incantations, and all our unnatural conventions, he rises up and reveals himself our master who was once our slave, and there shines forth nature's true justice.
Callicles

We are what we think, having become what we thought.
The Dhammapada

on the same principle the teacher who is able to train his pupils in this manner is not only wise but is also entitled to receive high pay from them when their education is finished. And in this sense it is true that some men are wiser than others, and that no one thinks falsely, and that you, whether you will or no, must . . . be a measure. Upon these positions my doctrine stands firm.[9]

PHILOSOPHICAL QUERY

Analyze Protagoras's speech. Has he convinced you? Explain. See if you can explain the trick used by both Protagoras and his pupil in the *Wager* (see pages 98–99).

Protagoras was a rather tame Sophist. He reasoned that the most intelligent thing to do is to accept the customs and beliefs of your own community. By understanding that the mores of the community are not universal absolutes, you will develop a relaxed, effective attitude about them. This in turn will allow you to use them rather than being controlled by them. Openly flouting convention is most likely to be counterproductive. With the rare exceptions of talented and charismatic individuals, *behaving in a generally conventional way affords us the most social power.*

Protagoras maintained that "each one of us is the measure." Is your reaction to the sumo wrestlers more negative than to the model? If so, why is one extreme more desirable than the other? If you do not care for either extreme, is your prefer-ence more "reason-able," "healthier," or just your preference?

Dress the way that will get you promoted at work, or get you a date at the club. Write the kind of essay your teacher wants and you'll get a good grade; write your own creative masterpiece and you may not. Drive with the flow of traffic—neither too fast nor too slow—and you'll lower your in-surance rates. If you want to get elected, go to church and keep your hair neat and conservative.

PROTAGORAS'S WAGER

Among the consequences of the Sophists' emphasis on power, winning, and relativism are the aggressive competitiveness and boldness that flourish in such a climate. Because the Sophists chose to be public figures, seeking fame and influence, they were always eager to show off their abilities. They used their speaking skills to attack one another and attract students. Whenever possible, they spoke to large audiences, whether in the Assembly or in the public square. The average Athenian found these sparring matches entertaining at first. But as you will learn, the audience soon regarded the Sophists as disturbing and dangerous. A famous example of sophistic sparring is the story known as *Protagoras's Wager*.

Protagoras had a pupil named Eulathus, who arranged to take Protagoras's course in rhetoric and sophistry, a kind of law school, for partial tuition. So sure was Protagoras of his abilities as a teacher that he told Eulathus he did not have to pay the balance until Eulathus won his first court case. In fact, Protagoras guaranteed that Eulathus would win his first case.

Time dragged on and Eulathus neither paid up nor argued any cases in court. Not only was Protagoras out the money, he looked bad to his students and to other Sophists. After all, if winning is what counts, and if appearance is reality, and if the pupil can outmaneuver the old master, why should anyone continue to pay his high fees? Protagoras was compelled to take action.

Confronting Eulathus (probably in a public place where he could use his crowd-

---

The majority of just acts according to the law are prescribed contrary to nature. For there is legislation about the eyes, what they must see and what not; and about the ears, what they must hear and what not; and about the tongue, what it must speak and what not; and about the hands, what they must do and what not; and about the feet, where they must go and where not. And about the soul, what it must desire and what not.

Antiphon

Tradition has it that Protagoras did not always follow his own advice. The story goes that at the home of a friend, Protagoras gave a reading of one of his own treatises called *On the Gods*. This particular work applied the principle of relativism to religious belief, apparently holding religion to the pragmatic standard. There was no separation of church and state in Athens at this time. Failure to believe in and respect "the gods of the state" was considered to be a form of treason known as impiety. One of the other guests, a conservative army officer, was so offended by Protagoras's ideas that he consequently had Protagoras indicted for impiety. Protagoras was found guilty. All copies of *On the Gods* were confiscated and burned, and the authorities set out to confiscate Protagoras, too. Facing death or exile, he attempted to escape on a ship headed for Sicily. The ship was wrecked and Protagoras drowned.

MORAL REALISM

In contrast to Protagoras, the next generation of Sophists carried moral relativism to a more radical level, proposing a pragmatic social philosophy unfettered by any moral considerations. One of

pleasing skills), Protagoras demanded payment in the form of this dilemma: "Eulathus, you might as well pay me, since I am going to sue you for the rest of the tuition. If I win in court, the court will rule that you owe me the money; if I lose in court, you will have won your first case, and you will owe me the money. Either I win in court or I lose, so either you owe me the money or you owe me the money."

Protagoras, alas, was a good teacher, and Eulathus was ready for him. He shot back with a counterdilemma: "No, sir, you have it backwards. If you defeat me in court, then I have lost my first case and so do not owe the money; if I defeat you, the court will rule that I do not owe you the money. Either I defeat you or you defeat me. In either case, I do not owe you the money."

Who won? The story does not say. And besides, Sophists being what they were, neither Eulathus nor Protagoras would have wanted to lose big in a highly publicized trial. *Protagoras's Wager* gives us an instructive glimpse of sophistry in action. Such encounters were common, as Sophists vied for students and reputation. To the general citizenry, they were sometimes amusing entertainment. Men like Protagoras lived rather mild lives considering what they taught and the reactions their excitable pupils had to their ideas. But when the same kinds of tricks were used for high stakes, say to convict innocent citizens, to control democracy, to wrest property away from people, no one laughed. Sophistry's reputation grew darker.

them, **Thrasymachus (c. 450 B.C.)**, is an archetype of the kind of Sophist who is less interested in theories and philosophy than in political and social action. In *The Republic*, Plato paints a vivid portrait of the volatile, aggressive style Thrasymachus used in confronting his opponents.

Thrasymachus the Moral Realist

We meet Thrasymachus in the first book of *The Republic*. *The Republic* consists of a series of dialogues between Socrates, Plato's late, beloved teacher, and various individuals. The chief question of *The Republic* concerns the nature of justice. After Socrates rejects some early attempts to define justice, Thrasymachus literally bursts into the scene. With energy and sarcasm, he categorically denies that any one moral standard can be equally applicable to rich and poor, strong and weak, "superior" and "inferior."

By skillful questioning, Socrates has already revealed that conventional views of morality are confused and "muddleheaded." Thrasymachus goes well beyond this position and rejects conventional notions of morality altogether. Plato's portrait reflects Socrates' critical opinion of such an extreme point of view. Plato's Thrasymachus is loud, offensive, and often on the

We do not want a thing because we reason; we find reasons for anything because we want it.

G. W. F. Hegel

Sometimes it seems as if might does indeed make right—at least that's what some observers of the 1992 Los Angeles riots claim. They argue that the riots brought attention, financial aid, business loans, and so forth to the riot-torn communities. Do you agree with this assessment?

verge of resorting to force. From the very start, we know we are in for an interesting experience as Thrasymachus disrupts the courteous, "philosophical" tone of the discussion. He transforms moral relativism into a hard-edged moral realism, contending that an unsentimental view of life shows quite clearly that *might makes right.*

Speak softly but carry a big stick.

Theodore Roosevelt

Whether we like it or not, according to the moral realist, the values that prevail in all areas of life—economic, political, racial, educational—reflect the interests of the strong. Certain values dominate not because they are in some absolute sense "right," but because they are the views preferred by the most powerful individual or group. And since nature rewards power, the powerful individual is the superior type, the "true individual," gloriously free in his or her indifference to morality.

Best-selling contemporary author Robert J. Ringer expresses the moral realist's view in *Winning Through Intimidation*:

> In general, I, like everyone else, wished that the game of business took place on a nursery school playground; the reality, however, was that the game of business is [*sic*] played in a vi-

cious jungle. I decided that I must either accept that reality or, for my own well-being, get completely out of the game.[10]

Thrasymachus would have understood this attitude. Plato makes the case for the moral realist in a speech attributed to Thrasymachus:

> "Listen then," [Thrasymachus] replied. "I define justice or right as what is in the interest of the stronger party. Now where is your praise? I can see you're going to refuse it."
>
> "You shall have it when I [Socrates] understand what you mean, which at present I don't. You say that what is in the interest of the stronger party is right; but what do you mean by interest? For instance, Polydamas the athlete is *stronger* than us, and it's in his *interest* to eat beef to keep it; we are *weaker* than he, but you can't mean that the same diet is in our *interest* and so *right* for us."
>
> "You're being tiresome, Socrates," he returned, "and taking my definition in the sense most likely to damage it."
>
> "I assure you I'm not," [Socrates] said; "you must explain your meaning more clearly."
>
> "Well then, you know that some states are tyrannies, some democracies, some aristocracies? And that in each city power is in the hands of the ruling class?"
>
> "Yes."
>
> "Each ruling class makes laws that are in its own interest, a democracy democratic laws, a tyranny tyrannical ones and so on; and in making these laws they define as 'right' for their subjects what is in the interest of themselves, the rulers, and if anyone breaks their laws he is punished as a 'wrongdoer.' That is what I mean when I say that 'right' is the same thing in all states, namely the interest of the established ruling class; and this ruling class is the 'strongest' element in each state, and so if we argue correctly we see that 'right' is always the same, the interest of the stronger party.
>
> ". . . Consider how the just man always comes off worse than the unjust. For instance, in any business relations between them, you won't find the just man better off at the end of the deal than the unjust. Again, in their relations with the state, when there are taxes to be paid the unjust man will pay less on the same income, and when there's anything to be got he'll get it all. Thus if it's a question of office, if the just man loses nothing else he will suffer from neglecting his private affairs; his honesty will prevent him appropriating public funds, and his relations and friends will detest him because his principles will not allow him to push their interests. But quite the reverse is true of the unjust man . . . the man . . . who can

Based on my interpretations of reality and relativity, the techniques I used were not "brutal," either. I merely fought fire with fire: the techniques were no more brutal than the realities they were intended to reckon with. And realities are nothing more than "things"—not "good" or "bad," not "brutal" or "comforting"—they just are.
Robert J. Ringer

We may have been talking about you, but I have always been thinking about myself.
Oscar Wilde

THE RING OF GYGES

The technical name for the view that all morality reduces to self-interest is *egoism*. It is usually associated with moral skepticism, since it is the only source of values left for the moral skeptic. One of the earliest and most interesting presentations of the egoist's position occurs in Plato's *Republic*:

Even those who practise justice do so against their will because they lack the power to do wrong. This we would realize if we clearly imagined ourselves granting to both the just and the unjust the freedom to do whatever they liked. We could then follow both of them and observe where their desires led them, and we would catch the just man redhanded travelling the same road as the unjust. The reason is the desire for undue gain which every organism by nature pursues as good, but the law forcibly sidetracks him to honour equality. The freedom I just mentioned would most easily occur if these men had the power which they say the ancestor of the Lydian Gyges possessed. The story is that he was a shepherd in the service of the ruler of Lydia. There was a violent rainstorm and an earthquake which broke open the ground and created a chasm at the place where he was tending sheep. Seeing this and marvelling, he went down into it. He saw, besides many other wonders of which we are told, a hollow bronze horse. There were window-like openings in it; he climbed through one of them and caught sight of a corpse which seemed of more than human stature, wear-

Because my philosophy was based on reality, all of my techniques were either directly or indirectly aimed at the most important reality of all: the necessity of getting paid.
Robert J. Ringer

Winning isn't everything, it's the only thing.
Attributed to Vince Lombardi

make profits in a big way: he's the man to study if you want to find how much more private profit there is in wrong than in right. . . . *So we see that injustice, given scope, has greater strength and freedom and power than justice; which proves what I started by saying, that justice is the interest of the stronger party, injustice the interest and profit of oneself"* [emphasis added].[11]

PHILOSOPHICAL QUERY

Statistically, poorer, less educated people make up a disproportionate segment of our prison population. Just how relevant to Thrasymachus's position is it that white-collar and celebrity criminals are often punished less severely than poor or obscure defendants? Other studies suggest that physically attractive job candidates are most likely to be hired. Have you ever noticed how some students seem to get by mostly on cleverness and charm? Should we draw conclusions about the nature of justice from these cases or just chalk them up to the way things sometimes go? Try to separate our lip-service moral values from those we practice. Try to separate a storybook conception of life from a realistic one. Are the Sophists onto something or not? Explain.

ing nothing but a ring of gold on its finger. This ring the shepherd put on and came out. He arrived at the usual monthly meeting which reported to the king on the state of the flocks, wearing the ring. As he was sitting among the others he happened to twist the hoop of the ring towards himself, to the inside of his hand, and as he did this he became invisible to those sitting near him and they went off talking as if he had gone. He marvelled at this and, fingering the ring, turned the hoop outward again and became visible. Perceiving this he tested whether the ring had this power and so it happened: if he turned the hoop inwards he became invisible, but he was visible when he turned it outwards. When he realized this, he at once arranged to become one of the messengers of the king. He went, committed adultery with the king's wife, attacked the king with her help, killed him, and took over the kingdom.

Now if there were two such rings, one worn by the just man, the other by the unjust, no one, as these people think, would be so incorruptible that he would stay on the path of justice or bring himself to keep away from other people's property and not touch it, when he could with impunity take whatever he wanted from the market, go into houses and have sexual relations with anyone he wanted, kill anyone, free all those he wished from prison, and do other things which would make him like a god among men.

Plato
The Republic, trans. G. M. A. Grube (Indianapolis: Hackett, 1974), p. 32ff.

Might Makes Right

The laws of every society, says the moral realist, turn out to reflect the interests of those in power. The U.S. Constitution, for example, places great emphasis on property rights and protections because most of its chief architects were landed gentry: persons with property. Hence their view of the "ideal" state reflected and furthered their material interests. Each new Supreme Court reflects the values of the majority of its members, now liberal, now conservative. The "right" view is the view held by those currently in power. The rest of us, says Thrasymachus, ultimately obey because we have to; we have no other choice: Regardless of whether we believe that what is legal is also right, the average person obeys anyway because he or she lacks sufficient power (and courage) not to obey.

From a certain perspective, history seems to support the view that might and power determine right. But what about counterexamples like the civil rights movement of the 1960s? Here "right" finally prevailed, even against centuries of custom and habit supporting racist practices. This example seems to show that moral progress is possible and that not everyone acts from limited self-interest.

A contemporary Thrasymachus could point out, however, that civil rights changes occurred in this country only after members of the powerful

And how many legions does the Pope have?
Joseph Stalin, at Yalta

Calvin and Hobbes. Copyright 1991 Universal Press Syndicate. Reprinted with permission.

Convention is the ruler of all.

Pindar

white middle class began to support the position of the racial minorities. The view of the most powerful faction of the time won: Civil might made civil rights. The same is true of women's rights. Women's rights have increased in proportion to women's power. African Americans, Hispanic Americans, Asian Americans, and other groups have rights in direct proportion to their might. The elderly will have more rights in the future because by the year 2000 they will outnumber members of other age groups. And so it goes. Your philosophy instructor has more power over your philosophy course than you do. Thus—ultimately—her interpretation of your test is more "right" than yours. Her answers are more "useful" than yours. Parents are "right" about many things simply because they have more power than children. Whoever has power gets to be right.

PHILOSOPHICAL QUERY

Is "might makes right" the only explanation for social changes like the civil rights movement? Could other factors besides self-interest account for a shift in basic social values? What factors? Is anything lost by accepting a might-makes-right interpretation? Is anything gained?

THE DOCTRINE OF THE SUPERIOR INDIVIDUAL

Not everybody willingly submits to those in power or depends on a group for clout. Those who do not are well represented by a Sophist named **Callicles (c. 435 B.C.)**. His point of view goes by different names: the doctrine of the superior individual, the true man, the natural man, the superman. You may recognize foreshadowings of Nazism and racism in it. It is always elitist, but it is not always a racial doctrine. Indeed, in its most compelling form it is highly individualistic. A person is superior not because of racial or cultural background but only because of individual virtues and traits. (We will study one of the most notorious expressions of this view in Chapter 16.)

The moral realist distinguished what is right by nature from what is right by convention. In the following selection from Plato's *Gorgias*, Callicles asserts that by nature the strong dominate the weak, whereas conventional morality tries to restrain the superior, the strong, the truly powerful individual. In nature, the survival of the fittest is the rule. This, said such Sophists, shows that power is the ultimate value, and that *the superior and powerful individual has a natural right to dominate others. All people are no more created equal than all animals are.*

> For to suffer wrong is not the part of a man at all, but that of a slave for whom it is better to be dead than alive, as it is for anyone who is unable to come either to his own assistance when he is wronged or mistreated or to that of anyone he cares about. I can quite imagine that the manufacturers of laws and conventions are the weak, the majority, in fact. It is for themselves and their own advantage that they make their laws and distribute their praises and their censures. It is to frighten men who are stronger than they and able to enforce superiority that they keep declaring, to prevent aggrandizement, that this is ugly and unjust, that injustice consists in seeking to get the better of one's neighbor. They are quite content, I suppose, to be on equal terms with others since they are themselves inferior.
>
> This, then, is the reason why convention declares that it is unjust and ugly to seek to get the better of the majority. But my opinion is that nature herself reveals it to be only just and proper that the better man should lord it over his inferior: it will be the stronger over the weaker. Nature, further, makes it quite clear in a great many instances that this is the true state of affairs, not only in the other animals, but also in whole states and communities. This is, in fact, how justice is determined: the stronger shall rule and have the advantage over his inferior. . . .
>
> . . . Now, my dear friend, take my advice: stop your [philosophy], take up the Fine Art of Business, and cultivate something that will give you a reputation for good sense. Leave all these over-subtleties to someone else. Should one call them frivolities or just plain nonsense? They'll only land you in a

Where there is no vision, the people perish; where there is no framework of moral reasoning, the people close ranks in a war of all against all.
Cornel West

"What is right in one group is wrong in another," he says. But what exactly is a group? and which group is one to select? Every person is a member of many different groups—his nation, his state, his city, his club, his school, church, fraternity, or athletic association. Suppose that most of the people in his club think that a certain kind of act is wrong and that most of the people in his nation think it is right; what then?
John Hospers

There are two sides to every question.
Protagoras

house where you'll be the only visitor! You must emulate, not those whose very refutations are paltry, but men of substance and high repute and everything else that is good.[12]

PHILOSOPHICAL QUERY

Is some part of you stirred by all this talk of power and superiority? The Sophists would say that if you can be honest, you'll answer in the affirmative. What might prevent you (in the Sophists' view) from admitting that you agree with them? Are they correct? Even if you personally reject Callicles' position, how common do you think it is? What's your evidence?

COMMENTARY

The questions raised by the Sophists are important, not just in the dusty archives of scholarly concerns but also for the continuing influence sophistic ideas exert on our lives and beliefs. Sophists helped free the Greeks to think on new, less restricted levels. From this beginning emerged a nonreligious (amoral) scientific method as well as a philosophic method of questioning, both of which are free to pursue knowledge for its own sake and wherever it leads. In other words, the Sophists helped break the shackles of dogma and superstition. For that we remain in their debt. They laid the cornerstone for the scientific study of human behavior—what would become the social, psychological, political, and anthropological sciences.

The Sophists' emphasis on the individual as determiner of value and the challenges they posed to the possibility of a moral absolute were contributing factors to increasing democracy in Athens. Thus, the Sophists were perceived as a direct threat by the "establishment" of privileged aristocrats.

The youth of Athens responded with gusto to these ideas as a call to unrestrained self-assertion and personal freedom. It was stimulating to challenge the stuffy, square, straight, uptight values of the establishment. The glorification of the "superior individual" or "natural man" has always appealed to adolescent cravings for power, fame, freedom, and identity. Logic and the rhetorical devices refined by the Sophists were liberally applied to legal maneuvering, politics, techniques of manipulation, and control of the marketplace. By the third generation, Sophists no longer claimed to be sophistai, teachers of wisdom, but advertised shortcuts to guaranteed social, political, financial, and personal success. These were the forerunners of today's how-to-succeed, you-can-have-it-all books, courses, and techniques. Freed of any moral anchor, the Sophists were often deadly and effective. They took no responsibility for the ways people might use their ideas, as the great Sophist Gorgias reminds us:

> And if a man learns rhetoric, and then does injustice through the power of his art, we shall not be right, in my opinion, in

If ethical relativism is correct, it is clearly impossible for the moral beliefs of a society to be mistaken because the certainty of the majority that its beliefs were right would prove that those beliefs were right for that society at that time. The minority view would therefore be mistaken, no matter what it was. Needless to say, most people who state that "in morals everything is relative" and who proceed to call themselves ethical relativists are unaware of these implications of their theory.

—John Hospers

DARROW'S CIGAR

An apocryphal story about the legendary lawyer Clarence Darrow circulates among law students: Darrow had to defend an especially unsavory client. This was a hard case to make. As the prosecutor ranted and raved to the jury about the heinous nature of the crime and the plight of the suffering victims, Darrow paid him close and courteous attention, puffing distractedly on a large cigar. The ash grew, an eighth of an inch, a quarter, a half, an inch or more— yet did not fall. Darrow didn't seem to notice. He just politely concentrated on the prosecutor's words. But the jury noticed. Instead of paying full attention to the prosecutor, they were drawn again and again to Darrow's cigar—into which he had secretly inserted a thin piece of wire.

detesting and banishing his teacher. For while the teacher imparted instruction to be used rightly, the pupil made a contrary use of it. Therefore, it is only right to detest the misuser and banish and kill him, not his teacher.[13]

Although they were attacked by Plato and others on moral grounds, most Sophists were actually amoral (nonmoral) rather than immoral. Like the caricature of a mob attorney who uses all her persuasive skills to vigorously and lucratively defend known drug dealers and Mafia bosses, the Sophists made no moral judgments. They were concerned only with "what worked." They saw the world as hard and brutal, a jungle. Because the restraints and inhibitions of morality weaken us, they refused to acknowledge them. In contemporary terms they were masters of "effective" thinking, communicating, and acting.

Many sophistic techniques, like Darrow's (see box), are genuinely clever and clearly effective. The Sophists of ancient Athens inspired mixed feelings of awe and admiration, anger and disgust. They raised vital, ongoing questions: When the stakes are high, is playing fair the smart thing to do? Just how important is winning? And how should we be judged? On the conventional morals most of us profess? Or on the values we actually practice and (secretly?) admire: strength, power, daring, attractiveness, social contacts, success? Can we ever have objective knowledge or escape the limits of culture? In the absence of certainty, might it be better to allow more individual choice rather than less?

As you reflect on the archetype of the Sophist, think about its place in today's world. As you are probably realizing, the similarities between the cultural climate of ancient Athens and that of America in the 1990s are widespread and deeply rooted. The Sophists represent one side of the timeless struggle between "the world" and wisdom. We all face this struggle. So we're not just learning about the past, about dead ideas. We are learning about living issues.

Go about with your middle finger up and people will say you're daft; go about with your little finger out, and they will cultivate your company.

Diogenes

Probably most people who call themselves ethical relativists are not so at all, for they believe in one moral standard which applies in different ways to different societies because of the various conditions in which they live. One might as well talk about gravitational relativism because a stone falls and a balloon rises; yet both events are equally instances of one law of universal gravitation.

John Hospers

As the original Sophists grew in numbers and boldness, they attracted more and more enemies. Unable to distinguish sophistic philosophies from other forms, the citizens of Athens began to agree with each other that philosophy itself was unacceptably subversive. Philosophy's reputation for being somehow unpatriotic and dangerous was established. Into this breach stepped perhaps the single most influential and arresting philosopher of all, the first major philosopher of the West: Socrates.

SUMMARY OF MAIN POINTS

As Athens grew in influence it attracted more and more people from other city-states and countries. Those who considered themselves to be "original, true Athenians" grew uncomfortable and defensive. They became increasingly ethnocentric. Ethnocentrism includes the often unconscious tendency to consider one's own customs, foods, and social patterns as superior to all others. This leads the ethnocentric person to condemn other customs as "unnatural."

The emergence of a new middle class combined with opportunities for a growing number of Athenians to speak before the Assembly created a demand for formal, specialized higher education in subjects such as letters, rhetoric, science, statesmanship, and philosophy.

Social and cultural changes also affect philosophy. Competing points of view criticized one another, yet failed to withstand criticism. Overwhelmed by so many conflicting theories and cultural viewpoints, a new kind of *sophos* emerged known as a *Sophist*.

Sophists concluded that if good reasoning could lead to inconsistent results, then the difference between a "good" argument and a "bad" argument was just a matter of the starting point. And the only difference between one starting point and another, according to the Sophists, was custom and individual preference.

The Sophists were a group of wandering teachers who were the first professional teachers, charging a fee to teach any who wished to study with them. They made Athenian education democratic at least in the sense that all who could pay were equal.

The Sophists believed that virtually nothing is good or bad by nature, but that good and bad are matters of custom and preference. They claimed that although different individuals desire different things, everyone seeks some form of power. The Sophists taught that so-called truth is subservient to power.

The early Sophists argued that the truth is relative. They were relativists who believed that knowledge is determined by specific qualities of the observer—for example, place of birth, family habits, personal abilities and preferences, religious training, age, and so forth control an individual's beliefs, values, and even perceptions.

There are two basic variants of what is known as *moral relativism*: cultural and individual. Cultural relativism is the belief that all values are culturally determined. Individual relativism carries the logic of cultural relativism to a more refined conclusion: Even in the same place and time, right and wrong are relative to the unique experiences and preferences of the individual.

Protagoras of Abdera was one of the most influential of the Sophists. Protagoras said that morals are nothing more than the social traditions, or mores, of a society or group. Therefore, following the mores of one's place is the best way to live successfully and well—in that place. According to Protagoras, the task of the truly wise observer is to record accurately and describe without bias what works and what does not work. Hence his famous remark: *Man is the measure of all things*.

The next generation of Sophists carried moral relativism to a more radical level, proposing a social philosophy unfettered by any moral considerations. Thrasymachus transformed moral relativism into a hard-edged moral realism based on the doctrine that might makes right.

According to the moral realist, the values that prevail in all areas of life—economic, political, racial, educational—reflect the interests of the strong. Certain values dominate not because they are in some absolute sense "right," but because they are the views preferred by the most powerful individual or group. Moral realism distinguishes what is right by "nature" from what is right by "convention."

Callicles was a Sophist associated with an aspect of moral realism known as the doctrine of the superior individual. He asserted that by nature the strong dominate the weak, whereas conventional morality tries to restrain the superior, truly powerful individual. In nature, the "survival of the fittest" is the rule. This, Callicles claimed, shows that the superior and powerful individual has a natural right to dominate others.

STUDY QUESTIONS

1. What is ethnocentrism? Give a few current examples from your own experience.

2. Describe the circumstances that led to the change from *sophos* to *Sophist*.

3. What is a Sophist?

4. Identify and explain three or four specific sophistic ideas.

5. Make a convincing case that advertisers are sophists. Are they? What would nonsophistic advertising be like?

6. Is there any merit to the claim that modern colleges and universities are sophistic in their attempts to compete for students? What other trends in contemporary education might be viewed as sophistic? Analyze.

7. Briefly distinguish different kinds of relativism.

8. Is there something logically peculiar about the claim that *all* values are relative? Analyze carefully.

9. If all opinions are true, as Protagoras claimed, why discuss them? What grounds does a relativist have for being angry when others dispute her beliefs? Does she need any grounds? If not, what follows?

10. Discuss Protagoras's notion that disagreements can be "cured."

11. What's wrong with believing whatever makes you happy? Are there any truly harmful consequences to believing in astrology or crystal power? How can we question the beliefs of others just because we haven't had similar experiences?

12. On the one hand, it seems as if we should not base a moral position on how people actually behave. If we did, we'd have to condone lying regularly, cheating now and then, and so forth. On the other hand, it seems foolish, and perhaps cold and arrogant, to ignore our basic conduct and weaknesses. What do you think? Explain. (Note: This is an important ethical issue that we will see again.)

13. Do you think that society stifles the "superior individual"?

14. Is there a contradiction involved in the way the Sophists present their doctrine that "justice is in the interest of the stronger"? Can you present a better version of it?

15. Is there any way to refute the idea that might makes right? Explain why or why not.

16. Are lawyers Sophists? Do the ends justify the means? Discuss.

17. Try to find a few current examples of sophistry. What do you think of them and why?

18. Today, the term *sophist* is often used as a criticism. Have the Sophists been given a bad rap? Why or why not?

CHAPTER FIVE

The Wise Man: Socrates

SOCRATES: Tell me, Euthydemus, have you ever gone to Delphi?

EUTHYDEMUS: Yes, twice.

SOCRATES: And did you observe what is written on the temple wall—"Know thyself"?

EUTHYDEMUS: I did.

SOCRATES: And did you take no thought of that inscription, or did you attend to it, and try to examine yourself, and ascertain what sort of character you are?

XENOPHON

Socrates

*Never mind the manner,
which may or may not be
good, but think only of the
truth of my words, and give
heed to that: let the speaker
speak truly and the judge
decide justly.*

Socrates

ou are about to meet one of the most powerful, intriguing, annoying, inspiring, widely known and yet misunderstood figures in the history of philosophy: **Socrates (c. 470–399 B.C.)**. He has been called the greatest of philosophers and also the cleverest of Sophists. Stoics, Hedonists, and Cynics (each of whom we shall study in other chapters) have all claimed him as their chief inspiration and model. He was a pagan who is seen by many Jews and Christians as a man of God. His Holiness Tenzin Gyatso, the fourteenth Dalai Lama of Tibetan Buddhism, has expressed respect for him as an enlightened individual. Socrates claimed to have devoted his life to serving his country but was executed as a traitor. He attracted faithful and adoring admirers and was idolized by many young followers, yet the second charge at his trial was "corrupting the youth of Athens." Although he wrote no philosophy himself, he taught and inspired one of the two most influential philosophers in Western history, who in turn taught the other: Plato and Aristotle.

In his impressive book *Socrates*, the renowned classical scholar W.K.C. Guthrie says, "Any account must begin with the admission that there is, and always will be, a 'Socratic problem.'"[1] In the first place, Socrates wrote nothing. (Or at least nothing philosophical. In *Phaedo*, Plato asserted that Socrates wrote a hymn to Apollo and versified some of Aesop's fables while in prison.[2]) Our two main sources of information about Socrates are the dialogues of his most brilliant and famous pupil, Plato, and the anecdotes and memoirs of the less philosophical soldier, Xenophon. Additionally, briefer references to Socrates appear in Aristotle, Aristophanes, and elsewhere. The "Socratic problem" is compounded because Socrates' philosophy was nearly inseparable from the way his whole personality was reflected in his spoken teachings and the conduct of his life. Guthrie says, "In spite of the most scientific methods, in the end we must all have to some extent our own Socrates, who will not be precisely like anyone else's."[3]

What will *your* Socrates be like? Perhaps you too will be "stung" by the man who referred to himself as a gadfly (horsefly) sent by "the god" to keep his drowsy fellows alert. Perhaps you too will give birth to a brainchild with the aid of this ancient *sophos* who claimed to "teach nothing" but merely to act as a "kind of midwife," helping others draw out the wisdom hidden within them. Or perhaps you too will be annoyed—even angered—at the sophistic arrogance and logical tricks of a dangerous enemy of conventional morality, democracy, and religion. These are just some of the documented reactions to Socrates.

"The fact is," Guthrie says, "that no one was left indifferent by this altogether unusual character: everyone who has written about him was also reacting to him in one way or another."[4] It is still possible to get a basic picture of Socrates, however. For example, even though Plato and Xenophon present almost completely different views of him, we can treat their accounts as honest reflections of Socrates filtered through the minds and experiences of two completely different admirers. Neither account is "inaccurate" so much as incomplete and perhaps exaggerated. By comparing and evaluating various accounts of Socrates, we can get some idea of the man as well as the philosophy. So let me introduce you to my Socrates.

THE GENERAL CHARACTER OF SOCRATES

As noted above, it is almost impossible to separate what Socrates taught from his whole personality. This accounts for much of his influence and charisma. Not only were his teachings challenging and powerful, he actually seemed to live up to them. Put in today's terms, he seems to have practiced what he preached.

The psychological term for this is *integration*. The opposite of an alienated or fragmented person, an integrated person has a clear sense of identity. She knows what she values and why, and is therefore strong. When we don't know who we really are or what is most important to us, we keep changing our minds. We get something we wanted very badly and then decide we don't like it. We have trouble making decisions because we are afraid of losing out on something better later. Living in a society that gives us many choices makes it especially difficult to find a clear identity. But it has never been easy. That is why Socrates' guiding motive of "Know thyself" has been so challenging to people all over the world and in all historical periods. Socrates struggled with one of the great problems of our time: Who am I? How can I discover my true identity? How shall *I* live?

Plato presents Socrates as an integrated, essentially unambivalent individual. He stood clearly for some values and clearly against others. Then, as now, such personal clarity, such strong sense of direction and purpose were attractive to young (or any) people confused as to who they are or want to be. Then, as now, his consistent respect for justice, integrity, courage, temperance, decency, beauty, and balance was especially appealing in a cultural climate of dizzy excesses, crass materialism, and cut-throat competition for money, power, and prestige. In a complex, sophisticated society in which old values were under siege, the simplicity and clarity of an individual with Socrates' obvious abilities were intriguing, even when it was upsetting.

The Ugliest Man in Athens

Against the popular notion of his time (and ours), Socrates taught that beauty and goodness should be determined by usefulness and fitness of function, rather than by mere appearance or personal feelings of delight. An interesting illustration of this can be found in his own appearance. He was

It is not the knowledge of the wise we acknowledge to be special but the value they place and invite us to place on it. In some sense, the recognition of wisdom is the recognition of that which we, the unwise, not only have known but should have known all along.
Stanley Godlovitch

In spite of being in sympathy with the sages, I am well aware of not having been one of them. As a person I was too self-indulgent and not heroic enough: as a writer I was too miscellaneous: as a thinker I was born at the wrong time and bred in the wrong way.
George Santayana

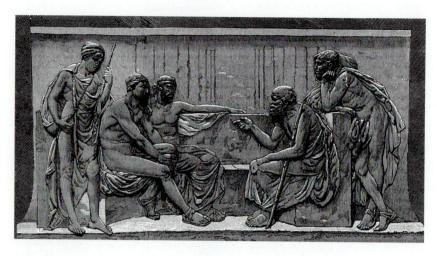

This nineteenth-century sculpture of Socrates teaching in the agora shows the contrast between Socrates' inner beauty and outer ugliness.

universally acknowledged to be "extraordinarily ugly"—so ugly, in fact, that he fascinated people.

His most notable physical features were a broad, flat, turned-up nose, protruding, staring eyes, thick, fleshy lips, and a belly which he himself characterized in Xenophon's *Symposium* as "a stomach rather too large for convenience,"[5] and which he elsewhere announced plans to "dance off." His friends compared him to a satyr or an electric eel.

He made his appearance serve him well. His humorous references to it reflect his good nature and modesty, as well as his hierarchy of values. After all, if, as he taught, the true self is not the body but the soul (psyche), and if all *virtue* implies *excellence of function*, then the appearance of the body is less important than how well it functions. True beauty will be inner beauty, beauty of spirit and character. Socrates' friends certainly came to see the "true Socrates," and so, for them, the beauty of who he was transcended and transformed the ugliness of his body.

In Plato's *Gorgias*, Socrates says that we cannot know whether a person is happy just because his external condition is attractive to us. He insists that happiness, like goodness, is a matter of inner qualities:

> Then doubtless you will say, Socrates, that you do not know that even the Great King is happy.
>
> Yes, and I shall be speaking the truth; for I do not know how he stands *in point of interior formation* and justice.
>
> Why, does happiness entirely consist of that?
>
> Yes, by my account, Polus; for a good and honorable man or woman, I say, is happy, and an unjust and wicked one is wretched.[6]

Beauty in things exists in the mind which contemplates them.
David Hume

PHILOSOPHICAL QUERY

Everyone I like and love seems quite "attractive" to me. Yet one of my friends resembled Socrates. Before I ever met him I had noticed him in the college cafeteria. I thought he was one of the most unfortunate-looking persons I had ever seen. He was friends with some acquaintances of mine, and so I eventually met him. I initially felt uncomfortable even being around him because of his looks, I'm sorry to say. But slowly I discovered an intelligent, funny, kind, strong, and courageous man. Over the years of our friendship, I actually lost the capacity to *see* him as ugly. Sadly, the converse has been true in my experience as well. A beautiful or handsome countenance that belongs to a slothful or self-centered or shallow or cruel person over time becomes less handsome or beautiful to me. Have you noticed this pattern? Analyze it, if you have.

Don't think Socrates was a prude. He was not. He was tempted by physical attractiveness, but he governed his life according to "true beauty and goodness," preferring a good and beautiful soul to a pleasing body that housed a lesser self.

An informative and humorous passage from Chapter 5 of Xenophon's *Symposium* illustrates how Socrates could incorporate philosophy into anything, even joking around with friends. Socrates is engaged in a good-natured "beauty contest" with a handsome young man named Critobulus. Critobulus has challenged Socrates to use his famous question-and-answer method (we'll look at this shortly) to prove that Socrates is "more beautiful" than Critobulus.

> Critobulus: All right, but which of our noses is the more beautiful?
> Socrates: Mine, I should say, if the gods give us noses to smell with, for your nostrils point to earth, but mine are spread out widely to receive odours from every quarter.
> Critobulus: But how can a snub nose be more beautiful than a straight one?
> Socrates: Because it does not get in the way but allows the eyes to see what they will, whereas a high bridge walls them off, as if to spite them.
> Critobulus: As for the mouth, I give in, for if mouths are made for biting you could take a much larger bite than I.
> Socrates: And with my thick lips don't you think I could give a softer kiss?
> Critobulus: By your account I seem to have a mouth uglier than an ass's . . . I give up. Let's put it to the vote, so that I may know as quickly as possible the forfeit I have to pay.[7]

I'm tired of all this nonsense about beauty being only skin deep. What do you want—an adorable pancreas?
Jean Kerr

Many are ruined by admirers whose heads are turned by the sight of a pretty face; many are led by their strength to attempt tasks too heavy for them, and meet serious evils; many by their wealth are corrupted, and fall victims to conspiracies; many through glory and political power have suffered great evils.
Socrates

When I think of both the wisdom and nobility of this man [Socrates], I cannot refrain from writing of him nor, in writing of him, from praising him.
Xenophon

When the votes were counted, Socrates lost unanimously, prompting him to accuse Critobulus of bribing the judges.

Barefoot in Athens

Socrates was also well known for his indifference to fashion and ordinary comforts. He was usually barefoot and apparently had only one tattered coat, about which his friends joked. His enemies accused him of being "unwashed," and even his friends admitted that it was a surprise to see Socrates freshly bathed.

One of his most noted characteristics was hardiness, reflected in remarkable self-control, or *temperance*. Temperance in this sense means indifference to both the presence and absence of material pleasures; it does not mean total abstinence from pleasure or extreme asceticism. In Xenophon's *Memorabilia*, Socrates put it like this:

> You seem, Antiphon, to imagine that happiness consists in luxury and extravagance. But my belief is that *to have no wants is divine; to have as few as possible comes next to the divine*; and as that which is divine is supreme, so that which approaches nearest to its nature is nearest to supreme [emphasis added].[8]

Should not every man hold self-control to be the foundation of all virtue, and first lay this foundation firmly in his soul?
Xenophon

Socrates' self-control included indifference to fear. During a battle at Delium he is said to have been the last Athenian soldier to give way before the advancing Spartans. In the Potidaean military campaign, Socrates is reported to have walked about barefoot on the icy winter ground of Thrace, dressed as he customarily was back home. In Plato's *Symposium*, Alcibiades claims that this irritated the other soldiers, who, bundled and muffled against the fierce winter with their feet wrapped in felt and sheepskin, thought Socrates was trying to humiliate them.

In Xenophon's *Memorabilia*, Socrates talks about self-control and self-discipline with his friend Euthydemus. He uses the term *incontinence* in its original sense to mean lack of self-control, especially concerning appetites and passions. Socrates argues that self-control—not self-indulgence and weakness of will—leads to pleasure. Lack of self-control, he asserts, prevents us from the finest expressions of pleasure in eating, drinking, resting, and making love. If we gratify every urge as soon as it arises, we must often settle for fast food, cheap drink, sleeping all day, or crude sexual encounters. We will be little more than animals. Without self-control we have no hope of learning how to moderate ourselves and our lives:

> "The delights of learning something good and excellent, and of studying some of the means whereby a man knows how to regulate his body well and manage his household successfully, to be useful to his friends and city and to defeat his enemies—knowledge that yields not only very great benefits but very great pleasures—these are the delights of the self-controlled;

THE SOPHOS AT LARGE

When Socrates prayed, he asked only for "good gifts, for the gods know best what things are good."

According to Diogenes Läertius, Socrates' style of arguing was sometimes so intense that his opponents frequently attacked him with their fists or tore his hair out, "yet he bore all this ill-usage patiently."

When Alcibiades offered Socrates a large site on which to build a house, he replied, "Suppose, then, I wanted shoes and you offered me a whole hide to make a pair, would it not be ridiculous of me to take it?"

Socrates used to say that he most enjoyed the food which was least in need of seasoning, and the drink which made him feel the least desire for another drink, adding that he was as the gods because he had few wants.

When someone asked Socrates whether he should marry or not, the *sophos* replied, "Whichever you do you will repent it."

When Socrates invited some rich men to dinner, his wife Xanthippe said she was embarrassed by the meal she had prepared. "Never mind," he said. "If they are reasonable they will put up with it, if they are good for nothing, we shall not trouble ourselves about them."

When someone said, "Socrates, you are condemned by Athens to die," he responded, "So are you, by nature."

but the incontinent have no part in them. For who should we say has less concern with these than he who has no power of cultivating them because all his serious purposes are centered in the pleasures that lie nearest?"

"Socrates," said Euthydemus, "I think you mean that he who is at the mercy of the bodily pleasures has no concern whatever with virtue in any form?"

"Yes, Euthydemus," said Socrates.[9]

Part of Socrates' appeal comes from the fact that he had the same desires as the rest of us. They may even have been more intense. So we respond to the effort he must have exerted to keep all his appetites and passions under strict control. His philosophical searching was, consequently, based on a full involvement with life. It was not the product of a withered, passionless mentality. Nor was it based on a naive goody-goody view of the human condition. He knew and loved life at its fullest, wrestling with it and challenging others to join his "enduring quest."

PHILOSOPHICAL QUERY

What do you think of Socrates' views on self-control? Does the current concern with healthy diets, exercise, and so on seem to be in line with what Socrates thought? Discuss.

There is no doubt that in one form or another, Socrates and Buddha, Jesus and St. Paul, Plotinus and Spinoza, taught that . . . without renunciation of many of the ordinary appetites, no man can really live well.

Walter Lippmann

A Most Unusual Father and Husband

Socrates was married to Xanthippe and had three sons. He was seventy years old at the time of his execution; his oldest son was not yet twenty, and the youngest was said to be a small child.[10] We know relatively little of Socrates' home life, but Xanthippe probably had aristocratic connections.

Although he was probably apprenticed as a stonecutter or sculptor by his father, Socrates worked only now and then. He lived off a modest inheritance from his father, consisting of a house and some money, which his best friend Crito invested for him.[11] And while he never took money for teaching (as the Sophists did), he occasionally accepted gifts from his wealthy friends and admirers.

His well-known contempt for indiscriminate social approval made it a simple matter for him to live comfortably without shoes and with an old coat. But what effect would Socrates' uncommon values have had on his wife and sons? Here was an obviously brilliant, physically powerful man who spent his time wandering about the marketplace asking philosophical questions all day. He seems to have had ample opportunity to eat and drink and mingle with the movers and shakers of Athens, yet he refused to seek political, social, or financial influence. Even (especially?) today it is easier to preach nonmaterialistic spiritual and philosophical values than to actually live as if the soul is more important than the body.

Imagine a philosophy professor today being indifferent to prestige, salary, and possessions. Also consider the effect this might have on her unphilosophical husband. Imagine the effect on her children: "Mommy cannot afford to buy you new shoes, she's busy searching for the meaning of life." Although a bit oversimplified, the point is important. An encounter with Socrates, likened to an "electric shock," is centered at just such tension: His life and teachings are at once inspiring and frustrating to us, as they were to his contemporaries.

PHILOSOPHICAL QUERY

How might we explain the fact that many churches and schools are luxurious? Don't both educators and preachers (not to mention gurus and therapists) *say* that material success does not guarantee happiness? Don't many of them *say* that the life of the mind or soul is most important? Why, then, do they *look* as if they don't believe it? There are plenty of famous examples of this inconsistency. Discuss one or two of them. If the Socratic view is wrong, why do so many people give it lip service?

The Archetypal Individual

The combined portraits of Plato and Xenophon reveal Socrates as a master teacher, a man of awesome intellectual force, possessing an integrated self,

---

In the world, one cannot have it both ways. If he wants to maintain his good reputation, he must not think of pursuing status and wealth. But if he wants status and riches, he must bear in mind that it will be at the expense of his integrity.

Lie Zi

Asked what was very difficult, Thales replied: "To know thyself." Asked what was very easy, he answered: "To give advice."

whose charisma and personal power sprang from more than either mere intellect or personality. In other words, Socrates is a genuine **archetypal individual**, or, in a term coined by philosopher and psychologist Karl Jaspers, a **paradigmatic individual**. Jaspers applied the term to a special class of teachers, philosophers, and religious figures whose nature becomes a standard by which a culture judges the "ideal" human being.

An archetypal or paradigmatic individual is a rare human being whose very nature represents something elemental about the human condition. "The historical reality of [the paradigmatic individual]," says Jaspers, "can be discerned only in [his] extraordinary impact on those who knew [him] and in [his] later echoes."[12] In any encounter with an archetypal individual, the power or force of the whole person is galvanic. This power does not come from a rational argument. It is an experience that almost goes beyond words and cannot be ignored. It triggers not just personal but deep philosophical and spiritual responses in others.

These human paradigms possess a timeless quality, according to Jaspers. They serve as *archetypal images* for their cultures, and usually speak to other cultures as well. Although different cultures and eras produce different archetypes (Jaspers used as his examples Socrates, Confucius, Buddha, and Jesus), *the archetypal individual's very nature demands a response*: What is it to be a human being? What is most important? What is good? How should *I* live?

Jaspers says:

> A radical change is experienced and demanded [by paradigmatic individuals]. They are stirred to their depths, by what we do not know. They express what there is no appropriate way of saying. They speak in parables, dialectical contradictions, conversational replies. . . .
>
> Socrates seeks himself and his relation to other men. By his extreme questioning he arouses a real, living certainty that is *not mere knowledge* of something. He transcends the world without negating it. He forges total knowledge, total judgments, contenting himself with a nonknowledge in which truth and reality are actualized [emphasis added].[13]

That is, Socrates continued to develop and grow as a person because of his philosophical search. He did not "fragment" himself into two parts, the thinker and the real person. He did not force himself to stick to a rigid theory. He responded anew to each experience. When Jaspers refers to "a nonknowledge" he means that Socrates always insisted that his "wisdom" lay in knowing what he did not know. (We'll look at this important concept shortly.)

PHILOSOPHICAL QUERY
Although complex political reasons lay behind some of the animosity that led to Socrates' execution, it is likely that bad feelings of a deeper, more primitive nature were also important factors.

ARCHETYPAL INDIVIDUAL or PARADIGMATIC INDIVIDUAL
A special class of teachers, philosophers, and religious figures whose nature becomes a standard by which a culture judges the "ideal" human being; a rare human being whose very nature represents something elemental about the human condition.

I will tell you something, Socrates [said Aristides, the son of Lysimachus and grandson of the great Aristides], something quite incredible but true. I have never learned a single thing from you, as you know yourself; but whenever I was with you I improved, even if I was only in the same house but not in the same room. . . .

Plato, *Theages*

Whatever reasons there may have been for trying Socrates on capital charges, recall that he was seventy years old at the time of his trial. What is the significance of this fact? Why bother to try, convict, and execute a seventy-year-old man whose behavior had been remarkably consistent and publicly observed for perhaps fifty years? There was nothing "new" about Socrates. So what was it?

THE TRIAL AND DEATH OF SOCRATES

Socrates' philosophy cannot be separated from his life. Neither can it be separated from his death. As with other great sages, much of what Socrates *said* has wide appeal. The difficulty, as many of us know, is trying to live in accordance with what we say we believe. Socrates not only lived his philosophy, he died for it. And in the act of dying, he reaffirmed it one more time.

For most of his long life Socrates was able to function as a critic at large, questioning Athenian values and occasionally annoying important and powerful people in the process. He acquired a mixed reputation, being viewed on the one hand as a harmless, irrelevant eccentric, and on the other as a dangerous social critic and "freethinker"—in short, a Sophist. Socrates' philosophic method consisted of raising question after question, calling into doubt cherished, often unchallenged beliefs to see if they were worthy of allegiance. Many Athenians found this skeptical attitude disrespectful and threatening; they preferred unwavering loyalty to the status quo and to conventional beliefs. To these citizens, the very process of questioning fundamental values was subversive, perhaps even traitorous.

Socrates' status changed from mere annoyance to overt threat as a result of events associated with the bitter Peloponnesian Wars between Athens and Sparta. One of Socrates' students, Alcibiades, went to Sparta, where he advised the Spartans during the war. In some people's minds, as the teacher, Socrates was responsible for the student's act of betrayal.

Socrates further alienated himself from powerful Athenians when he resisted efforts to judge eight Athenian generals accused of poor military strategy as a group, rather than as individuals, as was their right under the Athenian constitution. Socrates was the one member of the Committee of the Senate of Five Hundred to refuse. The other 499 members initially agreed with Socrates' position, but backed down when aggressive prosecutors threatened to add to the indictment the names of Committee members who refused to ignore the constitution. The threat worked, the generals were found guilty, and the six who were already in custody were executed on the same day. This is another example of Socrates' willingness to put his principles above all other considerations (including, perhaps, his family's).

Sparta defeated Athens in 404 B.C., and set up a Commission of Thirty to form a new Athenian government. The Thirty turned out to be a ruthless dictatorship which executed supporters of the earlier Periclean democracy and greedily confiscated their property. The Thirty lasted about a year before being removed from power by force. Unfortunately for Socrates, among the Thirty were his close friends Critias and Charmides. Once again, in the minds of many Athenians, Socrates was guilty of treason by association.

Finally, resentment, distrust, and hostility against Socrates grew to such proportions that he was brought to trial for "not worshiping the gods of the state," and "corrupting the young." These were potentially capital offenses, and Socrates' prosecutor, Meletus, demanded death. At the time, it was customary for individuals charged with such crimes to submit to voluntary exile. Had Socrates chosen this option, there would have been no trial. Socrates, however, remained to answer his accuser before a jury of his peers.

Athenian trials consisted of two parts. First, the jury determined whether or not the accused was guilty as charged. If guilty, the second stage of the trial determined the most appropriate punishment. Socrates' jury consisted of 501 members. There was no way such a large group could reasonably debate various penalty options, so if a defendant was convicted, the prosecutor proposed a penalty and the defendant proposed a counterpenalty. Then the jury voted once more, choosing one or the other. The hope was that both sides would be moderate in their demands.

Socrates defended himself and was judged guilty by a rather close vote. The custom of the time was for those convicted to show some contrition. The greater the prosecutor's proposed penalty, the more remorse the condemned man was expected to express. In cases where death was asked, the proposed counterpenalty was supposed to be stiff. It might include leaving Athens forever and giving up most or all of one's property as fines. Public humiliation was also part of the price of escaping death. Defendants were expected to tear at their clothes, roll on the ground, and throw dirt on themselves while crying and wailing. They would usually have their wives and children and friends cry and plead for their lives. An important function of the trial involved making peace with those one had offended.

Instead of following custom, Socrates pointed out that it would be undignified at his age to grovel for life. He refused to allow his friends and family to crawl either. To make things even worse, he reminded the jury that many of them believed he was not guilty and had been falsely convicted. Thus Socrates offered to redeem the jury! At one point, he considered that since he had given up opportunities to make money because he was trying to help others, he should perhaps be given free meals for the rest of his life. Ultimately, he made only a modest, inadequate concession to the jury by offering to let his friends pay a fine for him. His conviction did not upset him, for a divine sign had led him throughout:

> O my judges—for you I may truly call judges—I should like to tell you of a wonderful circumstance. Hitherto the divine faculty of which the internal oracle is the source has constantly been in the habit of opposing me even about trifles, if I was

If I had engaged in politics, I should have perished long ago . . . for the truth is, that no man who goes to war with you or any other multitude, honestly striving against the many lawless and unrighteous deeds which are done in a state, will save his life; he who will fight for the right, if he would live even for a brief space, must have a private station and not a public one.
Socrates

And this, O men of Athens, is the truth and the whole truth; I have concealed nothing, I have dissembled nothing. And yet, I know that my plainness of speech makes them hate me, and what is their hatred but a proof that I am speaking the truth?
Socrates

Either acquit me or not; but whichever you do, understand that I shall never alter my ways, not even if I have to die many times.
Socrates

going to make a slip or error in any matter; and now you see there has come upon me that which may be thought, and is generally believed to be, the last and worst evil. But the oracle made no sign of opposition, either when I was leaving my house in the morning, or I was on my way to the court, or while I was speaking, at anything which I was going to say; and yet I have often been stopped in the middle of a speech . . . What do I take to be the explanation of this silence? I will tell you. It is an intimation that what has happened to me is good, and that those of us who think that death is an evil are in error. For the customary sign would surely have opposed me had I been going to evil and not to good.[14]

Though we cannot know the exact nature of Socrates' "divine sign," we know that he took it seriously. One result was that Socrates himself had a clear sense of purpose, a vocation. His teaching was part of the whole person; it was not a way to *make* a living, but a way *of* living.

At his trial he said, "My service to the god has brought me into great poverty." Just as for Socrates real beauty was beauty of soul, real riches were riches of soul. Socrates appeared poor only by conventional standards. By his own sense of things, his service to the god brought real riches, rather than apparent ones.

Wise men profit more from fools than fools from wise men; for the wise men shun the mistakes of fools, but fools do not imitate the successes of wise men.
Cato the Elder

PHILOSOPHICAL QUERY
Some people argue that Socrates committed suicide by provoking the jury. By insisting that he was right and by refusing to show fear or at least some repentance, he drove them to execute him. He knew they would get carried away and yet he insulted them. So it is his own fault that he was executed. What do you think? Is there a defense for Socrates' actions? Who is responsible for the vote?

The Death of Socrates

Socrates could not be executed on the day of the trial, as was customary, because the trial had lasted longer than usual, extending into late afternoon, the beginning of a holy period. Socrates was put in prison to await the end of the holy period, in this case about a month. While there, he continued to pursue his philosophical questions. He was offered the opportunity to escape, the officials going so far as to make it clear they would not stop him. He refused, until finally the holy period ended and word came that Socrates must die before sundown.

A number of Socrates' friends visited him in prison on the last day of his life. He discussed the nature of the soul with them and told a mythical story about the soul's immortality. When his friend Crito asked how they should bury him, Socrates jokingly replied, "In any way you like; but you must get hold of *me*, and take care that I do not run away from you." Plato described what happened next:

> Then he turned to us and added with a smile:—I cannot make Crito believe that I am the same Socrates who has been talking and conducting the argument; he fancies that I am the other Socrates whom he will soon see, a dead body—and he asks, How shall you bury me? And though I have spoken many words in the endeavour to show that when I have drunk the poison I shall leave you and go to the joys of the blessed. . . . I shall not remain, but go away and depart; . . . I would not have [you] sorrow at my hard lot, or say at the burial, Thus we lay out Socrates, or, Thus we follow him to the grave or bury him; for false words are not only evil in themselves, but they infect the soul with evil. Be of good cheer then, . . . and say that you are burying my body only, and do with that whatever is usual, and what you think best.[15]

Socrates went to bathe, while his friends talked about what he had said. Plato reported that his friends felt as if they were losing a father and would be orphans for the rest of their lives. After Socrates' bath, his children and the women of his household were brought in. When he finally sent the women and children away, it was close to sunset—the end of the day, by which time he was officially supposed to be dead. The jailer came in while he was talking, and said that it was time. Most condemned men resisted drinking the hemlock until late into the evening, getting drunk and putting off the inevitable for as long as they could, but Socrates asked that the poison be prepared and brought to him. Socrates' jailer noted how different Socrates was and, weeping, he thanked Socrates for talking with him and treating him as a friend. Crito begged him to delay, but Socrates said that there was nothing to be gained by it. Rather, there was much to lose by degrading himself. To evade and fear death would have made a mockery out of his entire life, for Socrates had long taught that death was not an evil.

When the jailer returned with the cup, Socrates asked what he had to do and was told to just drink it and then walk around a bit. Plato's account continues:

> Then raising the cup to his lips, quite readily and cheerfully he drank off the poison. And hitherto most of us had been able to control our sorrow; but now when we saw him drinking, and saw too that he had finished the draught, we could no longer forbear, and in spite of myself my own tears were flowing fast; so that I covered my face and wept, not for him, but for the thought of my own calamity in having to part with

His martyrdom, and the genius of Plato, made him a secular saint, the superior man confronting the ignorant mob with serenity and humor. This was Socrates' triumph and Plato's masterpiece. Socrates needed the hemlock, as Jesus needed the Crucifixion, to fulfill a mission. The mission left a stain forever on democracy. That remains Athens' tragic crime.
I. F. Stone

When Rabbi Bunam lay dying his wife burst into tears. He said: "What are you crying for? My whole life was only that I might learn how to die."
Martin Buber

Jacques-Louis David's 1787 painting *The Death of Socrates* is perhaps the most famous artistic depiction of that significant event. Does it reflect your conception of Socrates' death?

If you think that by killing men you can prevent someone from censuring your evil lives, you are mistaken; that is not a way of escape which is either possible or honorable; the easiest and the noblest way is not to be disabling others, but to be improving yourselves. This is the prophecy which I utter before my departure to the judges who have condemned me.

Socrates

such a friend. Nor was I the first; for Crito, when he found himself unable to restrain his tears, had got up, and I followed; and at that moment Apollodorus, who had been weeping all the time, broke out in a loud and passionate cry which made cowards of us all. Socrates alone retained his calmness: What is this strange outcry? he said. I sent away the women mainly in order that they might not misbehave in this way, for I have been told that a man should die in peace. Be quiet then and have patience. When we heard his words we were ashamed, and refrained our tears; and he walked about until, as he said, his legs began to fail, and then he lay on his back, according to the directions, and the man who gave him the poison now and then looked at his feet and legs; and after a while he pressed his foot hard, and asked him if he could feel; and he said, No; and then his leg, and so upwards and upwards, and showed us that he was cold and stiff. And he felt them himself, and said: When the poison reaches the heart, that will be the end. He was beginning to grow cold about the groin, when he uncovered his face, for he had covered himself up, and said—they were his last words—he said: Crito, I owe a cock to Asclepius [the god of healing]; you will remember to pay the debt? The debt shall be paid, said Crito; is there anything else? There was no answer to this question; but in a minute or two a movement was heard, and the attendants uncovered him; his eyes were set, and Crito closed his eyes and mouth.

Such was the end . . . of our friend; concerning whom I may truly say, that of all the men of his time whom I have known, he was the wisest and justest and best.[16]

> *Wherefore, O judges, be of good cheer about death, and know of a certainty, that no evil can happen to a good man, either in life or after death. He and his are not neglected by the gods. . . .*
>
> Socrates

THE TEACHER AND HIS TEACHINGS

Now that we have learned a little about Socrates' life and general character, let's take a look at some of the basic components of Socratic philosophy.

The Dialectic

Socrates argued that one of the chief reasons many people cannot think clearly is that they do not even know what they are talking about. Consequently, the first order of business is to define our terms. The early dialogues of Plato reveal a Socrates constantly pushing and searching for clearer and more precise definitions of key terms. Time after time he lures a confused individual from one muddled definition to another. Then, using skillful (some would even say loaded or leading) questions, he attempts to guide his "opponent" closer to the truth by allowing him to experience the logical inconsistencies in the opponent's stated positions. Socrates was so effective with this method of philosophical teaching and inquiry that it came to be known as the **Socratic dialectic**, also known as the **Socratic method**.

The Socratic method begins with the assumption that the function of education is to draw the truth out of the pupil rather than "fill an empty vessel." In practice, it is a series of guided questions known as the dialectical method of inquiry. Claims are continually refined, definitions required for all key terms, logical inconsistencies brought to light and resolved. A vital aspect of Socratic teaching is the active involvement of the audience (pupils, listeners), hence the use of questions rather than straight lectures.

The dialectical process as Socrates practiced it was dynamic and hopeful. At worst, the participants learned that although they may not have found *the* answer, or *the* meaning of justice, *the* good life, or courage, they were each at least a bit clearer than before. At any rate, this was Socrates' experience—others were often angered and frustrated, if not humiliated, as their confusion and ignorance were exposed.

Socrates believed that the truth was somehow in each of us. The teacher's role, then, isn't to put knowledge into an empty mind, but to draw wisdom and clarity out of a disordered and confused soul. Just as a midwife does not herself give birth, but aids the mother, Socrates claimed to aid others

SOCRATIC METHOD or SOCRATIC DIALECTIC Question-and-answer technique perfected by Socrates to draw truth out of his pupils often by means of achieving a clearer, more precise definition of a key term or concept.

in giving birth to their own insights by *drawing out what was already there*. And just as a midwife is of no help until the mother has conceived a child, Socrates was of no help until the other person had conceived at least a sketchy idea.

For Socrates, the most important order of business was to *engage* the pupil. The Socratic method in full form is more than just questions and answers. It is a highly personal activity, guided by one who knows both the general direction of the inquiry (but not "the answers") as well as the nature and needs of the individual student. It works only if the student actively listens and responds.

Socratic Irony

A key element in keeping his pupils engaged, and calling attention to meaning, was Socrates' use of **irony**, a way of communicating on more than one level. An ironic utterance has at least two levels of meaning, *the literal level*, also known as the obvious level, and *the hidden level*, also known as the real level. As a rule, the two meanings are near opposites, as in the case of the sarcastic professor who writes on a woefully inadequate term paper: "Beautiful job! You've never done better!"

By using words in unexpected ways, by meaning more than one obvious, surface-level thing, Socrates hoped to keep his listeners alert. Further, the use of irony underscored his belief that things are not always as they first appear, that there is a deeper reality than may be apparent. Socrates used irony to keep his listeners on their toes and to avoid putting answers in their mouths. For instance, he begins his *Apology* (his defense at his trial) by referring to the "persuasive" abilities of his immediate accusers, who are Sophists. Of course, his remark is actually an ironic way of showing that these Sophists have not persuaded him of anything. His use of irony in his opening remarks gets the audience's immediate attention:

> How you, O Athenians, have been affected by my accusers, I cannot tell; but I know that they almost made me forget who I was—so persuasively did they speak; and yet they have hardly uttered a word of truth. But of the many falsehoods told by them, there was one which quite amazed me;—I mean when they said that you should be upon your guard and not allow yourselves to be deceived by the force of my eloquence. To say this, when they were certain to be detected as soon as I opened my lips and proved myself to be anything but a great speaker, did indeed appear to me most shameless—unless by the force of eloquence they mean the force of truth; for if such is their meaning, I admit that I am eloquent. But in how different a way from theirs! Well, as I was saying, they have

IRONY
Communication on at least two levels, a literal or obvious level and a hidden or real level; favored by Socrates as a technique for keeping his listeners alert and involved.

I do not suppose that I know.
Socrates

WHAT AN EXTRAORDINARY EFFECT HIS WORDS HAVE HAD ON ME . . .

In Plato's *Symposium*, Alcibiades notes the staggering power of Socrates:

. . . when we listen to you, or to someone else repeating what you've said, even if he puts it ever so badly, and never mind whether the person who's listening is man, woman, or child, we're absolutely staggered and bewitched. And speaking for myself, gentlemen, if I wasn't afraid you'd tell me that I was completely bottled, I'd swear on oath what an extraordinary effect his words have had on me—and still do if it comes to that. For the moment I hear him speak I am smitten with a kind of sacred rage . . . oh, and not only me, but lots of other men.

. . . He makes me admit that while I'm spending time on politics I am neglecting all the things crying for attention in myself. So I just refuse to listen to him—as if he were one of those Sirens, you know—and get out of earshot as quick as I can, for fear he will keep me sitting listening till I'm positively senile.

And there's one thing I've never felt with anybody else—not the kind of thing you'd expect to find in me, either—and that is a sense of shame. Socrates is the only man in the world that can make me feel ashamed. Because there's no getting away from it, I know I ought to do the things he tells me to, and yet the moment I'm out of his sight I don't care what I do to keep in with the mob. So I dash off like a runaway slave, and keep out of his way as long as I can, and the next time I meet him I remember all that I had to admit the time before, and naturally I feel ashamed. There are times when I'd honestly be glad to hear that he's dead, and yet I know that if he did die I'd be more upset than ever—so I ask you, what is a man to do?

Plato, *Symposium*, 215D–16C, in Edith Hamilton and Huntington Cairns, eds., *Plato: The Collected Dialogues*, trans. Michael Joyce (New York: Pantheon Books, Bollingen Series 71, 1966), p. 567.

scarcely spoken the truth at all; but from me you shall hear the whole truth: not, however, delivered after their manner in a set oration duly ornamented with words and phrases . . . at my time of life I ought not be appearing before you, O men of Athens, in the character of a juvenile orator—let no one expect it of me.[17]

Ironic communication confuses those who are inattentive or not in on the key to the hidden meaning. For instance, most members of Socrates' jury would have been familiar with his wranglings with Sophists and with sophistic emphasis on the arts of persuasion. A smaller group would have also responded to the irony of Socrates, whose life was devoted to following the command "Know thyself," forgetting who he was. Irony was both a crucial component of Socrates' method and a contributing factor to his ultimate trouble, since to many observers it was just another sophistic trick.

PHILOSOPHICAL QUERY

See how many ironic references to Sophists you can find in the preceding passage from the *Apology*.

The Unexamined Life

Among Socratic teachings, the most persistent command was "Know thyself." The significance to Socrates of this command is underscored by the fact that he stressed its importance to his life and mission during his *Apology*. Facing the end of a long life, Socrates uttered one of the most famous statements in the history of ideas: "The unexamined life is not worth living." By this he meant, among other things, that a life devoid of philosophical speculation is hardly a *human life*. That is, it is incomplete; it is not fully functioning and so lacks virtue or excellence.

Socrates believed that the human psyche is the essence of humanness. The **psyche** was a combination of what we think of as the mind and soul: consciousness, the capacity to reason, and the ability to reflect, known as *reflective thinking*. An "unexamined" life is, in a sense, an unconscious life. It is lived on the minimal level: Thinking never rises above practical concerns; desires are rarely pondered; custom, habit, and unquestioned beliefs substitute for reflection and assessment. Consequently, it is possible for a very intelligent, materially successful individual to live an unexamined life.

Giovanni Reale says, "As has recently come to light, no one prior to Socrates had understood by *soul* what Socrates understood by it, and after Socrates the whole of the West . . . the soul for Socrates was identified *with our consciousness when it thinks and acts with our reason and with the source of our thinking activity and our ethical activity.* In short, for Socrates the soul *is the conscious self, it is intellectual and moral personhood.*"[18]

An unexamined life is a life that takes the psyche for granted. It ignores the "true self." Interestingly, using Socrates' case as an example, we discover that the examined life does not produce "all the answers." Instead, it results in a life devoted to knowing more; a life in which progress means shedding false beliefs; a life in which pretense is continually reduced. The examined life is lived in conscious awareness of the human condition; it is not merely spent in an uncritical attempt to satisfy various needs and desires.

PHILOSOPHICAL QUERY

The relationship of reason to faith is a troublesome question for many. Do some informal research among your friends to get a sense of some contemporary conceptions of the soul. Compare and contrast what you discover with Socrates' conception of the

PSYCHE
Greek for "soul"; in today's terms, combination of mind and soul, including capacity for reflective thinking.

Calvin and Hobbes. Copyright 1993 Watterson. Reprinted with permission. All rights reserved. Dist. by Universal Press Syndicate.

psyche. How might a person's conception of the soul influence his or her response to this issue?

Socratic Ignorance

When Socrates was probably in his thirties, his friend Chaerephon went to the Oracle at Delphi with a question: Is anyone wiser than Socrates? The Oracle was believed to have the gift of prophecy. Either through divine guidance or cleverness, it gave this famous, ambiguous reply: *No man is wiser than Socrates.* This can be taken to mean either (a) Socrates is the wisest man in Athens, or (b) even though Socrates is not very wise, he is as wise as anybody gets. The first interpretation makes Socrates unique. The second makes him an archetype of the human condition.

Socrates took the Oracle's reply quite seriously, claiming that it was the turning point in his life. His first reaction to hearing the god Apollo's reply was confusion:

> I said to myself, What can the god mean? and what is the interpretation of his riddle? for I know that I have no wisdom, small or great. What then can he mean when he says that I am the wisest of men? And yet he is a god, and cannot lie; that would be against his nature. After long consideration, I thought of a method of trying the question. I reflected that if I could only find a man wiser than myself, then I might go to the god with a refutation in my hand. I should say to him, "Here is a man wiser than I am; but you said I was the wisest." Accordingly I went to one who had a reputation of wisdom, and observed him—his name I need not mention; he was a politician whom I selected for examination—and the result was as follows: When I began to talk with him, I could not

I am not wise.

Socrates

I found that the men in most repute were all but the most foolish; and that others less esteemed were really wiser and better.

Socrates

help thinking that he was not really wise, although he was thought wise by many, and still wiser by himself; and thereupon I tried to explain to him that he thought himself wise, but was not really wise; and the consequence was that he hated me, and his enmity was shared by several who were present and heard me. So I left him, saying to myself, as I went away: Well, although I do not suppose that either of us knows anything really beautiful and good, I am better off than he is—for he knows nothing, and thinks that he knows; I neither know nor think that I know. In this . . . , then, I seem to have slightly the advantage of him. Then I went to another who had still higher pretensions to wisdom, and my conclusion was exactly the same. Whereupon I made another enemy of him, and of many others besides him.[19]

One of the most intriguing aspects of Socrates' teachings is his profession of ignorance. (This is what Jaspers meant by "nonknowledge.") Plato's portrait of him suggests that Socrates continually reached "negative" conclusions of the form "This idea is faulty," or "That definition is inadequate." As we have seen, Socrates used the dialectical method to draw wisdom out of the minds of his listeners.

What point could Plato have been making? Clearly—it seems—Socrates possessed some kind of wisdom. Just as clearly—it seems—he was a basically good and honest man. He must have believed in his own ignorance, since he alluded to it on many occasions. If we allow for an element of irony in this, it then becomes clear that Socrates was challenging our notions of wisdom and knowledge. To certain sorts of people, Socrates' statements will remain clouded, perhaps beyond comprehension. Among them are young people whose "minds have not conceived at all," or older ones whose thoughts are already so firmly set that they can see only a phony technique used to avoid answering questions. Such people cannot conceive of their own ignorance. They are firmly convinced that they know everything important. To the Sophists, Socrates' use of "fake ignorance" was merely a clever psychological ploy to keep them off balance and on the spot. It's the sort of thing that made Thrasymachus so angry (Chapter 4).

Since the Socratic method employs guided questions, we can conclude that Socrates *does* have some ideas about the general direction the search for answers will take and the adequacy of certain lines of analysis. But he refuses to reveal these in dogmatic form. Socrates' "ignorance" was part of his whole mission, which he saw as bringing home to others *their own* intellectual needs. Once that was accomplished, they were invited to join the search for truth using the dialectical method of question and answer. The essence of the Socratic method is to convince the learner that, although he thought he knew something, in fact he may not.

Socrates was also sharing his own honest doubt. Even if he knew more than he let on, he was much more aware of the uncertain nature and limits

Socrates is guilty of rejecting the gods acknowledged by the state and of bringing in strange deities; he is also guilty of corrupting the youth.

Indictment brought against Socrates

Shall I tell you what knowledge is? It is to know both what one knows and what one does not know.

Confucius

of knowledge (his own included) than most of us probably are. In this, he was wiser than the average person in two ways. First, many of us tend to think that we know much more than we do. Second, all human knowledge is tentative and limited: we are not gods, though we sometimes act as if we were.

The Power of Human Wisdom

Perhaps the best way to glimpse the power of Socratic ignorance is to look once more to the *Apology*, this time where Socrates makes tantalizing statements regarding his "wisdom."

> I dare say, Athenians, that some of you will reply, "Yes, Socrates, but what is the origin of these accusations which are brought against you; there must have been something strange which you have been doing? All these rumours and this talk about you would never have arisen if you had been like other men: tell us, then, what is the cause of them, for we should be sorry to judge hastily of you." Now I regard this as a fair challenge, and I will endeavour to explain to you the reason why I am called wise and have such evil fame. Please to attend then. And although some of you may think that I am joking, I declare that I will tell you the entire truth. Men of Athens, this reputation of mine has come of a certain sort of wisdom which I possess. If you ask me what kind of wisdom, I reply, wisdom such as may perhaps be attained by man, for to that extent I am inclined to believe that I am wise; whereas the persons to whom I was speaking have a superhuman wisdom, which I may fail to describe, because I have it not myself; and he who says I have, speaks falsely, and is taking away my character.[20]

The Socratic distinction between "human wisdom" and "more-than-human wisdom" is a powerful one. Similar distinctions are made in Buddhist and Taoist philosophies (see Chapter 2).

In his effort to understand why the god said no one was wiser than he, Socrates discovered how easy it is to become deluded by our own special skills. The modern tendency to compartmentalize rather than integrate our lives, combined with the respect we have for specialized skills and knowledge, may make us especially susceptible to self-delusion. Television talk shows are a parade of individuals expressing their "insights" and "discoveries" in all areas of life. Psychologists discuss morals, entertainers lecture on food additives, preachers propose legislation, all sorts of people write books generalizing from their own experience to the human condition. They— and we—seem to assume that if you have a degree, sell lots of books, get rich, have a television or radio show, or become famous, you *must know*

But I shall be asked, Why do people delight in continually conversing with you? I have told you already, Athenians, the whole truth about this matter: they like to hear the cross-examination of the pretenders to wisdom; there is amusement in it.

Socrates

The oldest sage would admit at the close of a life of study his wisdom was as a raindrop to the sea. Nor is this idea new. . . . anthropologists have traced its presence in the legends and indigenous ideas of nearly every country in the world.

Christmas Humphreys

**How can we distinguish between self-help and self-delusion?
Between wisdom and mere opinion? How can a confused person
select a guide? Does it take wisdom to recognize wisdom?**

what you're talking about no matter what you're talking about. Things haven't
changed:

> At last I went to the artisans, for I was conscious that I knew
> nothing at all, as I may say, and I was sure that they knew
> many fine things; and here I was not mistaken, for they did
> know many things of which I was ignorant, and in this they
> certainly were wiser than I was. But I observed that even the
> good artisans fell into the same error as the poets—because
> they were good workmen they thought that they also knew
> all sorts of high matters, and this defect in them overshad-
> owed their wisdom; and therefore I asked myself whether I
> would like to be as I was, neither having their knowledge nor
> their ignorance, or like them in both; and I made answer to
> myself and to the oracle that I was better off as I was.
>
> This inquisition has led to my having many enemies of the
> worst and most dangerous kind, and has given occasion to

**Talk show hosts like Oprah Winfrey and Phil Donahue sometimes
go beyond functioning as moderators and become commentators
on a wide range of issues. How do you think they would fare with
Socrates as a guest?**

many calumnies. And I am called wise, for my hearers always
imagine that I possess the wisdom which I find wanting in
others; but the truth is, O men of Athens, that God only is
wise; and by his answer he intends to show that the wisdom
of men is worth little or nothing; he is not speaking of Socrates, he is only using my name by way of illustration, as if
he said, He, O men, is wisest, who, like Socrates, knows that
his wisdom is in truth worth nothing. And so I go about the
world, obedient to the god, and search and make enquiry
into the wisdom of anyone, whether citizen or stranger, who
appears to be wise; and if he is not wise, then in vindication
of the oracle I show him that he is not wise; and my occupation quite absorbs me, and I have no time to give either
to any public matter or interest or to any concern of my
own, but I am in utter poverty by reason of my devotion to
the god.[21]

*To know what you do
not know is best.
To pretend to know what you
do not know is a disease.*
Lao-tzu

Reprinted with permission of King Features Syndicate, Inc.

PHILOSOPHICAL QUERY

Have you ever met a highly educated specialist (physician, biochemist, psychologist, philosophy teacher, preacher) who thinks nothing of pontificating on the economy, sex education, and how you should raise your child? Discuss in light of Socratic statements concerning human wisdom.

THE PHYSICIAN OF THE SOUL

Socrates' entire teaching mission centered on his conviction that *we are our souls*. That is, the "real person" is not the body, but the *psyche*. Perhaps the most important passage in the *Apology* concerns Socrates' sense of himself as a kind of "physician of the soul." In Socrates' sense, "seeking my own welfare" means "seeking the welfare of my soul." Note how in the following passage Socrates implies that he does indeed know something (that the most important thing is care of the soul) and that he views his whole public career as a teacher in light of his expanded notion of the self as the soul:

> Men of Athens, I honour and love you; but I shall obey God rather than you, and while I have strength I shall never cease from the practice and teaching of philosophy, exhorting any one whom I meet and saying to him after my manner: You, my friend,—a citizen of the great and mighty and wise city of Athens,—are you not ashamed of heaping the greatest amount of money and honour and reputation, and caring so little about wisdom and truth and the greatest improvement of the soul, which you never regard or heed at all? And if the person with whom I am arguing, says: Yes, but I do care; then I do not leave him or let him go at once; but I proceed to interrogate and examine and cross-examine him, and if I think that

He who enjoins a knowledge of oneself bids us become acquainted with the soul.

Plato

he has no virtue in him, but only says that he has, I reproach him with undervaluing the greater, and overvaluing the less. And I shall repeat the same words to everyone I meet, young and old, citizen and alien, but especially to the citizens . . . For know this is the command of the God; and I believe no greater good has happened to this state than my service to the God. For I do nothing but go about persuading you all, old and young alike, not to take thought for your persons or your properties, but first and chiefly to care about the greatest improvement of your soul. I tell you that virtue is not given by money, but that from virtue comes money and every other good of man, public as well as private. This is my teaching.[22]

PHILOSOPHICAL QUERY

Compare Socrates' attitude toward the soul with your own. With your church's, if you go to church. What do you see as the main differences? What are some advantages and disadvantages of Socrates' view?

Socratic Egoism

The fundamental Socratic imperative "know thyself" takes on special significance in light of Socrates' *psychological egoism*, the view that human beings always seek what they perceive to be their own welfare and cannot deliberately do otherwise, and Socratic *ethical egoism*, the view that we *ought* to seek only our own welfare. In the *Gorgias*, Socrates points out that when people do what appear to be bad or distasteful things, it is always with some ultimate good in mind:

> So it is for the sake of the good that people do all these [distasteful] actions?
> Yes, it is.
> And we have admitted that when we act for any purpose, we do not desire the action itself but the object of the action?
> Yes.
> Then we do not desire . . . these [distasteful] actions themselves; but if they are advantageous, we desire to do them; and if they are harmful, we do not. For we desire what is good . . . but things that are neither bad nor good we do not desire, nor things that are bad either.[23]

For Socrates, the good (advantage) or harm in question is always determined by what benefits or harms the soul. In order to seek my soul's welfare I have to "know myself." And in order to "know myself," I have to know what kind of thing I am. Without this knowledge, I cannot know what is really good for me.

SOCRATIC EGOISM
Socratic belief that human beings always seek what they perceive to be their own welfare and cannot deliberately do otherwise (psychological egoism), and that they ought to seek only their own welfare (ethical egoism); for Socrates, the welfare in question was always the welfare of the soul.

In the *Protagoras*, Socrates reinforces his conviction that no one willingly does evil:

> For no wise man, I believe, will allow that any human being errs voluntarily, or voluntarily does evil or base actions; but they are very well aware that all who do evil and base things do them against their will.[24]

PHILOSOPHICAL QUERY

Do you agree that no one willingly does evil? Explain. What is your opinion of egoism—both kinds? You might want to read the box about the Ring of Gyges in Chapter 4 and the discussion of egoism in Chapter 14 before you answer.

Virtue Is Wisdom

VIRTUE
From the Greek *arete*, meaning "that at which something excels," or "excellence of function."

The Sophists claimed to be "teachers of human excellence," with excellence meaning "excellence of function" or **virtue** (*arete* in Greek). Too often, however, the result, as we saw in Chapter 4, was might-makes-right moral relativism and a radical this-worldly egoism—in contrast to Socratic egoism, which centers on the soul as the real self. The Sophists looked outward for markers of well-being and success, whereas Socrates looked inward at character.

Socrates believed that human excellence (virtue for short) is a special kind of knowledge that combines technical understanding with the skill and character to apply that knowledge. One of the words Socrates used for this kind of knowledge was **techne**, the Greek term for practical knowledge of how to do things. At various times, *techne* meant art, skill, craft, technique, trade, system, or method of doing something. It is the root of English words such as technique, technical, and technology. Techne is knowledge of what to do and how to do it. Thus, it is knowledge of both means and ultimate ends. Plato accused the Sophists of developing persuasive skills (rhetoric) without acquiring a corresponding knowledge of what ought to be done or avoided—that is without knowledge of ultimate ends.

TECHNE
From the Greek for "art," "skill," "craft," "technique," "trade," "system," or "method of doing something"; root of English words such as "technique," "technical," and "technology"; term Socrates used when he asserted that virtue (*arete*) is knowledge or wisdom (*techne*).

According to Socrates, a knowledgeable physician, for example, has both theoretical understanding and practical skill. Her techne is manifest by the fact that she makes her patients well. If she made them worse, we would conclude that she was not really a physician, that she lacked medical knowledge. Techne is not like a knowledge of a cake recipe; it requires certain skill (character) to bake a good cake.

According to Socrates, the Sophists lack of techne was evident because their teachings made people worse. Their own pupils attacked them and tried to cheat them out of their fees or engaged in corrupt business practices and destructive political schemes. Thus, the Sophists lacked knowledge of human excellence, or virtue.

In other words, for Socrates, knowledge of virtue is wisdom; it goes beyond theoretical understanding of justice or right and wrong, and includes *living* justly, living honorably and well in the highest sense. In the following passage from the *Meno*, Socrates argues that virtue is wisdom and that all things "hang upon" wisdom:

Socrates: The next question is, whether virtue is knowledge or of another species?

Meno: Certainly.

Socrates: Do we not say that virtue is good? . . .

Meno: Certainly. . . .

Socrates: Then virtue is profitable?

Meno: That is the only inference. . . .

Socrates: And what is the guiding principle which makes [things] profitable or the reverse? Are they not profitable when they are rightly used, and hurtful when they are not rightfully used?

Meno: Certainly.

Socrates: Next, let us consider the goods of the soul: they are temperance, justice, courage, quickness of apprehension, memory, magnanimity, and the like?

Meno: Surely.

Socrates: And such of these as are not knowledge, but of another sort, are sometimes profitable and sometimes hurtful; as, for example, courage wanting prudence, which is only a sort of confidence? When a man has no sense he is harmed by courage, but when he has sense he is profited?

Meno: True.

Socrates: And . . . whatever things are learned or done with sense are profitable, but when done without sense they are hurtful?

Meno: Very true.

Socrates: And in general, all that the soul attempts or endures, when under the guidance of wisdom, ends in happiness; but when she is under the guidance of folly, the opposite?

Meno: That appears to be true.

Socrates: If then virtue is a quality of the soul, and is admitted to be profitable, it must be wisdom or prudence, since none of the things of the soul are either profitable or hurtful in themselves, but they are all made profitable or hurtful by the addition of wisdom or folly; and therefore if virtue is profitable, virtue must be a sort of wisdom or prudence?

Meno: I quite agree. . . .

Socrates: And is this not universally true of human nature? All other things hang upon the soul, and the things of the

I think that all men have a choice between various courses, and choose and follow the one which they think conduces most to their advantage.
Socrates

To live is not itself an evil, as has been claimed, but to lead a worthless life is.
Diogenes

Every man is enlightened, but wishes he wasn't.
R. H. Blyth

*Yes, Socrates, I stand in
amazement when I reflect on
the questions that men ask.
By the Gods, I do! I want to
know more and more about
such questions, and there
are times when I become
almost dizzy just thinking
about them.*

Plato

INTELLECTUALISM
Term used to refer to
the claim that behavior is
always controlled by beliefs
about what is good and
the means to that good.

soul herself hang upon wisdom, if they are to be good;
and so wisdom is inferred to be that which profits—and
virtue, as we say, is profitable?

Meno: Certainly.

Socrates: And thus we arrive at the conclusion that virtue is
either wholly or partly wisdom?

Meno: I think that what you are saying, Socrates, is very true.[25]

All Evil Is Ignorance

Socrates believed that knowledge (wisdom) always produces behavioral results, because behavior is always guided by beliefs. For instance, if I believe
that the glass of water in front of me is poisoned, I will not drink it—unless
I also believe that dying will be better for me than living, given my present
circumstances, say terminal cancer of a painful sort. This rationalistic view
that behavior is always controlled by beliefs about what is good and the
means to that good is sometimes called **intellectualism**. Intellectualism
differs from egoism in its emphasis on cognitive states (beliefs) whereas egoism is usually expressed in terms of desires.

Socrates' intellectualism, combined with his psychological egoism, committed him to the unusual claim that no one knowingly does wrong. According to Socrates, when we "admit" (state) that our choices are wrong,
we are playing word games. To take an extreme example, a satanist who
glories in "choosing" evil really believes in the superiority of what he is calling evil. Perhaps according to Jews or Christians what he is choosing is
wrong, but to the satanist, it is *really good*. If he honestly believed (knew)
that X was wrong (fatal to his soul), our hypothetical satanist could not
choose X, according to Socrates.

In other words, there is no such thing as *weakness of will*. We are, implies Socrates, psychologically incapable of knowing what is good and not
doing it. Conversely, we are psychologically incapable of doing what we really know (and believe wholeheartedly) will harm us. Socrates' egoism and
intellectualism led him to the conviction that all evil is a form of ignorance,
because no one knowingly wills harm to herself.

Socrates: . . . Do not all men . . . desire the good?

Meno: I think not.

Socrates: There are some who desire evil?

Meno: Yes.

Socrates: Do you mean that they think the evils which they
desire, to be good; or do they know that they are evil and
yet desire them?

Meno: Both, I think.

Socrates: And do you really imagine, Meno, that a man knows
evils to be evils and desires them notwithstanding?

Meno: Certainly I do.

Socrates: And desire is [for] possession?

Meno: Yes, [for] possession. . . .

Socrates: Well, and do those who, as they say, desire evils, and
think that evils are hurtful to the possessor of them,
know that they will be hurt by them?

Meno: They must know it.

Socrates: And must they not suppose that those who are hurt
are miserable in proportion to the hurt which is inflicted
upon them?

Meno: How can it be otherwise?

Socrates: But are not the miserable ill-fated?

Meno: Yes, indeed.

Socrates: And does any one desire to be miserable and ill-fated?

Meno: I should say not, Socrates.

Socrates: But if there is no one who desires to be miserable,
there is no one, Meno, who desires evil; for what is misery but the desire and possession of evil?

Meno: That appears to be the truth, Socrates, and I admit that
nobody desires evil.[26]

*The cause of error is igno-
rance of the better.*

Democritus

PHILOSOPHICAL QUERY

What do you think of Socrates' claim that all evil is ignorance? Do
you think it is possible to knowingly choose (will) evil? If all evil is
ignorance, can we ever justly punish evil doers? Discuss.

*The striving to find meaning
in one's life is the primary
motivational force
in man.*

Viktor Frankl

COMMENTARY

Although Socrates was probably correct in his belief that
no normally reasonable person willingly does himself
harm, he was surely wrong in his rejection of the possibility of weakness of
will. His limited knowledge of the complexities of human psychology prevented him from recognizing what is a very common experience for most
of us: We lack the will to do the good we know or to resist the bad that
tempts us. Jesus' oft-quoted line that "the spirit is willing, but the flesh is
weak" probably comes closer to our experiences than Socrates' intellectual-
istic optimism.

Socrates was, after all, quite an optimist. He was convinced that genuine knowledge would make us good. The social qualities of the dialectic
are predicated on the belief that by working together, two or more honest,
well-meaning, and reasonable people can move steadily from ignorance to
virtue (goodness and happiness).

Perhaps the best way to approach the seeming paradoxes of Socrates'
rejection of the weak will and insistence that virtue is knowledge lies in not

imposing our contemporary sense of the soul and lack of respect for wisdom on the ancient *sophos*. The common counterexamples used to show that we often know the good but choose what we know is bad (smoking, acts of malice, dishonesty) are only counterexamples when we separate knowledge from wisdom.

If by "know the good," we mean, for example, to cognitively understand that smoking leads to impaired health, then it is possible to know the good and do the bad. But if by "know the good" we mean value and love the soul, then perhaps Socrates is correct. Perhaps we choose to smoke or lie in ignorance of their effects on our souls.

We might also find Socrates' ideas difficult to accept because—like the Sophists and many Greeks of his time—we grant primacy to the external physical and social world rather than to the soul. We more easily recognize harm to our reputations and physical health than we do harm to our souls. Using the physical and deductive sciences as our paradigms of knowledge makes it difficult to recognize the possibility of wisdom.

When Socrates said that "human wisdom" is "worthless," his point was that while the benefits of technical knowledge are apparent, its limits often escape us. It might be a fine thing to discover the physical origin of the universe or develop safer automobiles, and so forth. But does that kind of knowledge help our psyches, does it help us be better and happier people? Cures for AIDS and cancer will bring a certain peace of mind to us, because living longer seems to be a good thing. But how long? Would you like to live three hundred years, trying to plan for your retirement in another two hundred and fifty years? How will living longer make your life better if you are often bored or lonely now? Will more of the same be an improvement?

Contemporary psychologists are rediscovering both the soul and wisdom. Thomas Moore's book *Care of the Soul* was a surprise best seller in 1993. Solomon Schimmel's *The Seven Deadly Sins*, Robert J. Sternberg's *Wisdom: Its Nature, Origins, and Development*, and T. Byram's *Wisdom in the Practice of Psychotherapy* are three of the most significant recent books by clinical and research psychologists dealing with wisdom. Whether this new interest will result in actually taking better care of the soul remains to be seen, but at least wisdom is once again being taken seriously outside the academy.

Human wisdom rests on the courage to change what should be changed combined with the maturity and insight to accept what cannot be changed. I have no hope of doing either until I know myself. This, of course, means that I must discover the difference between what I cannot do and what I so far have only failed to do. So long as I think that I know more than I know, I will learn less than I can. The unexamined life—whatever its causes—is always a tragedy.

By professing his ignorance, Socrates has achieved a kind of immortality. He is one of the few great philosophers to whom people of many cultures, eras, abilities, and interests have looked for wisdom. The Socratic mission has not ended. Socrates' power to provoke, challenge, and awaken lives on.

Reason or a halter.

Diogenes

If, as they say, I am only an ignorant man trying to be a philosopher, then that may be what a philosopher is.

Diogenes

One ought not to talk or act as if he were asleep.

Heraclitus

For me, Socrates remains fresh. I return to him repeatedly. Slow learner that I must be, I am again and again caught up short by the force of his insight into *human* wisdom. Like Athens, I doze, forgetting to question myself. In a dreamlike condition, I imagine that I know what I do not know. I may fool myself. Perhaps I even fool others. But I cannot fool the old *sophos*. In moments of clarity, I long for human wisdom.

SUMMARY OF MAIN POINTS

Socrates is the first major Western philosopher. He wrote no philosophy, and what we know of him comes chiefly from his pupils Plato and Xenophon.

Socrates challenged the Sophist doctrines of relativism, moral realism, and might makes right. He also insisted that no one who took money for teaching could teach the truth.

Socrates' teaching and life were so fully integrated that the power or force of his whole person galvanized others. Socrates possessed a power that went beyond rational argument. An encounter with him could trigger not just personal, but deep philosophical and spiritual responses in others. Individuals of this sort are known as paradigmatic or archetypal individuals, rare human beings whose very nature represents something elemental about the human condition.

Socrates' dialectical encounters with powerful Sophists, his use of irony, his disdain for the trappings of material success, and his contempt for paid teachers angered and offended Sophists and those whom they taught. Many Athenians thought that Socrates was just another Sophist. In 399 B.C. he was condemned and executed.

Socrates perfected a style of philosophical inquiry known today as the Socratic method or Socratic dialectic. The method is based on the assumption that the function of education is to draw the truth out of the pupil rather than "fill an empty vessel." A series of guided questions continually refines the ideas under scrutiny; definitions are required for all key terms and logical inconsistencies brought to light and resolved. Because the active involvement of the audience is essential, questions are preferred to straight lectures.

Socrates used irony to encourage active listening by his pupils or dialectical partners. An ironic utterance is a way of communicating that has at least two levels of meaning, the literal level, also known as the obvious level, and the hidden level, also known as the real level.

Among Socratic teachings, the most persistent command was "know thyself." By this he meant, among other things, that a life devoid of philosophical speculation is hardly a human life, because only philosophical reflection can help us discover what is real and important from the standpoint of the psyche, the uniquely human soul-mind. The unexamined life takes the psyche for granted.

Socrates insisted that his only wisdom consisted of a kind of "nonknowledge": He knew what he did not know. Acknowledgment of ignorance, Socrates taught, is a fundamental characteristic of the examined life.

Socrates saw himself as a kind of "physician of the soul." He believed that we are our souls, that the "real person" is not the body, but the *psyche*.

Socratic egoism has two components: (1) psychological (human beings always seek what they perceive to be their own welfare and cannot deliberately do otherwise) and (2) ethical (we ought to seek only our own welfare). In Socrates' sense, "seeking our own welfare" means "seeking the welfare of the soul."

Socrates believed that human excellence or virtue is a special kind of knowledge (*techne*) that combines technical understanding with the skill and character to apply that knowledge. *Techne* is knowledge of what to do and how to do it.

Socrates believed that knowledge (wisdom) always produces behavioral results, because behavior is always guided by beliefs. This view is sometimes called intellectualism. Intellectualism differs from egoism in its emphasis on cognitive states (beliefs) whereas egoism is usually expressed in terms of desires.

Socrates' intellectualism combined with his psychological egoism committed him to the unusual claim that no one knowingly does wrong. In other words, there is no such thing as weakness of will. We are, implies Socrates, psychologically incapable of knowing what is good and not doing it.

STUDY QUESTIONS

1. Discuss what is meant by the "Socratic problem." Be sure to include strategies for dealing with it.

2. What do you see as the relevance of Socrates' life to his teachings? Explain.

3. Suppose it were discovered that Socrates secretly violated many of his teachings. How would this affect your attitude toward his philosophy? Which do you see as more important, the man or the ideas? Explain.

4. Explain how Socrates used his physical appearance to support his general theory of virtue.

5. Explain Socrates' views of self-control. Reconstruct his argument in your own words.

6. Use Socratic principles to defend Socrates against the charge of being a bad husband and father.

7. Explain what Jaspers meant by a paradigmatic individual. Then think about meeting one. Would it be a pleasant experience?

8. Thoroughly describe the Socratic dialectic. Then explain its significance to Socrates' claims of ignorance.

9. What is irony? Give one or two examples. Explain its function in the Socratic method.

10. Many Athenians thought that Socrates was a Sophist. Point out ways in which Socrates and the Sophists were alike. Then make your case that he was or was not a Sophist. Be sure to justify it with specific examples.

11. Analyze Socrates' claim that "the unexamined life is not worth living." What did he mean? Was he correct? Why or why not?

12. Explain "human wisdom."

13. What is Socratic egoism? Socratic intellectualism? How do they relate to Socrates' rejection of weakness of will and belief that evil is ignorance?

14. Fully explain what Socrates meant when he said that virtue is knowledge. What kind of knowledge? What is virtue?

15. What is the function of ignorance in Socratic philosophy?

16. In your own words, describe Socrates' mission.

17. How are Socrates' ideas about wealth and possessions connected to other aspects of his teaching?

18. Socrates thought it very important not to teach for money. Why? What kind of teaching did he mean? Was he right? Can this principle be extended to priests, rabbis, and preachers? Explain.

19. What individual or group (if any) provides a Socratic function for our society? Explain. If none, explain that.

The feeling of wonder is the touchstone of the philosopher, and all philosophy has its origins in wonder.

Plato

Democracy is the best form of government. Can there be any doubt? One of the great traditions of American history has been that "any boy can grow up to be president." And certainly our history suggests a continuous (if sometimes painfully slow) movement toward extending greater and greater choices and opportunities to all our citizens. Now it's no longer "any *boy* can grow up to be president," but "any *person*." Visible and invisible barriers of race, creed, and social class are being removed. Increasingly, the only limits on our dreams are our own. And someday even these barriers may be removed by educators, scientists, and therapists who seek special techniques and discoveries to abolish as many disadvantages of birth or background as possible.

As citizens of a democracy, we are free to seek any position we wish in society. The highest public office has only three entrance requirements: citizenship, age, and a majority of the votes. If in practice our presidents come from the wealthier, more educated classes, they still do not need to meet any stringent requirements of self-discipline, character, or wisdom. Nor do we who elect them. This is the glory of democracy.

Picture now a November morning. A line of voters waits to elect the next president of the United States. You have spent weeks studying the televised debates (you've even read the written transcripts). You've subscribed to liberal and conservative magazines and newspapers in order to get as complete a picture of the candidates' records and the issues as you can. You've read those long political editorials in the newspaper, as well as your voter's pamphlet. Because there are a number of lesser offices, bond issues, and legislative amendments on the ballot, you've brought a written list of your carefully reasoned decisions with you to the polls.

Patiently waiting your turn, you overhear a small group of people standing in line behind you. A woman announces, "I'm voting for X. She's a woman, and that's good enough for me." Someone else says, "My dad always voted Republican, so I'm voting Democrat!" A third person chimes in, "I'm not voting for Y, he's a jerk." Someone asks about "all those propositions and stuff," and the group laughs. "Who cares," someone else snaps. "None of that stuff makes any difference." "Yeah," another responds, "there are too many to keep straight anyway. I just vote yes, no, yes, at random." Yet another says, "As a single parent, I'm only interested in Prop M, since I need money for child care. I'll just guess at the rest."

Disturbed by this, you suddenly notice that the man in front of you is weaving. You ask if he's sick, and he laughingly answers, with the unmistakable smell of beer on his breath: "Heck no. I'm loaded. It's the only way to vote." You vote anyway, but can't shake your anger for a long time. It doesn't seem fair that these irresponsible votes should equal your carefully researched and reasoned decisions. They might even cancel your vote out. It's worse than unfair. It's dumb. It's not *reasonable*, you think. There should be *some* requirement for voting. Not anything unfair or "discriminatory," just *reasonable*. And come to think of it, there should be some kind

CHAPTER SIX

The Philosopher-King: Plato

Until philosophers are
kings, or the kings and
princes of this world
have the spirit and
power of philosophy . . .
cities will never have
rest from their evils . . .
nor the human race . . .
and then only will our
State . . . behold the
light of day.

PLATO,
THE REPUBLIC

of test or something for politicians. They're a pretty unethical and dumb lot, too.

If you have ever had thoughts like this, your disgust and annoyance at "the way things are run around here" have probably triggered a desire for a "more ideal" society. As we all know, however, no such ideal society exists in this world, so where did you get the idea for it? It's as if you have seen beyond the way things are, seen a *higher* possibility.

Anyone who has visualized a fairer, more ideal society has already shared at least some ideas with perhaps the greatest, and certainly one of the most imposing and influential, philosophers in the Western world: Plato.

> *The truth is that the common man's love of liberty, like his love of sense, justice and truth, is almost wholly imaginary.*
>
> H. L. Mencken

PHILOSOPHICAL QUERY

Americans have reason to be wary of requirements for voting. In the past they have been used to prevent women and people of certain ethnic groups from voting. On the other hand, a case might be made that by not having some minimal standard of preparedness and awareness, we make a mockery of "choosing." How can an ignorant voter "choose" anything? Discuss from both sides.

PLATO'S LIFE AND WORK

Our chief source of information regarding Plato's philosophy is Plato himself. We still have all the works attributed to him by ancient scholars. The most important of these are philosophical dialogues. We have already seen material from some of these in Chapters 4 and 5: the *Apology*, *Crito*, *Phaedo*, *Theaetetus*, *Timaeus*, *Gorgias*, *Protagoras*, *Meno*, and *The Republic*. We also have the summaries and analyses of some of Plato's doctrines left by his greatest student, Aristotle. We probably have more biographical information about Plato than of any other ancient philosopher, much of it from Diogenes Läertius's *Life of Plato*. Last is a controversial collection of thirteen letters and some dialogues whose authenticity some scholars dispute. One of these, *Letter: VII*, is of special interest because of its comments regarding the mature Plato's attitudes toward democracy in view of the way Socrates was treated by it.

> *Plato has exerted a greater influence over human thought than any other individual with the possible exception of Aristotle.*
>
> Raphael Demos

Probably no single work of philosophy has been read by as many people as Plato's *Republic*. It is considered by most philosophers to be Plato's most impressive and important work because it presents his overall philosophy in a dramatic, organized, and brilliant form. We'll use *The Republic* as the basis for our introduction to this genuinely great archetype of the philosopher-king, but first let us start with a brief sketch of Plato's life.

The Aristocrat

Plato (c. 427–348 B.C.) is actually the nickname of Aristocles, the son of one of the oldest and most elite Athenian families. Through his mother's

Plato

family he was related to a celebrated lawgiver named Solon. His father's family traced its lineage to the ancient kings of Athens and even further back to Poseidon, the god of the sea. His given name, Aristocles, meant "best, most renowned." He is said to have done well at practically everything as a young man: music, logic, debate, math, poetry. He was attractive and made his mark as a wrestler. In the military he distinguished himself in three battles, and even won a prize for bravery.[1] His nickname, Platon, means "broad" or "wide"; one story is that he had wide shoulders, another that he had a wide forehead.

Plato was born two years after the death of Pericles, the great architect of Athenian democracy. Athens was fighting Sparta in the Peloponnesian Wars, which lasted more than twenty years. During all that time Athens was in a state of turmoil, not unlike America during the Vietnam War. Great energy and expense were drained off by the war itself, as well as by disagreements over whether Athens should continue to fight, and if so, how. As we learned in Chapter 5, Athens finally surrendered to Sparta in 404 B.C.

The Spartan army supported a group of nobles, known as the Thirty, who overthrew the democracy and ruled Athens for a short time. Plato's family were members of this group. This is the same Thirty Socrates resisted when ordered to condemn and execute Leon of Salamis in violation of the Athenian constitution. Looking back on this time, Plato recalled:

> Of course I saw in a short time that [the Thirty] made the former government look in comparison like an age of gold. Among other things they sent an elderly man, Socrates, a friend of mine, who I should hardly be ashamed to say was the justest man of his time . . . against one of the citizens. . . . Their purpose was to connect Socrates to their government whether he wished or not. . . . When I observed all this—and some other similar matters of importance—I withdrew in disgust from the abuses of those days.[2]

The impact of these events never left Plato, who was in his early twenties at the time. The nobles who formed the Thirty had no doubt been disturbed by changes in Athenian society brought about by the long war and the loss of elitist privilege that accompanied increased democracy: the breakdown of tradition; the Sophists' use of debaters' tricks to sway the mob; the rule of passion and emotion. In a democracy, the cleverest, most persuasive, and most attractive speakers could control the state. The great privileges of being born into a special class disappeared. Moreover, the emerging business class had created a power base built on money and aggressiveness rather than tradition and social status.[3]

The Thirty, however, failed in their efforts to restore rule by an elite based on bloodlines, not character or wisdom. Their reign lasted only about three years before democracy was restored. It was the restored democracy, however, that tried and condemned Socrates.

Do you think I would have survived all these years if I were engaged in public affairs and, acting as good man must, came to the help of justice and considered this the most important thing? Far from it . . . nor would any other man.

Socrates

Plato's Disillusionment

This turmoil caused Plato to become discouraged by both the "mob" and the status "elite." The mob, represented by the jury at Socrates' trial, was irrational and dangerous; it was swayed by sophistic appeals to emotion, not by reason. Rule by the status elite, represented by the behavior of the Thirty, was cruel, self-centered, and greedy. When Plato saw that neither the aristocracy nor the common citizenry was capable of superior rule, his "disillusionment [was] fearful and wonderful to behold."[4]

Plato concluded that most people are unfit by training and ability to make the difficult and necessary decisions that would result in a just society. The "average person" lacks wisdom and self-restraint. As Plato saw things, most people make emotional responses based on personal gain and sentiment, rather than rational choices based on an objective, long-term view of what is genuinely good for the individual and society. What, he wondered, could be clearer proof of the mob's deficiencies than its utter failure to recognize the truth of Socrates' message? The trial and death of Socrates showed Plato what happens when "justice" is reduced to a majority vote.

> Now as I considered these matters, as well as the sort of men who were active in politics, and the laws and the customs, the more I examined them and the more I advanced in years, the harder it appeared to me to administer the government correctly. . . . The result was that I, who had at first been full of eagerness for a public career, as I gazed upon the whirlpool of public life and saw the incessant movement of shifting currents, at last felt dizzy, and . . . *finally saw clearly in regard to all states now existing that without exception their system of government is bad* [emphasis added].[5]

Socrates would be avenged—but by philosophy rather than by political action.

After the revolt of the Thirty and the execution of Socrates, Plato left Athens and wandered for nearly twelve years. He studied with Euclid (the great pioneer of geometry) and possibly with the hedonist Aristippus (Chapter 8). He seems also to have gone to Egypt. During his travels he studied mathematics and mysticism, both of which influenced his later philosophy. He studied Pythagorean philosophy and was deeply influenced by its emphasis on mathematics as the basis of all things.

The Academy

Plato was probably forty years old when he founded the Academy (around 388 B.C.). Ironically, considering the importance and influence the Academy was to exert, we have no solid evidence concerning when it was founded, how it was organized, what exactly was studied, or what educational techniques were used. Most of Plato's writing seems to have been

The status of Plato as the greatest of Western philosophers lies not in the soundness of the answers he provides, but rather in his unequaled perception of what questions must be asked, in his shaping of the language to allow the asking, and in the vast range of possibilities suggested in his exploration of every problem.
Alexander Sesonske

How can any man be a democrat who is sincerely a democrat?
H. L. Mencken

Plato's Academy was created as a school for philosopher-kings.

finished before he founded the Academy, with the exception of a few works completed when he was an old man. His chief function at the Academy was probably as a teacher and administrator.[6] Here Plato lived for another forty years, lecturing "without notes," until he died.

The chief purpose of the Academy was probably to educate people who would be fit to rule the just state. Plato's ideal educational program was a progressive one in which the study of mathematics, geometry, music, and so forth, introduced discipline into the student's overall character, and order into the mind. Only after the mind and soul were disciplined were a select few allowed to study ultimate philosophical principles.

Because, in Plato's view, "no present government [was] suitable for philosophy," the Academy was established as a philosophic retreat, isolated from the turmoil of Athenian politics, safe from the fate of Socrates. Let's see what philosophy Plato thought could produce the just state.

PLATO'S EPISTEMOLOGY

Socrates' death, the revolt of the Thirty, sophistic abuses, and other factors convinced Plato that a corrupt state produces corrupt citizens. He thus turned to the development of a theory of knowledge that could refute sophistic skepticism and moral relativism. Plato believed that if he could identify and articulate the difference between mere opinion and genuine knowledge, it would then be possible to identify the structure of the ideal state, a state based on knowledge and truth rather than the mere appearance of truth and personal whim.

Plato correctly understood that before he could provide satisfactory answers to ethical, social, political, and other philosophical questions, he must first tackle the problem of knowledge. We have seen how the conflicting opinions of the Presocratics first led to philosophical confusion and then to ethical and political abuses in the hands of the most extreme of the Sophists. Socrates' heroic effort to refute ignorance and relativism was most successful in its exposure of error and inconsistency. It was less successful in establishing any positive knowledge.

Thus, Plato could not avoid the challenge of sophistic skepticism or ignore philosophy's reputation for generating ludicrous doctrines that contradicted each other—and themselves. Though the Presocratics, the Sophists, and Socrates had all made use of the distinction between appearance and reality, the exact nature of reality and clear rational criteria for distinguishing reality from appearance had eluded them.

Attempts to explain how one kind of thing changes into another generated ambiguities and seeming contradictions: How could "one thing" somehow change into something else? In what sense can my twelve-year-old dog Daiquiri be the "same" dog she was five years ago? Does this mean that Daiquiri is both the same dog she was *and* a different dog? In what sense did the "same person" change from an infant into a philosophy student?

Plato recognized the full importance of being able to explain how things change, how reality "becomes" appearance, how appearances are related to reality, and other fundamental issues. The relation between appearance and reality, the problem of "the one and the many," and the nature of change needed to be clarified before any answer to the sophistic assault on rationality was possible.

For as all nature is akin, and the soul has [already] learned all things, there is no difficulty in . . . learning . . . all the rest, if a man is strenuous and does not faint; for all enquiry is but recollection.

Plato

Plato's Dualistic Solution

Plato concluded that the solution to the basic problem of knowledge lay in acknowledging that both Heraclitus and Parmenides were partially correct in their efforts to characterize reality. Recall that Heraclitus asserted that the "one" is some kind of orderly cycle or process of change. He said that "change alone is unchanging." Parmenides, in contrast, referred to the "one" as *being*. Parmenides argued that being is perfect and complete or "whole." It cannot

Plato's genius is exhibited in the fact that he succeeded in eliciting from his observations of the Athenian state reflections on society and government that are true everywhere.

Raphael Demos

Wise men say . . . that heaven and earth, gods and men, are held together by the principles of sharing, by friendship and order, by self-control and justice; that, my friend, is the reason they call the universe "cosmos," and not disorder or licentiousness . . . what a mighty power is exercised, both among men and gods, by geometrical equality.

Plato

move or change. Parmenidian being is material, "it is the being of the visible cosmos, immobilized, and to a great extent purified, but still clearly recognizable." (See Chapter 3.)

According to Plato, Heraclitus and Permenides probably thought they were discussing things that could be sensed or perceived as part of the physical world. (We can refer to such things as "sensibles," for short.) The Sophists' skeptical arguments were also aimed at contradictions and difficulties generated by problems of sensation and perception. (See Chapter 4.)

Suppose, Plato wondered, that reality is not a single thing (a monism) but is rather a dualism. One reality might be Heraclitean and another Parmenidian; one reality in constant change and the other eternally changeless.

Of course a supposition is not evidence. Plato needed to prove the dual nature of reality. Part of the "proof" seemed easy enough: it seems obvious that the world of "sensibles" exists. And the sensible world certainly seems to be one of change: growth cycles, soil erosion, flowing rivers, wear and tear of the implements of daily living, and so on. Further, this change is orderly: the same seasons follow the same seasons, dogs do not give birth to stones, objects fall down not up, and so forth. So, as far as the world of sensibles is concerned, Heraclitus seems to be basically correct.

But a completely Heraclitean world of observable change, for all its "obviousness," would be a world devoid of the possibility of knowledge and certainty, according to Plato. Such a world would be a world of appearances only, a realm of opinion, not knowledge. Plato called this condition the world of *becoming*.

Knowledge and Being

According to Plato, the very essence of time is change but the very essence of knowledge is unchanging. What is true is always true. Therefore, whatever is relative and always changing cannot be true. The Sophists could not discover truth because they were only concerned with the Heraclitean world of sensibles, the world of ever-changing perceptions and customs. Truth and knowledge are found in another realm of reality: the level of being that Parmenides tried to characterize.

Plato believed that this second reality, while closely related to the world of becoming, exists independently of it. This other reality has many of the qualities Parmenides ascribed to the one (being): It is not physical and it is not affected by space and time.

What is eternal is *real*; what changes is only *appearance*. Thus, we can have *knowledge* of what is eternal; of appearances there can be only *opinions*. Opinions change; knowledge is timeless. Plato insisted that whatever is permanent is superior to whatever is not. Reality is superior to appearance, and knowledge is superior to opinion, in Plato's view.

THE FORMS

In Plato's metaphysics, the level of being consists of timeless essences or entities called *forms*. Such a metaphysics is sometimes called transcendental because it asserts that there is a plane of existence "above and beyond" our ordinary existence. To transcend anything is to go so far beyond it as to reach a qualitatively different level.

The **Platonic forms** are independently existing, nonspatial, nontemporal "somethings" that cannot be known through the senses. Known in thought, the forms are the objects of thought—though they are not ideas in the usual sense. Thinking is always about forms.

It may be helpful to think about other meanings of the word form. By form we may mean the shape or manner or style or type of something. We make forms from which to mold dishes or statues, for example. We fill in business forms. The very notion of form implies something that provides general or essential order, structure, or shape for a particular instance. Thus, the form of something is sometimes called its structure or essence, or even its "basic nature." Many of these everyday meanings involve the essence of a thing, the quality that makes it what it is. In Platonic terms, a thing's form is what it uniquely and essentially is.

Knowledge and Opinion

For Plato, *thoughts* (as opposed to feelings, visions, images, and perceptions) and *knowledge* (as opposed to opinions) are always of forms. A science thus consists of necessary and universal truths about the objects (forms) that science studies. In all subject areas, the physical objects, particular individuals, societies, or types of government studied represent forms. Particular things (sensibles) are never "as real" as the forms they participate in.

Remember that, for Plato, that which changes is less real than that which does not. That which changes is "lower" than that which does not. And all sensibles change. When Protagoras said that the individual is "the measure," he was talking about the level of becoming, about perceptions of sensibles, about the private and individual rather than about the public and universal.

According to Plato, *knowledge of particulars is impossible*. What we often think of as knowledge, Plato thought of as *recognition* or *opinion*.

Becoming is the level of change: growth and decay, life and death. Here opinions can evolve toward true belief. Because I live in time (in becoming), I can have more—or less—correct opinions today than I did yesterday. I can become smarter—or more foolish. But truth and knowledge themselves cannot change.

Opinions about what's true change, not the truth itself. The Sophists failed to understand this. For instance, a first grader may be utterly certain that 4 times 4 equals 18. But 4 times 4 is simply 16, for all time, for all people,

PLATONIC FORMS Independently existing, nonspatial, nontemporal "somethings" known only through thought and that cannot be known through the senses; independently existing objects of thought; that which makes a particular thing uniquely and essentially what it is.

It is hard, too, to see how a weaver or a carpenter will be benefitted in regard to his own craft by knowing this [a form], or how the man who has viewed the Idea itself will be a better doctor or general thereby. For a doctor seems not even to study health in this way, but the health of man, or perhaps rather the health of a particular man; it is individuals that he is healing.

Aristotle

regardless of our opinions. For Plato, by definition, knowledge is always of things in their unchanging, eternal form, knowledge of their essence. Opinion, by contrast, is like perception: limited by physical conditions and perspectives, the reliability of our senses, our personal backgrounds and cultural experiences. Disagreement is possible only in the world of becoming. In the *Timaeus* Plato says:

> We must make a distinction and ask, What is that which always is and has no becoming, and what . . . is always becoming and never is? That which is apprehended by intelligence and reason is always in the same state, but that which is conceived by opinion with the help of sensation and without reason is always in a process of becoming and perishing and never really is.[7]

There are more things in heaven and earth, Horatio, Than are dreamt of in your philosophy.
Shakespeare

Throughout *The Republic* Plato repeatedly distinguishes between knowledge and opinion, warning against even true opinions which lack grounding in knowledge. Here's a typical passage:

> "But I don't think it's right, Socrates . . . for you to be able to tell us other people's opinions but not your own, when you've given so much time to the subject."
>
> "Yes, but do you think it's right for a man to talk as if he knows what he does not?"
>
> "He has no right to talk as if he knew; but he should be prepared to say what his opinion is, so far as it goes."
>
> "Well," I [Socrates] said, "haven't you noticed that opinion without knowledge is blind—isn't anyone with a true but unthinking opinion like a blind man on the right road?"
>
> "Yes."[8]

In *The Republic*, Plato used three different comparisons to help express various aspects of the theory of forms: the Divided Line, the Simile of the Sun, and the Allegory of the Cave. We will study each of them. Each illustration clarifies different but interconnected aspects of the theory of forms. Do not worry if you need to take extra time with this material. Allow each of Plato's illustrations to help you better grasp the whole.

To understand Plato is to be educated; it is to see the nature of the world in which we live. The vitality of what he has to say is due to one factor. He took his starting point from what is and not from what man wants.
Huntington Cairns

THE DIVIDED LINE

Plato used the concept of a divided line to illustrate the relationship of knowledge to opinion, reality to appearance, metaphysics and epistemology, and the worlds of being and becoming. The Divided Line shows that both knowledge and opinion deal with forms, though in different ways.

The Divided Line consists of two basic sections, each unevenly divided into two segments. The four segments illustrate four ways of apprehending

OBJECT OF AWARENESS   MENTAL STATE

METAPHYSICS	EPISTEMOLOGY
Higher forms Example: The Good	A Understanding
Lower forms Example: Form Human	B Reasoning
Sensible objects Example: Mother Teresa	C Perception
Images Example: Mother Teresa's reputation	D Imagination

BEING

BECOMING

KNOWLEDGE

OPINION

A + B = World of Forms (Being)

C + D = Physical World (Becoming)

Segments **A, B, C, D** represent decreasing degrees of truth. Each degree of truth corresponds to a different kind of thinking and different level of reality.

A: This is the level of pure intelligence or understanding. Here the soul directly apprehends truth at its highest level.

B: This is the level of reasoning; specifically, mathematical thinking and deductive reasoning.

C: This is the level of belief or common opinions about physical objects, morals, politics, practical affairs.

D: This is the level of illusion, dominated by secondhand opinions and uncritical impressions.[9]

FIGURE 6.1   **Plato's Divided Line**

four components of reality; two each of being and becoming. Here's a representation of the Divided Line to refer to as you read Plato's presentation of it. Note how the four metaphysical levels of reality correspond to four epistemological ways of apprehending them.

With Figure 6.1 as a guide, let's take a look at what Plato said about the Divided Line. In this passage Socrates is describing a conversation he had with Plato's older brother, Glaucon:

> "Well, take a line divided into two unequal parts, corresponding to the visible and intelligible worlds, and then divide the two parts again in the same ratio, to represent degrees of

*Out of Plato come all things
that are still written and
debated among men of
thought. Great havoc makes
he of our originalities. We
have reached the mountain
from which all these drift
boulders were detached.*

Ralph Waldo Emerson

clarity and obscurity. In the visible world, one section stands for images: by 'images' I mean first shadows, then reflections in water and other close grained, polished surfaces, and all that sort of thing if you understand me."

"I understand."

"Let the other section stand for the objects which are the originals of the images—animals, plants and manufactured objects of all kinds."

"Very good."

"Would you be prepared to admit that these sections differ in their degree of truth, and that the relation of image to the original is the same as that of opinion and knowledge?"

"I would."

"Then consider next how the intelligible part of the line is to be divided. In one section the mind uses the originals of the visible world in their turn as images, and has to base its inquiries on assumptions and proceed from them to its conclusions instead of going back to first principles: in the other it proceeds from assumption back to self-sufficient first principles, making no use of the images employed by the other section, but pursuing its inquiry solely by means of Forms. . . .

" . . . it treats assumptions not as principles, but as assumptions in the true sense, that is, as starting points and steps in the ascent to the universal, self-sufficient first principle; when it has reached that principle it can again descend, by keeping to the consequences that follow from it, to a final conclusion. The whole procedure involves nothing in the sensible world, but deals throughout with Forms and finishes with Forms."[10]

Levels of Awareness

The lowest level of awareness, **D** on Figure 6.1, is the level of illusion. Virtually no one inhabits this level all the time, but we can occasionally slip into states of illusion. We slip into **D** on purpose and for fun when we go to

Many admire, few know.

Hippocrates

magic shows or watch movies (which are really just light, shadows, and sound creating the illusion of depth and action). This is known as the "willing suspension of disbelief." But we can also slip into illusion without being aware of it when we hold opinions based solely on appearances, unanalyzed impressions, uncritically inherited beliefs, and unevaluated emotions. The image—opinion—I have of Mother Teresa is an example of Level D awareness. It is based on photographs I have seen, news clips on television, and part of a speech she gave to the United Nations, which I watched on the C-Span cable network.

C on Figure 6.1 represents the second or informed level of awareness. It involves a wider range of opinions about what most of us probably think of as reality. At this level of informed awareness, we attempt to distinguish appearance from reality, but in a kind of "everyday way." For example, I believe that my desk looks solid but it is actually made up of countless molecules and atoms in motion. I believe that the sun looks small because of its distance from earth, but in fact, it is much larger. Strictly speaking, I do not *know* these things. I have had some science classes, looked through microscopes and telescopes, and so forth, but I do not have a scientist's sophisticated knowledge built upon rigorous deductive reasoning. At the same time, my Level C opinions are based on observations and perceptions of physical objects, not just photos or representations of them. On this informed level we realize that the way things appear may not be the way they are. Most of us spend much of our lives dealing with more or less informed opinions about most things. If I ever get to meet Mother Teresa, perhaps my Level D image of her will become a more accurate Level C informed opinion.

The next level of awareness (**B**) takes us out of the realms of becoming and opinion (**D** + **C**) and into the world of being and the first stage of knowledge acquired through deductive reasoning. If, as Plato believed, truth is changeless, eternal, and absolute, then knowledge doesn't grow or decay, it just *is*. Since Mother Teresa the individual does grow and change, however, Level B knowledge must be of a form, say the Form Human. The Form Human does not change—grow or decay—according to Plato.

At the highest level of reality (**A**), the soul has no need for perception or interpretation. Plato says that it "directly apprehends" the "absolute form of the Good." At the highest level, reason does not—indeed it cannot—deduce the forms. The higher forms are directly understood, apprehended without any mediating process or principles.

THE SIMILE OF THE SUN

Plato compared the "absolute form of the Good" to the sun: Just as the sun (light) is necessary for vision and life, so, too, the Good makes Reality, Truth, and the existence of everything else possible. The Good exists beyond becoming at the highest reaches of being. The Good cannot be observed with the five senses and can be known only by pure thought or intelligence. The Good is the source of both the value and the existence of all other forms.

Comprehension of the Good is unlike other forms of knowing. It is holistic, not partial. The soul must deliberately work its way up from the lowest level of becoming to enlightenment. Experience of the Good so far transcends all other experiences that it cannot be clearly described, so Plato uses a comparison or simile to allude to the Good. We can represent Plato's comparison of the Good to the Sun as shown in Figure 6.2.

Human insight requires a turning around. . . . But when it is a question of thinking in earnest, when an . . . eternal truth . . . makes a claim on independent thinking, then there is something in man that rebels against the rigors of responsible self-clarification. He does not want to wake up but go on sleeping.
Karl Jaspers

VISIBLE WORLD (C + D)	INTELLIGIBLE WORLD (A + B)
The Sun	The Good
Growth	Reality
Light	Truth
Visibility	Intelligibility

FIGURE 6.2   Figure 6.2 shows the hierarchy of being and knowledge reflected in Plato's simile of the sun. *A* = pure understanding; *B* = deductive thinking; *C* = common opinion; *D* = uncritical impressions.

In the following extended passage from *The Republic,* Plato (in the character of Socrates) compares the Good to the sun, and apprehension of the Good to seeing. Note how strongly he expresses his ultimate regard for the Good:

> "Well, [the sun] is the child of the Good . . . The Good has begotten its own likeness, and it bears the same relation to sight and visibility in the visible world that the Good bears to intelligence in the intelligible world."
>
> "Will you explain that a bit further?"
>
> "You know that when we turn our eyes to objects whose colours are no longer illuminated by daylight, but only by moonlight or starlight, they see dimly and appear to be almost blind, as if they had no clear vision."
>
> "Yes."
>
> "But when we turn them on things on which the sun is shining, then they see clearly and their power of vision is restored."
>
> "Certainly."
>
> "Apply the analogy to the mind. When the mind's eye rests on objects illuminated by truth and reality, it understands and comprehends them, and functions intelligently; but when it turns to the twilight world of change and decay, it can only form opinions, its vision is confused and its beliefs shifting, and it seems to lack intelligence."
>
> "That is true."
>
> "Then what gives the objects of knowledge their truth and the mind the power of knowing is the Form of the Good. It is the cause of knowledge and truth, and you will be right to think of it as being itself known, and yet as being something other than, and even higher than knowledge and truth. And just as it was right to think of light and sight as being like the

There seems to be nothing in the study of chemistry that makes you feel like a superior order of being, but you study Plato and you begin to believe you're a philosopher.

S. I. Hayakawa

sun, but wrong to think of them as being the sun itself, so here again it is right to think of knowledge and truth as being *like* the Good, but wrong to think of either of them as being the Good, which must be given still a higher place of honor."

"You are making it something remarkably exalted, if it is the source of knowledge and truth, and yet itself higher than they are. For I suppose you can't mean it to be pleasure?"

"A monstrous suggestion," I replied. "Let us pursue our analogy further . . . The sun, I think you will agree, not only makes the things we see visible, but causes the process of generation, growth and nourishment, without itself being such a process. . . . The Good therefore may be said to be the source not only of the intelligibility of the objects of knowledge, but also of their existence and reality; yet it is not itself identical with reality, but is beyond reality, and is superior to it in dignity and power."[11]

Toward the end of the discussion of the Good, Glaucon remarks that the process of escaping from shadows to enlightenment "sounds like a long job." Plato-Socrates agrees, adding:

And you may assume that there are, corresponding to the four sections of the line, four states of mind: to the top section [**A**] Intelligence, to the second [**B**] Reason, to the third [**C**] Opinion, and to the fourth [**D**] Illusion. And you may arrange them in a scale, and assume that they have degrees of clarity corresponding to the degree of truth and reality possessed by their subject-matter.[12]

Just as people born blind have different meanings for color words than those who have seen colors, those on one level of reality cannot recognize what is being said by those on a higher level. They have no comparable experience. Those who see the Good are forever transformed; they are en-light-ened—filled with light. And the relationship between the enlightened and the un-enlightened is at the heart of Plato's whole philosophy.

THE ALLEGORY OF THE CAVE

One problem common to any enlightenment philosophy involves the gap between what the wise master knows and the pupil's initial ignorance. Different levels of experience can create communication and comprehension gaps.

We see a similar kind of difficulty in interactions between adults and young children. Most of us—at least as we mature— have no difficulty with the concept of degrees of awareness and knowledge between adults and children. We even accept the fact that there are levels of knowledge and

With [the Good], it is not the same as with other things we learn: it cannot be framed in words, but from protracted concentration devoted to [it] and from spending one's life with it, a light suddenly bursts forth in the soul as though kindled by a flying spark, and then it feeds on itself.
Plato

The parable [of the Cave] is unforgettable. It is a miracle of philosophical invention, providing an approach to thoughts that do not lend themselves to direct statement.
Karl Jaspers

FIGURE 6.3   **The Allegory of the Cave illustrates Plato's vision
of the ascent of the mind from illusion (level D) to opinion (level
C) to reasoned knowledge (level B) to enlightenment (level A).
These levels of awareness correspond to the segments of the
Divided Line illustrated in Figure 6.1.**

experience dividing adults with some form of mental impairment and those
of average or better mental capacities.

But what about differences between average and so-called wise or enlightened people? Do such differences really exist? If they do, are they indi-
cators of different levels of "awareness" or are they just unprovable claims
made by people who think they know more than the rest of us? What reasons do we have for believing Plato's claims about levels of being and the
Good? Why should we discount the views and experiences of the vast majority of people and listen to the outlandish claims of one person?

Plato responded to this important challenge by telling a story with a
lesson, an allegory, in Book VII of *The Republic*. This allegory is offered not
as a conclusive proof, but as a suggestive possibility. It is the summation of
the exposition of Plato's theory of forms that includes the Divided Line and
the Simile of the Sun.

The Divided Line expresses Plato's hierarchical view of reality and wisdom. The Simile of the Sun characterizes the act of apprehending highest truth in the form of the Good. In the Allegory of the Cave, Plato compares the level of becoming to living in a cave, and describes the ordeal necessary for the soul's ascent from shadowy illusion to enlightenment.

The levels of awareness identified in the Allegory of the Cave correspond to the segments of the Divided Line referred to above and in Figure 6.1: those chained to the wall of shadows are imprisoned in the shadowy world of imagination and illusion (**D**); those loose within the cave occupy the "common sense" world of perception and informed opinion (**C**); those struggling through the passageway to the surface are acquiring knowledge through reason (**B**); the rich surface world of warmth and sunlight is the highest level of reality, directly grasped by pure intelligence (**A**).

The allegory illustrates the ascent of the mind from illusion to enlightenment, and alludes to the obligation of the enlightened wise person to return to the world of becoming in order to help others discern the forms.

Socrates presents the allegory as part of his continuing conversation with Glaucon:

> "I want you to go on to picture the enlightenment or ignorance of our human conditions somewhat as follows. Imagine an underground chamber, like a cave with an entrance open to the daylight and running a long way underground. In this chamber are men who have been prisoners there since they were children, their legs and necks being so fastened that they can only look straight ahead of them and cannot turn their heads. Behind them and above them a fire is burning, and between the fire and the prisoners runs a road, in front of which a curtain-wall has been built, like the screen at puppet shows between the operators and their audience, above which they show their puppets."
>
> "I see."
>
> "Imagine further that there are men carrying all sorts of gear along behind the curtain-wall, including figures of men and animals made of wood and stone and other materials, and that some of these men, as is natural, are talking and some not."
>
> "An odd picture and an odd sort of prisoner."
>
> "They are drawn from life," I replied. "For, tell me, do you think our prisoners could see anything of themselves or their fellows except the shadows thrown by the fire on the wall of the cave opposite them?"
>
> "How could they see anything else if they were prevented from moving their heads all their lives?" . . .
>
> "Then if they were able to talk to each other, would they not assume that the shadows they saw were real things?"
>
> "Inevitably."

Learning without thought brings ensnarement. Thought without learning totters.
Confucius

Every man takes the limits of his own field of vision for the limits of the world.
Arthur Schopenhauer

"And if the wall of their prison opposite them reflected sound, don't you think that they would suppose, whenever one of the passers-by on the road spoke, that the voice belonged to the shadow passing before them?"

"They would be bound to think so."

"And so they would believe that the shadows of the objects we mentioned were in all respects real."

"Yes, inevitably."

"Then think what would naturally happen to them if they were released from their bonds and cured of their delusions. Suppose one of them were let loose, and suddenly compelled to stand up and turn his head and look and walk towards the fire; all these actions would be painful and he would be too dazzled to see properly the objects of which he used to see the shadows. So if he was told that what he used to see was merely illusion and that he was now nearer reality and seeing more correctly, because he was turned towards objects that were more real, and if on top of that he were compelled to say what each of the passing objects was when it was pointed out to him, don't you think he would be at a loss, and think that what he used to see was more real than the objects now being pointed out to him?"

"Much more real."

. . . "And if, . . . he were forcibly dragged up the steep and rocky ascent and not let go till he had been dragged out into the sunlight, the process would be a painful one, to which he would much object, and when he emerged into the light his eyes would be so overwhelmed by the brightness of it that he wouldn't be able to see a single one of the things he was now told were real. . . . he would need to grow accustomed to the light before he could see things in the world outside the cave. . . . The thing he would be able to do last would be to look directly at the sun, and observe its nature without using reflections in water or any other medium, but just as it is."

"That must come last."

"Later on he would come to the conclusion that it is the sun that produces the changing seasons and years and controls everything in the visible world, and is in a sense responsible for everything that he and his fellow-prisoners used to see."

"That is the conclusion which he would obviously reach."[13]

Bodily exercise, when compulsory, does no harm to the body; but knowledge which is acquired under compulsion obtains no hold on the mind.

Plato

PHILOSOPHICAL QUERY

The Allegory of the Cave has intrigued students of Plato since it first appeared. Do you think it accurately expresses the way we experience knowledge? For instance, in childhood, everything is black and white, but with experience, we discover rich nuances and hues, as it were.

What level are you on? Society in general? The world? Explain. Do you believe in levels of reality? In enlightenment? Why or why not?

THE RULE OF THE WISE

Plato's fundamental vision is hierarchical and aristocratic, rather than egalitarian and democratic. His epistemology and metaphysics reflect and encourage this kind of highly discriminating orientation. Today, any nondemocratic position is likely to be called "elitist." If you believe in the fundamental equality of all people, you may be suspicious of Plato's belief in the superiority of those who have supposedly escaped the Cave and seen the Good. If you are skeptical about the possibility of any human being discovering "the truth," you will probably have difficulty with the idea that only these exceptional, enlightened individuals are fit to govern.

Such concerns are well-founded. We are all aware of the abuses committed by Nazis, racist supremacists, and all sorts of "true believers" who are convinced that they alone know the truth and are thus superior to the rest of us.

Plato's aristocracy of wisdom, however, is not based on gender, national origin, and the like, at least in theory. It is built on Plato's conviction that enlightenment is real and that it is more than intellectual ability isolated from moral character. With rare exceptions, Platonic enlightenment is the product of careful training, directed desire, hard work, and luck (being raised in an environment that does not prevent us from escaping the Cave).

At the end of the Allegory of the Cave, Plato echoes the teachings of the two other enlightenment philosophies covered in this text, Buddhism and Taoism. They insist that enlightenment is always accompanied by a desire to help others escape the bonds of illusion and ignorance. (See Chapter 2.)

As the Allegory of the Cave draws to a close, Plato-Socrates expresses the love-based obligation of the wise person to guide and teach those less wise, helping them escape the Cave:

> "And when he [who escaped the cave] thought of his first home and what passed for wisdom there, and of his fellow-prisoners, don't you think he would congratulate himself on his good fortune and be sorry for them?"
>
> "Very much so." . . .
>
> "And if he had to discriminate between the shadows, in competition with the other prisoners, while still blinded and before his eyes got used to the darkness—a process that might take some time—wouldn't he be likely to make a fool of himself?

Plato is philosophy, and philosophy Plato. . . . No wife, no children had he, and the thinkers of all civilized nations are his posterity and are tinged with his mind.
Ralph Waldo Emerson

Among the disciples of Socrates, Plato was the one who shone with a glory which far excluded that of the others and who not unjustly eclipsed them all.
St. Augustine

And they would say that his visit to the upper world had
ruined his sight, and that the ascent was not worth even attempting. And if anyone tried to release them and lead them
up, they would kill him if they could lay hands on him."

"They certainly would."

"Now, my dear Glaucon," I went on, "this [allegory] must
be connected, throughout, with what preceded it [the Divided
Line and Simile of the Sun]. The visible realm corresponds to
the prison, and the light of the fire in the prison to the power
of the sun. And you won't go wrong if you connect the ascent
into the upper world and the sight of the objects there with
the upward progress of the mind into the intelligible realm—
that's my guess, which is what you are anxious to hear. The
truth of the matter is, after all, known only to God. But in my
opinion, for what it is worth, the final thing to be perceived in
the intelligible realm, and perceived only with difficulty, is the
absolute form of the Good; once seen, it is inferred to be responsible for everything right and good . . . And anyone who
is going to act rationally either in public or private must perceive it."[14]

Although we cannot fully describe being, Plato wrote *The Republic* to show
that the levels of reality correspond to three types of people. The highest
type is the philosopher-king. This remarkable individual is fit to rule because he (or she) has glimpsed the Good. Thus, *The Republic* is Plato's answer to who should rule, based on his theory of reality.

THE REPUBLIC

At the beginning of *The Republic*, Socrates and his friend
Glaucon have spent the day at a festival and are on their
way home when another friend, Polemarchus, stops them. The dialogue begins with good-natured banter among friends.

"Socrates," said Polemarchus, "I believe you are starting off on
your way back to town."

"You are right," I [Socrates] replied.

"Do you see how many of us there are?" he asked.

"I do."

"Well, you will either have to get the better of us or stay
here."

"Oh, but there's another alternative," said I. "We might persuade you that you ought to let us go."

"You can't persuade people who won't listen," he replied.[15]

*Plato . . . knew that our
reason, if left to itself, tries
to soar up to knowledge to
which no object that experience may give can ever
correspond; but which is
nonetheless real, and by no
means a cobweb of the brain.*
Immanuel Kant

*The safest general character-
ization of the European philosophical tradition is that it
consists of a series of footnotes
to Plato.*
Alfred North Whitehead

You can't persuade people who won't listen. Plato is no doubt referring in part to the people who executed Socrates. But he may also be giving us a key to the rest of *The Republic*.

Socrates believed in the pursuit of wisdom through the dialectical method of question-and-answer. This required participants willing to listen actively and to respond intelligently. But what about people who cannot or will not listen? What about people who are satisfied with life in the Cave? What good is being reasonable in the face of ignorance? Will a mob listen to reason?

Plato thought not. He came to believe that there were different types of human beings, with different strengths and weaknesses corresponding to each type. Not everyone is capable of participating in rational dialogue. Some people lack the intellect. Some lack the will. Some may even lack both. Thus it is that a wise and wonderful individual who has escaped from the Cave, like Socrates, can be brought down by his moral and intellectual inferiors who are still in it. In Plato's view, Socrates made a mistake in going to "the people" at all. Socrates himself had even said that in matters of virtue and wisdom, the majority is usually wrong, while only a few are wise.

Concerning the essentials I have written no book nor shall I write one.
Plato, *Letter: VII*

The Search for Justice

Plato argued that a reciprocal relationship exists between the individual and the kind of society he or she lives in. That means a certain kind of society produces a certain kind of individual, and certain kinds of individuals produce certain kinds of societies. In fact, he thought the relationship between the two was so close that a clear understanding of the just (ideal) society would yield a clear understanding of the just (healthy) individual. In *The Republic* he refers to society as "the individual writ large." *The Republic* is, consequently, a study of Plato's ideal society and, by extension, a study of types of individuals.

The first book of *The Republic* begins with a discussion of justice. But justice in this context doesn't mean quite what it does today. Philosophy translator H. D. P. Lee says that the Greek roots of what is usually translated as *justice* cover a cluster of meanings that no single English word does. According to Lee, *justice* in *The Republic* is a broad term covering right conduct or morality in general; the verb from the same root can mean to act "rightly" or "justly."[16] For Plato, justice involved much more than fairness under the law; it went beyond a legalistic limit. Historian of ancient Greece B. A. G. Fuller says that what Plato is interested in is nothing less than "the whole sphere of moral action, both external and internal."[17]

Various limited and specific definitions of justice are offered during the course of *The Republic*. The first one is that justice is paying our debts and telling the truth. Over the course of the dialogue a variety of modifications and alternatives are discussed and rejected.

Philosophy's first promise is a sense of participation, of belonging to mankind, being a member of society.
Seneca

Function and Happiness

The Republic contrasts two views of morality. One asserts that right and wrong must be determined by the consequences our acts produce, and the other holds that they can be understood only in terms of their effect on our overall functioning as human beings. The first view is called an **instrumental theory of morality**. Right and wrong are treated as *means to, or instruments for, getting something else.* Be good, get X. Be bad, get Y. Plato characterizes the instrumental view:

> For fathers tell their sons, and pastors and masters of all kinds urge their charges to be just not because they value justice for itself, but for the social prestige it brings; they want them to secure by a show of justice the power and family connexions and other things which [were] enumerated, all of which are procured by the just man of good reputation.[18]

Plato, by contrast, argues for a **functionalist theory of morality** in which each kind of thing (including human beings) has a "natural purpose or function." Renowned Plato scholar A. E. Taylor says that in *The Republic*, "Happiness depends on conformity to our nature [function] as active beings."[19] In other words, only virtuous people can be happy. The Greeks viewed happiness as being more than a matter of personal satisfaction. *Happiness was the result of living a fully functioning life.* It involved balance and wholeness. It required being pleased by what is good and being displeased by what is bad. For instance, under such a view, no cigarette smoker can be "happy" regardless of the pleasure derived from smoking. The reason is that no fully functioning, maximally healthy human being will enjoy polluting his or her body. (For a fuller treatment of this view of happiness, see Chapters 7 and 8.)

The rest of *The Republic* reveals Plato's view of "our nature as active beings" and what human nature needs to function properly. A good life can be lived only in a good society. No one can live the best possible life controlled and crushed by a repressive, irrational society. Conversely, no one can live a truly good life without having some social activities, obligations, and concerns. Thus a life of extreme individualism is as imbalanced as a life of individual repression. Plato's goal was to identify the kind of society that nurtures the essential nature of each individual.

The Ideal State

Plato said that society originates because no individual is self-sufficient. The most basic function of society is to provide necessities like food, shelter, and clothing. The just or ideal state meets three basic categories of needs: (1) nourishing needs (food, shelter, clothing); (2) protection needs (military, police);

(3) ordering needs (leadership and government). These needs are best met by members of three corresponding classes of people: (1) workers (butcher, baker, truck driver); (2) warriors (soldiers, police officers, fire fighters); (3) guardians (philosopher-kings).

The just state functions fully. An unjust state is dysfunctional; it is not meeting some essential need. Only when all classes of people are virtuous *according to their natures* is the state whole, healthy, balanced, and just. *The good life is nothing more than each individual functioning well according to his or her own nature, in a state which is well-ordered and wisely ruled.*

Injustice is a form of imbalance for Plato. It occurs whenever a state does not function properly. Some imbalance always results when one part of the state tries to fulfill the function of another part. Thus, countries in which the military governs are unjust in the Platonic sense. Justice, happiness, and the good life are interrelated *functional results* of order. Because the essence of a thing determines its proper order, function, and care, only those who have seen the forms and seen the Good can know what this essence is for the state or for individuals.

Besides, this at any rate I know, that if there were to be a treatise or a lecture on the [ideal society], I could do it best.
Plato

The Parts of the Soul

For Plato, **virtue** is excellence of function (which reflects form). We must identify a thing's function before we can fully evaluate it. The human soul resembles the state in that it too is divided into three parts. The healthy, good, or virtuous soul is one in which all parts function harmoniously. The three parts of the soul are *reason, spirit,* and *appetite*.

Plato disagreed with Socrates' belief that "to know the good is to do the good." He believed in weakness of will. According to Plato, we most clearly encounter each part of our souls when we're faced with a difficult choice. Suppose you are on a date with someone who wants to go dancing and stay out late. You, on the other hand, have an important test early the next morning. Your *reason* says: "Go home, review your notes, rest. You can go dancing another time, but you cannot make up this important test." Your *appetite* says: "I'd love a pizza. I'd love to party." Your *spirit*, which is concerned with honor, says: "This is awful! I hate it! I don't know what to do. I sort of want to study—but I'd really like to go out. Oh my, oh my!"

Most of us are intimately familiar with what can be characterized as "parts" of ourselves. Plato called them parts of the soul. In the *Phaedrus* Plato compares the soul to a chariot being pulled by two horses. One horse needs no touch from the whip, responding instantly to whispers and spoken commands. The other horse is full of "insolence and pride," and "barely yields to whip and spur." The charioteer knows where he wants to go but needs the help of both horses to get there. The driver, of course, corresponds to *reason*; the horse that responds to the merest whisper corresponds to *spirit* (or will); and the bad but powerful horse represents *appetite*.

VIRTUE (PLATONIC)
Excellence of function.

The greatest griefs are those we cause ourselves.
Sophocles

Perhaps the strongest evidence supporting Plato's belief in the three-part psyche comes in the form of everyday struggles between reason and appetite or desire—a struggle faced by many a student caught up in the throes of a strong desire to daydream.

If the charioteer is unable to control both horses, he will be dragged all over the place by the stronger horse. It is the *function* and therefore the *duty* and the *right* of the charioteer to control the horses. In *The Republic*, Plato says:

> So the reason ought to rule, having the ability and foresight to act for the whole, and the spirit ought to obey and support it. And this concord between them is effected, as we said, by a combination of intellectual and physical training, which tunes up the reason by intellectual training and tones down the crudeness of natural high spirits by harmony and rhythm.[20]

The Cardinal Virtues

Plato identifies four "cardinal virtues" as necessary for a good society and for a happy individual. Cardinal virtues are essential, basic virtues that provide optimal functioning for the human soul.

Temperance is another name for self-control and moderation. It is important for the worker classes, but necessary for all three classes of people. The state, too, must control itself, not yielding either to the unjust demands of other states or to a lust for expansion or power. It must not give in to an excess of liberty or repression. The healthy state resembles the healthy person. Both are moderate and self-disciplined, and guided by reason. The healthy soul is not controlled by appetites.

Courage is the essential virtue of the warrior class. Courage is necessary to protect the community and to enforce the just laws of the guardians. In the individual, courage is a quality of will, an essential drive which provides a person with stamina and energy.

Wisdom is the virtue associated with the guardians who are called the philosopher-kings. In the individual, wisdom is present when the rational part of the soul is healthy and in control. Wisdom is found only in a community ruled by those fit by nature and training to guide it: the philosopher-kings who have seen the Good.

Justice is the result of the other three cardinal virtues, in much the same way that bodily health is the result of the proper functioning of all organs and systems. **Justice** is excellence of function for the whole: Each essential element works well, and together all elements blend into a balanced system in the just state and in the just individual.

For Plato, justice extends far beyond a legal system. The just state is well, whole, vital. It nurtures each individual by providing a lifestyle appropriate to him or her.

PHILOSOPHICAL QUERY

Consider the family as a functional system: If young children are allowed to spend the money, determine bedtimes, and so on, the whole family suffers. If the parents try to live like children, the whole family suffers. If every family member is free to pick and choose what he or she feels like doing or not doing every day, there can be no family. You might try similar analyses of marriages, churches, schools, or factories. Discuss the need for hierarchy, authority, and a governing order.

SOCIETIES AND INDIVIDUALS

Plato's *Republic*, and a later dialogue called *Laws*, outline **utopias**, that is, perfect, ideal societies. (Although Plato originated the idea, the word *utopia* was coined by Thomas More in 1516.)

Can we create a good society that will encourage and foster inner harmony for ourselves and social harmony for the whole community? As Jesus said, "The spirit . . . is willing but the flesh is weak." Plato might add "and reason is absent." A Platonic utopia would be enormously difficult, perhaps impossible, to achieve. But a consideration of Plato's program for a utopia will prove to be worthwhile on many counts.

For Plato, the ideal form of government is the rule of philosopher-kings, not democracy. Because our current culture is democratic and individualistic in so many respects, many of us view democracy as the ideal form of

---

Then the master passion runs wild and takes madness into its service; any decent options or desires and any feelings of shame still left are killed or thrown out, until all discipline is swept away, and madness usurps its place.
Plato

JUSTICE (PLATONIC)
Excellence of function for the whole; in a just society each individual performs his or her natural function according to class; in a just individual, reason rules the spirit and the appetites.

UTOPIA
Term for a perfect or ideal society derived from Sir Thomas More's 1516 novel of the same name; the word was created from the Greek root meaning "nowhere."

government without giving any other possibilities serious consideration. For that reason alone, consideration of an elitist alternative can be illuminating. It may help us to better identify the virtues of our own society— and we may get a clearer look at its shortcomings. Let's complete this survey of Plato by looking at his vision of a better, "ideal" way of life.

The Origin of Democracy

In Book VIII of *The Republic* Plato discusses different kinds of governments and the types of souls they produce. He argues that democracy grows out of a form of government called *oligarchy*, the rule of a wealthy few. Because the chief aim of the oligarchs is to get rich, they create a constitution and form of government that encourage the acquisition of property.

Oligarchy: A government resting on a valuation of property, in which the rich have power and the poor man is deprived of it.
Plato

But just having property isn't enough. Plato asks, "Doesn't oligarchy change into democracy because of lack of restraint in the pursuit of its objective of getting as rich as possible?"[21] The seeds of democracy, according to Plato, are the love of property and riches, and the corresponding need for a free economy. So the oligarchs must encourage trading in real estate, heavy borrowing, and lack of self-control. The "money people" need to stimulate irrational but constant consumption by everyone else. Plato declares, "It should then be clear that love of money and adequate self-discipline in its citizens are two things that can't co-exist in any society; one or the other must be neglected."[22]

PHILOSOPHICAL QUERY

Can you spot any symptoms in our society of the pattern Plato attributes to injustice in individuals and the state? Can you identify individuals or groups that "fall into sickness and dissension at the slightest provocation"? What—if anything—does justice (or a lack of justice) have to do with these reactions? Explain.

In Plato's diagnosis, as the rich get richer, the poor grow angrier until they somehow overthrow the rich, either through armed revolt or by social and legal pressure. Resentful over their status, the poor initiate a program of equality.

Poverty in a democracy is as much preferable to so-called prosperity in an autocracy as freedom is to slavery.
Democritus

Then democracy originates when the poor win, kill or exile their opponents, and give the rest equal rights and opportunity of office. . . . There is liberty and freedom of speech in plenty, and every individual is free to do as he likes. . . . That being so, won't everyone arrange his life as pleases him best? . . . a democracy is the most attractive of all societies. The diversity of its characters, like the different colours in a patterned dress, make it look very attractive . . . perhaps most people would, for this reason, judge it to be the best form of society . . . [if they] judge by appearances.[23]

A democratic state, Plato says, will contain every type of human temperament. But the predominant characteristic of democracy is lack of guidance and self-control, lack of wisdom, and lack of temperance. Swayed by opinion rather than grounded in knowledge, the democratic state is in a state of constant flux, always *becoming*. It is hostile to the possibility of a fixed hierarchy of being.

> In a democracy . . . there's no compulsion either to exercise authority if you are capable of it, or to submit to authority if you don't want to; you needn't fight if there's a war, or you can wage a private war in peacetime if you don't like peace. . . . It's a wonderfully pleasant way of carrying on in the short run, isn't it?[24]

Not only is it pleasant, Plato points out that even those convicted of a crime in a democracy can continue "to go about among their fellows." H. D. P. Lee paraphrases Plato's description of the democratic type as "versatile but lacking principle."[25]

Most damning of all, Plato says, democracy violates the principle of functional order and rule by reason. He asserts that only very rare and exceptional individuals can grow up to be good people without good training from infancy, in a good environment. But democracy lacks the order and balance to provide this.

Plato says that at its most extreme, the disordered, democratic soul resists all limits, both internal and social:

> All pleasures are equal and should have equal rights. [Such a character] lives for the pleasure of the moment. One day it's wine, women, and song, the next bread and water; one day it's hard physical training, the next indolence and ease, and then a period of philosophic study. . . . There's no order or restraint in [this] life and [such a person] reckons [this] way of living is pleasant, free, and happy. . . . It's a life which many men and women would envy, it has so many possibilities.[26]

Thus the only sort of liberty that is real under democracy is the liberty of the have-nots to destroy the liberty of the haves . . .

H. L. Mencken

The Pendulum of Imbalance

Ancient philosophers were aware that one extreme often produces another, nearly opposite, extreme in a never-ending effort to achieve balance. In Plato's view, the chief objective of democracy is "excessive liberty." For Plato, the built-in excesses of democracy already contain the seeds of tyranny. **Tyranny** is a form of government in which all power rests in a single individual, the tyrant.

In one of the more interesting and perhaps prophetic passages in *The Republic*, Plato describes the effects "too much liberty" will produce. As you read what he said so long ago, take note of parallels to our own culture.

TYRANNY
Form of government in which all power rests in a single individual, known as the tyrant.

It becomes the thing for the father and son to change places, the father standing in awe of his son, and the son neither respecting nor fearing his parents, in order to assert his independence; and there's no distinction between citizen and alien and foreigner. And there are other more trivial things. The teacher fears and panders to his pupils, who in turn despise their teachers and attendants; and the young as a whole imitate their elders, argue with them and set themselves up against them, while their elders try to avoid the reputation of being disagreeable or strict by aping the young and mixing with them on terms of easy good fellowship. . . .

You would never believe—unless you had seen it for yourself—how much more liberty the domestic animals have in a democracy. Love me love my dog, as the proverb has it, and the same is true of horses and donkeys as well . . . Everything is full of this spirit of liberty. . . .

What it comes to is this, . . . that the minds of the citizens become so sensitive that the least vestige of restraint is resented as intolerable, till finally, as you know, in their determination to have no master they disregard all laws, written or unwritten.[27]

Each individual is his own center, and the world centers in him.
Søren Kierkegaard

One form of shamelessness is an exaggerated sense of honor. In this condition, the individual is always "ready to take offense." Every restriction or social limit is taken personally: "The least vestige of restraint is regarded as intolerable."

Plato makes the case that "from an extreme of liberty one is likely to get, in the individual and in society, a reaction to an extreme of subjection." That is, an extreme of liberty will create a corresponding demand for law and order; it will result in an extreme of control.

Democracy . . . is a system where anything, or almost anything, can happen. The worst, but also the best. In it one may encounter all types: the sophist and also the philosopher. That is the unique advantage of this way of life.
Andre Koyré

Certainly in the last few years we've seen some reaction against the permissiveness of the '60s and '70s, the "winner take all" excesses of the '80s, and the politically correct early '90s. As society becomes troubled by increased abuses of personal liberty in the form of high rates of venereal diseases, drug casualties, white-collar crime, and so forth, we witness demands for more restrictive sexual standards, more pressure to abstain from drugs and alcohol, more disciplined diets, more people convicted of fraud, embezzlement, and so on. As "shock jocks" push the bounds of free speech on the radio, and artists and musicians test the limits of their various media, we witness efforts to censor or ban what's on the radio, what's on television, records, and tapes, and even what's in art museums.

In our daily lives we see people become more undisciplined and abusive of their liberties, infringing upon one another's happiness. If we all talk in the movie theater, none of us can hear. If I insist on putting a megawatt stereo in my car and booming through your neighborhood, you will insist on laws to stop me. If bankers and real estate brokers continue to make exorbitant profits while growing numbers of families cannot buy homes, the state will be forced to exert stricter controls on everybody. If great hordes of us continue to exercise our liberty by commuting to work in our own vehicles, traffic will come to a stop and the sky will turn brown from the smog of excessive liberty.

PHILOSOPHICAL QUERY

What do you see as the good and bad points of "democratic families" in which the parents and children have essentially the same rights? What about school relationships in which teachers are "buddies" with students and the classroom is run democratically?

Are we making everything equal, including animals and the environment? Can you find support for Plato's observation about animal rights in a democracy?

Do you think absolute equality of opportunity is desirable or possible? Discuss fully.

The Tyranny of Excess

The ills of democracy were aggravated for Plato by a pattern of increasing self-indulgence, which he thought would pass from generation to generation. Sooner or later, pleasures and excesses would actually control the soul—they would tyrannize it.

> Isn't this the reason . . . why the passion of sex has for so long been called a tyrant? . . . And isn't there also a touch of the tyrant about a man who's drunk? . . . And the madman whose mind is unhinged imagines he can control gods and men and is quite ready to try. . . . Then a precise definition of a tyrannical man is one who, either by birth or habit or both, combines the characteristics of drunkenness, lust, and madness. . . . And how does he live? . . . When a master passion has absolute control of a man's mind, I suppose life is a round of holidays and dinners and parties and girl-friends and so on. . . . And there will be a formidable extra crop of desires growing all the time and needing satisfaction. . . . So whatever income he has will soon be expended, and he'll start borrowing and drawing on capital.
>
> . . . When these sources fail, his large brood of desires will howl aloud. . . . He *must* get something from somewhere or his life will be torment and agony.[28]

PHILOSOPHICAL QUERY

Compare Plato's description of the tyrannical soul to the life of a hard-core drug addict. The "fix" certainly *tyrannizes* the addict's

No educated man stating plainly the elementary notions that every educated man holds about the matters that principally concern government, could be elected to office in a democratic state, save perhaps by a miracle. His frankness would arouse fears, and those fears would run against him; it is his business to arouse fears that will run in favour of him.

H. L. Mencken

Plato thought that excessive liberty always leads to its own destruction because demands for increasing individual freedom result in counter-demands for more restrictions and control.

soul. Identify and discuss other common examples of this tyrannical pattern.

What begins as unlimited freedom ends up as the tyranny over reason by the lower parts of the soul. The spoiled and undisciplined person grows used to playing now and paying later. When he cannot pay his own way, he turns to his parents to gratify his desires. He sees their estate as "his due," and "if they don't give in to him," Plato says, "he'll try first to get his way by fraud and deceit." But "if his old mother and father put up a resistance and show fight . . . [he will not] feel any hesitation about playing the tyrant with them."

Ultimately, enough such people (even if they are not the majority) corrupt the whole state as "they become thieves, burglars, pick-pockets . . . they turn informers and false witnesses and take bribes." Fed up with this turn of events, the majority demands more law and order. As more and more individuals get in one another's way, each demands protection from the others.

To speak much is one thing, to speak well is another.
Sophocles

For Plato, the most imbalanced type of personality is the tyrant. Plato believed that happiness and goodness were inseparable, as were unhappiness and wickedness. Thus the most wicked person is the most unhappy, because he is the most imbalanced. A tyrant is always a slave to his own strong passions and desires. The tyrant who is controlled by drugs or lust is obviously a slave. But so is the politically powerful leader who is a slave to power and domination. Once again, things are not as they initially appear. What looks like power is in truth a form of enslavement. The Hitlers and Stalins and small-town bosses of the world live restricted, imbalanced lives. A "control freak" is not a happy person.

The only cure for excesses of either liberty or tyranny is justice. If the state is not just, then at least perhaps a fortunate "happy few" individuals can impose order on their own souls through the rule of reason aided by moderate appetites and a healthy spirit.

The state, if once started well, moves with accumulating force like a wheel. For good nurture and education implant good constitutions [temperaments], and the good constitutions taking root in a good education improve more and more, and this improvement affects the breed in man as in other animals.
Plato

COMMENTARY

The most damning charge that can be leveled at all enlightenment philosophies is that no matter how initially intriguing or appealing they seem, they remain impractical and unrealistic in the world as most of us experience and understand it.

In Plato's case, we might ask ourselves whether we have any supportable firsthand evidence for believing in actual levels of reality. Does a story like the Allegory of the Cave really help us determine who is enlightened and who is deluded? Do the Divided Line and Simile of the Sun do anything besides reflect common psychological states?

On the other hand, who can doubt the need for order and balance in both the individual and society? Further, it would not be difficult to make Plato's case against the "excesses of democracy" using trends and events from our own time. We might even find some merit in his idea that letting each individual choose his or her occupation based solely on strength of desire and ambition leads to great overall unhappiness.

When we rank occupations by income and prestige, most of the tasks needed for a good society are less desirable than a few glamorous, less useful ones. Which, then, does more lasting harm: letting everyone who wishes scramble for the top of the heap, or carefully matching people's basic abilities and personalities with various levels of education and occupation? We might find Plato's three categories of people, guardians, warriors, and workers, too restricting, but does that rule out a more realistic division?

Lastly, Plato's general portrait of the soul (psyche) might be worth looking into. There is much to be said for living a well-rounded life. That includes, of course, being individually balanced. But a society that values narrow specialists and puts as much emphasis on material success as ours does makes personal growth more difficult than a society that encourages fuller personal development.

The decrees of the people are in large measure repealed by the sages.
Seneca

Plato is dear to me, but dearer still is truth.
Aristotle

Interestingly, even though Plato's great pupil Aristotle turns away from his theory of forms, he follows the direction in which his great teacher pointed and makes perhaps the finest case for the fully functioning, whole, balanced human being. He is the subject of the next chapter.

SUMMARY OF MAIN POINTS

Plato was a member of the Athenian aristocracy and Socrates' most famous and important pupil. Socrates' trial and death convinced him that Athenian democracy was irrational mob rule. His experiences with the Thirty convinced him that rule by a greedy, cruel social elite was no better than mob rule.

Plato founded his famous Academy to educate wise rulers. His progressive educational program included mathematics, geometry, music, and philosophy.

In Plato's metaphysics, the highest level of reality consists of timeless "essences" or entities called ideas or forms. Such a metaphysics is sometimes called transcendental because it asserts that there is a plane of existence "above and beyond" our ordinary existence.

Plato divided reality into three levels. The highest level of reality is being. Being is eternal and changeless. The other two levels together make up the level of becoming, the level of change, which includes growth and decay, life and death. For Plato, knowledge is always of things in their unchanging, eternal form, of their essence. Opinion, by contrast, is like perception: limited by our individual senses, backgrounds, and cultural experiences. Disagreement is only possible on the lower level of becoming.

According to Plato, the very essence of knowledge is unchanging. Therefore, whatever is relative and always changing cannot be true. The Sophists could not discover truth because they were only concerned with the Heraclitean world of sensibles, the world of ever-changing perceptions and customs. Truth and knowledge are found in another realm of reality: the level of being that Parmenides tried to characterize. Plato's theory of forms was part of his refutation of sophistry.

Plato used the concept of the Divided Line to illustrate the relationship of knowledge to opinion, reality to appearance, and the worlds of being and becoming. The Divided Line consists of two basic sections, each unevenly divided into two segments. The four segments illustrate four states of mind or ways of apprehending four components of reality: (1) pure intelligence or understanding, (2) reasoning, (3) informed belief or ordinary opinions, and (4) illusion and imagination, dominated by secondhand opinions and uncritical impressions.

Plato compared the "absolute form of the Good" to the sun: Just as the sun (light) is necessary for vision and life, the Good makes the existence of everything else possible. The Good exists beyond becoming at the highest reaches of being. The Good cannot be observed with the five senses and can be known only by pure thought or intelligence. The Good is the source of both the value and the existence of all other forms.

In the Allegory of the Cave, Plato characterizes three levels of awareness by referring to three distinct levels of reality: two levels of becoming, the literal and the informed, and one qualitatively unique and ultimate level of being—the enlightened level. The lowest level of reality is the literal level, which is inhabited by people with little or no imagination. The informed level of reality involves a wider range of basic understanding. People on this level distinguish appearance from reality. The enlightened level is the level of truth and reality. On this level the soul has no need for perception or interpretation. Plato says that it "directly apprehends" the form of the Good.

In *The Republic*, Plato describes the just or ideal state. Plato argued that there is a reciprocal relationship between the individual and the kind of society he or she lives in.

The Republic contrasts two views of morality. The instrumental theory of morality asserts that right and wrong must be determined by the consequences our acts produce, and the functionalist theory of morality holds that right and wrong can only be understood in terms of the way they affect our overall functioning as human beings. Plato is a functionalist, and *The Republic* is Plato's attempt to identify the kind of society that nurtures the essential nature of various types of individuals.

The just state functions fully. An unjust state is dysfunctional; it does not meet some essential need. Only when all classes of people are virtuous according to their natures is the state whole, healthy, balanced, and just. The good life consists of each individual functioning well according to his or her own nature, in a state that is ordered and wisely ruled.

The just or ideal state meets three basic categories of needs: (1) nourishing needs; (2) protection needs; (3) ordering needs. These needs are best met by members of three corresponding classes of people: (1) artisans; (2) warriors; (3) guardians or philosopher-kings.

The human soul resembles the state in that it too is divided into three parts: reason, spirit, and appetite. The just (healthy, good, or virtuous) soul is one in which all parts function harmoniously. The just society is one ruled by guardians in a way that each class functions at its best.

Plato identifies four cardinal (essential, basic) virtues necessary for a good society and for happy individuals. He defined virtue as "excellence of function." The virtue of temperance is important for the worker classes but necessary for all three classes of people and the state itself. Courage is the essential virtue of the warrior class; in the individual, courage is a quality of will, an essential drive that provides a person with stamina and energy. Wisdom is the virtue associated with the guardians and the rational part of the soul. Justice, the result of the other three cardinal virtues, is excellence of function for the whole: Each essential element works well, and together all elements blend into a balanced system in the just state and in the just individual.

Plato rejected democracy as unjust because rule by the majority usurps the rightful role of the guardian class. The result is an excess of liberty and rule by impulse, appetite, and emotion in which all classes suffer. Democracy violates the principle of functional order and rule by reason.

Plato thought that the excessive liberty found in democracies contains the seeds of an opposite impulse known as tyranny, a form of government in which all power rests in a single individual, the tyrant. Extreme liberty creates a corresponding demand for extreme control. For Plato, the most imbalanced type of personality is the tyrant.

STUDY QUESTIONS

1. Discuss some of the personal experiences that shaped Plato's overall idealism.

2. What is meant by Plato's "disillusionment"?

3. What was the Academy? Where did it get its name? What was its chief purpose?

4. How did Plato distinguish between knowledge and opinion?

5. What is meant by calling Plato's philosophy transcendental?

6. What are forms?

7. How do forms differ from ideas?

8. Illustrate the Divided Line and relate each segment to Plato's epistemology as it is characterized in the Allegory of the Cave.

9. How did Plato use the sun to help explain the Good?

10. Identify and explain the three basic levels of reality.

11. Distinguish the realm of being from the realm of becoming.

12. Identify and characterize the levels of reality.

13. Tell the Allegory of the Cave in your own words. Then carefully explain its purpose.

14. What is the Good?

15. What is the "key" Plato reveals at the opening of *The Republic*? What is its significance to his basic attitude toward democracy?

16. How is Plato's use of the word *justice* different from ours?

17. Explain in what sense Plato's theory of justice is "functionalist." What kind of moral theory is contrasted with functionalism?

18. How is the Greek concept of happiness different from our contemporary concept? Compare and evaluate them.

19. Describe the general structure of the ideal state as Plato presents it in *The Republic*.

20. List and discuss the cardinal virtues.

21. What is special about justice as a virtue?

22. Carefully explain the relationship of the individual to the state in *The Republic*.

23. What are the three parts of the soul and how are they related?

24. Briefly explain the origin and nature of democracy according to Plato.

25. What is the democratic soul like, according to Plato? Do you agree? Justify your answer.

26. What is the relationship between democracy and tyranny as Plato saw it? Identify some current evidence that supports his view. On balance, do you agree with him or not? Explain.

27. What does Plato see as the most unjust type of person and state? Why? Do you agree? Explain.

28. Write a general assessment of contemporary American culture from a Platonic perspective.

29. In your opinion, what is Plato's greatest philosophical weakness? Explain.

30. In your opinion, what is Plato's greatest philosophical insight? Explain.

The Naturalist:

Aristotle

There is perhaps nothing
worse than reaching the
top of the ladder and
discovering that you're
on the wrong wall.

JOSEPH
CAMPBELL

ne of the most frustrating aspects of college can be choosing a major. Sometimes students are encouraged to decide without having had much exposure to a variety of disciplines, and some of us may just not really know who we are yet. (This condition is not confined to students or persons of any particular age!) As a result, we may change our minds as sophomores or juniors or seniors, when we realize that our initial choice was wrong for the real us. Outside the campus environment, more and more people seem to be making significant career changes at mid-life or later.[1]

What prompts a forty-five-year-old person to leave a secure job, giving up seniority and retirement benefits and medical insurance, to open a cookie shop? What makes a social worker quit work and go to law school? What drives a middle-aged man or woman to leave his or her family, lose weight, buy a sports car, and become a poet? What makes a pre-med major just nine units short of graduation drop out of school and join the Peace Corps? There are many reasons; some of them may be unwise, but perhaps some of them are good reasons.

Did you ever feel that you weren't really being yourself? What does that mean? Aren't you always yourself, even if that self is confused or inconsistent or phony? Maybe that's just who you are? On the other hand, maybe the "real you" is being denied or starved. Perhaps people who walk away from their jobs or families have been false to their "true selves" for years. Does that seem possible?

Aristotle would have thought so, even though he would not have suggested that we "find ourselves" by returning to adolescence or a self-indulgent escape from responsibility. But he did believe in a natural development of the soul/self based on an inner identity or goal. He believed that the good life involves balance and fullness. And though each of us may have individually different "selves" to develop, in his view all human beings share a common nature that makes it possible to identify the general outline of the best possible life.

The good life, according to Aristotle, is broad and rich, involving full emotional, intellectual, spiritual, and physical development and health. Thus it is entirely possible to wake up one day and realize that we have grown too much in some areas and too little in others. Such a realization may explain radical changes in our lives. We may be seeking balance and completion.

But unlike many modern theorists of self-realization and balance, Aristotle did not think that each individual is free to be whoever he or she chooses to be. Instead, he advocated self-emergence according to a natural order. He attempted to base his moral and social philosophy on a practical and empirical study of human behavior. His *Nicomachean Ethics* is among the most influential books ever written on self-realization and related moral and social factors. Rather than concentrate on an "ideal world" as Plato did, Aristotle turned to a study of the natural world and our place in it.

WORKS

Aristotle is said to have written twenty-seven dialogues on a level comparable to Plato's, and it is through these dialogues that he was best known in the ancient world.[2] Unfortunately, they were all destroyed when the barbarians sacked Rome in the year 400. What we know today as the "writings of Aristotle" are really a collection of notes. These apparently include notes Aristotle made for his lectures and possibly notes taken by students who attended his lectures. Of 360 works mentioned by Diogenes Läertius, 40 survive today.

Aristotle's works include *Organon*, a collection of six logical treatises; *Physics; On Generation and Corruption; De Anima (On the Soul); On the Heavens; The History of Animals; On the Parts of Animals; Metaphysics; Politics; Rhetoric; Poetics;* and the *Nicomachean Ethics*.

What remains of Aristotle's work is complex, stiffly written, and often dry. But in spite of that, these notes reflect a genius whose range of interests, wonder, insight, and effort stands as a most remarkable testament to the human mind and spirit.

ARISTOTLE'S LIFE

The son of a court physician, **Aristotle (384–322 B.C.)** was born in Stagira, a Greek community in Thrace. What little we know of him comes primarily through Diogenes Läertius's compilation of the lives of ancient philosophers.

Aristotle probably learned basic anatomy and dissection from his father before he was sent to study at Plato's Academy in Athens at the age of eighteen. When he arrived, practically everyone noticed him, in part because he was something of a dandy. Plato is reported to have said that Aristotle paid more attention to his clothes than was proper for a philosopher. In order to be fashionable, he cultivated a deliberate lisp, the speech pattern that the Greek elite used to separate themselves from the masses. (In a similar way, some people today think of an English accent as being "higher class" than a Southern drawl or Brooklyn accent.)

Despite his affectations, Aristotle almost immediately earned a reputation as one of the Academy's finest students. Diogenes Läertius says that on one occasion when Plato read aloud a difficult treatise about the soul, Aristotle "was the only person who sat it out, while all the rest rose up and went away."[3] Aristotle remained with Plato for perhaps twenty years, and Plato is supposed to have humorously remarked that his Academy consisted of two parts: the body of his students, and the brain of Aristotle. Although Aristotle disagreed with Plato on important philosophical matters, he built an altar to Plato at his teacher's death.

Aristotle, thirty-seven years old when Plato died, expected to be the next master of the Academy. But when the trustees of the Academy picked

Aristotle

All men by nature desire knowledge.
Aristotle

The development of philo-
sophic science as science, and,
further, the progress from the
Socratic point of view to the
scientific, begins with Plato
and ends with Aristotle. They
of all others deserve to be
called teachers of the human
race.

G. W. F. Hegel

a native Athenian instead, because they saw Aristotle as a "foreigner," he waited for the first good opportunity to leave Athens. As it turned out, a former classmate who had become a kind of philosopher-king over a rather large area in Asia Minor invited Aristotle to be his adviser.

Apparently Aristotle had little effect on his friend's rulership, but he did manage to marry the man's adopted daughter in 344 B.C. She had a large dowry, which Aristotle happily invested. Aristotle's life was disrupted the same year, however, when his political benefactor offended the king of Persia. Shortly after Aristotle and his wife fled to the island of Lesbos, Aristotle's friend was crucified by the Persian king. While on Lesbos, Aristotle studied natural history, and his wife died giving birth to their daughter. Aristotle later lived with a woman named Herpyllis. Their long, happy relationship produced Aristotle's son Nicomachus, to whom he dedicated the *Nicomachean Ethics*.

In 343 B.C. King Philip of Macedon invited Aristotle to train his thirteen-year-old son Alexander. The boy was wild and crude, but Aristotle was able to smooth his rough edges and instill in him respect for knowledge and science. As Alexander the Great, Aristotle's famous pupil ordered his soldiers to collect specimens of plant, marine, and animal life from faraway places for his old teacher.

In 340 B.C. Philip sent Aristotle back to his hometown, so that Aristotle could write a code of laws to help restore the community, which had been disrupted by a war. Aristotle did well enough that Stagira celebrated a yearly holiday in his honor. In 334 Aristotle at last returned to Athens, where he founded his own school, possibly with money from Alexander.

THE LYCEUM

Aristotle named his school after the god Apollo Lyceus. The Lyceum was built near some of the most elegant buildings in Athens, surrounded by shady groves of trees and covered walkways. Socrates used to visit the same groves, remarking on what a wonderful spot they made for reflection.

Aristotle's students were known as the *peripatetic* philosophers because he often discussed philosophy while strolling with them along tree-covered walkways called the Peripatos. In addition, Aristotle's curriculum included technical lectures for limited audiences and popular lectures of more general interest. Aristotle collected hundreds of maps, charts, and documents, forming the first important library in the West. For instance, he collected and studied 153 political constitutions.

Leadership of the Lyceum rotated among certain members of the school according to rules drawn up by Aristotle. Once a month he held a common meal and symposium at which one of the members was picked to defend a philosophical idea against criticism from everyone else. Aristotle continued to lecture and research for his entire tenure at the Lyceum.[4]

The actuality of thought
is life.

Aristotle

**This medieval print reflects Aristotle's status as "the Philosopher"
to the scholars and scientists of the Middle Ages. Notice how the
four scholars stand behind and follow Aristotle's lead.**

The Lyceum's students tended to be from the middle class, whereas the Academy's were more aristocratic. For a short while the two schools were bitter rivals, but as each concentrated on its own particular interests this rivalry died down. The Academy stressed mathematics and "pure" understanding, while Aristotle's students collected anthropological studies of barbarian cultures, chronologies of various wars and games, the organs and living habits of animals, the nature and locations of plants, and so on.[5]

Alexander the Great died in 323 B.C. Athens had smarted under a Greek unification program begun by his father Philip and continued under Alexander. With Alexander dead, Athens openly expressed its hostility and resentment toward all things Macedonian. Because of his long and favored place under the protection of both Philip and Alexander, Aristotle found himself in an uncomfortable position. He left Athens and the Lyceum the next year after being legally charged with not respecting the gods of the state—one of the same charges leveled at Socrates. Rather than stand trial like the crusty old *sophos*, Aristotle fled to the island of Euboea (his mother's birthplace), in his words, "lest Athens sin twice against philosophy."

In 322 B.C. the man who had created the first important library, tutored the greatest ruler of the ancient world, invented logic, and shaped the thinking of an entire culture died. So great was his influence on later thinkers that for hundreds of years all educated persons knew him simply as *the Philosopher*.

When Alexander the Great met the Cynic Diogenes, he is reported to have said: "If I were not Alexander, I would be Diogenes."

THE NATURALIST

Aristotelian philosophy is so complex in treatment and scope that no introductory survey can do justice to all of it. A good place to begin, however, is with a look at his ethics and psychology, for in addition to presenting a powerful and challenging doctrine of happiness as self-realization and personal growth, they rest on Aristotle's naturalistic metaphysics.

In Plato we saw one significant expression of the search for the good life: evaluating this life by comparing it to some ideal standard and then trying to perfect this world. In a sense, Aristotle brings to full maturity a second major expression of the search for the good life: attempting to acquire facts without bias and then using that information to make this a better world.

Although Aristotle loved and respected Plato, he saw dangers in Plato's failure to begin with a clear assessment of actual facts. Partly as a reaction to Plato, and partly as a consequence of his own temperament, Aristotle brought philosophy down to earth. He combined the study of humanity and nature to a degree which was not possible again, because after Aristotle no single individual could seriously hope to contribute to so many distinct fields in a major way.

Aristotle stands alone as an archetype of the philosophical naturalist. Basically, **naturalism** is the belief that reality consists of the natural world. The naturalist's universe is ordered in that everything in it follows consistent and discoverable *laws* of nature; everything can be understood in terms of those fundamental laws. Nothing escapes cause and effect. Nature always acts with a purpose, and the key to understanding anything lies in determining its essential purpose.

Philosophical naturalists deny the existence of a separate supernatural order of reality. They believe that *human beings, although special, are part of the natural order and behave according to fixed laws and principles.* Thus a clear understanding of nature is necessary to any clear conception of human behavior. Ethics and political (social) science must be based on the actual facts of life, carefully observed and collected by a scientific method—not on speculative, rationalistic schemes.

NATURALISM
Belief that reality consists of the natural world; denial of the existence of a separate supernatural order of reality; belief that nature follows orderly, discoverable laws.

Aristotle based his philosophical positions on close scrutiny of particular, actual things, not on the isolated contemplation of mathematical laws or "pure ideas." Let's see what Aristotle discovered in the teeming natural world.

ENTELECHY

Aristotle identified what he called an "inner urge" in each living thing to become its unique self. The acorn has an inner urge to become an oak tree, the baby has an inner urge to become an adult, and so forth. Aristotle characterized this inner urge to become what a thing is "meant to be" as "having its end within itself." The Greek word for this is **entelechy**.

Aristotle thought that entelechy explained nature. Certainly the concept frames his entire practical philosophy. *Entelechy means that things do not just happen—they develop according to natural design.* That is, nature is ordered and guided "internally." Sometimes Aristotle refers to entelechy as a "creative drive." "Such principles," he says, "do not all make for the same goal, but each inner principle always makes for the same goal *of its own [kind]*, if nothing interferes" [emphasis added].[6]

Plato erred by separating the forms from the rest of reality, Aristotle asserted. There are, to be sure, forms, laws, orders, or patterns that shape and govern this life, but they are *in* it, they are *of* it. They are not part of some supernatural level of reality. We see this natural order and purpose everywhere: Cats do not give birth to puppies; cornstalks do not yield turnips. Life, reality, is not just matter and it is not just soul. It is clearly both, and neither can be understood in isolation from the other. Soul is a natural force, not a supernatural entity.

The acorn will become an oak if nothing stops it, but it lacks the power to ensure that all its needs are met. It may fall upon rocky soil, get too much or too little water, and so forth. It might become a pretty pathetic oak tree—but it will never become any kind of cedar. Human beings, however, are more complex. And though we must remain human beings, we may fail (for reasons to be discussed) to follow our own entelechy. We may never become our true selves.

Psyche

Formless existence is not possible, according to Aristotle. Things exist according to some pattern, some form. As noted earlier, the Greek term for soul is psyche. We get the term *psychology* from it. For Aristotle, *soul is the form of the body*. Just as we cannot even imagine a soul going to Atlanta without a body, so too one's body is only a thing, a remnant—but not a human being without a human soul, in Aristotle's view.

Soul is entelechy. For Aristotle, it is impossible to affect the body without affecting the soul or to affect the soul without affecting the body. There is no way to reach the soul except through the bodily organs (including the brain/mind), and there is no way for the soul to act or communicate except bodily. Recently, some scientists have lent support to the view that the mind plays a role in altering the course of various autoimmune diseases, that laughter and positive attitudes have healing power. Such ideas reflect Aristotle's insistence on the organic, holistic, inseparable union of body and the natural soul. (African, Amazonian, Indian, and other tribal cultures have long accepted this as a fact.)

ENTELECHY
From the Greek for "having its end within itself": according to Aristotle, an inner urge that drives all things to blossom into their own unique selves; inner order or design which governs all natural processes.

I am convinced that each human being is unique and that he has a right to be his own separate self.
Aaron Ungersma

We must have richness of soul.
Antiphanes

Human beings are not the only *besouled* creatures (to use Aristotle's beautiful word), and each kind of substance requires a different kind of study.

The Hierarchy of Souls

Aristotle thought that although various kinds of souls are different enough that no single definition of soul can cover them all, they are similar enough that we can still recognize a common nature in all their varieties.[7]

Aristotle taught that there are three kinds of soul, which constitute a hierarchy. Each higher level on the continuum of souls contains elements of the lower levels—but the lower levels do not contain the higher. This hierarchy is based on the capacities or *potentialities* possessed by each level of animal life. The more "potentiality" a thing has, the higher its place in the hierarchy.

The hierarchy of souls progresses from the simplest life functions to more complicated ones. Thus the lowest soul is called the *vegetative*, or *nutritive*, soul. This is the minimal level of life (animate matter). *The nutritive soul absorbs matter* from other things (as food is absorbed and transformed into blood or tissue). The second level is the level of sensation; here we find the *sensitive*, or *sentient*, soul. *The sensitive soul registers information* regarding the form of things, but does not absorb or become those things (as when we look at or touch something). Human souls include a third, higher level of entelechy called the *rational* soul, which includes the nutritive and sensitive souls, as well as capacities for analyzing things, understanding various forms of relationships, and making reasoned decisions (called *deliberation*).

Human beings—as human beings, not as specific individuals—have the potential for scientific and philosophical knowledge and insight. The lowest level of life has the most limited potential; think, for instance, of single cells or worms. At the top of the hierarchy of souls, we observe greater capacities for discriminating among various aspects of the environment, for overriding impulse and instinct with rational deliberation based on goals and ends. We note a capacity for understanding the nature (form) of what's going on, and a capacity for creative and self-conscious intelligence. These capacities are lacking in lower life forms.

One way to understand this concept of a continuum of souls is to focus on the word *animated*, which comes from the Latin word for soul, *anima*. The more animated a thing is, the more it moves. Now add to that the notion that the more animated a thing is, *the more moves it has*. A person who has lots of moves is creative. He or she can respond to a variety of situations. A great basketball player is full of new moves, for example, and is always one move ahead of other players. A person who doesn't have many moves repeats the same mistakes, has little variety in his or her life, is often tripped up by circumstances.

Today we sometimes use the word *self* to mean what Aristotle meant by *soul*. So in more contemporary terms, Aristotle might have said that human beings have more potential self than snails. Snails seem (to me, at least) to

---

Nature, like mind, always acts for a purpose, and this purpose is its end [goal]. That it should be so is according to nature; for every part of a living body is an organ of the soul. Evidently then, all such parts are for the sake of the soul, which is their natural end.

Aristotle

For Aristotle, the great philosopher of the classical period, reared to accept slavery and pursue self-centeredness, the Greek was human. The European barbarians were not human, because they were unskilled; nor were Asians human, because they lacked strength and character; women were not human either; women were halfway human and children were only potentially human. The human being par excellence is the free man of the polis *of Hellas.*

Enrique Dussel

"THE MEANING OF OUR EXISTENCE IS NOT INVENTED BUT DETECTED."

What is called self-actualization is, and must remain, the unintended effect of self-transcendence; it is ruinous and self-defeating to make it the target of intention. And what is true of self-actualization also holds for identity and happiness. It is the very "pursuit of happiness" that obviates happiness. The more we make it a target, the more widely we miss.

It may now have become clear that a concept such as self-actualization, or self-realization, is not a sufficient ground for a motivational theory. This is mainly due to the fact that self-actualization, like power and pleasure, also belongs to the class of phenomena which can only be obtained as a side effect and are thwarted precisely to the degree to which they are made a matter of direct intention. Self-actualization is a good thing; however, I maintain that man can only actualize himself to the extent to which he fulfills meaning. Then self-actualization occurs spontaneously; it is contravened when it is made an end in itself. . . .

We have to beware of the tendency to deal with values in terms of the mere self-expression of man himself. . . . If the meaning that is waiting to be fulfilled by man were nothing but a mere expression of self, or no more than a projection of his wishful thinking, it would immediately lose its demanding and challenging character; it could no longer call man forth or summon him. . . . I think the meaning of our existence is not invented by ourselves, but rather detected.

Viktor E. Frankl
Man's Search for Meaning: An Introduction to Logotherapy (New York: Pocket Books, 1963), pp. 35–36; p. 8; pp. 156–57.

---

have less self, less individual identity than, say, dogs. Dogs have a higher level of soul than snails. But no dog, no matter how lovable and intelligent, has the capacity for self that the simplest, minimally rational human being has. Aristotle's ethics is built on this concept of a hierarchy of souls. It is sometimes classified as an ethic of "self-realization," but a much better term would be "soul-realization."

Although limited by the biases of classical Greek culture, the *Nicomachean Ethics* is still readable and instructive. More than a thousand years after Aristotle, the great scholar Thomas Aquinas recognized the value of Aristotle's classical virtues for medieval Christians (see Chapter 10). A case can be made today for another serious look at an ethics of *ensoulment*. If you are already familiar with the concept of self-realization from psychology, New Age metaphysics, or Eastern religions, I think you may be surprised by Aristotle's concept of self-realization. It is more complete than many contemporary systems using the same label. A good way to get a basic sense of Aristotle's self-realization ethic is to take a look at the concept of happiness expressed in the *Nicomachean Ethics*.

May God grant me power to struggle to become not another but a better man.
Samuel Taylor Coleridge

NATURAL HAPPINESS

For the classical Greeks, as has been noted, goodness or virtue was excellence of function. Happiness was also understood in terms of function: A thing was "happy" when it functioned fully and well according to its own nature. A virtuous thing was a happy thing. In Aristotelian terms, happiness is the state of actualizing or realizing a thing's function, its *entelechy*. *A good life is one that provides all the necessary conditions and opportunities for a person to become fully him- or herself—and one in which the person has the character to do so.*

For Aristotle, happiness is a quality of life here and now, not something for the hereafter. It is neither entirely material nor entirely spiritual. His is a philosophy of moderation in the fullest sense, based on common experience, stripped of sentimentality: Wealth is not enough to give us happiness, but poverty makes happiness impossible. Mental attitude is important, but so is physical health. No one can be happy *in the fullest sense* who is chronically ill or mentally deficient. Unattractive people are not as happy as attractive ones. No matter how great our efforts, happiness always contains an element of luck. A person raised well from infancy is a happier person than one who is not. A good life can be marred by a bad death.

PHILOSOPHICAL QUERY

As an example of the importance of luck in the good life, think about this Aristotelian maxim (derived from Solon): "Count no man happy until he is dead." Aristotle taught that a good life can be marred by a bad death. Discuss this general idea and then tie it to our present attitudes toward death, dying, and euthanasia.

The Good

Whereas for Plato the Good was the highest form of Being (an Idea), for Aristotle the good is "that at which all things aim." In other words, the good for anything is the realization of its own nature: *the good at which all things aim is their own entelechy.* When we use the expressions "for your own good," or "that's not good for you," we may have something similar in mind. "The good," then, is what's good for something's full functioning. It encourages its true nature.

Because human beings are complex, consisting of all three elements of soul, it is possible to develop physically or emotionally or intellectually and still fail to realize our entelechy. It is also possible to lack the ability to achieve it, either because the external circumstances of our lives inhibit our full development or because some imbalance in our own character prevents us from fully developing.

Before we go any further, it's important to be clear about the distinction between "aging" and "developing." We're probably all familiar with people who grow old without growing up. We must not confuse biological growth and maturation with personal development. Aristotle linked the two: A *fully* functioning, *completely* happy person will be mentally, physically, spiritually, financially, professionally, creatively, and socially healthy and well-rounded.

As noted above, Aristotle's classical values add an objective component to happiness. This means that entelechy is not determined by the individual. Aristotle's view differs from those self-realization or self-fulfillment theories that claim "you can be anything you want to be." Such a claim would have struck him as ridiculous. It is as irrational and "unworthy" for a human being to try to live like an animal, for example, as it is for an acorn to try to be an ear of corn.

"Know thyself" has become
"Do whatever you please."
Bruno Bettelheim

PHILOSOPHICAL QUERY

Discuss some of the common obstacles to becoming a fully functioning, balanced individual.

Teleological Thinking

According to Aristotle, observation of the natural world (which includes human behavior) reveals:

> Every art and every scientific inquiry, and similarly every action and purpose, may be said to aim at some good. Hence the good has been well defined as that at which all things aim. . . .
>
> As there are various actions, arts, and sciences, it follows the ends are also various. Thus health is the end of medicine, a vessel of shipbuilding, victory [is the end] of strategy, and wealth [is the goal] of domestic economy. . . .
>
> . . . If it is true that in the sphere of action there is an end which we wish for its own sake, and for the sake of which we wish everything else . . . it is clear that this will be the good or the supreme good. Does it not follow that the knowledge of this supreme good is of great importance for the conduct of life, and that, *if we know it*, we shall be like archers who have a mark at which to aim, we shall have a better chance of attaining what we want?[8]

The strongest principle of
growth lies in human choice.
George Eliot

The technical name for this kind of thinking is *teleological*, from the Greek root *telos*, meaning end, purpose, or goal. (*Entelechy* comes from the same root.) **Teleological thinking** is a way of explaining or understanding a thing in terms of its ultimate goal. For example, in teleological terms, infancy is understood as a stage on the way to mature adulthood. Adulthood is the *telos* of infancy. Teleological thinking also refers to understanding things functionally in terms of the relationship of the parts to a whole—for

TELEOLOGICAL THINKING
Way of explaining things in terms of their ultimate goals; understanding things functionally in terms of the relationship of the parts to the whole.

"Can Mommy borrow your baby-blue pinafore tonight, sweetie?"

Drawing by M. Stevens, © 1994 *The New Yorker Magazine*, Inc.

example, considering a vehicle's transmission in terms of the vehicle's ultimate function: speed, traction, comfort. Both Aristotle's ethic and conception of virtue are teleological.

The Science of the Good

The knowledge of the soul admittedly contributes greatly to the advance of truth in general, and, above all, to our understanding of Nature, for the soul is in some sense the principle of animal life. Our aim is to grasp and understand, first its essential nature, and secondly its properties.

Aristotle

In the first book of the *Nicomachean Ethics* Aristotle makes a famous and insightful proclamation:

> Our statement of the case will be adequate if it be made with all such clearness as the subject-matter admits; for it would be wrong to expect the same degree of accuracy in all [subjects]. . . . [Due to the nature of our subject] we must be content to indicate the truth roughly and in outline; and as our subjects and premises are true generally *but not universally*, we must be content to arrive at conclusions which are generally true.[9]

Aristotle was aware that moral considerations involve practical judgments of particular circumstances. We might characterize his position as "formal relativism." That means that even though there is an underlying structure, or form, of happiness for human beings, the specific way in which a particular human being realizes that form varies with his or her circumstances.

Let's use Aristotle's example to see the point: A wrestler and a young child do not eat the same kinds of foods or the same amounts. But this does not mean that the laws of nutrition are relative in the Sophists' sense of being radically determined by the individual or society. Indeed, the same laws apply to wrestlers and babies: minimum protein, fat, carbohydrate, and fluid levels must be met for good health. Appropriate caloric intake should be based on actual energy output, not on a merely theoretical model, and so on. But since individual metabolisms vary, since local temperature affects metabolism, since the quality of food varies, and so forth, we must modify each person's actual diet: "We must be content to indicate the truth roughly and in outline," Aristotle reminds us.

We can identify the general outline of conduct that will lead to the best possible life, but we cannot give a precise prescription for any individual's good life. Still, Aristotle says, we can arrive at a valuable approximation of the "good life" based on human nature and the good we each seek.

According to the *Nicomachean Ethics*, the good to which all humans aspire is happiness:

> As [all] knowledge and moral purpose aspires to some good, what is in our view the good at which the political science aims, and what is the highest of all practical goods? As to its name there is, I may say, a general agreement. The masses and the cultured classes agree in calling it happiness, and conceive that "to live well" or "to do well" is the same thing as "to be happy." But as to the nature of happiness they do not agree, nor do the masses give the same account of it as the philosophers.[10]

The *Nicomachean Ethics* is a careful survey of a variety of opinions regarding what constitutes "living well" in the best, fullest sense. Although Aristotle concludes that the best life is the life of philosophical contemplation, the heart of his ethics is a philosophy of moderation, fulfillment, activity, and balance.

Eudaimonia

The word Aristotle used that is so often translated as "happiness" is **eudaimonia**. English does not have a good one-word equivalent for *eudaimonia*. *Happiness* is almost too bland, although it's probably the answer most of us would give if asked what we want from life (or the afterlife, in many conceptions of heaven).

Eudaimonia implies being really alive as opposed to just existing: fully aware, vital, alert. It is more than being free of cares or worries. Rather,

---

The general movement, we may say, was from other-worldliness towards an intense interest in the concrete facts both of nature and history, and a conviction that the "form" and meaning of the world is to be found not apart from but embedded in its "matter."

Sir David Ross

EUDAIMONIA
Often translated as happiness; term Aristotle used to refer to fully realized existence; state of being fully aware, vital, alert.

eudaimonia implies exhilaration—great suffering and great joy, great passions. It implies a full life, not a pinched, restricted one.

A life devoted solely to pleasure, says Aristotle, is "a life fit only for cattle." Pleasure is not the *goal* of life; it's the natural companion of a full and vigorous life. If you have ever seen an athlete or scholar or artist working very hard at what she loves, you know what Aristotle meant: deep and satisfying pleasure *accompanies* doing what we are meant to do. But the pursuit of pleasure as an end is shallow:

> Ordinary or vulgar people conceive [the good] to be pleasure, and accordingly approve a life of enjoyment. . . . Now the mass of men present an absolutely slavish appearance, as choosing the life of brute beasts, but they meet with consideration because so many persons in authority share [such] tastes.[11]

According to Aristotle, a life devoted to acquiring wealth is also a limited one. Its focus is too narrow to nourish the natural soul's full complement of qualities and needs. Think of people who work long, stressful hours to get rich—and then think of how much life they miss in the process. They never "stop to smell the roses." Even with all the money in the world, a person still needs self-discipline and the knowledge to use his or her riches wisely. The unhappy rich person is common enough to be a stereotype. Aristotle says, "The life of money-making is in a sense a life of constraint, and it is clear that wealth is not the good of which we are in quest; for it is useful in part as a means to something else."[12]

Aristotle also rejected fame and public success as leading to eudaimonia because he believed that the more self-sufficient we are, the happier we are; and the famous are less self-sufficient than most: They need bodyguards, managers, financial advisers, public adulation, and so forth. There is greater peace of mind, security, and satisfaction in knowing that I can provide for my needs than there is in depending on others, as any adolescent or convalescent knows. If one's happiness depends on fame it depends on the whims of a fickle public:

> But [the love of fame] appears too superficial for our present purpose; for honor seems to depend more upon the people who pay it than upon the person to whom it is paid, and we have an intuitive feeling that the good is something which is proper to a man himself and cannot be easily taken away from him.[13]

The Good Life Is a Process

The highest and fullest happiness, according to Aristotle, comes from a life of reason and contemplation—not a life of inactivity or imbalance, but a rationally ordered life in which intellectual, physical, and social needs are all met under the governance of reason and moderation. The "reasonable" per-

Eudaimonia results when pleasure is the natural companion of a fully functioning life, rather than the goal of life. Artisans working at their true calling—such as this glassblower—combine hard work and happiness in a vital, rich way.

son does not avoid life: he or she engages in it fully. A rich and full life is a social life. "No one," Aristotle says in the *Ethics*, "would choose to live without friends, and no one would choose to have every conceivable good thing on the condition that he remain solitary, for man is a political (social) creature designed by nature to live with others."

The rational person alone knows how to engage in life fully, since he or she alone has fully realized all three souls: the nutritive, sensitive, and rational—according to the basic form or entelechy of human beings.[14] *The good life must be lived fully; it is a process, an activity, a becoming, not a static condition*. Not even moral virtue is adequate for happiness by itself, because virtue, ". . . it appears, lacks completeness; for it seems that a man may possess virtue and yet be asleep or inactive throughout life, and, not only [that], but he may experience the greatest calamities and misfortunes. But nobody would call such a life a life of happiness unless he were maintaining a paradox."[15]

Practicing a philosophy of *fully functioning* moderation is quite difficult, for it often requires that we stretch beyond those talents and areas of life we are currently satisfied with. Aristotle understood this, and attempted to present practical advice that could help us come closer to living a richer, more

Continued observations of this basic dynamic nature of happiness, especially in clinical psychological practice, leads almost inevitably to the conclusion that deeper and more fundamental than sexuality, deeper than the craving for social power, deeper even than the desire for possessions, there is a still more generalized and more universal craving in the human makeup. It is the craving for knowledge of the right direction—or orientation.

William H. Sheldon, M.D.

virtuous life: "The purpose of this present study is not . . . the attainment of theoretical knowledge; we are not conducting this inquiry in order to know what virtue is, but in order to become good, else there is no advantage in studying it."[16]

PHILOSOPHICAL QUERY

Consider Aristotle's position carefully here. It may conform more closely to our true feelings about virtue than our sentimental and idealistic platitudes imply. We may be taught that "virtue is its own reward," but how many of us *really* think as highly of a "good" person who hides away from the world as we do of someone who has faults and makes mistakes, but gets out there and gets involved in life? Is being "good" really enough?

HITTING THE MARK

There are, perhaps, two ways to avoid mediocrity. The first is probably the most common today: to excel or fail at something in a big way. The other, it seems, is rarer, probably because it is so difficult for many of us: to live the fullest life possible, developing and nurturing *all* good and necessary qualities while avoiding all character defects.

Now, clearly the second way constitutes an impossible goal for a human being to meet completely. No one seems likely to avoid all defects of character. That does not, however, rule out the desirability of trying to hit this difficult mark. It's one thing to say "I can't be expected to get perfect scores on all my assignments," and quite another to jump to the conclusion "So there's no point in studying at all." Such a reaction is already extreme.

We saw that temperance was one of the cardinal virtues in Plato's *Republic*, and that it was a key virtue for Socrates. Aristotle goes so far as to base his entire moral philosophy on moderation: "First of all, it must be observed that the nature of moral qualities is such that they are destroyed by defect and by excess."[17]

The Principle of the Mean

SOPHROSYNE
Wisdom as moderation; hitting the mark; quality of finding the mean between excess and deficiency.

The concept of moderation, what the Greeks called **sophrosyne**, seems dull and depriving to many people. It implies a life of rigid rules, no fun, playing it safe and avoiding any risks. But, as we have seen, Aristotle did not regard a narrow, boring, play-it-safe life as good. Indeed, the idea that moderation is boring is itself the product of an extreme view! The attitude that only living on the edge, "going for the gusto," abandoning self-restraint, can make life interesting is one-sided.

Aristotelian moderation is based on the concept of wisdom as *hitting the mark* between too much and not enough. If you study a target, you will no-

To attain any assured knowledge of the soul is one of the most difficult things in the world . . . if there is no . . . single and general method of solving the question of essence, our task becomes still more difficult . . . with what facts shall we begin our inquiry?

Aristotle

Compulsive dedication to something may result in excellence at that particular something. But Aristotle cautions that great effort in the service of anything less than the goal of well-balanced thriving results in imbalance and overall dysfunction. Do you think these bodybuilders would agree?

tice that only a small circle in the center is the bull's-eye. There is more room on the target to miss the mark than there is to hit it.

A life completely devoted to playing it safe would be off the mark. Living that way actually limits opportunities to grow and fully experience life. Living on the edge, going from extreme to extreme, will not produce a good, full life either. The great artist who lives only for her work is not living a good, full life, since she indulges her work at the expense of other vital parts of herself. The scholar who hides in research does likewise. So, too, the compulsive jogger or bodybuilder. People who spend all their time doing charity work, praying, and reading holy scriptures are not balanced human beings. (Moral virtue, remember, is not enough, according to Aristotle.)

The happy man lives well and does well; for we have practically defined happiness as a sort of good life and good action.
Aristotle

*Assume the virtue, even
if you have it not,
For use almost can change
the stamp of nature.*
Shakespeare

Aristotelian moderation is the crux of becoming a whole person. Achieving it may require that we do more of the things that are difficult for us and less of those we enjoy. Just as a proper diet is relative (the overeater must eat less than he is used to or wants to, the anorexic must do the opposite), the goal for each is a bull's-eye.

Each person's prescription for self-realization must be determined by his or her own actual condition. Some of us must become more social, others less so. Some students need to study less to become balanced human beings, others need to study more. If we see the call to moderation in terms of *who we are right now* and what it would take to make us fuller, more balanced, more "alive" and vibrant people, it is anything but a call to boring mediocrity.

> But let us first agree that any discussion on matters of action cannot be more than an outline and is bound to lack precision. . . . And if this is true of our general discussion, our treatment of particular problems will be even less precise, since these do not come under the head of any art which can be transmitted by precept, but the agent must consider on each different occasion what the situation demands, just as in medicine and in navigation. But although this is the kind of discussion in which we are engaged, we must do our best.[18]

Character and Habit

CHARACTER
From the Greek *charakter*, a word derived from *charassein*, "to make sharp" or "to engrave," character refers to the sum total of a person's traits, including behavior, habits, likes and dislikes, capacities, potentials, and so on; a key element of Aristotelian ethics and psychology, meaning the overall (generally fixed) nature or tone of a person's habits.

Central to Aristotle's ethics is the notion of character. By **character** Aristotle referred to the overall nature or tone of a person's habits. My character is the habitual or predictable and usual way I behave: my characteristic way of acting in different circumstances. A courageous person is characteristically brave. A slothful one is characteristically lazy.

Moral virtues, according to Aristotle, must be ingrained in us by training. We are not born with them.

> Moral virtue comes to us as a result of habit. . . . The virtues we first get by exercising them, as also happens in the case of the arts as well. For the things we have to learn before we can do them, we learn by doing them, e.g., men become builders by building. . . . So too we become just by doing just acts, temperate by doing temperate acts, brave by doing brave acts. . . . If this were not so, there would have been no need of a teacher, but all men would be born good or bad at their craft. . . . Thus in one word, states of character arise out of like activities. That is why the activities we exhibit must be of a certain kind; it is because the states of character correspond to the difference between these. It makes no small difference,

then, whether we form habits of one kind or another from our very youth; it makes a very great difference, or rather all the difference.[19]

The coward cannot wait for courage, or he will remain a coward. The coward must first act courageously if he wishes to become brave. The poor student cannot wait for motivation, but must first *act the way the disciplined student acts* in order to become a better student. Aristotle anticipated a number of contemporary psychological schools with this emphasis on behavior as the prime element in shaping the human character.

Aristotle distinguishes practical wisdom from theoretical understanding and other forms of knowledge. He links practical wisdom to deliberation. This means that practical wisdom involves choosing the right goals *and* acting on them. But he reminds us that "our ability to perform such actions is *in no way enhanced by knowing them,* since the virtues are characteristics [that is, fixed capacities for action, acquired by habit]" [emphasis added].[20]

This reminds me of a saying a friend uses as a rule of thumb: "You can act yourself into right thinking, but you can't think yourself into right acting." Like all such sayings, this one needs to be taken with the proverbial grain of salt, but it does emphasize an Aristotelian point: *Happiness requires action.*

Knowing what is good and healthy does not—by itself—usually lead to doing what is good and healthy, as most of us realize. Aristotle thought that good habits ingrained in childhood produced the happiest, best life. He said it was better to "overtighten the bow string" in youth, because aging would naturally loosen it. Practical wisdom can help those of us lacking good habits to develop them. "A man fulfills his proper function only by way of practical wisdom and moral excellence or virtue: virtue makes us aim at the right target, and practical wisdom makes us use the right means."[21] Here, too, however, individual cases vary. According to Aristotle, not everyone is salvageable. But on the assumption that you and I are not yet lost, let us examine one of the more important tools in the *Nicomachean Ethics*: the mean.

Application of the Mean

A **mean** is the midpoint between two other points. On a line, it is the exact middle. *Aristotle characterized moral virtue as a mean between too little and too much.* In his terms, the mean is located between deficiency and excess. We might visualize it like this:

```
vice ——————— virtue ——————— vice
deficiency ——————— mean ——————— excess
```

Practical wisdom helps us determine where a given action falls on this continuum. One advantage of a visual aid like this is that it shows us an action

MEAN
From the Latin *medius*, the midpoint between two other points; for Aristotle, moral virtue was characterized as a mean between too little (deficiency) and too much (excess).

TABLE 1. ARISTOTELIAN VIRTUES AND VICES

Deficiency/Vice	Mean/Virtue	Excess/Vice
Cowardice	Courage	Foolhardiness
Anorexia	Moderation	Gluttony
Stinginess	Generosity	Profligacy
Standoffishness	Friendliness	Obsequiousness
Shyness	Pride	Vanity
Pessimism	Realism	Optimism
Celibacy	Monogamy	Promiscuity
Dullness	Well-roundedness	Wildness

can be *more or less* virtuous or vicious (meaning that it's a vice, not that it's necessarily cruel). Depending on the area encompassed by the mean, there is a certain amount of room within the general area of virtue, but there is even more room in the range of the extremes. Thus it is easier to go wrong than right.

Aristotle realized that some actions are excessive by their very nature; they can have no mean. For instance, there is no moderate, appropriate way to commit adultery. Other kinds of actions admit of degree, and so can have a mean. Some examples are shown in Table 1. Aristotle illustrated his point with a lengthy analysis of courage, which he placed between the deficiency of cowardice and the excess of foolhardiness, both of which are vices.

Aristotle points out that some vices are closer to the mean than others, because they reflect more of the virtue. In this case, foolhardiness is closer to courage and so is less a vice than cowardice. But it is still a vice. This is why the coward—who is further from the mean—is more easily recognized as flawed than the foolhardy person who takes too many or the wrong kind of risks. Movie characters like Rambo and Dirty Harry are more foolhardy than they are courageous in Aristotle's value system. In real life, they are not the people to emulate. An army cannot tolerate a platoon of Rambos any more than a police force can tolerate a division of Dirty Harrys.

One possible benefit of reflecting on the mean is a broadened sense of virtue. Thinking only in terms of right *or* wrong can lead to a perception of virtues and vices as simple opposites, whereas Aristotle's system treats them as part of an organic whole, in which each element affects the others and the overall functioning of the organism.

The wealthiest person on earth is not truly happy with high blood pressure or anorexia nervosa. Sadly, the media regularly report the tragic lives of physically strong athletes who succumb to drugs, promiscuity, or financial mismanagement. A brilliant scholar whose professional life is full and rewarding will not be *living as well as possible*, according to Aristotle, if she is

So, as . . . Aristotle . . . insisted, wisdom is to be contrasted with cleverness because cleverness is the ability to take the right steps to any end, whereas wisdom is related only to good ends, and to human life in general rather than to the ends of particular arts.

Philippa Foot

physically decrepit from lack of exercise or socially inept from years of being buried in books. Such examples show how great virtue or talent in one or two areas cannot outweigh significant deficiencies in other areas if we take an organic view of life.

We can easily find many examples of excess or deficiency being mistaken for valuable character traits. An Aristotelian analysis of human activity as an organic complex affected by our characteristic virtues and vices can enrich our sense of possibilities. It can also improve our moral perspective.

> It is moral virtue that is concerned with emotions and actions, and it is in emotions and actions that excess, deficiency, and the median are found. Thus we can experience fear, confidence, desire, anger, pity, and generally any kind of pleasure and pain either too much or too little, and in either case not properly. But to experience all this at the right time, toward the right objects, toward the right people, for the right reason, and in the right manner—that is the median and the best course, the course that is a mark of virtue.[22]

According to Aristotle, we become our best selves in the process of becoming fully functioning human beings. *Aristotelian self-realization, like happiness, is a by-product of living a well-balanced life.*

PHILOSOPHICAL QUERY

Study and discuss Table 1, Aristotelian Virtues and Vices, using principles from the *Nicomachean Ethics* and the concept of the mean. Then add and discuss your own examples.

CONTEMPORARY SELF-REALIZATION

Self-realization or self-actualization theories are enjoying considerable popularity today. In our society, psychologists and "spiritual metaphysicians" have embraced the concept of self-realization much more than philosophers. A major difference between many of these self-realization theories and Aristotle's version centers on exactly what it is that we are trying to "realize."[23] Aristotle's position is that our individuality will emerge in the process of actualizing our basic human essence. A number of contemporary self-realization theories assert the contrary: They claim that our basic humanness will emerge as we actualize our true individuality.

Abraham Maslow and Carl Rogers

Psychologists **Abraham Maslow (1908–1970)** and **Carl Rogers (1902–1987)** were among the most important contemporary advocates of individualistic self-realization. Whereas Aristotle said "Aim for greatness of soul,"

Under favorable conditions man's energies are put into the realization of his own potentialities. Such a development is far from uniform. . . . But whatever course it takes him, it will be his given potentialities which he develops.
Karen Horney

they say "Be yourself." The difference in emphasis is not trivial, for by stressing our *freedom* to be whoever we choose, individualistic self-realization radically shifts our focus from moderation through self-restraint and rationality to self-expression. As Maslow put it:

> The key concepts in the newer dynamic psychology are spontaneity, release, naturalness, self-choice, self-acceptance, impulse-awareness, gratification of basic needs. They *used* to be control, inhibition, discipline, training, shaping, on the principle that the depths of human nature were dangerous, evil, predatory, and ravenous.[24]

Maslow's emphasis, then, is *away from the rule of reason*. But this part of his position rests on a common error, which confuses an irrational attempt to deny or bury unpleasant emotions with being rational in the fullest sense. The unfortunate consequence of this error is to view rational self-control and deliberate management of expression as being identical with neurotic repression and defensiveness. Aristotle did not advocate the rigid rule of reason *against* emotions and appetites, however. Nor did he view the "depths of human nature" as any more dangerous or evil than any other natural force. Rather, he saw the lower parts of the soul as part of the natural order. (See the discussion of ways of knowing in Chapter 20 for more on this.)

What replaces rational, balanced self-discipline and training in the newer dynamic psychologies is trust of one's feelings and openness to experience. Carl Rogers speaks of the "fully functioning person" in terms that reflect this free-flowing openness and trust:

> The good life, from the point of view of my experience, is the process of movement in a direction which the human organism selects when it is inwardly free to move in any direction, and the general qualities of this selected direction appear to have a certain universality.[25]

The universal pattern of development Rogers has in mind can be summed up as from defensiveness to openness. The philosophical question, then, concerns whether or not openness per se is a virtue. As Rogers sees it, the more "actualized" we become, the less "judgmental and inhibited" we become. He says, "The process seems to involve an increasing openness to experience. This phrase has come to have more and more meaning for me. It is the polar opposite of defensiveness." He continues:

> Thus, one aspect of this process which I am naming "the good life" appears to be a movement away from the pole of defensiveness toward the pole of openness to experience. The individual is becoming more able to listen to himself, to experience what is going on within himself. He is more open to his

The unforgivable sin is [to not] become all that you can as a human being, given the circumstances of life that we have to accept.

R. D. Laing

feelings of fear and discouragement and pain. He is also more open to his feelings of courage, and tenderness, and awe. He is free to live his feelings subjectively, as they exist in him, and also free to be aware of these feelings. He is more able to fully live the experiences of his organism rather than shutting them out of awareness.[26]

Perhaps the greatest difference between self-realization as Aristotle saw it and as it is commonly understood today lies in the abandonment of reason as a reliable guide; this in turn results in the loss of a moral center. Maslow and Rogers, for instance, have no clear criteria for rejecting or accepting different life choices. A killer may be as fully functioning as a saint. Reflecting the values of classical Greece, Aristotle would reject most of the newer dynamic psychologies as unfit for human beings because they degrade the *essentially human* part of the soul by replacing reason with feeling as the chief guide.

> *Why do people feel so crowded? Because each wants to occupy the place of the other.*
> Rabbi Abraham Yaakov of Sadagora

PHILOSOPHICAL QUERY

Is it possible that my "true self," the one I dare to become, is a liar or worse? What map shall I use when, in Rogers's words, I "launch myself fully into the stream of life"?

Thomas Merton

The Trappist monk and Roman Catholic philosopher **Thomas Merton (1915–1968)** expressed an interesting variation of a self-realization ethic in his book *New Seeds of Contemplation*. By tying individual entelechy to God's will, Merton avoided the problem of relativism. His position has some of the contemporary feel of Maslow and Rogers, but with the added moral limits of Roman Catholic Christian values. Merton's work is a blend of philosophy, religion, and psychology. The following passage is typical:

> Many poets are not artists for the same reason that many religious men are not saints: they never succeed in being the particular poet or the particular monk they are intended to be by God. They never become the man or the artist who is called for by all the circumstances of their individual lives.
>
> They waste their years in vain efforts to be some other poet, some other saint. For many absurd reasons, they are convinced that they are obliged to become somebody else who died two hundred years ago and who lived in circumstances utterly alien to their own.
>
> They wear out their minds and bodies in a hopeless endeavor to have somebody else's experiences or write somebody else's poems or express somebody else's spirituality.[27]

> *As long as you have to defend the imaginary self that you think is important, you will lose your peace of heart. As soon as you compare that shadow with the shadows of other people, you lose all joy, because you have begun to trade in unrealities, and there is no joy in things that do not exist.*
> Thomas Merton

PHILOSOPHICAL QUERY

Thomas Merton's basic point is worth thinking about. It may apply to the writer hoping to be "another Hemingway" or "another Alice Walker," as well as to children desperately trying to become their parents—or desperately trying not to be anything like them. On the other hand, having a model or hero can be inspiring, and even Aristotle used the "good man" as a model. Discuss.

COMMENTARY

For Aristotle, self-realization was part of a natural process which could be understood only in terms of the whole. It was not directed by a personal God, nor was it a function of free-flowing self-expression. Aristotle saw limits as set by nature, not the individual. He thought that he had identified a fixed, natural hierarchy within the human soul. The rational soul is "designed" to control and guide—but not crush—emotions and appetites. Just as some actions (adultery, for instance) cannot hit a mean because their very nature is imbalanced, so, too, some personalities cannot be actualized because their very essences are excessive or deficient.

The simple call to "be yourself" may sound appealing, but it proves to be insubstantial without solid philosophical grounding. While it is possible to be too self-controlled, no substantial good can come from realizing whatever self we happen to feel like—and this includes a self based only on religious, moral, or personal feelings.

Aristotle, like Plato, extended the range of philosophic inquiry beyond the *sophos'* earliest search for wisdom. Basing his philosophy on observation and experience, he added the scientist's acuity to the *sophos'* sense of wonder. Aristotle did not abandon the search for wisdom; he enriched it by bringing it down to earth. The *Nicomachean Ethics* remains one of the most complete expressions of practical wisdom in the tradition of philosophy in the original sense. The spirit of the *sophos* rings throughout the *Ethics*, no more forcefully than when Aristotle says: "The purpose of this present study is not . . . the attainment of theoretical knowledge; we are not conducting this inquiry in order to know what virtue is, but in order to become good, else there is no advantage in studying it."

It is difficult to judge Aristotle's conception of the self-realized, superior person today. Clearly, his classical model of "human excellence" is alien to a culture that encourages the expression of virtually every emotion as healthy. His basic values are alien to a culture that prizes youthful spontaneity and natural talent over mature self-mastery and self-discipline. The modern self, it seems, is set free without a clear direction. The Aristotelian self is crafted according to standards of excellence discovered through philosophical contemplation.

A great Hasidic rabbi by the name of Zusya once said: When I die, God will not ask me, "Why were you not Moses?" When I die, God will ask me, "Why were you not Zusya?"

SUMMARY OF MAIN POINTS

Aristotle was Plato's most illustrious pupil and tutor of Alexander the Great. His interests included philosophy, logic, natural and social science, poetry, and drama. Aristotle founded his school known as the Lyceum.

Aristotle saw dangers in Plato's failure to begin from a clear assessment of actual facts. In contrast to Plato's rationalistic approach, Aristotle brings to full maturity a second major approach to the study of the good life: collecting of facts and using factual information to make this a better world.

Aristotle is a philosophical naturalist. Naturalism is the belief that reality consists of the natural world and that the universe is ordered. Everything follows consistent and discoverable *laws* of nature, and can be described in terms of fundamental laws. Nature always acts with a purpose, and the key to understanding anything lies in determining its essential purpose. There is no separate supernatural order of reality, no world of Platonic forms.

Aristotle identified what he called an "inner urge" in every living thing, a drive to become its unique self. He called this inner urge *entelechy*, meaning "having its end within itself." Aristotle thought that entelechy explained nature: Things do not just happen—they develop according to natural design. Nature is ordered and guided "internally."

Aristotle taught that there are three kinds of soul and that they constitute a hierarchy. Each higher level of soul contains elements of the lower levels—but the lower levels do not contain the higher. This hierarchy is based on the capacities or potentialities possessed by each level of animal life. The more potentiality a thing has, the higher its place in the hierarchy.

The lowest soul is called the vegetative, or nutritive, soul. This is the minimal level of life (animate matter). The second level is the sensitive, or sentient, soul. The sensitive soul registers information regarding the form of things, but does not absorb or become those things (as when we look at or touch something). Human souls include a third,

higher level of entelechy called the rational soul, which includes the nutritive and sensitive souls plus capacities for analyzing things, understanding various forms of relationships, and making reasoned decisions.

According to Aristotle the good is "that at which all things aim." The good at which all things aim is their own entelechy. Because human beings are complex, consisting of all three elements of soul, it is possible to develop physically or emotionally or intellectually and still fail to realize our entelechy. The technical name for this kind of thinking is *teleological*, from the Greek root *telos*, meaning end, purpose, or goal.

The word Aristotle used that is so often translated as "happiness" is *eudaimonia*. Happiness is almost too bland, however, for *eudaimonia* implies being really alive as opposed to just existing—being fully aware, vital, alert. *Eudaimonia* implies exhilaration—great suffering and great joy, great passions, a fully realized life.

Aristotelian moderation is based on the concept of wisdom as hitting the mark (*sophrosyne*) between too much and not enough. Virtue consists of hitting the mark of moderation, and vice consists of being off by too much (excess) or too little (deficiency). Virtue is the mean between either extreme.

Aristotle taught that happiness requires activity and the happy person must develop good habits and learn practical wisdom. Knowing what is good cannot make us happy unless we have the character (habit) of acting wisely and moderately.

Self-realization theories remain popular today. Influential contemporary psychologists Abraham Maslow and Carl Rogers advocate self-realization but differ from Aristotle in their emphasis on feelings rather than reason. The Trappist monk Thomas Merton went beyond naturalism and attempted to link individual entelechy to God's will. So far, however, Aristotle's concept of self-realization remains the most thoroughly developed.

STUDY QUESTIONS

1. What is unusual about the nature of the writings attributed to Aristotle?

2. What do scholars mean by saying that Aristotle brought philosophy down to earth? How does this relate to Plato?

3. What is naturalism?

4. What is entelechy and how is it significant to Aristotle's ethics?

5. Describe teleological thinking. Give an example of a teleological explanation.

6. What, according to Aristotle, is the relationship between soul and body?

7. Describe the hierarchy of souls.

8. How does the hierarchy of souls relate to self-realization?

9. What is "the good," according to Aristotle?

10. Discuss Aristotle's use of the term *happiness*. Contrast it with the most common contemporary notion of happiness. Evaluate both.

11. What is *eudaimonia*? Is it the same thing as happiness? Explain.

12. In what sense can Aristotle's position be termed "formal relativism"? Is Aristotle a relativist? Explain.

13. What did Aristotle identify as the highest kind of life? Explain fully.

14. Explain the importance of sophrosyne to happiness.

15. What is the "principle of the mean"? Give one or two examples of using it to evaluate a course of action or moral choice.

16. How do character and habit affect happiness and virtue, according to Aristotle?

17. Give several examples of activities for which there is no mean.

18. Analyze one or two ranges of activity to show how some vices are more virtuous than others.

19. Critics accuse Aristotle of circular reasoning when he attempts to identify goodness by first looking at the good man. How does he solve the problem of studying virtue objectively?

20. Discuss the relationships among action, practical wisdom, and happiness in Aristotle's philosophy.

21. Compare and contrast classical Aristotelian self-realization with contemporary self-realization theories.

22. How does Thomas Merton try to balance personal self-realization with fully human self-realization? What would Aristotle think of his solution? Explain.

23. "The modern self, it seems, is set free without a clear direction. The Aristotelian self is crafted according to standards of excellence discovered through philosophical contemplation." Explain.

24. In your own words, describe the "fully functioning" human being.

25. Using your own educational experiences as a general basis, analyze public education from an Aristotelian perspective.

CHAPTER EIGHT

The Epicurean:

Epicurus

Nothing is sufficient to
someone for whom little
is not enough.

EPICURUS

What do you want most? If you're like most people, you probably want "to be happy." And what makes you happy? Good grades? Friends? A loving family? Sex? Food? Cars? Clothes? Beaches or mountains? Power? Success? Attention? Although each of us might compose a different list, our lists will all contain things that give us *pleasure*. If we each composed a second list, of things that make us unhappy, it would contain things that cause us *pain*.

An acquaintance of mine has a T-shirt that says "Live To Party!" Cyndi Lauper sprang to fame singing "Girls just want to have fun!" Madonna boasted, "I'm a material girl living in a material world." In commercials, the television camera lingers lovingly on beer in wet, frosty mugs, with thick foam running down the sides. And then there are all those other advertisements, songs, music videos, movies, and books with sensual or luxurious themes.

In 1988 President Ronald Reagan declared drug abuse "the number one problem" in America. Substance abuse remains such a serious problem that in 1993 President Clinton included treatment for it in his proposed plan for national health care. Obviously, most people do not start abusing alcohol or other drugs intending to become addicted. They begin for the promise of pleasure or to numb pain and worry. So even though substance abuse is a serious problem in our society, it is rooted in a common desire to have pleasure or to avoid pain.

PHILOSOPHICAL QUERY

The years 1989 and 1990 saw remarkable changes in Eastern Europe. The Berlin Wall was torn down; Romania, Hungary, Poland, Czechoslovakia, and Yugoslavia saw restrictive, communistic governments and dictators overthrown. For many years, the most desired items on the Soviet black market have been Levis, rock-and-roll recordings, and other luxury goods. Now as the Soviet Union appears to be opening itself to greater freedoms, Pepsi Cola, Domino's Pizza, and McDonald's (among others) have been invited to establish franchises there. New York governor Mario Cuomo has been quoted as saying: "They're running away from communism toward our way of life because of television and basketball. You play basketball in this country for a month, you go back, you're never going to be happy waiting in line for a potato."[1] Today much of Asia, Mexico, Central and Latin America, and other developing areas are looking more and more like the United States.

Discuss these developments in light of the pursuit of happiness. Can you make any connection between pleasure and these changes in the developing nations? Is a desire for more pleasure

---

I have never searched for happiness. Who wants happiness? I have searched for pleasure.
Oscar Wilde

Make haste and enjoy life while you have it. Why care what happens when you are dead?
Lie Zi

That pleasure is the goal is proved by the fact that from our youth up we are instinctively attracted to it and when we obtain it seek for nothing more and shun nothing so much as its opposite, pain.
Bruno Bettelheim

and less pain an adequate explanation for such a fundamental shift from communistic to more capitalistic systems of government? Explain.

THE PURSUIT OF HAPPINESS

The Declaration of Independence begins with the announcement that "life, liberty, and the pursuit of happiness" are among our most basic rights. So important was "the pursuit of happiness" to the founders of America that it is characterized as an "inalienable right." An *inalienable* right is the strongest kind there is: it flows from our very nature. Free speech, economic choice, religious liberty, private property, and equality of opportunity are guaranteed in the Constitution *because each is essential to the pursuit of happiness.*

The nature and conditions of happiness have concerned philosophers throughout history. Among the earliest and most persistent responses to the search for happiness is hedonism.

There is no such thing as pure pleasure; some anxiety always goes with it.
Ovid

THE HEDONISTIC VISION

Hedonism, from the Greek root for "pleasure," *hēdonē,* is the general term for any philosophy that says pleasure = good, and pain = evil. For a strict hedonist, nothing that provides pleasure can be bad. Some hedonists stress the pursuit of pleasure and others emphasize avoiding pain.

Philosophers distinguish two main forms of hedonism. **Psychological hedonism** is the belief that all decisions are based on considerations of pleasure and pain, that it is psychologically impossible for human beings to do otherwise. Even acts of self-sacrifice are hedonistic: the self-sacrificer either derives pleasure from being able to sacrifice something for a purpose or else fears the guilt, pain, or damnation that would accompany any other course of action. We may lose sight of the importance of pain and pleasure in our motivations because we use terms like *good* and *bad* or *right* and *wrong* to talk about pleasure and pain.

Ethical hedonism is the belief that although it is possible to deliberately avoid pleasure or choose pain, it is morally wrong to do so. We have a general moral obligation to seek pleasure and avoid pain. We *ought* to enjoy ourselves as much as possible.

Simply put, the hedonist sees the happy life as one possessing the most possible pleasure accompanied by the least possible pain. The pursuit of pleasure, says the hedonist, is our birthright. The baby in its cradle coos when it is cuddled, fed, or played with. It cries when it is uncomfortable. No baby has to be taught this; it "comes with the territory." We have to learn

HEDONISM
From the Greek root for "pleasure," the general term for any philosophy that says pleasure = good and pain = evil.

PSYCHOLOGICAL HEDONISM
The belief that all decisions are based on considerations of pleasure and pain because it is psychologically impossible for human beings to do otherwise.

ETHICAL HEDONISM
The belief that although it is possible to deliberately avoid pleasure or choose pain, it is morally wrong to do so.

SUICIDE AND SOUP

What would you think of the proposition that the pleasures of a good soup can overcome thoughts of suicide? That's the thrust of the following anecdote reported by one of the most elegant hedonistic writers of the early twentieth century, the Chinese-American scholar Lin Yutang.

Lin writes that one of the greatest of the ancient Chinese poets, Ch'u Yuan (343–290 B.C.), once went through a period of depression so deep that he had to struggle against suicide. He wrote a poem to persuade himself that it was good to be alive. In it he urged his soul to return and not leave his body. Among other things, he reviewed for his soul many of the good things of life: food, wine, beautiful girls, and music. According to Lin Yutang, one of Ch'u's most convincing arguments is based on the infinite variety of food. Here's part of Arthur Waley's translation:

Oh Soul, come back to joys beyond telling!
Where thirty cubits at harvest-time

Never before has the seductive market way of life held such sway in nearly every sphere of American life. This market way of life promotes addictions to stimulation and obsessions with comfort and convenience. Addictions and obsessions—centered primarily around bodily pleasures and status rankings—constitute market moralities of sorts. The common denominator is a rugged and ragged individualism and rapacious hedonism in quest of a perennial "high" in body and mind.

Cornel West

to be honest, to work hard, to delay gratification, but we do not have to be taught to seek pleasure and avoid pain. On the contrary, we have to be forced to go against our basic hedonistic natures.

Ironically, even when we are being discouraged from hedonistic living, we are trained and educated according to hedonistic principles! *Pain* (spanking, detention, no supper) and *pleasure* (hugs, allowances, gifts) are used to control us. Psychological hedonists cite such patterns as evidence that no one escapes the rule of pain and pleasure. We just alter their sources.

Our hedonistic nature is even reflected in most concepts of heaven and hell. Hell is bad because it is associated with pain and suffering. Heaven is good because in heaven we no longer suffer: our bodies are perfect; we never have to say good-bye to those we love; we don't have boring jobs. Some pictures of heaven even include golden streets, mansions, clear brooks, delightful food. All include the indescribable *pleasure* of being in God's presence. Many religions see God as a source of pleasure or protection from pain. And according to most religious beliefs, God uses hedonistic principles to reward the good with eternal happiness and punish the bad with eternal pain.

There is ample evidence of our hedonistic natures in other aspects of our lives. We want the pleasures of relationships—not the hassles. In books and magazines, on television, and in psychotherapy, we're counseled to leave our marriages or jobs if they don't make us happy. College courses are often chosen not on the basis of their substance and content, but on how easy or difficult they are. In poor neighborhoods throughout this country people wear designer jeans and jackets; they carry boom boxes and

The corn is stacked;
Where pies are cooked of millet and
    bearded-maize.
Guests watch the steaming bowls
And sniff the pungency of peppered herbs.
The cunning cook adds slices of bird-flesh,
Pigeon and yellow heron and black-crane.
They taste the badger stew.
O Soul, come back to feed on foods you
    love!
Next are brought
Fresh turtle, and sweet chicken cooked in
    cheese

Pressed by the men of Ch'u.
And pickled suckling-pig
And flesh of whelps floating in liver-sauce
With salad of minced radishes in brine;
All served with that hot spice of southern-
    wood
The land of Wu supplies.
O Soul, come back and choose the meats
    you love!

Arthur Waley, *Translations from the Chinese*
(New York: Knopf, 1919, 1941).

---

portable stereos. Students on financial aid wear Air Jordans or Nikes and buy the latest Dr. Dre or Mozart CD.

There are many ways to explain such a voracious appetite for entertainment, fashion, and luxury items. Hedonists see it as evidence that the pursuit of pleasure is natural and universal. After all, no matter how dismal our lives, we put enormous energies and whatever money we can into pleasure-producing activities. But if the pursuit of pleasure is "natural" and universal and unavoidable, what is there to philosophize about?

The difference between *philosophical* hedonism and the instinctive pursuit of immediate pleasure rests, among other things, on the possibility that while most people *think* they know what they need to be happy, a cursory look around makes it clear that many of us don't. We may be able to provide ourselves with *momentary distractions* or *isolated pleasures*; but that's not the same thing as *being happy*.

So powerful is the desire for happiness through seeking pleasure or avoiding pain that influential and able examples of the archetype of the hedonist can be found in virtually every historical period and culture. But experience suggests that for most people, life remains full of frustration and suffering despite their great efforts to be happy. Thus the hedonistic philosopher argues that the pursuit of pleasure and flight from pain may be universal, but the experience of genuine happiness is not. It does not occur naturally for most people, but is the result of intelligent reflection and careful selection based on practical wisdom. We may all want to be happy, but too few of us achieve our goal. We'll see why as we take a close look at two related archetypes of the hedonist: the Cyrenaic and Epicurean.

Because we cannot relate to the sensuous and material present we are most happy when good things are expected to happen, not when they are happening. We get such a kick out of looking forward to pleasures and rushing to meet them that we can't slow down enough to enjoy them when they come. We are therefore a civilization which suffers from chronic disappointment—a formidable swarm of spoiled children smashing their toys.
Alan Watts

Does fabulous wealth always encourage hedonism? What do you think accounts for our fascination with the very wealthy? Based on his media image, would you classify Donald Trump as a hedonist?

ARISTIPPUS

Aristippus

Aristippus was only concerned with the body, as though we did not somehow have a soul.
Cicero

Aristippus (c. 430–350 B.C.) lived in the town of Cyrene on the coast of North Africa in what is now Libya. Cyrene was founded by Greek colonists on the edge of a plateau near the Mediterranean coast. The soil and climate made the area rich in flowers, fruits, and lush vegetation. By the time Aristippus was born, Cyrene was a prosperous city, noted for its marble temples, its opulent public square, and the huge, luxurious homes of its wealthiest citizens. Like ancient Athens, Cyrene's strategic location helped make it a wealthy and exciting trading center.

Aristippus was born with all the advantages such a place had to offer, so perhaps it is not surprising that he was the first philosopher to make a direct statement of hedonism. In fact, from what we know of it, Aristippus's version is probably the purest, most uncompromising statement of the hedonistic vision.

Aristippus was a friendly and clever young man, fond of pleasures of all sorts. He heard about Socrates while attending the Olympic Games with a friend, and was so impressed that he rushed to Athens to meet Socrates. He quickly became a member of the closest, most involved group of his follow-

The archetype of the Cyrenaic hedonist can be found in all historical periods—usually with disastrous results.

ers, and eventually did some teaching himself. He annoyed some of his Socratic friends, who thought he was behaving like a Sophist, when he began to travel about teaching and collecting higher and higher fees.

Ultimately, Aristippus returned home and opened a school of philosophy in Cyrene. His form of hedonism, called **Cyrenaic hedonism**, takes its name from his hometown. As you get a fuller picture of this philosophy, see if you don't recognize elements of the Cyrenaic archetype all around us.

CYRENAIC HEDONISM

As noted in Chapter 5, Socrates evaluated pleasures in terms of their relationship to goodness and truth, and their effect on the soul. Knowledge of goodness and truth was of the highest value for him. Aristippus, on the other hand, was utterly convinced that physical benefits are the highest possible good. As Aristippus observed life in lush Cyrene, he concluded that *pleasure is the principal motive for living* and that *pleasure is always good—regardless of its source.*

CYRENAIC HEDONISM
Philosophy that advocates the unreflective pursuit of intense, immediate pleasure; makes no qualitative distinctions among pleasures.

The Meaning of Life Is Pleasure

Aristippus thought it was obvious, to anybody who cared to see it, that all people seek pleasure (whether they are aware of it or not). He argued that the meaning of life must be discerned by observing our *actual behavior*. Doing so reveals that the meaning of life is pleasure. The simple, healthy, proper course of life, according to Aristippus, is to follow our natural desires openly, without guilt or apology, and learn how to most enjoy ourselves. Since pleasure is the natural goal of all life, we should try to have as much intense, sensual pleasure as we can. The Chinese-American philosopher **Lin Yutang (1895–1976)** expresses the sensual quality of hedonism especially well:

> Just as it is impossible for me to say whether I love my children physically or spiritually when I hear their chattering voices or when I see their plump legs, so I am totally unable to distinguish between the joys of the flesh and the spirit. Does anybody ever love a woman spiritually without loving her physically? And is it so easy a matter for a man to analyze and separate the charms of the woman he loves—like laughter, smiles, a way of tossing one's head, a certain attitude toward these things?[2]

The Cyrenaics asserted that because sensory pleasures are more intense than mental or emotional ones, they are the best of all. Therefore, physical pleasure is superior to all other things. Only physical pleasures make life exciting, dynamic, worth living. Not only that, but actual pleasures of the moment are much more desirable than potential pleasures that may (or may not) occur in the future. In the first place, we are certain only of the present; the future may not even come. And besides, things may be different for us in the future. Today I may think that I would love to have a Porsche. Suppose I save my money, work extra hours—in short, suffer now for the pleasure of a Porsche later. I might die before I get my Porsche. Then what good was my suffering? My tastes might change while I struggle to save my money, so that by the time I can have my Porsche it no longer pleases me. Or the way Porsches are made might change so that I don't enjoy mine once I have it. Thus the wisest course is to choose the most pleasure right now, and buy the most enjoyable car I can today.

Knowledge and Pleasure

Cyrenaic hedonists were not interested in anything that wasn't directly related to the pursuit of pleasure. Consequently, they were not interested in the study of nature or mathematics, and their only interest in logic was a very basic concern with the subjective nature of experience.

One of the worst sins Dante could think of was to sulk in the sunlight. To those who did he assigned the eternal punishment of wallowing in the mud.
Irwin Edman

It is a hard matter, my fellow citizens, to argue with the belly, since it has no ears.
Cato the Elder

Men who are devoid of integrity and who live for food and nothing else . . . surely they are no better than beasts? If you are no better than a dog or chicken, others will not rely on you. Danger and disgrace will then befall you.
Lie Zi

"WHAT'S THE SENSE OF HAVING A GOOD TIME IF YOU DON'T KNOW YOU HAD A GOOD TIME?"

Reprinted with special permission of King Features Syndicate, Inc.

The Cyrenaics taught that our subjective sensations are knowable, but that a complete understanding of their objective causes is impossible. The belief that we can *know* what pleases or displeases us at the moment but only *speculate* on their objective natures is known as the problem of **subjectivism**. Perhaps the simplest way to understand the problem of subjectivism in relation to hedonism is in reference to tastes in food. Many people like licorice or chickory or grits or jalapeño peppers, for instance. Many others do not. Now, certain questions can be raised in regard to what any one of these foods *really* tastes like. I may find this jalapeño jelly mild. You may insist that it's hot. Are we both having the same taste experience but giving it different names? Or are we each actually tasting something quite different? Even if we both call the same thing "sweet," how can we be sure that "sweet" refers to the same sensation?

Walter Pater (1839–1894), an influential critic, philosopher, essayist, and hedonist in the latter part of the nineteenth century, wrote an ambitious novel, *Marius the Epicurean*, about a young man's search for a philosophy of life in ancient Rome. Here Pater elegantly expresses the problem of subjectivism:

> But can we be sure that things are at all like our feelings? Mere peculiarities in the instruments of our cognition, like the little knots and waves on the surface of a mirror, may distort the matter they seem but to represent. Of other people we cannot truly know even the feelings, nor how far they indicate the same modifications, each one of a personality really unique, in using the same terms as ourselves . . . how natural the determination to rely exclusively upon the phenomena

SUBJECTIVISM
Belief that we can know only our own sensations, not their objective causes.

Would you count as a human being (I will not say a true man) one whose supreme good consists of flavors and colors and sounds? He should be crossed off the roster of the noblest of all living species.
Seneca

of the senses, which certainly never deceive us about themselves, about which alone we can never deceive ourselves![3]

The consequence of such a view is that *whatever feels good is good*. Lacking any objective standard of comparison, the Cyrenaic hedonist concludes
that the individual is the measure: of that which is pleasure, that it is pleasure; of that which is pain, that it is pain. And since any pleasure is by definition good, it follows that I ought to be doing whatever I enjoy doing. The
principle of maximizing pleasure and minimizing pain is known as **hedonistic utility**.

The idea of deliberately maximizing pleasure and minimizing pain
transforms psychological hedonism into ethical hedonism. Although we
are, by nature, predisposed to seek pleasure and avoid pain, some of us become confused and our instincts and habits get corrupted. Hence we attempt to stifle the pursuit of pleasure because we see it as somehow sinful
or immoral. We may actually add pain to our lives if we think that by suffering we become purified or ennobled. Our natural hedonism may be sub-
dued by childhood training, religious indoctrination, or a puritanical culture. Thus, the ethical hedonist argues, it makes sense to advise people that
they *ought* to do what they are by nature trying to do: enjoy themselves.

PHILOSOPHICAL QUERY

Do you ever feel guilty about being too happy? Why do people
justify indulging themselves? Why do we feel the need to ration-
alize buying things, eating sinful desserts, watching lots of TV,
partying during finals week, and so on? Is "sinful" dessert just an
expression, or does it reflect a basic attitude toward pleasure?
Discuss contemporary attitudes toward pleasure.

All Pleasures Are Equal

The Cyrenaics considered all pleasures to be of equal kind; they had no hierarchy of pleasures. Any distinction between "good" and "bad" pleasures was
as absurd and contradictory as distinguishing between good and bad sins or
good and bad virtues. The only difference among pleasures, then, is their
intensity: *Whatever pleases me most at the moment is the highest good there can be.*
Perhaps this is part of what's implied by the beer commercial that advises:
"You only go around once, so grab all the gusto you can get." No pleasure
can be "sick" in such a value system. Only being victimized and controlled
by any pleasure is "sick." No enjoyment can be wrong. No passion is evil in
itself. Only loss of self-control is wrong, for loss of self-control leads to less
pleasure.

One of the most famous examples of the idea that no enjoyment can be
wrong is a doctrine that flourished in nineteenth-century France and England. **Aestheticism** is an amoral form of the pursuit of pleasure that fo-

---

HEDONISTIC UTILITY
Principle of maximizing
pleasure and minimizing
pain.

*Do not craze yourself with
thinking, but go about your
business anywhere. Life is
not intellectual or critical,
but sturdy. Its chief good is
for well-mixed people who
can enjoy what they find,
without question.*
Ralph Waldo Emerson

AESTHETICISM
Amoral form of the pursuit
of pleasure that focuses on
the worship of beauty and
beautiful objects.

cuses on the worship of beauty and beautiful objects; its advocates are known as **aesthetes**. Pater's Marius is an intelligent aesthete. Perhaps the most famous real-life aesthete was the Irish poet, novelist, and playwright **Oscar Wilde (1854–1900)**. Wilde believed that "there is no such thing as morality or immorality in thought. There is immoral emotion."[4] He considered "immoral" any painful or ugly emotion.

For Wilde, and to a certain extent Pater, the pursuit of "beautiful pleasures" required a willingness to experience "dangerous and exotic" practices. These included smoking opium, drinking absinthe (a powerful, hallucinogenic liqueur made from wormwood), sexual indulgence (but only with beautiful partners), and the acquisition of fine art objects, clothes, houses, food, and drink. Although the aesthetes talked about higher and lower pleasures, all values were subservient to pleasure, and the subjective experience of "beautiful moments" was seen as the highest pleasure. Although not purely Cyrenaic hedonists, the aesthetes made a religion out of the pursuit of pleasurable moments and actively opposed the introduction of moral values into the calculation of possible pleasures.

Wilde himself lived extravagantly, practicing what he preached. He ate and drank only the finest foods and wines and generally lived a life devoted to art and pleasure. He viewed conventional morality as being in "bad taste" because it preached repression, restraint, and self-sacrifice. Wilde saw himself and the other aesthetes as living in the realm of pure beauty, "beyond right and wrong." Any beautiful or pleasant experience was judged good.

Wilde was ultimately convicted of sodomy and served two years at hard labor in the notorious Reading Gaol. To many moralists of the day, Wilde's fate proved that unchecked hedonism always results in pain and unhappiness. But such an objection is itself hedonistic and shows, at most, that the pursuit of pleasure must be controlled. The objection is forceful only when the unchecked pursuit of pleasure results in unhappiness. It leaves open the possibility that once in a while we might be lucky enough or clever enough to enjoy causing pain to others. According to Cyrenaic hedonism, such pleasure is as good as any other equally intense "beautiful moment."

PHILOSOPHICAL QUERY

Consider what it means to say that *all* pleasure is good and *no* pleasure can be immoral. Do you agree? Why or why not?

Now think about your answer. Is it based on any negative reaction to the idea that no pleasure is wrong? Is your position determined by whether or not the idea of hedonism pleases or pains you? Can you ever make a decision that is *not* hedonistic?

The Self Is Utterly Free

In *The Culture of Narcissism* (1979), history professor Christopher Lasch discusses what he calls the "new narcissists," individuals who live only for

---

AESTHETES
Individuals who live according to the doctrines of aestheticism.

I can resist everything except temptation.
Oscar Wilde

Give me luxuries, and anyone can have the necessities.
Oscar Wilde

Self-sacrifice is a thing that should be put down by law.
Oscar Wilde

themselves and for the moment. The "new narcissists" feel free to walk away from social roles such as parent, student, or citizen whenever they become too confining or boring and pursue "self-fulfillment," "personal growth," and so forth, as they wish. Lasch writes:

> Having no hope of improving their lives in ways that matter, people have convinced themselves that what matters is psychic self-improvement: getting in touch with their feelings, eating health food, taking lessons in ballet or belly-dancing, immersing themselves in the wisdom of the East, jogging, learning how to "relate," overcoming the "fear of pleasure." . . .
>
> *To live for the moment is the prevailing passion—to live for yourself, not for your predecessors or posterity.* We are fast losing the sense of historical continuity [emphasis added].[5]

We can compare Lasch's observation with a conversation Xenophon reported in which he, Socrates, and Aristippus discussed the nature of the city-state. Socrates believed in an ordered city-state in which some command and others obey. Aristippus rejected both roles. He wanted no part of being in control, since political power and responsibility only create problems and obligations. He also rejected being controlled:

> "No," replied Aristippus, "for my part I am no candidate for slavery; but there is, as I hold, a middle path in which I am desirous of walking. That way leads neither through control nor slavery, but through liberty, which is the royal road to happiness. . . . My plan for avoiding such treatment is this. I do not shut myself up within a city-state, but am a stranger in every land."[6]

In other words, participation in public life is a "hassle." Being a fully involved citizen usually interferes with the Cyrenaic's pursuit of enjoyment. The only reason for people to get into politics is if they derive pleasure from it. We have no social or civic obligations, according to Aristippus.

To be a "stranger in every land" is to be a free *individual*. By extension, the Cyrenaic can also claim to be "a stranger in every relationship." Why should I try to work through the difficult spots in marriage or parenting if my only purpose in life is to achieve as little pain and as much pleasure as possible, *now, for me? My only obligation is to enjoy every moment.*

PHILOSOPHICAL QUERY

Do you know any "new narcissists"? Can you identify any social patterns that encourage or reflect such an attitude? What are some of them? Do you think this "new narcissism" is the wave of the future or is it only a temporary condition, not worth worrying about? Explain.

The problem about appealing ultimately to human desires is that this appears to exclude rational criticism of ethical motivations at the most fundamental level.

Thomas Nagel

But myself, I classify with those who wish for a life of the greatest ease and pleasure that can be had.

Xenophon

My duty as a gentleman has never interfered with my pleasures in the smallest degree.

Oscar Wilde

EPICURUS

Though **Epicurus (341–270 B.C.)** was born in the Asia Minor city of Samos, he was an Athenian citizen because his father had moved to Samos as an Athenian colonist. When he was eighteen years old, Epicurus went to Athens in order to complete the two years of military service required of Athenian males. The Macedonian king of Greece, Alexander the Great, had just died, and the Athenians, who had resented his rule, revolted against the regent Alexander had imposed on them. It took less than a year for this revolt to be crushed, but Epicurus drew an important lesson from it: Political activities and ambitions are pointless.

Epicurus remained in Athens for a time, and studied with major followers of both Plato and Aristotle. He never accepted Plato's philosophy and came to reject Aristotle's as well. He referred to himself as self-taught and never acknowledged any philosophical teacher or master. He saw himself as a moral reformer who had discovered a brand-new message, one that could save others from unhappiness:

> Vain is the word of a philosopher which does not heal any suffering of man. For just as there is no profit in medicine if it does not expel the diseases of the body, so there is no profit in philosophy either if it does not expel the suffering of the mind.[7]

Epicurus left Athens and for some years taught in outlying cities. But Athens remained the cultural and intellectual center of the Greek-influenced world. The two most important schools of the era were there: Plato's Academy and Aristotle's Lyceum. They attracted the finest minds of the time. It is not surprising, then, that Epicurus returned to Athens to establish his own school.[8]

Epicurus, then thirty-five years old, had refined and developed his philosophy and had already established an impressive reputation as a teacher. By the mere fact of moving his school to Athens, he directly challenged and provoked the philosophical establishment represented by Plato and Aristotle. His move signaled the beginning of a genuine intellectual revolution.[9] Epicurus was convinced that he had something brand-new to present. He viewed Platonic and Aristotelian philosophies as outdated, overly theoretical, and hence irrelevant to daily life and happiness. Epicurus's attack was aided by the internal quarreling and disagreements weakening those schools.

The Garden

Epicurus called his school the Garden. A serene retreat from the social, political, and even philosophical turmoil of Athens, Epicurus's Garden became as well known for good living and pleasant socializing as it was for its philosophy.

Epicurus

And so we speak of pleasure as the starting point and the goal of the happy life because we realize that it is our primary native good, because every act of choice and aversion originates with it, and because we come back to it when we judge every good by using the pleasure feeling as our criterion.
Epicurus

Epicurus.—Yes, I am proud of the fact that I experience the character of Epicurus quite differently from perhaps everybody else. . . . Such happiness could be invented only by a man who was suffering continually.
Friedrich Nietzsche

Guest, thou shalt be happy here, for here happiness is esteemed the highest good.

Motto hung over the entrance to the Garden

One of the unusual features of the Garden was that it welcomed everyone. It was one of the very few places in Greece where women were allowed and encouraged to interact with men *as equals.* By taking as obvious the essential equality and dignity of women, Epicurus's Garden provided a truly unique experience for *both* men and women, since elsewhere men, as well as women, were denied the opportunity to experience equality. Epicurus also made no distinctions based on social status or race. He accepted all who came to learn: prostitutes, housewives, slaves, aristocrats. His favorite pupil was his own slave, Mysis.[10] Epicurus took as his mistress a courtesan (a kind of prostitute) named Leontium, and under his nurturing influence she wrote several books.

As you might expect, rumors were rampant about exactly what went on in the Garden. We can lose sight of the truly radical nature of Epicurus's understanding and tolerance if we judge it only in light of today's more enlightened attitudes. But in his time, the mere acceptance of all races, sexes, and social classes would have been enough to brand Epicurus as a dangerous and ungrateful rebel, regardless of his philosophical ideas. Yet he went well beyond theoretical tolerance, actively welcoming and encouraging all comers. Even in our own time, such an attitude is often met with fear and criticism.

PHILOSOPHICAL QUERY

Are you aware of any groups or institutions today that are as genuinely gracious and open to *all* comers as Epicurus's Garden seems to have been? What do you see as some of the advantages and disadvantages of such openness? Discuss.

Epicurus the Sage

Faith in immortality was born of the greed of unsatisfied people who make unwise use of the time that nature has allotted us. . . . For the wise man one human life is sufficient, and a stupid man will not know what to do with eternity.

Epicurus

Epicurus was generous and friendly in other matters as well. He regularly contributed his own money to the group and had a reputation for being a sympathetic companion and reasonable adviser.[11] Epicurus himself lived a simple and moderate life. He took as his motto "Live unobtrusively" (*lathe biosas*). He sought peace of mind, called *ataraxia.* He avoided the commotion of political involvement and remained detached from the hubbub of the world. It was reported that his regular diet consisted of modest amounts of bread, cheese, a little wine, and water.

His enemies claimed that he overindulged when he could get away with it and lived modestly only when others were watching and for show, but Diogenes Läertius disputes this. Epicurus himself was quite eloquent in this regard: "My body exalts in living delicately on bread and water and it rejects the pleasures of luxury, not in themselves, but because of the trouble that follows upon them."[12]

More than just a thinker or teacher (though he did write many books), Epicurus was regarded as a sage by his friends and pupils. He taught in the

Garden by example as well as by word for thirty-six years. His followers memorized his "golden maxims" and tried to model their lives after his. Many of them were inspired by his courage in the face of chronic ill health; he was apparently unable even to walk for many years because of gout. His disciples said that he continued to practice his philosophy and teach wisely right up to his death at the age of seventy-one. Even in his last, painful hours he thought of his friends, writing from his deathbed:

> I write to you on this happy day which is the last of my life. The obstruction of my bladder, and the internal pains, have reached the extreme point, but there is marshaled against them the delight of my mind in thinking over our talks together. Take care of Metrodorus' [his most famous pupil] children in a way worthy of your lifelong devotion to me and to philosophy.[13]

How many things I can do without!
Socrates

The Roman philosopher Seneca said that Epicurus's pupils saw him as a god among men, and that after his death their motto was "Live as though the eye of Epicurus were upon thee." He left his property to the Garden, in the hope "that all those who study philosophy may never be in want . . . so far as our power to prevent it may extend."[14] All in all, he was a gentle, friendly philosopher, who practiced what he believed to be true and tried to share his wisdom with others.

EPICUREAN PHILOSOPHY

Epicurus had studied the ideas of the materialistic philosopher **Democritus (c. 460–370 B.C.)**, which were based on the principle "Nothing can come from nothing." Following Democritus, Epicurus reasoned along these lines: If it were possible for something to come from nothing, then there would be no order in nature. A shoe might come from a stone, a pig from a daffodil. Put another way, to say that something can come from nothing amounts to saying that things can just pop into existence out of nowhere for no reason. Further, Epicurus reasoned, "Nothing can be dissolved into nothing." If things could break down into nothing (no-thing whatsoever), the universe would disappear, since each dying and decaying thing would ultimately disappear.

Epicurus says:

> The sum total of things was always such as it is now, and such as it will ever remain. For there is nothing into which it can change. For outside the sum of things there is nothing which could enter into it and bring about change.[15]

This means that all existence shares a common base: material atoms. Even gods and souls are made of matter. According to Epicurus, it is logically absurd to speak of existence without speaking of existing in some space.

The idea of a Being who interferes in the world is absolutely impossible. . . . A God who rewards and punishes is unthinkable because man acts in accordance with an inner and outer necessity, and would, in the eyes of God, be as little responsible as an inanimate object for the movements it makes.
Albert Einstein

And it is equally absurd to speak of existing "immaterially," without a bodily component (no matter how submicroscopic):

> Hence those who maintain that the soul is incorporeal [spiritual or non-material] speak foolishly: if it were so, it could neither act nor be acted upon, while we can clearly see both these properties [the power to act and to be acted upon] in the soul.[16]

Epicurus was not an original thinker in this area. He agreed in essence with Democritus and used his materialistic doctrine to make philosophical and psychological points. (See Chapter 3.)

Democritus had claimed that if *everything*—including soul or spirit—is really material, then God is too. If nothing can exist outside of the sum totality of things, the whole, then God must be part of the natural order. According to this line of reasoning, it is unintelligible and self-contradictory to speak of God, or anything, existing apart from nature. Where could God be? If the soul (or mind) is not physical, how, for example, can drinking beer (a physical act) intoxicate it?

Lin Yutang expresses this sense of the union of "spirit and flesh" exceptionally well:

> The most obvious fact which philosophers refuse to see is that we have got a body. Tired of seeing our moral imperfections and our savage instincts and impulses, sometimes our preachers wish that we were made like angels, and yet we are at a total loss to imagine what the angel's life would be like. We either give the angels a body and a shape like our own—except for a pair of wings—or we don't. . . . I sometimes think that it is an advantage even for angels to have a body with the five senses. If I were to be an angel, I should like to have a school-girl complexion, but how am I going to have a school-girl complexion without a skin? I still should like to drink a glass of tomato juice or iced orange juice, but how am I going to appreciate iced orange juice without having thirst? How would an angel paint without pigment, sing without the hearing of sounds, smell the fine morning air without a nose? How would he enjoy the immense satisfaction of scratching an itch, if his skin doesn't itch? And what a terrible loss in the capacity for happiness that would be! Either we have to have bodies and have all our bodily wants satisfied, or else we are pure spirits and have no satisfactions at all. All satisfactions imply want.
>
> I sometimes think what a terrible punishment it would be for a ghost or an angel to have no body, to look at a stream of cool water and have no feet to plunge into it and get a delightful cooling sensation from it, to see a dish of Peking or Long

It is not what earnest people renounce that makes me pity them, it is what they work for. . . . So much tension is hysterical and degrading; nothing is ever gained by it worth half what it spoils. Wealth is dismal and poverty cruel unless both are festive. There is no cure for birth and death save to enjoy the interval.

George Santayana

Island duck and have no tongue to taste it, to see crumpets and have no teeth to chew them, to see the beloved faces of our dear ones and have no emotions to feel toward them. Terribly sad it would be if we should one day return to this earth as ghosts and move silently into our children's bedroom, to see a child lying there in bed and have no hands to fondle him and no arms to clasp him, no chest for his warmth to penetrate to, no round hollow between cheek and shoulder for him to nestle against, and no ears to hear his voice.[17]

No civilized man ever regrets a pleasure, and no uncivilized man ever knows what a pleasure is.
Oscar Wilde

PHILOSOPHICAL QUERY

One of the most interesting and important timeless philosophical questions centers around the points raised here: Can we even conceive of nonmaterial, disembodied existence? Is the existence of a purely spiritual entity even comprehensible, much less possible or provable? Since this issue will recur in our survey of philosophical archetypes, you might as well begin to wrestle with it now. First, state the issue in your own words. Then see if you can clear it up. Finally, explain its significance to many of our most common beliefs.

Freedom from Religion

Epicurus believed that happiness results from peace of mind, or tranquillity. As he studied the world around him, he concluded that perhaps nothing was more confusing and disturbing to others than fear of death and fear of the gods. Epicurus rejected both concerns on "scientific grounds." As a *strict materialist*, he rejected the possibility of a supernatural (nonmaterial) existence.

Epicurus saved mankind from religion.
Lucretius

Apart from any logical difficulties with theories about the supernatural, just raising theological issues is frustrating and disturbing to most people. People have always argued with, lectured, tortured, and condemned one another over theological disagreements. If the purpose of life is the happiness that flows from a serene mind, then what could be more important than to free ourselves from this distressing quality of religion? Epicurus did not deny the existence of God (or gods). What he did, however, was just as upsetting to many: He rejected the most common conceptions of God.

From the time of Homer, the Greeks believed that good or bad circumstances resulted from the favor or disfavor of the gods. The gods of Olympus had to be worshiped, bribed, and flattered when they decided to meddle in human affairs. The struggle between moral skepticism and conventional morality that we saw in the chapters on the Sophists and Socrates continued during Epicurus's time.

One common reaction to political upheaval, social unrest, and intellectual doubt (such as that occurring in Greece at the time) is a renewal of religious fervor among some groups, often accompanied by an increase in

Since 1986, Sikh and Hindu extremists have clashed in India. In this 1987 picture, anti-Sikh rioters protest the killing of 34 Hindu bus passengers by Sikh terrorists. Today, religious disagreements exacerbate tensions in Eastern Europe, the Middle East, parts of Africa, and, of course, the United States. Such "holy wars" led Epicurus and Lucretius to seek to "free humankind from religion."

superstitious beliefs and practices. Many Greeks attributed practically every-thing to divine punishments or rewards. Everything was "prophetic," every decision full of risk: If the soul is immortal, then any failure to appease the gods could result in horrible punishment now or after death. So the be-liever had to be very sure that his or her choice of belief and practice was correct. As Epicurus saw it, religion created disagreement, anxiety, and fear. And this is why he considered his first task to be freeing us from the tyranny of religion.

Epicurus argued that the qualities attributed to the gods—jealousy, fa-voritism, inconsistency, susceptibility to praise and flattery, and so on—are too much like the qualities attributed to human beings.

> The gods do indeed exist, since our knowledge of them is a matter of clear and distinct perception; but they are not like what the masses suppose them to be, because most people do

not maintain a pure conception of the gods. The [sacrilegious] man is not the person who destroys the gods of the masses but the person who imposes the ideas of the masses on the gods. The opinions held by most people about the gods are not true conceptions of them but fallacious notions, according to which awful penalties are meted out to the evil and the greatest of blessings to the good. The masses, by assimilating the gods in every respect to their own moral qualities, accept deities similar to themselves and regard anything not of this sort as alien.[18]

If there are gods, Epicurus reasoned, surely they are happy. If they are incapable of being happy they cannot be gods. And if the gods are to be happy, they cannot depend on human behavior or beliefs, which are unreliable and inconsistent. Further, the gods cannot be concerned with rewarding or punishing human beings, since that would add worry to their own lives and so detract from their peace of mind. So, Epicurus concluded, the gods must be indifferent to human affairs if they are to be happy. Therefore, the gods do not interfere in the daily affairs of human beings.

The very first of Epicurus's *Leading Doctrines* is:

> The blessed and indestructible being of the divine has no concerns of its own, nor does it make trouble for others. It is not affected by feelings of anger or benevolence, because these are found where there is lack of strength.[19]

In other words, the divine nature is not troubled of itself and it causes no trouble for others. The divine nature is not influenced by either anger or favoritism, since to be influenced by others is characteristic only of the weak and unhappy. It is easier for us to be happy when God is indifferent to us than when He takes an interest in us. Epicurus has kept his promise. Given his radical conception of God, he has indeed freed us from religion.

PHILOSOPHICAL QUERY

Do you think of successes or calamities as rewards or punishments for doing or not doing God's will? If you do, how can you be *sure* that you're doing the True God's True Will instead of making a mistake? Answer carefully, trying to go beyond "I have faith" or "I just know." After all, other sincere people have faith that God's nature and will are otherwise.

Quality versus Quantity

Neither life nor death is good or bad of itself, Epicurus said; only the quality of our pleasures or pains is important. This is a major departure from Cyrenaic hedonism's emphasis on intensity (quantity). Rather than seek to have

The blessed and indestructible being of the divine has no concerns of its own, nor does it take trouble for others.
Epicurus

As for me, when you want a laugh, you will find me in fine fettle, fat and sleek, a hog from Epicurus's herd.
Horace

the most of anything, including the longest possible life span, the wise and sophisticated person chooses to have the finest.

Most people, however, recoil from death as though it were the greatest of evils; at other times they welcome it as the end-all of life's ills. The sophisticated person, on the other hand, neither begs off from living nor dreads not living. Life is not a stumbling block to him, nor does he regard not being alive as any sort of evil. As in the case of food he prefers the most savory dish to merely the larger portion, so in the case of time, he garners to himself the most agreeable moments rather than the longest span.[20]

Philosophers distinguish between what is desired and what is desirable. Practically anything can be desired by someone somewhere. But that does not mean that it is desirable. This distinction goes beyond Aristippus's "go for the gusto" to a much more disciplined and subtle concept. In Epicurus's words:

> Because of the very fact that pleasure is our primary and congenital good we do not select every pleasure; *there are times when we forgo certain pleasures, particularly when they are followed by too much unpleasantness. Furthermore, we regard certain states of pain as preferable to pleasures, particularly when greater satisfaction results from our having submitted to discomforts for a long period of time. Thus every pleasure is a good by reason of its having a nature akin to our own, but not every pleasure is desirable.* In like manner every state of pain is an evil, but not all pains are uniformly to be rejected. At any rate, it is our duty to judge all such cases by measuring pleasures against pains, with a view to their respective assets and liabilities, inasmuch as we do experience the good as being bad at times and, contrariwise, the bad as being good [emphasis added].[21]

Less Is More

A life of extremes almost always causes avoidable sufferings. Some are obvious: obesity or anorexia, sloth or stress, bankruptcy, unrelenting pressures to "keep up with the Joneses," and ultimately even boredom. A life of disciplined moderation avoids the excesses of overindulgence or asceticism (denying all pleasures). In the long run, according to Epicurus, the quiet pleasures of moderation produce the finest life.

> We consider limitation of the appetites a major good, and we recommend this practice not for the purpose of enjoying just a few things and no more but rather for the purpose of enjoying

TRULY HAPPY MOMENTS

To me, for instance, the truly happy moments are: when I get up in the morning after a night of perfect sleep and sniff the morning air and there is an expansiveness in the lungs, when I feel inclined to inhale deeply and there is a fine sensation of movement around the skin and muscles of the chest, and when, therefore, I am fit for work; or when I hold a pipe in my hand and rest my legs on a chair, and the tobacco burns slowly and evenly; or when I am travelling on a summer day, my throat parched with thirst, and I see a beautiful clear spring, whose very sound makes me happy, and I take off my socks and shoes and dip my feet in the delightful, cool water; or when after a perfect dinner I lounge in an armchair, when there is no one I hate to look at in the company and conversation rambles off at a light pace with the world; or when on a summer afternoon I see black clouds gathering on the horizon and know for certain a July shower is coming in a quarter of an hour, but being ashamed to be seen going out in the rain without an umbrella, I hastily set out to meet the shower halfway across the fields and come home drenched through and through and tell my family that I was simply caught by the rain.

Lin Yutang
The Importance of Living (New York: John Day, 1937), p. 127.

those few in case we do not have much. We are firmly convinced that those who need expensive fare least are the ones who relish it most keenly and that a natural way of life is easily procured, while trivialities are hard to come by. Plain foods afford pleasure equivalent to that of a sumptuous diet, provided that the pains of [abject poverty] are wholly eliminated. Barley bread and water yield the peak of pleasure whenever a person who needs them sets them in front of himself. Hence becoming habituated to a simple rather than a lavish way of life provides us with the full complement of health; it makes a person ready for the necessary business of life; it puts us in a position of advantage when we happen upon sumptuous fare at intervals and prepares us to be fearless in facing fortune.[22]

No one was ever better for sexual indulgence, and it is well if he be no worse.
Epicurus

Friendship

Epicurus founded the Garden to teach that only the wise, fully aware individual will be truly happy. Happiness cannot come from the gods, nor can it come from society or political action. The only truly useful and effective bond among individuals is friendship. Epicurean friendship is a free bond uniting individuals who share similar feelings, values, and lifestyles.[23] In

Although no words are spoken, there can be tacit understanding of another. A friend after one's own heart is hard to find. If you have got such a friend, what more can be lacking?

Lie Zi

true friendship, nothing can be imposed which is not natural and proper for each individual. In this way, nothing violates the essence of the individual. As Giovanni Reale notes, "Epicurus sees almost another self in the friend."[24] Epicurus transformed the notion of friendship into a way of bringing out the true self in each individual.

Even though everything Epicurus wrote fell under the law of hedonistic utility (maximize pleasure, minimize pain), he took care to treat friendship as something special:

> The virtuous man cultivates above all wisdom and friendship; and of these the one is a mortal good, the other is immortal.[25]

> Every friendship is *desirable of itself* even if it has begun from utility.[26]

> He is no friend who is continually asking for help, nor he who never associates help with friendship. For the one barters kindly feelings for a practical return and the other destroys the hope of every good for the future.[27]

> Friendship can go around the earth, proclaiming to us all to wake up in order to give joy to each other.[28]

The Epicurean Fallacy

Perhaps you associate the term *epicurean* with expensive tastes, exotic food and drink, elegant clothing, and a life devoted to the pursuit of such pleasures. If so, you are not alone. Even in Epicurus's time, many people mistakenly thought that Epicureanism was a philosophy of expensive self-indulgence. The **Epicurean fallacy** is the error of confusing the active pursuit of specialized pleasures with disciplined moderation and restraint. But for Epicurus, the highest pleasures are intellectual, and the greatest good is peace of mind, not intense or exquisite physical pleasure.

> Thus when I say that pleasure is the goal of living I do not mean the pleasures of libertines or the pleasures inherent in positive enjoyment, as is supposed by certain persons who are ignorant of our doctrine or who are not in agreement with it or who interpret it perversely. I mean, on the contrary, the pleasure that consists in freedom from bodily pain and mental agitation. The pleasant life is not the product of one drinking party after another or of sexual intercourse with women and boys or of the seafood and other delicacies afforded by a luxurious table. On the contrary, it is the result of sober thinking—namely, investigation of the reasons for every act of choice and aversion and elimination of those false ideas about the gods and death which are the chief source of mental disturbances.[29]

EPICUREAN FALLACY
Error of confusing the active pursuit of specialized pleasures with Epicurus's philosophy of disciplined moderation and restraint.

The only sin today seems to be moderation.

COMMENTARY

There is a problem with Cyrenaic hedonism which you may already have identified: the unreflective pursuit of pleasure tends to backfire. Living for the moment sounds good, but more often than not, tomorrow tends to arrive with a hefty price tag. Partying students tend to flunk out of school or end up in dead-end jobs or are arrested for driving under the influence or become burned out and depressed. One day I turn off the football game and notice that my wife no longer loves me and my children are in trouble. Beer and pizza no longer cut it. What then?

Contemporary hedonists point out that most of us actually do a pretty poor job of pursuing pleasure. The drawbacks of unrefined Cyrenaicism are obvious. Such a life is little more than an animal existence, reduced to the indiscriminate satisfaction of urges as they arise. Who but a glutton would prefer lots of fast food to a smaller amount of gourmet fare? What kind of person would prefer hundreds of sexual partners to one fine friendship? More is not necessarily better; instant is often inferior; the pleasures of the moment often have some long-term negative consequence.

More significant, the hedonist can point to the rather shabby quality of life we settle for. Crowded highways, noisy cities, and a polluted environment rob us of pleasurable experiences. Yet even when we consciously try to add pleasure to our lives, we may be overwhelmed by mediocrity. We can embark on a cross-country odyssey but repeat the limited experiences

Think about these and related matters day and night, by yourself and in company with someone like yourself. If you do, you will never experience anxiety, waking or sleeping, but you will live like a god among men. For a human being who lives in the midst of immortal blessings is in no way like mortal man!

Epicurus

THE PHILOSOPHICAL ENTERTAINER

Alan Watts (1915–1973) was an interesting figure who rose to prominence in the 1960s. After becoming an Episcopal priest, he gradually turned to Eastern philosophy and religion, founding the American Academy of Asian Studies in San Francisco during the 1950s. After leaving the priesthood, Watts became a popularizer of Zen Buddhism and then Taoism. Referring to himself as a "philosophical entertainer," Watts lived an increasingly hedonistic life. He advocated free love and Asian attire, praising, for example, the sensuous joys of the kimono's freedom and its silky, colorful beauty. He contrasted this with the "uptight," "unnatural," restrictive nature of Western dress, comparing the comfort of sandals to the torture of oxfords and high heels.

Watts is at his best in "Murder in the Kitchen," in *Does It Matter?* An excerpt follows:

. . . For the perfect accomplishment of any art, you must get the feeling of the eternal present in your bones—for it is the secret of proper timing. No rush. No dawdle. Just the sense of flowing with the course of events in the same way that you dance to music, neither trying to outpace it nor lagging behind. Hurrying and delaying are alike ways of trying to resist the present. . . . To try to have time, that is, to move as quickly as possible into the future gives you abstract food instead of real food. Instant coffee, for example, is a well-deserved punishment for being in a hurry to reach the future. So are TV dinners. So are the warmed over nastinesses usually served on airplanes, which taste like the plastic trays and dishes on which they are served. So is the meat which is not roasted but heated through in thirty-second electronic ovens. So are mixtures of grape juice and alcohol, prepared in concrete vaults, pretending to be wine. . . .

Abstractionists would, if possible, save time by eating the menu instead of the dinner. . . .

Happiness, I have discovered, is nearly always a rebound from hard work. . . . For happiness must be tricked!
David Grayson

we have at home by staying at bland motel chains, eating at franchised coffee shops and fast-food outlets, watching the same TV shows we do at home, listening to nearly identical radio stations, and shopping for the same brands in St. Louis that are available in Boise. Would a real hedonist prefer this safety, predictability, mediocrity?

Most of us choose our pleasures poorly. Lin and Watts (see box) were both convinced that America would be a much saner, healthier place if it were honestly and openly and wisely hedonistic. That is, rather than waste our time eating pap, listening to repetitive, copycat music, wearing the same clothes as everyone else, a gloriously, richly hedonistic society would reflect variety, quality, and joy—genuine diversity.

It is difficult to classify Lin Yutang, Alan Watts, or Walter Pater as strictly Epicurean or Cyrenaic hedonists, because both systems are probably inadequate guides to the good life. Epicureanism robs us of too much vigor and variety. It is a philosophy of retreat, one might even say of fear. The Epi-

Another way of eating the menu is preferring money to wealth—a psychic disorder directly related to the hallucination that time is a physical reality. To be fair, there are still some substantial and excellent products for sale in our supermarkets, but if you are bewitched by money, what happens? You take your loaded cart to the cashier, who clicks out a long strip of paper and says, "Thirty dollars and twenty-five cents, please!" You are suddenly depressed at having to part with so much "wealth"—not realizing that your wealth is now in the shopping bags and that you are going to walk out with it. For the money was a future, a "promise to pay," an abstraction now converted into present and substantial reality—and you are unhappy because you have exchanged the expectation of good things to come for actual goods!

Thus I have promised myself that when I reach the age of seventy, I shall retire to a mountain slope near the ocean and raise a small garden of herbs—culinary, medicinal, and psychedelic. Beside the garden I shall build a redwood barn where bunches of drying plants will hang from the beams, and where long shelves will be lined with jars and bottles of dulcamara and spikenard, ginseng and aloeswood, lobelia, mandragora, and cannabis, pennyroyal, horehound, and meadowsweet. There also I shall maintain an alchemist's laboratory-cum-kitchen with a library, and if the world presses too much in on me, my wife will respond to unwanted visitors in the words of Chia Tao's poem "Searching for the Hermit in Vain":

> The Master's gone alone
> Herb-picking, somewhere on the
>   mount,
> Cloud-hidden, whereabouts unknown.

Alan Watts
"Murder in the Kitchen," in *Does It Matter?* (New York: Vintage, 1970), pp. 33, 34, 35, 36, 55.

curean's efforts to avoid pain can lead to a withdrawal from life, a leveling of emotion that extracts a high price for tranquillity.

Cyrenaicism, on the other hand, provides a balance against living vicariously. When we reduce our lives to a mad dash to save time, when most of our experiences come from television, and we avoid the touch and taste and smell of life, we rob ourselves.

Why must we choose between safety and excess? If hedonism can be made into a viable philosophy, it will probably have to be as a balance between Cyrenaicism and Epicureanism. But there remain serious objections to hedonism in either form.

Aristippus was indifferent to social and political concerns, and Epicurus was perhaps too tempted by the Garden—tendencies that severely limit their philosophies. They also have the same problem the Sophists had: There is no criterion for condemning behavior that harms others. The only prohibition the hedonist can offer is trivial: We shouldn't harm others if doing so

When someone brought his son as a pupil, [Aristippus] asked a fee of 500 drachmae. The father objected, "For that sum I can buy a slave." "Then do so," was [Aristippus's] reply, "and you will have two."

Diogenes Läertius

will cause us pain. But this position is amoral by most standards, since the moral dimension of life is usually thought to include duties and obligations to ourselves *and* others. And wisdom, as the *sophos* knew, always includes a moral dimension.

Why advocate hedonism if by nature we all seek pleasure and avoid pain? There is no more point to advising us to do this than there is to advising us to eat. The hedonist might respond that just because we are compelled by nature to eat, it does not follow that we eat wisely or well. Similarly, there is much to gain from learning how to pursue pleasure wisely. This leads to a last comment.

Moral philosophers talk about the **hedonistic paradox**: The harder we try to be happy, the harder it is to be happy. Put differently, if I make having a good time the most important thing in my life, it becomes more difficult to do than if I pursue a variety of interests and goals, and have a good time along the way. We have probably all had the experience of anticipating some special occasion to such a degree that once the event arrived we were somehow disappointed.

Philosophers and armchair psychologists have long known that the most fulfilling lives are rarely hedonistic. Happiness seems to be a by-product of other things. That is not to say that hedonism has no merit, for it is as easy to lose sight of what is genuinely pleasurable as it is to be hypnotized by the mindless pursuit of pleasure.

HEDONISTIC PARADOX
The harder we try to be happy, the harder it is to be happy.

SUMMARY OF MAIN POINTS

Hedonism is the general term for any philosophy that says that pleasure is identical with good and pain is identical with evil. Hedonists stress either the pursuit of pleasure or the avoidance of pain.

The principle of hedonistic utility advocates maximizing pleasure and minimizing pain.

Philosophers distinguish two main forms of hedonism: Psychological hedonism is the belief that it is psychologically impossible for human beings not to base all decisions on seeking pleasure or avoiding pain. Ethical hedonism is the belief that it is possible to deliberately avoid pleasure or choose pain, but that it is morally wrong to do so.

Aristippus was the founder of Cyrenaic hedonism, the doctrine that pleasure is always good regardless of its source, and that pleasures can be compared only in terms of intensity. Because the strongest

pleasure is the best, physical pleasures are better than mental or emotional pleasures.

Cyrenaic hedonism rests on a subjectivist epistemology that we can know only what pleases or displeases us at the moment; knowledge of objective causes is impossible.

Strict Cyrenaic hedonists believe that all pleasures of the same intensity are equal. They deny the possibility of qualitative differences among pleasures.

Aestheticism is an amoral form of hedonism that focuses on the worship of beauty and beautiful objects. Oscar Wilde and Walter Pater were advocates of aestheticism.

Christopher Lasch coined the term "new narcissists" to refer to individuals who live only for themselves and for the moment, who feel free to walk

away from social roles whenever they become too confining or boring in order to pursue self-fulfillment, personal growth, and so forth, entirely on their own terms.

Epicurean hedonism is a more refined doctrine than Cyrenaic hedonism. Epicurus advocated the intelligent avoidance of pain rather than the pursuit of intense pleasure. He pointed out that intense pleasures tend to come at the price of significant pain: hangovers, financial problems, health problems, legal problems, and so forth.

Epicurus based his philosophy in part on the materialist philosophy of Democritus. He denied the existence of a supernatural world and disputed common conceptions of the gods, claiming that because no one knows for sure what the gods want, attempts to do their will produce anxiety and worry. He reasoned that even if there are gods they will be indifferent to human beings, because worrying about us would cause the gods to suffer. Epicurus said that his philosophy freed us from the worries of religion.

Epicurus believed in qualitative differences among pleasures, distinguishing what is commonly desired from what is truly desirable. Having made this distinction, he argued that the quiet pleasures of moderation produce the finest life.

According to Epicurus, friendship is a most important virtue because through genuine friendship the true self of each friend emerges. He founded the Garden as a haven for friends to gather and share intelligent conversation and quiet pleasures.

Identifying philosophical Epicureanism with expensive self-indulgence results in the Epicurean fallacy, the error of confusing the active pursuit of specialized pleasures with disciplined moderation and restraint.

STUDY QUESTIONS

1. What is hedonism? What are psychological and ethical hedonism?

2. Identify some hedonistic elements in Judeo-Christian beliefs.

3. What was Aristippus's relationship to Socrates?

4. Construct a brief debate between Aristippus and Socrates. Use actual statements made by both philosophers.

5. Characterize Cyrenaic hedonism.

6. In your own words, give a Cyrenaic argument in favor of living for the moment.

7. Make a convincing counterargument against living for the moment.

8. What was the Cyrenaic's basic epistemology?

9. Analyze the claim that all pleasures are equal.

10. What is the "new narcissism"? Analyze it.

11. What kind of hedonist was Walter Pater? Justify your response.

12. Make your own case supporting the claim that we live in a Cyrenaic society.

13. What is Epicureanism, and how does it differ from Cyrenaicism?

14. What was so special about the Garden?

15. What is the Epicurean fallacy?

16. Discuss Epicurus's attitude toward religion. Do you agree with it? Why?

17. Compare and contrast Epicureanism and Cyrenaicism in terms of how each views pleasure.

18. Compare and contrast the Epicurean and Cyrenaic views of the good life.

19. What would Alan Watts and Lin Yutang say about pleasure in today's society?

20. *Is* this a hedonistic society? Make your case either way.

21. Are the psychological hedonists right? Explain.

CHAPTER NINE

The Stoic:

Epictetus and

Marcus Aurelius

You shame yourself, my soul, you shame your-self, and you will have no further opportunity to respect yourself; the life of every man is short and yours is almost fin-ished while you do not respect yourself but allow your happiness to depend upon . . . others.

MARCUS AURELIUS, EMPEROR OF ROME

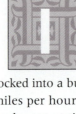t's the Friday before a three-day weekend and you are looking forward to a romantic vacation on the beach with your special friend. You get off work a bit late and head for the bank to get some cash. Pulling onto the freeway, you're immediately locked into a bumper-to-bumper mass of vehicles, lurching along at fifteen miles per hour. Forty-five minutes later, still a couple of miles from the bank, you notice that you're low on fuel. You begin to steam. Someone tries to cut in front of you and you explode in a rage, shaking your fist and shouting obscenities. When you finally get to the bank, there's no place to park.

After circling the parking lot for twenty minutes, you manage to park. The line in the bank looks endless and there are only three tellers. The man in front of you has a bag of checks and cash from his business. You continue to steam. It seems like every customer chats with the tellers. And the tellers! It takes them forever to do anything. As you inch along in line you glare at various bank officers in order to let them know how angry you are at the inefficient way they run their bank.

By the time you get out of the bank, you're behind schedule and it's rush hour—pre-holiday, Friday-afternoon rush hour. You race out of the parking lot, squealing your tires as you cut into traffic. Rushing through an intersection at high speed, you catch the attention of a police officer. It's not enough that you get a ticket for reckless driving, the officer takes forever checking out your license and writing the ticket. When you finally get going again, you feel like a bomb about to go off.

If you have ever had an experience anything close to the one just described, you've shared the nearly universal sense of frustration, anger, and anxiety caused by "stupid people" and "events beyond our control." This kind of reaction to external events is so common that a school of philosophy sprang up to deal with just such experiences, among other things. Yet its basic tenets go against the grain for most people, at least initially. It is called **Stoicism**, and those who practice it are called **Stoics**.

Stoicism initially emerged as a reaction against hedonism. Whereas the hedonist seeks pleasure or avoids pain, the Stoic seeks serenity (peace of mind) through self-discipline. Stoicism asserts that seeking anything but self-control results in *avoidable* unhappiness. Happiness comes only through detachment from all "externals." Put another way: Everything is a matter of attitude. The disciplined, reasonable person can be happy under any and all conditions.

Stoics believe that *nothing can make you happy or unhappy without your consent*. All unhappiness is the result of bad thinking, poor character, and confusing what we can control with what we cannot control. Regarding the opening story, a Stoic would diagnose your frustration and anger as self-induced. Traffic jams, lines and crowds, little brothers, dumb sweethearts, and cars

STOICISM
Philosophy that counsels self-control, detachment, and acceptance of one's fate as identified by the objective use of reason.

STOIC
Individual who attempts to live according to Stoic doctrine.

running out of gas are normal, common aspects of life. There is nothing new or surprising in anything that happens to you. In fact, nothing "happens to you." *You* are the problem.

PHILOSOPHICAL QUERY

Stop for a moment and reflect on this: Is it possible to be calm under all circumstances? Or do certain circumstances *force* us to be distressed and agitated? How, then, can we explain the incredible feats of Hindu yogis who can control their blood pressure, heart rates, even whether they bleed?

Why do some people seem happy in horrible circumstances, while others suffer in the midst of being loved, healthy, and financially well-off?

Do you think happiness is all a matter of attitude or not? Discuss.

Your medicine is in you,
and you do not observe it.
Your ailment is from yourself,
and you do not register it.
Hazrat Ali

THE CYNICAL ORIGINS OF STOICISM

The origins of Stoicism go back to the Cynics. **Cynicism** was a philosophic "school" only in the loosest sense. Founded by **Antisthenes (c. 455–360 B.C.)**, its most famous proponent was **Diogenes (c. 412–323 B.C.)**. As a philosophical school, Cynicism existed from the fourth century B.C. until the sixth century A.D., although by the first century A.D. its reputation had seriously diminished.

Although the Cynics revolted against the rigidly ordered philosophies of Plato and Aristotle, they admired Socrates. Socrates was the model on which Antisthenes built his philosophy, and, by extension, Socrates was a model for the Stoics. It is said that Antisthenes walked almost five miles every day to hear Socrates.

Antisthenes was apparently more impressed with Socrates' lifestyle and character than with his philosophical ideas, though he, too, sought to base his life on the rule of reason. Socrates' disdain for fashion, his ragged, functional clothing, lack of shoes, ability not to sleep or eat for long periods, his physical toughness and forthright honesty made a tremendous impression on the young Cynic.

After Socrates' death, Antisthenes founded a school called the Cynosarges (the Silver Dog). The word **Cynic** comes from the Greek word for "dog," and this label was later given to Diogenes because he "lived like a dog." That is, he was unwashed and rough-looking; he scrounged for food; and refused to follow conventional standards of dress and behavior.

Because Antisthenes attended some lectures of Gorgias the Sophist, and because he stayed so close to Socrates, it is not surprising that he was especially affected by Socrates' stinging attacks on such sophistic values as power,

CYNICISM
Philosophy based on the belief that the very essence of civilization is corrupt and that civilization destroys individuals by making them soft and subject to the whims of fortune.

CYNIC
Individual who lives an austere, unconventional life based on Cynic doctrine.

"A SOCRATES GONE MAD"

Diogenes studied under Antisthenes, who, by the way, hated students. Diogenes took his master's teachings to heart and went him one better. Being called a dog was not enough for him; he actually lived with a pack of stray dogs.

Alexander the Great (356–323 B.C.), having heard of Diogenes, made a point of meeting him. Diogenes was sitting on the seashore when the magnificent, handsome young king of Greece and conqueror of the known world rode up on his powerful charger. Looking down on the reclining Cynic, he said:

"I am Alexander the Great."
"I am Diogenes, the dog," replied the Cynic.

"The dog?"
"I nuzzle the kind, bark at the greedy, and bite louts."
"What can I do for you?" asked the Ruler of the World.
"Stand aside, you're blocking my light."

So impressed was Alexander with the uncompromising character of Diogenes that he later said, "If I were not Alexander, I would be Diogenes."

This sketch is based on material in Guy Davenport's *Herakleitos and Diogenes* (San Francisco: Grey Fox Press, 1979), pp. 35–37.

Discourse on virtue and they pass by in droves; whistle and dance the shimmy, and you've got an audience.
Diogenes

I can see Antisthenes' vanity through the holes in his cloak.
Plato

celebrity, prestige, wealth, and clever deception. The Cynics despised the widespread hedonism and hypocrisy that they saw throughout Athens. They believed that the very essence of civilization is corrupt: manners are hypocritical and phony; material wealth weakens people, making them physically and morally soft; the desire for success and power produces dishonesty and dependency; flattery, fashion, and convention destroy the individual and make him or her vulnerable to the whims of fortune. And as the tragic death of Socrates underscored, not even the wisest person can control other people or external events.

So the less an individual needs to be happy, the less vulnerable he or she is. Diogenes, for example, lived in an abandoned wine barrel on the beach, and once said: "When I saw a child drinking from his hand, I threw away my cup." The Cynics lived austere, unconventional lives. They distrusted luxury as a "hook" which always brought complications and ultimately frustration into people's lives. What happiness was possible, according to the Cynics, came from self-discipline, rational control of all desires and appetites, and minimal contact with conventional society.

The hedonist Epicurus also emphasized a simple life and the avoidance of pain, rather than a mad rush to acquire pleasures and luxuries. For example, Epicurus said that "all bodily suffering is negligible; for that which causes intense pain has a brief duration, and that which endures long in the flesh causes mild pain."[1] But the Cynics still found Epicureanism too

Diogenes preferred the free rent of an abandoned wine barrel and the company of dogs to the softening corruptions of sophisticated pleasures and the degradation of currying favor with so-called important people.

soft, too conventional, and too dependent to suit them. The Epicureans relied too much on their friends and certain "proper" pleasures. Cynicism was rough-and-tumble. Its most famous advocates were sarcastic and hostile toward conventions and institutions. They relied only on themselves.

Few Cynics exhibited the moral or intellectual virtues of Antisthenes or Diogenes, and eventually Cynicism fell into disrepute. The popular image of the Cynic was a hostile, arrogant individual who despised everyone else and hated the society in which he lived. Indiscriminate scorn and contempt for practically everything replaced penetrating social criticism.

Today the terms *cynic* and *cynical* are commonly used to refer to a general attitude of basic contempt for people, an excessively hostile or critical stance, or a tendency to distrust other people's motives.

The Stoics, however, agreed with the original Cynics' assessment of Socrates. They accepted the basic Cynic premise that excessive desires always lead to unhappiness. Like the Cynics, the Stoics valued self-control, courage, and dignity. The Stoic Epictetus characterized the "true Cynic, the free open-air spirit," as one saying to himself:

> "Henceforth, my mind is the material I have to work on, as the carpenter has his timber and the shoemaker his leather: my business is to deal with my impressions aright. My wretched body is nothing to me, its parts are nothing to me. Death? Let it come when it will, whether to my whole body or part of it. Exile? Can one be sent into exile beyond the Universe? One cannot. Wherever I go, there is the sun, there is the moon, there are the stars, dreams . . . conversation with the gods." The true Cynic when he has ordered himself thus . . . must know that he is sent as a messenger from God to men concerning things good and evil, to show them that they have gone astray and are seeking the true nature of good and evil where it is not to be found.[2]

Let us see how the Stoics built on basic Cynic principles.

Plato winces when I track dust across his rugs: he knows that I'm walking on his vanity.

Diogenes

THE SLAVE AND THE EMPEROR

Though the philosophical school known as Stoicism was founded in Greece by **Zeno (c. 334–262 B.C.)** around 300 B.C., it flourished in Rome. Zeno used to lecture at a place called the *stoa poikile*, or painted porch; the term *Stoic* comes from *stoa*—originally Stoics were "men of the porch."

Under Alexander the Great, Greece conquered the Persian empire (what is now Iran and Iraq) and established Greek rule over a large area of the Near East and Egypt. As a result, Greek culture became more sophisticated and cosmopolitan, absorbing ideas and customs from the cultures it conquered. As the Greek empire expanded, the importance of individual city-states such as Athens and Sparta diminished and people identified themselves as part of a larger, more international community.

Alexander's empire was unstable, however, and began to fall apart almost immediately after his death. For most of the third century B.C. no single dominant power emerged in the Mediterranean regions. By the middle of the second century B.C., Rome had destroyed what was left of Alexander's kingdom and annexed Greece as a Roman province called Achaia. By 100 B.C., Rome essentially controlled the entire Mediterranean area.

The Romans were not particularly interested in abstract, speculative thinking. Pragmatic and religiously tolerant, they borrowed heavily from Greek culture, including philosophy. Given their interest in establishing social order, the Romans were especially attracted to the Stoics' emphasis on duty and self-control. It especially appealed to the Romans' sense of *virility*.

To the Romans, virility meant manliness, courage, and moral strength. It did not, as it does today, refer to "macho" qualities or masculine sexuality. The English word *virtue* comes from the same root as *virile*.

The two most philosophically influential Stoics are a Roman slave and a Roman emperor: Epictetus and Marcus Aurelius. The Roman senator Seneca, although not a particularly original thinker, was one of the finest Stoic writers. We will be using some of his *Discourses* and Moral Letters to supplement our two main sources.

For many years, Stoic literature has been some of the most popular of all philosophical writings. Let us see why as we encounter the archetype of the Stoic in two radically different forms: a slave and an emperor.

Epictetus: From Slave to Sage

Stoicism appealed to Romans living in times of great uncertainty under emperors of widely differing abilities and virtues. It spread throughout the Roman world because it was advocated by three important public figures: **Cicero (106–43 B.C.), Cato (95–46 B.C.)**, and **Seneca (c. 4 B.C.–A.D. 65)**. But, ironically, one of the most important Stoic philosophers was a former slave named **Epictetus (c. A.D. 50–130)**. Perhaps because a slave's life is not his own, Epictetus acquired special insight into the major issue of Stoicism: controlling what we can and accepting what is beyond our control.

Epictetus

We do not know much about Epictetus's early life. His mother was a slave living in Hierapolis, a city in the Asia Minor province of Phrygia. Epictetus was brought to Rome as the slave of a former slave named Epaphroditus, who seems to have been Nero's administrative secretary. Epictetus must have demonstrated unusual abilities, for Epaphroditus sent the youth Epictetus to study with Musonius Rufus, the most powerful Stoic since the days of Zeno. Even so, Epictetus never lost sight of the fact that he could be bought or sold, pampered or tortured, at his owner's whim. As a slave, he was constantly reminded that what happened to him had no bearing on his own wishes or behavior. As a slave, the only absolute control Epictetus had was over his own reactions to what happened. His motto was *Anechou kai apechou*: Bear and forbear.

Epictetus was once so badly tortured—for another slave's mistake—that his broken leg did not heal properly, and he limped for the rest of his life. The story goes that as his leg was being twisted, Epictetus reminded his master that a person's leg was likely to break under such torture. Epaphroditus ignored this, and when his leg finally broke, Epictetus said, "See, it's just as I told you." He later said, "I was never more free than when I was on the rack." He had learned that he could control his attitude, but that fate controlled his life:

> If the captain calls, let all those things go and run to the boat without turning back; and if you are old, do not even go very

For we come into the world with no innate conception of a right-angled triangle or of a semi-tone, but we are taught what each of these means by systematic instruction. . . . On the other hand every one has come into the world with an innate conception as to good and bad, noble and shameful, becoming and unbecoming, happiness and unhappiness, fitting and inappropriate, what is right to do and what is wrong.

Epictetus

Lameness is an impediment to the leg, but not to the Will; and say this to yourself with regard to everything that happens. For you will find such things to be an impediment to something else, but not truly to yourself.

Epictetus

far from the boat, so that when the call comes you are not left behind.[3]

Ultimately freed sometime after Nero's death in the year 68, Epictetus became a well-known teacher. Sometime around the year 90, all the philosophers were ordered out of Rome by the emperor Domitian, who was angry about the encouragement certain Stoics had given to those who opposed him. Epictetus fled to Nicopolis in northern Greece, where he taught until he was very old. He was a popular teacher, and his schools in both Rome and Nicopolis throve during his lifetime.

A modest man, famed for his sweetness and simplicity, Epictetus lived in a sparely furnished house, content with a straw mat and pallet for a bed and a clay lamp (after his iron one was stolen). He was especially loving toward children, and he was charitable toward all those who came to him for advice and guidance. Following the example of Socrates, he published nothing. His ideas have come down to us in the form of the class notes of his student Flavius Arrianus, called the *Discourses*, and a truly remarkable set of excerpts from them called the *Enchiridion*, also known as the *Manual* or *Handbook* (because it was made into hand-sized books that were carried into the field by Roman soldiers.)[4]

Marcus Aurelius: Philosopher-King

Marcus Aurelius

To pursue the unattainable is insanity, yet the thoughtless can never refrain from doing so.

Marcus Aurelius

Marcus Aurelius Antoninus (A.D. 121–180) was bound by duty. By temperament a scholar and a recluse, he lived surrounded with commotion, deception, and crowds. Marcus so impressed the emperor Hadrian that he advised Marcus's uncle Aurelius Antoninus (commonly known as Antoninus Pius) to adopt Marcus. When Marcus was forty, Antoninus Pius, then emperor, appointed him heir, over Pius's other adopted son, Lucius Verus. From the beginning of his reign, Marcus faced calamity and disruption.

When Pius died in 161, Marcus generously named his stepbrother Verus co-emperor—against the wishes of the senate—but got little help from him. All the serious work of governing was done by Marcus. As emperor, he was obliged to contend with flatterers, liars, and enemies. He was regularly dragged away from Rome to deal with uprisings and barbarian invasions along the frontiers. He was betrayed by a trusted general, and spent the last years of his life away from home on a difficult military campaign. He suffered through the deaths of four of his five sons, and even endured unsubstantiated rumors that his wife took many lovers in his absence and that his sole surviving son was not his own. To himself, he wrote:

> Everywhere and at all times it is in thy power piously to acquiesce in thy present condition, and to behave justly to those who are about thee, and to exert thy skill upon thy present

thoughts, that nothing shall steal into them without being examined.[5]

Marcus was loved by many Romans for his kindness and mercy. He refused to turn away from his incompetent stepbrother, choosing instead to carry out both their duties until Verus died in 169, after which Marcus ruled alone. He convinced the senate to pardon the family of the traitorous general, when other emperors would have destroyed it. He stood by his wife as cruel rumors about her virtue spread everywhere and his own soldiers mocked his masculinity. He went so far as to promote those accused of being her lovers when doing so was good for Rome.

> Let it make no difference to thee whether thou art cold or warm, if thou art doing thy duty; and whether thou art drowsy or satisfied with sleep; and whether ill-spoken of or praised; and whether dying or doing something else. For it is one of the acts of life, the act by which we die: it is sufficient then in this act also to do well what we have in hand.[6]

Marcus Aurelius was the last truly great figure of Imperial Rome, combining classical philosophy with a spiritual quality that foreshadowed the Christian-influenced Scholasticism of the Middle Ages. He was also one of the kindest, wisest, and most virtuous philosophers.

> Only attend to thyself, [Marcus,] and resolve to be a good man in every act which thou doest; and remember. . . . Look within. Within is the fountain of good, and it will ever bubble up, if thou wilt ever dig.[7]

His last years were hard and lonely, spent on a military campaign along the Danube. Yet rather than succumb to bitterness or lash out at others, he sought solace in philosophy. Late at night, after his public duties were done, he did his duty to his soul, sitting alone in his tent writing what are popularly known as his *Meditations*, but which he addressed "To Myself." This journal is one of the finest, most widely read examples of both Stoic thought and personal reflection in Western literature.

On this last campaign, Marcus Aurelius, a man once described as "by nature a saint and sage, by profession a warrior and ruler," died at the age of fifty-nine, worn down by fatigue and toil.[8]

THE FATED LIFE

Though fate is an important aspect of their philosophy, the Stoics were rather imprecise about what it meant in specific terms. In some mysterious way, the actual course of our lives is directed by the *Logos*, which the Stoics thought of as World Reason or Cosmic Mind

---

People find no rest because of four pursuits—long life, reputation, office, possessions. Whoever has these four goals dreads spirits, fears other men, cowers before authority, and is terrified of punishment. I call him "a man in flight from things." He can be killed, he can be given life; the destiny which decides [his state of mind] is outside him.
Yang Zhu

For humans, a life of hardship is the norm and death is the end. Abiding by the norm, awaiting my end, what is there to be concerned about?
Rong Qiqi

Misfortune is not fate but providence.
Sarvepalli Radhakrishnan

WHY SHOULD ANYWHERE I GO NOT BE ALL RIGHT?

One of the great joys of learning is the discovery of common themes and threads. This is especially so in matters of wisdom. The great sages are at their most powerful when they speak of acceptance in the face of great hardship. Sometimes, it seems as if one spirit speaks with many voices and accents. Compare this passage from Chuang-tzu with the passage from Marcus Aurelius on page 248.

Tzu-lai fell ill, was gasping for breath and was about to die. His wife and children surrounded him and wept. . . . He said, "Don't disturb the transformation that is about to take place." Then, leaning against the door, he continued, "Great is the Creator! What will he make of you now? Where will he take you? Will he make you into a rat's liver? Will he make you into an insect's leg?"

Tzu-lai said, "Wherever a parent tells a son to go, whether east, west, south, or north, he has to obey. The yin and yang are like a man's parents. If they pressed me to die and I disobeyed, I would be obstinate. What fault is theirs? For the universe gave me the body so I may be carried, my life so I may toil, my old age so I may repose, and my death so I may rest. Therefore, to regard life as good is the way to regard death as good.

"Suppose a master foundryman is casting his metal and the metal leaps up and says, 'I must be made into the best sword. . . .' The master foundryman would certainly consider the metal as evil. And if simply because I possess a body by chance, I were to say, 'Nothing but a man! Nothing but a man!' the Creator will certainly regard me as evil. If I regard the universe as a great furnace and creation as a foundryman, why should anywhere I go not be all right?"

Chuang-tzu
In Wing-Tsit Chan, trans. and comp., *A Source Book in Chinese Philosophy* (Princeton, N.J.: Princeton University Press, 1963), p. 197.

To live under the false pretense that you will forever have control of your station in life is to ride for a fall; you're asking for disappointment. So make sure in your heart of hearts, in your inner self, that you treat your station in life with indifference, *not with contempt, only with* indifference.
James Bond Stockdale

(see Chapter 3). Sometimes the Logos is referred to as God, Zeus, Nature, Providence, Cosmic Meaning, or Fate. Seneca says:

> We are all chained to [fate]. . . . All of us are in custody, the binders as well as the bound . . . some are chained by office, some by wealth; some weighed down by high birth, some by low; some are subject to another's tyranny, some to their own; some are confined to one spot by banishment, some by a priesthood. All life is bondage.[9]

The Stoics learned, as many of us do, that our lives are not entirely our own. This discovery did not, at least in the cases of Epictetus and Marcus Aurelius, lead to despair or escapist indulgence, but to a shift in the focus of responsibility. Rather than complain about what they could not control, the Stoics chose to master what they could: their own minds. By mastering their thoughts, they believed, they could master their feelings. Serenity comes to that individual whose will is in accord with the World Reason, the Logos, for right thinking leads to a reduction of frustration and anxiety. In the words of Epictetus:

> Remember that thou art an actor in a play, of such a kind as the author may choose: if short, a short one; if long, a long one: if he wishes you to act the part of a poor man, see that you act the part naturally: if the part of a lame man, of a magistrate, of a private person (do the same). For this is your duty, to act well the part that was given to you; but to select the part belongs to another.[10]

The Stoic Logos

Under the guidance of the Logos the universe remains rational and ordered. Epictetus said, "Events do not just happen, but arrive by appointment." Everything that occurs is connected to everything else. Everything that exists is connected to the Logos. Our individual minds are "emanations" or "sparks" from the Logos, which is sometimes characterized as "fire." (The Stoics borrowed this idea from Heraclitus.) Our finite human reason is, thus, a small reflection of divine reason. Seneca puts it like this:

> We do not need to lift our hands to heaven . . . God is near you, with you, inside you. Yes . . . there is a holy spirit abiding within us. . . . No man is good without god.[11]

The ideas of a rationally ordered universe and our intimate relation to the Logos are central aspects of Stoicism. If the universe is divinely ordered, then there is a plan. Things happen to us for a reason—a divinely ordained reason.

If this is true, then nothing that happens can be "wrong" or "bad," since everything that happens is part of God's rational plan. When I truly grasp this, I will no longer fear for the future nor complain about the past or present, but can remain calm like Zeno when he heard that all his possessions were lost in a shipwreck and said, "Fortune bids me philosophize with a lighter pack."

What can I do, then, if the course of my life's events is beyond my control? The Stoic answers that I can concentrate on developing an attitude of courageous acceptance. My efforts should be directed toward that part of my life over which I exert absolute control: my attitudes, or my will.

PHILOSOPHICAL QUERY

Do you agree that the test of faith is anxiety? Are the Stoics correct in insisting that one who truly realizes that *everything* is governed by a divine plan will lose all fear and anxiety? Justify your position.

LOGOS (STOIC)
According to Stoic doctrine, World Reason, also referred to as Cosmic Mind, God, Zeus, Nature, Providence, Cosmic Meaning, and Fate; force that governs the universe; also see Chapter 3.

Reason or a halter.
Diogenes

*Do to me what is worthy
of Thee
And not what is worthy
of me.*
Saadi

Either belief in God is unconditional or it is not belief at all.
Viktor E. Frankl

The Disinterested Rational Will

If we are "bits" of the Logos, it follows that our virtue and happiness will consist in being as much like the Logos as possible. Being perfectly rational, the Logos is not partisan; that is, the Logos is objective. It is calm and serene, viewing events with "disinterest." Seneca says:

> Just as the rays of the sun do indeed warm the earth but remain at the source of their radiation, so a great and holy soul is lowered to earth to give us a nearer knowledge of the divine; but though it is in intercourse with us, it cleaves to its source . . . it looks toward it, it seeks to rejoin it, and its concern with our affairs is superior and detached.[12]

Glory be to that God
Who slays our wives and
destroys our children
And Whom withal we love.
Prayer of Attar

To be *disinterested* is to have no *personal* attachments or motives. For example, a judge or a teacher should be disinterested when she passes sentence or grades papers—she should not play favorites. Marcus Aurelius was disinterested when he promoted the men accused of being his wife's lovers.

The Stoics make an intriguing case that our best chance for happiness is to adopt a disinterested attitude toward our own lives, as well as toward all life. The Stoics thought such a perspective would result not in a world of self-centered isolationists, but in a sense of universal communion and duty. Turning to the Logos meant looking beyond the particular laws, customs, and prejudices of one's self and society and rejecting them if they deviate from Nature/Logos. Unlike the hedonist's evaluation of the welfare of others only in terms of one's own happiness, the Stoics viewed all humans as citizens of a "universal city," a *cosmopolis*. The hedonist is indifferent to others; the Stoic is indifferent to self. When our duties are dictated by disinterested reason, not custom or personal preference, we become members of a community, a human fellowship.

Marcus Aurelius alludes to universal fellowship in this beautiful passage:

Which of you by worrying
can add a moment to his
life-span?
Jesus, Matthew 6:26

> It is man's peculiar distinction to love even those who err and go astray. Such a love is born as soon as you realize that they are your brothers; that they are stumbling in ignorance, and not willfully; that in a short while both of you will be no more; and, above all, that you yourself have taken no hurt, for your master-reason has not been made a jot worse than it was before.
>
> Out of the universal substance, as out of wax, Nature fashions a colt, then breaks him up and uses the material to form a tree, and after that a man, and next some other thing: and not one of these endures for more than a brief span. As for the vessel itself, it is no greater hardship to be taken to pieces than to be put together. . . .
>
> Only a little while, and Nature, the universal disposer, will change everything you see, and out of their substance will

make fresh things, and yet again others from theirs, to the perpetual renewing of the world's youthfulness.[13]

PHILOSOPHICAL QUERY

Discuss the advantages and disadvantages of disinterestedness. When is it a virtue? When is it not? Give some examples, and explain them.

What is the fruit of your Stoic doctrines, someone once asked Epictetus. "Tranquility, fearlessness, and freedom," he answered.

Whereas other philosophies distinguished between good and bad emotions according to various criteria, the Stoics rejected emotion to the extent it was humanly possible. The best attitude, they claimed, was rational, detached acceptance.[14] Seneca says:

> Philosophers of our school reject the emotions; the [Aristotelian] Peripatetics keep them in check. I, however, do not understand how any half-way disease can be either wholesome or helpful. . . .
>
> "But," you object, "it is natural for me to suffer when I am bereaved of a friend; grant some privileges to tears which have the right to flow! It is also natural to be affected by men's opinions and to be cast down when they are unfavourable; so why should you not allow me such an honorable aversion to bad opinion?"
>
> There is no vice which lacks some plea. . . . we are in love with our vices; we uphold them and prefer to make excuses for them rather than shake them off. We mortals have been endowed with sufficient strength by nature, if only we use this strength. . . . The real reason for failure is unwillingness, the pretended reason, inability.[15]

Controlling your emotions is difficult but can be empowering.
James Bond Stockdale

STOIC WISDOM

By the time of Marcus Aurelius, Stoicism had a religious quality that made it especially attractive to the growing Christian community in the Roman world. As we have seen, classical philosophies were naturalistic: they placed rational humanity at the center of things. By contrast, Christian values place a personal God at the center. Though the Stoics were classical in their emphasis on the impersonal Logos as being material, and on reason and self-control of the human will as the means to salvation, they also anticipated Christianity in their emphasis on the divine will and on our submission to it. As you will see, many of the Stoics' specific lessons also have a decidedly Judeo-Christian flavor to them. Thus Stoicism stands as the most influential transitional philosophy between classical and Christian values.

[T]he lecture-room of the philosopher is the hospital; students ought not to walk out of it in pleasure, but in pain.
Epictetus

Some things are up to us and some are not up to us. Our opinions are up to us, and our impulses, desires, aversions. . . . Our bodies are not up to us, nor are our possessions, our reputations, our public offices.

Epictetus

Begin the morning by saying to yourself, I shall meet with the busy-body, the ungrateful, arrogant, deceitful, envious, unsocial. All these things happen by reason of their ignorance of what is good and evil. But I who have seen the nature of the good that it is beautiful, and of the bad that it is ugly, and the nature of him who does wrong, that it is akin to me . . . I can neither be injured by any of them, for no one can fix on me what is ugly, nor can I be angry with my kinsman, nor hate him. For we are made for co-operation, like feet, like hands, like eyelids, like the rows of the upper and lower teeth. To act against one another then is contrary to nature; and it is acting against one another to be vexed and to turn away.

Marcus Aurelius

Control versus Influence

Given the Stoic position that our lives are fated but that our wills remain free, our first task must be to distinguish what we can control from what we cannot control. *Control* is a most important concept. Because Stoic literature is often imprecise and inconsistent, it will help the modern student of Stoicism to consider the distinction between *control* and *influence*.

Even though the Stoics believed in destiny or fate, they also talked about choosing appropriate actions, in addition to just controlling our attitudes. This suggests that a given individual's fate is painted in broad strokes: X will not get into medical school; Y will marry Z. But X may have the freedom to apply to medical school, and Y may be free to break up with Z two or three times. There appear to be gaps in our fate. For instance, in the first section of the *Enchiridion* Epictetus says:

> If then you desire . . . great things, remember that you must not (attempt to) lay hold of them with small effort; but you must leave alone some things entirely, and postpone others for the present.[16]

Later he says:

> When you are going to take in hand any act, remind yourself what kind of act it is. If you are going to bathe, [remind] yourself what happens in the [public] bath; some splashing the water, others pushing against one another, others abusing one another, and some stealing.[17]

Elsewhere, he talks about choosing to be a philosopher or deciding to train for the Olympics. Thus Epictetus implies that we have at least some degree of influence over our actions. We *must* have influence over more than just our attitudes; otherwise, such advice is illogical. Advice makes sense only where there is some choice.

Although the Stoics are theoretically inconsistent when they counsel accepting fate on the one hand and then advise us to live moderately and wisely on the other, their position contains merit because *it is consistent with common experience.* A careful survey of the human condition reveals that many of us expend a great deal of effort trying to control things that we cannot control while nearly ignoring those areas over which we do have control. This insight, I think, reflects the genius of Stoicism.

A common example will make the point. Technically speaking, you cannot *control* your grades in school, although you have considerable *influence* over them. No matter how carefully you listen to instructions, no matter how good your notes, how thorough your studying and grasp of the material, you cannot *guarantee* a passing grade in any course. Your professor may have a personal grudge against you or be depressed or ill while grading your work. A clerical error may alter your grade in a class, and the sys-

There's certainly nothing wrong with taking reasonable precautions to manage our lives and protect our property, but the Stoics remind us not to confuse exerting influence with having control. All the bicycle locks in the world won't give us control over even one bicycle, if the Stoics are correct.

tem may refuse to correct it. By the same token, you cannot even guarantee a failing grade. Another clerical record may result in an A for a class you haven't attended for weeks. The professor may confuse your name with that of another student, for example.

We are foolish when we exert no effort on our own behalf. We all know that. But, the Stoic reminds us, we are also foolish to believe that we *control* our GPAs. Rather than trying to control our grades, we should work wisely to *influence* them and should make sure to *control our attitudes* toward them.

This difference may be difficult to grasp in a culture that pronounces "You can be anything you want to be if you work hard enough." From the Stoic point of view it is misleading to talk about controlling our lives (or grades); we can only influence them up to a point. And we must remember this warning: *The results of our efforts are out of our hands.*

Off campus we see this as well. Jim Fixx, the running enthusiast, ate sensibly and exercised regularly, yet died in his forties of an inherited heart condition. The film genius Orson Welles ate what he wished, never exercised, smoked cigars, and weighed over four hundred pounds when he died—at age seventy. Such an example is not an excuse for self-indulgence,

Show me a man who though sick is happy, who though in danger is happy, and I'll show you a Stoic.

Epictetus

but a hard fact of life: *We do not control our destinies; we influence them just enough so that we should do our best to behave responsibly.*

This is the crux of Stoicism. The inconsistencies in Stoic writing are due, in part, to our ignorance of precisely when influence becomes control in a particular case. There are ways to learn what to try and what to avoid, but in all cases the Stoic remains aware that the Logos ultimately rules the universe. The individual's task is to identify the Logos's will and then put his or her will in harmony with it. While we may not have control over the events in our lives, we do have control over our happiness. The wise person is easy to identify: He or she is the serene individual who lives courageously and responsibly, who graciously accepts everything that happens, be it good or bad, without becoming bitter or broken.

Some Things Are Not in Our Control

Do not be distressed, do not despond or give up in despair, if now and again practice falls short of precept. Return to the attack after each fail- ure, and be thankful if on the whole you can acquit yourself in the majority of cases as a man should.

Marcus Aurelius

To achieve serenity and wisdom, we must remain clear about what is not in our control:

> Not in our power are the body, property, reputation, offices . . . and in a word, whatever are not our own acts . . . the things not in our power are weak, slavish, subject to restraint, in the power of others. Remember that if you think the things which are by nature slavish to be free, and the things which are in the power of others to be your own, you will be hindered, you will lament, you will be disturbed, you will blame both the gods and men.[18]

"Not in our power" means not under our control. If I realize that these things are not under my control, I can adopt a healthy attitude toward them. For instance, since my reputation is not totally up to me, I can quit trying so hard to make everyone like me. I cannot *make* anyone like me or dislike me. My family likes me even when I'm a fool, and some of my students don't like me no matter how hard I try to be likable. Instead of directing my efforts where they are ineffective, I can devote them to what I have more control over: myself. In practical terms, this means that I take appropriate action and then mentally let go of the results.

All wisdom can be stated in two lines:

What is done for you— allow it to be done.

What you must do your- self—make sure you do it.

Khawwas

Once I realize that how long I live, who likes me or doesn't, and my so- cial status are beyond my total control, I can quit being obsessively fearful. I can manage my health with moderation, but will not be bitter if after watch- ing my diet and exercising daily I develop cancer. Bitterness will not get me well. Bitterness, or envy, or resentment are never my fate; they are always my choice.

Not getting into the university of my choice might be my fate. Resent- ing it for the rest of my life is not—it's my choice. I can ask you to marry me, and marry you if you say yes, but I cannot make you happy. I cannot make you stay with me. If you leave, my anger and despair are not my fate—they are my choice.

PHILOSOPHICAL QUERY

Reflect on letting go in the sense of doing what seems right and then relaxing. Provide a few of your own examples of how fear of consequences and an obsession with control can affect us. Discuss ways for identifying and striking a balance between letting go in a wise way and in an irresponsible way.

Some Things *Are* in Our Control

What is in our power is our free will. Epictetus insists, contrary to what we may believe, that we alone control our feelings. We control our feelings because we control our thinking. We can reason out that other people's likes and dislikes are beyond our total control. This should free us from depending on other people's opinions of us for self-esteem or happiness.

> In our power are opinion, movement towards a thing, desire, aversion; and in a word, whatever are our own acts. And the things in our power are by nature free, not subject to restraint or hindrance . . . if you think that only which is your own to be your own, and if you think of what is another's, as it really is, belongs to another, no man will ever compel you, no man will hinder you, you will never blame any man, you will accuse no man, you will do nothing . . . against your will, no man will harm you, you will have no enemy, for you will not suffer any harm.[19]

I wonder how many hours of human suffering can be chalked up to trying to control how others feel about things. I also wonder how hard we try to control our own thoughts. For example: Mike suffers and worries every time Lina is annoyed with him. He buys her flowers, is distracted at work, agonizes until she likes him again. If he had control over how she felt, he would never let her be annoyed. Since she gets annoyed and he doesn't want her to be annoyed, it follows logically (and causally) that he *cannot* control her feelings. But—irrationally—he tries to, again and again.

Suppose that Mike reads Epictetus. Now, instead of trying to make Lina feel a certain way, he tries to control his own thoughts and behavior. When he starts to worry, he consciously, and with great effort at first, forces himself not to dwell on Lina. He may not be able to stop worries about her from popping into his mind, but he can stop himself from dwelling on them. He can exert his *will* over his own thinking. He is not responsible for his first thoughts, but he is responsible for his second thoughts.

That which happens to . . . every man is fixed in a manner for him suitable to his destiny. . . . For there is altogether one fitness and harmony. . . . And so accept everything which happens, even if it seems disagreeable, because it leads to this, to the health of the universe and to the prosperity . . . of the whole.
Marcus Aurelius

All that happens without us knowing why is destiny. For the man who trusts destiny, there is no difference between long life and short. For one who trusts his mind, there is nothing which is agreeable or offensive.
Lie Zi

ADDICTED TO UNHAPPINESS

Let's face it: Reality often stinks. People don't always act the way we would like them to act. This doesn't seem to be the best of all possible worlds. . . . Moreover, society often gets worse: seems *more* polluted, economically unfair, burdened with ethnic prejudices, politically oppressive, violence-filled, superstitious, wasteful of natural resources, sexist, and ultraconformist.

But you *still* don't have to feel desperately unhappy. Unkind reality doesn't de-

press millions of humans. What does? Their unthinking addiction to . . . *the idea that people and things should turn out better than they do and that you must view it as awful and horrible if you do not find good solutions to life's grim realities.* An idiotic idea . . .

Albert Ellis and Robert A. Harper
A New Guide to Rational Living (North Hollywood: Wilshire Book Co., 1978), p. 177.

This is a difficult lesson. It may be especially difficult to accept today, when we place so much importance on relationships, and when we have been told that inadequate parents and abusive spouses are often responsible for our unhappiness. Epictetus has something interesting to say about relationships.

Relationships

Relationships must be evaluated with the same disinterested detachment as everything else. *According to the Stoics, we suffer to the extent that we take our own lives personally.*

Attachment is the great fabricator of illusions; reality can be attained only by someone who is detached.
Simone Weil

Duties are universally measured by relations. Is a man a father? The [duty] is to take care of him, to yield to him in all things, to submit when he is reproachful, when he inflicts blows. But suppose he is a bad father. Were you then by nature [guaranteed] a good father? No; [just] a father. Does a brother wrong you? Maintain then your own position towards him, and do not examine what he is doing, but what you must do [in order] that your will shall be [in accord with] nature. For another will not damage you, unless you choose; but you will be damaged when you shall think that you are damaged. In this way then you will discover your duty from the relation of a neighbor, from that of a citizen, from that of a general, if you are accustomed to contemplate [your relationships].[20]

This is an excellent example of applying disinterested reason to daily affairs. The Stoics believed that a disinterested study of life shows that no one is *entitled* to good, healthy parents, loving, supportive brothers and sisters, obedient children, or sexy, interesting, loyal boyfriends, girlfriends, or spouses. If the Logos provides *everything we need* to be happy, then it is clear that no one needs good parents, and so on. The reason is obvious: Not everyone gets them. They are not things to which we are entitled, or the Logos would have provided them.

The only way to grasp this point is to set our *feelings* aside and apply *disinterested reason* to relationships. For example, the traditional marriage vow commits each spouse to the other "for richer or poorer, in sickness and in health." This means that the essence of my relationship to my wife is simply that: She is my wife. As a husband—not as an individual—I have obligations, regardless of how my wife behaves, which stem from the nature of the marital relationship. They are not based on the personalities or preferences of the individuals involved. Similarly, as a son, I have duties toward my father whether or not I "like" him and whether or not he is a good father.

This interpretation of relationships seems overly simplistic given our sophisticated psychological knowledge of the damage that bad, abusive relationships can cause. So it will be necessary to modify Epictetus's strict position. But to give him his due, there is much to be learned from adopting a grown-up attitude toward relationships. What can I gain by resenting my childhood, for example? All my righteous indignation over some parental lack, all the suffering and bitterness in the world cannot make up for whatever I missed in childhood. That truly is beyond my power.

In Epictetus's time, social roles were less flexible than they are now. But even today, I can still be a Stoic without being a martyr. I can remind myself that so long as I am in this marriage or have this job, for instance, *I* have duties that are not contingent on other people fulfilling *their* duties. What kind of teacher would I be if I did not prepare my lessons carefully just because many of my students come to class unprepared? What kind of student would you be if you whispered and passed notes to your friend just because your teacher was not interesting?

As the Stoics remind us, our spouses, friends, teachers, and bosses are not the real causes of our happiness or unhappiness. When we look at relationships only in terms of how others behave toward us or whether they "make" us happy or unhappy, we fail to grasp one of the most fundamental aspects of life.

PHILOSOPHICAL QUERY

Discuss the preceding passage from Epictetus about relationships. What lessons might it have regarding our relationships and the things that make us unhappy?

Everything Has a Price

One reason we may be frustrated by events is that we tend to focus on the object of our desire while ignoring its cost. Yet everything has a clearly

You cannot judge by annoyance.
Idries Shah

What you're supposed to do when you don't like a thing is change it. If you can't change it, change the way you think about it.
Maya Angelou

"These sons belong to me, and this wealth belongs to me"—with such thoughts a fool is tormented. He himself does not belong to himself; how much less sons and wealth?
The Buddha

The athlete with the fine physique has paid the price of training and discipline. As Epictetus said: "You will be unjust and insatiable, if you do not part with the price in return for which . . . things are sold." If we remember this stoic principle, we will not envy or resent those who have paid the price when we have not.

marked price tag. The athlete with a fine physique has paid the price of training and discipline, perhaps giving up a broad education or full social life. The ambitious character at the office has paid the price of flattering the boss and working late while you did not have to "kiss up" and were home enjoying your family life. The A student has paid the price of missing many parties and other kinds of socializing.

We suffer unnecessarily when we try to have things without paying the price:

Do not value either your children or your life or anything else more than goodness.
Socrates

> You will be unjust then and insatiable, if you do not part with the price, in return for which . . . things are sold, and if you wish to obtain them for nothing. Well, what is the price of lettuces? An obulus perhaps. If then a man gives up the obulus and receives the lettuces, and if you do not give up the obulus and do not receive the lettuces, do not suppose that you receive less than he who has got the lettuces; for as he has the lettuces, so you have the obulus which you did not give . . . you have not been invited to a man's feast, for you did not give the host the price at which the supper is sold; but he sells it for praise (flattery), he sells it for personal attention. Give him the price, if it is for your interest, for which it is sold.

But if you wish both not to give the price, and to obtain the things, you are insatiable and silly. Have you nothing then in place of the supper? You have indeed, you have the [satisfaction of] not flattering . . . him . . . whom you did not choose to flatter; you have [not had to put up with him].[21]

What would you think of someone who screamed and turned red with rage when asked to pay for a basket of groceries at the market? He or she would be "silly," to say the least. How is this different from the couple who once eagerly desired a baby and now resent the infant's demands? Or the married man who chafes at his obligations? Or the woman who has a job, a social life, and three children and is surprised that she feels tired and run down? As obvious as the notion of a price seems, many of us seem to be stunned when we are expected to pay.

Suffering and Courage

Stoicism is a "mature" philosophy. Its appeal seems to increase with experience, that is, with frustration and disappointment. The process of growing up emotionally and philosophically involves adopting realistic expectations and accepting one's limits. The challenge of maturity is how to do this without becoming overly negative or giving in to inertia. How can I develop an attitude of Stoic detachment and acceptance and still have hopes and take action?

The key seems to involve seeing ourselves as part of the whole, in perspective—as opposed to seeing ourselves as a special part of the universe. If we can do this, we become members of the cosmopolis. We gain peace of mind from recognizing that illness, death, and disappointment are as much a part of everyone's life as are joy and delight. Shared suffering is diminished suffering.

The Stoics sometimes compared the Logos to a parent or teacher. They pointed out that suffering can be viewed as a gift, if we understand that the best teachers are strictest with those pupils in whom they see the most ability. They also noted that suffering cannot be bad by nature, or else good men like Socrates would not have suffered. In other words, who am I that I should escape the ordinary trials of life? The goal isn't to avoid them, but to use them to become a good person. Seneca said, "The greater the torment, the greater shall be the glory." He adds:

> Prosperity can come to the vulgar and to ordinary talents, but to triumph over the disasters and terrors of mortal life is the privilege of the great man. To be lucky always and to pass through life without gnawing of the mind is to be ignorant of the half of nature. You are a great man, but how can I know, if Fortune has never given you a chance to display your prowess? You have entered the Olympic games but have no

Whether you like it or not, you'd better accept reality the way it occurs: as highly imperfect and filled with most fallible human beings. Your alternative? Continual anxiety and desperate disappointment.
Albert Ellis and Robert Harper

Let others practice lawsuits, others study problems, others syllogisms; here you practice how to die, how to be enchained, how to be racked, how to be exiled.
Epictetus

The Stoics placed great value on strength of character, courage, enduring suffering without bitterness, and accepting one's fate. Epictetus said, "You can play your part badly or well, but the choice of which part you play belongs to Another."

Some in ten years, some in one hundred, we all die. Saints and sages die, the wicked and foolish die. In life they were Yao and Shun, in death they were rotten bones. In life they were Jie and Zhou, in death they were rotten bones. Rotten bones are all the same, who can tell them apart?
Yang Zhu

rival; you gain the crown but not the victory . . . I can say . . . "I count you unfortunate because you have never been unfortunate. You have passed through life without an adversary; no man can know your potentiality, not even you." For self-knowledge, testing is necessary; no one can discover what he can do except by trying.[22]

What of the unfortunate soul who tries to get out of everything difficult, who takes only easy courses or ends relationships at the first sustained period of responsibility? What of the poor characters whose careers suffer because they change jobs as soon as they are challenged, and so never get promoted? Or the person who lingers in an inferior job or bad relationship out of fear and inertia? Since there is really no way to avoid pain, it is especially tragic to see those who try, for not only are they doomed to failure, they suffer additionally because they lack character. They live at the whim of circumstances. Seneca says:

> So god hardens and scrutinizes and exercises those he approves and loves; but those he appears to indulge and spare he is only keeping tender for disasters to come. If you suppose

LIFE IS DIFFICULT

This is one of the greatest truths. It is a great truth because once we truly see this truth, we transcend it. Once we truly know that life is difficult—once we truly understand and accept it—it is no longer difficult. Because once it is accepted, the fact that life is difficult no longer matters.

Most do not fully see this truth that life is difficult. Instead they moan more or less incessantly, noisily or subtly, about the enormity of their problems, their burdens, and their difficulties as if life were generally easy, as if life *should* be easy. They voice

their belief, noisily or subtly, that their difficulties represent a unique kind of affliction that should not be and that has somehow been especially visited upon them, or else upon their families, their tribe, their class, their nation, their race or even their species, and not upon others. I know about this moaning because I have done my share.

M. Scott Peck
The Road Less Traveled: A New Psychology of Love, Traditional Values and Spiritual Growth (New York: Simon & Schuster, 1978), p. 15.

---

anyone is immune you are mistaken. . . . Why does god afflict every good man with sickness or grief or misfortune? Because in the army, too, the most hazardous duties are assigned to the bravest soldiers. . . . In the case of good men, accordingly, the gods follow the plan that teachers follow with their pupils; they demand more effort from those in whom they have confident expectations. . . . What wonder, then, if god tries noble spirits with sternness? The demonstration of courage can never be gentle. Fortune scourges us; we must endure it. It is not cruelty but a contest.[23]

Thus, the Stoics say, our misfortune on this earth is not a result of God's disfavor, but possibly His respect or understanding of what we need to endure but would avoid if left to our own devices. Certainly faith in a divine will seems to obligate us to reach such a conclusion. Even without belief in God, we can still ask the Stoic's question: Which is more reasonable, to endure inescapable hardship and to suffer mental torment, or to endure inescapable hardship but accept it with courage and gratitude? As I have framed the question, it answers itself. Without trivializing it, we can say that Stoicism comes down to this: *While making reasonable efforts to get what we want, it is wise to learn to be happy with what we get.*

If you regard yourself as a man and as a part of the whole, it is fitting for you now to be sick and now to make a voyage and run risks, and now to be in want, and on occasion to die before your time. Why, then, are you vexed? . . . For it is impossible in such a body as ours, that is, in this universe that envelops us, among these fellow-creatures of ours, that such things should not happen, some to one man, some to another.

Epictetus

STOICISM TODAY

As we saw in the discussion of self-realization (Chapter 7), psychologists sometimes devise practical applications for wisdom philosophies. Stoicism forms the basis of certain cognitive (rationalistic) psychological therapies. Three of the most influential are William Glasser's *reality therapy*, Albert Ellis's *rational-emotive therapy*, and Viktor Frankl's *logotherapy*. All three systems are based on controlling emotions by controlling irrational thinking. Consequently, they deny the primacy of emotions, but do not condemn feelings as the Stoics did. Like Stoicism, these therapeutic approaches emphasize self-control; they stress clearly stating accurate observations of reality; and they call for maturity and courage from their clients.

Reality Therapy: William Glasser

In his book *Reality Therapy: A New Approach*, contemporary psychiatrist William Glasser presents a theory of psychotherapy which shares certain fundamental values with both Cynicism and Stoicism. Reality therapy attempts to make people more realistic and responsible. This requires self-control and a rational assessment of actual conditions that directly contradicts Cyrenaic hedonism.

Glasser claims that cloudy thinking and poor character are the chief sources of suffering. He agrees with the Stoic emphasis on character:

> Very few of us realize how much we choose the misery in our lives. Even when we do, we still go ahead with the disastrous choice because we are convinced that we don't have the strength to choose better. A child doesn't give up in school, or a wife on her marriage, because each believes it's a good move. They give up because they no longer have the strength to keep up the struggle. . . . Weakness is the cause of almost all the unfortunate choices we make.[24]

Rational-Emotive Therapy: Albert Ellis

Although a Stoic thread in Glasser's reality therapy is clear, Albert Ellis's rational-emotive psychotherapy is even more directly stoically oriented. Ellis, executive director of both the Institute for Rational Living and the Institute for Advanced Study in Rational Psychotherapy, teaches that we are almost completely responsible for our fate. As a practicing psychologist, Ellis grew disenchanted with other therapies which, he thought, encouraged people "to focus upon great masses of irrelevant information" about themselves and engendered confusion, weakness, and dependency.[25] According to Ellis, nonrational forms of psychotherapy asume that

> . . . events and experiences are of paramount importance in a person's life, that he cannot help being traumatized by the unpleasant occurrences of his earliest years, and that if he truly

understands the origins of these occurrences he will overcome their noxious influences. Actually, as Epictetus demonstrated some two thousand years ago, humans are not bothered by the things that happen to them but by their *view* of these things.[26]

Ellis's work shows a clear philosophical influence. In the following passage, Ellis and co-author Robert A. Harper cite examples of philosophers to illustrate their belief that correct use of reason can radically change our lives for the better:

> History gives us several outstanding instances of those who changed themselves and helped change others by hardheaded thinking. Zeno of Citium, for example, who flourished in the third century B.C., and founded the Greek Stoic school of philosophy. The Greek philosopher Epicurus; the Phrygian Epictetus; the Roman emperor Marcus Aurelius; the Dutch Jew Baruch Spinoza. These and other outstanding rational thinkers, after reading about the teaching of still earlier thinkers (Heraclitus and Democritus, among others), and doing some deep thinking of their own, enthusiastically adopted philosophies radically different from their original beliefs. More to the point for purposes of our present discussion, they actually began to *live* these philosophies, to *act* in accordance with them.
>
> All this, mind you, without benefit of what we today would call formal psychotherapy. Granted, of course, these individuals performed outstandingly—and held rare places in human history. But they did see the light of another's reasoning and use it for their own saner living.[27]

In the following excerpt, note the strong influence of Epictetus:

> Whether you like or not, you'd better accept reality the way it occurs: as highly imperfect and filled with most fallible human beings. Your alternative? Continual anxiety and desperate disappointment. . . .
>
> We do have the power to change and control ourselves to a considerable degree (if we work hard and long enough at modifying our own beliefs and actions); we do not have a similar power to control the behavior of others. . . . If, therefore, you get unduly aroused over the way others act, instead of paying more attention to how you respond to their actions, you upset yourself over an outside event beyond your control. This seems akin to tearing out your hair because a jockey, a prizefighter, or an actor does not perform the way you would like. Very silly business indeed!
>
> If you control your own destiny, by the proper cultivation of your own emotional garden, the most harrowing things

It may seem strange, but most people . . . elect not to continue with their life journeys—to stop short by some distance to avoid the pain of giving up parts of themselves. If it does not seem strange, it is because you do not understand the depth of the pain that may be involved. In its major forms, giving up is the most painful of human experiences.

M. Scott Peck

It is the mind which moulds man's destiny, action being but precipitated thought. It follows that one's lightest thought has vast effects, not only on the thinker, but on all that lives.

Christmas Humphreys

that happen will not perturb you too much and you may even help change things and people for the better. But if you unduly upset yourself over outside happenings, you will inevitably consume so much time and energy that you will have little left for the proper cultivation of your own garden.[28]

Logotherapy: Viktor E. Frankl

Perhaps the most philosophical, and certainly the most Stoic, psychology today is Viktor E. Frankl's logotherapy. During World War II, Frankl, an Austrian Jew, was imprisoned for three years in the Nazi concentration camp at Auschwitz. In addition to the suffering and degradation he suffered there, upon his release he discovered that his whole family had been destroyed. Based on his personal and clinical experiences with suffering on a scale few of us can even imagine, he developed his own psychological school.

Logotherapy, as you might sense, means Logos-based healing. Frankl used the definition of Logos as "meaning" and felt that the individual's struggle to find a meaning in life is a primary motivation. He stated that the "will to meaning" is as strong as the will to pleasure or the will to power. Logotherapy combines the insights of Stoicism with contemporary psychology's more sophisticated understanding of the relationship of feeling to thinking. Frankl's firsthand experiences with utter loss—and the power of the will to give that loss meaning—make logotherapy especially interesting to the student of Stoicism.

His most famous book is *Man's Search for Meaning*. If you have not read it, I recommend it to you. Let's see how Frankl talks about Stoicism:

> Whenever one is confronted with an inescapable, unavoidable situation, whenever one has to face a fate that cannot be changed, e.g., an incurable disease, such as inoperable cancer, just then one is given a last chance to actualize the highest value, to fulfill the deepest meaning, the meaning of suffering. For what matters above all is the attitude we take toward suffering, the attitude in which we take our suffering upon ourselves.[29]

> Suffering ceases to be suffering in some way at the moment it finds a meaning, such as the meaning of a sacrifice. . . . It is one of the main tenets of logotherapy that man's main concern is not to gain pleasure or avoid pain, but rather to see a meaning in his life. That is why man is ready to suffer, on the condition, to be sure, that his suffering has a meaning.[30]

> What a man has done cannot be undone . . . [but] through the right attitude unchangeable suffering is transmuted into a heroic and virtuous achievement. In the same fashion a man

We can only bow our heads in the presence of those broken beneath the burden of their destiny. The capacity of the human soul for suffering and isolation is immense.

Sarvepalli Radhakrishnan

To bear pain, to endure suffering, is the quality of the strong in spirit. It adds to the spiritual resources of humanity.

Sarvepalli Radhakrishnan

who has failed by a deed cannot change what happened but by repentance he can change himself. Everything depends on the right attitude in the same way and manner as in the case of suffering. The difference lies in the fact that the right attitude is, then, a right attitude to himself.[31]

PHILOSOPHICAL QUERY

Discuss this passage from *Man's Search for Meaning*: "Has all this suffering, this dying around us [in the concentration camps], a meaning? For, if not, then ultimately there is no meaning to survival; for a life whose meaning depends upon such a happenstance—whether one escapes or not—ultimately would not be worth living at all."[32]

Epictetus in Vietnam

Perhaps the greatest testimonies to the merit of Stoicism come from those who have suffered greatly, as Frankl reminds us. One of the most interesting and compelling arguments for the practical value of a good philosophical education came from an unexpected source: a highly trained United States Navy fighter pilot.

What we know as the *Enchiridion* of Epictetus can be a powerful consolation and support to people undergoing the severest trials. In fact, James Bond Stockdale, a former vice admiral in the United States Navy, credits his education in the humanities—and Epictetus in particular—with helping him survive eight years as a prisoner of war in North Vietnam, four years in solitary confinement. Stockdale was awarded the Congressional Medal of Honor after his release.

In April 1978 the *Atlantic Monthly* published a remarkable article by this unusual soldier-philosopher called "The World of Epictetus." Stockdale describes the brutal conditions the POWs were kept in, and his own fear and despondency. As he reviewed his life from his solitary cell, Stockdale "picked the locks" to the doors of his past experiences. He recalled cocktail parties and phony social contacts with revulsion as empty and valueless. "More often than not," he said, "the locks worth picking had been old schoolroom doors."

In this passage, Stockdale testifies to the real-life value of Epictetus's *Enchiridion*:

> The messages of history and philosophy I used were simple.
>
>   The first one is the business about life not being fair. That was a very important lesson and I learned it from a wonderful man named Philip Rhinelander. . . . He said, "The course I'm teaching is my personal two-term favorite—The Problem of Good and Evil—and we're starting our second term." He said

Love only that which happens to thee and is spun with the thread of thy destiny. For what is more suitable?

Marcus Aurelius

The judge will do some things to you which are thought to be terrifying; but how can he stop you from taking the punishment he threatened?

Epictetus

For wherever a man's place is, whether the place which he has chosen or that in which he has been placed by a commander, there he ought to remain in the hour of danger; he should not think of death or of anything but disgrace. And this, O men of Athens, is a true saying.

Socrates

James Bond Stockdale credits the lessons he learned from Epictetus's *Enchiridion* with helping him survive eight years in a North Vietnamese prison camp, confirming the Stoic belief that through great effort of will we can transform total loss into "heroic and virtuous achievement."

What's important is not fame, nor glory, but the ability to endure, to be able to bear one's cross and have faith.
Anton Chekhov

For it is better to die of hunger, exempt from fear and guilt, than to live in affluence with perturbation.
Epictetus

the message of his course was from the Book of Job. The number one problem in this world is that people are not able to accommodate the lesson in the book.

He recounted the story of Job. It starts out by establishing that Job was the most honorable of men. Then he lost all his goods. He also lost his reputation, which is what really hurt. His wife was badgering him to admit his sins, but he knew he had made no errors. He was not a patient man and demanded to speak to the Lord. When the Lord replied in the whirlwind, he said, "Now, Job, you have to shape up! Life is not fair." That's my interpretation and that's the way the book ended for hundreds of years. I agree with those of the opinion that the happy ending was spliced on many years later. . . . People couldn't live with the original message.

Rhinelander also passed on to me another piece of classical information which I found of great value. On the day of our last session together he said, "You're a military man, let me give you a book to remember me by. It's a book of military ethics." He handed it to me, and I bade him goodbye with great emotion. I took the book home and that night started to read it. It was the *Enchiridion* of the philosopher Epictetus, his "manual" for the Roman field soldier.

As I began to read, I thought to myself in disbelief, "Does Rhinelander think I'm going to draw lessons for my life from this thing? I'm a fighter pilot. I'm a technical man. I'm a test pilot. I know how to get people to do technical work. I play golf; I drink martinis. I know how to get ahead in my profession. And what does he hand me? A book that says in part, 'It's better to die in hunger, exempt from guilt and fear, than to live in affluence and with perturbation.'" I remembered this later in prison because perturbation was what I was living with. When I ejected from the airplane on that September morn in 1965, I had left the land of technology. I had entered the world of Epictetus, and it's a world that few of us, whether we know it or not, are ever far away from.[33]

The lessons that the old Roman slave learned on the rack gave comfort and courage to a solitary prisoner of war two thousand years later in the rice paddies of Southeast Asia.

COMMENTARY

This summary glance at Stoicism shows up inconsistencies and difficulties. The nature of fate remains ambiguous: How detailed is my life "script"? Has the Logos determined that I drop a pencil or make a typing mistake as I write this? Or is my fate painted in broader strokes? If so, in what sense is it fate? Are all emotions "bad"? Is it *reasonable* to be so detached, if it's even possible? Can a disinterested person have a motive, or are motives emotional?

Such immediately obvious problems result partly from the Stoics' near indifference to everything but the issue of how to live the least disturbed life possible. They were not concerned with providing a completely worked-out philosophical *system*. Even so, Stoicism retains an appeal that rests on genuine insights into the causes of much suffering and unhappiness. The Stoics were highly practical "moral psychologists," whose chief interests were ethics and psychology. As such, the most insightful of them offer sage counsel and inspiration which is as pertinent and helpful today as it was when first presented over two thousand years ago.

When I first encountered Stoicism as an undergraduate, I found it annoying. The ideal Stoic seemed to be a bland, emotionless vegetable—certainly not the kind of person I wanted to be. I needn't have worried. Stoic self-control and discipline were unlikely to stifle my great emotions. And so I spent too many years fuming over traffic, long lines, the way the world behaved, my teachers, my students, being alone, not being alone—life.

Today, I recognize the depth of passion behind the words of Marcus Aurelius and Epictetus. They certainly were not bland, unfeeling people. I

I consider it a dangerous misconception of mental hygiene to assume that what man needs in the first place is equilibrium or . . . a tensionless state. What man actually needs is not a tensionless state but rather a striving and struggling for some goal worthy of him.

Viktor E. Frankl

understand how much of my own frustration has come from not looking carefully for the price tag before I rushed to the checkout.

Given the condition of our society and basic human nature, I see enough merit in Stoic wisdom to compensate for certain ambiguities and inconsistencies in its expression. If nothing else, it sometimes helps me go to the bank on Friday afternoon without fuming and complaining—or helps me stay home without fuming and complaining.

Stoicism provides a counterbalance of sorts to today's love affair with instant gratification and emotional expressiveness. In its lessons on relationships and suffering, it wisely reminds us that what cannot be changed *must* be accepted graciously if we are ever to be happy. We live in a time when people seek external solutions to nearly every sort of predicament. Many will be found. But no external solution can make us happy or unhappy, for, as a late friend used to remind me, "Happiness is an inside job."

After his 1973 release from prison, James Bond Stockdale served as president of the Naval War College in Newport, Rhode Island, and president of the Citadel, the military college of South Carolina. Since 1981, he has been a senior research fellow at the Hoover Institution, located at Stanford University. In 1992, third-party presidential candidate Ross Perot asked Stockdale to be his vice presidential running mate. During an election-year debate among the three vice presidential candidates, Stockdale began, as Socrates might have, with two timeless questions: "Who am I? Why am I here?" Though the philosophical thrust of the questions was missed by most people, Stockdale's philosophical vision attracted national attention to Stoicism in general and Epictetus in particular.

Stockdale remains one of our most remarkable contemporary philosophers in the original sense. The lessons of wisdom he has learned are particularly compelling because they come from as broad a spectrum as is humanly possible—the extremes of defeat, degradation, torture, and isolation, on the one hand, and the heights of influence, national prominence, and academic recognition, on the other. Few of us experience such extremes in either direction; fewer yet in both. Thus, Stockdale provides us with a rare contemporary example of the Stoic sage. Who better to have the last word in our survey of one of the most influential archetypes of wisdom? Stockdale says:

> Stoicism is certainly not for everybody, and it is not for me in every circumstance, but it is an expression in philosophical terms of how people find purpose in what they have every right to see as a purposeless world. . . . [Stoicism] speaks to people everywhere who persist in competing in what they see as a buzz-saw existence, their backs to the wall, their lives having meaning only so long as they fight for pride and comradeship and joy rather than capitulate to either tyranny or phoniness. . . .

We grow older. But it is by no means certain that we shall grow up.
Walter Lippmann

Giving up comforts and trying to carry out efforts. That is the practice of the Sufi.
Bayazid Bistami

. . . We who are in hierarchies—be they academic, business, military, or otherwise—are always in positions in which people are trying to manipulate us, to get moral leverage on us. The only defense is to keep yourself clean—never to do or say anything of which you can be made to feel ashamed. . . .

Am I personally still hooked on Epictetus's Principle of Life? Yes, but not in the sense of following a memorized doctrine. I sometimes become amused at how I have applied it and continue to apply it unconsciously. An example is the following story about myself.

As the months and years wear on in solitary confinement, it turns out each man goes crazy if he doesn't get some ritual into his life. I mean by that a self-imposed obligation to do certain things in a certain order each day. Like most prisoners, I prayed each day, month after month, continually altering and refining a long memorized monologue that probably ran to ten or fifteen minutes. At some point, my frame of mind became so pure that I started deleting any begging of God and any requests that would work specifically for my benefit. This didn't come out of any new Principle of Life that I had developed; it just suddenly started to seem unbecoming to beg. I knew the lesson of the book of Job: life is not fair. What claim had I for special consideration? And anyway, by then I had seen enough misery to know that He had enough to worry about without trying to appease a crybaby like me. And so it has been ever since.[34]

What is the result at which all virtue aims? Serenity. Epictetus

In this day and age, the greatest devotion, greater than learning and praying, consists in accepting the world exactly as it happens to be. Rabbi Moshe of Kobryn

SUMMARY OF MAIN POINTS

Antisthenes was the founder of a philosophical school known as Cynicism and Diogenes was its most famous advocate. The Cynics believed that the very essence of civilization is corrupt, that manners are hypocritical, that material wealth weakens people, and that civilization destroys the individual and makes him or her vulnerable to the whims of fortune.

According to the Cynics, the death of Socrates showed that not even the wisest person can control other people or external events. They concluded that the less an individual needs to be happy, the less vulnerable he or she will be. Cynics live austere, unconventional lives.

Founded in Greece by Zeno, Stoicism grew out of Cynicism and achieved widespread influence in first-century Rome, ultimately spreading throughout Christianized Europe. The Roman slave Epictetus, the Emperor Marcus Aurelius, and the senator Seneca are the most influential Stoic writers.

Stoics advised learning to want whatever we get by willing ourselves to accept whatever circumstances we are in without resentment. They believed that the cosmos is wisely governed by the Logos (World Reason) and that everything happens as part of a divine plan. The wise person anticipates and goes along with fate, the foolish one wishes things were otherwise.

According to the Stoics, human beings are bits of the Logos because we have rational souls. Happiness comes from the effective use of reason to alter the will. Based on their concept of a disinterested World Reason, the Stoics taught that it is wise to minimize personal attachments and motives. One way to do this is to evaluate things in terms of the goal of a universal harmony rather than from an individualistic view.

The Stoics rejected emotion to the extent it was humanly possible, favoring detached, rational acceptance over personal, emotional involvement.

Central to Stoicism is the distinction between control and influence. Though the Stoics believed that life is fated, they understood this in a loose sense. Because we cannot know precisely what our fate is, we must take reasonable action without pinning our happiness on a particular result.

According to the Stoics, we can control our ideas and attitudes but we cannot control "externals" such as reputation, social status, relationships, health, and wealth. A great deal of Stoic literature concerns learning how to identify what we cannot control and exercising control over our will.

Stoic virtues include strength of will, courage, dignity, and maturity.

According to Stoic doctrine, everything has a price that reason can reveal. The ultimate price of happiness is personal detachment from external conditions; peace of mind comes from indifference to everything except accepting the will of the Logos.

The Stoics looked upon suffering as a test of character and praised the ability to accept unavoidable suffering without bitterness or complaint. They taught that only great struggle could produce greatness of character.

Stoicism remains influential today in the form of various schools of cognitive psychotherapy. Three of the most important are William Glasser's reality therapy, Albert Ellis's rational-emotive therapy, and Viktor Frankl's logotherapy. The philosopher-warrior James Bond Stockdale continues to define Epictetus's Principle of Life and communicate it to a growing audience.

STUDY QUESTIONS

1. What is Cynicism?

2. Explain how Cynicism influenced Stoicism. Be specific.

3. What is the relationship of Socrates to Cynicism and Stoicism?

4. Compare and contrast Hedonism, Cynicism, and Stoicism.

5. Discuss how the social climate of ancient Rome encouraged the emergence of Stoicism.

6. Discuss the relationship of the lives of Marcus Aurelius and Epictetus to their philosophies.

7. What is the Logos?

8. How are the Logos and fate related in Stoicism?

9. Identify and discuss possible problems with the Stoic notion of fate.

10. Stoicism was quickly absorbed into Christianity. Identify and comment on any similarities you are aware of.

11. What is the disinterested rational will, and why is it important to Stoic doctrine?

12. Explain and defend the Stoic view of emotions. Then analyze it.

13. What do the Stoics think falls under our control? What do the Stoics think does not fall under our control? Do you agree? Why or why not?

14. Analyze the relationship between influence and control.

15. Discuss the difference between avoidable and unavoidable suffering. How can we tell which is which? Why does it matter?

16. State the essence of Stoicism in twenty-five words or less.

17. Explain the Stoic attitude toward relationships. How does it differ from today's attitudes? Explain.

18. Using a not-too-embarrassing example from your own life, illustrate the principle of paying the price.

19. How do the Stoics interpret suffering? What do you think of their view?

20. What does Seneca mean when he says "I count you unfortunate because you have never been unfortunate"?

21. Can you find additional examples of Stoicism today?

22. Do you know any Stoics? If so, describe them.

23. What do you think of Stockdale's claim that a good philosophical education is highly practical? Give his position and then comment on it.

CHAPTER TEN

The Scholar:

Thomas Aquinas

Now among the inquiries that we must undertake concerning God in Himself, we must set down in the beginning that whereby His Existence is demonstrated, as the necessary foundation of the whole work. For, if we do not demonstrate that God exists, all consideration of divine things is necessarily suppressed.

THOMAS AQUINAS

once watched a television news reporter interview a sobbing woman who sat on the pile of rubble that had once been her small mobile home. Everything she owned had been destroyed by a tornado. Through her tears, the victim expressed her gratitude to God for saving her life. As she explained it, she was preparing supper when she "mysteriously" had the urge to go to the corner market for a loaf of bread. She was gone for only a few minutes, but in those minutes the tornado struck. "If I hadn't gone for that bread," she said into the camera, "I would be dead now. God told me to go get that bread in order to save my life."

Does this mean that God *wanted* those people who were not warned to die? Suppose the woman's neighbor had been planning to go to the store but got a phone call just as he started for the door. Should we conclude that God arranged the timing of the call to make sure he didn't escape the tornado?

After all, if God is the cause of *everything* that happens, *everything* includes tornadoes and torture, as well as salvation and joy. If God knows *everything*, does He know your grade on your philosophy final right now? But if God knows things before they happen, how can we be held responsible for them? If God knew before you were born that you would get a C minus in philosophy, isn't *He* the cause of your grade, not you? And if there is even one thing that He does not know, even one thing, how can He be all-wise?

These and related questions are of more than just academic interest. They are vitally important to anyone who attempts to reconcile faith with reason. One "solution" to such problems has been to hold a *dual-truth point of view*. This is the position that there is one small-t truth on the finite, human level, and another, superior, capital-T Truth for God. Another strategy is to declare that these problems demonstrate that the ways of God are a "mystery" to human beings. In both cases, inconsistencies and ambiguities are not so much confronted as they are evaded.

Many believers and nonbelievers alike feel cheated when asked to accept inconsistent beliefs or simply to dismiss the most vital questions of faith. If you doubt this, wander through the sections of your college library's stacks dealing with theology and religious philosophy. You will find a large number of books and articles attempting to reconcile faith with reason. If you have ever seriously wrestled with the problem of evil (How can a good, loving, wise, powerful God allow evil?) or the problem of moral responsibility (If God gave Adam and Eve a corrupt nature, how can they—and we—justly be held responsible?), you have entered a timeless struggle.

Our culture has been heavily influenced by an ongoing clash between Christian values and the values established in classical Greece. In the classical view, human beings, despite our many faults, represent the most important life-form. The classical philosopher believed that objective knowledge and logic could unlock the keys to the universe, improving our lives in the process. The good life was seen as being a product of reason. Reason was valued over faith, because knowing was thought to be more useful than believing.

The Christian view presents a completely different picture. Human beings are seen as fallen and corrupt creatures, finite and ignorant. Christian theology teaches that we are incapable of avoiding sin and the punishment of hell through our own efforts. Only the undeserved grace and sacrifice of a loving God can save us. Obedience to the revealed word of God is also necessary for salvation. Faith is valued more highly than reason, because salvation is more important than worldly progress or success in a life that is relatively brief compared to the afterlife—where we will spend eternity in heaven (if we are saved) or hell (if we are not). As a result of its emphasis on the afterlife, Christian theology is sometimes characterized as *otherworldly*.

> *I inquired, "Whence is evil?" and found no result. . . . What torments did my heart then endure!*
> **St. Augustine**

THE GOD-CENTERED UNIVERSE

Are faith and reason inevitable enemies? Can the human mind know God through reason? Does being a "good Christian" prohibit questioning and trying to understand certain things? Why did God give us the ability to reason if we are asked to ignore what reason reveals? When conflicting religious beliefs all claim to rely on divine authority and revelation, how can we choose among them? These are among the great questions of the Middle Ages.

Whereas the classical mind was predominantly secular, the medieval mind was chiefly theological. **Theology**, from the Greek *theos* (God) and *logos* (study of), means "talking about God" or "the study or science of God." The Middle Ages saw philosophers turn from the study of man and nature to "otherworldly" inquiries and the study of God. Rather than *discover* the truth through reason and science, the scholar studied church dogma and theology in order to *explain* what God chose to reveal.

The great transition from the classical to the medieval worldview occurred in a series of steps. Late Stoicism, especially in the *Meditations* and *Letters* of Marcus Aurelius, marks the beginning of the shift from pagan to Christian philosophy. Though pagan himself, Marcus in the *Meditations* expresses values and interests that will become hallmarks of Christian philosophy: devaluing of this life and its temporary nature, a strong sense of duty, and the idea that human beings are related to the Logos (see Chapter 9). But Marcus differed from his medieval successors in his view of humans as social and political beings.[1]

THEOLOGY
From the Greek *theos* (God) and *logos* (study of); "talking about God" or "the study or science of God."

The Seeds of Change

The Christian religion arose after the death of Jesus Christ, through the efforts of the early apostles and disciples, especially Paul. Christianity originally consisted of scattered groups of believers anticipating the Second Coming of Christ, which would signal the end of the world. Thinking that they would soon be in heaven, early Christians saw no need to develop political

Can there be a future good so great as to render acceptable, in retrospect, the whole human experience, with all its wickedness and suffering as well as all its sanctity and happiness? I think that perhaps there can, and indeed perhaps there is.

John Hick

interests. Similarly, they were uninterested in science and philosophy and remained indifferent to much of what went on around them. Their chief concern was salvation through faith. Expecting that the risen Christ would return at any moment, they were understandably impatient with the affairs of this world. Thus they devoted themselves to converting non-Christians and to preparing their own souls for judgment. In a major contrast with the classical view of life, they saw no time or need to fashion philosophical, social, or moral theories.

When Christianity was new, its primary energies lay in survival and expansion. As time passed and the world did not end, Christians found it increasingly difficult to avoid dealing with problems of the here and now. Principles and rules for interpreting the basic teachings of Christ collected as the New Testament became necessary when it grew clear that the Second Coming might not occur until well into the future.

Interpreting revealed sacred dogma is always dangerous, however, for once the inevitability of interpretation is accepted, the door is open to competing interpretations. If *every* claimed interpretation is reliable, God's revealed will is going to appear chaotic, inconsistent, contradictory, and capricious. There must be criteria for distinguishing revelation from delusion and dogma from error. And there must be criteria for choosing criteria. And criteria for choosing criteria for choosing criteria. . . .

Some reinterpretation of Christian teachings was clearly called for if the Second Coming might be generations away. Giving all our goods to the poor is one thing when we expect to be in heaven in the immediate future; practical considerations complicate matters if the final judgment may be years away. As the centuries passed and the Second Coming did not occur, Christianity continued to expand until Christians dominated Europe. As Christian doctrine increased in complexity, theological issues added to practical complications.

The Need to Reconcile Faith and Reason

My life is still governed by a faith I no longer have.

Ernest Renan

The great paradoxes of faith are sometimes superficially dismissed by people who have never really grappled with them. Their religious training may have given them simple answers to the problems of free will, evil, predestination, God's nature, and others. Or they may have been taught to exalt faith by condemning reason. It is easy to *say* that faith surpasses understanding until you fully grasp the complex depths and significance of these problems. Whatever our individual religious beliefs, most of us are also rational creatures for whom it is somehow unsatisfying to accept contradictions and serious inconsistencies concerning something as important as our religious faith. Most of us are uncomfortable when we learn that we are violating rational principles.

The basic **principles of reason**—also called **rules of inference**—define the limits of rationality. That is, consistently violating them moves us to

PRINCIPLES OF REASON or RULES OF INFERENCE Principles (such as the law of contradiction) that define the limits of rationality by their very structure and that cannot be rationally refuted since we rely on them in order to reason.

The dominant theme of the Middle Ages was the God-centered universe. In this illustration, though God and Satan struggle over a dead man's soul, it is clear that God holds the supreme, central place.

the realm of the irrational or illogical. They are true by their very structure (by definition). They cannot be rationally refuted, since we rely on them in order to reason. Contemporary logicians recognize several rules of inference. One of the most important is the law of contradiction.

The **law of contradiction** (sometimes known as the law of noncontradiction) says: *No statement can be both true and false at the same time and under the same conditions.* Or to use symbols (as philosophers who study logic often do), p cannot be both p and not-p *at the same time.* For example: Either this is a philosophy book or it is not a philosophy book. It cannot be both a philosophy book and *not* a philosophy book. It can, however, be a philosophy book *and* a doorstop at the same time. There is no contradiction involved in asserting that it is a philosophy book and more. The contradiction occurs in the mutually exclusive assertions: "This is a philosophy book" *and* "This is not a philosophy book."

Take a moment to reflect on the law of contradiction. See if you can get a sense of just how basic it is to rationality. Because it is a fundamental principle of reasoning, we are usually disturbed to discover that our ideas are contradictory, for such awareness commits us to resolving the contradiction or holding irrational ideas.

Avoiding the possibility of contradiction by claiming that the human mind is finite and unable to understand God and His ways is ultimately

LAW OF CONTRADICTION (sometimes known as the law of noncontradiction) Rule of inference that says no statement can be both true and false at the same time and under the same conditions.

unsatisfying, for it removes us from meaningful communication with God. If we can never fully comprehend God, if we must trust that things *are not at all what they seem* (for instance, that evil only *appears to be evil* from our level but is *really* good from God's), then our "solution" may not be what it appears to be, either. The mere assertion of human limitations reduces all theology and religion to the realm of the unknowable, or it leaves us where we started: If we can know *some* things about God, *which* things, and how do we know? Like it or not, we are susceptible to principles of reason.

Scrutinized according to logical principles, the most commonly accepted attributes of God—all-knowing, all-good, all-powerful—generated problems concerning the suffering of innocents, the existence of evil, and the possibility of free will. Efforts to resolve these contradictions resulted in such doctrines as Original Sin, the elect, and the sin of intellectual pride. Once the idea of a personal God replaced the impersonal Logos of the Greeks, new questions arose for those willing to face them.

PHILOSOPHICAL QUERY

Have you ever felt that you had to choose between "hard" scientific and rational evidence and "soft" faith or intuitive religious belief? We also may encounter this tension in regard to our beliefs about psychic experiences, astrology, reincarnation, and other supernatural events. Why do people get so upset when someone points out inconsistencies or contradictions in their beliefs? If faith is higher than understanding, why do inconsistencies matter? What could count as evidence for such beliefs?

THE LIFE OF THOMAS AQUINAS

Thomas Aquinas

Every saint has a past and every sinner a future.
Oscar Wilde

Thomas Aquinas (c. 1225–1274) was born near Naples.[2] His father, who was related to the count of Aquino, planned for Thomas to achieve a position of importance in the Catholic church. To this end he enrolled Thomas in the Benedictine abbey school at Montecassino when Thomas was around five. The Benedictines are Roman Catholic monks famed for their modest lifestyle, which involves physical labor as well as spiritual discipline. As a general rule, Benedictines remain in one monastery for life. While under their care, Thomas was well grounded in basic religious knowledge, academic skills, and good study habits.

The monks of Montecassino taught by emphasizing close scrutiny of Scripture, careful reading and writing, and rote memory of long and complicated passages. Years later, when he was a famous scholar, Thomas drew upon what he had learned at Montecassino in answer to a request for advice on how to study:

> Make up your mind to start on small streams rather than to plunge into the sea; for one should progress from easier matters to those that are more difficult. . . .

. . . Do not be concerned about what speaker you are listening to; instead, when something good is said, commit it to memory. Be sure that you understand whatever you read. Make sure you know the difficulties and store up whatever you can in the treasure-house of the mind; keep as busy as a person who seeks to fill a vessel.[3]

The Dominican

The spiritual authority of the Benedictine monasteries of the time had begun to decline, in great part due to their wealth and prosperity. In 1239, Thomas was sent to study at the Imperial University of Naples, where he made friends with some Dominican monks. Dominicans were dedicated to education and to preaching to common people. They took vows of poverty, chastity, and obedience. Unlike the Benedictines, who tended to establish their monasteries in the country, the Dominicans established themselves in the towns. They quickly became the intellectual elite of the thirteenth century.[4] Thomas was so attracted to the Dominican way of life that he decided to join the order. This decision disturbed his family, who had been looking forward to enjoying the advantages of being related to a powerful priest or bishop. That Thomas would become a poor monk was not in their plans.

Nonetheless, Thomas entered the Order of Preachers, as the Dominicans are known, in 1243 or 1244. His mother was so unhappy about it that she sent a distress signal to his older brothers, who were soldiers at the time. Thomas was traveling with other Dominicans when the brothers tracked him down and ordered him to remove his Dominican habit. When he refused, they kidnapped him. His family held him captive for several months. They applied various arguments and pressures but did allow him to wear his Dominican habit and to study—though they kept him confined to his room. One biographer reports the interesting but unlikely story that his family sent a provocatively dressed girl into his room one night while Thomas slept: "She tempted him to sin, using all the devices at her disposal, glances, caresses and gestures."[5] The saint in Thomas proved stronger than temptation, and he prayed until the girl left. He even managed to write a treatise *On Fallacies* while in family captivity. Finally, convinced of Thomas's sincerity and strength, his family released him. Soon after, the Dominicans sent him first to Cologne to continue his studies with the acclaimed teacher Albertus Magnus and then to the University of Paris.

The University of Paris

What we know today as universities began as medieval cathedral schools, though cathedral schools lacked central libraries and clusters of special buildings. Cathedral schools were religious in nature, originally consisting of masters and students under the authority of the supporting cathedral.

You can say that you trust God anyway—that no arguments can undermine your faith. But that is just a statement describing how stubborn you are; it has no bearing whatsoever on the question of God's goodness.

B. C. Johnson

It is clear from what has been said that there is a substance which is eternal and unmovable and separate from sensible things.

Aristotle

These independent schools were associated with cathedrals and monasteries in such cities as Cluny, Tours, Chartres, and Paris. Notre Dame eventually supported more than one school. They spread from France to England and throughout Europe.

As the number of schools increased, they vied to possess the best libraries and faculty, as well as competing over the quality and drama of the great public debates (called disputations) they held. Associated with both the Dominicans and Franciscans, these individual schools, which were clustered about Paris, tended to specialize in copying and commenting on selected texts, in consolidating oral teachings into unified written form, or in subject areas such as rhetoric or theology. In time, the individual schools merged into the University of Paris, which was closely supervised by the bishop of Paris, the chancellor of Notre Dame, and the pope.

As they developed, universities became centers of medieval learning, based in part on the quality of their faculties and in part on the availability of important new translations of philosophical texts. Most notable among these was the work of Aristotle; also significant were the great commentaries on Aristotle made by Arabian scholars from Baghdad and Spain, and original Arabic and Jewish works of epistemology, metaphysics, and ethics by al-Farabi, ibn-Gabriol, Avicenna, and Averroës.

Only the clergy could study and teach at the universities, and Latin was the universal language of church and school. It is not surprising, then, that for the first time the unification, organization, and synthesis of knowledge became major philosophic tasks, strengthened by the authority and firm hierarchy of the church. The fundamental philosophical and social movement of the thirteenth century was toward the synthesis and consolidation of a single spiritual truth.[6]

Much of the teaching was conducted in the great public debates, the disputations, so the universities sought great debaters who could enhance the school's reputation by the quality of their disputations. The Dominicans were renowned debaters, and by 1231 they held two faculty positions in theology at the University of Paris.[7]

On disputation days all other classes were suspended. One type of disputation was the *disputed question*, which consisted of two sessions. In the morning session bachelors in theology (the equivalent of graduate students today) carefully studied a set of problems (the question) and then, under the guidance of their teacher, publicly stated complications, ambiguities, and contradictions in the form of numbered objections. The student was required to demonstrate familiarity with important works bearing on the topic by citing various authorities and quoting their positions. Lastly, the student suggested the best solution he could to the original question. This was all done before a large audience of other students, faculty, and distinguished guests.

In the afternoon session, the master of the school of theology summarized the morning session and, going through the objections one by one, provided his own final answer to the questions, together with his reply to

I maintain that all attempts to employ reason in theology in any merely speculative manner are altogether fruitless.

Immanuel Kant

Thomas Aquinas was a master of the "disputed question." Medieval disputations sometimes lasted for days and have been characterized as philosophical combat.

the objections. The master would eventually write and publish a summary known as a *disputed question*. The basic structure of these oral disputations—statement of the question, detailed list of objections and commentaries on the objections, and final resolution—is the basic model on which Aquinas constructed his *Summa Theologica*.

Medievalist Martin Grabmann characterizes these public debates as tournaments for the clergy. Priests of all ranks and any church officials who happened to be in town attended. The time, place, and topic of the dispute were announced in all the schools of the university. The bachelor being tested responded to questions formulated by the masters present. If necessary, the student could be prompted by the teacher who had helped him prepare for the dispute. Grabmann says:

> These disputations exercised enormous attraction upon
> teacher and pupil alike. They provided a continuous coming
> together between the master and his scholars, they spurred

Theology is an effort to ex-
plain the unknowable in
terms of the not worth know-
ing. . . . [It] is not only op-
posed to the scientific spirit;
it is opposed to every other
form of rational thinking.
H. L. Mencken

the ambitions of the young, and stretched their intellectual capacities to the limit. In the disputation the personal capability of the student appeared most articulately and publicly. The disputations also exhibited a certain dramatic interest. They were a kind of tournament, a contest or duel with the weapons of the mind. The alternating movement of these duels, the gradual development and complication of problems, the blow for blow presentation of suggestions and solutions, questions and answers, distinctions and negations, the various sophisms and entrapments in which one tried to entice the adversary— all these, and other moments too, were well calculated to keep the interest and expectation of both the participants in, and spectators of, such exercises of disputation at the highest tension and suspense.[8]

Albertus Magnus: The Universal Teacher

While at Cologne, Thomas was encouraged in the search for philosophical unity by his teacher **Albertus Magnus (Albert the Great) (c. 1200– 1280)**, who was among the first scholars to realize the need to ground Christian faith in philosophy and science. If this were not done, the church would lose influence in the face of great advances in secular and pagan knowledge. Rather than ignore the huge quantity of learning made available by the Crusades, Albert chose to master it. He read most of the Christian, Arabian, and Jewish writers, and wrote continuously about what he read. Albert was called the "Universal Teacher" because of the breadth of his knowledge and because he tried to make Aristotle accessible by paraphrasing many of his works.

Although Albert has been criticized for not being creative and consistent, his efforts at synthesis laid a foundation for Thomas Aquinas. Albert quoted extensively and without alteration, and from this Thomas learned the value of broad knowledge and extensive documentation. In his own work, however, Thomas went beyond his teacher by using his sources to construct a coherent philosophy of his own. Still, his scholarly skills owe a great deal to Albert, who recognized his ability while Thomas was still a young man, as a famous anecdote reveals: When Thomas first arrived in Paris, his rural manners, his heavyset, farm-boy physique, and slow, quiet ways earned him the nickname of "the Dumb Ox," and his handwriting was so bad that others could barely read it. Yet he studied hard and remained good-natured as the other students laughed at him—until the day he answered one of Albert the Great's questions with such stunning brilliance that the master said to the others: "We call this man the Dumb Ox, but someday his bellow will be heard throughout the whole world."

The Task of the Scholar

Shortly before Thomas was born, the church had forbidden the teaching of Aristotle's natural science and *Metaphysics*. His Unmoved Mover was an impersonal, natural force, not a loving, personal God. Entelechy (soul) was part of nature, inseparable from the body that housed it, and so it seemed that Aristotle denied the possibility of personal immortality. Yet the thorough, systematic quality of Aristotle's work on scientific thinking, logic, and nature gradually won more and more medieval converts. As Aristotle's influence spread throughout the University of Paris, questions arose regarding both the relationship of Aristotle's classical naturalism to orthodox Christianity and the accuracy of newly arrived Arabian commentaries on Aristotle. The faculty realized that Aristotle would have to be integrated into Christian theology. This task became the great, courageous accomplishment of Tommaso d'Aquino, "the Dumb Ox of Sicily."

In 1252 Thomas received his master's degree from the University of Paris, where he was also lecturing. He taught theology at the papal court in Rome in 1259, and from 1268 to 1272 lectured in Paris once more. During the twenty years that he was an active teacher, Thomas wrote disputations on various theological questions, commentaries on books of the Bible, commentaries on twelve works of Aristotle and others, and nearly forty other miscellaneous notes, sermons, lectures, poems, and treatises. His crowning achievements are the multivolume summaries of arguments and theology known as the *Summa Theologica* and *Summa contra Gentiles*.

Thomas was sent to Naples to establish a Dominican school in 1272, and in 1274 he was commanded by Pope Gregory X to attend the Council of Lyons. He died on the trip to Lyons on March 7, 1274. As reported by Brother Peter of Montesangiovanni, his last hours reflected his submission to the authority of the church.

THE WISDOM OF THE SCHOLAR

The term **Scholasticism** refers to the mainstream of Christian philosophy in medieval Europe from about 1000 to about 1300, just after the death of Aquinas. It comes from the Greek *scholastikos*, meaning "to enjoy leisure" or "to devote one's free time to learning."

Scholastic philosophy rested on a strong interest in logical and linguistic analysis of texts and arguments for the ultimate purpose of producing a systematic statement and defense of Christian beliefs. As the revealed word of God, the Bible was central to this project, but always interpreted in accord with the authority of the church and the wisdom of selected earlier Christian writers.

A central effort of Scholastic philosophers was the attempt to reconstruct Greek philosophy in a form that not only was consistent with but supported

SCHOLASTICISM
Christian philosophy that dominated medieval Europe from about A.D. 1000 to 1300, stressing logical and linguistic analysis of texts and arguments in order to produce a systematic statement and defense of Christian beliefs.

The creationist, whether naive Bible-thumper or an educated bishop, simply postulates an already existing being of prodigious complexity. If we are going to allow ourselves the luxury of postulating organized complexity without offering an explanation, we might as well make a job of it and simply postulate the existence of life as we know it!

Richard Dawkins

and strengthened Christian doctrine. An important aspect of this effort was the imposition of a hierarchy of knowledge, in which the highest place was held by revelation, as interpreted by the church; next were faith and theology; philosophy came last, subordinated to both faith and revelation.[9]

Medieval scholars were the first professors of philosophy; their task was to teach, to expound on texts, to write about them, to debate in class and in public, and to publish great educational summations of official doctrine.[10] Generally viewed as the most complete realization of medieval Scholasticism, Thomas Aquinas is the archetype of the scholar. Unlike modern professional philosophers, Thomas was not free to *pursue* the truth wherever it led; he *started from the truth*—always ultimately supporting Christian doctrine.

In Scholastic philosophy, the *way* a case was made and analyzed became an integral part of what was being claimed. Method remains an important concern to today's scholars. Logic and linguistic analysis were vital elements in proving a case—as they are today. Scholarly, intellectual standards were developed for documenting an argument with citations from approved sources—standards that any student who has ever written a research paper will recognize. In fact, in the first twelve questions of the *Summa Theologica*, Thomas refers to other authors 160 times.

Scholastic philosophers had to present their arguments publicly and defend them against all comers—a precursor to the modern professor's obligation to publish and present and defend papers. Subject matter became specialized, and a universal impersonal, technical, scholarly style of writing was developed to communicate with a select audience of students and teachers devoted to mastering an elaborate professional technique.[11]

Thomas reflects a move away from the importance of a particular philosopher, away from the *sophos* whose work closely reflected his life, to a less personal view of the individual thinker as a part of a scholarly community. Thomas's work reflected his life, but the product of his work is scholarly and technical in ways unlike anything produced before. He says:

A philosopher is a blind man in a dark room looking for a black cat that isn't there. A theologian is the man who finds it.

H. L. Mencken

> That which a single man can bring, through his work and his genius, to the promotion of truth is little in comparison with the total of knowledge. However, from all these elements, *selected and co-ordinated and brought together*, there arises a marvelous thing, as is shown by the various departments of learning, which by the work and sagacity of many have come to a wonderful augmentation [emphasis added].[12]

Although many of the issues that troubled Thomas are closely tied to the medieval worldview, his arguments for the existence of God, and his discussions of fate, free will, evil, and God's nature transcend the Middle Ages, speaking to timeless questions about our relationship to God. Thomas's stature as a philosopher is independent of his importance as a medieval Catholic theologian, for he addresses eternal, truly catholic (universal) questions for anyone who takes seriously the existence of a loving, powerful, personal God—and polls report that nearly 90 percent of all Americans do.[13]

Now, as in Thomas's time, there are conflicting claims about the meaning and authenticity of sacred texts, and disagreements regarding Christian authorities. The proper use of reason is an important part of the search for divinely inspired wisdom today, as it was in the thirteenth century.

Christian philosophy, like Jewish, Islamic, or Buddhist philosophy, often resembles theology. Any religion-based philosophy walks a fine line between intellectual rigor and doctrinal orthodoxy. Christian doctrine is complex, encompassing teachings concerning the Creation, the Fall, Original Sin, the nature of evil, angels and demons, grace, predestination, the elect, sacraments, disputes over ritual, and authoritative texts, to list only some. But, of course, these issues are unimportant if there is no God. Thomas's efforts to prove the existence of God are among the most widely studied parts of his philosophy.

When a Sophist asked St. Augustine what God was doing before the Creation, the Saint answered: "He was creating Hell for people like you."

PROVING THE EXISTENCE OF GOD

Any religious philosophy faces the problem of proving the existence of God. The believer may be content with faith, but the philosopher is obligated to present rational and/or empirical evidence. Although Thomas believed in God, he also thought God's existence could be demonstrated by natural reason. To this end he offered five proofs for the existence of God. Each proof follows a basic pattern, beginning with some effect that we are all familiar with, such as movement or growth. Thomas then tries to show that the only possible explanation for this effect is God. *The Five Ways are cause-effect arguments, beginning with our experience of effects and moving toward their cause, God.*

The Five Ways are most effective if viewed as part of a single argument. The first three ways deal with avoiding an infinite chain of causes in nature. Their conclusion is that an Unmoved Mover/Uncaused Cause must exist, that is, a being whose existence depends only on its own essence and not on anything external to itself. But Aristotle said much the same thing without concluding that a personal god exists; such an impersonal cause could just as easily be basic matter and energy. The fourth and fifth ways are thus crucial. They are needed to introduce some quality into the overall description of causes and effects that can transform them into a personal God.

The First Way: Motion

The Five Ways begin with the argument Thomas thought was the easiest to understand, the **argument from motion**. Starting with the indisputable observation that things are moving, the argument points out that motion must be given to each object by some other object that is already moving. For instance, a rack of balls at rest on a billiard table is set in motion only after being struck by the *already moving* cue ball. In turn, the cue ball is set in motion after being struck by the tip of the *already moving* cue stick. But

ARGUMENT FROM MOTION Attempt to prove the existence of God based on the reasoning that in order to avoid an infinite regress, there must be an Unmoved Mover capable of imparting motion to all other things; Aristotelian argument that forms the basis for the first of Thomas Aquinas's Five Ways.

the cue stick cannot move unless something *already moving* moves it: a gust of wind, an earthquake, a cat, or Minnesota Fats.

It *might* be possible to keep imagining an infinite chain of things already in motion moving other things. But no such infinite regress can account for the fact that things *are actually in motion*. Given that things are moving, we know that some *first already moving thing* had to move other not-yet-moving things. Thomas reasoned that some "first mover" had to exist, some force or being with the ability to move other things without itself needing to be moved by any outside force. God is just such an Unmoved Mover. Here is Thomas's argument:

> Therefore, whatever is moved must be moved by another. If that by which it is moved be itself moved, then this also must needs be moved by another, and that by another again. But this cannot go on to infinity, because then there would be no first mover, and, consequently, no other mover, seeing that subsequent movers move only inasmuch as they are moved by the first mover; as the staff moves only because it is moved by the hand. Therefore it is necessary to arrive at a first mover, moved by no other; and this everyone understands to be God.[14]

PHILOSOPHICAL QUERY

Is there any other explanation for motion besides an "unmoved mover"? If so, what is it? If not, is Thomas's conclusion sound?

My father taught me that the question "Who made me?" cannot be answered, since it immediately suggests the further question "Who made God?"

John Stuart Mill

The Second Way: Cause

The explanation given above for the motions of billiard balls is incomplete. We can still ask what accounts for the existence of billiard balls, cue sticks, and Fats. Thomas answered with a second argument, similar in pattern to his first, but based on the Aristotelian concept of cause. Because the second argument concerns the ultimate cause of the entire universe, it is called the **cosmological argument**, from the Greek word *kosmos,* meaning "world," "universe," or "orderly structure."

In a nutshell, the cosmological argument asserts that it is impossible for any natural thing to be the complete and sufficient source of its own existence. In order to cause itself, a thing would have to precede itself. Put another way, in order for me to be the source of my own existence, I would have to exist before I existed. This is as absurd as it is impossible.

In broad strokes, my existence is explained by my parents' existence, and theirs by my grandparents' existence, and so on. But if *every* set of parents had to have parents, there could never be any parents at all. At least one set of parents must not have had parents. In the Bible, this is Adam and Eve. But even Adam and Eve did not cause their own existence. They were created by God, who creates but is uncreated. This is why it is said that "God always was, is, and will be."

COSMOLOGICAL ARGUMENT From the Greek word *kosmos,* meaning "world," "universe," or "orderly structure"; argument for the existence of God that since it is impossible for any natural thing to be the complete and sufficient source of its own existence, there must be an Uncaused Cause capable of imparting existence to all other things; Aristotelian argument that forms the basis for the second of Aquinas's Five Ways.

In Thomas's understanding of things, any series or system of causes and effects requires an originating cause. In order to avoid an infinite regress of causes, which he thought was impossible, there had to be an Uncaused Cause.

The cosmological argument is based on Aristotle's concept of *efficient cause*. Efficient cause is the force that initiates change or brings about some activity. The efficient cause in the development of a human fetus, for example, is the entire biochemical process of changes in the mother's womb that nurtures the growing fetus. In the case of an acorn, the efficient cause that produces an oak tree consists of rain, sun, soil, and temperature interacting to initiate growth and development. Thomas argues:

> In the world of sensible things we find there is an order of efficient causes. . . . Now in efficient causes it is not possible to go on to infinity, because in all efficient causes following in order, the first is the cause of the intermediate cause, and the intermediate is the cause of the ultimate cause, whether the intermediate cause be several, or one only. Now to take away the cause is to take away the effect. Therefore, if there be no first cause among efficient causes, there will be no ultimate, nor any intermediate, cause. . . . Therefore it is necessary to admit a first efficient cause, to which everyone gives the name God.[15]

PHILOSOPHICAL QUERY

Discuss the cosmological argument. Is Thomas's reasoning sound or not? Are you comfortable with the possibility that there is no "first cause"? If there isn't, can we explain the existence of the universe at all? Discuss.

The Third Way: Necessity

Thomas's third proof, the **argument from necessity**, may seem odd to you. It is based on the difference between two classes of things: those whose existence is only contingent or *possible* and those whose existence is *necessary*. Contingent things might or might not exist, but they do not have to exist, and they all eventually cease to exist. You and I do not exist of necessity: we just happen to exist given the particular history of the world. Our existence is contingent, dependent on something else. This is true, in fact, of every created thing in the universe. It is even possible and imaginable that the universe itself never existed, or that it someday will cease to exist. In other words, the universe is also contingent.

But, Thomas pointed out, it is not possible to conceive of a time in which nothing whatsoever existed. There would be no space; time itself would not exist. There would be no place for something to come into existence from or to. There would be nowhere for anything to move, if there were anything to move, which there would not be. Without movement, there would

Supposing science ever became complete so that it knew every single thing in the whole universe. Is it not plain that the questions, "Why is there a universe?" "Why does it go on as it does?" "Has it any meaning?" would remain just as they are?

C. S. Lewis

ARGUMENT FROM NECESSITY Argument for the existence of God based on the idea that if nothing had ever existed, nothing would always exist; therefore, there is something whose existence is necessary (an eternal something); Aristotelian argument that forms the basis for the third of Aquinas's Five Ways.

be no passage of time. If no time passes, nothing happens. *Thus, if nothing had ever existed, nothing would always exist.* But all around us we see things in existence. Therefore, there was never no-thing. Getting rid of the double negatives, this becomes: There was always something—or there is something that always existed and always will. (See Democritus, Chapter 3.)

In other words, there must be something whose existence is necessary and not just possible. There needs to be some reason that what is possible actually happens. In short, God's existence is necessary. As Thomas puts it:

[Religious ideas], which are given out as teachings, are not precipitates of experience or end-results of thinking; they are illusions, fulfill-ments of the oldest, strongest and most urgent wishes of mankind.

Sigmund Freud

> We find in nature things that are possible to be and not to be, since they are found to be generated, and to be corrupted, and consequently, it is possible for them to be and not to be. But it is impossible for them always to exist, for that which can not-be at some time is not. Therefore, if everything can not-be, then at one time there was nothing in existence. Now if this were true, even now there would be nothing in existence, be-cause that which does not exist begins to exist only through something already existing. . . . Therefore, we cannot but admit the existence of some being having of itself its own necessity, and not receiving it from another, but rather causing in others their necessity. This all men speak of as God.[16]

PHILOSOPHICAL QUERY

Scholastic arguments often hinged on whether or not something was conceivable (clearly imaginable). One cardinal principle held that no one could even conceive of absolute nothingness. Do you agree? Explain. Whether or not you agree, do you find the argu-ment from necessity convincing? Discuss.

The Fourth Way: Degree

The first three arguments for the existence of God fail to establish the exis-tence of a good and loving being. They only deny the possibility of an infi-nite series of causes and effects. Even if some element or entity functions as an ever-existing Prime Mover or Uncaused Cause, these characteristics alone do not describe God. In the fourth and fifth arguments, Thomas makes a qualitative shift in his proofs.

ARGUMENT FROM GRADATION Argument for the existence of God based on the idea that being progresses from inanimate objects to increas-ingly complex animated creatures, culminating in a qualitatively unique God; Aristotelian argument that forms the basis for the fourth of Aquinas's Five Ways.

The fourth way rests on the idea of qualitative differences among kinds of beings. Known as the **argument from gradation**, it is based on a meta-physical concept of a hierarchy of souls (see Chapter 7). In ascending order, being progresses from inanimate objects to increasingly complex animated creatures. (For instance, a dog has more being than a worm, and a person more than a dog.) Thomas believed that what contemporary philosopher Arthur Lovejoy called "the great chain of being" continued upward through angels to God.

According to the principle of gradation, the man in this photo has more "being" than the dog, which has more than the tree. Does such a view reflect reality or does it foster a kind of arrogance in which we see ourselves as superior to—rather than a part of—the natural world? Which attitude does the way the dog is looking at the man seem to support?

This chain of being, Thomas thought, is reflected in the properties of individual things, as well as in the kinds of things that exist. For example, there are grades of goodness, going from the complete lack of goodness (evil) to pure goodness (God), from the complete lack of honesty to complete honesty, from utter ugliness to sublime beauty, and so forth. In very general terms, existence flows downward from perfection and completeness to varying lower stages, each descending level possessing less being.

Of the Five Ways, the significance of this argument can be especially difficult for contemporary thinkers to grasp because it rests on a metaphysical worldview that is alien to many of us today. Yet we cannot just dismiss it as a quirk of the medieval mind-set. The Five Ways form a cumulative argument. The first three arguments cannot establish the existence of *a qualitatively different kind of being*. The fifth argument, as we shall see, only establishes that the universe is ordered. Without the argument from gradation,

If God did not exist it would be necessary to invent him.
Voltaire

Thomas can make a case only for an eternal something that follows orderly patterns. But this "something" is almost a contemporary scientist's description of the universe; it is certainly not a description of God. Without the introduction of qualitatively different kinds of entities, Thomas cannot establish the existence of God by rational argument.

Here is Thomas's argument from gradation:

> Among beings there are some more and some less good, true, noble, and the like. But *more* and *less* are predicated of different things according as they resemble in their different ways something which is the maximum, as a thing is said to be hotter according as it more nearly resembles that which is hottest; so that there is something which is truest, something best, something noblest, and, consequently, something which is most being, for those things that are greatest in truth are greatest in being. . . . Therefore there must also be something which is to all beings the cause of their being, goodness, and every other perfection; and this we call God.[17]

PHILOSOPHICAL QUERY

Do you have any sense of grades of being? Is there anything in your own experience that supports Thomas's argument? Discuss the argument from gradation.

[T]here is no escape from the conclusion that it is unlikely that God is all good. Thus the problem of evil triumphs over traditional theism.

B. C. Johnson

The Fifth Way: Design

Thomas's **teleological argument**, also called the argument from design, is one of the most widely known and used arguments for the existence of God. Teleological thinking, as we learned in Chapter 7, is a way of understanding things in terms of their telos, or end. For example, infancy is understood in relationship to adulthood: The adult is the telos of the infant; the oak tree is the telos of the acorn. When archaeologists uncover some ancient artifact unlike anything ever seen before, they often "recognize" that it was made for a purpose, a telos, even if they do not know what specific purpose. In other words, they infer the existence of a designer who shaped the mysterious object.

Thomas asserts that the entire natural world exhibits order and design. Water behaves in orderly ways, as do rocks, crabs, clouds, reindeer, and people. Today, we are even more aware of the complex interrelatedness of the natural world than Thomas was: Rain forests in the Amazon basin scrub the atmosphere in ways that affect the whole earth; this is their telos. Cells and chromosomes, molecules, atoms, and subatomic particles exhibit order with each performing a specific function, a telos. On inspection, the universe reveals order; otherwise, we could not quantify scientific laws.

Order, Thomas argued, implies intelligence, purpose, a plan. Here again he follows the pattern of starting with common observations and searching

TELEOLOGICAL ARGUMENT Also called the argument from design, this widely known argument for the existence of God claims that the universe manifests order and purpose that can only be the result of a conscious intelligence (God); Aristotelian argument that forms the basis for the fifth of Aquinas's Five Ways and the basis of William Paley's watchmaker argument..

for principles to explain them. In this case, Thomas held that the order we observe in inanimate nature cannot come from matter itself, since matter lacks consciousness and intelligence. Design, by its nature, implies conscious intent. Thus, if the world exhibits evidence of design, it follows logically that there must be a Designer:

> We see that things which lack knowledge, such as natural bodies [matter and inanimate objects], act for an end, and this is evident from their acting always, or nearly always, in the same way, so as to obtain the best result. Hence it is plain that they achieve their end, not fortuitously, but designedly. Now whatever lacks knowledge cannot move towards an end, unless it is directed by some being endowed with knowledge and intelligence; as the arrow is directed by the archer. Therefore some intelligent being exists by whom all natural things are directed to their end; and this being we call God.[18]

PHILOSOPHICAL QUERY

Is order the same thing as design? Does the universe seem to be ordered and well designed? Discuss. (For more on this intriguing topic, see Chapter 12.)

Commentary on the Five Ways

Thomas's arguments begin with empirical observations and then attempt to show that the only logically consistent, adequate explanation for them requires the existence of God. If other equally plausible arguments can account for these observations, then Thomas has not conclusively proved the existence of God; he has at best shown that God's existence is possible or probable.

Underlying Thomas's first three arguments is his conviction that an infinite series of events (motions or causes) is impossible, even inconceivable. But is it? Not according to modern science and mathematics. The simplest example of an infinite series is the positive numbers. No matter what number you reach, you can always add +1. If one infinite series is possible—and it is—then another is possible. So to the extent that Thomas's arguments rely on the impossibility of any infinite series, they fail.

It is certainly possible to argue that nature exhibits as much ugliness and disorder as it does design and purpose. What's the telos of starving children or freak accidents? Where is the hand of the most good, most noble designer in poverty and inequity? Perhaps Thomas only *projected* his own sense of order onto the world, rather than *observing* order in it. Many observers simply deny the presence of design; they fail to see the world as well ordered.

But don't be too quick to reject Thomas's proofs. Historian of philosophy W. T. Jones points out that the force of Thomas's arguments rests on

---

Creation produces myriad forms. Whatever one's form, one should cherish and take care of it and use it to live well.
Lie Zi

Science has not killed God— quite the contrary. It is clearer now than ever that what we can learn from science is limited to what is abstract and quantifiable. Because of what science has achieved, the unresolved (and undoubtedly unresolvable) dilemmas of what Unamuno called the "man of flesh and bone; the man who is born, suffers, and dies"—above all, who dies"—are more poignant, the mysteries deeper. God is needed now more than ever.
René J. Muller

whether or not they "account for" motion, cause, goodness, and design. He distinguishes between explanations *inside* a system and explanations that account for the system *as a whole*.[19] Ignorance of this difference is a chief source of conflict between science and religion. Scientific explanations are explanations within systems; Thomas, on the other hand, was attempting to account for the universe as a whole. Let us examine this difference.

In 1953, Stanley Miller, a biochemist at the University of Chicago, provided the first empirical evidence for the possibility that organic life could evolve from inorganic matter. Miller tried to replicate conditions as they could have been soon after the earth formed. He put methane, ammonia, and hydrogen—elements believed to have been present in the early atmosphere—into a glass container. As the chemicals were mixed with steam from boiling water, they passed through glass tubes and flowed across electrodes that were constantly emitting a spark. At the end of a week, a soupy liquid had formed in the container. This liquid contained organic compounds and amino acids—building blocks for organic matter and life-forms. In the decades since Miller's experiment, many of these building-block chemicals have been produced in laboratory conditions thought to mimic conditions during various stages of the earth's history.

Such experiments might explain the origins of life *within* the universe, understood as a system composed of basic matter and energy. But they cannot address certain kinds of questions regarding the universe *as a whole*. Where did the matter and energy come from? In his experiment, Miller *acquired* matter and energy, he did not *create* them from nothing. He "created" only in the sense that an artist creates—by transforming what is already there. Interestingly, experiments like Miller's can be used to support Thomas's arguments. Miller had to design his experiment, being careful in his selection of gases. Then he had to provide a fitting environment and introduce motion/cause in the form of electrical impulses. The existence of the experimenter and the need for carefully controlled conditions can be interpreted as demonstrating the need for the intervention of the Designer. If the analogy is carried further, the scientist represents the need for God to get the whole thing going.

Which interpretation is correct, the Thomistic or the scientific? The question cannot be answered without qualification. Scientific explanations enable us to understand and control events within the natural order. Even if scientists agree on the steps that produced the universe, such explanations cannot account for the existence of matter and energy themselves. All they can account for is the behavior of matter and energy, *given their existence and given how they exist*.

Thomas's arguments, though beginning with empirical observations, attempt something else. They address questions about the whole. For many people, science—with all its virtues—cannot satisfy a need to understand where we came from and why. Thomas the Scholar stands between science and religion, attempting to reconcile faith, reason, and experience.

Religions are the great fairy-tales of the conscience.
George Santayana

Take from your scientific work a serious and incorruptible method of thought, help to spread it, because no understanding is possible without it. Revere those things which go beyond science which really matter and about which it is so difficult to speak.
Werner Heisenberg

THE ONLY PERSON RESPONSIBLE ESCAPED

To proceed with the Biblical curiosities. Naturally you will think the threat to punish Adam and Eve for disobeying was of course not carried out, since they did not create themselves, nor their natures nor their impulses nor their weaknesses, and hence were not properly subject to anyone's commands, and not responsible to anybody for their acts. It will surprise you to know that the threat *was* carried out. Adam and Eve were punished, and their crime finds apologists unto this day. . . .

As you perceive, the only person responsible for the couple's offense escaped; and not only escaped but became the executioner of the innocent.

In your country and mine we should have the privilege of making fun of this kind of morality, but it would be unkind to do it here. Many of these people have the reasoning faculty, but no one uses it in religious matters.

Mark Twain
"Letters from Earth," in *What Is Man? And Other Philosophical Writings*, ed. Paul Baender (Los Angeles: University of California Press, 1973), Letter III.

Given Thomas's intentions, and taken together, the Five Ways are persuasive and suggestive, even if they are not conclusive. Some religions tend to dismiss or even mock attempts to prove God's existence as unworthy of the faith that "surpasses all understanding." Some scientists and philosophers tend to dismiss and even mock attempts to answer timeless "why questions" as naive or irrational. To the true believer, faith is enough. To the pure scientist or analytic philosopher, the fact that the universe is here is enough. Both approaches, in their extreme forms, repress some of the most powerful, important aspects of the human experience.

COMPLICATIONS FOR NATURAL THEOLOGY

If Thomas's arguments are difficult and unconvincing to you, keep in mind, though, that he was applying what he called "natural reason" to a complex theology. Part of the difficulty he, or any philosopher who attempts such a task, faces is that various articles of faith seem to contradict each other and appear inconsistent with common experience. Had Thomas been able to follow either faith *or* reason, he could have avoided certain inconsistencies and confusions more easily. Instead, he struggled with the most difficult questions facing the Christian philosopher. (Similar difficulties face Jewish and Muslim philosophers as well.) To get a clearer sense of the complexities involved, we'll look at Thomas's analysis of the problem of reconciling free will and evil with God's omnipotence and foreknowledge.

If God is the wise and good First Cause, it follows that He wills everything that happens, including the existence of each individual. Nothing occurs by chance. Chance is merely the name we give to events that occur in a causal sequence unclear or unknown to us. Since *all* causal sequences lead back to the First Cause, everything happens "for a reason," or, more accurately, "nothing happens unless God causes it." It would seem to follow, then, that because of God's foreknowledge and the fact that He causes everything to happen, every event *must* occur exactly as it does.

In Thomas's language, every event that occurs does so out of *necessity*—nothing that happens can be merely *possible*. If everything that happens must happen exactly as it does, how can humans be free? Yet free will—the freedom to choose our own actions—is a necessary condition for moral responsibility. We cannot *justly* be held responsible for events over which we have no control.

If there were not a Devil, we would have to invent him.
Oscar Wilde

The Problem of Evil

I think the **problem of evil** is the most important theological question for any religion or philosophy that asserts the existence of an all-powerful, all-wise, all-good God. The problem in its basic form: *If God can prevent the destructive suffering of the innocent, yet chooses not to, He is not good. If God chooses to prevent the suffering, but cannot, He is not omnipotent. If God cannot recognize the suffering of the innocent, He is not wise.*

The problem of evil is a timeless question that confronts nearly every thinking person. It is often cited as a barrier to faith in the Judeo-Christian-Islamic God by agnostics and atheists. Quick answers to the problem of evil are usually worse than no answers because they involve obvious absurdities or suggest a callousness that's inconsistent with charity. If someone answers that suffering builds character, I offer you the starvation, molestation, or torture of children: Modern psychology has clearly shown that the damage caused by childhood suffering is often severe enough to last a lifetime. If someone answers that we are unable to understand the ways of God, I remind you that this gap of comprehension must apply to *everything else* about God if we are to be consistent. But these are distractions.

The real force of the problem of evil always comes back to justifying preventable evil and suffering. Given the qualities attributed to the Judeo-Christian God, how can He not be responsible for evil? Thomas himself deplored contradictions. Is it not contradictory to assert that God is the cause of everything, and then to say that He is not responsible for the existence of evil (just everything else)?

Thomas reasoned that God willed the universe in order to communicate His love of His own essence, in order to "multiply Himself." Now of course, this does not mean that God created other Gods, for as we have seen, God must be a unique essence. It means that God created the universe as a reflection of His love.

PROBLEM OF EVIL
If God can prevent the suffering of the innocent, yet chooses not to, He is not good. If God chooses to prevent the suffering, but cannot, He is not omnipotent. If God cannot recognize the suffering of the innocent, He is not wise.

Even that which is called evil, when it is regulated and put in its own place, only enhances our admiration of the good; for we value and enjoy the good more when we compare it with the evil.

St. Augustine

Perhaps the greatest theological question of all is the problem of evil. Is there any way to reconcile the suffering of the innocent (especially children) with the existence of an all-wise, all-good, all-powerful God?

Evil, in Thomas's view, is not a positive, created entity, however. Rather, it is a lack of goodness, which he calls a "privation," and as such, it is not "creatable." Instead, evil is a kind of necessary *by-product* of free will. But it is not a product of the informed human will: *No one can deliberately will evil who fully recognizes it as evil.* For example, Thomas points out that an adulterer is not *consciously willing a sin*, but is willing something that appears to be good, say, sensual pleasure. In this case, however, the pleasure is sought in a way that lacks goodness. To lack goodness is to be evil.

Even the most deliberate, diabolical willing of evil—the most blatant defiance of God—is not really *chosen as evil.* Even if the person uses the word *evil* to describe an action, it is misperceived as being something desirable, something good. In the last few years we've seen an increase in concern about satanism and the occult. Satanists seek power, *which they view as good.* If they use the word *evil* to shock the rest of us, that does not alter the fact that *to them "evil" is good.* Satan himself thought it was bad to be second to God and viewed his rebellion as *good for himself.* No one can choose evil as evil.

PHILOSOPHICAL QUERY

Do you agree that no one *can* choose evil as evil? Why or why not? Explain. Compare Thomas's position with Socrates' position in Chapter 5.

Has all this suffering, this dying around us, a meaning? For, if not, then ultimately there is no meaning to survival; for a life whose meaning depends upon such a happenstance—whether one escapes [suffering] or not— ultimately would not be worth living at all.
Viktor E. Frankl

But God surely foresaw the evil that would occur in His creation. Is He not responsible for it, then, since He went ahead with the Creation? Thomas argued that God willed the creation of a universe in which His love could be multiplied. In His wisdom, He chose to do this through a rich natural order that allowed for the possibility of physical defect and suffering. Physical suffering is not the same as moral evil. God did not directly will suffering, He willed sensitive, rational creatures.

> Now it is necessary that God's goodness, which in itself is one and simple, should be manifested in many ways in His creation; because creatures in themselves cannot attain the simplicity of God. Thus it is that for the completion of the universe there are required diverse grades of being, of which some hold a high and some a low place in the universe. That this multiformity of grades may be preserved in things, God allows some evils, lest many good things should be hindered.[20]

This is an interesting point. It means that the inescapable price for awareness and feeling is the possibility of pain. The eye that is exquisitely sensitive to beauty, for example, will be equally sensitive to ugliness. The only way we could suffer less is if we loved less. It is the nature of love to experience both happiness and sadness. To use Thomas's logic, to think of love without thinking of concern for our loved ones is contradictory. Can I love my family and friends and not miss them when they are away or dead? Is it love if I never let my children leave home, to spare myself missing them? Can I love others and not suffer when they suffer? We all realize that love without suffering is not possible. Feeling and awareness, Thomas argued, involve both pleasure and pain; they are inseparable.

According to Thomas, God could not have fully manifested His nature if He had created a universe of limited choices in which we were forced to love Him and do His will. God, Thomas says, is worthy of love freely given. If we had no choice but to love God, it would no longer be love. It would not be worthy of God. Besides, love under coercion is one of those contradictions Thomas said could not exist. Therefore, since God chose to create a universe in which we could love, He *had* to give us the freedom necessary for love. "Freedom" that prohibits certain choices is not freedom; it is another contradiction.

This, then, is Thomas's solution to the problem of evil: *Though God did not deliberately will evil, He willed the real possibility of evil: evil must always be possible when love and goodness are free choices.* God wills the good of the whole universe. From the standpoint of the whole, a universe containing free moral choices is better than a restricted universe without love and responsibility. We are more like God with freedom than without it.

According to Thomas, the overall perfection of the universe requires a range of beings, some of which get sick, decay, die, and so on. By virtue of being human, as a union of body and soul, we are subject to physical pain

WOULD YOU CONSENT?

"Tell me yourself, I challenge you—answer. Imagine that you are creating a fabric of human destiny with the object of making men happy in the end, giving them peace and rest at last, but that it was essential and inevitable to torture to death only one tiny creature—the baby beating its breast with its fist, for instance—and to found that edifice on its unavenged tears, would you consent to be the architect of those conditions? Tell me, and tell me the truth."

"No, I wouldn't consent," said Alyosha softly.

Fyodor Dostoevsky
The Brothers Karamazov, trans. Constance Garnett (London: Heinemann, 1912).

and suffering. God could have created beings that do not suffer physical death and pain (like angels), but they would not be human. He could not create *humans* who do not suffer.

God willed us freedom that we might love Him in this world, not so we could use it for moral evil. But He could not give us the freedom to choose good without also letting us choose evil. God wills our free choice of good by allowing us the free choice of good or evil. Mature parents understand this. At some point, the child's greatest good must be purchased at the risk of letting him or her make bad decisions. Some of these can have terrible consequences. But love of the child requires the risk.

PHILOSOPHICAL QUERY

Reflect on the idea that God chose to allow evil in order to allow free will and love. Do you think freedom with the real possibility of abuse is better than forced limitation, no matter how "good" the reasons for limitations? What might this imply about forms of government? About censorship? About banning books or rock and roll or drugs? Which is more godlike, protecting people for their own sakes or letting them do harm? Has Thomas provided a satisfactory solution to the problem of evil? Discuss.

COMMENTARY

Perhaps you find Thomas's arguments not quite convincing. Why doesn't God make His existence clearly indisputable to everyone? Why require proofs anyway? Why didn't God use His wisdom and omnipotence to create us so that we do not suffer or do wrong? These are always unanswerable questions, for they amount to asking why did God create *this* universe?

As a Christian philosopher, Thomas pursued his natural theology as far as he could, but he refused to speculate on God's ultimate motives. In the end, he accepted the limits of the human mind when it confronts the infinite. There's even a tradition that Thomas turned toward mysticism late in his life. He is supposed to have said that everything he had written was "as straw"—but he wouldn't say what he "saw" that taught him that.

Thomas's philosophy is alive today as a vital component of Roman Catholicism, but the impact of his great efforts extends beyond the church. He is the first philosopher to have actually produced a comprehensive, logically ordered synoptic (holistic) science, when science is understood as *organized knowledge*. That is, he fulfilled the promise of Aristotle and actually produced a cohesive *system* that included all the known sciences of his time.

Of course, the fragmentation and specialization of knowledge today make such an achievement virtually impossible. That does not reduce the desirability, and perhaps the need, for a cohesive, consistent, all-encompassing philosophy, even if it must be less grand. From Thomas we can learn more than the Scholastic method. In his great effort we see that faith need not be a substitute for philosophical rigor. We see that in spite of the confusions and problems in his arguments, it is still preferable to balance faith with reason rather than to believe, not in humility, but in ignorance.

The logical and theoretical questions Thomas faced still confront basic Christian doctrine. Questions about ultimate causes remain beyond the scope of science, but they do not disappear just because scientists cannot answer them. In Thomas Aquinas we encounter a rare, magnificent attempt to blend faith, reason, and experience into wisdom. If so comprehensive a system is no longer possible, it does not follow that no comprehensive vision is possible. The very effort to construct a consistent, coherent philosophy may be worth more than any risk to our faith in science or religion.

Thomas squarely faced the tension between reason and faith and, without abandoning either, gave faith his ultimate allegiance. The next major figure in the history of philosophy, René Descartes, faced the same tension, but gave himself to reason. In so doing, he ushered in the modern era.

Of all the pursuits open to men, the search for wisdom is more perfect, more sublime, more profitable, and more full of joy.

Thomas Aquinas

SUMMARY OF MAIN POINTS

Scholastic philosophy was a product of a hierarchical society based on a God-centered view of the universe.

Scholastic philosophy developed out of efforts to reconcile Aristotle's naturalism with the increasingly complex theological problems that developed when it became clear the Second Coming of Christ might not occur for generations.

The reconciliation of faith and reason was based, in part, on the law of contradiction: No statement can be both true and false at the same time and under the same conditions.

Scholastic philosophy rested on a strong interest in logical and linguistic analysis of texts and arguments for the ultimate purpose of producing a systematic statement and defense of Christian beliefs.

Thomas Aquinas introduced new levels of thoroughness, scholarship, and methodical rigor to philosophy in the form of his massive summaries known as *summas*.

Thomas's efforts to prove the existence of God using the Five Ways are among the most widely studied examples of Scholastic thinking.

The Five Ways are: the argument from motion; the cosmological argument; the argument from necessity; the argument from gradation; and the argument from design.

In spite of their limits, the Five Ways recognize a common desire to account for the whole of existence. Though science may be able to identify and explain the causal patterns of the universe and the systems it contains, scientific thinking may not be able to account for the existence of the universe itself.

The problem of evil derives from the apparently inescapable conclusion either that God cannot prevent evil, and is therefore not all-powerful, or that God will not prevent evil, and is therefore not all-good.

Thomas answers the problem of evil from two directions: First, he argues that evil is not a positive thing, but a lack of goodness. Hence, it cannot come from God. Evil, like love, is a necessary by-product of free will.

Second, Thomas returns to the importance of love, asserting that God created the universe in order to multiply His love. Because it involves caring, love always involves suffering. Because love cannot be forced, it always requires freedom of choice.

Genuine freedom of choice includes the real possibility of evil. God does not will evil; He wills freedom and love.

STUDY QUESTIONS

1. Compare and contrast the classical worldview with the medieval.

2. What is theology? Distinguish between natural and revealed theology.

3. What basic conditions led to the development of Christian philosophy? Where did the need for interpretation come from?

4. What does it mean to say that human beings are susceptible to principles of reason?

5. What is the significance of Albertus Magnus to Thomas Aquinas?

6. State the law of contradiction. What is its connection to the origins of Scholastic philosophy?

7. In your own words, give a brief description of Scholasticism and describe the chief characteristics of scholarship.

8. In what ways is the medieval scholar the forerunner of the modern professor?

9. In summary—but thorough—form, state Thomas's Five Ways for proving the existence of God.

10. Which of the Five Ways do you think is the weakest? Explain why.

11. Discuss the influence of Aristotle in Thomas's philosophy.

12. Compare and contrast scientific attempts to explain the origin of the universe with theological or philosophical ones.

13. What is evil, according to Thomas?

14. State the problem of evil.

15. Explain how the traditional Judeo-Christian concept of God generates the problem of evil.

16. What is the relationship of free will to love?

17. How does Thomas solve the problem of evil? What do you think of his solution?

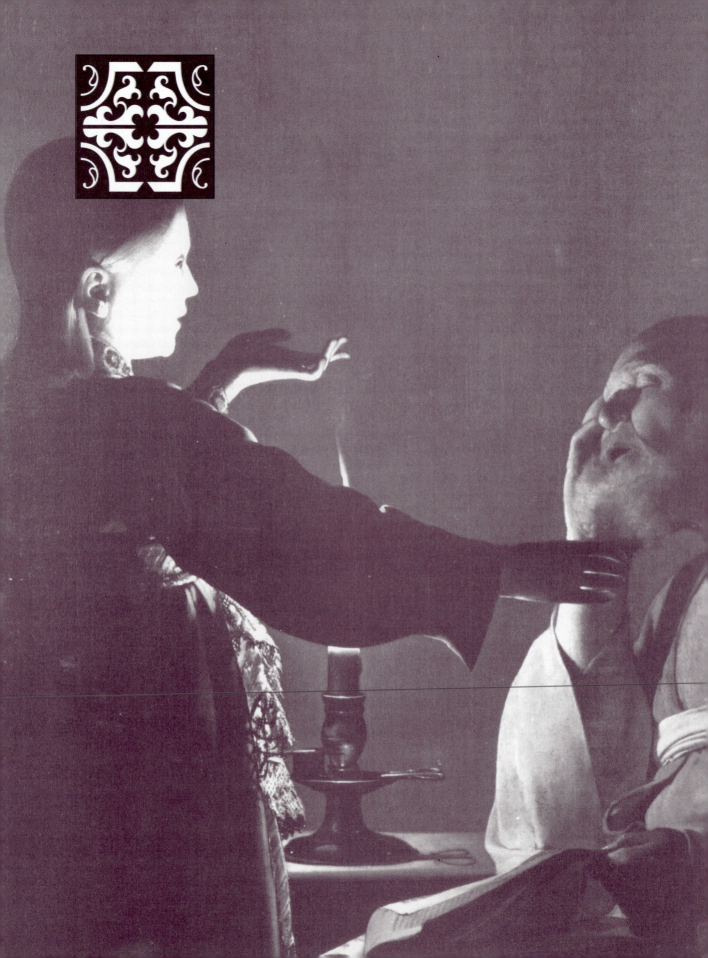

CHAPTER ELEVEN

The Rationalist:

René Descartes

But what then am I?
A thing which thinks.

RENÉ DESCARTES

It's a glorious Sunday morning and you go outside to watch the sun rise. Glancing at the paper, you happily note that your horoscope is favorable. Later you hurry on to church, where you teach Sunday school. The sermon is on Genesis 1:31–2:3:

. . . and God saw all that he had made, and it was very good. Evening came, and morning came, the sixth day.

Thus, the heavens and earth and everything in them were completed. On the sixth day God brought to an end all the work he had been doing; on the seventh day, having finished all his work, God blessed the day and made it holy, because it was the day he finished all his work of creation (Revised Standard Bible).

After a pleasant day, you watch a multicolored sunset, looking forward to tomorrow. It's the first day of the new term, and you've just been awarded tenure at the university. Your field is paleontology, your specialty is evolution. You are quite happy.

And yet your life is full of fundamental inconsistencies and superstitions. In your daily affairs, you forget that the sun neither rises nor sets—the rotation of the earth only makes it appear to move. Relying on your horoscope conflicts with both your religious beliefs and scientific education, but you continue "just for fun." As a paleontologist you teach that it took billions of years for the earth to form and life and consciousness to emerge, yet you also believe that the Bible is the unerring word of God.

You are not alone. Like many others, you have mastered the knack of compartmentalizing your beliefs so that possible inconsistencies are not so obvious. On the rare occasions when you acknowledge inconsistencies, you brush them aside with a variety of strategies: "The Bible is written in the language of faith. Science has its own language. They're both saying the same thing in different ways. The Bible says creation took 'six days,' and biblically that's true. Science says evolution took 'billions of years,' and that's true too—just from a different perspective. And there must be something to astrology. Millions of people believe in it. Besides, it's possible that God is the author of our horoscopes."

Although vaguely dissatisfied with the inconsistencies among your beliefs, you never get around to resolving them. Why should you? We live in an era that fosters rather than discourages such fundamental confusions. We turn to science for medical cures and environmental solutions, yet some of us also turn to crystals and trance channelers, psychics and astrologers. The same person who lobbies against abortion because "life is sacred" may also lobby against higher taxes for education, Medicare, and welfare.

What has come to be known as the modern era of philosophy began when a solitary French philosopher attempted to resolve similar difficulties and contradictions. Modern philosophy began with a new vision of the cosmos and our place in it.

This illustration from Martin Luther's Bible shows God as the orderer of the Ptolemaic universe. So convinced was Luther of the accuracy of this picture of the heavens that he called Copernicus "that fool [who would] reverse the entire art of astronomy. . . . Joshua bade *the sun* and not the earth to stand still."

THE ORIGIN OF THE MODERN MIND

The medieval mind transformed natural order into a divine purpose that was reflected in a hierarchy of authority throughout the entire universe. In the medieval worldview, everything was understood in terms of its place in the whole scheme of things. God ruled the universe, the pope ruled the church, the king ruled the state, and so on down through lords, merchants, craftsmen, and serfs. People accepted that this hierarchy came from God and therefore accepted as legitimate the authority

For many people it is, more than anything else, the appalling depth and extent of human suffering, together with selfishness and greed which produce so much of this, that makes the idea of a loving creator implausible.
John Hick

of the church and the pope. As institutional authority declined, reliance on individual reasoning and experience increased. Whereas the medieval mind was authoritarian, the modern mind is much more individualistic.

By the fourteenth century, the authority of the Roman Catholic church and of the pope had eroded. The credibility of the papacy was severely damaged by a series of disputes and scandals, as popes began to keep church offerings for their own use, and to sell offices and ecclesiastical titles. These abuses led to cries for reform.

Martin Luther

The most famous reformer of the era was **Martin Luther (1483–1546)**, a monk who became disenchanted with the church. Luther challenged the entire medieval and Scholastic worldview by asserting that the individual's channel to God was "justification by faith" rather than by "works" (that is, living a good life in accord with the teachings of the church). In *A Treatise on Christian Liberty* he says:

> You ask, What then is this Word of God, and how shall it be used, since there are so many words of God? I answer, The Apostle explains . . . "The just shall live by faith." . . . Hence it is clear that, as the soul needs only the Word for its life and righteousness, so it is justified by faith alone and not by any works; for if it could be justified by anything else, it would not need the Word, and therefore it would not need faith. . . .
>
> It is clear then that a Christian man has in his faith all that he needs and needs no works to justify him.[1]

In rejecting "works," Luther included the sacraments and confession. Moreover, if, as Luther claimed, the institution and authority of a church are unnecessary, then "every believer is a priest." Luther publicly challenged church authority when he nailed ninety-five theses, which were criticisms of church teachings, to the door of the church in Wittenberg. Although he was ultimately labeled a heretic for his statements, Luther had enough political support in Germany that the church was reluctant to use force against him. He went on to establish his own church—which, ironically, very quickly institutionalized its own rigid requirements and began ejecting heretics.

There is nothing in the world over and above those entities which are postulated by physics.
J. J. C. Smart

The philosophical significance of Luther's move lay in its implication that individual experience and interpretation are more truly Christian than unquestioning acceptance of an official, authoritative position. Luther's revolt against institutionalized authority is one of the markers of the decline of the medieval worldview. As doubts grew about the legitimacy or necessity of the institutional hierarchy, the individual became increasingly significant.

PHILOSOPHICAL QUERY

Today, some people claim to be "spiritual" rather than "religious." They seem to be making a distinction between faith (spirituality) and works (religion). Can there be "a church" if "every individual is a priest"? Is the individual the ultimate authority on matters of faith? If so, is faith relative? If the individual is not the ultimate authority on matters of faith, how can we resolve competing religious or spiritual claims?

The Copernican Revolution

In the Middle Ages, the natural, physical world was thought to be a reflection of a spiritual order. The universe was carefully created by a God of harmony and design, and human beings were the centerpiece, the very purpose, of Creation. The heavens reflected this belief: God made the sun and moon to shine upon us, and placed the earth so that the rest of the universe *revolved around us*. This geocentric worldview is both comforting and reassuring. It physically manifests a sense of order and purpose.

But as it became clearer and more widely known that the earth is a sphere, with no fixed "up" or "down," the old worldview began to totter. Once Luther's contemporary Nicolaus Copernicus mapped the heavens, it toppled.

Some ancient Greek astronomers—in particular, the philosopher Aristarchus of Samos (third century B.C.)—had concluded that the earth revolves around the sun. However, most of Aristarchus's writings were lost, and later astronomers rejected his ideas, in part because they seemed contrary to common experience and in part because they conflicted with Aristotle's teachings. Aristotle believed the earth was the unmoving center of the universe and that the sun, moon, and planets moved in semiregular "epicycles" around it. Ptolemy, an astronomer of the second century A.D., gave Aristotle's ideas even more weight by designing a mathematical model that seemed to predict planetary motions quite well.

By the fifteenth century, however, calculations using the Ptolemaic model no longer matched the observed positions of the planets. This inspired **Nicolaus Copernicus (1473–1543)** to look for a more accurate model. His proposal that the sun is the center of the solar system set in motion a revolution in thinking. He made his case in such a way that knowledgeable astronomers realized the entire Ptolemaic model had to be revised.

Aristotle believed that the earth was the center of the universe, so Copernican astronomy directly refuted Aristotle. Because Thomas Aquinas and the church were so closely tied to Aristotelian philosophy and science, any major threat to Aristotle threatened church authority. If the church—guided by God—was in error here, where else might it be in error? Copernicus was sensitive enough to the church's attitude toward criticism and unofficial doctrines that he withheld publication of his discoveries until shortly before he died.

Once his work was known, the earth was cut loose from its central place of honor, both physically and psychologically, and became just one more planet revolving around the sun. If the earth was reduced in significance, what about us? This major change in perspective did not *feel right* to either

Our own universe, of which we see only a small part today, may not be unique. Its beginning is not the beginning of everything. Other universes may exist at an earlier stage.

Victor Weisskopf

That truth was not worth the stake. Whether the earth or the sun revolves around the other is a matter of profound indifference.

Albert Camus

The Copernican Revolution began when Copernicus showed that the earth is not the center of the universe. As Kierkegaard put it, "Since Copernicus man has been rolling toward X." These sixteenth-century drawings represent pre-Copernican (above) and Copernican (opposite) views of the universe.

Catholic or Protestant theologians. Thus Martin Luther called Copernicus "that fool [who would] reverse the entire art of astronomy. . . . Joshua bade *the sun* and not the earth to stand still."[2]

PHILOSOPHICAL QUERY

Scientific descriptions of reality are often at odds with everyday experience. For example, the sun seems to move across the sky each day, yet "everybody knows" that the earth, not the sun, is moving. So how can we know when to rely on our own experiences, or on the beliefs of the majority, or on the claims of science when the three do not immediately agree? Can you think of any criteria to use?

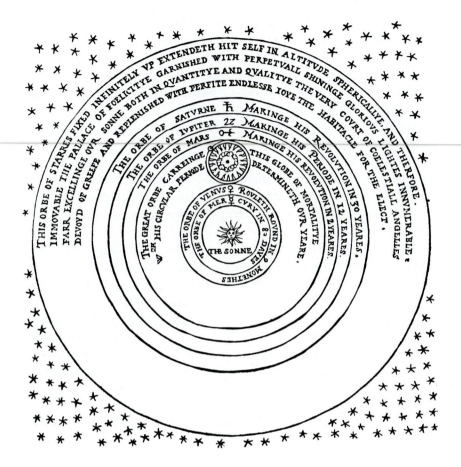

Luther's opinion notwithstanding, Copernicus was no fool. Although the details of his model were inaccurate (for instance, he thought the earth's path around the sun was a circle, but it really is an ellipse), his hypothesis that the earth is part of a sun-centered system was correct, and he achieved it by applying careful calculations to careful observations. The danger in his position can be clearly observed if we speak bluntly: Copernicus rendered both church authority and the consensus of unqualified nonastronomers irrelevant. His careful application of reason and observation began revolutions in both astronomy and philosophical thought.

RENÉ DESCARTES:

THE SOLITARY INTELLECT

René Descartes (1596–1650) was born into an old and respected family in the French province of Touraine. His mother died of tuberculosis a year after his birth, and Descartes believed he

René Descartes

inherited a frail constitution from her. His father was a famous lawyer, whose career kept him away from home for months at a time.

When he was approximately nine or ten years old, Descartes was sent to the Jesuit college at La Flèche, where his physical weakness and mental strength were both acknowledged—he was allowed to sleep later than the other students (a lifelong habit). At La Flèche Descartes studied Greek, Latin, history, liberal arts, science, mathematics, and philosophy, in addition to music, dancing, and fencing.

Descartes spent the next few years living the life of the young gentleman he was. He practiced his fencing, rode horses, and—already in love with mathematics—briefly took up gambling to see if he could devise a system to break the bank. At the University of Poitiers he earned degrees in civil and canon law.

In 1618, when Descartes was twenty-two years old, the Thirty Years' War broke out. To the surprise of his friends, a strong, healthy Descartes first enlisted in the army of the Prince of Nassau, and later joined the army of the Duke of Bavaria. It is not clear whether he ever saw combat.

All the while, Descartes continued to study, being especially fond of mathematics. On November 10, 1619, he had a revelation which would transform him, and ultimately change entirely the direction of Western philosophy. As he later wrote, "I remained the whole day shut up alone in a stove-heated room, where I had complete leisure to occupy my thoughts."[3] There, Descartes says, he "discovered the foundations of a wonderful new science." The next night, full of excitement and anticipation over his discovery, he had three dreams, in one of which he heard a clap of thunder. He took it to be "the Spirit of Truth descending to take possession" of him. Descartes believed he had been divinely encouraged to establish a universal method of reasoning, based on mathematical principles, which, if followed carefully enough, would guarantee the absolutely certain truth of its results.

After this remarkable experience, Descartes' outward life seemed little changed. His inheritance, first from his mother and then from his father, had freed him from the need to make a living, so he traveled, studied, conversed, and wrote. He lived alone most of his life, except for his servants, and during a twenty-year period lived in twenty different houses.

Solitary and secretive, Descartes preferred to avoid the distractions and commotion of city life and social involvements. Most of his philosophical discourse took the form of letters. There were times when he didn't want his friends to know where he was; he even asked them not to write to him for a while. Descartes thought he worked better this way, completely free to devote all his energy, at his own pace, to his studies. In a letter to a friend, Descartes wrote from Amsterdam: "And thus in this large city where I now am, since I seem to be practically the only one here who is not a merchant or in trade; all are so bound up in their profitable business transactions that

I could remain here my entire life without being noticed by anyone."[4] Living this way, Descartes was able to study philosophy, geometry, physics, optics, circulation, and other subjects. Conducting experiments and dissections, as well as making important discoveries in mathematics, he rejected the Scholastic model of science and philosophy, turning instead to firsthand observations and deductions.

In 1635 Descartes had an illegitimate daughter (who died at the age of five) with a servant girl. Later, he referred to the episode as "a dangerous commitment" from which he had "extricated" himself. He was not entirely immune to the charms of women, however. He had a close six-year correspondence with Princess Elizabeth, daughter of the dethroned queen of Bohemia. At nineteen the princess read his *Discourse on Method*, and was surprised and delighted to discover philosophy written in clear, everyday language.

Through a friend who had become the French ambassador to the court of Queen Christina of Sweden, Descartes was ultimately convinced in September 1649—against his better judgment—to join her court in Stockholm. He was not happy there. He had little time for his experiments, and the queen forced him to break his lifelong habits of sleeping late and working at leisure—she wanted to be tutored in philosophy at five in the morning! This forceful woman even managed to get Descartes to write a ballet. The cold weather and austere conditions had a weakening effect on his frail health. By the end of January 1650, he was ill with pneumonia. He died February 11, two months before his fifty-fourth birthday.

In his bold reliance on the disciplined use of his own reason; in his refusal to accept as true anything that did not square with what he had personally verified as true; in his exaltation of the thinking, conscious self as the foundation of all certainty, René Descartes stands not only as the "father of modern philosophy," but as the original archetype of the modern rationalist.

DESCARTES' PROPOSAL

Most philosophers agree that modern philosophy began with Descartes. His remarkable revolution was not so much a shift in the content of philosophical problems as it was a radical new orientation toward the *method* by which philosophy is practiced. His rather uninteresting life is completely overshadowed by his work—just as today a scholar's work may be his or her life.

Modern philosophy emphasizes methodology, technique, and personal, social, and historical detachment. Its origins lie in the decline of a stable social order, the loss of central authority by the church, and the proliferation of scientific advances. More sophisticated mathematics and improved scientific instruments resulted in discoveries that challenged and contradicted Aristotelian naturalism. Scientists were able to move beyond metaphysical

He has lived well who has lived secretly.
Ovid (adopted by Descartes as a motto)

Above all, Descartes admired almost nothing and no one.
C. Adam

Method consists entirely in the order and disposition of the objects toward which our mental vision must be directed if we would find out any truth. We shall comply with it exactly if we reduce involved and obscure propositions step by step to those that are simpler, and then starting with the intuitive apprehension of all those that are absolutely simple, attempt to ascend to the knowledge of all others by precisely similar steps.
René Descartes

speculations to careful observations. No authority—church or political—could refute what the individual observer *saw* or the individual mind *calculated* for itself.

Descartes was a Catholic, but his argument that each individual possesses the "natural light of reason" and needs no intervening authority to interpret "the great book of the world" may remind you of Luther's claim that each person can go directly to God without the church as an intermediary. In other words, Descartes set aside the so-called accumulated wisdom of the past, insisting that each person must examine what is true and false afresh.

Descartes had been educated in the Scholastic tradition. As we saw in Chapter 10, Thomas Aquinas and the other Scholastic philosophers gave great weight to the authority of the church, Plato, Aristotle, and other classical and religious figures. Creative reasoning was possible—but always with an eye toward what was accepted as authoritative.

Reliance on authority is often appropriate and unavoidable in a complex world, but authority is always a secondary source of knowledge. Authoritative claims should always be accepted with caution, subject to rejection or modification in light of our own experiences.

FALLACY OF FALSE AUTHORITY
The error in reasoning that results from accepting the word of experts who are speaking outside their proper fields or uncritically relying on the testimony of others without checking it against our own experiences and reason.

We make an error in reasoning called the **fallacy of false authority** when we accept the word of experts who are speaking outside their proper fields, or when we uncritically rely on the testimony of others without checking it against our own experiences and reason. Some everyday examples would be letting your parents pick your spouse, turning to a pastor for medical advice, or giving uncritical acceptance to whatever the majority of a group decides.

Descartes' scientific interests led him to observe and experiment for himself, however, and he soon discovered that Aristotle's writings on nature contained many errors.

> But so soon as I had achieved the entire course of study at the close of which one is usually received into the ranks of the learned, . . . I found myself embarrassed with so many doubts and errors that it seemed to me that the effort to instruct myself had no effect other than the increasing discovery of my own ignorance. And yet I was studying at one of the most celebrated schools in Europe.[5]

Descartes has transformed wisdom into a work, a project, a making, a determinate problem, for he denies that he can work with anything else.
Robert E. Meagher

In Descartes' time, the distinction between science and philosophy was not clear. His interests and abilities in philosophy, mathematics, and science made this confusion especially intolerable to him. He expected scientific claims to be provable by appeals to observation and clear thinking. So he made a radical proposal: Let's start fresh, throwing out everything we think we know, and build a system of knowledge based entirely on ideas whose truth can be clearly and distinctly known—to us, firsthand.

Rationalism

Descartes' proposal puts him among the ranks of the rationalist philosophers. Chapter 6 defined rationalism as an epistemological position in which reason is the primary source of all knowledge. Reason is said to be superior to sense evidence. Reason alone can distinguish reality from illusion and give meaning to all other kinds of experience.

In general, rationalists believe that abstract reasoning can produce undeniable, absolutely certain truths about nature, existence, the whole of reality. Many of these important, ultimate truths can be discovered without observation, experiment, or even experience. These are called **a priori** or, sometimes, **innate ideas**. Thus, to the rationalists, reason—not empirical observation—is the ultimate test of truth.

According to this so-called **coherence theory of truth**, new or unclear ideas are evaluated in terms of rational or logical consistency and in relation to already established truths. The ultimate criteria for basic, originating truths are clarity and distinctness. Once fundamental truths are established, the rationalist uses a deductive, mathematical/logical method to test and establish other, more complex ideas. True ideas are coherent (rationally consistent) with each other, and the rationalist's aim is to achieve absolute certainty of the sort possible in mathematics. "My method," said Descartes, "contains everything which gives certainty to the rules of arithmetic."

The coherence theory of truth is in direct opposition to the correspondence theory of truth (in Chapter 12) and differs from the other major theory of truth, the pragmatic theory (in Chapter 17).

A PRIORI IDEAS
(or INNATE IDEAS)
Truths that are not derived from observation or experiment, characterized as being certain, deductive, universally true, and independent of all experience.

COHERENCE THEORY OF TRUTH
Truth test in which new or unclear ideas are evaluated in terms of rational or logical consistency and in relation to already established truths.

Against Authoritarian Thinking

Descartes' first philosophical work was *Rules for the Direction of the Mind*. The twenty-one principles contained in *Rules* reappear in Descartes' major philosophical works, *Discourse on Method* and *Meditations on First Philosophy*.

Rule 3 advises: *Once we have chosen a subject to study, we should confine ourselves to what we can clearly intuit and deduce with certainty for ourselves*. We must not rely on what others have thought or on our own as-yet-untested beliefs. We must look for ourselves, with new eyes and new understanding. Referring to the Scholastics, among others, Descartes cautions that "in a too absorbed study" of the works of earlier thinkers, we become "infected with their errors, guard against them as we may."

This is a general caution against authoritarian thinking, in which we give more weight to the opinions of others than to our own experience and clear thinking. When we accept views *solely* on the weight of the authority or prestige of those who hold them, or because of loyalty to a cause or belief structure, we become nonrational at best. We are memorizers, not thinkers. Loyalty becomes more important than honesty and truth.

I shall not say anything about Philosophy, but that, seeing that it has been culti-vated for many centuries by the best minds that have ever lived, and that nevertheless no single thing is to be found in it which is not the subject of dispute, and in conse-quence which is not dubious, I had not enough presump-tion to hope to fare better there than other men had done. And also, considering how many conflicting opin-ions there may be regarding the self-same matter, all sup-ported by learned people, while there can never be more than one which is true, I esteemed as well-nigh false all that only went as far as being probable.

René Descartes

Descartes points out that it is common to overlook clear, simple truths (intuitions) when we do encounter them. We quickly complicate them with cloudy but elaborate "explanations." He speculates that we surround the truth with ambiguities because we are afraid that the simplicity of our dis-coveries will make them seem unimportant. He adds:

> For we shall not, e.g., turn out to be mathematicians though we know by heart all the proofs others have elaborated, unless we have an intellectual talent that fits us to resolve difficulties of any kind. Neither, though we may have mastered all the arguments of Plato and Aristotle, if yet we have not the capac-ity for passing solid judgment on these matters, shall we be-come Philosophers; we should have acquired the knowledge not of a science, but of history.[6]

PHILOSOPHICAL QUERY

Use Descartes' distinction between memorizing ideas and under-standing them to examine your own education. Give examples of both. Describe the distinction between learning to love psychol-ogy or literature and becoming a *historian* of psychology or litera-ture in Descartes' terms. Speculate on ways this distinction might be used to reform education.

Addressing the fact that we are bombarded with conflicting knowledge claims, Rule 4 succinctly states: *There is need of a method for finding the truth.*

> So blind is the curiosity by which mortals are possessed, that they often conduct their minds along unexplored routes, hav-ing no reason to hope for success. . . . it were far better never to think of investigating truth at all, than to do so without a method. For it is very certain that unregulated inquiries and confused reflections of this kind only confound the natural light and blind our mental powers. . . . In [method] alone lies the sum of all human endeavour, and he who would approach the investigation of truth must hold to this rule. . . .[7]

Descartes' concern over lack of method remains relevant today. For ex-ample, in 1989 we knew about highly sophisticated genetic modeling, an airplane that is almost invisible to radar, computers that talk—and we dis-covered that the president of the United States scheduled important speeches and meetings on the advice of his wife's astrologer. The scientific under-standing of the general populace continues to decline, yet millions of peo-ple still read their horoscopes, consult psychics, and devote years of effort and thousands of dollars to what Descartes referred to as "blind curiosity." Some religious groups still evaluate scientific conclusions on theological grounds. Students are taught to memorize information and techniques,

More than three hundred and fifty years after Descartes complained that we "investigate the most difficult questions with so little regard to order," many educated people consult astrologers, tarot card readers, palm readers, and such without taking the time to learn about scientific method as used in astronomy, physics, chemistry, psychology, and medicine.

rather than to seek understanding. Perhaps we should be applying a more rational method to our present madness.

PHILOSOPHICAL QUERY

People who have little or no scientific education sometimes engage in fierce debates about evolution. Individuals who don't keep up with world events nonetheless express opinions about foreign affairs, balancing the federal budget, or the meaning of the First Amendment. Have you ever been guilty of investigating "the most difficult questions with so little regard for order"? Did your investigation pay off or not? Discuss the general advantages of "method," and identify one or two current areas of controversy that might benefit from "method."

THE METHOD OF DOUBT

Descartes believed that a mathematically precise method was the only reliable way to discover the truth about the

Descartes' success is indicated by the extent to which the central notions of his philosophy became the common conception of man and the universe for nearly three centuries.

Alexander Sesonske
and Noel Fleming

universe. He proposed to use the new spirit of scientific inquiry and mathematical rigor to reexamine—everything! His effort not only marks the beginning of an entirely new philosophical orientation, it is fascinating and relevant to our times.

Descartes attacked earlier philosophy on the grounds that it did not demand rational comprehension from the individual intellect. It did not rest *solely* on ideas known through "the clear light of natural reason."

> I thought that the sciences found in books—and those at least whose reasonings are only probable and which have no demonstrations, composed as they are of the gradually accumulated opinions of many different individuals—do not approach so near to the truth as the simple reasoning which a man of common sense can quite naturally carry out respecting the things which come immediately before him.[8]

"Common sense," which Descartes also referred to as *natural reason*, is the ability to think found in all normal human minds. It does not depend on divine revelation or special education—at least according to Descartes. Though not everyone has the talent or interest to do every kind of refined thinking, Descartes believed all reasoning individuals could apply his method to basic (timeless) questions concerning human nature, truth, the existence of God, and so forth.

If I write in French which is the language of my country, rather than in Latin which is that of my teachers, that is because I hope that those who avail themselves only of their natural reason in its purity may be better judges of my opinions than those who believe only in the writings of the ancients . . . those who unite good sense with study . . . alone I crave for my judges.

René Descartes

Good sense is of all things in the world the most equally distributed, for everybody thinks himself so abundantly provided with it, that even those most difficult to please in all other matters do not commonly desire more of it than they already possess. It is unlikely that this is an error on their part; it seems rather to be evidence in support of the view that the power of forming a good judgment and of distinguishing the true from the false, which is properly speaking what is called Good Sense or Reason, is by nature equal in all men. Hence too it will show that the diversity of our opinions does not proceed from some men being more rational than others, but solely from the fact that our thoughts pass through diverse channels and the same objects are not considered by all. For to be possessed of good mental powers is not sufficient; the principal matter is to apply them well. The greatest minds are capable of the greatest vices as well as of the greatest virtues, and those who proceed very slowly may, provided they always follow the straight road, really advance much faster than those who, though they run, forsake it.[9]

PHILOSOPHICAL QUERY

Comment on the preceding passage. Do you agree with Descartes? Why? Is common sense the same thing as good sense? Analyze the notion of common sense. Do you really think there is such a thing? What is your evidence either way?

The Cartesian "I"

Descartes did not write in Latin, the "universal language of scholars," but in everyday French. His aim was to reach beyond the confines of the university and church to a wider audience of European intellectuals. Descartes cast all his works in the first person to describe his own thinking, both his *conclusions* and his *thinking process*. He wanted to call our attention to the reasoning mind itself. Until Descartes, philosophers tended to focus on the content of ideas and on their logical relations to each other, not on the mind itself. Although "reason" was discussed and referred to, often cited as the guide by which we should live, the "reasoning thing" itself was not directly studied.

As we study Descartes' ideas, don't always interpret the "I" as referring to Descartes—allow it also to refer to you while you are reading (and, I hope, thinking along with) the words Descartes wrote. By occasionally becoming the "I" yourself, you can participate in the *conscious flow* of Descartes' reasoning in a way that will help you evaluate his arguments as if they were your own. You will be reflecting and meditating on your own conscious mind.

There does seem to be, so far as science is concerned, nothing in the world but complex arrangements of physical constituents. All except for one place: consciousness.

J. J. C. Smart

Methodic Doubt

Descartes was convinced that he could apply a mathematically oriented method to the most fundamental problem of all: How can I know that I know anything?

In geometry, Descartes pointed out, we begin with self-evident truths such as "A straight line is the shortest distance between two points." More complex theorems based on these truths are then called upon to prove less-evident truths. Descartes proposed to apply this basic method to philosophy. In his *Rules*, he stated that *we must not accept anything we can doubt at all.*

His first task, then, was to find a self-evident, independent truth to start from. For instance, we *know* with *rational certainty* that *if* $A = B$ and *if* $B = C$, then $A = C$. Can we know anything besides mathematics and logic with such certainty? Can our grasp of any factual idea ever be as certain as our understanding of a deductive principle? Since Descartes had a mathematical model in mind, he could not settle for any lesser degree of certainty.

In his effort to base his philosophy on an absolutely certain foundation, Descartes had a brilliant, culture-altering insight. He discovered **methodic doubt**. Simply put, *methodic doubt involves deliberately doubting everything it is possible to doubt in the least degree. Whatever remains will be known with absolute certainty.* In order to apply methodic doubt, Descartes had to rely on a standard of truth that could tell him whether or not it was reasonable to doubt something.

METHODIC DOUBT
Cartesian strategy of deliberately doubting everything it is possible to doubt in the least degree so that what remains will be known with absolute certainty.

Standard of Truth

No matter what method we employ in a search for truth, we must have some criterion for distinguishing truth from falsity. Descartes proposed that we "might assume as a general rule that the things which we conceive very clearly and distinctly are all true." He defined *clear* as "that which is present and apparent to an attentive mind," and *distinct* as "that which is so precise and different from all other objects that it contains within itself nothing but what is clear." We might say that for Descartes, knowledge requires precision and detail.

Throughout his philosophical writings Descartes appeals to clear and distinct knowing as the ultimate standard to be used in accepting or rejecting ideas. To produce the most certain conclusions possible, he rejected *anything* he did not know "clearly and distinctly." He also believed that certain very basic propositions *need only to be understood* to be recognized as true. To understand something clearly and distinctly, according to Descartes, is a matter of perceiving that there are no reasonable grounds on which it can be doubted. In other words, *to recognize something clearly and distinctly is to know that it is true.*

Some philosophers are troubled by Descartes' standard of truth. They claim that *the standard itself* is ambiguous and subjective and thus cannot be known with clarity and distinctness! Their point is that "clear and distinct" vary from individual to individual; I might be convinced I know something clearly and distinctly and still be wrong about it. In other words, they accuse Descartes of basing his rationalism on the subjective states of the perceiver; they interpret this to mean that, in spite of his talk about reason, Descartes actually bases his philosophy on his feelings and moods.

> *It must always be recollected, however, that possibly I deceive myself, and that what I take to be gold and diamonds is perhaps no more than copper or glass.*
> René Descartes

PHILOSOPHICAL QUERY

A common criticism of Descartes' standard of truth is that he failed to apply it to itself: *Do we know with clarity and distinctness that only what we know with clarity and distinctness is true? Can we know it?* Not if, as critics claim, Descartes' position is itself unclear and ambiguous. Do you have a clear and distinct idea of Descartes' criteria? How can we tell when an inability to perceive something clearly and distinctly is the fault of the individual or of the quality of the idea? Discuss carefully.

Innate Ideas

As you wrestle with these issues, keep in mind that getting started is the most difficult part of establishing a new or original philosophical orientation. We must begin with initially unquestioned assumptions and basic principles. To a certain extent, these must be known before we can know anything else. That is, they must be first or *prior* to knowing everything else. Such ideas are called *a priori*. A priori ideas are characterized as being certain, deductive, universally true, innate, or independent of all experience.

A priori knowledge is derived from reason without reference to sense experience. Truths of reason and laws of logic are usually thought to be a priori. Examples include: "All triangles contain 180°" and "Every event has a cause." A priori knowledge contrasts with **a posteriori knowledge**, that is, empirical knowledge derived from sense experience. This kind of knowing comes from the accumulation of experience. It is not regarded as certain or necessary, because the conditions under which it is acquired change, perceivers vary, and factual relationships change. For example, the statement "My shirt is white" can be true for a particular set of circumstances today and false tomorrow. It is not universally or eternally true in the way that "Every event has a cause" is. A posteriori truths are called factual truths or truths of fact, as opposed to rational truths. (Not all philosophers agree that a priori truths exist. The empiricists—whom we will meet in Chapter 12— insist that all knowledge comes from sense experience.)

As a brilliant geometer, Descartes was familiar with the axioms for geometric proofs, which he characterized as a priori ideas. He believed we are born with certain ideas "implanted" in us by God. For example, we are born with the idea of a triangle in our minds. When we see triangles or triangular-shaped objects, we are reminded of this innate idea. Descartes often appeals to the standard of clarity and distinctness as if its truth should be obvious to us with a bit of reflection. All we need is to be "reminded" of it to recognize its truth.

> A PRIORI KNOWLEDGE
> Derived from reason without reference to sense experience. Examples include: "All triangles contain 180°" and "Every event has a cause."
>
> A POSTERIORI KNOWLEDGE
> Empirical knowledge derived from sense experience and not regarded as universal because the conditions under which it is acquired change, perceivers vary, and factual relationships change.

PHILOSOPHICAL QUERY

Is Descartes correct? What about seemingly sincere, rational, and intelligent people who say they do not, perhaps cannot, see the truth of *this* idea about innate ideas? Compare Descartes' problem here with Plato's problem of accounting for levels of ignorance of the forms. Do you think forms are innate ideas? Are innate ideas forms? (See Chapter 6.)

THE CARTESIAN GENESIS

Descartes wanted to find an absolutely certain, indubitable starting point for his philosophy. He chose a form of deliberate, methodological skepticism which we have labeled *methodic doubt*. As we will see in Chapter 12 from the work of David Hume, there are levels of skepticism, progressing from total doubt about everything to temporary or particular doubt invoked just for the process of analysis. Descartes' skepticism is part of his method, and is, consequently, of the temporary—but still serious—sort. This means he does not really doubt everything he challenges in his *Meditations*; systematically doubting is the process of Cartesian

> *Descartes'* Meditations *probably rivals Plato's* Republic *as the work most frequently read or recommended as an introduction to philosophy.*
> **Alexander Sesonske and Noel Fleming**

inquiry, it is not the end result. Descartes hoped to use skepticism to establish complete certainty.

In the six *Meditations*, Descartes begins by seeing whether it is rationally possible to doubt everything. He reasons that by doing this, he will quickly discover if there is any certain, undoubtable truth. In the course of the *Meditations* Descartes tears down the old world of Scholastic philosophy, unquestioned beliefs, and ambiguous ideas, and attempts to create a brand-new, certain, clearly proved, rational order. He suggests that his readers reflect on one meditation a day, reading carefully and leisurely. After six days, Descartes, like God in the biblical book of Genesis, will have finished with his own creation. The attentive, rational reader, by becoming the Cartesian "I" in the manner noted earlier, will also have torn down and rebuilt his or her previously unquestioned house of beliefs on a solid, rational foundation. Let's look at some of the more interesting and important stages of this Cartesian Genesis.

The Doubting Self

Descartes begins the *Meditations* by giving his methodic doubt the widest possible scope. He calls Meditation I *Of the things which may be brought within the sphere of the doubtful*. In the first two paragraphs Descartes invokes the skeptical method and introduces the standard of clarity and distinctness. He quickly points out that it would be impossible to examine every belief he currently holds. Instead, he will examine the origins and foundations of basic kinds of beliefs. If there is *any* possibility, however remote, that they could be mistaken, Descartes will reject them and every idea that depends on them:

> It is now many years since I detected how many were the false beliefs that I had from my earliest youth admitted as true, and how doubtful was everything I had since constructed on this basis; and from that time I was convinced that I must once and for all seriously undertake to rid myself of all the opinions which I had formerly accepted, and commence to build anew from the foundation if I wanted to establish any firm and permanent structure in the sciences. . . .
>
> Now for this object it is not necessary that I should show that all of these are false—I shall perhaps never arrive at this end. But inasmuch as reason already persuades me that I ought no less carefully to withhold my assent from matters which are not entirely certain and indubitable than from those which appear to be manifestly false, if I am able to find in each some reason to doubt, this will suffice to justify my rejecting the whole. And . . . owing to the fact that the destruction of the foundations of necessity brings with it the downfall

After the guarantee of the criterion of clear and distinct ideas has been elaborated, however, it turns out that the relations apprehended by reason are but misleading representatives of the true relations whose basic nature must remain a mystery to us. There is a powerful and basic undercurrent of irrationalism in Descartes, the first of the modern rationalists.

Leonard G. Miller

Even if life and all of you and everything is like just a dream I'm having, I still figure I'm going to need all the money I can lay my hands on.

Reprinted by permission of Chronicle Features, San Francisco, CA.

of the rest of the edifice, I shall only in the first place attack those principles upon which all my former opinions rested.[10]

PHILOSOPHICAL QUERY

How carefully have you examined your own fundamental beliefs? What—if anything—is wrong with trusting beliefs handed down by others? Why not rely on the testing of others, trusting their conclusions? Discuss. Also comment on the opposite extreme from Descartes: the tendency to believe something if it could possibly be correct. What is the relationship between *possible* and *plausible*, and what might it have to do with this entire issue? Explain.

Maybe It's All a Dream?

Like most of us, Descartes had uncritically assumed that the most true and certain things known come from the senses. For example, it is obviously true that my computer exists as I type this sentence, and it is obviously true that the book you are reading exists. What can be more certain than simple, direct sensations and perceptions of our immediate environment?

But our senses sometimes deceive us. For example, we may think we are looking at an airplane and later discover that it is a bird. Witnesses to

BEYOND INTELLECT THERE IS YET ANOTHER STAGE

In 1091, the Persian philosopher **Abu Hamid Muhammad al-Ghazali (1058–1111)** was appointed professor of Islamic theology at the Nizamiyah College in Baghdad. In 1095, al-Ghazali, by then a man of great influence, suffered a spiritual crisis and nervous breakdown which resulted in a speech impediment that prevented him from lecturing. He left the college and ultimately embraced a mystical form of Islam known as *sufism*. Al-Ghazali briefly returned to teaching, but eventually quit for good and founded a monastic community in Tus, the city of his birth. The passage that follows is from his work *The Deliverance from Error*. Note how al-Ghazali's work anticipates Descartes' first Meditation by five hundred years. Whereas Descartes exalted reason over faith, al-Ghazali "transcended" reason with the mystic's direct and immediate experience of God (Allah).

To thirst after a comprehension of things as they really are was my habit and custom from a very early age. . . . as I drew near the age of adolescence the bonds of mere authority . . . ceased to hold me and inherited beliefs lost their grip upon me, for I saw that Christian youths always grew up to be Christians, Jewish youths to be Jews and Muslim youths to be Muslim. . . .

I therefore said within myself: "To begin with, what I am looking for is knowledge of what things really are, so I must undoubtedly try to find what knowledge really is." It was plain to me that sure and certain knowledge is that knowledge in which the object is disclosed in such a fashion that no doubt remains along with it, that no possibility of error or illusion accompanies it, and that the mind cannot even entertain such a supposition. Certain knowledge must also be infallible. . . . Thus, I know that ten is more than three. Let us suppose that someone says to me: "No, three is more than ten, and in proof of that I shall change this rod into a serpent": and let us suppose that he actually changes the rod into a serpent and that I witness him doing so. No doubts about what I know are raised in me because of this. The only result is that I wonder how he is able to produce this change. Of doubt about my knowledge there is no trace.

---

crimes disagree over descriptions of perpetrators, and we think we recognize the figure coming down the sidewalk only to be wrong. Even so, aren't we always sure of immediate sensations? Though our senses may deceive us about distant events, there are many other things we know through our senses "as to which we cannot reasonably have any doubt." Descartes cites an example:

In the interplay of reality and illusion, how can you be sure that you are now not dreaming and that events seen during a state of dream may be closer to the truth?

Lie Zi

> At the same time I must remember that I am a man, and that consequently I am in the habit of sleeping, and in my dreams representing to myself the same things or sometimes even less probable things, than those who are insane do in their waking moments. How often has it happened to me that in the night I dreamt that I found myself in this particular place, that I was

After these reflections I knew that whatever I did not know in this fashion and with this mode of certainty is not reliable and infallible knowledge; and knowledge that is not infallible is not certain knowledge. . . .

Thereupon I investigated the various kinds of knowledge I had, and found myself destitute of all knowledge with this characteristic of infallibility except in the case of sense-perception and necessary truths. . . .

I proceeded therefore with extreme earnestness to reflect on sense-perception and on necessary truths, to see whether I could make myself doubt them. The outcome of this protracted effort was that I could no longer trust sense-perception either. . . .

. . . "Do you not see," [my ego] said, "how, when you are asleep, you believe things and imagine circumstances, holding them to be stable and enduring, and, so long as you are in that dream-condition, have no doubts about them? . . . Why then are you confident that all your waking beliefs, whether from sense or intellect, are genuine? They are true in respect of your present state; but it is possible that a state will come upon you whose relation to your waking consciousness is analogous to the relation of the latter to dreaming. In comparison with this state your waking consciousness would be like dreaming! When you are in this state, you will be certain that all the suppositions of your intellect are empty imaginings. . . ."

It became clear to me . . . that what is most distinctive about mysticism is something which cannot be apprehended by study, but only by immediate experience . . . by ecstasy and by a moral change. What difference between *knowing* the definition of health and satiety . . . and *being* healthy and satisfied! . . .

Beyond intellect there is yet another stage. In this another eye is opened, by which he beholds the unseen, what is to be the future, and other things which are beyond the ken of intellect.

Abu Hamid Muhammad al-Ghazali
The Deliverance from Error, in *The Faith and Practice of Al-Ghazali*, trans. W. Montgomery Watt (London: George Allen and Unwin, 1953), pp. 21–68.

dressed and seated near the fire, whilst in reality I was lying undressed in bed! At this moment it does indeed seem to me that it is with eyes awake that I am looking at this paper; that this head which I move is not asleep, that it is deliberately and of set purpose that I extend my hand and perceive it; what happens in sleep does not appear so clear and distinct as does all this. But in thinking over this I remind myself that on many occasions I have in sleep been deceived by similar illusions, and in dwelling carefully on this reflection I see so manifestly that there are no certain indications by which we may clearly distinguish wakefulness from sleep that I am lost in astonishment. And my astonishment is such that it is almost capable of persuading me that I now dream.[11]

*All that is comes from
the mind.*

The Dhammapada

With this example, Descartes rejects sense knowledge as a sufficient foundation for certainty. In so doing, he also rejects the primacy of the external, physical world. It is *possible* that the whole so-called real world is nothing but an elaborate mental construct, a hallucination. Remember, in the interest of constructing a flawless philosophy, Descartes is being ultracautious. He has dispensed with considering degrees of probability. Whether or not you consider it *probable* that your world is a dream, it is *possible*, according to Descartes.

But even if the world is a dream, it still has regularity, predictability, and so on, doesn't it? Maybe the world is just a dream implanted in the mind by God.

PHILOSOPHICAL QUERY

How can we know the difference between a dream or hallucination and reality? Seriously consider how a confused person might verify that he or she was or was not dreaming.

The Evil Genius

Perhaps, like Descartes, you are having some trouble seriously doubting your experiences of the real world. Descartes says, "These ancient and commonly held opinions [that I am not dreaming] still revert frequently to my mind." To test his beliefs, he decides to allow himself deliberately "to be deceived, and for a certain time pretend that all these opinions are entirely false and imaginary." Descartes is in no danger of losing his bearings; this is still methodic doubt, not real confusion or delusion. He even says not to worry about giving in to too much doubt and distrust, since he is "not considering the question of action, but only of knowledge."

At this point, Descartes introduces one of the most intriguing figures in the history of philosophy, the *evil genius:*

What is important is not liberation from the body but liberation from the mind. We are not entangled in our own body, but entangled in our own mind.

Thomas Merton

> I shall then suppose, not that God who is supremely good and the fountain of truth, but some evil genius not less powerful than deceitful, has employed his whole energies in deceiving me; I shall consider that the heavens, the earth, colours, figures, sound, and all other external things are nought but the illusions and dreams of which this genius has availed himself in order to lay traps for my credulity; I shall consider myself as having no hands, no eyes, no flesh, no blood, nor any senses, yet falsely believing myself to possess all these things; I shall remain obstinately attached to this idea, and if by this means it is not in my power to arrive at the knowledge of any truth, I may at least do what is in my power [i.e., suspend my judgment], and with firm purpose avoid giving credence to any false thing, or being imposed upon by this arch deceiver, however powerful and deceptive he may be.[12]

This cold possibility of ultimate delusion concludes the first Meditation. Descartes has reduced his world to himself and one all-powerful, all-evil source of deception. He reasons that if he can find one anchor point of undoubtable certainty in the midst of the possibility of error in *all* quarters of his life, he will have found his unshakable foundation.

PHILOSOPHICAL QUERY

Before reading any further, stop for a moment and play with Descartes' idea of an evil genius. Try to get into the spirit of doubting as much as you can. Do not be limited by what you actually doubt; this is an intellectual exercise, not a personal confession. See if you can extend the range of what might on the remotest possibility be false or other than you think it is. Can you be *absolutely sure* that there is no evil genius?

Cogito, ergo sum

Could the evil genius so arrange things that nothing is as I think it is? In the physical realm he could. He could trick me into thinking that I have a body when I don't, that things have shapes, colors, and so on, when they really don't. Descartes says that—as difficult as it is to imagine—he might even be able to deceive me regarding certain innate, a priori ideas, so that maybe 7+5 does not really equal 12 or triangles don't have three sides. Is there anything the evil genius cannot trick me about? If I can be tricked into thinking things exist that do not exist, and if I can be fooled into thinking things do not exist when they really do, then maybe I am being deceived about my own existence. Maybe I don't exist at all. Is that possible?

> Not at all; of a surety I myself [must] exist since I persuaded myself of something [or merely because I thought of something]. But [what if] there is some deceiver or other, very powerful and very cunning, who ever employs his ingenuity in deceiving me. Then without doubt I exist also if he deceives me, and let him deceive me as much as he will, he can never cause me to be nothing so long as I think that I am something. So that after having reflected well and carefully examined all things, we must come to the definite conclusion that this proposition: I am, I exist, is necessarily true each time that I pronounce it, or that I mentally conceive it.[13]

This is the famous "cogito," from the Latin sentence **Cogito, ergo sum**, meaning *I think, therefore I am*. In some ways, this Cartesian insight, more than anything else, marks the beginning of the modern worldview.

Note the difference between "Descartes thinks, therefore he exists" and "I think, therefore I exist," where the "I" refers to whoever speaks or thinks the sentence. The cogito must be understood in the first person. In that

COGITO, ERGO SUM
Latin version of Descartes' famous sentence "I think, therefore I am."

form, it meets Descartes' conditions for being utterly unshakable. No rational person can doubt his or her own existence as a conscious thinking entity—while being aware of thinking about anything.

Descartes interprets this to mean that while bodily existence may seem more solid and certain than ideas, mental existence is in actuality more certain. He goes on:

> I find here that thought is an attribute that belongs to me; it cannot be separated from me. I am, I exist, that is certain. But how often? . . . to speak accurately [at this stage of the Meditations] I am not more than a thing which thinks, that is to say a mind or soul, or an understanding, or a reason, which are terms whose significance was formerly unknown to me. I am . . . a real thing and really exist; but what thing? I have answered: a thing which thinks.
>
> . . . What is a thing which thinks? It is a thing which doubts, understands, [conceives], affirms, denies, wills, refuses, which also imagines and feels.[14]

Descartes argues that we identify and know everything—including bodily and material things—through the mind. He grounds all knowledge in mental states, in awareness. Thus the foundation of Descartes' philosophy and, to a considerable extent, of the modern worldview is the thinking self. Although Descartes was a rationalist, the thrust of the cogito is not *reasoning* but *self-awareness*. St. Augustine had a similar formula: "I doubt, therefore I am," and in *Nausea* (Chapter 18) Jean-Paul Sartre wrote, in effect, "I am nauseated, therefore I exist."

So far, Descartes has established that the thinking thing possesses absolute certainty of its own existence as a consciously thinking thing. So there is one rather limited fact I know with certainty. Do any other insights follow from this bedrock experience of self-consciousness? Can Descartes move from it to re-create the external world?

PHILOSOPHICAL QUERY

When I was a student I felt compelled to challenge anything presented to me as being *irrefutable*. As soon as I heard about the cogito I assumed I would be able to refute it, to show that it was not necessarily true. That proved easier said than done. Try for yourself; it is interesting, and it is the only way to grasp Descartes' point. Discuss your efforts.

THE INNATE IDEA OF GOD

Descartes begins the third Meditation still treating everything he thinks of as part of himself as merely "percep-

For those who like a dramatic and specific date, the simple but far-reaching phrase of Descartes, "I think, therefore I am," will do very well for the beginning [of the Age of Reason]: 1657.
Crane Brinton

When a person is in any state of consciousness it logically follows that he is not sound asleep.
Norman Malcolm

tions and imaginations" from his own mind. That being so, his next step is to survey his own thoughts, to see whether there might be something he has overlooked or been unaware of so far. He reasons that the most important issue is the existence of God: "I must inquire whether there is a God as soon as the occasion presents itself; and if I find that there is a God, I must also inquire whether He may be a deceiver; for without a knowledge of these two truths I do not see that I can ever be certain of anything."[15]

In other words, if Descartes can establish the existence of God, he will have a foundation for truth concerning other ideas. If God is not an evil deceiver, Descartes argues, He will have created the reasoning mind to seek and know the truth. Rationally verifying the existence of God will not only guarantee the possibility of knowledge with certainty, it will bridge the gaps between religion and science and between the imagination and reality. If God is the source of reason, then it follows that He wills the use of reason in pursuit of truth. If so, then God is the impetus behind science. If God is not a deceiver, then He will have given Descartes the ability to distinguish the real from the merely imagined. Thus the issue of God's existence and nature is crucial to Descartes' entire rationalistic enterprise.

The Perfect Idea of Perfection

Clearly, Descartes says, the *idea* of God exists. He notes the obvious: Such an idea does exist—he has it. But does it follow that an *object* corresponding to this idea exists?

> Hence there remains only the idea of God, concerning which we must consider whether it is something which cannot have proceeded from me myself. By the name of God I understand a substance that is infinite [eternal, unchangeable], independent, all-knowing, all-powerful, and by which I myself and everything else, if anything else does exist, has been created. Now all these characteristics are such that the more diligently I attend to them, the less do they appear capable of proceeding from me alone; hence, from what has been already said, we must conclude that God necessarily exists.[16]

Descartes' position amounts to this: I have in me the clear and distinct idea of a perfect being. Where could I, an imperfect creature, ever get the idea of perfection? A perfect being is not just a bigger, stronger, quantitatively improved Descartes. If my idea of God were merely of a kind of superhuman being, then I might have created it out of wishful thinking. But how could I even have a notion of perfection, or want to be more perfect myself, "unless I had within me some idea of a Being more perfect than myself, in comparison with which I should recognize the deficiencies of my nature?"[17] In other words, because of its very uniqueness, the idea of God must come from God. To clearly and distinctly understand the idea of God is—at the same instant—to know with certainty that God exists.

This line of reasoning is known as an ontological argument. The term *ontology* derives from the Greek roots *onta*, "truly real," and *logos*, "study of." An **ontological argument** is an attempt to prove the existence of God by referring either to the meaning of the word *God* when it is understood a certain way, or by referring to the purportedly unique quality of the concept of God.

The purest form of the ontological argument first occurs in the *Proslogion* of St. Anselm (1033–1109). A Benedictine monk who eventually became the archbishop of Canterbury, Anselm attempted to provide a rational basis for Christian doctrine. He asserted that the very idea of God "contains existence" because *by definition* God is "that than which nothing greater can be conceived." And of any two things, a real one is "greater" than an imaginary one. Hence, an existing God is greater than a merely imaginary God. Therefore, by definition, the term *God* refers to a real, existing being. When we use *God* to refer to a fantasy being, we have changed its meaning.

Descartes' similar argument says that no ordinary accumulation of knowledge can account for the idea of God as a perfect being. This issue hinges on whether or not the idea of God is qualitatively different from other ideas. For example, it is sometimes argued that God is nothing more than a bigger, smarter, tougher, more virtuous version of ourselves. What's so different about that? Since I know people can live to be ninety or a hundred years old, why can't I imagine one who lives forever? I can do some things. Why can't I fantasize about a being who can do all things?

Descartes, for all his dislike of Scholastic philosophy, follows a Scholastic line in his analysis of these matters. He seems to be saying that not only is God a perfect being, the idea of God is a "perfect idea." If it is, he reasons, where could it come from? Imperfect creatures such as ourselves can imagine only imperfect ideas; we could not come up with the idea of a *perfect* anything without help. Where could the idea of perfection come from? Only from a mind more perfect than ours.

Maybe the evil genius gave me the idea of perfection? But where would an imperfect, evil being get the idea? Only from a being more perfect yet. Ultimately, the existence of the *idea of perfection* can come only from an already perfect source: the perfect being.

Cogito ergo non dormio.
(*I think, therefore I am not asleep.*)

> It is perfectly evident that there must be at least as much reality in the cause as in the effect; and thus since I am a thinking thing, and possess an idea of God within me, whatever in the end be the cause assigned to my existence, it must be allowed that it is likewise a thinking thing and that it possesses in itself the idea of all the perfections I attribute to God. . . . But if it derives its existence from some other cause than itself, we shall again ask, for the same reason, whether this second

cause exists by itself or through another, until from one step to another, we finally arrive at an ultimate cause, which will be God.[18]

Descartes determines that he cannot have "received" the idea of God through the senses, nor has it suddenly burst upon his consciousness. He cannot have imagined it, for he lacks the ability to improve upon or to detract from it. Consequently, he says, "the only alternative is that it is innate in me, just as the idea of myself is innate in me."[19]

Descartes' argument is crucial to the Cartesian Genesis. His conception of God as a perfect being includes the qualities of all-knowing, all-powerful, all-loving, all-good. Descartes posits that such a God would not let him be constantly deceived by either himself or some evil genius. If, the argument goes, God gave us reason and faculties of perception, they must be basically accurate and reliable.

> And the whole strength of the argument which I have here made use of to prove the existence of God consists in this, that I recognize that it is not possible that my nature should be what it is, and indeed that I should have in myself the idea of a God, if God did not veritably exist—a God, I say, whose idea is in me, i.e., who possesses all those supreme perfections of which our mind may indeed have some idea but without understanding them all, who is liable to no errors or defect [and who has none of all those marks which denote imperfection]. From this it is manifest that He cannot be a deceiver, since the light of nature teaches us that fraud and deception necessarily proceed from some defect.[20]

PHILOSOPHICAL QUERY

Some philosophers insist that ontological arguments beg the whole question by defining God in terms of existing. In the case of Descartes' argument, there is also the question of whether or not we really do have a clear and distinct (precise) idea of God in the first place. Reflect on the idea of God. Is it clear and distinct? Do you have a clear and distinct idea of perfection—in beings or automobiles or marriages or anything? Does the ontological argument persuade you? Does Descartes' argument?

*Hamlet did think a great
many things; does it follow
that he existed?*
Jaako Hintikka

Reconstructing the World

Having shown that one mind and God exist, Descartes proceeds to reestablish knowledge of the objective existence of the rest of the world:

> Nothing further now remains but to inquire whether material things exist. . . . And certainly I at least know that these may

There is no simple entity that you can point to and say: this entity is physical and not mental.
Bertrand Russell

exist. . . . For there is no doubt that God possesses the power to produce everything that I am capable of perceiving with distinctness.[21]

Descartes reasons that since he has a clear and distinct idea of himself *both as a mind and as having a body*, he must of necessity be both a mind and a body. But the idea of being both mind and body is not innate or known to be true with deductive certainty. Thus the idea of the body must originate outside Descartes' mind.

> And . . . because I know that all things which I apprehend clearly and distinctly can be created by God as I apprehend them, it suffices that I am able to apprehend one thing apart from another clearly and distinctly in order to be certain that one is different from the other, since they may be made to exist in separation at least by the omnipotence of God. . . . On the one side, I have a clear and distinct idea of myself inasmuch as I am only a thinking and unextended thing, and as, on the other, I possess a distinct idea of body, inasmuch as it is only an extended and unthinking thing, it is certain that this I [that is to say, my soul by which I am what I am], is entirely and absolutely distinct from my body and can exist without it.
> . . . But, since God is no deceiver, it is very manifest that He does not communicate to me these ideas immediately and by Himself. . . . I do not see how He could be defended from the accusation of deceit if these ideas were produced by causes other than corporeal objects. Hence we must allow that corporeal things exist.[22]

The relation between the body and the mind is so intimate that, if either of them got out of order, the whole system would suffer.
Mohandas Gandhi

Descartes reasoned that his own ideas of body and mind must be basically sound, since God allowed him to know clearly and distinctly that he is both.

At this point, the Cartesian Genesis is essentially complete. All that remains are the details of reconstructing knowledge of the world on a solid base by carefully following the rules of method.

MATERIALISM
(also known as *behaviorism, mechanism,* or *reductionism*) Belief that everything is composed of matter (and energy), and can be explained by physical laws, that all human activity can be understood as the natural behavior of matter according to mechanical laws, and that thinking is merely a complex form of behaving: the body is a fleshy machine.

THE CARTESIAN BRIDGE

Descartes was a devout Catholic who took his religion seriously. He was aware of the challenge to religion posed by advances in physics and astronomy and the reemergence of **materialism** (also known as *behaviorism, mechanism,* or *reductionism*). Other philosophers, most notably **Thomas Hobbes (1588–1679)**, were arguing that everything is composed of matter (and energy) and can be explained by physical laws. This means all human activity can be understood as the natural behavior of matter according to mechanical laws. Thus, thinking is merely a complex

DARROW'S TRIP TO GOOFVILLE

If I am told that next week I shall start on a trip to Goofville; that I shall not take my body with me; that I shall stay for all eternity: can I find a single fact connected with my journey—the way I shall go, the part of me that is to go, the time of the journey, the country I shall reach, its location in space, the way I shall live there—or anything that would lead to a rational belief that I shall really take the trip? Have I ever known anyone who has made the journey and returned? If I am really to believe, I must try to get some information about all these important facts.

Clarence Darrow
"The Myth of the Soul," *The Forum* 80 (October 1928).

form of behaving, and the body is a fleshy machine. The so-called mind can be reduced to the brain, and thinking and acting can be reduced to biochemical brain states and stimulus-response reactions. Since the laws of physics are universal, there can be no such thing as a free will. If everything is material, there can be no such thing as an immaterial soul. (This point of view, which is still held by many scientists and philosophers today, will be discussed more fully in Chapters 12 and 14.)

Like the theologians, Descartes was alarmed by the amoral, secular nature of this particular view of the universe. Yet, as we have noted, he was a scientist himself, and his philosophy was designed to bridge the growing gap between the "new science" and religion. By showing that the mind is different in kind from the body, Descartes hoped to prove that the discoveries of the physicists posed no threat to free will or the existence of an incorporeal soul. The laws of physics apply only to matter, but the mind (soul) is an incorporeal thinking substance. Mind and body are two completely different kinds of substances. Thus science turns out to be the language of bodies; it cannot address minds or souls, so it is no threat to the church or basic Christian theology.

Cartesian Dualism

Any philosophical position that divides existence into two completely distinct, independent, unique substances or kinds of things is a form of **dualism.** The distinction may be between mind and body, natural and supernatural, spirit and matter, soul and body, good and evil, and so on. (**Monism** is the general name for the belief that everything consists of only one, ultimate, unique substance, such as matter; **pluralism** is the name for the belief in more than one substance.)

DUALISM
Any philosophical position that divides existence into two completely distinct, independent, unique substances.

MONISM
General name for the belief that everything consists of only one, ultimate, unique substance such as matter or spirit.

PLURALISM
The belief that there exist many realities or substances.

Such a dualistic mode of perception not only impedes a holistic theory of liberation, but it is also substantially responsible for constructing the very world of alienation from which we seek liberation . . . operating on three levels: (1) alienation from oneself; one's own body; (2) alienation from one's fellow person in the "alien" community; (3) alienation from the "world": from the visible earth and sky.

Rosemary Radford Ruether

Cartesian dualism refers to Descartes' conviction that human beings are a mysterious union of mind (soul) and body, of incorporeal substance and corporeal substance, with each realm operating according to separate sets of laws. The mind follows the laws of reason, but otherwise is free. The body is governed by the laws of physics and falls under the rule of cause and effect: The human body is no freer than any other material thing. The soul is somehow dispersed to all parts of the body, but thinking enters the brain through the pineal gland.

> And as a clock composed of wheels and counter-weights no less exactly observes the laws of nature . . . if I consider the body of a man as being a sort of machine so built up and composed of nerves, muscles, veins, blood, and skin, that though there were no mind in it at all, it would not cease to have made the same motions as at present, exception being made of those movements which are due to the direction of the will, and in consequence depend upon the mind.[23]

We can understand thinking without ever referring to the body, and we can understand the body without ever referring to the mind/soul. So, Descartes concluded, minds and bodies are essentially independent of each other. Science can study bodies and the natural world without ever treading in theology.

Initially, this rationale seems satisfactory. Indeed, it fits the "common-sense" view of Christian theology and ordinary experience. Cartesian dualism allows for the doctrine of the soul's continued existence after the body's death. Further, by defining himself as *thinking substance* rather than corporeal, Descartes reaffirms the primacy of the soul over the body. Human beings are essentially spiritual beings who happen to inhabit bodies. As a devout believer, Descartes has salvaged his faith from the threats of science. As a scientist, he has freed science to progress without church interference, since scientific discoveries are about the body and have no real bearing on the nature of the soul.

The Mind-Body Problem

Dualism generates one of the most tenacious timeless (and timely) questions: What is the relationship of the mind to the body?

So appealing is dualism to philosophers, preachers, psychologists, and most of the rest of us that in his influential and controversial book *The Concept of Mind*, contemporary philosopher Gilbert Ryle refers to it simply as "the official doctrine." Ryle says:

> The official doctrine, which hails chiefly from Descartes, is something like this. With the doubtful exceptions of idiots and infants in arms every human being has both a body and

a mind. Some would prefer to say that every human being is both a body and a mind. His body and his mind are ordinarily harnessed together, but after the death of the body his mind may continue to exist and function.[24]

Versions of the "official doctrine" are obvious in beliefs about the immortality of the soul and reincarnation. It is implicit in psychological theories that view the mind as something other than the brain, and that differentiate mental states from bodily conditions and behavior. It is reflected in ordinary language when we talk about *having* a body, and in common experience when we feel as if "we" are somehow *in* our bodies. Religious and metaphysical versions of the official doctrine often compare the soul to a driver and the body to a car. At death, we get out of the car or—if you believe in reincarnation—trade the old body in for a new one.

Descartes rejects the car-driver type of analogy and unites mind and body into "one whole."

> Nature also teaches me by these sensations of pain, hunger, thirst, etc., that I am not only lodged in my body as a pilot in a vessel, but that I am very closely united to it, and so to speak so intermingled with it that I seem to compose with it one whole. For if that were not the case, when my body is hurt, I who am merely a thinking thing, should not feel pain, for I should perceive this wound by the understanding only, just as a sailor perceives by sight when something is damaged in his vessel; and when my body has need of drink or food, I should clearly understand the fact without being warned of it by confused feelings of hunger and thirst. For all these sensations of hunger, thirst, pain, etc., are in truth none other than certain confused modes of thought which are produced by the union and intermingling of mind and body.[25]

(The "union" or "intermingling" occurs, as noted earlier, in the pineal gland. Descartes apparently devoted some time to dissecting animal carcasses in order to study this mysterious gland.)

Dualism *feels consistent* with certain common experiences, but inconsistent with others: If I hit my thumb with a hammer, I experience no mind-body split. Yet there are serious consequences if we reject dualism in favor of a materialistic, behavioristic monism: When we reduce mental states to physical states, do we lose the possibility of free will, moral responsibility, and the possibility of survival after death? Such beliefs are important to the very meaning of life for many people, real enough and important enough so that any difficulties of *explaining* mind-body interaction pale beside the consequences of rejecting dualism.

But the fact that millions of people believe something does not make it true. Cartesian dualism—indeed, metaphysical speculation itself—stands in

Here I confess that I have been suffering from a deception. For I believed that I was addressing a human soul, or that internal principle by which a man lives, feels, moves from place to place and understands, and after all I was only speaking to a mind.

Pierre Gassendi

It is to be noticed also that you seem to fail to understand, O flesh, what it is to employ reason.

Descartes' reply to Gassendi

From the "I conquer" applied to the Aztec and Inca world and all America, from the "I enslave" applied to Africans sold for gold and silver acquired at the cost of the death of the Amerindians working in the depths of the earth, from the "I vanquish" of the wars of India and China to the shameful "opium war"— from this "I" appears the Cartesian *ego cogito. . . .*

Enrique Dussel

direct opposition to another major modern philosophical archetype: the skeptical questioner who turns to experience rather than to the mind for knowledge.

PHILOSOPHICAL QUERY

How plausible is this "official doctrine"? On Descartes' own terms, how "clearly and distinctly" do we understand the relationship of the mind to the body? How can a *completely* nonphysical thing interact with a *completely* physical thing? To ask Mark Twain's insightful question, How come the mind gets drunk when the body does the drinking? Why does my mind react to what happens to my body with such intensity if it's not part of my body?

THE EPISTEMOLOGICAL TURN

As a general rule, allowing for the specialized concerns of individual philosophers, Western philosophy was dominated by metaphysical issues until the seventeenth century. These concerned the nature of ultimate reality, soul and substance, God, and levels of being. It was not until Descartes defined knowledge in terms of certainty and refined the use of methodic doubt that the importance of epistemology was fully recognized.

Prior to Descartes' inquiry into the foundations of knowledge, philosophers distinguished between good and bad reasons, and established standards of proof, but they did not directly study the *process of thinking* in the way Descartes did. He began what Robert Paul Wolff refers to as the *epistemological turn*.[26] Wolff points out that this major transformation in the character of philosophy took a century and a half to complete, culminating with Immanuel Kant's *Critique of Pure Reason* (Chapter 13).

To put it another way, we can say that whereas earlier philosophers sought knowledge about the good life, nature, the soul, God, the ideal society, and so forth, modern philosophers increasingly devoted themselves to acquiring knowledge about knowledge. This, we shall see, led them to emphasize the precise meaning of terms and standards of evidence. This important general principle seems obvious once it is expressed: *Before we can reasonably evaluate any beliefs about reality, we must inquire into the nature of the "instrument" we use to observe it.* Contemporary philosophy has followed this lead, and all major areas of the field have been dominated by epistemological concerns.

COMMENTARY

Descartes' rationalism was inspired by a vision and three dreams, which he interpreted as a divine calling to establish his method of rational inquiry. Through the innovative use of methodical doubt, he established one irrefutable certainty, the cogito. Descartes claimed that God's existence was the foundation for all knowledge and the general reliability of the "natural light" of reason, yet for the contemporary observer the cogito is more solidly grounded than the proof for God.

Thus the modern era is grounded in Cartesian self-consciousness, self-reflection, and self-analysis. In its emphasis on an individual's inquiry after truth rather than official answers, Cartesian rationalism seems to pave the way for social and political democracy. The irony in this is that we note a kind of cool, analytic detachment as Descartes makes himself the subject of study in a new way. As the modern era develops, purity of method ultimately takes precedence over the search for wisdom. This trend may be a consequence of the detached, depersonalized quality of rationalistic analysis that emerged in the work of Descartes.

The benefits of the Cartesian revolution include using clearer, simpler, ordinary language (an idea that significantly influenced subsequent philosophers). Descartes paved the way for psychological studies by showing that the "thinking thing" is not a neutral "window," but a dynamic entity whose very nature affects its observations and conclusions. He initiated the study of knowledge and the sources of knowledge that continues to this day. Even the rationalists' great epistemological opponents, the empiricists, found themselves in part responding to issues raised by rationalism.

Without intending to trivialize this most important philosophical question, our attitudes toward the mind-body problem and its solution seem to be greatly influenced by whether we focus on the wider or narrower view. By the wider view I mean the view that takes seriously both our (common?) *sense* of free will and cross-cultural reports of out-of-body experiences, belief in personal immortality in some form or other, and a recognizable difference between the spiritual and material realm. The narrower view is chiefly concerned with logical consistency, precise use of terminology, and demonstrable evidence, usually resting on an observable, empirical component.

I find myself drawn to the wider view for a number of reasons. Although I reject arguments based strictly and solely on the authority of custom, tradition, or numbers, I cannot ignore nearly universal, cross-cultural beliefs in a spiritual dimension of reality. Temperamentally preferring the certainty of observable evidence and the clarity of precise speaking, I am still not comfortable rejecting dualism just because it is difficult to express the exact nature of the mind-body relationship.

The mind-body problem remains. On the one hand, we have the problems of dualistic interaction. But a materialistic, reductionistic alternative renders as illusory and confused some of our most important, widely held beliefs. The average person has actually been rather receptive to bizarre-sounding scientific theories and discoveries, accepting without always understanding, for example, that the earth is a tiny sphere in a vast universe, that much of our behavior is inherited, that time and space are relative, and

It seems to me that the greatest lesson of adult life is that one's own consciousness is not enough.
Sir Fred Hoyle

Consciousness is a disease.

Miguel de Unamuno

so on. This demonstrates a willingness to accept changing ideas of reality. What, then, accounts for the persistence of dualism, given the dominance of reductionistic materialism in the scientific and philosophic communities? I can only think that dualism speaks more accurately of reality as most of us experience it than reductionistic alternatives.

Unlike others of his time (and ours), Descartes refused to bow before religious authority, choosing to accept only what he knew for himself. Consider the alternative: believing—or trying to believe—and devoting your life to ideas you cannot really understand or that you know to be inconsistent and contradictory. The temporary victory of the Inquisition over the spirit of honest inquiry and rational rigor was merely the victory of force over reason. It is no more praiseworthy than contemporary efforts to legislate the appropriateness of ideas on religious, social, or political grounds.

Descartes was one of those dangerous philosophers mentioned in Chapter 1. He stands out as an archetype of the rationalist for his unwillingness to settle for inconsistencies and contradictions between his faith and his intellect. If his notion of "clear and distinct" is itself cloudy; if his introduction of God is suspicious; and if his attempt to account for mind-body interaction is unsatisfying, he is nonetheless remarkable for squarely facing up to the need to reassess his belief system for himself. He tried not to believe what he could not clearly understand. That in itself is a remarkable achievement.

SUMMARY OF MAIN POINTS

A combination of factors, including Luther's Protestant Reformation and Copernicus's advances in scientific understanding and technique, led to the erosion of the hierarchical, authoritarian medieval worldview, and weakened the authority of Scholastic philosophy, which relied heavily on Aristotle.

Descartes' scientific and mathematical interests demanded clear, provable evidence of a sort lacking in Scholasticism's cumbersome reliance on authority, and resulted in a radical proposal: Start fresh; throw out everything we think we know and build a system based entirely on ideas whose truth can be clearly and distinctly known to us firsthand.

Reliance on reason as the ultimate source of knowledge is a form of rationalism. In general, rationalists believe that abstract reasoning can produce absolutely certain truths about reality, and that some important ultimate truths can be discovered without observation, experiment, or experience. Such truths are known as innate ideas or a priori

ideas. Ideas derived from experience are known as a posteriori ideas.

Rationalists rely on the coherence theory of truth: New or unclear ideas are evaluated in terms of rational or logical consistency and relation to already established truths.

Descartes replaced Scholastic authority with a rational method that restricts us to accepting as true only what we understand clearly and distinctly for ourselves.

Descartes' interest in the "thinking thing itself" was the first major step in a shift in emphasis in modern philosophy from metaphysics to epistemology.

Descartes recognized the need for orderly thinking, which he called *method*. This paved the way for the modern emphasis on technique (method) and marks a major shift from metaphysical, authoritarian medieval thinking to epistemological, technical modern thinking.

Descartes' method avoids the *fallacy of false authority:* an error in reasoning in which we accept the word of experts speaking outside their fields, or uncritically rely on the testimony of others without checking it against our own experiences and reason.

Descartes employed *methodic doubt* in his effort to find one absolutely certain and undoubtable idea. Methodic doubt is a form of skepticism that rejects any idea that could possibly be false, no matter how remote that possibility. Methodic doubt coupled with the concept of the evil genius led Descartes to raise questions about whether or not he was dreaming, and about the existence of his own body and of the entire external world.

Even an evil genius could not shake one fundamental idea: "I think, therefore I am." This is known as the cogito.

Having found an undoubtable truth, Descartes tried to build a reliable foundation for knowledge based on the innate idea of God. He did this by appealing to an ontological argument that attempts to prove the existence of God by showing that the idea "God" cannot be derived from human experience; it can only come from the existence of a perfect being.

Having established the existence of God to his satisfaction, Descartes believed he had clearly and distinctly demonstrated the reliability of reason and the possibility of certain knowledge, since if God is all-knowing, all-good, and all-powerful, He would not let us live in constant ignorance.

Descartes rejected the materialists' challenge to the notion of free will with Cartesian dualism, the belief that two completely different kinds of things exist, bodies and minds, and that human beings are a mysterious union of both. Dualism, however, generates the mind-body problem: What is the relationship of the mind to the body? How can a nonmaterial thing (mind) affect a material thing (body)?

STUDY QUESTIONS

1. In general terms, explain how the modern worldview differs from the medieval.

2. Explain the significance of Luther's notion that every believer is a priest.

3. What were some of the philosophical consequences of the Copernican revolution?

4. What was Descartes' proposal, and how did his Scholastic education influence it?

5. What is the coherence theory of truth?

6. What is the method of doubt? Give a brief summary of its function in terms of Descartes' overall effort to discover certain knowledge.

7. Discuss Descartes' standard of truth. Do you think it is chiefly rational or psychological? Explain.

8. Descartes asserted that whatever we recognize "clearly and distinctly" is true. Explain the criticism that this formulation fails to meet its own standard. Do you agree that Descartes' rationalism is based on subjective states rather than on reasons understood "clearly and distinctly"? Discuss.

9. What are innate ideas? Give one or two examples.

10. What is skepticism? How is it important to Cartesian philosophy?

11. What is the cogito? Is it refutable? Discuss.

12. What is the evil genius, and what is its significance to the Cartesian Genesis? Explain.

13. Give Descartes' argument for the existence of God in your own words, then analyze it. Is it convincing? Why or why not?

14. What is Cartesian dualism?

15. What is the mind-body problem? How does Descartes deal with it? Is he successful? Why or why not?

CHAPTER TWELVE

The Skeptic:
David Hume

We declare at the outset that we do not make any positive assertion that anything we shall say is wholly as we affirm it to be. We merely report accurately on each thing as our impressions of it are at the moment.

SEXTUS EMPIRICUS

friend of mine once told me that her third cousin could move objects by psychokinesis, that is, by "mind power." She insisted that she had seen him send ashtrays and glasses across a room, without touching them or leaving his chair, merely by concentrating very deeply. I was intrigued, because I had known this woman for years, and she seemed intelligent and sane to me—yet I had never seen such a phenomenon for myself. I asked to be allowed to witness this amazing feat, but was told that, sadly, this remarkable individual had died some years before. This did not surprise me, and I may have been too blunt in saying so. "You don't believe me, do you?" my friend said, obviously annoyed with me. "You never believe anything! You're too skeptical."

A **skeptic** is a person who demands clear, observable, *undoubtable* evidence—based on experience—before accepting any knowledge claim as true. The word *skepticism* (from the Greek *skeptesthai*, "to consider or examine") refers to both a school of philosophy and a general attitude. Originally, a skeptic was a special kind of doubter, one who withheld judgment while waiting for better evidence. Sextus Empiricus (c. 200) even devised a *skeptical grammar*, which ends every proposition with "so it seems to me at the moment." There are variations of skepticism, progressing from total doubt about everything to temporary or particular doubt invoked just for the process of analysis—what Descartes called "methodic doubt" (Chapter 11).

My friend's reaction was common: She took my demand for firsthand evidence personally. That is, she interpreted it as an attack on her integrity. She would have preferred that I accept her claim as true simply because we were friends. I have experienced this reaction many times, and am even guilty of it myself. Yet anyone who is seriously interested in the pursuit of truth in general, or in the truth of a specific claim, must demand more than the personal testimony of others, no matter how sincerely they may give it or how much we may care for them.

Standards of evidence vary with the conditions. The more important the issue is, the stricter our standards must be. And the more important the issue is, the greater is our obligation to demand evidence.

PHILOSOPHICAL QUERY

Have you ever been angry or insulted when someone pressed you for evidence? Or has anyone ever gotten angry with you for asking for evidence? Why do you suppose that is? Is it rude to ask "How do you know that?" or "Can you prove that?" when people make claims about important, or even not so important, things? Analyze this question and see if you can justify *not* asking for evidence.

There is also the matter of expertise and training, as well as time, interest, and ability in the matter of justifying our beliefs. Often we must rely on the testimony of qualified experts, but this differs considerably from relying on unqualified (or at least unverified) testimony. Ideally, we should accept

SKEPTIC

From the Greek *skeptesthai*, "to consider or examine"; a person who demands clear, observable, undoubtable evidence before accepting any knowledge claim as true.

A healthy dose of skepticism can save us from making big mistakes. Skepticism can be especially valuable when we really want to believe the claims made by those trying to sell us things (including ideas and beliefs).

as true only what we can verify for ourselves. My friend was not qualified to determine the genuineness of psychic experience. Further, accepting her claim at face value would have been unreasonable; I would be discounting my own experience without ever having seen the phenomenon for myself or even having read about incontrovertible, repeatable, carefully controlled cases of similar powers.

Yet consider how rarely we seem to demand good evidence for beliefs and knowledge claims. We buy so-called health foods on the recommendation of neighbors and fellow students. In recent years, books describing their authors' experiences as "channels" for "ancient entities" have sold quite well. Many of these books also discuss out-of-body experiences, past lives, and other psychic feats. How can the reader determine whether such claims are true? What could count as proof?

Political candidates make claims about nuclear energy, education, the environment, even moral values. Automobile manufacturers make claims

Scepticism, while logically impeccable, is psychologically impossible, and there is an element of frivolous insincerity in any philosophy which pretends to accept it.
Bertrand Russell

for the reliability and safety of their vehicles. Political action groups make claims concerning abortions, racial prejudice, toxic effects, crime rates, drugs, and so forth. How often have you asked for verification of such claims? When a salesperson makes claims about this refrigerator or that CD player, do you ask for supporting data?

All of these issues (and more) involve knowledge claims. In technical language, they are *epistemological issues*. The study of the theory of knowledge, epistemology, is the branch of philosophy concerned with the origins, quality, nature, and reliability of knowledge. Beginning with Descartes, philosophy has been dominated by epistemological issues, which concern us all. We want and need to *know* the truth about the sorts of claims noted above. The truth makes a difference to us in big and little matters. If nothing else, we need the truth in order to make informed choices.

PHILOSOPHICAL QUERY

Who is a qualified expert in areas such as psychic phenomena, miracles, nutrition, or philosophy? What is the relationship between the reports of experts and your own experience? When the two conflict, which should you trust? Why? How do you know? Discuss.

BRITISH EMPIRICISM

Attempts to answer fundamental epistemological questions gave rise to the two major orientations of modern philosophy. The first, as we learned in Chapter 11, is rationalism. The other dominant philosophical orientation rejected the primacy of reason and insisted that all knowledge comes from experience. It is known as **empiricism**, from the Greek root *empeiria*, meaning "experience."

Empiricists believe that all ideas can be traced back to *sense data*. Abstractions and complex beliefs are said to be combinations and mental alterations of original impressions and perceptions, as when, for example, we imagine a man with a horse's head. Reason is unable to provide knowledge of reality; that must be derived from experience. The strictest empiricists believe that even mathematical and logical principles are derived from experience.

A potent form of empiricism emerged with the advent of modern philosophy. Because its three founding philosophers were all British, it has come to be called *British Empiricism*.

John Locke

The earliest of the three British empiricists, **John Locke (1632–1704)**, was disturbed by the confusion and uncertainty surrounding seventeenth-century philosophy and theology. Like Descartes, he was troubled by Scholastic phi-

EMPIRICISM
Belief that all knowledge is ultimately derived from the senses (experience) and that all ideas can be traced to sense data.

John Locke

losophy (Chapter 10), which he had encountered as a student at Oxford. He was especially critical of its emphasis on formal disputations and debates, which he said were "invented for wrangling and ostentation, rather than to discover the truth." Locke's *An Essay Concerning Human Understanding*, published in 1690, established the groundwork for empiricism as it is generally understood today.

Educated as a physician, Locke was aware of the great changes and progress being generated by science. He was trained to rely on his own powers of perception. He pointed out that as a physician you cannot "wait until you have reached mathematical certainty about the correct treatment" before helping a patient. You have to observe and act based on what you perceive. You must turn to the facts.[1]

In the winter of 1670, Locke had a series of philosophical discussions concerning morality and religion with some friends. It wasn't long before the friends found themselves confused and puzzled. Their inability to reach clearly right or wrong answers—in the way a chemist or baker often can— had a profound effect on Locke. He realized he had to take a step back and examine the nature and limits of knowledge before trying to sort out the truth or falsity of specific ideas:

> After we had awhile puzzled ourselves, without coming any nearer a resolution of those doubts which perplexed us, it came into my thoughts that we took a wrong course; and that before we set ourselves upon inquiries of that nature, it was necessary to examine my own abilities, and see what *objects* our understanding were, or were not, fitted to deal with.[2]

Without some clear idea of the ultimate source of knowledge, we have little hope for resolving philosophical agreements. If you have ever been involved in a nearly endless, unsettled disagreement over social, moral, political, or religious issues at some casual gathering, you know what Locke experienced. Each person seems to have an unstated set of rules and assumptions regarding what is "obviously" true and what is "ridiculous," which sources of information are reliable and which are not. Without a clearly stated and agreed upon set of basic principles, such "discussions" often amount to nothing more than each person repeatedly affirming a set of favored beliefs and denouncing all others.

Locke proposed to study the origins of our ideas in order to better understand the nature and process of acquiring knowledge. He hoped he could thereby find a way to settle difficult issues.

The Tabula Rasa

Locke completely rejected the possibility of innate ideas. He believed that at birth the mind is like *a blank tablet*, which he sometimes referred to as a **tabula rasa**, its Latin equivalent.

Unless some things are certain, it is held, nothing can be even probable.
A. J. Ayer

TABULA RASA
Latin expression for a "clean slate," used by John Locke to challenge the possibility of innate ideas by characterizing the mind at birth as a blank tablet or clean slate.

Locke argued that all ideas derive from experience and that without experience, reason has no "ground," or standard, for distinguishing truth from fantasy. In a famous passage, Locke expressed his blank-tablet, or clean-slate, view of the mind at birth:

> *All ideas come from sensations or reflection*—Let us then suppose
> the mind to be, as we say, white paper, void of all characters,
> without any ideas:—How comes it to be furnished? . . .
> Whence has it all the *materials* of reason and knowledge?
> To this I answer, in one word, from EXPERIENCE. In that
> all our knowledge is founded; and from that it ultimately
> derives itself.[3]

Locke went on to develop the first modern empirical philosophy. Although his philosophy contains inconsistencies, it is a worthwhile attempt to counter important weaknesses in Continental rationalism. It introduced a stunning new philosophical emphasis on logical rigor and analytic precision that would shake the foundations of many of our most cherished beliefs.

Locke's Egocentric Predicament

Locke placed the origin of all ideas in *sensation* and *reflection*. He says we can think about things only after we have experienced them. Thus all ideas originate from sense data. For example, no one born blind can ever have an idea of color, according to this theory. Those of us who are sighted abstract the idea of color by reflecting on, say, red, green, yellow, and blue circles. We note that they have two common qualities, circularity and color. Our blind friend can trace their shape, and thus acquire sensations of circularity, but color, which is perceived through sight, will remain unknown.

Locke attempted to explain and classify different kinds of ideas and the ways we combine and reorganize our simple ideas into complex, increasingly abstract ones. He insisted that all ideas are *copies* of the things that caused the basic sensations they rest on. Ideas are less intense copies or images of sensations. Your idea, for example, of a baseball is a copy of the set of sensations and impressions you have received from seeing and handling actual baseballs. If your idea of a baseball includes the shape of a cube, it is a poor copy. It does not *correspond* to reality.

This is known as the copy theory or representation theory, or, most recently, correspondence theory of truth, a term attributed to contemporary philosopher Bertrand Russell. The **correspondence theory of truth** is a truth test that holds that an idea (or belief or thought) is true if whatever it refers to actually exists. An idea is defined as true if it corresponds to a fact. The procedure for checking the truth of an idea is called *confirmation* or *verification*.

Favored by empiricists, the correspondence theory of truth is in direct contrast with the coherence theory of truth favored by rationalists (see Chap-

CORRESPONDENCE
THEORY OF TRUTH
Truth test that holds that an idea (or belief or thought) is true if whatever it refers to actually exists (corresponds to a fact).

IF PHYSICS IS TO BE BELIEVED . . .

We think that the grass is green, the stones are hard, and the snow is cold. But physics assures us that the greenness of the grass, the hardness of the stones, and the coldness of snow are not the greenness, hardness, and coldness that we know in our own experience, but something very different. The observer, when he seems to himself to be observing a stone, is really, if physics is to be believed, observing the effects of the stone upon himself.

Bertrand Russell
Our Knowledge of the External World as a Field for the Scientific Method in Philosophy (Chicago: Open Court, 1915).

---

ter 11) and differs from the other major truth theory, the pragmatic theory (see Chapter 17).

But if all true ideas are copies, how can we ever verify the objective, independent existence of an external reality? It seems as if all I can know are my own experiences. As soon as I am aware of them, I have labeled and organized them. That is, they instantaneously become *ideas*. I don't ever seem to be able to actually *experience* raw sense data. If my ideas are "messages" from my senses, how can I verify where the messages come from? Locke himself asks, "How shall the mind, when it perceives nothing but its own ideas, know that they agree with things themselves?"

Locke answers that we "somehow know" mental and physical substances and an objective external reality exist. We just don't have a clear idea of the difference between minds and bodies or other aspects of ultimate reality:

> Sensation convinces us that there are solid extended substances [matter and bodies]; and reflection that there are thinking ones [minds, souls]; experience assures us of the existence of such beings; and that one has the power to move body by impulse, the other by thought; this we cannot have any doubt of. Experience, I say, every moment furnishes us with clear ideas both of one and of the other. But beyond these ideas, as received from their proper sources, our faculties will not reach.[4]

Locke's position is known as **epistemological dualism**, the view that knowing contains two distinct aspects: the knower and the known. Given Locke's basic premise that all knowledge comes from our own ideas based on our own sensations and perceptions, epistemological dualism presents the fundamental problem faced by any correspondence theory of truth: *If all knowledge comes in the form of my own ideas, how can I verify the existence of anything external to them?* This predicament has been termed the **egocentric predicament**, so named because we are placed in the position of being able to

EPISTEMOLOGICAL DUALISM The view that knowing consists of two distinct aspects: the knower and the known.

EGOCENTRIC PREDICAMENT Problem generated by epistemological dualism: If all knowledge comes in the form of my own ideas, how can I verify the existence of anything external to them?

know only a world of our own mental construction, an egoistic or self-limited world.

Locke tried to avoid the egocentric predicament by asserting that we *somehow* know a material reality exists to which our ideas correspond. Locke holds on to both a "commonsense" view of reality *and* his copy theory of truth, even though he cannot verify either by appealing to the copy theory. In spite of his major differences with Descartes, he draws surprisingly similar conclusions for similar reasons.

Both Locke and Descartes shied away from pursuing the logical consequences of their basic premises. Descartes was able to establish the momentary certainty of the cogito but had difficulty moving beyond his own mind when he attempted to provide a certain foundation for the external world and God's existence. Locke was able to demonstrate the importance of experience as an element of knowledge and show that many of our ideas are based on sensation and experience. He was also able to show the inadequacy of pure reason as a foundation for all knowledge. But, like Descartes, he was unable to move from direct knowledge of his own ideas to direct knowledge of external reality.

Pursued to its logical conclusion, Locke's empiricism seems to end in the egocentric predicament. If it does, not only are we denied knowledge of an external, independent reality, we are denied the possibility of knowing God, for what simple sensations and experiences can there be on which the idea of God rests? Locke chose, in the end, to affirm certain beliefs at the expense of philosophical consistency. The second of the British empiricists tried to be more consistent.

PHILOSOPHICAL QUERY

Reflect on the claim that ideas are copies of sensations by considering these ideas: love, God, perfection, wisdom. Can you identify the sensations they correspond to?

Berkeley's Tree

George Berkeley

George Berkeley (1685–1753) was an Anglican bishop who posed one of the most quoted and least understood questions in the history of ideas: Does a tree falling in the forest make a sound if no one is there to hear it? Berkeley's answer is no, and it is based on a clear sense of the predicament Locke's empiricism generated.

From a "commonsense" point of view it may seem absurd to deny the existence of a material world, but Berkeley pointed out that on closer examination it makes more sense to deny the existence of matter than it does to affirm it. Don't pass over this point too quickly. Taking empiricism a logical step further than Locke, Berkeley argues that the material world does

not exist. Only ideas exist, and ideas are mental states, not material objects. This makes Berkeley an **idealist** or **immaterialist**: The idea of matter existing without mental properties is self-contradictory, for there is no way to conceive of what an unperceived, unexperienced existence would consist of. We can conceive of things only in terms of the perceptions (ideas) we have of them.

Berkeley challenged Locke's copy theory of truth by pointing out that the so-called objects Locke thought our ideas correspond to lack any fixed nature. They are constantly changing. There is no "thing" to copy, Berkeley said, only a cluster of constantly changing perceptions:

> [Some hold that] real things, it is plain, have a fixed and real nature, which remains the same notwithstanding any change in our senses or in the posture and motion of our bodies; which indeed may affect the ideas in our minds, but it were absurd to think they had the same effect on things existing without the mind.
>
> . . . How then is it possible that things perpetually fleeting and variable as our ideas should be copies or images of anything fixed and constant? Or, in other words, since all sensible qualities, as figure, size, color, etc., that is, our ideas, are continually changing upon every alteration in the distance, medium, or instruments of sensation—how can any determinate, material objects be properly represented or painted forth by several distinct things each of which is so different from and unlike the rest? Or, if you say it resembles some one only of our ideas, how shall we be able to distinguish the true copy from all the false ones?[5]

According to Berkeley, all of the qualities we assign to material objects are relative to the perceiver. For example, the coffee I am drinking is hot or cold depending on my perception of it. It is absurd to ask if it is *really* hot or cold. But, you might point out, it has an objective temperature, say 120 degrees Fahrenheit. Only, however, when someone measures it, that is, only when someone perceives a thermometer registering 120 degrees Fahrenheit. Even so, you're probably tempted to respond, it *does have* a certain temperature regardless of whether or not someone is aware of it.

Does it? What kind of temperature is it if no one anywhere is aware of it? And how can we ever—*in fact* or *in theory*—verify the existence of a thing's temperature *when no one is aware of it*? Even if there is an "objective, real" temperature, we will never know it.

We can know things only in terms of our perception of them through the senses, or as ideas perceived by the mind. And this being so, Berkeley argued, we know only perceptions—not *things in themselves*, only *things as perceived*. What difference does it make to insist that things exist independently

IDEALISM (IMMATERIALISM)
Belief that only ideas (mental states) exist; the material world is a fiction, it does not exist.

The refutation of skepticism is the whole business of philosophy.
Rush Rhees

of perceptions? If they do, we have no awareness of them, and they have no effect on us, so they are of no importance to us. When they do affect us, we perceive them. Thus if no one or no thing were around to perceive the famous tree falling all alone in the forest, it would be absurd to say that it made a sound. In *Three Dialogues Between Hylas and Philonous*, written in 1713, Berkeley points out that there is no difference between sound as perceived by us and sound as it is in itself. We may define sound in terms of what is perceived: sensations, atmospheric disturbances, decibels, waves, marks on a graph, or whatever, but in all cases sound remains *something that is perceived*.

One has no knowledge of the sun but only of an eye that sees a sun, and no knowledge of the earth but only of a hand that feels an earth.
Arthur Schopenhauer

> Philonous: It should follow then, that, according to you, real sounds may . . . never [be] heard.
> Hylas: Look you, Philonous, you may, if you please, make a jest of my opinion, but that will not alter the truth of things . . . sounds too have no real being without the mind.[6]

Berkeley takes the radical—but logically correct—step of concluding that this is true of everything. We know things only as different kinds of ideas about them. Berkeleian ideas imply consciousness, perception. It is self-contradictory to discuss ideas we do not know we have.

Consider the implications of this position for psychological theories of the unconscious *mind*: If an unconscious mind exists, it can have nothing to do with us. Moods and emotional states like guilt or self-hate exist only as we perceive them; they, too, are ideas in Berkeley's sense. When we do not perceive them, they do not exist. The notion of an *unconscious mind* is self-contradictory, since by definition a mind is a thinking, perceiving, hence conscious, thing.

PHILOSOPHICAL QUERY

Think about the notion of mind as contrasted to the brain and brain states. It seems clear that our behavior, moods, and even thoughts can be influenced by factors we are unaware of. These might include fatigue, hunger, the effects of medication, allergies, neurological disorders, and so on. Could we also have ideas, motives, and emotions we are unaware of? That is, could we have an "unconscious *mind*"?

It is equally absurd to posit an independent, external reality, for if it exists, we cannot have anything to do with it. If we accept Locke's starting point that all knowledge derives from experience, Berkeley reasons, we must conclude that all knowledge is limited to ideas, because *we experience things only as ideas*. So-called material or physical *states* are perceptions, mental acts. Pain is a perception; sweet and sour are perceptions; the moon is a perception; my own body is known to me only as a series of perceptions. ***Esse est percipi***: To be is to be perceived.

As Descartes pointed out, there can be no doubt about my existence while I am aware of it: To think is to exist. Berkeley adds that to exist is to be thought about: Nothing, not even an unthinking thing, can exist unless something perceives it:

> The table I write on I say exists; that is, I see and feel it: and if I were out of my study should say it existed; meaning thereby that if I was in my study I might perceive it, or that some other spirit actually does perceive it. . . . This is all that I can understand by these and the like expressions. For as to what is said of the *absolute* existence of unthinking things [matter], without any relation to their being perceived, that to me is perfectly unintelligible. Their *esse* is *percipi*; nor is it possible they should have any existence out of the minds or thinking things which perceive them.[7]

Had Berkeley continued working out the logical consequences of his position, he would have had to accept a disturbing picture of reality: Only particular, immediate perceptions can be known to exist.

Berkeley stopped short of the skeptical conclusions implied by his premises. He introduced God as a guarantee that he had a continuing self, that he existed during deepest sleep, and that there was indeed an external world, safely encapsulated in the never-resting, all-perceiving mind of God. His successor, David Hume, did not stop, but pursued skeptical logic to unsettling consequences.

DAVID HUME: THE SCOTTISH SKEPTIC

David Hume (1711–1776) stands out in the history of ideas for the fearless consistency of his reasoning. I am aware of no other philosopher who so relentlessly and thoroughly follows the premises and principles on which his or her philosophy rests to such chilling and disturbing conclusions. Many great thinkers ultimately shied away from the logical conclusions of their ideas for personal, social, or religious reasons. Hume refused to do so. So powerful is his analysis that it effectively destroyed many important philosophies that went before it, and much of the philosophy, science, and "commonsense" beliefs that follow it. Ironically, the wielder of perhaps the sharpest philosophical ax was one of the sweetest, most accessible figures in Western philosophy.

David Hume

Hume was born in Edinburgh, Scotland, and raised by his mother under a strict Presbyterian regimen. He attended three-hour morning services, went back for an hour in the afternoon, and joined in family prayers every evening. His father died the year after he was born, leaving his son a small income. Hume enrolled in the University of Edinburgh when he was twelve years old, but after three years dropped out without a degree, planning to devote himself to philosophy and literature. A short time later, Hume admitted he had lost the faith of his childhood, writing that once he read Locke and other philosophers, he never again "entertained any belief in religion."[8]

The small income his father left allowed him only the barest existence, and Hume's family tried to persuade him to do something more practical and profitable than just study literature and philosophy. He studied law from 1726 to 1729, but the experience was so unpleasant that he had a breakdown and for a time lost interest in everything. In his own words, "The law appeared nauseous to me."[9]

Hume moved to London "to make a very feeble trial for entering into a more active scene of life," though he must have had a somewhat active social life in Scotland, for on March 5 and June 25 of 1734 he was twice accused of being the father of Agnes Galbraith's child. Hume escaped censure by the church because he was out of Scotland, but poor Agnes was required to wear sackcloth in front of the congregation and be put on public display in the pillory for three consecutive Sundays.

Americans especially might take their cue today from their forebears in the eighteenth century in making an approach to Hume's philosophy. For in 1787, when the statesmen of the new American republic were discussing for many arduous months their design of a new constitution for the United States, they alluded almost daily to various writings of Hume.
Charles W. Hendel

Meanwhile, Hume was working for a merchant in Bristol, but "in a few months I found that scene totally unsuitable to me." He moved to France, where living expenses were lower, finally settling near Descartes' old college at La Flèche. There the Jesuits allowed him full access to their first-rate library. Already his skeptical, questioning mind and discomfort in the face of any authority not supported by clear evidence stood out. One of the Jesuits described Hume as "too full of himself . . . his spirit more lively than solid, his imagination more luminous than profound, his heart too dissipated with material objects and spiritual self-idolatry to pierce into the sacred recesses of divine truths."[10]

The Skeptical Masterpiece

The Jesuits were correct in one aspect of their assessment of Hume, for they recognized a mind given to no allegiance but its own experiences interpreted in an unforgiving rational light. While in France, Hume had what contemporary philosopher Richard Watson calls a "skeptical crisis." In six weeks he gained sixty pounds, and remained a "fat, jolly fellow for the rest of his life."[11] He also completed the first two books of his powerful and disturbing *Treatise of Human Nature*.

In 1737 he returned to England hoping to publish the *Treatise* and immediately ran into objections from publishers. In December 1737 he wrote, "I am at present castrating my work, that is, cutting out its noble parts, . . . endeavoring it shall give as little offense as possible."[12] Hume found most

THIS MOPING METHOD OF STUDY

Learning has been [a] great . . . loser by being shut up in colleges and cells, and secluded from the world and good company. By that means every part of what we call *belles lettres* became totally barbarous, being cultivated by men without any taste for life or manners, and without that liberty and facility of thought and expression which can only be acquired by conversation. Even philosophy went to wreck by this moping recluse method of study, and became chimerical in her conclusions, as she was unintelligible in her style and manner of delivery; and, indeed, what could be expected from men who never consulted experience in any of their reasonings, or who never searched for that experience, where alone it is to be found, in common life and conversation?

David Hume
"Of Essay Writing," in *Of the Standard Taste and Other Essays*, ed. John W. Lenz (Indianapolis: Bobbs-Merrill, 1965), p. 39.

resistance to his analysis of miracles. He agreed to remove the most offensive passages, but did not destroy them. In this censored form, the two-volume *Treatise* was published anonymously in January 1739. Hume received fifty pounds and twelve copies as his total payment. At the age of twenty-seven he had written one of the major works of modern philosophy.

In the *Treatise* Hume makes compelling arguments *against* materialism, the possibility of a spiritual, supernatural reality and personal immortality—this in the watered-down version! Pushing beyond Locke and Berkeley, Hume argued that neither matter nor mind exists. (A standing joke at the time referred to Berkeley and Hume with the slogan "No matter; never mind.")

The uncensored *Treatise* does not stop there. Hume ultimately reduces reason to the "slave of the passions" and alters the conventional picture of the nature of science by denying cause and effect as they are generally understood. Thus Hume challenged established religious beliefs, moral judgments, reason and rationalism, earlier forms of empiricism, and the certainty of science. He denied the existence of a "fixed self," the possibility of personal immortality, and the questioned possibility of miracles. It would not be surprising if such a book provoked a great storm of controversy. Ultimately, it would, but not among the general public and not right away. The second edition of the *Treatise* was not published until after Hume's death.

Never [a] literary attempt was more unfortunate than my Treatise of Human Nature. *It fell dead-born from the press, without reaching such distinction as even to excite a murmur among the zealots.*
David Hume

An Honest Man

Unable to earn his living as a writer, Hume applied for a professorship at the University of Edinburgh, but was rejected. He took a somewhat humiliating job as the tutor of a young nobleman, who shortly went insane. Hume was ultimately dismissed and had to sue for his salary. He eventually secured a position as secretary to a general on a mission to Turin, Italy. Hume, having apparently gained more weight, began wearing a scarlet uniform. His appearance unsettled the young Earl of Charlemont, who wrote as follows: "His face was broad and fat, his mouth wide, and without any other expression than that of imbecility. . . . The corpulence of his whole person was far better fitted to communicate the idea of a turtle-eating alderman than that of a refined philosopher."[13]

Hume returned to London in 1748 and published *An Enquiry Concerning Human Understanding*. In 1749 he went back to Edinburgh and in 1751 published *An Enquiry Concerning the Principles of Morals*. These works reach the same conclusions as the *Treatise*, but in a softer tone.

The softer tone was not to last, for in about 1751 Hume wrote the most devastating, direct, and irreverent of his works, the *Dialogues Concerning Natural Religion*. In it Hume mounts an unrelenting attack on the argument from design (see Chapter 10) and other attempts to demonstrate the existence of or understand the nature of God. At the urging of friends, Hume withheld the *Dialogues* from publication. They were finally published in 1779, three years after his death.

Hume wearied of the heated discussion his philosophical reasonings provoked, and turned to politics and history. He finally achieved some success as an author with *Political Discourses* (1751) and *Essays on Various Subjects* (1753). The theory of economics discussed in the *Essays* was substantial enough to influence the great economist Adam Smith.

In 1752 Hume was elected keeper of the library for the Faculty of Advocates in Edinburgh. The pay was low, but Hume was delighted with the job because it gave him control of thirty thousand volumes. Taking advantage of this opportunity, he researched and wrote a *History of England*. He was a competent enough historian that Edward Gibbon, the author of *The Decline and Fall of the Roman Empire* (1776), cited him as an influence.

Hume published his *History* in six volumes, in reverse order, beginning with the years 1603–49 and ending with the period from Julius Caesar to Henry VII in 1485. His attitudes toward Parliament and Bonnie Prince Charlie were unorthodox, and the controversy aroused by the first volume was so intense that Hume grew depressed and planned to move back to France. But France and England were at war and the second volume was nearly done. So Hume revised the first volume and continued with the others. By the publication of the sixth volume Hume's popularity as a writer had soared. James Boswell referred to him as "the greatest writer in Britain," and Voltaire said Hume's work was "perhaps the best history ever written in any language."[14] (Today, hardly anyone reads Hume's *History of England*, but no truly educated person fails to read something of Hume's philosophy.)

In spite of his success, Hume remained troubled by the unrelenting attacks from ecclesiastical and other sources. Relief arrived in the form of an ap-

Upon the whole, I have always considered [David Hume], both in his lifetime and since his death, as approaching as nearly to the idea of a perfectly wise and virtuous man as perhaps the nature of human frailty will permit.

Adam Smith

I salute you, I love you, I revere you.

Denis Diderot, to David Hume

pointment as deputy secretary to the Earl of Hertford, ambassador to France. Hertford also arranged that Hume should receive a pension of two hundred pounds for life.

His writing was more popular in France than in England, and by the time he returned to France he was almost a cult figure. The aristocracy loved him (the ladies most of all) and he loved them (the ladies most of all). The Earl of Hertford found that Hume was more popular and respected than the earl was. Once at a party an envious French intellectual made fun of Hume's weight, quoting the Gospel verse "And the word was made flesh." One of Hume's many lady admirers quickly countered, "And the word was made lovable."

After Britain appointed a new ambassador to France in 1765, Hume worked for a time as undersecretary at the Foreign Office in London. He retired to Edinburgh in 1769, being, in his own words, "very opulent (for I possessed a revenue of £1,000 a year), healthy, and though somewhat stricken in years, with the prospect of enjoying long my ease, and of seeing the increase of my reputation."[15]

Hume's home (on, fittingly, St. David Street) became an intellectual salon for Scottish celebrities, including Adam Smith. Hume was a friendly, supportive, encouraging mentor, despite the rigor and iconoclasm of his intellect. He remained a popular guest, even if he occasionally broke a host's chair.[16] He once proposed a tax on obesity but thought its passage unlikely because it might put the church in danger, and he blessed Julius Caesar for preferring fat men.

Part of Hume's charm came from his personal modesty. These days rock stars and television "personalities" in their teens think nothing of writing a two or three hundred-page autobiography, yet one of the finest minds to have ever lived considered it sufficient to write an eight-page one—and then only shortly before he died. In it he wrote:

> In the spring of 1775 I was struck with a disorder in my bowels, which at first gave me no alarm, but has since, as I apprehend it, become mortal and incurable. I now reckon upon a speedy dissolution. I have suffered very little pain from my disorder; and what is more strange, have, notwithstanding the great decline of my person, never suffered a moment's abatement of my spirits; insomuch that were I to name the period of my life which I should most choose to pass over again, I might be tempted to point to this later period. I possess the same ardor as ever in my study, and the same gaiety in company. I consider, besides, that a man of sixty-five, by dying, cuts off only a few years of infirmities.[17]

In 1775 Hume lost seventy pounds due to his illness. In 1776 he was prepared to die "as fast as my enemies, if I have any, could wish, and as easily and cheerfully as my best friends could desire."[18]

Hume was a wonderful man. He and Benjamin Franklin used to have grand times together in Paris, eating and drinking and playing whist, and pulling bluestocking ladies down to sit on their fat laps.

Richard Watson

Even in his last hours, Hume was not spared the attentions of the devout. James Boswell was troubled that the agnostic Hume, whom many erroneously believed to be an atheist, could be so cheerful in the face of death. But Hume did not deny the existence of God, a position known as *atheism*; he adopted the agnostic view that we do not know enough to assert or deny the existence of God.

Happiness in the face of death was thought to be a virtue of the devout believer, not the skeptical agnostic. Unrelenting even at the end, Boswell asked the dying Hume if he did *now* finally believe in an afterlife. Hume answered, "It is a most unreasonable fancy that we should exist forever." Asked if he didn't at least think the possibility of another plane of existence was desirable, the dying skeptic answered, "Not at all; it is a very gloomy thought." A small parade of women visited Hume, begging him to believe, but he distracted them with humor.[19]

David Hume died free of much pain on August 25, 1776. The story goes that a large crowd attended his burial, despite heavy rain. Someone was heard to say, "He was an atheist." "No matter," a voice answered from the crowd. "He was an honest man."

HUME'S SKEPTICAL EMPIRICISM

Hume's philosophy rests on the rejection of overly abstract, obscure, bloated speculations. Hume found most metaphysical speculation irrelevant to the lives of ordinary people. Being poorly worded, unclear, and based on unverified assumptions, it was also, he observed, never-ending. No metaphysical issue was ever clearly and thoroughly settled. For each theory about the soul or nature or reality, there were opposing theories and modifications, apparently infinite in number.

Hume thought such "abstruse speculation" was useful only to individuals with some theological motive, who, "being unable to defend [their views] on fair grounds, raise these entangling brambles to cover and protect their weaknesses." The only way to rid ourselves of these pointless excursions, he claimed, is to inquire seriously and thoroughly into the nature of human understanding, "and show, from an exact analysis of its powers and capacity, that it is by no means fitted for such remote and abstruse subjects."

In other words, Hume continued the epistemological turn, moving further away from metaphysics than Locke and Berkeley. Although he said we must "cultivate true metaphysics with some care in order to destroy the false," Hume moved modern philosophy firmly into the realm of epistemology.

Impressions and Ideas

In *An Enquiry Concerning Human Understanding*, Hume set out to modify Locke's theory of ideas in a way that removed any metaphysical residue. He began by pointing out the very obvious difference between, say, the painful perception of excessive heat or the pleasure of comforting warmth, and the memory of such perceptions. There is also, he noted, a difference between anticipating a perception in the imagination and actually perceiving it. He says, "The most lively thought is still inferior to the dullest sensation." This kind of distinction also applies to "mental perceptions," such as anger and hate.

Hume thought Locke was correct in claiming that thought is a "faithful mirror, and copies objects truly." But he reminds us not to overlook a vital fact: The copies are always duller and fainter than the original perceptions they are based on.

Hume proposes that we distinguish "ideas" from "impressions":

> Here therefore we may divide all perceptions of the mind into two classes or species, which are distinguished by their different degrees of force and vivacity. The less forcible and lively are commonly denominated *Thoughts* or *Ideas*. The other species wants a name in our language, and most others. . . . Let us, therefore, use a little freedom, and call them *Impressions*; employing that word in a sense somewhat different from the usual. By the term *impression*, then, I mean all our more lively perceptions, when we hear, or see, or feel, or love, or hate, or desire, or will. And impressions are distinguished from ideas, which are the less lively perceptions, of which we are conscious, when we reflect on any of those sensations or movements above mentioned.[20]

More careful analysis of ideas, no matter how fanciful, creative, or original, reveals that "all this creative power of the mind amounts to no more than the faculty of compounding, transposing, augmenting, or diminishing the materials afforded us by the senses and experience." In other words, all ideas can be traced to impressions and thus are derived from experience, even if they become so abstracted and diluted that they no longer resemble any identifiable impressions. If you doubt this, Hume says the only way to refute him is to produce an idea not derived from impressions or from combining and altering the ideas that impressions generate.

From this basic position, which he took for granted, Hume proposed one of the most powerful, controversial, devastating ideas in modern philosophy: the empirical criterion of meaning.

The Empirical Criterion of Meaning

Modifying Locke's copy theory of ideas, Hume established an empirical test of meaning:

> When we entertain, therefore, any suspicion that a philosophical term is employed without any meaning or idea (as is a bit

No sooner do we depart from sense and instinct to follow . . . reason . . . but . . . we are insensibly drawn into uncouth paradoxes, difficulties, and inconsistencies, which multiply and grow upon us as we advance in speculation; till at length, having wandered through many intricate mazes, we find ourselves just where we were, or, which is worse, sit down in a forlorn Scepticism.

George Berkeley

too frequent), we need to enquire, *from what impression is that supposed idea derived*? And if it be impossible to assign any, this will serve to confirm our suspicion. By bringing ideas into so clear a light we may reasonably hope to remove all dispute, which may arise, concerning their nature and reality.[21]

The **empirical criterion of meaning** holds that all *meaningful* ideas can be traced to sense experience (impressions). Beliefs that cannot be reduced to sense experience are technically not "ideas" at all: they are *meaningless utterances*.

To understand how the empirical criterion works, imagine for a moment that we are with some fellow philosophers discussing the existence of God and related theological issues. We might argue all evening about whether or not Thomas Aquinas's proofs for the existence of God work. We might argue about whether or not we are born with the innate idea of God or acquire the idea of God from experience. Or we might argue about the problem of evil or whether God favors one religion over another. Whatever position we take on these issues, at least one thing seems clear: We have an idea of God. But do we?[22]

If, as Locke thought, all ideas are derived from experience and the mind begins as a clean slate, the idea of God must be empirically based; it cannot be innate. What *impressions* can justify an assertion like "God is eternal"? We never experience "eternity." At most we experience "long, long time." We say that God is *perfect*. Have we ever experienced absolute perfection in anything? I am not speaking metaphorically or poetically, but precisely and literally: Do we even have a clear *idea* of perfection?

With an idea as important and controversial as God, the empirical criterion of meaning is explosive. It causes us to look anew at the very *idea* of God before we can begin to discuss God's nature and existence. Experience alone cannot provide the idea of an all-perfect, eternal, all-powerful God, because nothing in our experience even remotely resembles perfection, eternity, or infinite power. Thus if we accept the empirical criterion of meaning, the idea of God is neither true nor false, it is *meaningless*. That is, talk about God conveys no information. It is simply a form of confusion resulting from not paying close enough attention to what we say.

Hume's precise, logically rigorous use of the empirical criterion of meaning led to other startling, uncomfortable conclusions about some of the most cherished, influential ideas in philosophy, theology, and science. Let's see what happens when strict empirical standards are applied to some of the ideas we have already studied.

EMPIRICAL CRITERION OF MEANING
Meaningful ideas are those that can be traced back to sense experience (impressions); beliefs that cannot be reduced to sense experience are not "ideas" at all, but meaningless utterances.

Nihil in intellectu quod prius non fuerit in sensu.
(Nothing is in the intellect which was not in the senses first.)
Thomas Aquinas

PHILOSOPHICAL QUERY

Do you agree that "talk about God conveys no information"? Explain. Apply the empirical criterion of meaning to such concepts as love, creativity, and intelligence. What, in general, do you see as the strengths and weaknesses of this criterion?

The Self

As we have seen, Descartes based modern philosophy on the thinking thing, the self. We seem intimately acquainted with a self. What could be more certain than the existence of my self? But what exactly does the word *self* refer to?

Hume says that we do not have any idea of self as it is commonly understood:

> For from what impression cou'd this idea be deriv'd? This question 'tis impossible to answer without a manifest contradiction and absurdity; and 'tis a question, which necessarily must be answer'd, if we wou'd have the idea of self pass for clear and intelligible. But self or person is not any one impression, but that to which our several impressions and ideas are suppos'd to have a reference. If any impression gives rise to the idea of self, that impression must continue invariably the same, thro' the whole course of our lives; since self is suppos'd to exist after that manner. But there is no impression constant and invariable. Pain and pleasure, grief and joy, passions and sensations succeed each other, and never all exist at the same time. It cannot, therefore, be from any of these impressions, or from any other, that the idea of self is deriv'd; and consequently there is no such idea.[23]

The solution to the problem of identity is, get lost.
Norman O. Brown

But if we have no such *impression* of self, what are we? Hume gives one of the most intriguing yet elusive answers in modern philosophy:

> For my part, when I enter most intimately into what I call *myself*, I always stumble on some particular perception or other, of heat or cold, light or shade, love or hatred, pain or pleasure. I never can catch *myself* at any time without a perception, and never can observe any thing but the perception. When my perceptions are remov'd for any time, as by sound sleep; so long am I insensible of *myself*, and may truly be said not to exist. And were all my perceptions remov'd by death, and cou'd I neither think, nor feel, nor see, nor love, nor hate after the dissolution of my body, I shou'd be entirely annihilated, nor do I conceive what is farther requisite to make me a perfect non-entity. If any one upon serious and unprejudic'd reflexion, thinks he has a different notion of *himself*, I must confess I can reason no longer with him. All I can allow him is, that he may be in the right as well as I, and that we are essentially different in this particular. He may, perhaps, perceive something simple and continu'd, which he calls *himself*; tho' I am certain there is no such principle in me.
>
> But setting aside some metaphysicians of this kind, I may venture to affirm of the rest of mankind, that they are nothing

but a bundle or collection of different perceptions, which succeed each other with an inconceivable rapidity, and are in a perpetual flux and movement.[24]

In such passages, Hume sounds very much like a Buddhist or Hindu. He has dissolved the self into a flickering series of perceptions with no underlying, constant *thing* to unite them. What has come to be known as Hume's **bundle theory of the self** is difficult for most of us to accept. Yet Hume's position is more consistent than some that are more comforting and popular.

BUNDLE THEORY OF THE SELF
Humean theory that there is no fixed "self," but that the "self" is merely a "bundle of perceptions"; a "self" is merely a habitual way of discussing certain perceptions.

PHILOSOPHICAL QUERY

Where and what are "you" in the midst of some exciting experience that totally absorbs your consciousness? That is, what happens to your "self" when you are not aware of it? What exactly are you aware of when you are self-conscious? A "self" or sweaty palms, uncomfortable desks, boring lectures? Discuss.

Personal Immortality

If we cannot speak clearly about the self, what happens to the common belief that the self (or the soul) survives after bodily death? If an *identity* of some sort survives bodily decay, what exactly does that identity find in the afterlife? Is the afterlife a place? How do we know that? And what do we mean when we talk of the soul going somewhere? Does such a concept have any clear content? Can we describe the soul's journey with the same detail and clarity as we recount a physical journey? I don't think we can.

Hume says, in his straightforward fashion, that there can be no persistent identity for us. We speak of "the oak tree" in the backyard, but in fact, each time we see it, "the oak tree" is different. It has a different number of leaves, it has grown, even when we cannot yet discern these changes. Any change in a thing changes its identity. In what sense can a two-hundred-pound man who has been married twice and fathered children be the "same person" who was once a fifty-pound third grader? In what sense are you the "same person" who began reading this book? Your mind has different ideas. Your body has different cells. As Heraclitus noted, "We cannot step twice into the same river, for the water into which we first stepped has flowed on."

Strictly speaking, nothing exists except sensations (and the minds which perceive them).

W. T. Stace

In other words, identity is not a property of things, but a mental act. Our minds *confer* identity on things; we do not perceive it.

The whole of this doctrine leads us to a conclusion, which is of great importance in the present affair, *viz.* that all the nice and subtle questions concerning personal identity can never possibly be decided, and are to be regarded rather as grammatical than as philosophical difficulties. . . . We have no just standard, by which we can decide any dispute concerning the

In what sense is the "self" negotiating the turbulent rapids of
Lava Falls in the Grand Canyon the same "self" that sat on a couch
reading a book the week before? What are "you" in the midst of
some all-absorbing, intense experience? Is there a "you" at all *during the peak moments of such experiences*?

time, when [things] acquire or lose a title to the name of identity. All the disputes concerning the identity of connected objects are merely verbal, except so far as the relation of parts
gives rise to some fiction or imaginary principle of union, as
we have already observ'd.[25]

In other words, a self is merely a habitual way of discussing certain perceptions.

Strictly speaking, Hume is correct. We do not *perceive identity*. Yet something gives order and continuity to our experiences, and Hume does not deny
that. Rather, he insists on clearer, more precise talking, reasoning, and thinking about this and other important matters. In the process, Hume reaches
the limits of reason, and, perhaps, of knowledge.

THE LIMITS OF REASON

In a sense, Hume is simply stopping at the first part of Berkeley's position. Hume says, "The mind has never anything

*Shall we esteem it worthy
the labour of a philosopher
to give us a true system of
the planets, and adjust the
position and order of those
remote bodies; while we affect to overlook those, who,
with so much success, delin-
eate the parts of the mind, in
which we are so intimately
concerned?*

David Hume

present to it but the perceptions, and cannot possibly reach any experience of their connexion with objects. The supposition of such a connexion . . . is, therefore, without any foundation in reasoning."[26] This means we have no way of empirically establishing the independent existence of an external world, or what many of us mean by "reality." The only world we can ever know is the world of our own perceptions, ideas, and experiences.

> As several impressions appear exterior to the body, we suppose them also exterior to ourselves. The paper, on which I write at present, is beyond my hand. The table is beyond the paper. The walls of the chamber beyond the table. And in casting my eye towards the window, I perceive a great extent of fields and buildings beyond my chamber. From all this it may be infer'd, that no other faculty is requir'd, besides the senses, to convince us of the external existence of body. But to prevent this inference, we need only weigh the three following considerations. *First*, That, properly speaking, 'tis not our body we perceive, when we regard our limbs and members, but certain impressions, which enter by the sense; so that in ascribing a real and corporeal existence to these impressions, or to their objects, is an act of the mind as difficult to explain, as that which we examine at present. *Secondly*, Sounds and tastes, and smells, tho' commonly regarded by the mind as continu'd independent qualities, appear not to have any existence in extension, and consequently cannot appear to the senses as situated externally to the body. . . . *Thirdly*, Even our sight informs us not of distance or outness (so to speak) immediately and without certain reasoning and experience, as is acknowledg'd by the most rational philosophers.[27]

Accurate and just reasoning is the only catholic remedy, fitted for all persons and all dispositions; and is alone able to subvert that abstruse philosophy and metaphysical jargon, which, being mixed up with popular superstition, renders it in a manner impenetrable to careless reasoners, and gives it the air of science and wisdom.

David Hume

If we were merely reasoning creatures, we could accept this conclusion. Yet belief in an external world is one of the strongest, most universal beliefs. If, as Hume thought, there is no rational evidence whatsoever for belief in an external reality, then why is the notion so popular?

Hume concludes that the very nature of imagination accounts for the universal notion of the independent existence of an external world. The imagination completes and fills in gaps between perceptions. If we regularly experience very much the same perceptions, say of the oak tree in the yard or our own face, we overlook the gaps between different perceptions. Hume says we "feign" or fabricate continuity. I assume that because my face looks "the same" this morning as yesterday morning, it has existed continuously all night and at other times when I had no perception of it.

Further, our experiences tend to occur with a kind of pattern or regularity, which Hume refers to as *coherence*. That is, when I turn my head to the left, my view in the mirror is a particular perception. When I tilt forward, I have a completely different perception, and so on. When I turn around and use a hand mirror to examine the thinning hair on the back of my head, I have yet another perception. What I never have is an impression of my whole head. But because my various views always follow a pattern, my imagination feigns or fabricates an idea of my whole head.

According to Hume, this process explains our belief in an external world. But it points to a startling conclusion: that a natural quality of the mind exists which is much more powerful than logical reasoning, and which always reasserts itself after being challenged on logical grounds.

> There is a great difference betwixt such opinions as we form after a calm and profound reflection, and such as we embrace by a kind of instinct or natural impulse, on account of their suitableness and conformity to the mind. If these opinions become contrary, 'tis not difficult to foresee which of them will have the advantage. As long as our attention is bent upon the subject, the philosophical and study'd principle may prevail; but the moment we relax our thoughts, nature will display herself, and draw us back to our former opinion. . . .[28]

If Hume is correct, nature and reason are adversaries: "Nature is obstinate, and will not quit the field, however strongly attack'd by reason; and at the same time reason is so clear in the point, that there is no possibility of disguising her." This explains why many people are indifferent to logical precision or rational evidence. It might also account for the ease with which we accept poorly justified beliefs. It might even explain why you can study only so much philosophy (or anything else) and then find yourself almost compelled to do something nonintellectual. Nature acts as a corrective and cure to reason.

By the same token, the human mind has a rational component. A completely nonrational life would be barely human. Even the most primitive, nontechnical, "natural" cultures depend on reason. What Hume suggests is a kind of fluctuating balance between reason and nature, or logic and emotion. We find such a position less disturbing today than philosophers did in the eighteenth century, for Hume's skepticism indicates that a completely rational view of reality is not possible, or at least not for more than brief, concentrated periods. It suggests that reason, the great ideal of so many philosophers, is, in fact, the slave of emotions, shaped by psychology and biology.

Reason is, and ought only to be the slave of passions, and can never pretend to any other office than to serve and obey them.
David Hume

PHILOSOPHICAL QUERY

Have you been able to take Hume's claims seriously? That is, have you seriously considered the *possibility* that we lack *knowledge* of the external world? Discuss some factors that make taking this idea seriously so difficult. Can you spot any errors in Hume's reasoning? Discuss.

THE LIMITS OF SCIENCE

Scientific reasoning rests on a pattern of **inductive reasoning**, which results in generalized rules or principles. Simplistically, we can say that it reasons from the particular to the general or from some to all. Conclusions about atoms or the behavior of iron filings or causes of rain are never based on experience with *all* things of a certain kind. Newton did not have to observe the behavior of all bodies to conclude they are subject to gravity. He based his conclusion on the behavior of just some bodies.

Scientists assume that such inferences are reliable because they identify *causal patterns*. In Hume's time, cause and effect were defined in terms of a *necessary connection*. That is, A was said to cause B if the occurrence of A *always and without exception* was followed by the occurrence of B. But if Hume's epistemology is correct, how can we perceive the actual connection, the causal relationship? Strictly speaking, all we actually observe is A followed by B. We observe constant conjunction; that is, a perception of A is always (or so far) followed by a perception of B. But that is a temporal sequence, not a necessary connection. Ironically, the great empiricist demonstrates, *on strictly empirical grounds*, that the very foundation of the empirical sciences is nothing more than a product of the human mind. According to Hume, there is no empirical evidence for the existence of cause and effect:

The mind is a kind of theatre, where several perceptions successively make their appearance; pass, re-pass, glide away, and mingle in an infinite variety of postures and situations.

David Hume

> We have sought in vain for an idea of power or necessary connexion in all the sources from which we could suppose it to be derived. It appears that, in single instances of the operation of bodies, we never can, by our utmost scrutiny, discover anything but one event following another, without being able to comprehend any force or power by which the cause operates, or any connexion between it and its supposed effect. The same difficulty occurs in contemplating the operations of mind on body—where we observe the motion of the latter to follow upon the volition of the former, but are not able to observe or conceive the tie which binds together the motion and volition, or the energy by which the mind produces this effect. The authority of the will over its own faculties and ideas is not a whit more comprehensible: So that, upon the whole, there appears not, throughout all nature, any one instance of connexion which is conceivable by us. All events seem entirely loose and separate. One event follows another; but we can never observe any tie between them. They seem *conjoined*, but never *connected*. And as we can have no idea of any thing which [is not based on an impression], the necessary conclusion *seems* to be that we have no idea of connexion or power at all, and that these words are absolutely without any meaning, when employed either in philosophical reasonings or common life.[29]

What *do* we observe that we call cause and effect? Hume answers that we observe a series of recognizable impressions, and that we come to expect the first part of the series to be followed by the second part. When we are correct, we assume the connection is causal. But we cannot observe that one event *must* follow the other. All we *know* is that one event *happens* to follow another. We may have observed this pattern countless times, but that does not logically justify inferring any sort of necessity.

In other words, the mind creates the ideas of causality and necessity; we do not observe them. The best we can do is take for granted that the future will resemble the past: there is no way to prove that it will or that it must. We are psychologically constructed so that we have no choice but to *believe in* cause and effect. For the most part, our inferences regarding the predictability and uniformity of experience have been borne out. But, Hume cautions us, we should not forget that the real origin of science lies in the operation of the human mind. We believe in an independent, external reality because we cannot help it.

Science is included in Hume's consistent skeptical conclusion: All *knowledge* is limited to our own impressions; everything else is a product of the imagination.

THE LIMITS OF THEOLOGY

Given his radical view of cause and effect, it is not surprising that Hume rejected all efforts to prove the existence of God based on cause. The cosmological argument and the argument from motion were meaningless for him. The ontological argument was meaningless as well, because the very qualities ascribed to God—perfection, omniscience, omnipotence, and so forth—do not correspond to specific impressions. They are empty noises.

Besides rejecting these arguments, Hume wrote perhaps the most devastating and complete critique of the argument from design, also known as the teleological argument (see Thomas Aquinas's fifth way in Chapter 10). After taking the briefest look at this compelling bit of logical analysis, we can understand why Hume withheld publication of his *Dialogues Concerning Natural Religion* during his lifetime.

Recall that the core of the argument from design is the belief that all about us we see evidence of God's handiwork. We perceive order and harmony and beauty throughout the universe. We sense the divine in a beautiful sunset or an ocean breeze; we feel God's presence in the miracle of childbirth or the renewing of the seasons. But as Hume points out, that's not the whole picture.

In the first place, we need to remind ourselves that the argument from design is an analogy in which God and Creation are compared to a craftsman and a crafted object (a watchmaker and a watch is the most famous

The whole conception of God is a conception derived from ancient Oriental despotisms. It is a conception quite unworthy of free men. . . . A good world needs knowledge, kindliness and courage; it does not need a regretful hankering after the past or a fettering of the free intelligence by the words uttered long ago by ignorant men.

Bertrand Russell

example). Let us grant the similarity for purposes of analysis. Careful reasoning produces a disquieting conclusion:

> But were this world ever so perfect a production, it must still remain uncertain, whether all the excellences of the work can justly be ascribed to the workman. If we survey a ship, what an exalted idea must we form of the ingenuity of the carpenter, who framed so complicated, useful, and beautiful a machine? And what surprise must we feel, when we find him a stupid mechanic, who imitated others, and copied an art, which, through a long succession of ages, after multiplied trials, mistakes, corrections, deliberations, and controversies, had gradually been improving? Many worlds might have been botched and bungled, throughout an eternity, ere this system was struck out: Much labor lost: Many fruitless trials made: And a slow, but continued improvement carried on during infinite ages in the art of world-making. . . .[30]

Moreover, we need to think carefully about the relationship between the designer and the finished product:

> Did I show you a house or palace, where there was not one apartment convenient or agreeable; where the windows, doors, fires, passages, stairs, and the whole economy of the building were the source of noise, confusion, fatigue, darkness, and extremes of heat and cold; you would certainly blame the contrivance, without any farther examination. . . . If you find many inconveniences and deformities in the building, you will always, without entering into any detail, condemn the architect. . . . Accurate and just reasoning is the only catholic remedy, fitted for all persons and all dispositions; and is alone able to subvert that abstruse philosophy and metaphysical jargon, which, being mixed up with popular superstition, renders it in a manner impenetrable to careless reasoners, and gives it the air of science and wisdom.[31]

Christianity does not—and cannot—explain how a God who is infinitely powerful and infinitely loving came to create a universe which turned out to be not very good.

Arnold Toynbee

The argument from design depends, in great part, on the nature of the universe (the designed thing). Why would God design a world such as ours which contains disorder, ugliness, injustice, and cruelty? Nature at best is inefficient: one part of the world drowns in torrential rains and another burns under drought; some regions have plenty and others starve. If this is "the best of all possible worlds," the critics argue, it only shows that God could not create a first-rate world.

There is even less reason to infer the existence of a good God once one takes a thorough, objective look at life:

> But allowing you, what never will be believed; at least, what you never possibly can prove, that animal, or at least human

happiness, in this life, exceeds its misery; you have yet done nothing: For this is not, by any means, what we expect from infinite power, infinite wisdom, infinite goodness. Why is there any misery at all in this world? Not by chance surely. From some cause then. Is it from the intention of the Deity? But he is perfectly benevolent. Is it contrary to his intention? But he is almighty. Nothing can shake the solidity of this reasoning, so short, so clear, so decisive. . . .

Look round this universe. What an immense profusion of beings, animated and organized, sensible and active! You admire the prodigious variety and fecundity. But inspect a little more narrowly these living existences, the only beings worth regarding. How hostile and destructive to each other! How insufficient all of them for their own happiness! How contemptible or odious to the spectator! The whole presents nothing but the idea of a blind nature, impregnated by a great vivifying principle, and pouring forth from her lap, without discernment or parental care, her maimed and abortive children.[32]

Based solely on our observations of human experience, we find insufficient evidence to assume the existence of a good, all-wise, all-powerful God. Imagine what kind of argument Hume could have made had he known of the Holocaust.

PHILOSOPHICAL QUERY

Take a moment to reconsider the argument from design in light of such twentieth-century horrors as chemical warfare, environmental disasters, AIDS, crack babies, crime rates, world hunger, and homelessness amid plenty. Do such examples refute the notion of design or not? Discuss.

Hume also pointed out that we have no real reason to compare the universe to a machine or crafted object in the first place. It makes as much, if not more, sense to view the universe as an organism:

> The world plainly resembles more an animal or a vegetable, than it does a watch or knitting-loom. Its cause, therefore, it is more probable, resembles the cause of the former. The cause of the former is generation or vegetation. The cause, therefore, of the world, we may infer to be some thing similar or analogous to generation or vegetation.[33]

At this point in the dialogue, Hume has the person representing orthodox belief object, asking, "What *data* have you for such extraordinary conclusions? And is the slight, imaginary resemblance of the world to a vegetable or an animal sufficient to establish [any] inference in regard to both?"

I said that I could not imagine being an atheist any time before 1859, when Darwin's **Origin of Species** *was published. "What about Hume?" replied the philosopher. "How did Hume explain the organized complexity of the living world?" I asked. "He didn't," said the philosopher. "Why does it need any special explanation?"*

Richard Dawkins

Hume replies with the most important and devastating point of all:

> Right. . . . This is the topic on which I have all along insisted. I have still asserted that we have no *data* to establish any system of cosmogony [theory of the origins of the universe]. Our experience, so imperfect in itself, and so limited both in extent and duration, can afford us no probable conjecture concerning the whole of things.[34]

Strictly speaking, our own little corner of the universe is too small to permit useful generalizations about the whole. To conclude yea or nay about God's existence and nature is beyond the limits of both reason and experience.

In a note added to the *Dialogues* just before his death, Hume stated that *"the cause or causes of order in the universe probably bear some remote analogy to human intelligence."* But he insisted that this analogy does not suggest that God exists, at least the God of Judeo-Christian-Islamic religions.

THE LIMITS OF RATIONALISTIC ETHICS

A s we have seen, Plato argued that reason's function is to rule the appetites and emotions. The Stoics attempted to control their passions through reason. Descartes attempted to replace the authority of the church with the authority of reason. Descartes was not alone in his vision of reason as the ground of all knowledge, including moral knowledge. The seventeenth and eighteenth centuries are sometimes characterized as the Age of Reason. Attempts to ground morals in reason continue in the present. But when Hume applied his empirical ax to moral philosophy, he challenged the role of reason in morality in an unprecedented way and achieved results similar to his critiques of theology and metaphysics.

As we shall see, Hume insisted that morality is grounded in sentiment, not reason. His devastating attack on any "metaphysic of morals" has had an enormous influence on modern and postmodern conceptions of morality, value judgments, and the possibility of moral knowledge. Immanuel Kant (Chapter 13) would refer to Hume's work as a "scandal in philosophy."

In his *A Treatise of Human Nature*, Hume asserts that "reason alone" can never provide a motive for any action:

> Nothing is more usual in philosophy, and even in common life, than to talk of the combat of passion and reason, to give the preference to reason, and to assert that men are only so far virtuous as they conform themselves to its dictates. Every rational creature, 'tis said, is oblig'd to regulate his actions by reason; and if any other motive or principle challenge the direction of his conduct, he ought to oppose it, 'till it be entirely subdu'd, or at least brought to a conformity with this common

I am uneasy to think I approve of one object, and disapprove of another; call one thing beautiful, and another deform'd; decide concerning truth and falsehood, reason and folly, without knowing upon what principles I proceed.

David Hume

principle. On this method of thinking the greatest part of moral philosophy, ancient and modern, seems to be founded; nor is there an ampler field, as well for metaphysical arguments, as popular declamations, than this suppos'd pre-eminence of reason above passion. . . .

In order to shew the fallacy of all this philosophy, I shall endeavour to prove *first*, that reason alone can never be a motive to any action of the will; and *secondly*, that it can never oppose passion in the direction of the will.[35]

Hume did not deny that reason plays a role in making moral judgments. Rather, he argued that reason's role is secondary to the role of moral feelings or *sentiments*, because reason can never provide ultimate ends:

It appears evident that the ultimate ends of human actions can never . . . be accounted for by *reason*, but recommend themselves entirely to the sentiments and affections of mankind, without any dependence on the intellectual faculties. Ask a man *why he uses exercise*; he will answer, *because he desires to keep his health*. If you then enquire, *why he desires health*, he will readily reply, *because sickness is painful*. If you push your enquiries farther, and desire a reason *why he hates pain*, it is impossible that he can ever give any. This is an ultimate end, and is never referred to any other object.[36]

According to Hume, although reason has a useful role to play in moral discernment, moral judgments themselves ultimately rest on

some internal sense or feeling which nature has made universal in the whole species. For what else can have an influence on this nature? But in order to pave the way for such a sentiment, and give it proper discernment of its object, it is often necessary, we find, that much reasoning should precede, that nice distinctions be made, just conclusions drawn, distant comparisons formed, complicated relations examined, and general facts fixed and ascertained.[37]

That is, reason helps us clarify experience. It helps us identify facts. It does not, however, evaluate them. Hume's most famous sentence summarizes this point: "Reason is, and ought only to be the slave of the passions, and can never pretend to any other office than to serve and obey them."[38]

PHILOSOPHICAL QUERY

Compare Hume's claim that reason is incapable of ruling the passions with Plato's belief that reason's very function is to rule over the appetites and spirit (will). Refer to your own experience, as well as to any psychological or scientific knowledge you have.

I found a certain boldness of temper growing on me, which was not inclined to submit to any authority in these subjects [philosophy and literature]. . . . When I was about eighteen years of age there seemed to be opened up a new scheme of thought, which transported me beyond measure, and made me, with an ardor natural to young men, throw up every other pleasure or business to apply myself entirely to it.

David Hume

The Facts, Just the Facts

Hume's analysis of moral judgments resembles his analysis of causality. Recall that, according to Hume, we do not perceive the fact of "necessary connection," but associate the feeling of necessity with certain related events (events constantly conjoined). Moral judgments are like causal judgments: they are mental associations or projections, not perceptions of facts. When we like a certain characteristic, we call it a virtue or label it "good" or "right." When we dislike something, we call it a vice or label it "wrong" or "bad." These evaluations are not derived from reason, but from experience. It is "just a fact" that a certain combination of conditions produces cold or heat; likewise, it is "just a fact" that we associate some experiences with good feelings (these are desired), and some with bad feelings (these are disliked). In other words, through experience, we learn to associate certain facts with positive sentiments (being good or desired) and other facts with negative sentiments (being bad or disliked). The facts themselves are value neutral.

In the important and influential Part I of Book III of his *Treatise*, Hume makes a crucial distinction between *facts* and *values* (evaluations of facts). According to Hume, *facts themselves are valueless*. Moral judgments (like all evaluations) are not judgments of facts but reports of moral sentiments or feelings. Hume's fact-value distinction has exerted tremendous influence on all moral philosophy since. In the *Treatise* he says:

> But can there be any difficulty in proving, that vice and virtue are not matters of fact, whose existence we can infer by reason? Take any action allow'd to be vicious: Willful murder, for instance. Examine it in all lights, and see if you can find the matter of fact, or real existence, which you call *vice*. In whichever way you take it, you find only certain passions, motives, volitions and thoughts. There is no matter of fact in the case. The vice entirely escapes you, as long as you consider the object. You can never find it, till you turn your reflexion into your own breast, and find a sentiment of disapprobation, which arise in you towards this action. Here is a matter of fact; but 'tis the object of feeling, not of reason. It lies in yourself, not in the object. So that when you pronounce any action or character to be vicious, you mean nothing, but that from the constitution of your nature you have a feeling or sentiment of blame from the contemplation of it. Vice and virtue, therefore, may be compar'd to sounds, colours, heat and cold, which according to modern philosophy, are not qualities in objects, but perceptions in the mind . . .[39]

Doubt is the nerve of all fresh and durable thinking. If Aristotle was right in the first book of his Metaphysics *when he said that philosophy began in wonder, philosophy could not have got very far if she had not doubted searchingly.*

Phillip P. Hallie

To fully grasp what Hume is saying, it helps to distinguish between *descriptive language* and *normative language*. Descriptive language—as the name suggests—is devoid of all subjective, evaluative characterizations. Using Hume's example of "willful murder," we might expect to find descriptive language in a police report: "Dean Fetters shot J. Scott Vargas in the chest six times. Vargas fell to the floor. He lost three quarts of blood and died at 6:15 p.m." and so on. No matter how precise and elaborate a purely factual description of the circumstance is, it will contain no moral judgments. Indeed, the moral judgment of murder is like the legal judgment of murder. Although we base both judgments on our beliefs about the facts, murder (in either the moral or legal sense) is an interpretation of the facts—not a description or observation. No one sees murder. We see Fetters shoot Vargas, and so forth. We do not see murder. In a court of law, we *decide* murder (or not). In the moral case, we react subjectively to the facts and feel murder (or not). Moral judgments, according to Hume, are like judgments about art or food—matters of moral taste or sentiment.

PHILOSOPHICAL QUERY

Hume's point here is very important. Don't rush by it. Take a moment and try to write a purely factual description of something you believe is immoral. Do you agree with Hume that the facts are value neutral and that all moral judgments are reports of feelings associated with certain facts? Discuss.

Moral Sentiments

Hume believed that the task before him was a "question of fact, not of abstract science" and that success was possible only by "following the experimental method, and deducing general maxims from a comparison of particular instances." Using the fact-value distinction, he attempted a "reformation" of moral philosophy, announcing that it was time to "reject every system of ethics, however subtle or ingenious, which is not founded on fact and observation."

Hume's efforts did, indeed, launch a revolution in moral philosophy. He helped establish a method of "ordinary language analysis" that became especially influential in the early part of the twentieth century, and whose influence is still significant. Notice how the empirical criterion of meaning affects Hume's language analysis in the following passage. Also note the role he gives reason.

> The very nature of language guides us almost infallibly in forming a judgment of [matters of Personal Merit]; and as every tongue possesses one set of words which are taken in a good sense, and another in the opposite, the least acquaintance with the idiom suffices, without any reasoning, to direct us in collecting and arranging the estimable or blamable qualities of [people]. The only object of reasoning is to discover the circumstances on both sides, which are common to these qualities; to observe that particular in which the estimable qualities agree on one hand, and the blamable on the other;

The intercourse of sentiments, therefore, in society and conversation, makes us form some general inalterable standard, by which we may approve or disapprove of characters and manners. And tho' the **heart** *does not take part with those general notions, or regulate its love and hatred by them, yet are they sufficient for discourse, and serve all our purposes in company, in the pulpit, in the theatre, and in the schools.*

David Hume

and thence to reach the foundation of ethics, and find those universal principles, from which all censure or approbation is ultimately derived.[40]

In all cases of moral judgment, what we call virtues are traits we, in fact, find agreeable. The feeling of agreeableness is what makes them virtues to us. We do not find them agreeable because they are virtues. We call them virtues because we find them agreeable. That's an important distinction.

We sometimes lose sight of the fundamental nature of all value judgments because we use different terms to distinguish among variations of experience.

Put another way, different pleasures are like different flavors; all the good flavors are pleasing, yet we call some sweet, some sour, some chocolate, some lime, some fruity, some salty, and so forth. Similarly, all unpleasant sentiments are alike, yet we call some disgusting, some ugly, some evil, some bad, some cowardice, and so forth.[41]

What, then, is unique to that "peculiar kind" of sentiment that Hume calls moral? Hume says that *moral sentiment is a disinterested reaction to character (motive)*. Moral virtue is *disinterested approbation* (liking or approval) of character or motive. Moral vice is *disinterested disapprobation* (disliking or disapproval) of character or motive. According to Hume, careful language analysis reveals that, *as a matter of fact*, moral judgments are disinterested judgments of character.

The Limits of Egoism

By asserting that moral judgments are "disinterested," Hume rejected egoism. (See Chapters 4, 5, 13, and 14 for more about the relationship of self-interest to morality.) In his forceful attack, he refers to egoism as "a principle . . . supposed to prevail among many." Hume characterizes egoism as the belief that

> . . . all *benevolence* is mere hypocrisy, friendship a cheat, public spirit a farce, fidelity a snare to procure trust and confidence, and that while all of us, at bottom, pursue only our private interest, we wear these fair disguises, in order to put others off their guard, and expose them the more to our wiles and machinations.[42]

Hume points out that egoism is utterly inadequate as an account of real life. A clear look at the facts makes it plain that we have other motives than these. He rejects egoism as factually inaccurate and overly simplistic, warning that the love of such contrived simplicity "has been the source of much false reasoning in philosophy." He says:

> The most obvious objection to the selfish hypothesis is that, as it is contrary to common feeling and our most unprejudiced notions, there is required the highest stretch of philosophy

The sceptic wishes, from considerations of humanity, to do all he can with the arguments at his disposal to cure the self-conceit and rashness of the dogmatists.

Sextus Empiricus

to establish so extraordinary a paradox. To the most careless observer there appear to be such dispositions as benevolence and generosity; such affections as love, friendship, compassion, gratitude. . . . As this is the most obvious appearance of things, it must be admitted, till [the selfish] hypothesis be . . . proved.[43]

Hume's attack on egoism is withering in its clarity and appeal to everyday experience. He rejects and ridicules the complications implicit in the belief that our "real" motives are always some form of narrow self-interest. He compares that kind of claim with the equally absurd claim that a horse-drawn wagon is "really" moved by "minute wheels and springs, like those of a watch."

Consider, Hume suggests, feelings of grief. Which is more absurd, to assume that all feelings of grief over the deaths of our loved ones are really disguised self-interest, or to accept them as we experience them? Are we, Hume asks, ready to believe that our loving pets are really motivated solely by self-interest? Obviously not. The most cursory glance at our actual experiences with animals shows that conditioning (or even instinct) does not adequately describe all acts of animal loyalty and affection. Does this mean that animals can express disinterested benevolence but human beings can't? Hume thought such an idea was preposterous.

According to Hume, pure self-love is another of the fictions that results from rationalistic thinking that loses touch with actual experience because it is not based on empirical facts. When we take our actual experience into account, self-love is not an adequate explanation of human motivation. Even the most common objects of so-called self-love, power, praise, revenge, and such, have no appeal without other sentiments. Hume claimed that if "there is no appetite of any kind antecedent to self-love, [self-love] could scarcely ever exert itself," because self-love by itself is too "slender" a sentiment. That is, motives to action always involve seeking or avoiding something according to some appetite (sentiment) that precedes the action. In simple terms, self-love is never the only motive to action.

Hume is at his best when he challenges the egoist's shriveled view of human motivation:

Where is the difficulty in conceiving, that . . . from the original frame of our temper, we may feel a desire of another's happiness or good, which by means of that affection, becomes our own good, and is afterwards pursued, from the combined motives of benevolence and self-enjoyments? Who sees not that vengeance, from the force alone of passion, may be so eagerly pursued, as to make us knowingly neglect every consideration of ease, interest, or safety; and, like some vindictive animals, infuse our very souls into the wounds we give an enemy; and what a malignant philosophy it must be, that will not allow to humanity and friendship the same privileges

which are indisputably granted to the darker passions of enmity and resentment.[44]

COMMENTARY

In the end, Hume compared full-blown skepticism to doubting the existence of an external reality, pointing out that the
issue cannot be settled logically and rationally. No one can actually live as a
skeptic:

> To whatever length anyone may push his speculative prin-
> ciples of scepticism, he must act . . . and live, and converse like
> other men. . . . It is impossible for him to persevere in total
> scepticism, or make it appear in his conduct for a few hours.[45]

Having reasoned carefully and thoroughly, without shying away from
what he discovered, no matter how alien to common sense or established
knowledge and custom, no matter how foreign to his heart's desire, the great
archetype of the skeptic expresses a timeless lament in his own fashion:

> Where am I, or what? From what causes do I derive my ex-
> istence, and to what condition shall I return? Whose favour
> shall I court, and whose anger must I dread? What beings sur-
> round me? and on whom have I influence, or who have influ-
> ence on me? I am confounded with all these questions, and
> begin to fancy myself in the most deplorable condition imag-
> inable, inviron'd with the deepest darkness, and utterly de-
> priv'd of the use of every member and faculty.
>
>   Most fortunately it happens, that since reason is incapable
> of dispelling these clouds, nature herself suffices to that pur-
> pose, and cures me of this philosophical melancholy and de-
> lirium. . . . I dine, I play a game of backgammon, I converse,
> and am merry with my friends; and when after three or four
> hours' amusement, I wou'd return to these speculations, they
> appear so cold, and strain'd and ridiculous, that I cannot find
> in my heart to enter them any farther.[46]

What, then, is the point of these difficult and frustrating skeptical inquiries if, in the end, not even Hume takes them seriously? Ah, but he does
take them seriously. Using careful observation and analysis, Hume raises important points about both the limits of reason and the needs of the human
heart.

Hume exposes cloudy and meaningless language and bogus theorizing.
He shows clearly the ultimate inadequacy of rational and empirical efforts to
prove God's existence or infer his nature. In Hume's own time a great scientific revolution had already established the force and usefulness of the sci-

*Scepticism is . . . a form of
belief. Dogma cannot be
abandoned; it can only be
revised in view of some more
elementary dogma which it
has not yet occurred to the
sceptic to doubt; and he may
be right in every point of his
criticism, except in fancying
that his criticism is radical
and that he is altogether a
sceptic.*

George Santayana

entific method. His analysis of cause and effect, as he acknowledges, does not destroy science but modifies a bit of what some see as its arrogance. Neither science nor theology can explain the ultimate origins of life or the ultimate nature of reality.

Hume has shown us how little we actually *know* of the most important and most common aspects of existence: self, personal identity, cause and effect, reality, the external world, the universe, and God. Read correctly, I think, Hume reveals that the power of logic and reason are, still and all, not *all*-powerful. He shows that the great theological beliefs to which so many are devoted are barely intelligible. In other words, Hume teaches us that neither the scientist, nor the philosopher, nor the priest has *the* method and *the* answer to timeless questions.

Hume shows us there is no absolute certainty in life, only enough uniformity to live reasonably well, if we are lucky. He shows that belief without reason is often meaningless, but that a life based solely on reason is not possible. We live and act on what George Santayana calls *animal faith*: a force within us that *trusts something* in spite of the limits of our experience and reason.

Additionally, Hume's use of the empirical method took root and ushered in a new and powerful philosophical movement that demanded increasingly clear use of language, precision of thought, and observable evidence.

Hume reminds us that though our search for absolute answers cannot be completely satisfied, our search for wisdom is not in vain. Hume sometimes makes progress the way Socrates sometimes makes progress: by exposing ignorance, by showing us what is not an adequate answer. Human intelligence and human experience cannot answer timeless questions with certainty. Does this necessarily lead to despair? I think not, though some may be despondent upon first hearing this, and others may be unable to face it. There is another possibility: to treat skepticism as a warning—a warning to avoid arrogant dogmatism; a warning to be tolerant of the other person's beliefs, since, in many cases, we have no better basis for our beliefs than she does for hers. Most of all, Hume reminds us that it is better to end in honest doubt than in dishonest belief.

Hume, the archetypal skeptic, suggests that a person will always be more than philosophy, religion, or science can hope to know:

> Man is a reasonable being; and as such, receives from science his proper food and nourishment: But so narrow are the bounds of human understanding, that little satisfaction can be hoped for in this particular, either from the extent of security or his acquisitions. Man is a sociable, no less than a reasonable being: But neither can he always enjoy company agreeable and amusing, or preserve the proper relish for them. Man is also an active being; and from that disposition, as well as from the various necessities of human life, must submit to business and occupation: But the mind requires

As a philosophical critic Hume has few peers. No one has challenged more sharply rationalism's central thesis that matters of fact can be known without recourse to experience; nor has anyone revealed more clearly the severe problems raised by insisting that all factual claims be empirically verified.
John W. Lenz

some relaxation, and cannot always support its bent to care and industry. It seems, then, that nature has pointed out a mixed kind of life as the most suitable to the human race, and secretly admonished them to allow none of these biases to *draw* too much, so as to incapacitate them for any other occupations and entertainments. Indulge your passion for science, says she, but let your science be human, and such as may have a direct reference to action and society. Abstruse thought and profound researches I prohibit, and will severely punish, by the pensive melancholy which they introduce, by the endless uncertainty in which they involve you, and by the cold reception which your pretended discoveries shall meet with, when communicated. Be a philosopher; but amidst all your philosophy, be still a [human being].[47]

SUMMARY OF MAIN POINTS

Skepticism is both a school of philosophy and a general attitude. A skeptic is a person who demands clear, observable, undoubtable evidence based on experience before accepting any claim as true.

Empiricism is the belief that all knowledge is ultimately derived from the senses (experience). Empiricists believe that all ideas can be traced to sense data. There are no innate ideas. At birth the mind is a clean slate, or tabula rasa.

John Locke, the first of the three British empiricists, claimed that all ideas are copies of the things that caused the basic sensations they rest on. Today Locke's copy theory is known as the correspondence theory of truth: an idea (or belief or thought) is true if whatever it refers to actually exists.

The correspondence theory generates what is called the egocentric predicament: If all knowledge comes in the form of my own ideas, how can I verify the existence of anything external to them?

Locke's successor, George Berkeley, rejected the copy theory, pointing out that ideas are constantly changing. There is no fixed "thing" to copy; we know only perceptions. Berkeley's formula is *esse est percipi*: to be is to be perceived. This view is known as idealism or immaterialism.

Perception, however, cannot account for ideas such as the self or the apparent continuity of experiences—for example, that a burning candle is shorter if we return to look at it after being away for a time. Berkeley shied away from the logical consequences of immaterialism and posited the existence of a universal perceiver (God) to account for the existence of the external world and regularity of nature.

The third British empiricist, David Hume, continued the epistemological turn by rejecting overly abstract, obscure, bloated metaphysical speculation as meaningless and irrelevant to the lives of ordinary people. He asserted that no metaphysical issue was ever clearly and thoroughly settled.

Hume modified Locke's theory of ideas by distinguishing between two kinds of perceptions: Ideas are faint copies of impressions, which are intense. All ideas can be traced to the impressions they are based on. All ideas are derived from experience.

Hume established the empirical criterion of meaning: All meaningful ideas can be traced to sense experience (impressions). Beliefs that cannot be traced to sense experience are technically not ideas at all; they are meaningless utterances. Strict application

of the empirical criterion of meaning led Hume to skeptical conclusions regarding some of our most fundamental beliefs. (Locke and Berkeley deviated from strict empiricism rather than accept skeptical conclusions.)

Applying the empirical criterion of meaning, Hume argued that we have no idea of the self; the self is only a bundle of impressions, and identity is a mental act, not a property of things. Therefore, personal immortality is a meaningless concept.

Hume thought that imagination, not reason or experience, accounts for the persistence of our belief in the independent existence of an external world. Imagination ultimately overrides reason, and we cannot help believing in an independent, ordered, external world. We can accept the strict limits of reason only temporarily; we cannot live by them alone.

Strictly considered, Hume argues, there are no empirical grounds for belief in cause and effect. We experience only constant conjunction. Cause and effect are products of imagination.

The empirical criterion of meaning renders the cosmological argument, the argument from motion, and the ontological argument meaningless. The argument from design (teleological argument) fails because human experience cannot provide sufficient evidence of order on earth, much less order in the universe. It also denies the possibility of rationalistic ethics and claims that all moral judgments are based on sentiments.

In the end, Hume claimed that no one can actually live as a skeptic: Reason is, and ought to be, the slave of the passions.

STUDY QUESTIONS

1. What is skepticism?

2. Explain what is meant by the "epistemological turn." Briefly outline the stages of the turn from Descartes through Locke and Berkeley to Hume.

3. What is empiricism?

4. In your own words, reconstruct the basic empirical critique of rationalism.

5. What is the tabula rasa? What is its significance to Locke's empiricism?

6. What was Locke's egocentric predicament?

7. What is epistemological dualism?

8. Explain the philosophical significance of the question "Does a tree falling in the forest make a sound if no one is there to hear it?"

9. What is immaterialism?

10. Was David Hume an atheist? Explain.

11. Explain how Hume distinguished between impressions and ideas. Why is the distinction important to his philosophy?

12. What is the empirical criterion of meaning? Explain by applying it to an example of your own choosing.

13. How does Hume explain the self?

14. In your own words, characterize Hume's position regarding personal identity and immortality.

15. How does Hume account for the external world?

16. Sketch Hume's analysis of cause and effect.

17. First summarize, then analyze Hume's critique of the argument from design.

18. Summarize Hume's critique of rationalistic ethics. Then construct a Humean analysis of some contemporary moral issue. What are the advantages of Hume's approach? The disadvantages?

19. What does Hume mean when he says, "I am ready to throw all my books and papers into the fire, and resolve never more to renounce the pleasures of life for the sake of reasoning and philosophy"?

The Formalist:

Immanuel Kant

Two things fill the mind
with ever new and in-
creasing admiration and
awe . . . the starry heavens above and the moral
law within.

IMMANUEL KANT

oral issues confront us daily. We live in a time troubled by intense moral controversies concerning abortion, euthanasia, affirmative action, capital punishment, substance abuse, monetary fraud, governmental deception, the environment, aid to the homeless, welfare, the rights of disabled persons, parental influence in the schools, pornography, AIDS, smoking in public, and sexual conduct. Such issues have political, financial, legal, religious, and psychological aspects. But in their moral dimensions they touch upon our most fundamental values concerning good and bad, personal worth and character, respect for ourselves and others—in sum, what it means to be a human being.

The word **moral** comes from the Latin *moralis*, meaning "custom," "manner," or "conduct." Moral refers to what people consider good or bad, right or wrong. There are two contrasting words: **nonmoral (amoral)** and **immoral**. The *moral-nonmoral* distinction is *descriptive*. It makes no value judgment and only distinguishes moral concerns from such nonmoral ones as economic, mechanical, nutritional, and so on. The *moral-immoral* distinction is *prescriptive*; it makes a value judgment about what we ought to do. The distinction between moral and immoral is equivalent to that between right and wrong or good and bad.

The moral dimension confronts us in courtrooms, classrooms, at work, and at home, as we try to determine who is or is not *responsible* for this or that act. Moral responsibility is different from the factual issue of determining who did what. It has to do with punishment or forgiveness; it affects whether we see a sexual offender as bad or sick, whether we scold a child or hug her, whether a criminal defendant is imprisoned, hospitalized, or released. Morality seems to be inseparable from responsibility.

Responsibility, in turn, implies freedom of choice, the ability to decide on one course of action over another, to think and behave one way instead of another way. For example, a person unwillingly drugged is not held morally accountable for actions performed under the influence of the drug, but a person who willingly gets drunk and then drives probably is.

Lawyers, theologians, psychologists, and parents continually wrestle with issues of free, responsible choice. Yet scientific evidence of causal patterns suggests that more and more conduct once labeled immoral may be beyond our control. We learn that some children who are abused grow up to abuse. Alcoholism may have a genetic component or at least a family pattern. Children raised without stable parental supervision seem to turn to crime more often than children from other backgrounds. Children whose families own and read lots of books tend to be better students than those whose families don't. Bio-psychologists and geneticists continue to discover physical and chemical "causes" of behavior. Studies reveal that identical twins separated at very young ages and raised without contact often grow up to get the same kind of job, marry people with the same name, have the same kinds of cars and pets, even like the same brand of toothpaste!

MORAL

From the Latin *moralis*, meaning "custom," "manner," or "conduct"; refers to what people consider good or bad, right or wrong; used descriptively as a contrast to amoral or nonmoral and prescriptively as a contrast to immoral.

NONMORAL (AMORAL)

Not pertaining to moral; a value-neutral descriptive claim or classification.

IMMORAL

Morally wrong, bad, or not right; a moral value judgment or prescriptive claim.

We cannot doubt the progress science has made since the seventeenth century in understanding human behavior. We can hardly doubt that some factors in our lives *make* us who we are. But if all nature is *governed* by laws of chemistry and physics, laws that admit of no exceptions, then I can no more be held responsible for helping you across the street than you can be held responsible for striking me with an ax because you're bored. If even our tastes in toothpaste are determined by genetic influences, how can we ever hold anyone responsible for anything? And if we cannot, how do we justify moral sanctions? If life loses its moral dimension, is it worth living? Stripped of the possibility of moral choice, how different am I from any other animal? What is the purpose of morally praising or blaming behavior if it *cannot be otherwise*?

PHILOSOPHICAL QUERY

Think for a moment about a nonmoral world, a world in which no one is held morally accountable. In such a world, every action would be viewed as the inevitable result of genetic, social, and historical causes. What are the advantages of such a view? The disadvantages? Think about some time when you made an excuse for yourself, claiming that you "couldn't help" doing or not doing something. What is gained and lost by making such excuses?

Without responsibility, there is no goodness. So, at least, feared and reasoned one of the most important philosophers of all time. (And the science of his day was much less sophisticated than today's science. Imagine his fears if he lived now.) Immanuel Kant attempted to meet the challenge of science to human freedom and responsibility by completing the epistemological turn begun by René Descartes and David Hume (see Chapters 11 and 12). He attempted to refute Hume's critique of rationalistic ethics by showing that morality is based on reason, not sentiment.

THE LITTLE PROFESSOR

Immanuel Kant (1724–1804) was born in Königsberg in what was then known as East Prussia. His parents were poor but devout members of a fundamentalist Protestant sect known as Pietism. Pietists rejected the idea of imposing a church and priests between the individual and God, preferring immediate personal appeal to God. They emphasized faith and repentance, and lived severe, puritanical lives.

When he was eight years old Kant was sent to a school founded by a local Pietist preacher. The regimen was exceptionally strict, beginning daily at five-thirty in the morning. Students received an hour's daily instruction in Pietism, and each class period concluded with a prayer. Sundays were

Immanuel Kant

devoted almost completely to religious activity. Later in life, Kant said that he resented the school's heavy emphasis on a theology of terror and piety—fear of hell and trembling before a vision of a wrathful God. Yet he never lost his regard for righteousness and moral severity. As an old man he spoke respectfully of his parents' faith, saying, "People may say what they will of Pietism. Those in whom it was sincere were worthy of honor. They possessed the highest thing that man can have—the quiet, the content, the inner peace, which no suffering can disturb."[1]

At the age of sixteen, Kant entered the University of Königsberg, where he studied for six years. Upon leaving the university, he refused a lucrative offer to become a Lutheran minister, choosing instead to continue his studies. For the next nine years he meagerly supported himself as a private tutor. In 1755, Kant received the equivalent of today's doctoral degree. This earned him the privilege of lecturing at the university as a *Privatdozent*, a private teacher whose salary was paid directly by his students. The more students he attracted and retained, the more money he earned. Kant became a popular lecturer, and in 1770, when he was forty-six, the university hired Kant as a professor of logic and metaphysics. Though the salary was small, Kant was pleased with his improved status.

The Solitary Scholar

For the most part, Kant's life is noteworthy for not being noteworthy. He probably never traveled more than sixty miles from his birthplace in his entire life. One biographer said, "Kant's life was like the most regular of regular verbs," to which another added, "But it was not a *conjugated* verb. For Kant never married."[2]

Despite his popularity as a lecturer, Kant remained relatively poor, and cited his poverty as the reason he never married, though he considered marriage on at least two or three occasions. One of the women was described as a "gentle, pretty widow," another as a "handsome Westphalian girl whose company he obviously liked." In the case of the pretty widow, Kant spent so much time calculating his income and weighing his decision that she finally gave up and married someone else. The "handsome Westphalian girl" was a lady's traveling companion; by the time Kant got around to visiting her, she had moved on with her employer.[3]

When I could have used a wife, I could not support one; and when I could support one, I no longer needed any.

Immanuel Kant

Kant was barely over five feet tall. He had a large head and a sunken chest, and was so thin that he invented an odd contraption to hold up his pants and socks, which consisted of bands that he passed up his pantlegs into his pockets "by means of springs contained in little boxes."[4] One description adds that his stomach protruded, while his right shoulder twisted back and his left one sloped downward (he suffered from curvature of the spine).

He lived most of his life on a rigid schedule. The poet Heinrich Heine described Kant's penchant for routine:

I do not believe that the great cathedral clock of this city accomplished its day's work in a less passionate and more regular way than its countryman, Immanuel Kant. Rising from bed, coffee-drinking, writing, lecturing, eating, walking, everything had its fixed time: and the neighbors knew that it must be exactly half past four when they saw Professor Kant, in his gray coat, with his cane in his hand, step out of his house-door, and move toward the little lime tree avenue, which is named after him, the Philosopher's Walk. Eight times he walked up and down that walk at every season of the year, and when the weather was bad, or the gray clouds threatened rain, his servant, old Lampe, was seen anxiously following him with a large umbrella under his arm like an image of providence.[5]

Kant is reported to have missed his walk only once, when he became so absorbed in reading Rousseau's *Emile* that he forgot to take it.

Kant was always in frail health, but not apparently seriously ill for the greater part of his life. A near obsession with living a long time, coupled with physical frailty, seems to have inclined him to hypochondria. A recent biographical sketch suggests that this, added to the severity of his early Pietist education, may account for Kant's famous need for order and regulation.[6] He kept favorite objects in exactly the same location, and could become severely upset if a pair of scissors or a coffee cup was not in its proper place.

Kant was physically and emotionally distant from his sisters and brother. Although he helped them financially, he appears not to have exchanged a single word with his sisters for some twenty-five years.[7] He was so embarrassed by them that he did not see them after his graduation until his weakened old age. When one sister came to take care of him, he did not recognize her; when he learned who she was, he apologized for *her* lack of breeding![8] Kant gave "lack of culture" as the reason he avoided his sisters, but he also avoided his brother, who was his cultural, if not his philosophical, equal.

On the other hand, Kant was friendly with younger scholars and other friends. As a younger man he was a welcome guest and enjoyed a modest reputation as a conversationalist in the Königsberg social set. He dressed as well as he could in carefully tailored, if inexpensive, clothes, and enjoyed playing cards and billiards. He was also something of a gossip. This social activity did not last very long, however.

Kant increasingly distanced himself from others, becoming more and more reclusive. The German language has two forms of the second-person pronoun (*you*). One is formal, the other is personal or intimate. Kant addressed only two or three friends in the personal way, and ultimately disliked using a personal tone even with them.[9] Yet he cared enough about his servant Lampe to have said, "Old Lampe must have a God, or else the poor man cannot be happy; and people really ought to be happy in this world.

The goodly burghers of Königsberg had an infallible way of setting their clocks. Every afternoon, precisely at three-thirty, Immanuel Kant left his house for his daily stroll.
Henry Thomas and Dana Lee Thomas

[Kant] is often pictured as an old bachelor whose every activity was scheduled with such precision that neighbors could set their watches when he stepped out of his house each day at half past four to walk up and down his small avenue eight times.
Samuel Enoch Stumpf

[Kant] arose at five every morning, was in bed by ten every night, and the towns-people used to set their watches by his three o'clock walk.
Burton F. Porter

Practical common sense *requires* it. Very well, then, let practical reason *guarantee* it."[10]

Seeds of Revolution

Kant's work became important and troubling, for it included devastating critiques of the dominant philosophical schools of the day (rationalism and empiricism), as well as popular theology. It is said that some clergymen called Immanuel Kant a dog, while others called their dogs Immanuel Kant.

It is indeed true that I think many things with the cleverest conviction, and to my great satisfaction, which I never have the courage to say, but I never say anything that I do not think.

Immanuel Kant

When Kant was over seventy, he was even threatened by Frederick William II, King of Prussia, with "unpleasant consequences for yourself" if Kant continued to "misuse your philosophy to undermine and debase many of the most important and fundamental doctrines of the Holy Scriptures and Christianity; how, namely, you have done this in your book, *Religion Within the Limits of Reason Alone.*"[11] Kant prudently informed the king that his work was meant for the scholarly community and not the general public but, nonetheless, promised to "refrain from all public statements on religion, both natural and revealed."[12] In the end, though, the Prussian state fell apart, whereas by 1800 Kant's work dominated German intellectual life.

The Writer

Kant was a prolific writer. His works include the difficult but revolutionary *Critique of Pure Reason* (1781 and a second edition in 1787), *Prolegomena to Any Future Metaphysics* (1783), *Foundations of the Metaphysics of Morals* (1785), *Critique of Practical Reason* (1788), *Critique of Judgment* (1790), and *Religion Within the Limits of Reason Alone* (1793).

The *Critique of Pure Reason* is one of the most difficult books ever written. Philosophy majors approach it with dread and then forever after boast proudly if they manage to read the entire thing. Kant once said that he did not fear being refuted; he feared not being understood. He had good reason to fear. On August 16, 1783, he wrote that his work was

> the result of reflection which occupied me for at least twelve years. I brought it to completion in the greatest haste within four or five months, giving the closest attention to its contents, but with little thought of the exposition, or of rendering it easy of comprehension by the reader—a decision which I have never regretted, since otherwise, had I longer delayed and sought to give a more popular form, the work would probably never have been completed at all.[13]

Kant admitted that he deliberately left out illustrative examples because they would just add length to an already massive work. Besides, he added, examples are only necessary for popular appeal "and this work can never be

A BELOVED TEACHER

I have had the good fortune to know a philosopher who was my teacher. In the prime of his life he possessed the joyous courage of youth, and this also, as I believe, attended him to extreme old age. His open, thoughtful brow was the seat of untroubled cheerfulness and joy, his conversation was full of ideas most suggestive. He had at his service jest, witticism, and humorous fancy, and his lectures were at once instructive and most entertaining. . . . No cabal or sect, no prejudice or reverence for a name, had the slightest influence with him in opposition to the extension and promotion of truth. He encouraged and gently compelled his hearers to think for themselves. . . . This man, whom I name with the greatest gratitude and reverence, is Immanuel Kant; his image stands before me, and is dear to me.

Johann Gottfried Herder (1744–1803) Quoted by Will and Ariel Durant in *Rousseau and Revolution*, vol. 10 of *The Story of Civilization* (New York: Simon & Schuster, 1967), p. 532.

---

made suitable for popular consumption."[14] When he sent the metaphysician Marcus Herz the manuscript of the *Critique of Pure Reason*, Herz sent it back only half read, saying, "If I finish it I am afraid I shall go mad."[15]

Kant's work was made difficult by another factor: Because he was trying to express new concepts, he felt that he had to invent new meanings for Latin terms or coin new phrases in German; he also gave his own unusual meanings to common terms and sometimes used the same term to mean different things. All of that notwithstanding, the little professor's big, difficult books forever altered Western thinking.

Kant retired from public lecturing in 1797, and although he physically declined, he remained a prolific writer. Immanuel Kant died a lonely old man who had never seen a mountain or the sea. Yet he shook the foundations of Western philosophy to such an extent that it has been said that whether or not philosophers agree or disagree with Kant, they must face him. Above his grave in the Königsberg cathedral his own words are inscribed, "The starry heavens above me; the moral law within me."

The philosopher-poet Friedrich Schiller, referring to the richness, complexity, and importance of Kant's philosophy, as well as its impact on the many philosophers whose work is in one way or another a response to Kant's, said, "See how a single rich man has given a living to a number of beggars."[16]

One of the mistakes oftenest committed, and which are the sources of the greatest practical errors in human affairs, is that of supposing that the same name always stands for the same aggregation of ideas.
John Stuart Mill

FROM ENLIGHTENMENT TO DESPAIR

The Enlightenment, sometimes called the Age of Reason, began in 1637 with Descartes' cogito: "I think, therefore I

This illustration of a print shop from Denis Diderot's *Encyclopédie*
illustrates the Enlightenment's optimistic faith in the spread of
knowledge through free exchange of ideas.

am."[17] This was an age shaped by the scientific revolution and by a shift in
emphasis in philosophy from metaphysics to epistemology. Historian of philosophy W. T. Jones says that *optimism* is the one word that best characterizes the Enlightenment of the seventeenth and eighteenth centuries.[18]

Enlightenment thinkers reduced God to the role of spectator, as they discovered more and more mechanical laws to explain the operations of nature. Their faith lay in the orderly, ultimately understandable workings of nature, and in human reason as the only tool necessary to ensure progress and improvement of the human condition. They assumed that the scientific method would unlock all the mysteries of the universe. Given the regularity of the heavens and the discovery of laws of physics and astronomy, it was a simple step to conclude that God (if there was a God) had created a universe of such regularity and order that He no longer bothered running it. Further, having imbued us with reason, God had no need to govern or rescue us.

Disagreeing over exactly what "reason" is, Enlightenment champions of reason were nonetheless convinced that all people (with the exception of "idiots") possessed an innate, virtually equal capacity for rational thinking. If this is true, they concluded, then a proper education will enable everyone to live well. You might recognize this optimistic faith in science, reason, and universal education as a fundamental principle of American thinking. Indeed,

*The life of Immanuel Kant
is hard to describe; he had
neither life nor history in the
proper sense of the words.*
Heinrich Heine

The products of reason are not uniformly beneficial. The French Revolution began with a universal declaration of human rights and ended in the Reign of Terror when the mob defeated reason.

the framers of our Constitution were children of the Enlightenment who believed that science and universal education would combine to produce a rational, free, ever-progressing society.

In his essay *What Is Enlightenment?* Kant eloquently expresses the age's equation of rational enlightenment with human freedom:

> *Sapere aude!*—Dare to reason! Have the courage to use your own minds!—is the motto of the enlightenment.
>
> Laziness and cowardice explain why so many men . . . remain under a life-long tutelage and why it is so easy for some men to set themselves up as the guardians of all the rest. . . . If I have a book which understands for me, a pastor who has a conscience for me, a doctor who decides my diet, I need not trouble myself. If I am willing to pay, I need not think. Others will do it for me.[19]

Kant's faith in rational intelligence was so great that he claimed a "race of devils" could produce a sound community if they were intelligent. All that was needed, he thought, was to apply reason to the problems of knowledge and conduct.

Alas, the products of reason are not uniformly beneficial. Then, as now, the technology made possible by scientific discoveries caused harm as well as benefit. For example, former peasants and farm laborers were drawn to large urban centers by the promise of employment; once there, they were easily exploited. The dirty, crowded slums that resulted made a stark contrast to the orderly serenity of the astronomers' heavens and the physicists' belief that nature never does anything without a purpose. The French Revolution, which began as a reasoned call to universal rights and freedoms in support of human dignity, ended in an irrational bloodbath, reason defeated by the mob. It was so horrible that we now know it as the Reign of Terror. In France and other parts of Europe, notably Kant's Prussia, rulers and rigid absolutists reasserted control over "freethinkers, skeptics, and atheists," often lumping all scientific or philosophic thinkers into one dangerous group.

The optimism that lay behind Descartes' faith in reason to produce certainty and behind science's faith in experience to produce knowledge seemed to lead only to confusion and despair. As Kant pointed out, philosophy—especially since Hume—was of little help in refuting the charges against it. It was, Kant said, "a scandal to philosophy and to human reason in general that the existence of things outside us . . . must be accepted merely on *faith*, and that if anyone thinks it good to doubt their existence, we are unable to counter his doubts by any satisfactory proof."[20]

> *If I am asked "What is good?" my answer is that good is good, and that is the end of the matter. Or if I am asked "How is good to be defined?" my answer is that it cannot be defined, and that is all I have to say about it.*
>
> G. E. Moore

A SCANDAL IN PHILOSOPHY

In Chapter 12, we saw how radical Hume's skepticism was. Because Hume was one of the most logically consistent philosophers of his or any time, his critique of empiricism led to such disturbing conclusions as we can never know cause and effect, the self, or the external world, and that moral judgments are somehow like matters of taste. Hume's withering *Dialogues Concerning Natural Religion* applied a strictly rational analysis to cherished arguments for the existence of God, and showed them to be illogical and unpersuasive. With his strict understanding of knowledge and reason, Hume concluded that reason is and ought to be "the slave of the passions." Hume's philosophy made the external world unknowable and rendered reason impotent to unlock the secrets of nature. His critique of rationalistic ethics seemed to show that reason was utterly incapable of motivating people. In other words, Hume undercut the very essence of Enlightenment thinking.

Kant was one of those rare thinkers who fully realized the consequences of Hume's relentless attack on the scope of reason. In the preface of his *Prolegomena to Any Future Metaphysics* he wrote:

> Since the origin of metaphysics so far as we know its history, nothing has ever happened which could have been more decisive to its fate than the attack made upon it by David Hume. He threw no light on this species of knowledge, but he certainly struck a spark by which light might have been kindled had it caught some inflammable substance and had its smouldering fire been carefully nursed and developed.
>
> . . . However hasty and mistaken Hume's inference may appear, it was at least founded upon investigation, and this investigation deserved the concentration of the brighter spirits of his day as well as determined efforts on their part to discover, if possible, a happier solution of the problem in the sense proposed by him. . . .
>
> But Hume suffered the usual misfortune of metaphysicians, of not being understood. It is positively painful to see how utterly his opponents . . . missed the point of the problem; for while they were ever taking for granted that which he doubted, and demonstrating with zeal and often with impudence that which he never thought of doubting, they so misconstrued his valuable suggestion that everything remained in its old condition, as if nothing happened.[21]

I freely admit it was David Hume's remark that first, many years ago, interrupted my dogmatic slumber and gave a completely different direction to my inquiries in the field of speculative philosophy.

Immanuel Kant

Kant knew he must somehow meet Hume's challenge and show that reason is potent, that our knowledge of causes and effects is real and not illusory, and that the external world and the self can be grounded in more than animal faith or wishful thinking.

The seeds of what Kant referred to as a "scandal" in philosophy actually were planted when Descartes doubted his own existence and divided everything into two completely distinct substances: minds and bodies. Descartes was never able to satisfactorily account for mind-body interaction or to establish with certainty the existence of an external, material world. Although Descartes refused to follow his rationalistic premises to their logical conclusions, the Continental rationalists who came after him did. Because their model of certainty was mathematical and geometric, they moved further and further away from experience. As a result, they established grand systems of logical relationships ungrounded in observation or perception.

The British empiricists chose another tack, viewing the human mind as the passive receiver of impressions and experiences. But this view leads to the unfortunate conclusion that all certain knowledge is confined to ideas. Ironically, beginning with experience, the empiricists were unable to get back to it. The result was Hume's admission that we must believe in an external world, in selves, and in causes and effects, without ever knowing them.

As it has so often in history, scientific progress challenged the dominant philosophies of the day. As Kant noted, something was drastically wrong with philosophy if between them the two major philosophical schools at the time denied the importance of perception, denied the possibility of knowledge of cause and effect, denied the verifiable existence of the external world, and rendered reason impotent as a motivator in human affairs, while science— not to mention common sense and everyday experience—clearly showed otherwise.

You might ask why Kant did not abandon philosophy, if it was so out of touch, so bizarre? Why not just accept the supremacy of science and let philosophy die of irrelevance? Kant found this course unsatisfying, for science was unveiling a mechanistic universe in which everything (at least once fully understood) would ultimately be shown to follow universal, unchanging laws of nature. If such a picture is complete and accurate, then God is unnecessary, free will is an illusion, and morality is impossible. If we have no choice but to follow "laws of nature," then values as they are usually understood disappear. Our behavior is only more complex than that of rocks or worms, it is not different in kind. The murderer and the saint are both following inescapable patterns of cause and effect.

How, Kant asked, could science, which clearly made progress, be headed for conclusions that reduced human life to blind mechanism? How could two radically different philosophies each reach such odd, unacceptable results? Was it possible to synthesize science with the good parts of rationalism and empiricism in a way that would give a rational account of the world without stripping us of moral worth and dignity? Surely there had to be better alternatives than the cold, unfree world of science or the unverifiable, impractical worlds of rationalistic and skeptical philosophy.

PHILOSOPHICAL QUERY

Do you think morality must disappear if everything we do can be explained according to scientific laws and patterns? Could there be another kind of morality based on laws of behavior and biopsychology? Why or why not? What is lost in the purely "scientific" view? Anything important? Explain.

KANT'S COPERNICAN REVOLUTION

In response to the "scandal in philosophy," Kant turned to an analysis (which he called a critique) of *how* knowledge is possible. In the process, he discovered an underlying *structure* imposed by the mind on the sensations and perceptions it encounters. We can think of this structure as the *formal* component of knowing. For this reason, Kant is known as a formalist. Kant theorized that neither reason by itself nor sensation by itself can give us knowledge of the external world. Knowledge is the result

of the interaction between the mind and sensation. Knowledge and experience are shaped, structured, or formed by special regulative ideas called *categories*. This theory is known as **Kantian formalism**, or *Kantian idealism*, or *transcendental idealism*.

Kant noted that Descartes' principal error began with a failure to understand scientific method. Galileo had changed science by establishing a "common plan of procedure," a method for studying phenomena. Though Descartes had understood the importance of method, he had not fully understood that the *scientific* method is *both* empirical *and* rational. Kant realized that the empiricists were guilty of a similar error of incompleteness by discounting the importance of reason. Knowledge, as the scientific method shows, consists of both a rational and a perceptual (empirical) component. It requires both a subject (a knowing mind) and an object (that which is known).

The common belief during Kant's time, however, was that truth occurs when ideas in the mind agree with external conditions or objects. For example, if I think this book has a red cover, my idea is true if the cover actually is red. But as Kant realized, if all knowledge fits that model, we could never discover general laws of nature. We could discover only that *this* apple falls, not that all bodies are subject to gravity, because we never experience all bodies. Hume understood this but was willing to limit the domain of knowledge to particulars, in the end asserting that we could *only believe in* the most important aspects of our existence: the regularity of experience, the existence of an external world, the existence of a unified self, cause and effect, and a moral order.

If we accept Hume's initial premises, his conclusions follow. However, close inspection of the way science is actually done shows that scientists make precisely the kinds of generalizations Hume's *theory* says we cannot make. As Kant pointed out, *when a theory results in conclusions that are clearly inconsistent with experience, real-world evidence must outweigh theoretical consistency.* And everyday experience shows that knowledge of causes and effects, the external world, the self, and so on, exists.

The scientific method is obviously more reliable and complete than Hume's philosophy. How do they differ? Kant pointed out that scientific thinking involves the *activity* of asking questions and framing hypotheses. It is not merely the passive recording of whatever happens; it requires the *active* setting up of controlled experimental conditions.[22] And this suggests that knowledge is a kind of *interaction*, a two-way street between the knower (the subject) and the known (the object).

Kant realized he was proposing to change fundamental assumptions about the structure of knowledge, just as Copernicus had changed our assumptions about the structure of the universe. After astronomers had failed for centuries to make consistent sense of an earth-centered universe, Copernicus proposed the revolutionary hypothesis: that the sun is at the center, that the earth is part of a solar system. This assumption dissolved the great difficulties of the past and produced new, predictable knowledge. Kant was

KANTIAN FORMALISM
(also known as *Kantian idealism* and *transcendental idealism*)
Theory that knowledge is the result of the interaction between the mind and sensation, and structured by regulative ideas called categories.

Hitherto it has been assumed that all our knowledge must conform to objects. But all attempts to extend our knowledge of objects by establishing something in regard to them by means of concepts have, on this assumption, ended in failure. We must, therefore, make trial whether we may not have more success if we suppose that objects must conform to our knowledge.

Immanuel Kant

proposing a Copernican revolution in philosophy: He would assume that *instead of the mind having to conform to what can be known, what can be known must conform to the mind.*

Critical Philosophy

Kant proposed "a critical inquiry into the faculty of reason with reference to all the knowledge which it may strive to attain independently of reason." That is, he was proposing a critical reexamination of metaphysics. Metaphysics, as distinct from science, is an attempt to acquire and systematize knowledge derived by reason, not experience. Kant referred to earlier metaphysical philosophies as *dogmatic*, by which he meant, among other things, that they were *uncritical efforts* to understand the nature of whatever lies beyond immediate experience.

Kant asked a profoundly basic question: *Is metaphysics possible?* Can we know things beyond immediate experience? That is, does the human mind have the capacity for a priori knowledge, knowledge derived from reason without reference to sense experience (see Chapter 11)?

Kant called his attempt to discover whether a priori knowledge is possible *critical philosophy*. Hume had insisted that all knowledge begins in experience with sense impressions. But Hume confused knowledge that is *triggered by* experience with knowledge that is *based on* experience. Kant raised the possibility that our "faculty of knowledge" (mind, for short) might add something to the raw data of experience. Because experience *triggers* and hence *accompanies* all knowledge, we may fail to notice the effects the mind has on experience:

> But though all our knowledge begins with experience, it does not follow that it all arises out of experience. For it may well be that even our empirical knowledge is made up of what we receive through impressions and of what our own faculty of knowledge (sensible knowledge serving merely as the occasion) supplies from itself. If our faculty of knowledge makes any such addition, it may be that we are not in a position to distinguish it from the raw material, until with long practice of attention we have become skilled in separating it.
>
> This, then, is a question which at least calls for closer examination, and does not allow of any offhand answer:—whether there is any knowledge that is thus independent of experience and even of all impressions of the senses. Such knowledge is entitled *a priori*, and distinguished from the *empirical*, which has its sources *a posteriori*, that is, in experience.[23]

CRITICAL PHILOSOPHY
Kant's term for his effort to assess the nature and limits of "pure reason," unadulterated by experience, in order to identify the actual relationship of the mind to knowledge.

Critical philosophy is an effort to assess the nature and limits of "pure reason," reason unadulterated by experience, in an effort to identify the actual relationship of the mind to knowledge. "Pure knowledge" is not morally

pure, but refers, rather, to *independent reasoning*, to knowledge *not derived from* the senses.

Descartes began the epistemological turn by focusing on the mind as a rational substance. But by concentrating on the mind's rational function he ignored its *organizing function*, and so was unable to avoid generating conclusions that do not square with experience. The British empiricists, concluding with Hume, took the second step and demonstrated both the importance of experience and the limits of reason. So strict was Hume's emphasis on experience as the sole source of knowledge that, coupled with the empiricists' view of the mind as a passive, neutral blank tablet, he was forced to conclude we cannot "know" that anything happens of necessity or even that we have a self.

Kant proposed a radical alternative, which we can think of as the third and final step of the epistemological turn: a critical analysis of what kind of knowledge we actually have based on a new view of the mind as actively interacting with impressions and perceptions.

Phenomena and Noumena

According to Kant, our knowledge is *formed* by two things: our actual experiences *and* the mind's faculties of judgment, called *categories of understanding*. This means we cannot know reality as it is. We can know reality only as it is organized by human understanding. **Phenomenal reality** is Kant's term for the world as we experience it. **Noumenal reality** is his term for reality as it is independent of our perceptions, what we commonly call "objective reality."

All we can *know*, Kant reminds us, is perceived reality. This is not the same thing as saying that we each have our own private, subjective reality. All other things being equal, Kant says, the human mind imposes uniform categories on reality. Because the faculty of understanding is uniform, all functioning minds impose the same basic order on experience. Thus we might think of Kant's distinction as between *human reality* and *pure reality*.

Although we never experience pure reality, we can know (understand) that our minds do not just invent the world. In Kant's language, the mind imposes order on a world of things-in-themselves. Things-in-themselves are *noumena*, things as they exist independently of us. We know they exist, but we can never know them, because in the act of imposing order, the mind changes things-in-themselves to a comprehensible form.

For example, the human ear cannot hear the noumena—the full spectrum of air vibrations known as sound. We cannot hear the highest-pitched sounds a dog hears or the lowest pitches an elephant hears. Human beings would not know that these other wavelengths of sound exist without the help of dog and elephant ears or sensitive instruments. In respect to knowledge, then, we can know only what our human faculty of understanding is capable of processing.

PHENOMENAL REALITY
Kant's term for the world as we experience it.

NOUMENAL REALITY
Kant's term for reality as it is, independent of our perceptions; what is commonly called "objective reality."

Why make such a distinction, since we will never experience noumena? Kant's response is twofold. First, the distinction shows us the limits of human understanding. Second, as we shall see, Kant uses the distinction to establish a foundation for his moral philosophy, one of the dominant ethical positions of modern and contemporary philosophy.

THE METAPHYSICS OF MORALS

You may have identified a basic strategy throughout Kant's philosophy so far. Kant shows great respect for powerful and persistent ways of thinking, even if they seem difficult to justify philosophically. I have in mind, for example, the persistence of belief in cause and effect, self-identity, the external world, and God. To establish his "metaphysics of morals," Kant starts with the hypothesis that somehow such ideas can be justified *because we keep relying on them*. They must have more than just the psychological value Hume assigned them, given how they work in our lives and their apparent universality. Kant thinks it is important to analyze the content of such beliefs, the form they take, and their possible sources. He uses this analysis to draw a picture of the active faculty of understanding.

Practical Reason

Although there is only one reason, one faculty of understanding, Kant distinguishes two functions of reason, which he called theoretical reason and practical reason. **Theoretical reason**, including scientific reasoning, is confined to the empirical, phenomenal world. Interaction with the world of experience produces laws of behavior that force reason to view everything mechanically. Theoretical reason thus concludes that human beings, like all phenomena, are governed by cause and effect in the form of inescapable laws of nature. Limited by the way the mind can understand the phenomenal world, we must accept that there is no freedom on that level. If freedom is necessary for morality, we must find our freedom elsewhere.

Using the distinction between the phenomenal world and the noumenal world, Kant asserts that it is possible to be both determined, or unfree (in the phenomenal world), and free (in the noumenal world). We have a phenomenal self which falls under the laws of nature and behavior and a noumenal self which is free. Thus, free will exists in the noumenal world. This means we are free and morally responsible even though from the empirical, scientific view of life, we cannot *experience* our freedom but only *think of it*. It is a mistake to attempt an empirical proof of human freedom. Science describes the phenomenal world, but it cannot deal with the noumenal world.

According to Kant, we use **practical reason** to move beyond the phenomenal world to the moral dimension. Practical reason begins with knowl-

THEORETICAL REASON
According to Kant, a function of reason confined to the empirical, phenomenal world.

PRACTICAL REASON
According to Kant, moral function of reason that produces religious feelings and intuitions based on knowledge of moral conduct.

METAPHYSICAL MOMENTS

The name metaphysics is apt to suggest something difficult, unusual, and remote. Yet it has its familiar side. Most of us have times at which, in reflection, we seem to be confronted not with any particular isolated problem or any particular aspect of our experience, but with experience, or life, or existence, *as a whole*. These might be called our metaphysical moments. It is not easy to give a detailed description of them and for our purpose it is not necessary. Indirectly and roughly, however, it is possible to identify them by saying that if they did not occur there would be no point in religion and little in many works of art and philosophy.

S. Körner
Kant (Baltimore: Penguin, 1955), p. 13.

edge about moral conduct and produces religious feelings and intuitions. Practical reason helps us deal with the moral freedom provided by free will. In *Critique of Practical Reason*, Kant says that no matter how many natural causes and sensations might "drive" a person, "they cannot produce [a state of] *being under obligation*, they cannot account for moral duty."[24] The feeling of duty comes from within; it comes from being rational.

Kant uses the term *practical* reason to indicate that we do not act on impulses and desires alone. We also act from *conscious choice* based on our general principles. In direct opposition to Hume's claim that reason cannot be a motivator, Kant argues that we can consciously act when no desire is involved at all.[25] Consider, for example, the kind of inner conflict you might experience between a strong desire to buy a new CD and your awareness of your duty to repay a friend you borrowed money from. You can choose to repay your friend because you ought to, even though you do not want to. (This is not the same thing as doing something to avoid feeling guilty: that does involve desire.)

PHILOSOPHICAL QUERY

What would a person be like who could choose only what he or she desired? Do you think it is possible to choose to do something if no desire whatsoever is involved? Explain.

The Moral Law Within

Imagine a world in which *no one* had any moral obligations. Would any rational creature desire to live in it? Kant answers with a resounding no! Therefore, he reasoned, morality is absolutely necessary for human relationships.

And thus I conclude the analytical solution of the main question which I had proposed: "How is metaphysics in general possible?" by ascending from the data of its actual use, as shown in its consequences, to the grounds of its possibility.

Immanuel Kant

But a moral code can't be discovered by simply conducting anthropological studies, that is, by looking at people's cultural and individual habits and tastes.

Empirical studies can identify only what people *actually do*, they cannot identify what we *ought to do*. Whereas Hume dealt with the is/ought (fact/value) issue by denying that "ought" refers to any fact (Chapter 12), it seemed obvious to Kant that the very essence of moral judgments involves *duty* or ideas of what we ought to do. Again, Kant begins his inquiry with awareness of and respect for the way we actually think. He notes that very few people consistently think of their own moral judgments as mere matters of custom or taste. Whether we actually live up to our moral principles or not, we think of moral judgments as concerned with how people ought to behave.

Thus, if we begin with the *actual form* of moral judgments as they occur in our lives, we see that they are judgments of universal duty. As an example, Kant offered the moral judgment "We ought to tell the truth," which he said has the same status as "Every change must have a cause." (Hume rejected the idea of cause.) Just as we cannot begin to think of or even experience anything without already assuming the principle of cause and effect, Kant thought that we cannot function without a sense of duty. Practical reason imposes the notion of *ought* on us.

Morality and practical reason rely on concepts that transcend particular facts and immediate experience. Practical reason deals with human behavior and relationships by continually monitoring how we ought to behave. Further, practical reason goes beyond merely addressing how we should behave in particular circumstances and generates universal principles that apply to everyone's behavior at all times in similar circumstances.

PHILOSOPHICAL QUERY

Psychologists have identified a character disorder that is labeled as either "sociopathic" or "antisocial personality disorder." One component of this diagnosis is that such people are amoral, lacking any conscience. Do you know people without any sense of moral duty? What are they like? Does the existence of such people mean there is no such thing as a necessary, universal moral law? Discuss.

For Kant, morality is a function of reason. Specifically, morality is based on our consciousness of necessary and universal moral laws (or rules, as Kant calls them). Moral rules of behavior differ from other, pragmatic rules because they alone have the quality of being thought of as universal and necessary. And since only a priori judgments are universal and necessary, moral judgments must be a priori. This is why the empiricists could not discover them.

Thus the moral law cannot be discovered in actual behavior. It is a function of reason, a component of how we think. From this it follows that only rational creatures can be moral or held morally accountable. It also follows that any and all rational creatures are moral beings. The capacity for reason is the source of morality. Reason imposes moral obligation.

The Good Will

Kant thought that virtually everyone has the capacity to make sound moral judgments. Valid moral principles will be the same for everyone, just as the truths of geometry or logic are. Thus, for Kant, goodness depends not on our behavior but on our will, on what we intend to do if circumstances do not prevent it. Though some erroneously evaluate morality on the basis of conduct and the results of our actions, Kant insisted that morality was entirely a matter of reason and good will.

It's important to note that Kant conceives of the good will as a component of rationality. He also believes that "ought implies can," by which he means it must be possible for human beings to live up to their moral obligations. Yet circumstances sometimes prevent us from doing the good we want to do. I may sincerely wish to minister to the sick, but be physically or financially unable. I may diligently try to love my neighbor, only to be rebuffed by him. Thus I must not be morally judged on the consequences of what I actually do. Put another way, morality is a matter of motives.

> A good will is good not because of what it performs or effects, not by its aptness for the attainment of some proposed end, but simply by virtue of the volition, that is, it is good in itself, and considered by itself is to be esteemed much higher than all that can be brought about by it in favour of any inclination, nay, even of the sum-total of all inclinations. Even if it should happen that, owing to special disfavour of fortune, or the niggardly provision of a step-motherly nature, this will should wholly lack power to accomplish its purpose, if with its greatest efforts it should yet achieve nothing, and there should remain only the good will (not, to be sure, a mere wish, but the summoning of all means in our power), then, like a jewel, it would still shine by its own light, as a thing which has its whole value in itself. Its usefulness or fruitlessness can neither add to nor take away anything from this value.[26]

We must not, of course, confuse a good will with rather halfhearted good wishes. After all, "The road to hell is paved with good intentions." I have the will to do something, in Kant's words, only when I "summon all the means within my power." This is much more than merely wishing to be good. It is certainly more than a cheerful expression of moral platitudes. My good will is based only and entirely on my realization that I have a moral duty to do X.

Morality is not properly the doctrine of how we should make ourselves happy, but how we should become worthy of happiness.
Immanuel Kant

The altruism which in my view underlies ethics is not to be confused with generalized affection for the human race. It is not a feeling.
Thomas Nagel

If I do X because it makes me happy, I am not acting from a moral motive. If I do it to avoid going to jail, I am making a pragmatic, not a moral, judgment. Moral judgments may bring other desired consequences along with them, but *there is only one moral motive: duty.*

PHILOSOPHICAL QUERY
Does the idea of good will help our analysis of the sociopath? Explain.

MORAL DUTY

Kant thought it was crucially important to distinguish moral motives from others. I might tell the truth to impress you or to avoid going to jail for perjury. Obviously, such considerations are not moral. I may give money to charity in order to cut my tax bill. I might do what I think God commands in order to go to heaven or to escape hell, but then my motive is hedonistic. Only when I do a thing solely because it is my duty do I have a good will.

What, then, is duty? Kant says, *"Duty is the necessity of acting from respect for the [moral] law."*[27] He goes on to explain that duty does not serve our desires and preferences (he calls these "inclinations"), but rather *overpowers* them. Put another way, duty excludes considerations of personal preference or profit and loss from moral calculation. For example, suppose I have criticized my boss to others. When she asks me whether I've done this, I decide to tell her the truth because I am not sure what my co-workers have already told her. Even though I do my duty, I cannot get moral credit for it, according to Kant, because my decision is based on something other than moral duty—it's based on not getting fired.

> Thus the moral worth of an action does not lie in the effect expected from it, nor in any principle of action which requires to borrow its motive from its expected effect. For all these effects—agreeableness of one's condition, and even the promotion of the happiness of others—could have been also brought about by other causes so that for this there would have been no need of the will of a rational being; whereas it is in this alone that the supreme and unconditioned good can be found. The preeminent good which we call moral can therefore consist in nothing else than *the conception of law* in itself, which certainly is only possible in a rational being, in so far as this conception, and not the expected effect, determines the will.[28]

If this seems unduly strict (and it has to many philosophers), keep in mind that decisions based on "inclinations" are often inconsistent and always relative. My inclination might be to renege on a loan or to be rude to a dirty, smelly customer. How can anyone rely on me if I only follow my inclina-

The way to appraise a "way of life" may well be by considering what's in it for you; the way to appraise the moral value of a course of action is by considering what's in it for everyone.

Jan Narveson

tions? My inclination on the day I asked you to dinner might have been to keep our date, but by Friday my inclination might be to stay home alone. And I might not be inclined to call and inform you of this, either. Imagine the chaos of a world in which our obligations were tied to our moods.

My moral obligations cannot be grounded in my whims and personal taste. Nor can yours. According to Kant, moral duty must be confined to considerations of the form: *What are the universal obligations of all persons in similar circumstances?* My duty cannot be based on what I want to do, what I like or don't like, whether or not the others involved are people I care about.

Having defined the good will in terms of acting only from duty, and having defined duty as acting from a conscious awareness of our obligations under rational, moral law, we now need a way to determine exactly what our duty is in this or that case. That is, we can at last ask, *What is the moral law?* Kant's answer is one of the most intriguing and widely debated principles in all moral philosophy. He calls it the *categorical imperative.*

PHILOSOPHICAL QUERY

Do you think it is possible to have only one motive for an action? Is it common to have only one motive? Is it important to distinguish moral motives from pragmatic ones? Why? Compare Kant with Hume on this issue.

Hypothetical Imperatives

Kant's position is that the moral quality of an act is determined by the *principle* to which the will consciously assents. If, for instance, I resolve to feed the hungry and mistakenly serve tainted meat at a charity dinner, my intention is praiseworthy even though my action results in sickness or death. If, on the other hand, I intend to poison my sick wife in order to inherit her fortune and mistakenly give her a chemical that cures her, I am morally guilty of murder, for that was what I consciously willed.

Since they affect behavior, moral principles are always framed as commands, according to Kant. He refers to commands by their grammatical designation as *imperatives*. Examples of imperatives are "Shut the door," "Always brush your teeth after eating," "Love your neighbor as yourself," and "Double-space your term paper."

Imperatives that tell us what to do under specific, variable conditions are called **hypothetical imperatives**. In logic, a hypothetical proposition takes the form "*If* this, *then* that." These are also called *conditional* propositions, because they set up a conditional relationship: *If* it rains, *then* postpone the picnic. The imperative "Postpone the picnic" is binding only in the condition of rain. According to Kant, all empirical or factual imperatives are hypothetical, because they are binding only so long as certain conditions apply.

There are a variety of *kinds* of hypothetical imperatives. Some are technical, applying to chemists or surgeons or bakers. Others are social, telling us

HYPOTHETICAL IMPERATIVES Propositions that tell us what to do under specific, variable conditions.

how to be popular or get dates. Some are legal, and so on. No hypothetical imperative is binding on everyone or even on one person all the time. When factual conditions change, so do hypothetical imperatives. No hypothetical imperative is a priori. All are relative.

In fact, Kant says, "the imperatives of prudence do not, strictly speaking, command at all."[29] No one has a necessary obligation to be practical, to make money, to eat wisely. Thus, though hypothetical imperatives can help us deal with life, they cannot be a basis for determining moral duty.

The Categorical Imperative

If moral duty must be universally—not conditionally—binding, how can we determine what to do? What principle can we follow that is not conditional? After considering the difference between telling the truth because it is a duty and telling it because of some payoff it might yield, Kant concludes that acting from duty is always based on the principle of a "conception of the law in general."

What Kant means can be characterized as *acting on the principle of acting on principle*. In the case of telling the truth, I tell the truth because I have a basic, general obligation to tell the truth—period. This obligation is general in the sense that I must not base it on particular considerations at all. I must not be partial to myself and my fears or my wants.

What is needed is a **categorical imperative**, a command that is universally binding on all rational creatures. This alone can guide the good will. Indeed, the good will is precisely that which summons all its powers in order to obey just such an imperative. Kant has stripped the good will of every Humean sentiment, every impulse, appetite, fear, preference, or other practical or person-specific consideration. What's left?

> There remains nothing but the universal conformity of [the will's] actions to law in general, which alone is to serve as its principle, *i.e.*, I am never to act otherwise than *so that I could also will that my maxim should become a universal law*. Here, now, it is the simple conformity to law in general, without assuming any particular applicability to certain actions, that serves the will as its principle, and must so serve it, if duty is not to be a vain delusion and a chimerical notion.[30]

Kant formulated the categorical imperative as *"Act as if the maxim of thy action were to become a universal law of nature."* In other words, we must act only according to principles we think should apply to everyone. Because a free will is a necessary condition of morality, Kant reminds us that the "universal law" in question comes from our own rational, willing assent—it is not imposed on us from the outside. Obeying God or nature or any other *overpowering force* out of fear or necessity is not moral. If we obey out of fear,

CATEGORICAL IMPERATIVE
According to Kant, a command that is universally binding on all rational creatures; the ultimate foundation of all moral law: "Act as if the maxim of thy action were to become a universal law of nature."

Calvin and Hobbes © Watterson. Dist. by Universal Press Syndicate. Reprinted with permission. All rights reserved.

our motive is partial and pragmatic; if we have no choice but to obey, we are not free. Moral law is obligatory because it springs from our own rational nature and becomes law only when we willingly assent to it.

By *maxim* Kant means the rule according to which an act is done. It is the principle behind my action, my rational motive. What happens if we try to apply the categorical imperative to a course of action? A survey conducted by the Carnegie Foundation for the Advancement of Teaching asserted that 40 to 90 percent of college students cheat on exams or papers.[31] Let us analyze college cheating.

Don't be in a hurry to conclude, "Yeah, yeah, we all know cheating is wrong. That's obvious. But just about everybody does it—the survey shows that. So it's not a big deal." By scrutinizing it along Kantian lines, we discover exactly why cheating is wrong and learn something about the nature of morality.

We must begin by asking whether a rational person could universalize cheating. That is, would I be willing to cheat if by doing so I created a new law of nature that would *force* everyone to cheat in similar circumstances?

Nowadays everyone in the world is deluded about right and wrong, and confused about benefit and harm. Because so many people share this sickness, no one perceives that it is a sickness.

Lao Zi

Kant held that, as conscious, rational creatures, we each possess dignity that deserves universal respect and that is not contingent on how likable we are, how attractive, successful, and so forth. In this photo, the caregiver's sense of dignity is apparent in the way he is helping another man find clothes that fit. His posture reflects patience and concern—as well as his own dignity.

Suppose the maxim under which I act is something like this: "Cheat only when necessary to get good grades in required classes outside your major that you think you'll never use in later life." Now suppose every college student *must* behave just as I do.

Reason reveals what such a world would be like. Here is an imaginative picture of a world in which my moral principle operates as a universal law of nature: One day, after I've graduated, I'm being prepped for surgery. Dozing under a mild sedative, I'm chatting with my nurse anesthetist as I'm waiting to be wheeled into the operating room. She casually mentions that she originally studied to be a pediatric nurse and decided to go into anesthesiology only when she couldn't get a job in pediatrics. As I'm wheeled into the operating room, it dawns on me that—having acted on *my* moral principle—she cheated in anesthesiology courses because when she took them they were not required in her major, and she thought she'd never use them!

In more general terms, no rational person can universalize cheating in school because as cheating becomes widespread, the value of everyone's education becomes doubtful and diminished. Employers will not trust college degrees, since, according to my own law, they will have been acquired by cheating. No one will feel secure relying on anyone else's expertise. Cheating in school cannot be justified without making myself an exception to the *general rule* not to cheat.

But we already know that. What's the point of mentioning it? This kind of analysis shows one way of using the categorical imperative to bolster what we already know, to help us will and do what we ought. Rational analysis can do this by making clearer exactly what is wrong with a course of action.

PHILOSOPHICAL QUERY

To get a clearer sense of the power of the categorical imperative to clarify the nature of various forms of behavior, formulate and then analyze the maxims that are required to justify: charging things on credit without being sure you can pay them off on time; enrolling in two different high-demand courses so that you can check them both out and drop the one you don't like; having sex without knowing if you are HIV positive; talking in the theater; forcing schools to teach the values of your religion.

The Kingdom of Ends

Kant held that as conscious, rational creatures, we each possess intrinsic worth. Because we are capable of reason and goodness, we possess dignity that deserves universal respect. We are more than mere objects to be used to further this or that end. We are persons competent to monitor and guide our own behavior according to principles. Our ability to reason carries with it an obligation to respect the rights of others to reason for themselves.

This intrinsic worth is not contingent on anything. It is not a function of how likable we are, how attractive, talented, clean, or even good we are. It is not contingent on how well we use our reason or on whether we use it at all. We possess worth because we *can* reason.

We have seen that, according to Kant, our basic obligations to one another cannot rest on inclinations or sentiments (desires), for that amounts to saying we have no moral obligations. Imagine a wedding in which the bride or groom promised to love, cherish, and respect the other "so long as I feel inclined to." The very concept of duty implies acting in an appropriate way regardless of our sentiments, regardless of convenience, comfort, or other personal factors. In Kant's terms this is an objective duty toward other rational beings—exactly what Hume denied:

> Man and generally any rational being *exists* as an end in himself, *not merely as a means* to be arbitrarily used . . . but in all his actions, whether they concern himself or other rational beings, must be always regarded at the same time as an end. All objects of inclination have only a conditional worth; for if the inclinations and the wants founded on them did not exist, then

their object would be without value. . . . Rational beings . . . are called *persons*, because their very nature points them out as ends in themselves. . . . These, therefore, are not merely subjective ends whose existence has a worth *for us* as an effect of our action, but *objective ends*, that is, things whose existence is an end in itself: an end moreover for which no other can be substituted . . . for otherwise nothing whatever would possess *absolute worth;* but if all worth were conditional and therefore contingent, then there would be no supreme practical principle of reason whatever.

If then there is a supreme practical principle or, in respect of the human will, a categorical imperative, it must be one which, being drawn from the conception of that which is necessarily an end for everyone because it is *an end in itself*, constitutes an *objective* principle of will, and can therefore serve as a universal practical law. The foundation of this principle is: *rational nature exists as an end in itself.*[32]

Kant uses a beautiful expression to describe the moral universe, the universe of all moral beings, of all creatures possessing intrinsic worth. He refers to it as the *kingdom of ends*, a kingdom in which everyone is an end in him- or herself and no one is just a means to be used and tossed aside.

PRACTICAL IMPERATIVE (or PRINCIPLE OF DIGNITY) Kant's formulation of the categorical imperative based on the concept of dignity: "Act in such a way that you always treat humanity, whether in your own person or in the person of another, never simply as a means but always at the same time as an end."

Kant formulates the categorical imperative around the concept of dignity in a way that is sometimes referred to as the **practical imperative** or **principle of dignity:** *"Act in such a way that you always treat humanity, whether in your own person or in the person of another, never simply as a means but always at the same time as an end."*[33] I confess I'm partial to this principle. It has, I believe, much to teach us.

If, for example, I view my students only as a way to make a living, or only as a captive audience to indoctrinate with my views, I treat them as means to an end without honoring their basic dignity as persons. We violate this principle of dignity when we hurl racial or gender insults at one another, for then we are treating other persons as means of venting rage or expressing feelings. No abusive parent or spouse treats the objects of his or her abuse as *persons*. In the kingdom of ends there are no slaves, no sweatshops, no terrorists, no bullies, no rude clerks or surly customers, no unprepared teachers or students, only respectful and respected *persons*.

Yet in fact, my students *are* a *means* to an income for me. I *am* a *means* to a degree or meeting a requirement for them. Bosses and employees are means to each other, and so on. Note that the principle does not preclude this. Rather, it adds a dimension of universal respect to all human relationships: We are means *and* ends. How often we seem to forget that others are *persons* when we use them as status symbols or see only their outward appearance or religious or political beliefs. Imagine a world in which clerks and medical doctors and parents and children and spouses and students and teachers and politicians and police officers and everyone else followed this principle.

If I can remember that I live in a kingdom of ends, I can transform my relationships from a sort of bartering for favors, or competing for power and success. I can elevate my life to something beyond a contest in which I and mine must struggle against a "different" and "inferior" them. In the kingdom of ends, it is always *us*.

PHILOSOPHICAL QUERY

Consider the actual case of the parents who conceived a child for the express purpose of producing a bone marrow donor for their nineteen-year-old daughter who has leukemia. Doctors advised the parents that a bone marrow transplant was the only hope of saving their daughter's life. Unable to find a compatible donor match, the parents took the desperate step of having another child, and in late May of 1991 bone marrow from the specially conceived child, then just over one year old, was transplanted to her nineteen-year-old sister. Can the parents' action be morally justified? Explain.

COMMENTARY

Kant remains *the* major figure in modern philosophy. His effort to understand how the mind knows has shaped a significant portion of the field. Kant is also a major influence in modern psychology. In fact, many of the epistemological issues he raised are now being addressed by the cognitive sciences, which are devoted to unraveling the mysteries of perceiving, learning, knowing, and thinking.

In the field of ethics, three imposing visions dominate modern philosophy. One is Kantian formalism, the second is Humean subjectivism, and the third is utilitarianism (the subject of Chapter 14). We will address some criticisms of Kantian ethics in the process of understanding the major alternative to it in the next chapter. Even so, some general remarks are in order.

In spite of the difficulty of his arguments and writing style, Kant's moral philosophy has proved to be influential beyond philosophical circles. Part of its power lies in a deep sense that it is wrong to make ourselves the exception in moral matters. If something is right (or wrong) for one person, it seems only fair that it be right (or wrong) for all persons in similar circumstances. We are offended when others make themselves or their loved ones exceptions. This may indeed stem from a sense of a "moral law within."

You may already have sensed that Kant's categorical imperative is a more refined and sophisticated version of the Golden Rule: "Do unto others as you would have them do unto you." Kant understood that a sloppy formulation of the Rule can be interpreted as saying "Treat others as you would *like* to be treated." Such a formulation generates what I call the Sadomasochistic Paradox, from an old joke in which a masochist says to a sadist, "Hurt me!" and the sadist replies, "No." The point, of course, is that how we *want* to be treated varies and is often determined by our individual tastes, background, personal beliefs, and temperament. It is certainly not a very reliable standard for treating others. If we have low self-esteem or some psychological quirk, we may want to be treated very poorly indeed. Kant's insistence that duty rise above inclination is meant to prohibit such individualistic interpretations of the Rule.

A common criticism of Kant's moral philosophy is that it promotes rash and irresponsible behavior by exempting us from responsibility for the consequences of our actions. After all, if the only truly good thing is a good will or motive, then all that matters morally is my intention—not the results of my behavior. Sophisticated Kantians point out, however, that any universalizable maxim must include concern for and consideration of the likely consequences of action. No defensible moral duty can condone indifference to what happens to others.

Another intriguing problem has to do with the conscience of a fanatic. By stressing the rational aspects of morality, Kant may have given too little weight to important psychological factors. A famous example involves a Nazi who is willing to universalize this maxim: "Always annihilate those whom you judge to be inferior and impediments to human progress." When it is pointed out that the Nazi may become the target of annihilation if he turns out to be an impediment to human progress, he is expected to see the "unreasonableness" of his maxim. If he still holds to it, knowing that it may result in his own destruction, he is said to be a "fanatic." But isn't this judgment based on our own inclinations (sentiments) and beliefs about what is reasonable? Yet how else can we determine what's rational? Didn't Kant merely use his own Western European Christian background to define "reasonable"? Is he, perhaps, guided by moral sentiment after all—as Hume thought? This is a complex and important problem, one the finest moral philosophers still struggle with.

The sociopath presents a dramatic example of the difficulties in determining what is rational. By most standards, sociopaths are intelligent and rational. Kant would not agree, because he sees the presence of a good will as a necessary condition of rationality. Thus, *by definition*, anyone lacking a good will is not rational. Kant's move seems arbitrary and circular, for it defines "reasonable" after the fact. In defense of Kant, we can offer the kinds of examples he uses in explaining the categorical imperative: repaying loans, keeping promises, telling the truth. It seems clear that social harmony and perhaps civilized life itself depend on such basic principles. But does that mean everyone must honor them? Clearly not, since we live in a society in which Kantian consistency is regularly ignored. The Sophists and egoists argue that it is perfectly rational to preach conformity to moral rules but to

Judaism would reject the Kantian axiom, "I ought, therefore I can": it would claim, instead, "Thou art commanded, therefore thou canst."

Abraham Joshua Heschel

make myself the exception when it's to my advantage. As a *rational* egoist, all I need care about is that most people are moral most of the time.

Perhaps the most serious charge against Kantian formalism concerns its overemphasis on motives. A morality that seems to trivialize the consequences of action is clearly inadequate. Is it really preferable for a woman to stay in an abusive marriage because of a promise she made on her wedding day? Can we afford to separate motives from consequences in the way Kant does? It seems wiser to acknowledge the importance of both motives and consequences. This would reflect our most common moral experiences: personal character and intentions, as well as the consequences of our acts, are important components of morality.

Being "rational" is clearly not all that matters, as the harm caused by "rational" criminals, frauds, toxic polluters, and others clearly demonstrates. Experience offers countless examples of dangerous, immoral schemes hatched by rational individuals lacking good will. Equally dangerous is the well-intentioned but shortsighted or incompetent individual whose motives are unassailable, yet whose actions generate harm. The best intentions must be combined with a certain minimum of intelligence, insight, and ability. Just as being rational is not a sufficient condition for being moral, neither is having a good will.

Further, attempting to apply the categorical imperative results in seemingly irresolvable difficulties, because we lack the ability to frame moral rules so clearly that they do not generate problems. Suppose you promise a friend to repay borrowed money whenever he requests it. One evening your friend and a drug dealer show up. Your friend demands the money to buy an ounce of heroin. Should you repay it? Which is more important, keeping a promise or looking out for a friend's welfare when he or she is unable to? Can a drug user be rational when compelled by a powerful addiction? Does treating my friends as ends entail protecting them from themselves or letting them make their own choices no matter how harmful the consequences?

Imagine that a frightened man dashes into your office one day and hides behind your desk. Before you can ask him what's going on, a hysterical woman with a shotgun looks in your door and asks, "Is my cheating husband in here?" Should you tell the truth, because telling the truth is universalizable? Which value is higher, truth telling or life saving? Can I frame a moral maxim to guide me in choosing between conflicting moral rules in such a case? I could add qualifications to my rules, but then what is the purpose or benefit of having rules? It is not clear there is *any* maxim that can be universalizable without qualification.

In the end, however, I remain especially impressed by Kant's pattern of starting with commonly accepted ideas like causality, the unitary self, and free will and then trying to determine how the mind can know them. Some of the greatest philosophers have painted themselves into "scandalous" corners by either ignoring or trivializing commonly held ideas. Kant does not

*Kant can justly be called the
father of modern philosophy,
for out of him stem nearly
all the still current and contending schools of philosophy:
Positivism, Pragmatism,
and Existentialism.*
William Barrett

uncritically validate "common sense"; rather, he respects some nearly universal ideas of his own culture. He assumes that certain basic thinking patterns
(as opposed to strongly held controversial beliefs) must have merit. They must
serve some inherent, preconscious purpose. He then proceeds to subject them
to his critical philosophy.

The result is certainly not a simplistic epistemology or moral philosophy.
Kant presented a radically new picture of the mind as an active organizer
and questioner of sensation. He identified important limits of empiricism
and rationalism, and identified vital questions that wait to be answered. His
insistence that "reason demands" a noumenal world beyond immediate experience and the reach of science remains a profound expression of a sense
shared by many people.

To the extent that we worship scientific knowledge as the only secure
kind, we remain somehow dissatisfied. Kant understood that we have within
us more than the "moral law." We feel a need for fairness, a hunger to become
good (or at least better), and an abiding sense of "something more," something just beyond the reach of science and theoretical reason.

SUMMARY OF MAIN POINTS

As Enlightenment thinkers discovered more and
more laws of nature, they came to view human
reason as the only tool necessary for progress. Faith
in reason turned to frustration and despair, however, as reason was defeated by the mob during the
Reign of Terror and technical progress was accompanied by slums and abusive working conditions.

Kant fully understood the serious implications
of the "scandal in philosophy" that resulted from
Hume's devastating use of the empirical criterion
of meaning and the failure of rationalism and empiricism to adequately account for knowledge of
the external world, cause and effect, and knowledge in general while science clearly showed
otherwise. Yet Kant did not want to abandon philosophy to science because science was unveiling
a mechanistic universe without God and which,
in its denial of free will, left no room for morality
or human dignity.

Kant developed a special kind of analysis called a
critique that combined reason and experience in
order to avoid the errors of rationalism and empiricism. Critical philosophy attempts to discover
whether a priori knowledge and metaphysics are
possible. Critical philosophy completes the episte-

mological turn in its efforts to assess the nature of
"pure reason" and identify the actual relationship
of the mind to knowledge.

Kant claimed that knowledge is formed by actual
experience and faculties of judgment called categories of understanding. We know reality only
as it is organized by human understanding (phenomenal reality), not reality as it is (noumenal
reality).

Kant distinguished between theoretical reason and
practical reason. Theoretical reason is confined to
the phenomenal world; practical reason moves beyond the phenomenal world to the moral dimension. Practical reason helps us deal with the moral
freedom provided by free will.

Practical reason reveals a moral dimension based
on our consciousness of necessary and universal
moral laws, which Kant calls rules or maxims.
Moral rules cannot be discovered empirically; reason imposes moral obligation. Reason reveals that
morality is a matter of moral duty (good will) rather
than consequences, since circumstances sometimes
prevent us from performing our moral duty.

Moral duty does not serve our sentiments and preferences, it overpowers them. Moral duty must be confined to considerations of the form: What are the universal obligations of all persons in similar circumstances? The moral quality of an act is determined by the principle to which the will consciously assents. Moral obligations are not hypothetical, dependent on individual circumstances, but categorical, universally binding on all rational beings.

Kant characterized moral duty as acting on the principle of acting on principle and identified the universal command that infuses all moral obliga-tions, which he called the categorical imperative: Act as if the maxim of thy action were to become a universal law of nature.

As rational creatures capable of goodness, we belong to what Kant called the kingdom of ends. Because we can reason, we have intrinsic worth, we are ends-in-ourselves, not mere means to other ends. A special formulation of the categorical imperative acknowledges this worth: Act in such a way that you always treat humanity, whether in your own person or in the person of another, never simply as a means but always at the same time as an end.

STUDY QUESTIONS

1. Briefly explain how Kant completed the epistemological turn.

2. Identify and discuss one or two major Enlightenment themes and their relationship to Kant's philosophy.

3. What did Kant mean by "a scandal in philosophy"?

4. Briefly explain Hume's significance to Kant.

5. What was Kant's "Copernican revolution in philosophy"?

6. What is critical philosophy?

7. Distinguish between phenomena and noumena. Give examples of each.

8. Why did Kant think it necessary to posit the existence of the noumenal world?

9. How does Kant answer Hume's bundle theory of the self? Do you think he's successful? Explain.

10. What is practical reason?

11. Describe the moral dimension as Kant understood it.

12. Explain the reasoning behind Kant's efforts to make morality a matter of motives, not consequences.

13. Why does Kant claim that the only thing good in itself is a good will?

14. What does Kant mean by duty?

15. What is the categorical imperative? Apply it to one or two cases of your own choosing.

16. What is the practical imperative?

17. What is the kingdom of ends?

18. In what sense are Hume and Kant both Enlightenment thinkers? Compare and contrast their views of reason. Which view do you think is more realistic? Why?

CHAPTER FOURTEEN

The Utilitarian:

John Stuart Mill

If all mankind minus one were of one opinion, and only one person were of the contrary opinion, mankind would be no more justified in silencing that one person than he, if he had the power, would be justified in silencing mankind.

JOHN
STUART
MILL

Life requires choices. The more complex a society, the larger and more diverse its population, the more difficult those choices become. Two competing tendencies struggle to control the general direction of any society: a desire for change and progress, and a desire for security and order. To do justice to both tendencies, a free society must try to balance individual rights and freedoms with the general social welfare.

You may have driven or ridden to work or school today on a roadway carved through what used to be a family farm. Let's call this family the Malones. When the community decided to build a highway across that land, it probably first offered to buy the land. Such an offer is technically only a courtesy, for virtually every community in this country can appropriate private land—at a "fair market price"—under what is called the right of eminent domain. If the Malones refused to sell, perhaps because three generations of Malones had lived and died on that land, the community could simply force them to leave (and pay them the price it determined was fair).

It's easy to sympathize with the Malones. We can all imagine how we would feel in similar circumstances. Such a use of government power seems almost un-American. In fact, however, it represents an application of one of the basic philosophical principles our society rests on. The principle is that individual rights and desires should be protected, but that ultimately the good of the majority must take precedence over the good for any individual. This is a tricky, difficult balance to reach. Granting our sympathy for the Malones, how can the desires of one family outweigh so much good for so many others? Whether the Malones like it or not, their displeasure is a small price to pay for so much happiness for so many people.

The same kind of reasoning, stated or not, is the foundation of laws restricting what you can do with your property. The "greatest-happiness principle" limits when your neighbors can run their loud leaf blowers. It prevents you from refusing to rent apartments in a building you own to people of races, sexes, or ages you don't like. In certain cases, we easily understand, accept, and favor this reasoning.

The greatest-happiness principle is a more sophisticated, modern version of hedonism (Chapter 8). First presented in its new form by the British philosopher Jeremy Bentham, it was modified and refined by John Stuart Mill as *utilitarianism*. From the moment Bentham's work became known, utilitarianism has been an influential moral and social philosophy.

JEREMY BENTHAM

Jeremy Bentham (1748–1832) was a child prodigy. He reportedly read an eight-volume history of England at age three, and at four he studied Latin grammar. He entered Oxford at twelve

I would have the dearest friend I have to know that his interests, if they come in competition with those of the public, are as nothing to me. Thus I would serve my friends—thus I would be served by them.
Jeremy Bentham

Jeremy Bentham

and received his bachelor of arts degree. After graduating, he studied law at Lincoln's Inn to please his father, but chose not to become a lawyer because the confusion and abstraction of the law offended him.

In December 1763, Bentham heard a lecture by the great British legal scholar Sir William Blackstone. Blackstone's "fallacy regarding natural rights" especially offended him, and the admiration with which Blackstone's cloudy reasoning was greeted by others frightened him. Bentham saw how the legal and political professions used abstractions about honor, duty, power, right, "natural rights," and so on, as clubs to oppress those beneath them in the social order. He called such obtuse abstractions "nonsense on stilts" and concluded that legal reform would be a long time coming. Thus was born in him a passion to bring reason, empirical evidence, consistency, and compassion to British law and society.

Bentham began to argue in favor of a natural, empirical ethic that would base both the law and individual conduct on the best interests of the whole community rather than on the desires of the elite classes. As a result, he made enemies among the most powerful, entrenched members of society: the church, the aristocracy, the legal profession, Parliament, the wealthy manufacturers.

Have I a genius for anything? What can I produce? . . . What, of all earthly pursuits, is the most important? Legislation. Have I a genius for legislation? I gave myself the answer, fearfully and tremblingly: "Yes."

Jeremy Bentham

The Malthusian Universe

The advent of efficient steam and water power made large factories practical. Cloth weaving, for example, had once been a cottage industry, but the textile mills rendered handwoven fabrics too expensive. Hordes of workers sought jobs in the mill towns, creating large urban slums. Between 1800 and 1831, Leeds, Sheffield, Manchester, and Liverpool nearly doubled in population. Shabbily constructed buildings rented at such high prices that they paid for themselves in five years. Of course, such high rents resulted in overcrowding, as poorly paid workers lived two and three families to an apartment. In Manchester in 1845, for example, twenty-seven cases were documented of up to seven people trying to sleep in one bed.[1]

In 1798, **Thomas Malthus (1766–1834)**, an Anglican minister, published a work titled *An Essay on the Principle of Population as It Affects the Future Improvement of Society*. In it, Malthus expressed grave doubts about the feasibility of social reform:

> I have read some . . . speculations, on the perfectibility of men and society, with great pleasure. I have been warmed and delighted with the enchanting picture which they hold forth. I ardently wish for such happy improvements. But I see great and, to my understanding, unconquerable difficulties in the way to them.[2]

The "great difficulties" Malthus feared were overpopulation and underproduction of food. He argued that although food production increases arithmetically (1 to 2 to 3 to 4 to 5 to 6, etc.), unchecked population growth progresses geometrically (1 to 2 to 4 to 8 to 16 to 32, etc.). Thus, according to Malthus, unchecked population inevitably outgrows the food supply.

Troubled both by the growing slums in the cities and by efforts to improve living conditions for the poor, Malthus concluded that there could be no justification for helping the disadvantaged. Raising wages would only enable the poor to marry younger and have even more children; population would outgrow food supply and poverty would return anyway. Welfare programs would only result in increased "idleness" and encourage large families—with the same result.

Malthus argued that the only way to avoid such harsh natural cures as epidemics and the historical cure of war or rebellion was to stop helping the poor and remove all restraints on the free enterprise system. Buyers, sellers, bosses, workers, and owners must be left to their own struggle. The law of supply and demand would make it more difficult for the poor to afford to marry early or support very many children, thereby checking the geometrical rise of population.

PHILOSOPHICAL QUERY

Think carefully about Malthus's argument. Can you think of any current evidence to support Malthus's view? Can you think of any evidence against it?

The conservative British ruling class eagerly embraced Malthusian principles. Factory owners and businessmen were able to justify low wages as their "duty." The evils of the Industrial Revolution could be rationalized away by blaming the miserable living and working conditions of the poor on the poor themselves. And certainly these conditions were discouraging.

In this context, Bentham's insistence that legislators take into account the greatest happiness of the greatest number of people can be seen as the radical philosophy it was. It directly threatened and challenged the owners, bosses, and the ruling classes: If "each counts as one and none more," privileges of class, wealth, and title lose their force. Bentham blasted those in power for pursuing their own narrow, socially destructive goals instead of wanting the greatest happiness for the greatest number. (Once again, we see how philosophy can be dangerous.)

Bentham's solution was to broaden the base of those in power—to establish democratic rule by the whole people, not a select class. If "the rulers are the people," the greatest-happiness principle will be followed almost naturally, Bentham reasoned. He believed "all government is in itself evil"; the only justification for government is to prevent worse evils. Thus the functions of government were social reform and establishment of the conditions most conducive to promoting the greatest happiness for the greatest number of people. This proved to be a nearly irresistible philosophy for many.

It is clear that any society where the means of subsistence increase less rapidly than the numbers of the population is a society on the brink of an abyss. . . . Destitution is fearfully prolific.

M. Louis Blanc

PHILOSOPHICAL QUERY

Research the arguments surrounding the debate over national health care. How does the "greatest happiness" figure into this issue? Does one group favor "greatest happiness" reasoning or do all groups? Discuss.

Bentham's Legacy

Bentham's *Introduction to Principles of Morals and Legislation*, published in 1789, was fairly popular, considering that it is awkwardly constructed, antagonistic to the book-buying classes, and secular in tone. The French were so taken by it that they made Bentham a French citizen in 1792, and leaders and scholars from throughout Europe wrote to him. In England, by contrast, his materialistic philosophy was condemned as unpatriotic and un-Christian. His use of the term *utility* was misunderstood to mean dull, unadorned, unattractive. He was incorrectly seen as advocating a cold, calculating philosophy in which family relationships and altruism were reduced to mechanical considerations. But his great successor, John Stuart Mill, recognized that Bentham's real importance lay in the foundation he set for a new way of dealing with social ethics and in the improvements he helped bring about in the general condition of Britain's working poor. Mill says

> the changes which have been made, and the greater changes which will be made, in our institutions, are not the work of philosophers, but of the interests and instincts of large portions of society recently grown in strength. But Bentham gave voice to those interests and instincts: until he spoke out, those who found our institutions unsuited to them did not dare to say so, did not dare to think so.[3]

True to his philosophy even in death, Bentham found a way to make his corpse useful to "the greatest number possible." He willed that he be dissected in front of his friends, providing them with knowledge. He left his entire estate to the University of London on the condition that "he" be present at all board of governors meetings. His cranium was filled and a wax head constructed from it, and his stuffed body, attired in a favorite outfit, sits upright in a glass case at the university, waiting for the next board meeting. (His actual head resides between his feet, preserved using methods similar to those of Amazonian headhunters.)

SIMPLE UTILITARIANISM

Much of nineteenth-century philosophy was a response to Kant's work, but with the notable exceptions of G. W. F. Hegel and Arthur Schopenhauer, most philosophers rejected both Kant's

Judgment is given to men that they may use it. Because it may be used erroneously, are men to be told that they ought not to use it at all?

John Stuart Mill

*Morality, the science of
human happiness, [is]
the principle which binds
the individual to the species,
and the inducements which
are calculated to persuade us
to model our conduct on the
way most conducive to the
advantage of all.*
William Godwin

elaborate systems and his transcendental metaphysics. They viewed meta-physics as cumbersome, irrelevant, and meaningless, unverifiable by science and unclear according to the empirical criterion of meaning (see Chapter 12). Philosophers' interest shifted from the search for transcendental truth or systemic coherence to practical remedies for the pressing problems of society. They explored social and political philosophy, empirically based ethics, and the application of scientific knowledge and thinking to immediate problems of human happiness.

Predictably, this secular, fact-oriented approach revived belief in the cultural relativity of values and beliefs. Philosophers no longer felt obliged to produce elaborate theories or systems, since they thought even their own theories had to be culturally limited. By contrast, particular strategies and factual information were thought to be reliable, provided they were "scientific" and "objective."

Moreover, the new scientific view of an evolving universe made elaborate metaphysical theories seem irrelevant. If the universe and everything in it is slowly changing, then any fixed "grand theory" would apply for only a brief time at best. Growing belief in evolution resulted in efforts to identify an evolutionary view of ideas, as opposed to a search for *the* static truth.

Lastly, the social change and turmoil generated by the Industrial Revolution, the French Revolution, and the Napoleonic Wars cast serious doubts on the adequacy of Kant's ethic of *motives*. Looking about them, philosophers noted that *what actually happens to people* is of supreme importance. A clear need for fact-based, humanistic reform emerged.

Science became the new hope, replacing Enlightenment conceptions of reason. Empirical awareness of the social, physical, and emotional factors of acting and deciding created a desire to identify and alter the actual causes of poverty, crime, ignorance, and other sources of widespread misery. Social and political issues eventually dominated metaphysical concerns. Epistemology was important only to the extent that it related to verifiable, immediate improvements in society. If the Enlightenment was the Age of Reason, the nineteenth century began as the Age of Reform. (How it ended is another story.)

The Principle of Utility

Bentham attempted to base his philosophy on careful consideration and observation of social conditions and actual human behavior. In other words, he looked in exactly the opposite direction from Kant, who would have dismissed Bentham's work as "anthropology," not moral philosophy. This is not likely to have distressed Bentham, since he was deliberately trying to avoid the errors of ungrounded metaphysics and construct a scientific system.

Bentham declared that careful observation of actual behavior makes it crystal clear that pain and pleasure shape all human activity. As he says in the famous opening passage of *An Introduction to Principles of Morals and Legislation*:

I. Nature has placed mankind under the governance of two sovereign masters, *pain* and *pleasure*. It is for them alone to point out what we ought to do, as well as determine what we shall do. On the one hand the standard of right and wrong, on the other the chain of causes and effects, are fastened to their throne. They govern us in all we do, in all we say, in all we think: every effort we can make to throw off our subjection will serve but to demonstrate and confirm it. In words man pretends to abjure their empire; but in reality he will remain subject to it all the while. The *principle of utility* recognizes this subjection and assumes it for the foundation of that system, the object of which is to rear the fabric of felicity by the hands of reason and of law. Systems which attempt to question it deal in sounds instead of sense, in caprice instead of reason, in darkness instead of light.[4]

It is vain to talk of the interest of the community, without understanding what is in the interest of the individual. A thing is said to promote the interest, or to be for the interest, of an individual when it tends to add to the sum total of his pleasures; or, what comes to the same thing, to diminish the sum total of his pains.

Jeremy Bentham

Bentham is both a psychological hedonist (pain and pleasure "determine what we shall do") and an ethical hedonist (pain and pleasure "alone . . . out what we ought to do"). Thus the principle of utility is also referred to as the *pleasure principle*.

The term *utility* has two related meanings. A thing's utility refers to its usefulness, to how well it performs its specific function. In this sense, a utilitarian automobile would have blackwall tires and only the most practical accessories like rear window defrosters or anti-lock brakes. Although this no-frills notion of utility enters into Bentham's meaning, he uses the term to mean *pleasure-producing or pain-avoiding*. We might simplify that to *pleasure-maximizing*—if we keep in mind that sometimes the best we can do to maximize pleasure is minimize pain. Bentham says:

> III. By utility is meant that property in any object, whereby it tends to produce benefit, advantage, pleasure, good, or happiness (all this in the present case comes to the same thing) or (what comes again to the same thing) to prevent the happening of mischief, pain, evil, or unhappiness to the party whose interest is considered: if that party be the community in general, then the happiness of the community; if a particular individual, then the happiness of that individual.[5]

Having asserted both ethical and psychological hedonism and described what he means by utility, Bentham made a move that revolutionized the concept of hedonism. He enlarged the ethical interests of the hedonist. And since he thought we are all hedonists whether we know it or not, this amounted to enlarging everyone's general ethical obligation:

> VI. An action may be said to be conformable to the principle of utility, or, for shortness sake, to utility (meaning with respect to the community at large) when the tendency it has to

augment the happiness of the community is greater than any it has to diminish it.[6]

PRINCIPLE OF UTILITY
Always act to promote the greatest happiness for the greatest number.

In this statement we have a basic formulation of the **principle of utility:** *Act always to promote the greatest happiness for the greatest number.* In Bentham's hands, hedonism became an influential social and ethical philosophy.

Although John Stuart Mill coined the term *utilitarianism*, philosophers sometimes refer to Bentham's philosophy as utilitarianism, also. To avoid confusion, we'll refer to Bentham's as *simple utilitarianism*, to distinguish it from Mill's more refined and elaborate version, which we'll refer to as *utilitarianism*.

The Hedonic Calculus

This, then, is our Bentham. He was a man both of remarkable endowments for philosophy, and of remarkable deficiencies for it: fitted, beyond almost any man, for drawing from his premises conclusions not only correct, but sufficiently precise and specific to be practical: but whose general conception of human nature and life furnished him with an unusually slender stock of premises.
John Stuart Mill

Bentham wanted to make ethics a science. To that end, he tried to base his philosophy on observations of actual conditions and to derive principles of behavior from facts. Bentham thought he had found a scientific way to calculate the precisely proper course of action for any circumstance. He called his technique the hedonic calculus. Mill sometimes referred to the calculus as Bentham's "method of detail," because it took a detailed look at various factors.

To introduce mathematical precision to the difficult task of weighing alternative courses of action, Bentham proposed the notion of "units" of pleasure or pain, which he called *hedons* or *lots*. (Some contemporary philosophers use the term *utiles*.) Thus, when contemplating an action, we add units of pleasure or subtract units of pain.

But actions are complex, and Bentham identified four elements that affect pleasure or pain themselves, two that affect action related to pleasure or pain, and one based on the number of people affected. The seven elements are:

1. *Intensity.* How strong is the pleasure?
2. *Duration.* How long will the pleasure last?
3. *Propinquity.* How soon will the pleasure occur?
4. *Certainty.* How likely or unlikely is it that the pleasure will occur?
5. *Fecundity.* How likely is it that the proposed action will produce more pleasure?
6. *Purity.* Will there be any pain accompanying the action?
7. *Extent.* How many other people will be affected?

Positive units of pleasure or negative units of pain can be attached to each of these seven elements. The resulting totals can then be compared, and if the balance is on the positive (pleasure) side, the proposed choice is good; if the balance is on the negative side (pain), the choice is bad. If a hedonic calculation results in more units of pleasure, we should perform the contemplated action; if more units of pain, we should not. Bentham says:

Take an account of the *number* of persons whose interests appear to be concerned; and repeat the above process with respect to each. *Sum up* the numbers expressive of the degrees of *good* tendency which the act has, with respect to each individual [to whom the balance is good] . . . do this again with respect to each individual, in regard to whom the tendency of it is *bad* upon the whole. Take the *balance*; which, if on the side of *pleasure*, will give the general *good tendency* of the act, with respect to the total number or community of individuals concerned; if on the side of pain, the general *evil tendency*, with respect to the same community.[7]

Bentham believed each of us already uses hedonic calculation on a commonsense, intuitive level; in his view, he was simply adding scientific rigor to our various informal methods of choosing pleasure and avoiding pain.

PHILOSOPHICAL QUERY

Apply the hedonic calculus to one or two decisions from your own experience. Does it work? That is, does it reflect the basic criteria you use when contemplating competing courses of action? Discuss its strengths and weaknesses.

The Egoistic Foundation of Social Concern

Bentham believed psychological egoism is natural and universal. Psychological egoism asserts that it is human nature for each of us to be interested chiefly in our own welfare. All decisions are made in terms of furthering or hindering what we want or need.

In hedonistic terms, my chief concern is my own pleasure or pain. That's not to say I don't care about anyone or anything else, but my caring is defined by how those things affect my feelings. Those I love give me pleasure, which is in my interest. Those I hate cause me pain, which is not in my interest. To those who cause me neither pain nor pleasure, I am indifferent.

Because by our psychological makeup we *must* always seek pleasure or avoid pain, all values and value systems are pleasure/pain based. Regardless of their terminology, all ethical systems attempt to produce pleasure. They may speak of right and wrong, good and bad, and so forth, but these terms all reduce to pleasure and pain. Reason is simply a tool whose function is to help determine the most likely consequences of our actions in terms of pain and pleasure. (Note how significantly this pragmatic, calculating concept of reason contrasts with Kant's metaphysical concept.)

Bentham thought that if people could be shown how a better society for others will result in less pain and more pleasure for *them*, genuine social reform would occur. Our natural self-interest provides an *egoistic hook* to show how our individual welfare is inseparable from social welfare. Thus the proper role of government must be to ensure that the *enlightened self-interest* of each

Overcome, you higher men, the petty virtues, the petty prudences, the sand–grain discretion, the ant–swarm inanity, the miserable ease, the "happiness of the greatest number!"
Friedrich Nietzsche

The utilitarian standard . . . is not the agent's own greatest happiness, but the greatest amount of happiness altogether, and if it may possibly be doubted whether a noble character is always the happier for its nobleness, there can be no doubt that it makes other people happier, and that the world in general is immensely a gainer by it. Utilitarianism, therefore, could only attain its end by the general cultivation of nobleness of character.

John Stuart Mill

individual is allowed to develop. Further, to promote the greatest possible happiness for the greatest number, laws and regulations must be fair and effective, and designed to motivate people to consider others' welfare as well as their own.

Bentham and other liberal, laissez-faire reformers made a stunning connection between the welfare of the individual and the welfare of the community. They attempted to *show* how clear-thinking "selfishness" could produce a better world. Rather than chastise us for being self-interested, Bentham sought to take advantage of it.

Let's examine Bentham's egoistic hook by considering an actual issue. During a heated debate over a severe cut in tax money available for schools, a number of letters to the editor of a local newspaper made this basic point: "I have paid my dues. My children are grown and I've paid taxes for years. Why should I pay to send someone else's children to school? Let their families pay." Such letters reflect a disappointing lack of enlightened self-interest. It is in every individual's self-interest—even individuals who don't have children themselves—to see that all children get a good education. Poorly educated people are much more likely to be unemployed or dependent on government assistance for survival than adequately educated ones. Moreover, if poorly educated people turn to crime for survival, the rest of us will have to live in fear and to pay for more judges, district attorneys, police officers, and jails; we'll see a general decline in our own social services. Thus it is clearly in every individual's interest for as many children as possible to grow up to be well-educated, productive members of society.

Bentham's move was motivationally brilliant. In one fell swoop he found a way to link individual self-interest and the good of the community. Egoistic utilitarian logic is concrete and practical, based on everyday concerns and foreseeable consequences. We need not be able to reason abstractly to understand the basic wisdom of the greatest-happiness principle.

But such reasoning, though effective, remains egoistic and potentially destructive, for whatever sense of community it creates is based chiefly on selfish concerns, not compassion or empathy. The full force of utilitarianism did not emerge until Mill went beyond Bentham to produce a more refined altruistic utilitarianism.

John Stuart Mill

PHILOSOPHICAL QUERY

Are you convinced by Bentham's reasoning? Do you think many people are? Discuss.

JOHN STUART MILL

John Stuart Mill (1806–1873), one of the most brilliant, interesting figures in philosophy, and in effect, the "son of utilitarianism," began life with nearly equal doses of favor and misfortune.

A lucid defender of individual liberty, his childhood was severely restricted, his emotional needs virtually ignored.

Mill's parents were estranged—in his words, living "as far apart, under the same roof, as the north pole from the south." Mill's contemporary biographer, A. Bain, described his father, James Mill, as unfeeling:

> Even in his most amiable moods, he was not a man to be trifled with. His entering the room where the family was assembled was observed by strangers to operate as an immediate damper. This was not the worst. The one really disagreeable trait in [James] Mill's character, and the thing that has left the most painful memories, was the way he allowed himself to speak and behave to his wife and children before visitors.[8]

James Mill believed that the best way to love his children was by identifying and prohibiting their "vices."[9]

Few but those whose mind is a moral blank, could bear to lay out their course of life on the plan of paying no regard to others except so far as their own private interest compels.
John Stuart Mill

The Experiment

John Stuart Mill's destiny was sealed when Jeremy Bentham befriended his father, who was one of Bentham's younger disciples. John Stuart later said his father was influential in shaping Bentham's version of utilitarianism.

From Bentham, James Mill came to believe that all minds are the same at birth. Thus proper education—begun early enough—would produce a healthy, rational child. The two of them decided to use little John Stuart to show just how effective Bentham's ideas were. They gave him a rigorous education, carefully planned to produce a champion of utilitarianism.

Basing their program in part on Bentham's own experiences as a child prodigy, the experimenters saw to it that John Stuart learned Greek and arithmetic at three, Latin, geometry, and algebra at eleven, and logic and philosophy at twelve. Though not everything went smoothly (young John Stuart had some trouble with Plato's *Theaetetus*), he was such a whiz at math that he had to teach himself once he had surpassed his father's abilities.[10] In an effort to refine John Stuart's thinking and to prevent "the mere cramming of the memory," James Mill forced him to try and learn everything for himself before James would even consider explaining it.

> Most boys or youths who have had much knowledge drilled into them have their mental capacities not strengthened, but overlaid by it. They are crammed with mere facts, with the opinions and phrases of other people, and these are accepted as a substitute for the power to form opinions of their own; and thus the sons of eminent fathers, who have spared no pains in their education, so often grow up mere parroters of what they have learnt, incapable of using their minds except in the furrows traced for them. Mine . . . was not an education

of cram. My father never permitted anything that I had learnt to degenerate into a mere exercise of memory. He strove to make the understanding not only go along with every step of teaching, but, if possible, precede it. Anything which could be found out by thinking, I never was told, until I had exhausted my efforts to find it out for myself.[11]

Because of his ultimate brilliance, John Stuart Mill's education has been viewed as a testimony to the power of education itself. Bentham and James Mill produced not just a champion of utilitarianism, but a true genius. John Stuart Mill said his education gave him a quarter of a century advantage over others his age—but added that any average, healthy boy or girl could achieve the same results with the same training.[12] The personal cost, however, was high: Mill's education robbed him of his childhood. His father's strict control, though typical of the time, nonetheless stifled any expression of emotion or spontaneity.

I was so much accustomed to expect to be told what to do, either in the form of direct command or of rebuke for not doing it, that I acquired a habit of leaving my responsibility as a moral agent to rest on my father, my conscience never speaking to me except by his voice.[13]

Later, a friend would say of Mill, "He had never played with boys; in his life he never knew any."[14]

In an early version of his *Autobiography*, Mill said: "Mine was not an education of love but of fear. . . . My father's children neither loved him, nor, with any warmth of affection, anyone else."[15] This is not true of Mill himself, for as we'll see, Mill dearly loved one woman his entire adult life.

Mill's Crisis

When he was twenty, Mill began to pay the high price of his hothouse education in earnest with a depression or breakdown he described as a "dry heavy dejection."

In the golden rule of Jesus of Nazareth, we read the complete spirit of the ethics of utility.
John Stuart Mill

I was in a dull state of nerves, such as everybody is occasionally liable to, one of those moods when what is pleasure at other times becomes insipid or indifferent; the state, I should think, in which converts to Methodism usually are when smitten by their first "conviction of sin." I seemed to have nothing left to live for. At first I hoped that the cloud would pass away of itself; but it did not. A night's sleep, the sovereign remedy for the smaller vexations of life, had no effect upon it. In vain I sought relief from my favourite books, those memorials of past nobleness and greatness from which I had always hitherto drawn strength and animation. I read them now without feeling, or with the accustomed feeling *minus* all its charm; and I became persuaded that my love of mankind, and of excellence for its own sake, had worn itself out.[16]

Mill blamed the strict, critical, analytic environment he was raised in for robbing him of his feelings by insisting that only facts and reasons, only the objective, mattered. But a finely honed analytic mind, unaided by emotion, cannot provide life with meaning:

> I was . . . left stranded at the commencement of my voyage, with a well equipped ship and rudder, but no sail; without any real desire for the ends which I had been so carefully fitted out to work for; no delight in virtue or the general good, but also just as little in anything else.[17]

Mill was eventually able to pull himself out of his depression and begin the process of becoming a more integrated person by studying music and Romantic poetry. After reading a passage about the way a father's death affected his son in the memoirs of a French writer, Mill had an emotional catharsis:

> A vivid conception of the scene and its feelings came over me, and I was moved to tears. From this moment my burthen grew lighter. The oppression of the thought that all feeling was dead within me was gone. I was no longer hopeless: I was not stock or stone.[18]

The catharsis broke the stranglehold Bentham and his father had maintained for so long. Finally open to a wider range of experience, aided by his superior intellect, Mill developed an insight into the human condition fuller and deeper than his two teachers knew. Although he had bouts of depression for the rest of his life, and although he is reported to have remained rather serious, John Stuart Mill became a compassionate champion of the oppressed and a brilliant defender of classical liberal principles.

Redemption and Balance

Mill's rigid training was also balanced and softened by his remarkable relationship with Harriet Taylor. The couple fell in love when Mill was twenty-four. Harriet was married to a merchant quite a bit older than she and much more conservative in his interests. The relationship began with discussions of Mill's writings and Harriet's plans (she wanted to be a writer also). As Mill began to spend all his free time at the Taylors' house, it eventually became obvious to Harriet's husband that the relationship was more than simple friendship.

Harriet's husband and some of Mill's friends advised the couple to end their relationship. Instead, they became more discreet about appearing in public. Ultimately an arrangement was worked out so that Mill could stay with Mrs. Taylor when her husband was away, and she could stay with him during the summer and on weekends. This arrangement lasted over fifteen years. Two years after Harriet's husband died, she and Mill were finally married. After seven years of marriage, Harriet Taylor Mill died suddenly, while the couple were in Avignon. A grieving Mill said, "The spring of my life is broken."

Mill credited his wife with influencing his work for the better, saying:

> What was abstract and purely scientific was generally mine; the properly human element came from her: in all that concerned the application of philosophy to the exigencies of human society and progress, I was her pupil. . . . Her mind invested all ideas in a concrete shape, and formed to itself a conception of how they would actually work: and her knowledge of the existing feelings and conduct of mankind was so seldom at fault that the weak point of any unworkable suggestion seldom escaped her.[19]

Others who knew them both suggested that Mill's vision of Harriet was more loving than it was objective. There may be some truth to that, but there can be no doubt that her relationship with Mill was beneficial and encouraging. Mill insisted that Harriet gave him a better sense of what truly mattered— and what did not—than he had on his own.

Mill's richer, fuller, and therefore *more useful* expression of utilitarianism clearly owes a major debt to his crisis and to his relationship with Harriet, to poetry, and to music. The emotional restrictions imposed by both Bentham and James Mill limited simple utilitarianism in much the same way that John Stuart Mill was emotionally blocked until his life opened up. As John Stuart Mill wrote of Bentham:

> He never knew prosperity and adversity: he never had even the experiences which sickness gives; he lived from childhood to the age of eighty-five in boyish health. He knew no dejection, no heaviness of heart. He never felt life a sore and weary burthen. He was a boy to the last. . . . Self-consciousness . . . never was awakened in him. How much of human nature slumbered in him, he knew not, neither can we know. . . . His own lot was cast in a generation of the leanest and barrenest men whom England had ever produced; and he was an old man before a better race came in with the present century. He saw accordingly in man little but what the vulgarest eye can see. . . . Man is never recognized by him as a being capable of pursuing perfection as an end. . . .[20]

Even so, Mill saw Bentham as a positive force for good. Mill stood, as it were, on the shoulders of Bentham, and so saw much deeper into life. He acknowledged his debt to Bentham, and to his father, and paid it with interest by producing a philosophy more solid, more fully human than they could ever have imagined.

Altruism itself depends on a recognition of the reality of other persons, and on the equivalent capacity to regard oneself as merely one individual among many.

Thomas Nagel

We should seek the general happiness because it will make us happier. No doubt Mill, like many others, thought that this was true as it may well be. But this is not relevant. For utilitarianism is out to show that we ought to have regard for the interests of other people on moral grounds.

Jan Narveson

MILL ON WOMEN'S RIGHTS

As I have already said more than once, I consider it presumption in anyone to pretend to decide [what] women are or are not, can or cannot be, by natural constitution. They have always hitherto been kept, as far as regards spontaneous development, in so unnatural a state that their nature cannot but have been greatly distorted and disguised; and no one can safely pronounce that if women's nature were left to choose its direction as freely as men's, and if no artificial bent were attempted to be given to it except that required by the conditions of human society, and given to both sexes alike, there would be any material difference, or perhaps any difference at all, in the character and capacities which would unfold themselves.

John Stuart Mill
"The Subjection of Women," in *Human Worth*, eds. Richard Paul Janaro and Darwin E. Gearhart (New York: Holt, Rinehart & Winston, 1972), p. 53.

The Reformer

Mill's writing shows the breadth and balance he worked so hard to develop: *System of Logic* (1843), *Principles of Political Economy* (1848), *On Liberty* (1859), *Representative Government* (1861), *Utilitarianism* (1863), the posthumous *Autobiography* (1873), and *Three Essays on Religion* (1874). His "On the Logic of the Moral Sciences" has been described as "the most enduring essay on the method of the social sciences which has ever been written."[21]

In the last years of his life Mill continued to press for universal suffrage and social harmony. In 1865, a group of supporters asked Mill to stand for Parliament. Mill made a fascinating reply:

> I wrote, in reply to the offer, a letter for publication, saying that I had no personal wish to be a member of Parliament, that I thought a candidate ought neither to canvass nor to incur any expense, and that I could not consent to do either. I said further, that if elected, I could not undertake to give any of my time and labour to their local interest. I made known to them, among other things, my conviction (as I was bound to do, since I intended, if elected, to act on it), that women were entitled to representation in Parliament on the same terms as men.[22]

To everyone's surprise, including his own, Mill was elected and served in Parliament, where he proposed legislation to give the vote to all women who met the same conditions then required of men. The proposal was defeated, but his vigorous advocacy of women's rights led to what became the National Society for Women's Suffrage.

In 1873, a fatigued Mill and Harriet Taylor's daughter Helen, who cared for Mill after Harriet's death, went to Avignon, where Harriet had died so suddenly in 1858. After an especially strenuous day, Mill developed a high fever and died at sixty-seven on May 7, 1873. He was buried in Avignon beside his beloved Harriet. So ended the remarkable life of this most competent, archetypal utilitarian, John Stuart Mill, a lover of liberty and equality, reason and feeling, who worked tirelessly to improve the lot of all people.

REFINED UTILITARIANISM

Mill could not accept Bentham's version of hedonism, for Bentham leveled all pleasures. He did not assign higher importance to moral, intellectual, or emotional pleasures. His only criteria are those included in the hedonic calculus. All other factors being equal, for Bentham, the crucial difference between two pleasures is merely intensity. "Prejudice apart, the [child's] game of push-pin is of equal value with the arts and sciences of music and poetry. If the game of push-pin furnish more pleasure, it is more valuable than either."[23]

Bentham even referred to a "moral thermometer," implying that the only difference among various kinds of behavior was the "degree" of pleasure they produced. John Stuart Mill, who had been salvaged and made whole by music and poetry, knew better. He knew from personal experience that pleasures differ in *kind* as well as in *degree* and identified with the Epicurean hedonists: "There is no known Epicurean theory of life which does not assign the pleasures of the intellect, of the feelings and imagination, and of the moral sentiments, a much higher value as pleasure than those of mere sensation."[24] Thus Mill modified and interpreted the simple Benthamite utilitarianism he started with until it had become a much richer moral doctrine.

By introducing the notion of *quality* into utilitarianism, Mill refuted the orthodoxy he had been raised to defend. He dismissed Bentham's hedonic calculus as crude and unworkable, and appealed instead to a wider vision of human happiness based on a broader range of values. Most significant was Mill's declaration that all pleasures are not, in fact, equal.

In his analysis of this crucial issue, Mill offers a most persuasive solution to a timeless question we have encountered before: *Is there any way to prove that supposedly "enlightened" opinions and judgments are more than mere opinions?* Mill doesn't address the issue directly in terms of wisdom and enlightenment, but he does address the heart of this timeless question: *Is there an objective way to settle disagreements involving "levels" of knowledge and value disputes?*

Having inherited a dislike of abstract theories and systems, and having been trained as a social empiricist, Mill approached this ancient problem in a straightforward way. He included an objective component in the assessment of pleasure. His argument begins:

> If I am asked what I mean by difference of quality in pleasures, or what makes one pleasure more valuable than another merely as a pleasure, except its being greater in amount,

It is better to be a human being dissatisfied than a pig satisfied; better to be Socrates dissatisfied than a fool satisfied. And if the fool, or the pig, is of a different opinion, it is because they only know their own side of the question. The other party to the comparison knows both sides.

John Stuart Mill

there is but one possible answer. Of two pleasures, if there be one which all or almost all who have experience of both give a decided preference, irrespective of any feeling of moral obligation to prefer it, even though knowing it to be attended with a greater amount of discontent, and would not resign it for any quantity of the other pleasures which their nature is capable of, we are justified in ascribing to the preferred enjoyment a superiority in quality, so far outweighing quantity as to render it, in comparison, of small account.[25]

Man does not strive for pleasure, only the Englishman does.
Friedrich Nietzsche

In other words, only those fully acquainted with two pleasures can decide which, if either, is better. If there is no consensus among them, then there is no objective difference in quality, only difference in taste or preference.

For example, only people well enough versed in two (or more) kinds of music actually know if one is qualitatively better than another. This is a necessary, *empirical criterion*. Many of us can only (honestly) say, "I don't like such and such, but then I've never really tried to understand it." If we really want to compare various kinds of music, we must either listen widely and carefully or ask those who know a great deal about music. If a consensus exists among those familiar with the types being compared, then on Mill's criterion, we have discovered a qualitative difference. Of course, the same pattern applies to comparing the competing pleasures/values of reading Shakespeare or romance novels, playing basketball or playing checkers, and so on.

PHILOSOPHICAL QUERY

Can you identify any pleasures "which all or almost all who have experience of both give a decided preference, irrespective of any feeling of moral obligation to prefer it, even though knowing it to be attended with a greater amount of discontent, and would not resign it for any quantity of the other pleasures which their nature is capable of"? Discuss.

Higher Pleasures

Mill proceeds to argue that there are *empirical grounds* for asserting that what we might call "refined pleasures" are preferable to and hence better than the "cruder pleasures."

Now it is an unquestionable fact that those who are equally acquainted with, and equally capable of appreciating and enjoying, both, do give a most marked preference to the manner of existence which employs their higher faculties. Few human creatures would consent to be changed into any of the lower animals, for a promise of the fullest allowance of a beast's pleasures; no intelligent human being would consent to be a fool, no instructed person would be an ignoramus, no

Mill claimed that some pleasures are qualitatively better than others. Is there any objective way to compare the qualities of playing the cello with playing video games?

person of feeling and conscience would be selfish and base, even though they should be persuaded that the fool, the dunce, or the rascal is better satisfied with his lot than they are with theirs. They would not resign what they possess more than he for the most complete satisfaction of all the desires which they have in common with him. If they ever fancy they would, it is only in cases of unhappiness so extreme that to escape from it they would exchange their lot for almost any other, however undesirable in their own eyes. A being of higher faculties requires more to make him happy, is capable probably of more acute suffering, and certainly accessible to it at more points, than one of an inferior type; but in spite of these liabilities, he can never really wish to sink into what he feels to be a lower grade of existence.[26]

This is an interesting argument. Consider typical reactions to individuals with diminished mental or emotional capacities. We love and, perhaps, pity the mentally retarded, but we do not wish to join them. Techniques to control emotional disturbances by removing the possibility for emotion are properly seen as a last resort. Though we may jokingly claim that ignorance is bliss, few of us would consciously choose bliss if the price is ignorance.

Not everyone agrees with Mill that the "higher" faculties and their pleasures are superior, however. Many people live as if their values regarding pleasures are just the opposite from Mill's. Not only are their lives not devoted to the use and development of their higher faculties, they seem actively to discourage them. Why are the "higher" pleasures unpopular if they are objectively superior?

PHILOSOPHICAL QUERY

What would we make of someone who did choose ignorance? Could such a person be sane and rational? Reflect on the following: To be considered sane and rational, a person must recognize the value of both sanity and reason. If so, then by definition no sane or rational person can choose a radical diminishment of an essential capacity such as knowledge. What do you think of this argument?

Lower Pleasures

Mill argues that there is no inconsistency between an appreciation of the superiority of the higher pleasures and succumbing to the temptation of more easily secured lesser pleasures. He recognizes that character and experiences are major components of our judgment and behavior:

> Men often, from infirmity of character, make their election for the nearer good, though they know it to be the less valuable; and this no less when the choice is between two bodily pleasures than when it is between bodily and mental. They pursue sensual indulgences to the injury of health, though perfectly aware that health is the greater good. It may be further objected that many who begin with youthful enthusiasm for everything noble, as they advance in years sink into indolence and selfishness. But I do not believe that those who undergo this very common change voluntarily choose the lower description of pleasures in preference to the higher. I believe that before they devote themselves exclusively to the one, they have already become incapable of the other. Capacity for the nobler feelings is in most natures a very tender plant, easily killed, not only by hostile influences, but by mere want of sustenance; and in the majority of young persons it speedily dies away if the occupations to which their position in life has devoted them, and the society into which it has thrown them, are not favorable to keeping that higher capacity in exercise.

The joy of understanding is a sad joy, yet those who have once tasted it would not exchange it for all the frivolous gaieties and empty hopes of the vulgar herd.
Anatole France

Men lose their high aspirations as they lose their intellectual tastes, because they have not time or opportunity for indulging them; and they addict themselves to inferior pleasures not because they deliberately prefer them, but because they are either the only ones to which they have access or the only ones which they are any longer capable of enjoying. It may be questioned whether anyone who has remained equally susceptible to both classes of pleasures ever knowingly and calmly preferred the lower; though many, in all ages, have broken down in an ineffectual attempt to combine both.[27]

The bad part of [Bentham's] writings is his resolute denial of all that he does not see, of all truths but those which he recognizes.

John Stuart Mill

When Mill speaks of character, he refers to socially conditioned habits. Though there are always exceptions, consider the enormous social pressures that can interfere with nurturing "higher" sentiments: Can we reasonably expect children raised in extreme poverty, violence, turmoil, and instability to develop their higher faculties in school, if every afternoon they return to an empty apartment or social jungle? Can we reasonably expect working parents to find time to work extra hours, raise healthy children, maintain their homes, and *then* develop and nurture their own higher faculties? It often seems as if our lives and culture conspire against the full, continuing development of the nobler faculties. Check any major bookstore and discover the dwindling proportion of fine literature and nonfiction as compared to pulp fiction and tabloid, self-help nonfiction. Compare the numbers of people flocking to inane but easily understood movies with those trickling into museums or art houses. Bombarded on all sides by seductive chemicals and toys, fatigued from self-imposed and inescapable pressures, we find that the lure of philosophy or literature or poetry can pale beside the temptations of a new mountain bike, Spielberg movie, relationship, or basketball game.

If we grant, at least for now, that there are "nobler sentiments" and that many factors conspire to crush them, must we just accept things as they are? Mill answers with a hearty no. Having added the notion of quality to utilitarianism, he expands Bentham's appeal to enlightened self-interest into a full-fledged altruistic social philosophy.

PHILOSOPHICAL QUERY

How many students continue to read philosophy or literature after graduating from college? How many high school graduates continue to read a variety of books? Why don't more of us pursue "higher" purposes? Discuss.

ALTRUISM AND HAPPINESS

We have seen the general utilitarian connection between our own happiness and the happiness of others expressed in Bentham's conception of enlightened self-interest. Mill's argument is less

TO BE LOGICAL MEN SHOULD NOT BE SELFISH

It seems to me that we are driven to this, that logicality inexorably requires that our interests shall not be limited. They must not stop at our own fate, but must embrace the whole community. This community, again, must not be limited, but must extend to all races of beings with whom we can come into immediate or mediate intellectual relation. It must reach, however vaguely, beyond this geological epoch, beyond all bounds. He who would not sacrifice his own soul to save the whole world is, as it seems to me, illogical in all his inferences, collectively. Logic is rooted in the social principle.

To be logical men should not be selfish.

Charles Sanders Peirce
Collected Papers of Charles Sanders Peirce, vol. 2, eds. Charles Hartshorne and Paul Weiss (Cambridge, Mass.: Harvard University Press, 1931–35), p. 398.

problematic than Bentham's, because it is based on a more solid relationship between the individual and the group. Mill asserts that, ultimately, utilitarianism rests on "the social feelings of mankind; the desire to be in unity with our fellow creatures." **Altruism**, from the Latin *alter*, "other," is the capacity to promote the welfare of others; altruism stands in clear contrast to egoism. According to Mill's altruistic utilitarianism, no individual's self-interest is *more* or *less* important than any other's.

> I must again repeat, what the assailants of utilitarianism seldom have the justice to acknowledge, that the happiness which forms the utilitarian standard of what is right in conduct is not the agent's own happiness, but that of all concerned. As between his own happiness and that of others, utilitarianism requires him to be as strictly impartial as a disinterested and benevolent spectator.[28]

Mill wanted to show that as civilization advances, the social spirit grows. In the effort, he made an eloquent defense of the importance of universal education to general happiness.

For Mill, the function of education is twofold: to instill the skills and knowledge necessary for an individual to live well and productively, and to create healthy, altruistic citizens. But to fulfill the second mandate, education must become a lifelong activity. People must be given opportunities to grow as part of their daily lives. They must be given fulfilling work and sufficient leisure to nurture more than their belly or bank account. The heart of such reform efforts must be widespread, good education.

An excellent example of utilitarian reasoning can be found in a brief examination of the rationale behind school desegregation and busing, which caused so much controversy beginning with the civil rights movement of the 1950s and lasting into the 1970s. (See Chapter 19.) At the time, some

ALTRUISM
From Latin for "other"; the capacity to promote the welfare of others; opposed to egoism.

Mill argued that education must be a lifelong process, and that a complete education nurtures altruistic feelings. Events like this fund-raising "AIDS Walk" are educational and altruistic. They are also controversial. How might the greatest-happiness principle be used to address controversial issues like those related to AIDS?

What Mill obviously thought needed advocating is that people have regard for other people's happiness, i.e., the general happiness.
Jan Narveson

people argued for "separate but equal" schooling for black and white children. Close analysis of actual conditions showed that "separate but equal" was not possible, because most entirely black schools were in communities with inadequate tax bases to support good schools. Wealthier communities attracted the best teachers because they could offer better salaries, facilities, equipment, and teaching conditions.

Mill had pointed out that we must act from solid knowledge, not idealistic hopes. How could modern education reformers use empirical information to improve education for all children? The answer was surprisingly simple, though difficult for many to accept; it has yet to be fully implemented. The utilitarian solution was to take advantage of the self-interest of those parents with the most social and political influence. How could this be done? By sending *their children* to schools in other neighborhoods. The corollary to this, of course, involved busing black children to white schools.

What is utilitarian about this? Mill argued that we must be dispassionate, impartial spectators to everyone's interest, our own included. When I am not thinking exclusively of my own child, for example, it's clear that everyone is better off if all children go to good schools. But if I cannot or will not think dispassionately and objectively, I must be given *a personally effective motive*, an egoistic hook. One way to hook me is to send my child to an inferior school, so that my self-centered interest *in my own child* can be tapped to improve the school's quality, which would benefit other people's children as well. Even if many families resent integration, in the long run their unhappiness will be balanced against a greater good for society as a whole.

Until we all possess "nobler sentiments," we must perhaps be moved to act for the general good by such appeals to self-interest. Believing that *consequences* matter at least as much as motives, the utilitarian can be satisfied with getting me to help improve the school system even if I am coerced to do so by law. This kind of forced stretching of my concerns also falls under the heading of education.

Each person possesses an inviolability founded on justice that even the welfare of the society as a whole cannot override.

John Rawls

PHILOSOPHICAL QUERY

Identify and discuss one or two current issues in which this kind of utilitarian appeal to altruism through self-interest might be effective. Elaborate on your reasoning, and discuss some of the details involved in implementing your suggestions.

Selfishness and Contentment

Mill distinguished between what he called happiness and "mere contentment." Contentment, as Mill meant it, is the condition of animals and those unfortunate people limited to enjoying lower pleasures. A major purpose of Mill's utilitarianism is to make as many people as possible as *happy* as possible, not as *content* as possible. What, then, is happiness?

> The ultimate end, with reference to and for the sake of which all other things are desirable (whether we are considering our own good or that of other people), is an existence exempt as far as possible from pain, and as rich as possible in enjoyments, both in point of quantity and quality. . . . secured to all mankind; and not to them only, but so far as the nature of things admits, to the whole sentient creation.[29]

Mill argued that the principal cause of unhappiness is selfishness. He believed that happiness requires a balance between tranquillity and excitement, and selfishness robs us of both. It robs us of tranquillity because it is never satisfied, and it diminishes our possibilities for excitement (or stimulation) by narrowing our range of interests. Could that be why so many people seem to need artificial or extravagantly orchestrated excitement?

> When people who are tolerably fortunate in their outward lot do not find in life sufficient enjoyment to make it valuable to them, the cause generally is, caring for nobody but themselves. To those who have neither public nor private affections, the excitements of life are much curtailed, and in any case dwindle in value as the time approaches when all selfish interests must be terminated by death; while those who leave after

One of the great drawbacks to the self-centered passions is that they afford so little variety. The man who loves only himself cannot, it is true, be accused of promiscuity in his affections, but he is bound in the end to suffer intolerable boredom from the invariable sameness of the object of his devotion.

Bertrand Russell

them objects of personal affection, and especially those who have also cultivated a fellow-feeling with the collective interests of mankind, retain as lively an interest in life on the eve of death as in the vigor of youth and health.[30]

PHILOSOPHICAL QUERY

Discuss the preceding passage in light of your own experience. Can you make any connection between periods of boredom and extreme self-interest? If Mill is correct, how could a bored individual become an interested one?

"A Mind Is a Terrible Thing to Waste"

Mill says that next to selfishness, the principal cause of an inability to be happy for an extended period is a lack of mental cultivation.

> A cultivated mind (and I do not mean that of a philosopher, but any mind to which fountains of knowledge have been opened, and which has been taught, in any tolerable degree, to exercise its faculties) finds sources of inexhaustible interest in all that surrounds it; in the objects of nature, the achievements of art, the imaginations of poetry, the incidents of history, the ways of mankind, past and present, and their prospects in the future. It is possible, indeed, to become indifferent to all this, and that too without having exhausted a thousandth part of it; but only when one has had from the beginning no moral or human interests in these things, and has sought in them only the gratification of curiosity.[31]

What a powerful, beautifully written description of one of the greatest of all tragedies: a wasted mind. A mind that has not been sparked to life and taught to wonder is condemned to shallow, limited satisfactions, dependent on the world to entertain it, since it has no momentum of its own.

Besides reducing life to ceaseless attempts at short-lived stimulation, a chronically bored mind at its worst can undertake a self-destructive quest for thrills. This restless searching for "something to do" deprives us of opportunities to synthesize our experiences, to reflect on ourselves, our relationships, our values, and our goals. Hence chronic boredom interferes with personal growth and may even prevent it.

Mill was convinced that science and clear utilitarian thinking could produce a better environment, one conducive to altruism as well as the mental, emotional, and physical development and well-being of individuals.

Mill's Vision

Mill thought that no insurmountable reasons or conditions existed that would prevent the emergence of a truly healthy society.

A DIMINISHING PREOCCUPATION WITH MYSELF

Perhaps the best introduction to the philosophy which I wish to advocate will be a few words of autobiography. I was not born happy. As a child, my favorite hymn was: "Weary of earth and laden with sin." At the age of five, I reflected that, if I should live to be seventy, I had only endured, so far, a fourteenth part of my whole life, and I felt the long-spread-out boredom ahead of me to be almost unendurable. In adolescence, I hated life and was continually on the verge of suicide, from which, however, I was restrained by the desire to know more mathematics. Now, on the contrary, I enjoy life; I might almost say that with every year that passes, I enjoy it more. This is due partly to having discovered what were the things that I most desired, and having gradually acquired many of these things. Partly it is due to having successfully dismissed certain objects of desire—such as the acquisition of indubitable knowledge about something or other—as essentially unattainable. But very largely it is due to a diminishing preoccupation with myself.

Bertrand Russell
The Conquest of Happiness (New York: Liveright, 1958), quoted in Robert F. Davidson, *The Search for Meaning in Life* (New York: Holt, Rinehart & Winston, 1962), p. 86.

Genuine private affections, and a sincere interest in the public good, are possible, though in unequal degrees, to every rightly brought up human being. In a world in which there is so much to interest, so much to enjoy, and so much also to correct and improve, everyone who has this moderate amount of moral and intellectual requisites is capable of an existence which may be called enviable; and unless such a person, through bad laws, or subjection to the will of others, is denied the liberty to use the sources of happiness within his reach, he will not fail to find this enviable existence, if he escape the positive evils of life, the great sources of physical and mental suffering—such as indigence, disease, and the unkindness, worthlessness, or premature loss of objects of affection.[32]

The chief task, then, of all right-thinking, well-intentioned people is to address those causes of misfortune that can be avoided or altered.

From Mill's (and Bentham's) great concern for society, we have acquired the concept of public *utilities*, welfare and other forms of assistance for the poor, mandatory minimum education standards, and laws that are more humane. Mill showed how necessary liberty of thought and speech is for the general happiness, since we can determine the truth only by an ongoing clash of opinions. He worried about "the tyranny of the majority," and warned against the very great, and often ignored, dangers of assigning too much weight to majority beliefs.

The only part of the conduct of anyone for which he is amenable to society is that which concerns others. Over himself, over his own body and mind, the individual is sovereign.

John Stuart Mill

**Mill argued that, for
our own peace of mind,
we need to provide
social support for those
in need—because we
never know when *we*
will need help. The
quality of life without
general assistance
would diminish for all
of us, Mill insisted.**

In the end, Mill remained an optimist who believed that by applying
reason and good will, the vast majority of humankind could live with dignity, political and moral freedom, and harmonious happiness. He believed
that "the wisdom of society, combined with the good sense and providence
of individuals," could extinguish poverty completely, and that scientific progress along with "good physical and moral education" could alleviate the scourge
of disease.

*Dissent and dissenters have
no monopoly on freedom.
They must tolerate opposition. They must accept dissent
from their dissent.*
Abe Fortas

As for the vicissitudes of fortune, and other disappointments
connected with worldly circumstances, these are principally
the effect of either gross imprudence, of ill-regulated desires,
or of bad or imperfect social institutions. All these grand sources,
in short, of human suffering are in a great degree, many of
them almost entirely, conquerable by human care and effort;
and though their removal is grievously slow—though a long
succession of generations will perish in the breach before the
conquest is completed, and this world becomes all that, if will
and knowledge were not wanting, it might easily be made—
yet every mind sufficiently intelligent and generous to bear a
part, however small and inconspicuous, in the endeavor will
draw a noble enjoyment from the contest itself, which he

would not for any bribe in the form of selfish indulgence consent to be without.[33]

Mill's optimism is based on his view of a social human nature and a deep, nearly universal, sense of connectedness. It is a vision that sees no inevitable competition between my needs and yours, between ours and everyone else's:

> The deeply rooted conception which every individual even now has of himself as a social being tends to make him feel it is one of his natural wants that there should be harmony between his feeling and aims and those of his fellow creatures. If differences of opinion and mental culture make it impossible for him to share many of their actual feelings—perhaps make him denounce and defy those feelings—he still needs to be conscious that his real aim and theirs do not conflict; that he is not opposing himself to what they really wish for, namely, their own good, but is contrary, promoting it. . . . This conviction is the ultimate sanction of the greatest happiness morality.[34]

In so many ways, our lives, and those of people in many other countries, have directly benefited from the seed Jeremy Bentham and James Mill planted in John Stuart Mill, clearly the finest archetype of a utilitarian social reformer so far.

A votary of ahimsa *[nonviolence against all living things] cannot ascribe to the utilitarian formula (of the greatest good of the greatest number). He will strive for the greatest good of all and die in the attempt to realize the ideal. . . . The utilitarian to be logical will never sacrifice himself.*

Mohandas Gandhi

PHILOSOPHICAL QUERY

Do you share Mill's optimistic belief that "all these grand sources, in short, of human suffering are in a great degree, many of them almost entirely, conquerable by human care and effort"? Make a case for and against Mill. Which is more persuasive? Why?

COMMENTARY

Simple utilitarianism shares with other forms of hedonism the belief that human behavior does seem to be pleasure-seeking. But is that *all* it is, and, in any event, *should* it be? Should our hedonistic urges be encouraged, discouraged, ignored, or modified? The basic appeal of Bentham's utilitarianism is obvious. You may wish to review the basic objections to hedonism found in the Commentary to Chapter 8.

Bentham's failure to consider the quality of pleasures is, I think, a fatal flaw. Moreover, the hedonic calculus is arbitrary and subjective, not scientific, as Bentham claimed. It is also probably unworkable.

Yet Bentham's attempt to base a social ethic on facts, on how people actually behave, is important and ultimately effective. It saves both Bentham and Mill from Kant's tendency to stress motives at the expense of actual consequences. It also promises a more feasible moral code for the average person than Kant's, since it relies less on abstract reasoning and more on such common practices as calculation of self-interest and desire for basic, identifiable happiness. Bentham's brilliant attempt to show the link between self-interest and the happiness of the community foreshadows the collectivist thinking of Karl Marx (Chapter 15).

There can be no such thing as ethical science . . . ethical judgments are mere expressions of feeling, there can be no way of determining the validity of any ethical system.

A. J. Ayer

The difficulties with Mill's philosophy, as might be expected, are more subtle. He fails to completely resolve the tension between hedonism and altruism, though his "altruistic hedonism" is truly different from Bentham's egoistic hedonism—if indeed Mill's position is hedonism.

Mill's consideration of quality is important and necessary if utilitarianism is to be anything more than another appeal to pleasure. His attempts to rate the quality of pleasures factually by the judgment of those who have experienced them is intriguing, but probably cannot be empirically supported. After all, couldn't there be some people well versed in, say, both art movies and slasher movies who prefer the latter? It's tempting to say that the general public has low taste, but is this anything but the opinion of an educated, culturally conditioned elite? Marx will argue that philosophers like Mill—who by influence, intellect, and training is, after all, an aristocrat—reflect only the values of their class. This raises the question of whether Mill's distinction between "higher" and "lower" pleasures reflects an inbred cultural bias. Though important, that criticism can be made of any philosopher.

Contemporary moral philosophers have uncovered interesting and troubling problems with utilitarianism in general. These stem from the possibility that an emphasis on the greatest happiness of the greatest number can result in immoral actions. Suppose, for instance, that the vast majority (the greatest number) of a community derives great pleasure (the greatest happiness) from harassing a small minority? There seem to be no clearly utilitarian grounds on which to condemn them. If enough Nazis derive enough pleasure from exterminating a Jewish minority, aren't they thereby generating the greatest happiness of the greatest number?

Mill could argue (as he did, in effect, in his essay *On Liberty*) that the rights of minorities must be protected from "the tyranny of the majority," since everyone is likely to be in a minority on some issue. But that's a factual prediction. What if the present majority doesn't believe Mill, or care? Are there any strictly utilitarian grounds for preventing their exploitation of the minority?

Problems arise when we treat the principle of utility as a form of *averaging out* "units" of happiness. Is there no difference between a community of fifty persons in which one hundred units of pleasure are distributed among twenty people and another fifty-person community in which everybody has two units? In both cases the totality of pleasure remains the same. To what extent can inequity be tolerated? Can utilitarianism offer any solution to the question of how happiness is distributed?

THE "SAINT OF RATIONALISM"

When we look for intellectual guidance today with respect to the problems of freedom in communist societies, the exhaustion of the environment, and the pressure of population, Mill is the only sociologist of the nineteenth century whose pages are not discolored with the acid of bias. Others claiming to prefigure the law of history were obsessed by the demon of making history; Mill held to the more modest ethic of acting as circumstances allowed on behalf of human happiness. In so doing, the "saint of rationalism" held to the conception of scientific truth with an integrity which the prophet-ideologists never approached.

Lewis S. Feuer
"John Stuart Mill as a Sociologist: The Unwritten Ethology," in Mill, *On Socialism* (Buffalo: Prometheus Books, 1987), p. 43.

One way out of all these dilemmas might be to introduce a Kantian, *formalistic moral dimension* into ethical deliberations. Although Mill had a more thorough sense of psychology than Bentham expressed, both of them tend to simplify moral motives. As in other cases of efforts to be systematically "neat," utilitarianism overemphasizes one aspect of morality. Some balance between Kant and Mill seems more promising and useful than either alone. Just as there is more to right and wrong than rational motives, so too there is more than an empirical assessment of consequences.

Even if we know an action will result in the greatest possible happiness for the greatest number, we can—and should—still ask, "But is it *right*?" The fact that such a question is meaningful shows that morality must be based on more than just considerations of happiness, even the happiness of everybody. Goodness, as Kant showed, is not the same as happiness. Kant was correct in his belief that the moral dimension always includes more than just considerations of happiness. Yet he erred by overlooking the equally important fact that responsible moral evaluation always includes a reasonable assessment of the effects any action is likely to have on people's happiness. Indifference to our own or others' happiness violates the Kantian principle of dignity; but so does a strictly utilitarian exclusion of everything but considerations of happiness.

All that being so, Bentham and Mill have given us one of the most important ethical philosophies of the modern era. If we look beyond their philosophies, we see two diligent social reformers whose lives certainly transcended hedonism. Both lived altruistically. Both reaffirm the pursuit of wisdom in their efforts to make philosophy matter. And time after time, Mill's strongest arguments move well beyond strictly defined utilitarian principles. Without directly referring to wisdom, Mill's educational philosophy is nonetheless a call to wisdom.

Among the great social thinkers of the nineteenth century, Mill was the only one who failed to write a system encompassing the evolution of humanity. . . . Mill alone tried to do justice to all the competing drives and motives of human nature; he would never banish from his consciousness the many-sidedness and many-leveledness of social reality.

Lewis S. Feuer

Consider, in closing, the following passage from Mill's *Autobiography*. Referring to the time of his crisis, it reveals that early on, Mill's wisdom was deeper than his utilitarianism could accommodate. His monumental effort to remain true to the philosophical orthodoxy of his father and Bentham hampered his philosophical expression, yet his great intellect and deeply compassionate moral sense found a voice anyway. As philosophers, we are obligated to note Mill's inconsistencies. As human beings, we can acknowledge and honor his great struggle for—and ultimately brilliant statement of—a most compelling case for the virtues of education, community, liberty, women's rights, concern for the disadvantaged, and freedom of speech.

I never, indeed, wavered in the conviction that happiness is the test of all rules of conduct, and the end of life. But now I thought that this end was only to be attained by not making it the direct end. *Those only are happy (I thought) who have their minds fixed on some object other than their own happiness; on the happiness of others*, on the *improvement of mankind*, even on some art or pursuit, followed not as a means, but as itself an ideal end. *Aiming thus at something else, they find happiness by the way.* The enjoyments of life (such was now my theory) are sufficient to make it a pleasant thing, when they are taken *en passant*, without being made a principal object. Once make them so, and they are immediately felt to be insufficient. They will not bear a scrutinizing examination. Ask yourself whether you are happy, and you cease to be so. The only chance is to treat, not happiness, but some end external to it, as the purpose of life.[35]

SUMMARY OF MAIN POINTS

The manufacturing techniques of the Industrial Revolution produced a new class of working poor forced to live in crowded urban tenements clustered around plants and factories. In Britain, the great majority of workers had little protection and virtually no representation in Parliament. A reform movement arose to improve working conditions and the overall quality of life for all citizens.

Jeremy Bentham resurrected hedonism, adding a social component. He reasoned that if pleasure is good, more pleasure is better. This led him to introduce the greatest-happiness principle (also known as the principle of utility): That action is best which produces the greatest happiness for the greatest number. The greatest-happiness principle was a direct challenge to the conservative ruling class in Britain, since, according to Bentham, "each counts as one and none more," worker and owner.

Known today as simple utilitarianism, Bentham's philosophy was an attempt to avoid the errors of irrelevant metaphysical theories by basing moral and social policies on experience and scientific principles. Bentham's hedonic calculus was a crude method of reducing issues to simple calculation of units of pleasure versus units of pain.

Simple utilitarianism is based on *psychological egoism*, the belief that each of us is interested chiefly

in his or her own welfare. Bentham attempted to take advantage of egoism by using reason to show that each individual's welfare is ultimately dependent on the welfare of the community. The appeal to self-interest as a way of improving overall social conditions is known as the *egoistic hook*.

John Stuart Mill coined the term *utilitarianism* and refined Bentham's principle of utility by distinguishing between pleasures on the basis of quality as well as quantity. Mill's concept of happiness is more complex than Bentham's and extends beyond simple concern with pleasure.

Mill discovered an ingenious empirical method for settling disputes concerning the quality of two competing pleasures. He argued that only those familiar with both pleasures could compare them. Mill noted that there are empirical grounds for the superiority of refined pleasures to crude ones: Those familiar with both consistently prefer refined pleasures (philosophical speculation, classical mu-

sic, poetry) to crude pleasures (eat, drink, and be merry).

Mill disagreed with Bentham's insistence that all motives are egoistic and based his refined utilitarianism on "the social feelings" of all people for unity with each other. Mill believed in the possibility of altruism, the capacity to promote the welfare of others.

Mill argued that lack of altruistic feelings and ignorance of the higher pleasures were products of poor education and harsh conditions, not qualities of human nature. He advanced the cause of social reform by advocating a wider base of representation in Parliament, including women, and universal education aimed at producing well-rounded human beings. According to Mill, selfishness and lack of mental cultivation are the chief causes of unhappiness, and both can be cured with a proper education.

STUDY QUESTIONS

1. Identify and discuss some of the social and economic factors that influenced Bentham's development of simple utilitarianism.

2. What is "the Malthusian universe"?

3. Who were the Philosophical Radicals?

4. Characterize simple utilitarianism.

5. What is the hedonic calculus?

6. What is the method of detail?

7. What is the greatest-happiness principle?

8. Discuss the "egoistic hook" that Bentham discovered, and explain its significance to his philosophy.

9. Distinguish refined utilitarianism from simple utilitarianism.

10. In your own words, present Mill's basic argument for qualitative differences among pleasures. Then analyze it.

11. How does Mill account for the predominance of lower pleasures? Do you agree? Why?

12. Why is education so important to Mill?

13. Distinguish between happiness and contentment, according to Mill. Explain the importance of the distinction to his utilitarian philosophy.

14. Express Mill's vision in your own words.

15. Is Mill a utilitarian? Explain why the question is raised at all and then answer it based on your understanding of the issue.

16. Compare and contrast Bentham's notion of self-interest with Mill's.

17. Compare and contrast Mill's altruistic self-interest with Hume's notion of benevolence (Chapter 12).

The Materialist:
Karl Marx

The philosophers have only *interpreted* the world in various ways: the point is to *change* it.

KARL MARX

ave you ever really resented your job, or where you live, yet felt trapped by economic circumstances, unable to improve the basic conditions of your life? Or perhaps your education is uninspiring, something you feel pressured to do in order to get a good—or just an adequate—job? Most of us probably have felt such frustration occasionally. Sometimes, our lives seem to be controlled by our jobs and the need to earn a "decent living." It seems as if money determines everything.

During a discussion about youngsters selling cocaine, a twelve-year-old drug dealer explained that his father had long ago abandoned the family and left this boy, his mother, and two sisters to fend for themselves. The young dealer's economic logic was impressive: "I make four or five hundred dollars a day—tax free. Now my mother and sisters have nice clothes and food. We can go to a good doctor. How else could we do that? Nobody helped us before." How can we reasonably expect this boy to listen when we say "Go to school, study hard. Learn to delay gratification and someday you can get a decent job, and so on, and so on, and so on"? Economic reality is more powerful than such middle-class logic.

We have learned how Bentham and Mill hoped to reform society by applying the greatest-happiness principle and an empirically based social hedonism. Mill, especially, hoped that providing decent living conditions and better education would mean a juster, more humane world.

Mill and Bentham were not the only social reformers inspired by the great inequities of the nineteenth century's fast-moving industrialization, however. Reform movements under the general banners of socialism and communism spread throughout France and Germany. English socialists whose views differed from Bentham's and Mill's also contributed to the overall climate of social analysis and criticism. What all these reformers had in common was a clear sense of injustice and increasing inequality. Where they differed, and often significantly, was on the exact causes of and hence the proper remedies to improve the dismal living conditions of the poor and working classes.

Besides utilitarianism, another, more influential theory emerged at roughly the same time. We know it today as Marxism. The most influential philosopher in history, if we judge influence by the numbers of people attempting to live by a philosophy, is its founder, Karl Marx. The sheer social and political impact of Marxism warrants a careful look at it. But, as you will discover, *philosophical Marxism* is not at all what we usually think of as Marxism or communism—and it is not what today's Marxists or Communists practice either. Let us see, then, what philosophical Marxism is, and what has made it so attractive to so many people.

The very idea of distributive justice, or of any proportionality between success and merit, or between success and exertion, is in the present state of society so manifestly chimerical as to be relegated to the regions of romance.

John Stuart Mill

THE PROPHET

Karl Marx (1818–1883) was born in Trier, Germany. His father was a respected lawyer, and both parents were Jewish. Marx's father eventually distanced himself from the local Jewish community and changed the family name from Levi to Marx, most likely for social and business reasons.

From early on, Karl Marx proved to be highly intelligent and obsessively interested in nearly everything. He was also very independent and hard to control. At seventeen Marx entered the University of Bonn to study law. He enjoyed himself, writing romantic poems, socializing, spending more money than he had, even fighting in a duel—not to mention getting arrested once for disorderly conduct. His conventional father was not at all happy with his son's behavior and insisted that he transfer to the more serious and prestigious University of Berlin.

Marx's stay at Berlin proved to be crucial to his later philosophical growth. Big, busy, and ugly, Berlin epitomized the nineteenth-century idea of a modern city. It was a magnet for social agitators, radicals, and other intellectuals. Imagine the impact such an environment would have on a bright, curious, somewhat rebellious young man from a conservative small-town background.

Karl Marx

All I know is that I am not a Marxist.

Karl Marx

Soaring with the Intellectual Spirit of the Age

One way or another, most philosophers have believed that truth exists, that it is knowable, and that whatever truth is, it is always the same for everyone. Yet, as we have seen, philosophers radically disagree about what can be known, about how to know it, and about the grand scheme of things. Sophists and skeptics even challenge whether there is any unchanging truth, questioning our ability to recognize it if there is.

Kant's effort to answer Hume's assault on reason was a direct influence on the idealist philosopher **Georg Wilhelm Friedrich Hegel (1770–1831)**, the dominant thinker being read in every major German university when Kant was a student. Though Hegel was primarily a philosopher, his influence spread across intellectual and artistic disciplines. One was either a Hegelian or an anti-Hegelian, but no serious German intellectual could ignore Hegel. Hegel's works include *The Phenomenology of Mind (or Spirit)* (1807), *Science of Logic* (1812, 1816), *Encyclopedia of the Philosophical Sciences in Outline* (1817), and *Philosophy of Right* (1821).

Hegel pushed Kant's claim that the mind imposes categories (concepts) on experience to its ultimate conclusion. Rather than appeal to unknowable *noumena* to avoid slipping into Humean skepticism, Hegel argued that Kant's *categories of thought* are actually *categories of being*. According to Hegel, whatever exists is knowable. Therefore, it is contradictory to assert that noumena are unknowable because to do so we must somehow know that noumena exist.

For Hegel, Kant's categories exist independently of any specific individual's mind. They are both mental processes and objective realities. In Hegelian philosophy, capital-R Reality is referred to as Absolute Thought, Mind, Spirit, or Idea. Hegel believed that it is the unique task of philosophy to discover the relationships of various aspects of Reality to the Whole (Absolute Mind or Absolute Spirit). These relationships can be understood as part of a monistic system consisting of a single, evolving substance known as Absolute Spirit. History is the all-encompassing Absolute Spirit self-actualizing into perfection. Consequently, Hegel's philosophy is sometimes called **absolute idealism**.

Hegel insisted that mind can only be recognized as "continuously developing consciousness." The pattern which all consciousness follows constitutes a "dialectical process." As Hegel uses the term, **dialectic** refers to a three-step pattern in which an original idea (thought or condition) known as a *thesis* is opposed by a contrary idea (thought or condition) known as the *antithesis*. The interaction or struggle between the thesis and antithesis produces a new idea (thought or condition) that combines elements from the others, known as the *synthesis*. Once established, the synthesis becomes the thesis for a new cycle until everything is realized in the infinite synthesis of Absolute Spirit. Each resulting level of consciousness includes its predecessors. The Hegelian Dialectic was supposed to represent the actual structure of reality, which for Hegel was the unfolding thought of the cosmic or absolute *Geist*, translated as Mind, or Spirit.

Hegel believed that it was possible to construct a complete picture of reality, a grand system that would incorporate all of philosophy, science, theology, art, history, and so on. In fact, he insisted that it is impossible to understand anything except as it relates to the Whole.

Thus, for Hegel, everything is always developing according to the dialectical process. Previous philosophers were unaware that they were working with a particular stage of the development of capital-R Reason as it unfolds in history. They were products of the *zeitgeist*, the "spirit of the age." By failing to recognize the *dialectical process* of which they were a part, these philosophers mistook something "abstracted" from the Whole for a fixed, independent entity. But nothing can be understood or even recognized this way. Things can only be understood when they are watched phenomenologically as they develop in relationship to the Whole, the Ultimate Synthesis toward which history is unfolding. For Hegel, history does not "just happen." It is the rational development of progressively inclusive stages toward realization in Absolute Spirit. This Absolute Spirit is the ultimate synthesis of what Hegel saw as a tension between the subjective (Idea) and the objective (Nature).

Hegel was a grand systematizer—some would say *the* grand systematizer—who thought that history is the unfolding of the Absolute Idea of God (Absolute Spirit). He saw philosophy as the attempt to construct a comprehensive picture of everything as it relates to everything.

ABSOLUTE IDEALISM (HEGELIAN)
Term used to identify Hegel's particular form of German idealism; a monistic philosophy which is based on an all-encompassing Absolute Spirit that is self-actualizing into perfection; Reality (Absolute Mind or Absolute Spirit) is independent of any individual's mind; not to be confused with Berkeleian idealism (immaterialism), in which objective reality is said to exist in the individual's mind.

DIALECTIC (HEGELIAN)
According to Hegel, a three-step pattern in which an original idea, known as a thesis, struggles with a contrary idea, known as the antithesis, to produce a new synthesis that combines elements of both.

The young Marx was deeply influenced by Hegel, from whom he derived the crucial concept of alienation and the notion of historical evolution as an ongoing struggle.

Back Down to Earth

During this time, Marx became acquainted with a number of radical "freethinkers." These excited young people spent hours arguing the finer points of Hegelian philosophy. Marx thrived on the heady combination of intellectual stimulation and radicalism. Despite all the time spent in coffeehouses and beer halls, Marx completed his doctoral work in philosophy with a dissertation on the materialistic philosophy of Democritus and Epicurus. He planned to practice that noblest of all occupations, professor of philosophy.

Fate had other plans, however. Marx had been living on money from his father. When his father died about the time of Marx's graduation, he left only enough to support Marx's mother and younger siblings. This would have been no real problem if Marx had been able to secure an appointment as a professor. But by now the Prussian government had grown wary of the young, radical Hegelians and issued a decree prohibiting them from university employment.

Fortunately, Marx was offered a job by a liberal publisher named Moses Hess. Hess, himself a Hegelian, wanted Marx to help him edit a new, vocal "democratic journal" called *Rheinische Zeitung*. Even at this early age, Marx was an impressive figure. Writing about Marx to a friend, Hess said:

> He is the greatest, perhaps the one genuine philosopher now alive and will soon draw the eyes of all Germany. Dr. Marx is still very young (about twenty-five at most) and will give medieval religion and politics their *coup de grace*. He combines the deepest philosophical seriousness with the most biting wit. Imagine Rousseau, Voltaire, Holbach, Lessing, Heine, and Hegel fused into one person—I say fused, not thrown in a heap— you have Dr. Marx.[1]

Marx's admiration for Hegel was altered by an article called *Theses on the Hegelian Philosophy* by **Ludwig Feuerbach (1804–1872)**. Feuerbach was a materialist who challenged Hegel's notion that the driving force behind historical eras was their *zeitgeist*, or unique spirit, the *spirit of the age*. Feuerbach argued that any given era was the accumulation of the actual, concrete material conditions of the time—not some abstract "spirit of the age." So important were material conditions, according to Feuerbach, that they controlled not just the way people behave, but *how they think* and *what they believe*. Different material conditions result in what we think of as different cultural eras. After reading Feuerbach, Marx retained Hegel's belief in the dialectics of history, and a single reality, but concluded that reality was material, not spiritual.

History does nothing, it "possesses no colossal riches," it "fights no battles"! Rather it is man, actual and living man who does all this, who possesses and fights; "history" does not use man as a means for its purposes as though it were a person apart; it is nothing but the activity of pursuing his ends.
Friedrich Engels

All official and liberal science defends wage-slavery in one way or another, whereas Marxism has declared relentless war on that slavery. To expect science to be impartial in a society of wage-slavery is as silly and naive as to expect impartiality from employers on the question as to whether the workers' wages should be increased by decreasing the profits of capital.
V. I. Lenin

A chance combination of events in a thinker's life sometimes has a lasting and profound effect on his or her later theories. In Marx's case, a series of articles he had been doing for Hess on the exploitation of peasants in the wine-growing Moselle Valley crystallized his understanding of Feuerbach's thesis. Observing the way the landowners repressed the workers, actively inhibiting and even punishing their efforts at self-improvement, Marx concluded that material conditions did indeed dominate all others.

The Wanderer

Like many social reformers and agitators, Marx paid a price for his outspoken concern for the downtrodden and his vehement attacks on those he saw as their oppressors. After Marx wrote a series of bitter editorials criticizing the Russian government, the rulers of Prussia—afraid of offending their powerful neighbor—shut down Hess's journal. This was April 1843, the same year Marx married Jenny von Westphalen.

Having a wife, no job, and no longer a Hegelian, Marx sought what he hoped would be a freer intellectual climate: He and Jenny moved to Paris. One of the social and political hubs of Europe at the time, Paris attracted thinkers and doers from around the world with its unique atmosphere of openness and encouragement. Naturally, such a climate attracted the most intense and talented freethinkers and radicals. It was not long before Marx was right at home.

In Paris, Marx discovered another congenial group of radical thinkers, this time centered around the economic ideas of the **Comte de Saint-Simon (1760–1825)**. Saint-Simon was especially interested in the emergence of a powerful new middle class, known as the bourgeoisie. He concluded that *economic conditions determine history*. More specifically, Saint-Simon argued that historical change is the result of *class conflict*: Those who control the material necessary for production are in a perpetual struggle with those who do not. This idea, as we shall see, had a major impact on Marx's thinking.

Marx also befriended various revolutionary groups of exiled German workers. These workers were on the periphery of and were influenced by an organized group of French laborers who agitated for radical changes in the conditions of workers and in the relationship between workers and owners. Because they wanted property held in common and shared by all, they were known as communists. Marx developed a keen sense of the proletariat, or working class. He now possessed the seeds of his own philosophy.

Within a year of moving to Paris, Marx was expelled from the city, and from 1845 to 1848 he and his family lived in Brussels. While there, he helped organize the German Workers' Union, which became part of an international Communist League in 1847. Its first secretary was Marx's friend and collaborator Friedrich Engels. Marx and Engels wrote the official statement of beliefs and doctrines of the Communist League, which was published in

It is not the consciousness of men that determines their existence, but on the contrary, their social existence determines their consciousness.

Karl Marx

1848 as *The Manifesto of the Communist Party* (now known simply as *The Communist Manifesto*). It may be the most important and influential revolutionary tract ever written.

Marx next went to Cologne to help agitate for a revolt of the German people. His timing was poor, however, as a more conservative tide was sweeping across France and Germany. Marx was formally expelled from Germany by the government and returned to Paris. Not yet thirty-two years old, he was already perceived as a dangerous revolutionary. He had barely returned to Paris when the French government again made him leave.

In August 1849, Marx's friends gave him enough money to move to London. England, in spite of the flaws Marx and Engels would find in its class structure and capitalist economy, proved a haven of freedom of thought and expression. Thus, in one of the ironies of history, the great critic of capitalism found the freedom to criticize capitalism only in a capitalistic environment.

Marx never left London. For almost a decade he spent long days in the reading rooms of the British Museum, researching some, but mostly writing. After returning home, he often continued working late into the night. He and his family lived a hand-to-mouth existence, moving from one shabby apartment to another, unable to pay rent. Once, they were evicted without anything when the landlord confiscated their few possessions in lieu of rent. Food and medicine were always scarce. Their poverty was so dire that two sons and a daughter died in childhood.

Vindication

At forty-two, Marx was thought of as an old man. Poverty and exile had worn him down, and his influence over revolutionary thinkers had begun when he was so young that he was seen as a member of the old guard. His influence grew, however, with the emergence of the militant German Social Democracy party. After Marx became their authority on socialist theory, his financial condition improved. Then, in 1864, the International Workingmen's Association was established by revolutionaries in France and England. They, too, turned to Marx, and he came to dominate their general council. He tolerated no deviance from his views, and used any means necessary to defeat those who dared challenge him.

During this time Marx began *Das Kapital*. The first of its three volumes appeared in 1867. This massive work established Marx's reputation as a philosopher. It eventually became what is sometimes referred to as "the Communist Bible," probably because of its nearly mythical status, and possibly because more people claim to give their allegiance to it than actually read it.

As his health and strength grew weaker, Marx was unable to devote the same care and attention to the two remaining volumes of *Das Kapital* that he had to the first. In fact, he never finished them. What we know as the second and third volumes were extensively edited by Engels in 1885

The teaching of Marx is all-powerful because it is true. It is complete and harmonious, providing men with a consistent view of the universe, which cannot be reconciled with any superstition, any reaction, any defence of bourgeois oppression. It is the lawful successor of the best that has been created by humanity in the nineteenth century—German philosophy, English political economy, and French socialism.

V. I. Lenin

and 1894, after Marx's death. In many ways they are inferior to the first volume. (What is called the fourth volume was ultimately compiled later.)

In 1881, Jenny died after a long and painful bout with cancer. The death of the woman who had stood by the exiled, reviled philosopher through poverty and the loss of three children broke his spirit. He lived for fifteen more months in a state of grief and despair. Karl Marx died sleeping in a favorite armchair on March 14, 1883, two months after the death of his oldest daughter. His funeral was attended by his family and a few friends. At the funeral of his old friend, Engels said:

> Just as Darwin discovered the law of development of organic nature, so Marx discovered the law of the development of human history: the simple fact that man must first of all eat, drink, have shelter and clothing, before he can pursue politics, science, art, religion, etc.; that therefore the production of the immediate means of subsistence, and consequently the degree of economic development of a given epoch, form the foundation on which state institutions, legal conceptions, art and even religious ideas have evolved and in the light of which they must, therefore, be explained.
>
> Marx was before all else a revolutionist. His real mission in life was to contribute, in one way or another, to the overthrow of capitalistic society, and to the liberation of the proletariat, which he was the first to make conscious of its own position and needs. Fighting was his element. And he fought with a passion, a tenacity and a success few could rival.
>
> His name will live through the ages, and so also will his work.[2]

FRIEDRICH ENGELS

Friedrich Engels

Friedrich Engels (1820–1895), the son of a wealthy German textile manufacturer, came to Paris to meet Marx, after sending him some articles Engels had written criticizing English economists. The meeting changed forever the lives of both men and the shape of the world. They remained friends and collaborators until Marx's death.

Engels was clearly a member of the bourgeoisie who enjoyed the pleasures and comforts provided by his father's money. He loved to hunt, write poems, and drink fine wines. Such a lifestyle did not please his strict Calvinist father, who sent young Friedrich off to learn the work ethic. Laboring on the docks of Bremen, Engels developed deep compassion for the condition of his less fortunate colleagues. He read radical literature, and was converted to communism by Marx's mentor, Moses Hess.

Engels tried a job in his father's Manchester, England, branch of the family business, but could not shake his interest in the working class. He spent more and more time studying slum conditions and noting the immense disparity between the conditions of the poor and the upper and middle classes. The utter degradation and despair he found in the slums squelched any lingering interest in becoming a businessman, and he began to write about what he saw.

In 1844, Engels published *The Condition of the Working Class in England*. His writing was strong, practical, and effective. He went on to write a series of attacks on the most important English economists of the day, accusing them of rationalizing and justifying the abuses the middle and upper classes heaped upon the poor. He saw their economic theories as capitalistic propaganda, not honest economic or historical research. As he and Marx discussed these essays, each realized that he had finally found someone who understood the power of economic and material conditions. It has been said that Marx was the deeper thinker and Engels added breadth and fire to his ideas.

Engels had a gift for acquiring the hard facts Marx needed to support his philosophical arguments, and for making Marx's often difficult and obscure thinking easier to follow. Thus he played a crucial role in the spread and acceptance of Marxist thinking. Engels and Marx worked together for over forty years, and Engels supported Marx and his family through the long years of poverty in London. When Marx died, Engels protected, advocated, and interpreted his philosophy for the rest of the world.

DIALECTICAL MATERIALISM

From Hegel, Marx took the ideas that there is only one uniform reality, and that history is an evolutionary cycle governed by an internal **dialectical process**, in which progress occurs as the result of a struggle between two opposing conditions. From Feuerbach, Marx concluded that reality is material, and that consequently the material conditions of life control it. And from Saint-Simon, he learned to observe the relationship between the owning/governing class and the producing/exploited class. Combining these elements with a deep concern for the conditions of workers and a keen awareness of the importance of economic conditions to other aspects of life, Marx constructed a social-political-economic philosophy known variously as Marxism, Communism, historical materialism, Marxian dialectics, historical dialectics, or dialectical materialism. We must take care not to confuse Marx's philosophy with various kinds of governments who claim to be Marxist, for as we shall see, the gap between Marx's philosophy and Marxist regimes can be significant.

According to Marx's dialectical materialism, history is the ongoing result of a constant tension between two classes, an upper class of rulers/owners and a ruled and exploited underclass. From the struggle between different economic interests emerges a brand-new economic structure. Marx saw conflicting economic interests in terms of two classes, the **bourgeoisie**, or

The society of money and exploitation has never been charged, so far as I know, with assuring the triumph of freedom and justice.
Albert Camus

DIALECTICAL PROCESS
(HEGELIAN)
Internally governed evolutionary cycle in which progress occurs as the result of a struggle between two opposing conditions.

BOURGEOISIE
All those who do not produce anything yet who own and control the means of production.

middle-class, and the **proletariat**, or working class. The bourgeoisie consists of those who do not produce anything yet who own and control the
means of production. The proletariat consists of all those whose labor produces goods and provides essential services, yet who do not own the means
of production.

Marx took Hegel's concept of the dialectical process and applied it to
historical stages, which he called "the five epochs of history." These epochs—
(1) primitive/communal, (2) slave, (3) feudal, (4) capitalist, (5) socialist/
communist—are named after their dominant economic system. Marx argued that as each epoch develops, its basic economic structure matures. In
the process, the success of the economic structure alters the material conditions of people's lives. These altered conditions ultimately lead to the creation of a new social structure.

*What else does the history
of ideas prove than that intellectual production changes
character in proportion
as material production is
changed? The ruling ideas
of each age have ever been
the ideas of its ruling class.
The Communist Manifesto*

At a certain stage in their development, the material productive forces of society come in conflict with the existing relations of production or—which is but a legal expression for
the same thing—with the property relations within which
they have been at work hitherto. . . . Then begins an epoch
of social revolution. With the change of the economic foundations, the entire immense superstructure is more or less
rapidly transformed. In considering such transformation a distinction should always be made between the material transformation of the economic conditions of production, which
can be determined with the precision of natural science, and
the legal, political, religious, esthetic, or philosophic—in short,
the ideological forms, in which men become conscious of the
social conflict and fight it out.

No social order ever perishes before all the productive forces
for which there is room in it have developed; and new higher
relations of production never appear before the material conditions of their existence have nurtured in the womb of the
old society itself. Therefore mankind always sets itself only
such tasks as it can solve; since, looking at the matter more
closely, it will always be found that the task itself arises only
when the material conditions for its solution already exist,
or are at least in the process of formation.[3]

In outline form, Marxian history looks like this: The original primitive
stage of history developed because the discovery of increasingly sophisticated agricultural techniques, tools, and simple metals required more labor.
Thus was born the slave economy (a thesis stage). Over time, the slave economy produced even more sophisticated skills and information. As a result,
people began to cluster around towns, where craft guilds emerged. A crude
form of specialization arose: As fewer people were needed to devote their
time to meeting basic agricultural needs, craftsmen were free to develop spe-

The German workers depicted grinding silverware in this 1887 engraving were typical of the alienated proletarians championed by Marx and Engels. Could they even afford to own the very utensils they worked so hard to produce?

cialized skills. These newer skills required more concentration of labor and a bit more freedom than slaves had. Thus a feudal system emerged in which great lords owned the land, and serfs in effect leased portions of it (an antithesis to the slave economy). As payment, the serfs owed the lord most of what they raised or produced. The serfs were allowed to keep only a small portion of the products of their labor. This was a period of semifreedom in which most people lived in semirural, semiurban towns.

The crafts guilds, especially, resulted in specialized manufacturing techniques. Soon, more and more goods were available. The demand for goods gave rise to increased trading and bartering, and capitalism began to grow out of feudalism (a synthesis of slave and feudal economies and a new thesis stage). Money became increasingly important, and with the spread of money as the medium of barter, financial brokers emerged. The demand for goods, coupled with new steam-powered manufacturing techniques, ultimately meant the death of feudalism. Feudalism was too cumbersome and inefficient to meet the needs and desires of the emerging capitalist middle class.

The technology of industrialization pulled people to areas with sources of sufficient power and transportation, near rivers or coal mines. Great cities developed. Mass production created more, cheaper goods, and demand continued to accelerate. A new class of middlemen who neither owned nor

What is competition from the point of view of the work man? It is work put up to auction.

M. Louis Blanc

produced grew in power. They invested and began to acquire capital. In Marx's view, the gap between the owners-investors and the workers will continue to grow as one class amasses more and more wealth at the expense of a larger, exploited class. This gap will eventually become intolerable, resulting in a violent revolution of the workers.

PHILOSOPHICAL QUERY

Do you think the gap between owners-investors and workers is closing or widening? Cite some contemporary examples to support your view.

Since the great injustices of capitalism (thesis) result from the private ownership of property, according to Marx, a new socialistic economy (antithesis) will eventually emerge in which private property is abolished. Society will ultimately be able to provide decent, meaningful lives to virtually everyone (synthesis). As a result, no one will need private property or wealth. Instead of having to compete for a good life, we will live harmoniously, doing creative, satisfying work that benefits us individually at the same time it benefits society collectively. There will be only one class, hence no class conflict. The economy will reach a state of balance, and history as such (not the world, just history as class struggle) will end.

Mystification and Materialism

Marx radically transformed Hegel's dialectic by confining it to the material world. He objected to excessively abstract philosophy, referring to it as **mystification**: the use of cloudy abstractions to create elaborate metaphysical systems that distract us from concrete material reality. Marx thought that instead of clarifying ideas, Hegel and other "abstractionists" and idealists make them "mysterious" and vague.

MYSTIFICATION
Use of cloudy abstractions to create elaborate metaphysical systems that distract us from concrete material reality.

Mystifying logic, like money, does not *produce* anything, it merely alters relationships. Hegel's great error, and that of philosophers in general, according to Marx, is *abstraction*. Thus most philosophy lacks substance. Like Bentham and Mill, Marx believed sweeping metaphysical systems and grand-sounding statements about human dignity and virtue pale beside the actual, concrete, *existing conditions* under which the poor barely survive.

In the *Manifesto*, Marx asserts that "man's ideas, views and conceptions, in one word, man's *consciousness*, changes with every change in the conditions of his material existence, his social relations, and his social life." When Marx talks about "material conditions" he means more than just natural physical and biological conditions. He includes economic and social relationships.

Thus Marxian materialism should not be confused with scientific materialism (Chapter 11), which leads to the conclusion that all behavior is governed by strict laws of cause and effect. Marx is a *social determinist*, not a *hard determinist*. Hard determinists deny the possibility of free will or free action. **Marxian materialism**, by contrast, sees a reciprocal relationship between individuals and their environment.

Marx criticized other forms of materialism for failing to understand just how important the role of human consciousness is in shaping society:

> The distinctive character of social development as opposed to the natural process of development lies in the fact that human consciousness is involved. . . . *Intelligent social action is creative action.* . . . By acting on the external world and changing it, man changes his own nature. . . . The material doctrine that men are products of circumstances and a changed upbringing forgets that it is men that change circumstance, and that the educator himself needs educating.[4]

This reciprocity between individuals and their circumstances is a dialectical relationship. Marx's materialism avoids the futility and degradation he saw in scientific materialism, while acknowledging the importance of the material conditions of our lives.

Engels referred to Marx's philosophy as *dialectical materialism*, but Marx himself referred to it as *naturalism*. Both characterizations are expressive of its overall thrust. Marx's emphasis, like that of his great utilitarian contemporary John Stuart Mill, is on the here and now. Like Mill, Marx refers to what he is doing as "social science." He believed his unique mixture of idealistic (Hegelian) and materialistic principles was the *only way* to understand and predict the course of history:

> We see here how consistent naturalism or humanism is distinguished from both idealism and materialism, and at the same time constitutes their unifying truth. We see also that only *naturalism* is able to comprehend the process of world history.[5]

According to Marx, the process of human history is shaped by inseparable social and economic conditions.

Economic Determinism

Philosophers and other intellectuals tend to attribute great power to ideas. They talk of the transforming power of profound ideas such as democracy or truth. Marx, by contrast, proposes a radical view of ideas, namely, that *the economic structure of a culture creates and forms its ideas*.

Marx uses the term **economic** to refer to the complete array of social relationships and arrangements that constitutes a particular social order. He assigns a crucial role to the material **substructure** (or base) **of society**, which consists of the means of production, the forces of production, and the relationships of production.

MARXIAN MATERIALISM Form of social determinism based on a reciprocal relationship between individuals and their environment; distinguished from strict materialism and hard determinism.

ECONOMIC (AS USED BY MARX) Term Marx used to refer to the complete array of social relationships and arrangements that constitutes a particular social order.

SUBSTRUCTURE OF SOCIETY In philosophical Marxism, the material substructure or base of society determines the nature of all social relationships, as well as religions, art, philosophies, literature, science, and government.

The **means of production** include natural resources such as water, coal, land, and so forth. The **forces of production** are factories, equipment, technology, knowledge, and skill. The phrase **relationships of production** refers to who does what, who owns what, and how this affects members of both groups. The relationships of production shape society.

The relationships of production constitute a complex system that shapes everything else. This material substructure determines the nature of all social relationships (parent-child, boss-employee, ruler-citizen, and so on), as well as religions, art, philosophies, literature, science, and government. According to Marx, the basic substructure of a society produces ideas and institutions that are compatible to it; these he referred to as the **superstructure of society**. The superstructure of a culture rests on and is determined by the substructure.

We can use a bit of what we have learned so far about the history of philosophy to see what Marx means. A sketchy Marxist survey of philosophy might go something like this:

Plato and Aristotle reflected the values of a slave economy. Plato's social hierarchy classified most people as warriors or artisans. Only an elite few, the guardians, were fit to rule. Aristotle's ethic of self-realization certainly did not apply to slaves and illiterate laborers and farmers. Both philosophies were shaped by the dominant social relationships of production at the time. The expanding Roman Empire needed strong, disciplined soldiers and citizens who could survive sometimes capricious emperors. Hence it nurtured just the right philosophy: Stoicism.

Thomas Aquinas's great summae reflect medieval Catholic theology, which justified the feudal order and excused the suffering of the exploited laboring classes as God's will. Such beliefs made the degradation of people acceptable, as it was part of our punishment for Original Sin, ordained by the will of God, and only "temporary" for those who would eventually escape servitude by going to heaven.

The more sophisticated methods of production whose arrival marked the beginning of capitalism required a less hierarchical, freer, more individualistic social structure. Technology began to replace human effort. The result of this economic shift was Descartes' emphasis on method, which is the philosophic version of technology, and his individualism, which followed the decline of the great feudal communities and guilds. This set the stage for the industrialization of Europe and the rise of capitalism. Further, Descartes' rationalism is clearly the product of an elitist gentleman.

The utilitarians' emphasis on universal education and praise of liberty are partly a justification of capitalism, which requires skilled, educated workers and entrepreneurs who are free from excessive government interference. Both Bentham and Mill express the growing tension and increasing inequality resulting from the Industrial Revolution. Their social policies reflect the changing nature of the relationships of production: Utilitarianism is a bourgeois philosophy that seeks to improve the conditions of the proletariat just enough to make them more efficient. It does nothing to significantly alter their basic state.

You may not agree with this Marxian analysis at all, but it does seem clear that social conditions affect art, literature, philosophy, and so on. Marx refined the notion of "social conditions," and insisted that the dominant, all-important social condition is the relationships of production.

Communism is a society where each one works according to his ability and gets according to his needs.

Pierre-Joseph Proudhon

> In the social production which men carry on they enter into definite relations that are indispensable and independent of their will; these relations of production correspond to a definite stage of development of their material powers of production. The sum total of these relations of production constitutes the economic structure of society—the real foundation on which rise legal and political superstructures and to which correspond definite forms of social consciousness. The mode of production in material life determines the general character of the social, political, and spiritual processes of life.[6]

The relationship between the economic structure of a society and the kinds of people, ideas, and institutions it produces will become clearer as we take an extended look at Marx's critique of capitalism.

PHILOSOPHICAL QUERY
Analyze your education from the standpoint of relationships of production. What values does public education really serve?

CRITIQUE OF CAPITALISM

Given the importance Marx placed on the economic structure of society, it is not surprising that he developed a detailed critique of the prevailing nineteenth-century relationship of production, **capitalism**. Although many of Marx's ideas are clearly revolutionary, and although he did predict a violent overthrow of capitalism, Marx never actually made a moral judgment of capitalism. He thought of his analysis as "pure social science." His aim was to describe current social and economic conditions objectively, identifying their causes and predicting the next historical change.

In Marx's opinion, tension under capitalism is increased as *inequities of distribution* destroy any correlation between how much an individual contributes or produces, and how much he or she receives. There is a fundamental contradiction at the heart of capitalism: The law of supply and demand determines prices, yet the large pool of workers keeps wages low. Manufacturers keep prices higher than the actual cost of production, so over time workers get less and less for their effort. The result is **surplus value**,

CAPITALISM
Economic system in which the means of production and distribution are all (or mostly) privately owned and operated for profit under fully competitive conditions; tends to be accompanied by concentration of wealth and growth of great corporations.

SURPLUS VALUE
Term Marx used to refer to the capital accumulated by owners; the result of keeping prices higher than the costs of production at the expense of workers.

which the owners accumulate in the form of capital. Those who contribute the least profit the most.

The bitter irony, Marx says, is that most of the people who suffer under capitalism have been conditioned by it to value it. They support a tax system that favors the rich, dreaming of the day when they, too, will be rich enough to benefit from it. Yet the laws determining who is allowed to own what, and who gets to keep what, are written by those who already own. Education is controlled by the same class, so the children of the most deprived grow up believing in free enterprise and "fair competition," only to be condemned to lives of poverty, or at least constant financial anxiety.

PHILOSOPHICAL QUERY

Compare kinds of contribution: Who contributes more, the builders who construct houses or the developers who finance them? Who contributes more, the president of a corporation or the secretaries? Are ideas contributions? Discuss.

The Bourgeoisie and the Proletariat

Marx's critique of capitalism rests on an analysis of the two classes that have emerged under capitalism. In *The Communist Manifesto* he characterizes the bourgeoisie as disdainful of everything but capital. The government is nothing but "a committee for managing the common affairs of the whole bourgeoisie." In other words, the government is not "of, by, and for the people," but "of, by, and for the important people." The bourgeoisie reduces everything to crude calculations of self-interest and personal wealth:

I think that there is nothing, not even crime, more opposed to poetry, to philosophy, ay, to life itself than this incessant business.

Henry David Thoreau

[The bourgeoisie] has left no other nexus between man and man than naked self-interest, than callous "cash payment." It has drowned the most heavenly ecstasies of religious fervour, of chivalrous enthusiasm, of Philistine sentimentalism, in the icy water of egotistical calculation. It has resolved personal worth into exchange value, and in place of the numberless indefeasible chartered freedoms, has set up that single, unconscionable freedom—Free Trade. In one word, for exploitation, veiled by religious and political illusions, it has substituted naked, shameless, direct, brutal exploitation.

The bourgeoisie has stripped of its halo every occupation hitherto honoured and looked up to with reverent awe. It has converted the physician, the lawyer, the priest, the poet, the man of science, into its paid wage earners.

The bourgeoisie has torn away from the family its sentimental veil, and has reduced the family relation into a mere money relation.[7]

According to Marx, one of the bitterest ironies of capitalism is that those who suffer the most under capitalism have been conditioned to value it. The old woman in this picture may have worked very hard her entire life, yet remained unable to purchase expensive clothes like those in the store window. Would Marx find that appalling? What do you think?

Expressions of frustration over the way doctors treat patients appear often in the media. We lament the demise of the family doctor who made house calls. We resent arriving on time for appointments only to be kept waiting and then having to pay high fees for a cursory examination, or a battery of tests whose chief purpose is to protect the doctor from a malpractice suit. Could this be an example of what Marx said happens when a profession is reduced to a means of making money?

PHILOSOPHICAL QUERY

We read that financial problems are perhaps the greatest cause of marital difficulties. If we marry after we have amassed some property, we are advised to protect ourselves by insisting on a

MILL THE SOCIALIST?

Since the human race has no means . . . of existence at all but what it derives from its own labor and abstinence, there would be no ground for complaint against society if everyone who was willing to undergo a fair share of this labor and abstinence could attain a fair share of the fruits. But is this the case? Is it not the reverse of the fact? The reward, instead of being proportioned by the labor and abstinence of the individual, is almost in inverse ratio to it: those who receive the least, labor and abstain the most. Even . . . the inadequate self-control exercised by the industrious poor costs them more sacrifice and more effort than is almost ever required of the more favored members of society.

John Stuart Mill
On Socialism (1879; reprint, Buffalo: Prometheus, 1987), pp. 69–70.

To be sure, labor produces marvels for the wealthy, but it produces deprivation for the worker. It produces palaces, but hovels for the worker. It displaces labor through machines, but it throws some workers back into barbarous labor and turns others into machines. It produces intelligence, but for the worker it produces imbecility and cretinism.

Karl Marx

carefully drawn-up prenuptial agreement. Is such thinking an example of reducing "the family relation into a mere money relation"? Is rewarding a child with money part of this pattern? Deciding not to have children because they are too expensive? Provide your own additional examples of reducing human relationships to "mere money relations." Can you find any evidence to refute Marx's basic contention that for the bourgeoisie, money matters most?

Marx and Engels claim that the bourgeoisie, with its hunger for more, cannot rest, cannot leave any corner of the world unexploited and unspoiled.

Constant revolutionising of production, uninterrupted disturbance of all social conditions, everlasting uncertainty and agitation distinguish the bourgeois epoch from all earlier ones. All fixed, fast-frozen relations . . . are swept away, all new-formed ones become antiquated before they can ossify. . . .

The bourgeoisie has through its exploitation of the world market given a cosmopolitan character to production and consumption in every country. . . . It compels all nations, on pain of extinction, to adopt the bourgeois mode of production; it compels them to introduce what it calls civilisation into their midst, i.e., to become bourgeois themselves. In one word, it creates a world after its own image.[8]

The bourgeoisie cannot actually produce all that it needs and wants, Marx pointed out. Its enormous wealth and comfort have resulted from the exploitation of a great underclass, the proletariat. These are the people who

Reprinted by permission: Tribune Media Services.

actually provide the goods and services society requires to function. Controlled by the bourgeoisie, they are even compelled to produce frivolous luxuries whose real purpose is to generate ever-escalating production. Not only are the workers paid as little as the bourgeoisie can get away with in order to maximize profit, they are seduced by bourgeoisie-controlled education and media to consume these overpriced, useless products. Thus the proletarians are trapped in a never-ending cycle of debt, denied significant influence over their own work, and tricked and coerced into furthering the power and advantage of their own exploiters. As *The Communist Manifesto* explains it:

> In proportion as the bourgeoisie, i.e., capital, is developed, in the same proportion is the proletariat, the modern working class, developed—a class of labourers, who live only so long as they find work, and who find work only so long as their labour increases capital. These labourers, who must sell themselves piecemeal, are a commodity, like every other article of commerce, and are consequently exposed to all the vicissitudes of competition, to all the fluctuations of the market.

Not only has the bourgeoisie forged the weapons that bring death to itself; it has called into existence the men who are to wield those weapons— the modern working class— the proletarians.
The Communist Manifesto

The rushed existence into which industrialized, commercialized man has precipitated himself is actually a good example of an inexpedient development caused entirely by competition between members of the same species. Human beings of today are attacked by so-called manager diseases, high blood pressure, renal atrophy, gastric ulcers, and torturing neuroses: they succumb to barbarism because they have no more time for cultural interests.

Konrad Lorenz

Owing to the extensive use of machinery and to division of labour, the work of the proletarians has lost all individual character, and, consequently, all charm for the workman. He becomes an appendage of the machine, and it is only the most simple, the most monotonous, and most easily acquired knack, that is required of him. Hence, the cost of production of a workman is restricted, almost entirely, to the means of subsistence that he requires for his maintenance, and for the propagation of his race. But the price of a commodity, and therefore, also of labour, is equal to the cost of production. In proportion, therefore, as the repulsiveness of the work increases, the wage decreases. . . . Not only are [the laborers] slaves of the bourgeois class, and of the bourgeois state; they are daily and hourly enslaved by the machine, by the overlooker, and above all, by the individual bourgeois himself. The more openly this despotism proclaims gain to be its end and aim, the more petty, the more hateful and the more embittering it is.[9]

If you have ever worked on an assembly line, or at picking fruits and vegetables, or in meat- or fish-packing plants, you will instantly understand the relationships of production that Marx and Engels are describing. Some of the most difficult and "repulsive" jobs are the most necessary to society, yet those who perform them are paid little and often respected less. Those who produce the least in Marxian terms work in air-conditioned offices, supported by hardworking staffs, and may receive salaries, bonuses, and stock options worth hundreds of thousands—if not millions—of dollars.

Marx and Engels were among the first modern philosophers to recognize the plight of women in modern society. When physical strength became less important, employment opportunities expanded for women and for men unable to do strenuous manual labor. But the work available and the pay offered were often substandard. Garment factories, for example, paid (and still pay) low piecework wages.

The less skill and exertion of strength implied in manual labour, in other words, the more modern industry becomes developed, the more is the labour of men superseded by that of women. Differences of age and sex no longer have any distinctive social validity for the working class. All are instruments of labour, more or less expensive to use, according to their age and sex.[10]

According to philosophical Marxism, the corruption of the worker's judgment is a predictable effect of the capitalist substructure. The reality is that workers are exploited, even if *they* do not realize it. The fact that a powerless group submits to economic exploitation willingly does not alter the nature of the exploitative relationship.

Just as an abused spouse or child may lose the ability to perceive reality and hence mistakenly see herself or himself as somehow causing or deserving abuse, so too exploited workers, after generations of capitalistic conditioning through schools and the media, may fail to recognize their actual social condition.

We have already seen how working-class and middle-class people can come to identify with the *possibility* of acquiring wealth rather than with their *actual chances* of doing so. In other words, we may identify with the *system* rather than with our true role in it. Marxists refer to this as being **co-opted**. You are co-opted when you are tricked, seduced, or somehow convinced to further interests that are to your ultimate disadvantage—and think that you do so willingly.

In the past, when labor unions made their initial approach to various industries, exploited workers often resisted, identifying more with their bosses' values than with their own actual condition. If Marx is correct, we cannot base an assessment of the relationships of production just on the desires or beliefs of the workers, who often (perhaps usually) express the dominant values of the substructure, even when these values are contrary to their well-being.

Bourgeois education fosters competitiveness in the scramble for grades, scholarships, and athletic trophies; it preaches individuality and teaches the doctrine of free choice in the marketplace—all capitalistic values. Bourgeois religion helps suppress workers by teaching them they are meant to suffer, that the love of money is the root of all evil, that hard work is a blessing and idle hands are the devil's workshop, that the meek shall inherit the earth. Capitalistic workers not only lose control of their time and the products of their work, since these belong to bosses and owners, they lose control of their beliefs. If Marx is correct, it is no wonder we find identifying with our true proletarian status so difficult.

Ultimately, Marx predicted, the proletariat expands; more and more of us join it. Whereas we once believed in "upward mobility," more and more citizens fear that the general direction will be "downward mobility" for increasing numbers—as Marx predicted.

> The lower strata of the middle class—the small tradespeople, shopkeepers, and retired tradesmen generally, the handicraftsmen and peasants—all these sink gradually into the proletariat, partly because their diminutive capital does not suffice for the scale on which modern industry is carried on, and is swamped in the competition with large capitalists, partly because their specialised skill is rendered worthless by new methods of production. Thus the proletariat is recruited from all classes of the population.[11]

As the ranks of the proletariat grow, the dialectical struggle with the bourgeoisie begins.

CO-OPT
In Marxian social analysis, co-option occurs when workers identify with the economic system that oppresses them by confusing the remote possibility of accumulating wealth with their actual living and working conditions; being co-opted also refers to anyone who is somehow convinced to further interests that are to her or his ultimate disadvantage.

Socialism will never destroy poverty and the injustice and inequality of capacities.
Leo Tolstoy

Differences of age and sex have no longer any distinctive social validity for the working class. All are instruments of labour, more or less expensive to use, according to their age and sex.
The Communist Manifesto

PHILOSOPHICAL QUERY

Economists are claiming that for the first time in decades, a generation of Americans is financially worse off than their parents. Many young adults have to live at home longer, have a more difficult time finding jobs, never become able to afford their own homes. Does this square with your experience? Does it support Marx's contention that more and more of us will slip into the proletariat? Is there another explanation? Discuss.

Class Struggle

All history, according to Marx and Engels, is the history of class struggle. In this struggle are the seeds of the next stage of history. The bourgeoisie has forged the instrument of its own destruction as it grows smaller but richer and more powerful. In our own time, social scientists are discussing the "shrinking middle class," the growing disparity between the haves and the have-nots. Escalating housing prices keep more and more young families from owning property. As the divorce rate remains high, working-class people suffer the economic (not to mention psychic) cost of supporting two separate households. Divorced mothers of young children face the dilemma of working and paying high child-care costs, or not working and living at or below the poverty level on state assistance or often inadequate child-support payments.

Medical insurance is now priced beyond the reach of so many working- and middle-class people that in 1993 President Bill Clinton began an unprecedented effort to fashion a federal health care program that would "guarantee" adequate care to all Americans. For the present, working- and middle-class people must use a continually increasing portion of their income to provide adequate health care for themselves and their families. This further diminishes their chances to save, invest, or buy a home. Yet the tax code remains full of breaks for those with business, investment, or real estate deductions. The wealthiest class in the country pays proportionally the smallest amount of taxes.

Marx and Engels said the overall situation cannot change until the proletariat becomes *fully aware* of itself. That is, so long as different segments of the population compete for raises and jobs, people whose class interests are identical will fail to see that they are.

The inherent vice of capitalism is the unequal sharing of blessings; the inherent virtue of socialism is the equal sharing of miseries.
Winston Churchill

At this stage the labourers still form an incoherent mass scattered over the whole country, and broken up by their mutual competition. If anywhere they unite to form more compact bodies, this is not yet the consequence of their own active union, but of the union with the bourgeoisie, which class, in order to attain its own political ends, is compelled to set the

whole proletariat in motion, and is moreover yet, for a time,
able to do so. At this stage, therefore, the proletarians do not
fight their enemies, but the enemies of their enemies . . .
every victory so obtained is a victory for the bourgeoisie.[12]

Under this interpretation, it is in the bourgeoisie's short-term interest for
different ethnic, gender, age, and religious groups to distrust and despise
each other, Marx and Engels point out. If poor Anglos and poor Hispanics
and poor people of color and poor Native Americans and poor Asian Americans and poor men and poor women spend their time blaming their own
poverty on each other, they fail to see what they *all* have in common: exploitation by the bourgeoisie. So, for instance, a Marxist might argue that
the bitter debate over affirmative action serves the bourgeoisie by obscuring
the fact *most people of all backgrounds are being kept out of the wealthy classes.* Indeed, for the bourgeoisie as a class, nothing could be better than for "token"
members of all disadvantaged groups to become publicly successful through
education and hard work. This will co-opt others in those groups to "behave" and work hard while dreaming of "making it."

Change will come only when the exploited identify with each other and
not with their race, religion, gender, or age, says *The Communist Manifesto*.

> This union is helped on by the improved means of communi-
> cation that are created by modern industry, and that place the
> workers of different localities in contact with one another. It
> was just this contact that was needed to centralise the numer-
> ous local struggles, all of the same character, into one national
> struggle between classes. But every class struggle is a political
> struggle. . . .
>
> This organisation of the proletarians into a class, and conse-
> quently into a political party, is continually being upset again
> by the competition between the workers themselves. But it
> ever rises up again, stronger, firmer, mightier. It compels leg-
> islative recognition of particular interests of the workers, by
> taking advantage of the divisions among the bourgeoisie it-
> self. . . . The bourgeoisie itself, therefore, supplies the prole-
> tariat with its own elements of political and general education,
> in other words, it furnishes the proletariat with weapons for
> fighting the bourgeoisie.[13]

PHILOSOPHICAL QUERY

Discuss the possibility that affirmative action and similar social
reform efforts actually serve the interests of an exploitative class
by creating increased consciousness of difference and division. Are
efforts to "honor diversity" aiding or hindering class consciousness? Is there a better solution to social inequality? Discuss.

*But whatever form they may
have taken, one fact is common to all past ages, viz.,
the exploitation of one part
of society by the other. No
wonder, then, that the social
consciousness of past ages, despite all the multiplicity and
variety it displays, moves
within certain common forms,
or general ideas, which cannot completely vanish except
with the total disappearance
of class antagonisms.*
The Communist Manifesto

As capitalism becomes increasingly efficient, it produces more than it can consume, and its technological progress renders large numbers of workers obsolete. Marxists say the result is an overburdened welfare state that provides barely enough sustenance—and no dignity—to its displaced workers.

> The modern labourer, on the contrary, instead of rising with the progress of industry, sinks deeper and deeper below the conditions of existence of his own class. He becomes a pauper, and pauperism develops more rapidly than population or wealth. And here it becomes evident that the bourgeoisie . . . is unfit to rule because it is incompetent to assure an existence to its slave within his slavery, because it cannot help letting him sink into such a state, that it has to feed him, instead of being fed by him. Society can no longer live under the bourgeoisie; in other words, its existence is no longer compatible with society. . . . The development of modern industry, therefore, cuts from under its feet the very foundation on which the bourgeoisie produces and appropriates products.[14]

Marx and Engels predicted that more and more workers would suffer as the bourgeoisie acquired capital at their expense, and that the workers' unhappiness, frustration, and indignation would erupt in violent revolution. After the revolution a new social order would emerge, from which all class distinctions, private ownership of the means of production, and exploitation would disappear forever.

What happened? Is the revolution behind schedule or is it not going to come at all? To address this issue, we need to look at one of the most important aspects of Marxist theory, one that is often overlooked by capitalistic critics of Marxism.

ALIENATION

One of Marx's most interesting and compelling insights centers on the concept of **alienation**, a term he derived from Hegel. Marx thought of alienation as the most destructive feature of capitalism. Indeed, he thought it revealed an inherent irrationality, an inherent evil in the very basis of capitalism. Alienation occurs when the worker no longer feels at one with the product of his or her labor. An alienated individual rarely feels at home with him- or herself, or with others. Alienation is a state of powerlessness, frustration, repressed resentment, and despair. It results from the transformation of a human being into a commodity.

Marx was convinced we are happiest not when we are idle but when we are engaged in meaningful work. Meaningful work can be work of virtually any kind so long as the worker has control over its products. This is necessary psychologically, not just morally. Imagine the suffering of a designer whose boss controls what brushes, pens, and colors the designer can

What the bourgeoisie therefore produces, above all, are its own gravediggers. Its fall and the victory of the proletariat are equally inevitable.
The Communist Manifesto

ALIENATION
According to Marx, condition of workers separated from the products of their labor; primarily an objective state, but can also refer to not feeling "at one" with the product of labor.

use; how much time can be devoted to each project; what is good enough (or not); what happens to the designs. No matter how much such a designer produces, he or she will suffer. Being detached from the work, prevented from exercising personal judgment and applying personal standards, the artist is alienated from his or her own work.

Large bureaucracies can also be alienating: we expect to get unclear answers to questions, wait in a long line at one window only to discover that it's the wrong window, and, worst of all, be greeted by hostile or indifferent employees. We feel alienated as they dehumanize us, but they are themselves dehumanized. Performing repetitive tasks without having any say in how things are done, boxed into a rigid hierarchy of rules, these workers become commodities, the human equivalent of data processors. The "existing individual" is lost. Marx would say their behavior is the result of alienation.

Anyone who takes a job *solely* on the basis of what it pays becomes alienated in Marx's sense by reducing himself or herself to a money-making machine. Alienation pervades education as teachers are compelled to teach outside their areas of interest and genuine competence or be fired. Even teachers lucky enough to teach in their own fields can become alienated as school districts base course loads on financial, not educational, considerations. Taxpayers who resist paying for adequate education help reduce *their own children* to commodities, because they make a "mere money relationship" the basis of their decision.

The common value system behind such examples is that possessions and money to buy them become more important than time to do things right, than the experience itself, and than the people involved. Soon the alienated worker sees those he or she works for or provides services to as the means to a paycheck, not full human beings. This is what Marx meant when he said, "The *increase in value* of the world of things is directly proportional to the *decrease in value* of the human world." And, of course, full functioning and eudaimonia are impossible in such conditions; this is a "kingdom of means," not a "kingdom of ends."

According to Marx, alienation even extends to our relationship with nature (as environmentalists remind us today). Nature provides the material basis for all work. Yet unchecked capitalism uses up nature, because the capitalist does not feel part of nature.

> The more the worker *appropriates* the external world and sensuous nature through his labor, the more he deprives himself of the *means of life* in two respects; first, that the sensuous world gradually ceases to be an object belonging to his labor, a *means of life* of his work; secondly, that it gradually ceases to be a *means of life* in the immediate sense, a means of physical subsistence of the worker.[15]

The alienated worker sees money as the means of life, not the natural world which provides bread and milk and fruit and wood. Alienated from nature,

To be alienated is to feel separated from the world as we experience it daily, from the "center" of ourselves, and from others who are having the same problem. Alienation is what a man feels when he has lost his sense of belonging to the world.

René J. Muller

we cannot see what we really depend on. Today we know the consequences of alienation from nature on a scale Marx could not have imagined.

Because so many of us must work to live, most of us spend the majority of our lives at our jobs. If we are alienated there, we are likely to be alienated elsewhere, for we cannot avoid being shaped by all those hours at work.

PHILOSOPHICAL QUERY

Discuss some examples of ways alienation spreads from the workplace into society at large, and the home in particular. Has it spread to your life? To school? Discuss.

Psychic Alienation

Marx describes alienation as *externalization*: work is seen as something I *do*, not as an expression of who I *am*. When I am in a state of alienation, I develop a habit of separating myself from nature and other people. I lose touch with myself, becoming alienated from who I really am, or at least from who I *ought to be*.

The less you are and the less you express of your life— the more you have and the greater is your alienated life.
Karl Marx

What constitutes the externalization of labor?

First is the fact that labor is *external* to the laborer—that is, it is not part of his nature—and that the worker does not affirm himself in his work but denies himself, feels miserable and unhappy, develops no free physical and mental energy but mortifies his flesh and ruins his mind. The worker, therefore, feels at ease only outside work, and during work he is outside himself. He is at home when he is not working and when he is working he is not at home. . . . External labor, labor in which man is externalized, is labor of self-sacrifice, of penance. Finally, the external nature of work for the worker appears in the fact that it is not his own but another person's, that in work he does not belong to himself but to someone else . . . the activity of the worker is not his own spontaneous activity. It belongs to another. It is the loss of his own self.

The result, therefore, is that . . . the worker . . . feels that he is acting freely only in his animal functions—eating, drinking, and procreating, or at most in his shelter and finery—while in his human functions he feels only like an animal. The animalistic becomes human and the human becomes animalistic.[16]

To the extent that Marx is correct, it is no wonder we are so interested in our weekends and vacations, in our leisure: only there do we feel fully free to be ourselves. Most of the week we sell our bodies and souls out of necessity: the capitalist machine demands that we work. Marx did not believe humans are by nature lazy. Quite the contrary; he believed we *want* and *need* meaningful work. Our obsessions with leisure, our absenteeism, our efforts to strike it rich or retire as early as possible only testify to the deep degree of alienation we must be experiencing in our work.

Marx distinguishes alienated life from species-life. **Species-life** is fully human life, life lived productively and consciously. **Alienated life**, in contrast, creates a sense of distance from nature and renders people unconscious of precisely how unhappy, unspontaneous, and unfulfilled they really are. In other words, alienation prevents us from being fully human. Thus alienation is anti-species or anti-human.

Marx, we see at last, is propounding not just an economic theory, but a sophisticated philosophy of *self-actualization*. He thinks that in the next historical stage, people will work to fulfill themselves, for the creative, self-actualizing joy of it. If that is difficult to believe, Marx says, it is because we are so alienated from human nature (our species) that we can conceive of work only in distorted, alienated terms.

Yet think of people with hobbies. Maybe you know a dentist who does woodworking in her spare time, or maybe you garden every chance you get. Other people write books or sew or knit or repair things around the house in their spare time or after they retire. These tasks take concentration and effort, yet we do not think of them as work. Students sometimes get distracted by interesting books they stumble on in the library and read them instead of their assignments. Yet they do not think of that reading as work. Why not?

What makes something "work" is not whether it is difficult or easy, but *how we relate to it*. If we are involved in and care about it, if, in Marx's expression, we are "at home," we do not look upon a task as work. If we have significant say over how we do something and do it for reasons we understand and for values we hold, we may not like what we do, but we are not alienated from it. If we act from love when we cut the grass for our parents or help a friend move furniture, we are not alienated.

Whenever we feel that what we do matters, we feel productive. We come alive. The more alive and conscious we are, the more fully we participate in species-life.

> The animal is immediately one with its life activity, not distinct from it. The animal is *its life activity*. Man makes his life activity itself into an object of will and consciousness. He has conscious life activity. It is not a determination with which he immediately identifies. Conscious life activity distinguishes man immediately from the life activity of the animal. Only thereby is he a species-being. Or rather, he is only a conscious being—that is, his own life is an object for him—since he is a species-being. Only on that account is his activity free activity. Alienated labor reverses the relationship in that man, since he is a conscious being, makes his life activity, his *essence*, only a means for his *existence*.[17]

SPECIES-LIFE
Fully human life lived productively and consciously; not alienated.

ALIENATED LIFE
Unconscious, unspontaneous, and unfulfilled life; deprived of fundamental conditions necessary for self-actualization.

The business of America is business.
Calvin Coolidge

The philosopher, who is himself an abstract form of alienated man, takes himself as the yardstick of the alienated world. The whole history of alienation . . . is . . . nothing but the history of the production of abstract thought.
Karl Marx

If capitalism were destroyed, Marx thought, we would revert to species-life. Once freed from the irrational, destructive pressure to survive only at the expense of others, we would be free to develop as human beings, to actualize ourselves as productive workers who find joy and fulfillment in personally meaningful work. If we are unable to accept that vision of ourselves right now, Marx would say it is because we are living alienated lives to one degree or another. Our distrust of Marx's utopia becomes a symptom of our distorted view of human nature. What we think of as human nature—people hustling for a buck, scheming to strike it rich, and looking forward to the day they can quit working—is not *human* nature at all: it is alienation.

One-Dimensional Man

We proceed from a **present** *fact of political economy.*

The worker becomes poorer the more wealth he produces, the more his production increases in power and extent. The worker becomes a cheaper commodity the more commodities he produces. The in-crease in value of the world of things is directly proportional to the decrease in value of the human world. Labor not only produces commodities. It produces itself and the worker as a commodity, and indeed in the same proportion as it produces commodities in general.

Karl Marx

Marxist and non-Marxist observers alike note that the violent overthrow of capitalism by the proletariat that Marx predicted has not occurred and seems less and less likely as we survey the world scene. Does this mean Marx was wrong in his critique of capitalism and alienation? It may not, for much of Marx's analysis remains persuasive and perceptive.

Marx's prediction was based on his belief that increased industrialization would lead to a greater and greater gap between the bourgeoisie and proletariat. The living conditions of the proletariat would become intolerable, and having "nothing to lose but their chains," they would revolt and destroy the system. An intriguing explanation of Marx's miscalculation on this score can be found in the book *One-Dimensional Man* by **Herbert Marcuse (1898–1979)**.

Marcuse, born and educated in Germany, came to America in 1934 to escape the Nazis. He taught philosophy at Brandeis University and the University of California at San Diego. In *One-Dimensional Man*, Marcuse argued that Marx was unable to anticipate the adaptive powers of capitalism. Specifically, he claimed that capitalist leaders have learned to manage the economy well enough to prevent the major disruptions (famines, shortages, depressions) Marx expected. Further, no one, Marx included, could have predicted the rapid, qualitative changes in technology which have altered the very nature of work for most people. Physical conditions of employment continue to improve for virtually all workers.

More important, many of us have been co-opted by a taste of the pie in the form of color television sets, stereos, nice cars, and so on. In other words, we are distracted from our true condition by being in a position to buy (or charge) technologically sophisticated, comforting goods. Yet we remain slave laborers, paying inflated prices for what we get, and still doing meaningless work. Marcuse thought our "economic prosperity" has been purchased by an irrationally large defense industry that is used to drive the economy, to keep it expanding.

Trapped in a cycle of consume-borrow-pay, we become one-dimensional people, not fully realized human beings consciously participating in our own species-life. Subtly conditioned by the media, we settle for immediate gratification and fail to notice or care about the gross and immoral inequities in the system—or, if we notice them, we are too tired, too frustrated, or too distracted by our own self-interest to attempt improving them.

> This society is irrational as a whole. Its productivity is destructive of the free development of human needs and faculties, its peace maintained by the constant threat of war, its growth dependent on the repression of the real possibilities for pacifying the struggle for existence—individual, national, international. This repression, so different from that which characterized the preceding, less developed stages of our society, operates today not from a position of natural and technical immaturity but rather from a position of strength. The capabilities (intellectual and material) of contemporary society are immeasurably greater than ever before—which means that the scope of society's domination over the individual is immeasurably greater than ever before. Our society distinguishes itself by conquering the centrifugal social forces with Technology rather than Terror, on the dual basis of an overwhelming efficiency and an increasing standard of living. . . .
>
> The fact that the vast majority of the population accepts, and is made to accept, this society does not render it less irrational and less reprehensible. The distinction between true and false consciousness, real and immediate interest still is meaningful. But this distinction itself must be validated. Men must come to see it and to find their way from false to true consciousness, from their immediate to their real interest. They can do so only if they live in need of changing their way of life, of denying the positive, of refusing. It is precisely this need which the established society manages to repress to the degree to which it is capable of "delivering the goods" on an increasingly large scale, and using the scientific conquest of nature for the scientific conquest of man.[18]

A maxim of revolutionists is that the group most likely to revolt is the group with the least to lose. Thus one way to keep people in submission is to give

All previous historical movements were movements of minorities, or in the interest of minorities. The proletarian movement is the self-conscious, independent movement of the immense majority, in the interest of the immense majority.

The Communist Manifesto

them just enough that their desire for change is tempered by fear of losing what they already have. Marcuse argues that contemporary capitalism has co-opted the proletariat and bought us off with possessions. Our moral sense is eroded. We tolerate gross inequities in income distribution and subhuman living and working conditions for some people, because our gadgets and toys mean more to us than a saner, more just society.

Gross misdistribution of the work force is a product of the inherent irrationality of society, Marcuse suggests: people gravitate toward high-paying, high-status jobs rather than toward personally and socially fulfilling work. The result is too many lawyers and too few grade school teachers, too many stockbrokers and not enough nurses.

Complete renunciation of one's possessions is a thing which very few . . . are capable of. All that can legitimately be expected of the wealthy class is that they hold their riches and talents in trust and use them for the service of society. To insist on more would be to kill the goose that laid the golden egg.
Mohandas Gandhi

PHILOSOPHICAL QUERY

Consider the possibility that in some areas, at least, society might actually benefit from less technology. For example, at some point it becomes irrational to continue to improve agricultural productivity through the use of chemicals and planting procedures that deplete topsoil when there are able-bodied, willing people looking for work. We could have healthier crops, preserve nature, and provide the satisfaction and dignity of meaningful work to those who seek it by making agriculture more "human," more labor-intensive. Discuss. Provide additional supporting examples if you can.

Alienated Love

Psychologist and "socialist humanist" philosopher **Erich Fromm (1900–1980)** wrote in a Marxian vein about self-actualization and love in his book *The Art of Loving.* Specifically, Fromm attempted to show how the structure of capitalistic society shapes our personal relationships. Of special interest to us is the way he characterized love as a form of commodity transfer in which we "exchange personality packages." This thesis rests on a Marxian conception of alienation. In sum, Fromm argued that alienated people cannot really love—themselves, one another, or God. Along the way he raised some disturbing questions about our society. See what you think of this contemporary Marxist analysis.

> Modern capitalism needs men who co-operate smoothly and in large numbers; who want to consume more and more; and whose tastes are standardized and can be easily influenced and anticipated. It needs men who feel free and independent, not subject to any authority or principle or conscience—yet willing to be commanded, to do what is expected of them, to fit into the social machine without friction; who can be guided

without force, led without leaders, prompted without aim—
except the one to make good, to be on the move, to go ahead.

What is the outcome? Modern man is alienated from himself, from his fellow man, from nature. He has been transformed
into a commodity, experiences his life forces as an investment
which must bring him the maximum profit obtainable under
existing market conditions. Human relations are essentially
those of alienated automatons. . . . Our civilization offers many
palliatives which help people to be consciously unaware of
this aloneness: first of all the strict routine of bureaucratized,
mechanical work, which helps people remain unaware of their
most fundamental human desires, of the longing for transcen-
dence and unity. Inasmuch as the routine does not succeed in
this, man overcomes his unconscious despair by the routine of
amusement, the passive consumption of sounds and sights offered by the amusement industry; furthermore by the satisfaction of buying ever more things, and soon exchanging them
for others. Modern man is actually close to the picture Huxley
describes in his *Brave New World*, well fed, well clad, satisfied
sexually, yet without self, without any except the most superficial contact with his fellow men, guided by slogans. . . .

The situation as far as love is concerned corresponds, as it
has to by necessity, to this social character of modern man.
Automatons cannot love; they can exchange their "personality
packages" and hope for a fair bargain. . . .

Just as automatons cannot love each other, they cannot love
God. The *disintegration of the love of God* has reached the same
proportions as the disintegration of the love of man. This fact
is in blatant contradiction to the idea that we are witnessing a
religious renaissance in this epoch. Nothing could be further
from the truth. What we witness (even though there are exceptions) is a regression to an idolatric concept of God, and
a transformation of the love of God into a relationship fitting
an alienated character structure. The regression to an idolatric
concept of God is easy to see. People are anxious, without principles or faith, they find themselves without an aim except the
one to move ahead; hence they continue to remain children,
to hope for father or mother to come to their help when help
is needed. . . .

. . . belief in God and prayer is recommended as a means to
increase one's ability to be successful. Just as modern psychia-
trists recommend happiness of the employee in order to be
more appealing to the customers, some ministers recommend
love of God in order to be more successful. "Make God your

*Under capitalism man ex-
ploits man; under socialism
the reverse is true.*
Polish proverb

*The oppressed are allowed
once every few years to decide
which particular representatives of the oppressing class
are to represent and repress
them.*
Karl Marx

*Communism, like any other
revealed religion, is largely
made up of prophecies.*
H. L. Mencken

partner" means to make God a partner in business, rather than to become one with him in love, justice and truth. Just as brotherly love has been replaced by impersonal fairness, God has been transformed into a remote General Director of the Universe, Inc.; you know that he is there, he runs the show (although it would probably run without him too), you never see him, but you acknowledge his leadership while you are "doing your part."[19]

PHILOSOPHICAL QUERY

Go through the Fromm passage carefully. What is the relationship between alienation and the transformation of human beings into commodities? What do you think of Fromm's notion that capitalism shapes personal relationships? Does it apply to your family, to your relationships with your teachers? What do you think of his assessment of love? Of capitalistic religion? Explain.

COMMENTARY

Here in the non-Communist world, we have tended to confuse the crude, degrading, dehumanizing efforts of the large Communist states with philosophical Marxism. Marx's vision of self-actualized people living species-life to its fullest cannot be realized in bread lines; secret police are certainly not elements of species-life. The revolt Marx predicted may not have to be violent. Perhaps we are seeing something very much like it in the ongoing struggles occurring in the former Soviet Union, where people are saying, "We have had enough. We want meaningful work, personal freedom, and bread," and in the growing dissatisfaction among people of other Eastern Bloc countries.

Marx seems to have confused the evils of industrialization with capitalism. His critique of capitalism has much to teach us about the relationship of the material conditions of people's lives to the ideas and beliefs they hold. His assessment of the evils of the bourgeoisie reminds us of the dangers of class disparity and the separation of reward from performance. His overall critique raises important questions about the meaning of work and human dignity.

But we must not overlook the fact that Marx's philosophy itself is—by his own criteria—a product of *his* material condition. He acknowledged this possibility but insisted he could overcome this limit and produce an objective analysis of history. Yet it is clear that his sense of class consciousness is tied to nineteenth-century social and economic conditions.

I find it difficult to overlook the strong strain of resentment and bitterness that runs through the work of Marx and Engels. This may be a reflection of their identification with the abused workers of the postindustrial

The Communists disdain to conceal their views and aims. They openly declare that their ends can be attained by the forcible overthrow of all existing social conditions. Let the ruling classes tremble at a Communist revolution. The proletarians have nothing to lose but their chains. They have a world to win. Working men of all countries unite! The Communist Manifesto

state. It may also help account for the fact that Marxism's greatest appeal is to people in underdeveloped countries. Contemporary political Marxism seems to derive much of its momentum from similar anger. That may be appropriate as an early reaction against exploiters, but anger alone cannot construct a healthy society. So far, Marxism has failed to appeal to the masses of workers in advanced capitalistic countries—precisely those it is aimed at.

Marx has been compared to an Old Testament prophet, and like a prophet he has taken us to task for our sins. These sins are indifference to gross inequities and injustice, the diminishment of the worth of people (ourselves included) for the exaltation of property and capital, alienation from nature and each other, and the sin of not being all that we can, of failing to live our species-life. He has shown us society in a new way, and called our attention to the importance of its substructure.

The state is not abolished, it withers away.
Friedrich Engels

But he has assigned too little importance to the role of ideas as causes of change. He has romanticized the proletariat and oversimplified the relations between classes. Marx did not allow for the possibility of societal self-correction and consciously guided change, nor did he fully anticipate the shape of the modern economy. He did not, as no one could, imagine the effects of the great technological revolution we are living through. Lastly, in spite of his concern for the alienated, degraded worker, Marx's emphasis on classes and class struggle does not pay enough respect to the individual. One of the major problems with political Marxism is its tendency to sacrifice the individual for the good of the collective.

Still, Marx's vision of a fuller, better life adds him to the list of champions of the oppressed and exploited. Like a prophet, he called us to account for our errors and, like a prophet, he indicated a general direction, though he was not able to provide a detailed map. Perhaps that is enough.

SUMMARY OF MAIN POINTS

Marx combined Hegel's dialectical view of history with Feuerbach's concept of a materialist *zeitgeist* (spirit of the age) to produce historical materialism, the view that history is the ongoing result of constant tension between two classes: the exploiters and the exploited. Engels helped Marx write *The Communist Manifesto* and spread historical materialism.

Dialectical process consists of an interaction between an original condition (thesis) and a contrary condition (antithesis) that produces a new condition containing elements of the thesis and antithesis (synthesis). The synthesis becomes the thesis for a new dialectical cycle.

Marx identified five "epochs of history" that comprise the dialectical development of history: (1) primitive/communal, (2) slave, (3) feudal, (4) capitalist, (5) socialist/communist. As each epoch develops, its basic economic structure matures and the material conditions under which people live change. According to Marx, ideas, values, and thinking itself are shaped by material conditions and social relations.

Marx argued that the economic structure of a culture creates and forms its own ideas. Most important is the material substructure, which consists of three components: (1) the means of production (natural resources); (2) the forces of production (factories, equipment, technology, and knowledge); (3) the relationships of production, which constitute a complex system that shapes everything else.

The material substructure produces ideas and institutions compatible to it. These constitute the culture's superstructure and include art, science, philosophy, religion, and government.

Marx was sharply critical of capitalism, which he saw as a stage on the way to a classless socialistic economy. In his view, the capitalist substructure contains a fundamental contradiction in the tension between the owners' desire to keep wages low while prices fluctuate according to the law of supply and demand. Marx predicted that as owners accumulated capital (surplus value), the condition of workers would decline.

Under capitalism, the two struggling classes are the bourgeoisie and the proletariat. The bourgeoisie consists of those who own the means of production but do not produce anything; it views everything in terms of money and self-interest. The proletariat consists of those who produce things but do not own the means of production (including their own time and labor).

Marx predicted that the demands of the bourgeoisie would result in an ever-growing proletariat whose living conditions would continue to decline until the proletariat would rise up in violent revolt and destroy the bourgeoisie and capitalism, leading to the next historical epoch, socialism.

The most destructive feature of capitalism, according to Marx, is alienation, which occurs when the worker no longer feels at one with the product of his or her labor; it is a state of powerlessness, frustration, and despair. Capitalism alienates people from one another, from nature, and from work.

Marx distinguished alienated life from species-life, which is lived productively and consciously. Species-life is fully human life, a product of self-actualization (which capitalism inhibits).

Herbert Marcuse argues that Marx failed to predict the adaptive powers of capitalism to make the expanding proletariat comfortable enough to prevent violent disruption of the entire economy. According to Marcuse, the modern capitalist economy creates one-dimensional people who do not fully participate in species-life.

Erich Fromm used the concept of alienated love to explain how the structure of capitalistic society shapes personal relationships. According to Fromm, alienated people cannot really love, so under capitalistic conditions love becomes an exchange of "personality packages."

STUDY QUESTIONS

1. Describe the social conditions that led Marx and Engels to write *The Communist Manifesto*.

2. What was Feuerbach's influence on Marx?

3. What was Hegel's influence on Marx?

4. What did Marx mean by saying that Hegel needed to be set "right side up"?

5. Explain why Marx's philosophy is sometimes called *historical materialism*.

6. What is the dialectical process of history? Explain in terms of the five epochs of history.

7. What does Marx mean by *mystification*? Give one or two examples.

8. Briefly explain the notion of economic determinism.

9. Identify the three components of the material base of society. Which is the most important, according to Marx? Why?

10. Distinguish between the superstructure and substructure of society.

11. Describe capitalism in terms of the relationships of production.

12. What is the bourgeoisie? Describe it; then discuss its significance to philosophical Marxism.

13. What is the proletariat? Describe it; then discuss its significance to philosophical Marxism.

14. Explain the significance of class consciousness and class struggle to Marxism.

15. What did Marx see as the inherent contradiction in capitalism? How is the contradiction related to his prophecy of violent revolution?

16. Thoroughly explain Marx's concept of alienation.

17. What is alienated labor? What is unalienated labor?

18. What is species-life? What roles do consciousness and alienation play in it?

19. What does Marcuse mean by the expression "one-dimensional man"?

20. How does Marcuse account for the failure of violent economic revolution?

21. In your own words, present Fromm's case that we are alienated from love of others and God.

CHAPTER SIXTEEN

The Individualist: Søren Kierkegaard and Friedrich Nietzsche

Who is most influential.—When a human being resists his whole age and stops it at the gate to demand an accounting, this must have influence. Whether that is what he desires is immaterial; that he can do it is what matters.

FRIEDRICH
NIETZSCHE

Just as desert travellers combine into great caravans from fear of robbers and wild beasts, so the individuals of the contemporary generation are fearful of existence, because it is God-forsaken; only in great masses do they dare to live, and they cluster together en masse *in order to feel that they amount to something.*

Søren Kierkegaard

H as it perhaps occurred to you that something fundamentally important seems to be missing from most (or all) of the philosophies we have studied so far? Has the ancient challenge to philosophy been answered for *you:* "Philosophy, what practical difference do you make to *me*?" What bearing does the categorical imperative have on your actual, day-to-day moral life? Can Thomas Aquinas's proofs of the existence of God provide you with a living faith, a relationship with a living God? What do the sterile inquiries of Hume or Descartes have to do with the concrete and immediate choices facing you as an *existing individual*? As seekers of wisdom, we might wonder whether a utilitarian calculus or Marxian assessment of history makes any real difference to the daily sufferings of real people. It seems as if philosophy has passed over the genuine concerns of individuals.

But then, from a certain perspective, our entire culture seems to be at odds with the genuine concerns of "existing individuals." Modern institutions have become increasingly massive, objectified, dehumanized, and impersonal. Science continues to reduce human suffering—and human achievement—to the effects of genetics and environmental conditioning. Bureaucracies reduce their employees to "fleshy automatons" whose every decision is guided by "company policy." Computerized assembly lines replace human workers. Mass production and prefabricated materials replace handmade goods and craftsmanship.

Though we profess to value individuality, we reward conformity. Our politicians look and talk alike. Our celebrities are uninspiring and unoriginal. We are consumed by one craze after another, as we strive to belong to this group or that. Yuppies conform; gangsters conform; rappers and rockers conform; Christians, Muslims, and Jews conform; even children, whom we might expect to be free spirits, succumb to fads and fashions.

Instead of seeing ourselves as individuals, we may think of ourselves as "types," as hyphenated Americans (Italian-Americans, Native Americans, African-Americans), or we may identify with our sexual preference (gay Americans) or our age (senior citizens) or our gender (National Organization for Women) or our religion. Our identity may come from membership in a group, gang, or club.

"Good and evil are the prejudices of God"—said the snake.

Friedrich Nietzsche

As we try to juggle a variety of roles—student, worker, spouse, parent, child—we learn, without always being conscious of it, to move from one discrete, disconnected experience to another. We become oblivious, perhaps, to the emptiness in our lives.

What if the key elements of our "identities" are only abstractions, lifeless concepts that do not encompass the real qualities of actual human existence? What, for instance, does it mean to *be* a woman? A Christian? A student? Can any objective description capture existence? We are understandably frustrated when a doctor sees only "the liver case" or "the preg-

Though we profess to value individuality, our most successful politicians and celebrities are surprisingly unoriginal and uninspiring. Sometimes, they even look very much alike—as this photo of CBS *This Morning* **anchor Paula Zahn (left) interviewing Tipper Gore (center) and First Lady Hillary Rodham Clinton (right) shows.**

nant diabetic" and does not see us as individuals. We feel deprived when we learn that we were chosen because "the company was looking for a Hispanic male."

We cope, it seems, only by a kind of self-deception, in which we attempt to convince ourselves that we are living the way we choose to, that we are living reasonably, "all things considered."

One of the most influential, intriguing, and arresting responses to the massing of society and the loss of respect for the individual goes under the name **existentialism**. Existentialism refers to any philosophy that says the most important philosophical matters involve fundamental questions of meaning and choice as they affect individuals. Existential themes include choice, freedom, identity, alienation, inauthenticity, despair, and awareness of our own mortality. Existentialists point out that objective science and rationalistic philosophy do not come to grips with the real problems of human existence: "What am *I* to do?" "To what can *I* commit myself?" "What does *my life* mean?" Existentialists believe that general answers, grand Hegelian-type metaphysical systems, and supposedly objective and rational theories cannot address the existential (living, concrete) concerns of individuals.

EXISTENTIALISM
Term used to refer to any philosophy that emphasizes fundamental questions of meaning and choice as they affect existing individuals; existential themes include choice, freedom, identity, alienation, inauthenticity, despair, and awareness of our own mortality.

The early existentialists were among the first to identify major issues unique to postindustrial, highly specialized, technical, "sophisticated" societies: increased loss of individuality; increased pressure to conform; the threat to human freedom and dignity from science and bureaucracy. Philosopher of history Samuel Enoch Stumpf says:

> Existentialism was bound to happen. The individual had over the centuries been pushed into the background by systems of thought, historical events, and technological forces. The major systems of philosophy had rarely paid attention to the uniquely personal concerns of individuals. Although Aristotle, for example, wrote a major treatise on ethics, Montaigne could say that "I can't recognize most of my daily doings when they appear in Aristotle." Nietzsche also wrote that "to our scholars, strangely enough, the most pressing question does not occur: to what end is their work . . . useful?" . . . [Traditional] philosophy for the most part dealt with technical problems of metaphysics, ethics, and the theory of knowledge in a general and objective manner, which bypassed the intimate concerns of [people] about their personal destiny. Historical events, particularly wars, showed a similar disregard for the feelings and aspirations of individuals. And technology . . . soon gathered a momentum of its own, forcing [people] to fit their lives into the rhythm of machines. Everywhere [people] were losing their peculiarly human qualities. They were being converted from "persons" into "pronouns," from "subjects" into "objects," from an "I" into an "it."[1]

Unfortunately, many scholars and authors talk about existentialism as if it were a clearly defined school of philosophy. It is not. Let us resist reducing the existentialists to an abstraction, to a category, by acknowledging that there is no such thing as an existentialist school of philosophy. Individual philosophers, poets, novelists, dramatists, and artists address the nature and quality of daily human existence in their work. When they do, they are "existentialists."

In this chapter, we take a look at two of the most important thinkers first associated with that label, Søren Kierkegaard and Friedrich Nietzsche. Although Kierkegaard was a Christian and Nietzsche was an atheist, both were fierce champions of the real, the concrete, the existing individual. In Chapter 18, we will look at contemporary existentialism.

PHILOSOPHICAL QUERY

Reflect back over your philosophical studies so far. Can you "recognize yourself" in the philosophies you've studied? In which ones? Discuss.

To dream here perhaps of equal rights, equal training, equal claims and obligations: that is a typical sign of shallow-mindedness.
Friedrich Nietzsche

Had I to carve an inscription on my grave I would ask for none other than "the individual."
Søren Kierkegaard

SØREN KIERKEGAARD

Søren Kierkegaard

The most important work of **Søren Kierkegaard (1813–1855)** was virtually ignored during his lifetime, in part because he wrote in Danish, in part because of what he wrote, in part because of his brilliant use of sarcasm and irony. Yet some 135 years later, Kierkegaard's journals and essays have a contemporary, living quality that still engages and disturbs many a reader. His work is not easy to fathom, but it is well worth the struggle.

Because he rebelled against the system and against objectivity, Kierkegaard's work confounds easy classification (which would delight him). His "unscientific" and "unsystematic" attacks on conventional Christian theology and dogma, on science, and on professional philosophy took the form of satirical essays, parables, anecdotes, real and fictional journals. Even after his works were translated into other languages and became widely known, Kierkegaard's reputation has remained mixed: Was he a philosopher? A writer of fiction? A theologian? A superficial wit?

What are scholars and philosophers to make of a writer who asserted that "truth is subjectivity" and "the System is a lie"? Can we criticize the inconsistencies and lack of a coherent philosophy in a writer who boldly denounced both systematic consistency and coherence? As we shall see, Kierkegaard's attack represented a radical shift in orientation from objectivity to subjectivity, from efforts to impose rational consistency to a search for authentic existence. Kierkegaard said, "The question is not what am I to *believe* [think, understand], but what am I to *do*?"

Kierkegaard saw himself as a disciple of Socrates. And like Socrates, his life and work make a seamless whole. We cannot know Kierkegaard the existentialist without meeting Kierkegaard the individual.

The Family Curse

Born in Copenhagen, Denmark, the youngest of seven children, Søren Kierkegaard was deeply and permanently influenced by his father Michael, a strict and devout Lutheran. One day, while herding sheep, young Michael cursed God over the conditions of his life. Until his death, he never forgot what he had done and never forgave himself for his youthful outburst. Though he grew up to become a successful merchant, Michael Kierkegaard remained consumed by what he saw as his unforgivable blasphemy. Years later, weakened by grief and loneliness, he had sexual relations with a housemaid immediately after his first wife died. Overwhelmed with guilt and sadness, consumed by his two "great sins," Michael lived without peace of mind or genuine hope, seeing himself only as a sinner.

The youngest son of an elderly father, Søren was his father's favorite. To him went Michael's legacy: a sense of despair and melancholy, an obsession

The real action is not the external act, but an internal decision in which the individual puts an end to mere possibility and identifies himself with the content of his thought in order to exist in it.
Søren Kierkegaard

with the nature and possibility of a finite individual's relationship with an infinite God. Unusually intelligent and sensitive, Søren had few close friends as a child and spent most of his formative years in the company of his father.

In 1830, Kierkegaard enrolled in the University of Copenhagen to study theology. The "unforgiven" father wanted his son to become a minister. Kierkegaard soon discovered, however, that theology did not interest him as much as philosophy and literature. He spent the next ten years living a collegiate life devoted primarily to drinking and attending the theater. He became known for his good taste in food, clothes, and other epicurean delights. During this time, he lost interest in religion and became estranged from his father.

Father and son made peace before Michael died in 1838, and Michael confessed the two great sins of his past to his son. Kierkegaard referred to the confession as "a great earthquake," and became consumed by its implications. He returned to the study of theology, passing his exams with honor in 1840. The next year he preached his first sermon and submitted a master's thesis on Socratic irony.

The Universal Formula

At the same time, at age twenty-seven, Kierkegaard fell in love with Regina Olsen, the attractive fourteen-year-old daughter of an important government official. When Regina turned seventeen, the couple became formally engaged, but almost immediately Kierkegaard broke the engagement. For the rest of his life, he struggled to understand, explain, and justify this action. In his *Journals* he wrote, "It was a time of terrible suffering to have to be so cruel and at the same time to love her as I did. She fought like a tigress. If I had not believed that God had lodged a veto, she would have been victorious."[2]

Kierkegaard may have had more than one motive for breaking up with Regina Olsen. He may have been afraid of committed marriage. He may have found her cheery temperament incompatible with his somber melancholy. He may have feared that his depressions would harm her. He may have been a cad, as the popular opinion in Copenhagen had it. Perhaps all these motives played a part.

But of special interest to us is Kierkegaard's later interpretation of his "sacrifice" of Regina Olsen. Two weeks after he broke the engagement, Kierkegaard fled to Berlin, where he wrote *Either/Or, A Fragment of Life* (1843), his first important work, and *Repetition: An Essay in Experimental Psychology* (1843), through which he hoped to re-establish his relationship with Regina. But before he could publish *Repetition*, Kierkegaard learned of Regina's engagement to a former boyfriend. Stunned, hurt, and despairing, Kierkegaard destroyed the last ten pages of his original manuscript, which addressed his hope of a reconciliation with Regina.

For the rest of his short life, Kierkegaard claimed he had "offered up" his love for Regina Olsen as a sacrifice to God, just as Abraham offered Isaac in the Old Testament story (Genesis 22). Kierkegaard had thought he had

I owe everything I am to the wisdom of an old man and the simplicity of a young girl.
Søren Kierkegaard

What I really lack is to be clear in my own mind what I am to do. The thing is to understand myself, to see what God really wants me to do; the thing is to find a truth that is true for me, to find the idea for which I can live and die.
Søren Kierkegaard

to choose *either* God *or* "the world," and that choosing one excluded the other entirely. Torn between a career as a minister and a comfortable, middle-class life with Regina, Kierkegaard thought he had discovered a way to have both. His solution was what he interpreted as the "universal formula" revealed in the story of Abraham and Isaac: Having finally blessed Abraham and Sarah with a son in their old age, God then tested Abraham's faith by sending an angel to him, demanding the blood sacrifice of Isaac. Abraham submitted to God's will in a supreme act of faith, resisting the pull of his love for Isaac and resisting the moral code of his time which forbade such human sacrifice. At the last moment God stopped Abraham, and returned Isaac to him. Kierkegaard interpreted this story to mean: If you give something up for God, you get it back *plus* the love and salvation of God. In other words, by giving something up, you get to keep it! Applying this "formula" to his predicament of "*Either* devote my life to God *or* live in comfort with Regina," Kierkegaard "reasoned" a way to have both. He was stunned when he lost her. What went wrong? Didn't Kierkegaard do just what Abraham had done? Was his reasoning somehow flawed?

In his later works, Kierkegaard wrestled with the basic existential problems exemplified in this episode from one individual's life: What am I to *do* when confronted with the awesome finality of any choice? Can I objectively and scientifically model my relationship with God after Abraham's? Or Paul's? Or Christ's? How can I know what God wants *me* to do? Can I *reason* it out? What do *universal principles* have to do with *this choice*? Kierkegaard learned that he was not Abraham. He concluded that universal principles must give way to individual predicaments.

The Christian

Struggling with the existential predicament of choice and commitment, Kierkegaard grew increasingly interested in what it means to be a Christian. He became convinced that institutionalized Christianity suffers from the same inauthenticity as other institutions. **Inauthenticity** results when the nature and needs of the individual are ignored, denied, obscured, or made less important than institutions, abstractions, or groups. **Authenticity** is the subjective condition of an individual living honestly and courageously in the moment without refuge in excuses, and without reliance on groups or institutions for meaning and purpose. Given the stakes—salvation or damnation—Kierkegaard turned his penetrating wit and scathing criticism to the task of distinguishing "institutionalized Christianity" from authentic Christianity. He published three important attacks on the Danish church, *The Sickness Unto Death* (1849), *Training in Christianity* (1850), and *For Self-Examination* (1851).

When his "attacks on Christendom" were largely ignored, Kierkegaard decided to make a clear, dramatic existential step: He had to break officially with the church. At the time of this decision, the head of the Danish church

If you are always profoundly occupied, you are beyond all embarrassment.
Friedrich Nietzsche

INAUTHENTICITY
Condition that results when the nature and needs of the individual are ignored, denied, and obscured or sacrificed for institutions, abstractions, or groups.

AUTHENTICITY
Subjective condition of an individual living honestly and courageously in the moment, refusing to make excuses, and not relying on groups or institutions for meaning and purpose.

was Bishop J. P. Mynster, who had been a close friend of Michael Kierkegaard. Because Søren himself respected and cared for the old man, he delayed his attack until Mynster died. Upon the bishop's death, however, he published his vehement attack on "false Christianity" in an article called "Was Bishop Mynster a Witness for the Truth?" Kierkegaard's answer was an unequivocal no. He argued that the bishop was a witness to an error, a witness to false Christianity.

Both the clergy and the general public rose to the defense of their beloved bishop as a symbol of a way of life. Kierkegaard continued to hammer away at what he saw as false Christianity, hypocrisy, inauthenticity, and "mere living." To these he opposed his famous "leap of faith," a complete commitment to God made each instant, made without guarantees, made alone, made in fear and trembling. He rejected an institutionalized religion of formulas, guarantees, security, and "group salvation."

On October 2, 1855, Kierkegaard was nearly broke. He visited his banker brother-in-law to withdraw the last of his money. On his way home, he fell to the street, paralyzed from the waist down. Destitute, helpless, and weak, Søren Kierkegaard died quietly November 11, 1855. He was only forty-two years old.

That Individual

Kierkegaard was buried in the huge Cathedral Church of Copenhagen. His eulogy was delivered to a crowd of both friends and enemies by his brother Peter, a respected member of the Danish church. Upset with the way the institution had violated the spirit of its great critic, his nephew caused a scene at the graveside. The irony of such a funeral would not have been lost on Kierkegaard.

The most interesting epitaph for Kierkegaard, however, is found in his own bitterly ironical words:

> The Martyrdom this author suffered may be briefly described thus: He suffered from being a genius in a provincial town. The standard he applied . . . was on the average far too great for his contemporaries; it raised the price on them too terribly; it almost made it seem as if the provincial town and the majority in it did not possess [absolute authority], but that there was a God in existence.
>
> Yet it is true that he found also here on earth what he sought. He himself was *that individual* if no one else was, and he became that more and more. It was the cause of Christianity he served, his life from childhood on being marvelously fitted for such a service. Thus he carried to completion the task of translating completely into terms of reflection what Christianity is, what it means to be a Christian. . . .

It is not so much a question of choosing the right as the energy, the earnestness, the pathos with which one chooses. Thereby the personality announces its inner infinity, and thereby, in turn, the personality is consolidated.

Søren Kierkegaard

> . . . he could not ascribe [the grand enterprise he under-
> took] to any man, least of all would he ascribe it to him-
> self; if he were to ascribe it to anyone, it would be to Provi-
> dence, to whom it was in fact ascribed, day after day and
> year after year, by the author, who historically died of a mor-
> tal disease but poetically died of longing for eternity, where
> uninterruptedly he would have nothing else to do but to
> thank God.[3]

TRUTH AS SUBJECTIVITY

Perhaps the major existential issue is "What am *I* to *do*?"
Not "How is an individual to live?" but "How am *I* to *exist*?"
As Kierkegaard pointed out, any choice, once made, rules out *all* other possibilities. To be fully conscious of this is to experience what Nietzsche called
fatefulness, the fact that our actions and choices create our individual destiny. Deciding to take a philosophy class—or deciding not to take one; deciding to marry that person—or not to marry that person; checking the air
in a car's tires—or not checking it: on such inescapable daily choices hang
the quality and shape of individual lives. The basic fact of Kierkegaard's *project*, as he referred to his existentialism, is the dilemma of lived choices:

> What I really lack is to be clear in my mind *what I am to do*, not
> what I am to know, except in so far as a certain understanding
> must precede every action. The thing is to understand myself,
> to see what God really wishes *me* to do; the thing is to find a
> truth which is true *for me*, to find *the idea for which I can live
> and die*. What would be the use of discovering so-called objec-
> tive truth, of working through all the systems of philosophy
> and of being able, if required, to review them all and show up
> the inconsistencies within each system;—what good would it
> do me to be able to explain the meaning of Christianity if it
> had *no* deeper significance *for me and for my life*;—what good
> would it do me if the truth stood before me, cold and naked,
> not caring whether I recognised her or not, producing in me
> a shudder of fear rather than a trusting devotion? I certainly
> do not deny that I still recognise an *imperative of understanding*
> and that through it one can work upon men, *but it must be
> taken up into my life*, and *that is* what I now recognise as the
> most important thing. That is what my soul longs after, as the
> African desert thirsts for water. That is what I lack, and that is
> why I am left standing like a man who has rented a house and
> gathered all the furniture and household things together, but
> has not yet found the beloved with whom to share the joys
> and sorrows of his life.[4]

*All our norms are nothing
but desires in disguise.*
Abraham Joshua Heschel

*For one thing is needful: that
a human being should at-
tain satisfaction with himself, whether it be by means
of this or that poetry and art;
only then is a human being
at all tolerable to behold.
Whoever is dissatisfied with
himself is continually ready
for revenge, and we others
will be his victims.*
Friedrich Nietzsche

PHILOSOPHICAL QUERY
How do you make life choices? Do you make them clearly and consciously, or do things just somehow happen? Does your religion or philosophy help you make concrete choices? Does a psychological theory?

Kierkegaard realized that no amount of objective, systematic Hegelian knowledge could ever provide a meaning for life. He did not deny the value of objective knowledge, which he refers to as an *imperative of understanding*, but he pointed out that the "objective facts" of a life cannot account for its existential quality. In *Either/Or*, he tells the story of a man who decides to scientifically and objectively study a Christian, in order to understand what it is to "be a Christian." Following his subject about, the observer notes what he eats, where he goes, when he reads the paper, what paper he reads, what brand of tobacco he smokes, and so on. After amassing quite a quantity of factual, objective data, the observer laments, "But he does just what I do!"

Kierkegaard's point, made ironically, is that objective information reveals facts or truths, not truth. What makes one individual a Christian and another a non-Christian, Kierkegaard claims, is not the objective conditions of their lives but their *inner condition: truth is a subjective condition, not an objective one.*

The implications of this claim—that scientific, or objective, impersonal, understanding can never pass beyond factual description—are radical. Objective understanding cannot reveal truth; it cannot give Kierkegaard—or any existing individual—reasons to live; it cannot answer the most important question: What am I to do? Objective, scientific, philosophical, and theological systems and arguments cannot provide *"the idea for which I can live and die."* In an era seduced by faith that science inevitably leads to "progress," Kierkegaard's existential critique challenges "science" ("the system" or "the establishment") to answer: What am I to do? Give *me* a reason for which *I* can live and die.

Kierkegaard wanted to pass from fragmentation to integration. In his terms, he wanted to alter his life from a "chance assemblage of mere details" into an existence with a "focus and center." The modern age, with its drive toward massive institutions, infatuation with objectivity, and reliance on the scientific understanding of human behavior, inhibits personal integration. Neither scientific, objective understanding nor elaborate, abstract philosophical systems can deal with *"that individual."* Systems and theories only identify patterns and abstractions. They never even see "the existing individual."

The story is told (by Kierkegaard) of the absent-minded man so abstracted from his own life that he hardly knows he exists until, one fine morning, he wakes up to find himself dead.

William Barrett

Objectivity as Untruth

Philosophers have traditionally agreed that arguments and evidence should be evaluated rationally and objectively; evidence of partiality or bias is usually considered a serious weakness in a philosopher's arguments. Scientists, too, see impartial, impersonal, objective evidence as a praiseworthy goal.

WE ARE BEING DESTROYED BY OUR KNOWLEDGE

Our culture is superficial today, and our knowledge dangerous, because we are rich in mechanisms and poor in purposes. The balance of mind which once came of a warm religious faith is gone; science has taken from us the supernatural bases of our morality, and all the world seems consumed in a disorderly individualism that reflects the chaotic fragmentation of our character. . . . We move about the earth with unprecedented speed, but we do not know, and have not thought, where we are going, or whether we shall find any happiness there for our harassed souls. We are being destroyed by our knowledge, which has made us drunk with our power. And we shall not be saved without wisdom.

Will Durant
The Mansions of Philosophy: A Survey of Human Life and Destiny (New York: Simon & Schuster, 1929), pp. vii, viii, xff.

Kierkegaard vehemently disagreed. He considered objectivity, impersonality, and impartiality as dangerous, insulting, and ugly delusions. That is, not only is impartiality impossible, but claims of objectivity and disinterest are always lies. In the first place, preferring objectivity and impartiality to subjective involvement is itself a bias: *favoring objectivity is a form of partiality*. Worse, our desire for objectivity deceives us by obscuring our individual (subjective) responsibility for our evaluations. The philosopher who says, "Reason demands that we must reject X because it is inconsistent" has herself *subjectively chosen* certain values: objectivity and consistency. Moreover, "reason" is a mere abstraction, a noble-sounding term that conceals an individual, subjective choice. But anything that obscures the existing individual interferes with authenticity, honesty, and passionate commitment.

The impersonal quality of objective language reduces the uniqueness of individual existence to generalizations, abstractions, and features in common. But the vital issues of existence confront the complex, individually existing self, not the general self of psychologists and philosophers, or Descartes' "thing which thinks," or Kant's "rational agent," or Hume's "bundle of perceptions." Objectivity, by its very nature, is cool, detached, impersonal. Existence is not:

> The difficulty that inheres in existence, with which the existing individual is confronted, is one that never really comes to expression in the language of abstract thought, much less receives an explanation. . . . Abstract thought . . . ignores the concrete and the temporal, the existential process, the predicament of the existing individual arising from his being a synthesis of the temporal and the eternal situated in existence. . . .

All logical thinking employs the language of abstraction. . . . It is easier to indulge in abstract thought than it is to exist.
Søren Kierkegaard

We do not err because truth is difficult to see. It is visible at a glance. We err because this is more comfortable.
Alexander Solzhenitsyn

. . . Existing is ordinarily regarded as no very complex matter, much less an art, since we all exist; but abstract thinking takes rank as an accomplishment. But to really exist . . . that is truly difficult.[5]

Descartes, and all those who followed his lead, reduced existence to believing: "I *think*, therefore I am." Abstract, rationalistic philosophies ignore the real predicament of actual existence: deciding what to do. Actual decisions are not the neat, reasonable calculations of philosophers, nor are they the products of systematic scientific thinking. Abstract philosophies and all metaphysical systems merely observe life from a distance; they do not take part in it.

The Present Age

Kierkegaard viewed the mid–nineteenth century as an era of passionless mediocrity and conformity. He lamented the *massing of society*, by which he meant both the diminution of the individual's role in the face of mass production and the press (mass media), and the loss of truth in the face of objectivity and abstraction. He included what he saw as the inflated reputation of science and technological solutions to human problems in the massing of society. In *Either/Or*, Kierkegaard began a profound and eloquent analysis of conformism and mediocrity:

> Let others complain that the age is wicked; my complaint is that it is wretched, for it lacks passion. Men's thoughts are thin and flimsy like lace, they are themselves pitiable like lacemakers. The thoughts of their hearts are too paltry to be sinful. For a worm it might be regarded as a sin to harbor such thoughts, but not for a being made in the image of God. Their lusts are dull and sluggish, their passions sleepy. They do their duty, these shopkeeping souls, but they clip the coin a trifle . . . ; they think that even if the Lord keeps ever so careful a set of books, they may still cheat Him a little. Out upon them! This is the reason my soul always turns back to the Old Testament and to Shakespeare. I feel that those who speak there are at least human beings: they hate, they love, they murder their enemies, and curse their descendants throughout all generations, they sin.[6]

Because the contemporary individual has no comprehensive picture of the social universe within which he lives and of the structure of modern society, he pays the price of meaninglessness and insignificance in his daily work and even a spiritual isolation from his fellows.

A. W. Levi

In an essay called *The Present Age* (1846), which, according to philosopher William Barrett, "has become the source of nearly all the Existentialist criticisms of modern society," Kierkegaard continued his attack on conformity.[7] "The crowd," he points out, overwhelms the individual, yet the individual feels frightened and lost without "the crowd." The mediocre, alienated individual needs a group to identify with, to provide "peer approval."

Yet, Kierkegaard insists, a collective identity is always somehow false; in order to belong, to fit in, we must betray some part of ourselves, must cease living our own lives and begin living "a kind of life."

PHILOSOPHICAL QUERY

During the 1993 trial of four men for allegedly attacking truck driver Reginald Denny during the Los Angeles riots triggered by the verdict in the first Rodney King beating trial, a sociologist testifying for the defense argued that the accused were not responsible for their actions because they were caught up in the "crowd contagion" of the moment. What do you think of such a defense? Analyze your behavior as part of a group or crowd. Do you find that it is always "somehow false"? Is it possible to be more yourself in a crowd than when alone? Discuss.

The intelligence of any group of people who are thinking as a "herd" rather than individually is no higher than the intelligence of the stupidest members.

Mary Day Winn

The Age of Equality

According to Kierkegaard's view of "the crowd," modern people are anonymous creatures dependent on experts to point the way to salvation or personal growth. Think about Kierkegaard's analysis in light of the many coalitions, committees, and other groups that continue to spring up in our own times as you read this passage:

> The present age tends toward a mathematical equality in which it takes so and so many to make one individual. Formerly the outstanding individual could allow himself everything and the individual in the masses nothing at all. Now everyone knows that so and so many make an individual, and quite consistently people add themselves together (it is called joining together, but that is only a polite euphemism) for the most trivial purposes. Simply in order to put a passing whim into practice a few people add themselves together, and the thing is done—they dare to do it. . . .
>
> The individual no longer belongs to God, to himself, to his beloved, to his art or to his science; he is conscious of belonging in all things to an abstraction to which he is subjected by reflection.[8]

In short, rather than being themselves, people conform to an image or idea associated with being a certain *type* of person. That's what Kierkegaard means by belonging to an "abstraction" (an image or idea) created by "reflection" (self-conscious thinking). Thus, for example, a woman tries to be "a Christian" or "a lawyer" based on some collective abstraction, some image or idea. She attempts to conform to a pattern. Today, many of us govern our lives by abstractions based on age, race, and gender.

[B]ecause man is always inclined to cling to isms, instead of seeking independent strength in himself, the danger arises that one makes father or mother out of the group and remains as infantile and insecure as before.

Marie-Louise von Franz

Those who claim to be hurt by words must be led to expect nothing as compensation. Otherwise, once they learn they can get something by claiming to be hurt, they will go into the business of being offended.
Jonathan Rauch

The abstract principle of leveling . . . like the biting east wind, has no personal relation to any individual, but has only an abstract relationship which is the same for everyone. There no hero suffers for others, or helps them; the taskmaster of all alike is the leveling process, which itself takes on their education. And the man who learns most from the leveling and himself becomes greatest does not become an outstanding man or hero—that would only impede the leveling process, which is rigidly consistent to the end; he himself prevents that from happening because he has understood the meaning of leveling: he becomes a man and nothing else, in the complete equalitarian sense.[9]

In courtrooms and classrooms, "abstractions" level us so that "everyone is treated the same." The press levels presidents and celebrities through exposés of their personal lives. The underlying message is "They're no different from us." Indeed, they are not, but the nature of these exposés, coupled with the sameness and mediocrity of the people we elect to office or turn into celebrities, seems to support Kierkegaard's conclusion that the modern age remains an era of increasing dullness, conformity, and lack of genuine individuals.

PHILOSOPHICAL QUERY

Identify some current examples of leveling, and discuss the general notion of leveling. Must efforts at furthering equality result in leveling? Is leveling possibly desirable?

Kierkegaard identified and addressed the most important issue of the contemporary world: how to become our true selves in an age dominated by sophisticated ways of influencing our thoughts, feelings, and actions. How can we find the passion to become ourselves in a world seduced by objectivity and conformity, and run by ever more massive institutions?

Friedrich Nietzsche continued the search for the authentic individual and identified the "perfect type"—which he called the *overman.*

Friedrich Nietzsche

FRIEDRICH NIETZSCHE

Perhaps no philosopher of modern times has provoked as much controversy as **Friedrich Nietzsche (1844–1900)**. Of small physical stature, so nearsighted he was nearly blind, plagued by headaches, nausea, loneliness, and depression, Nietzsche voiced an explosive philosophy that attracts and offends people nearly a century after his death. One of a handful of philosophers who can be called "best-selling" authors, Nietzsche has a poetic, confrontational style that is both exhilarating and disturbing.

Nietzsche was born in the Prussian village of Röcken. When he was four years old, his father, a Lutheran minister, died, leaving the pious little boy to the care of his mother, grandmother, two aunts, and sister. As the only man in the household, young "Fritz" became the center of attention, coddled and protected. Nietzsche's studious demeanor and religious piety earned him the nickname "the little pastor."

Nietzsche originally planned to follow in his father's footsteps and become a Lutheran minister, but in his late teens, something changed. The "good boy" lost interest in his studies. He questioned the existence of God and even sneaked away and got drunk—on a Sunday.

At twenty, Nietzsche enrolled in the University of Bonn. Freed from the pampering and domination of five women, faced with uncertainties about his faith and childhood plans for the future, Nietzsche, like Kierkegaard, went through a period of rebellious high living.

He tried his best to fit into the raucous life of late-nineteenth-century German students: drinking, boisterous singing, romantic pursuits, duels. Nietzsche joined a student club, caroused, and even fought a halfhearted duel. Yet, for all his efforts, Nietzsche was not "one of the guys." He was personally disgusted with drunken excess, smoky beer halls, and the "coarse, Philistine spirit" of his fellows. The little pastor found that kind of student life intolerable and ultimately suffered a nervous collapse.

Insofar as we believe in morality we pass sentence on existence.

Friedrich Nietzsche

The Outsider

Nietzsche left Bonn and enrolled in the University of Leipzig. There he had the good fortune to meet Professor Friedrich Ritschl, who kindled in him a passion for philology, the study of classical philosophy and literature. Ritschl recognized that Nietzsche was a brilliant scholar, and encouraged and stimulated his genius.

Despite his academic brilliance, however, Nietzsche was already a lonely man, basically an outsider. When he first moved to Leipzig, he was still shaken by his disillusionment with Bonn and by the emptiness he felt having lost his religious faith. He went through the motions of being actively interested in his life, but found himself torn by doubts. Hedonistic pursuits left him disgusted and depressed, yet the way of the church remained closed off to him.

While in this state, Nietzsche came across the work of **Arthur Schopenhauer (1788–1860)**. Schopenhauer's philosophy is known as **pessimism**, the belief that life is disappointing and that for every satisfied desire, ten new unsatisfied ones emerge; our only hope is detachment and withdrawal. In his book *The World as Will and Idea*, Schopenhauer argued that life is nothing more than a constant will to survive. We are pawns of a life force, and our best hope is to detach our individual will from the cycle of wanting–getting–wanting more. Life, in Schopenhauer's vision, is an irrational, purposeless striving for a pointless existence. According to Schopenhauer, what

PESSIMISM
Schopenhauer's theory that life is disappointing and that for every satisfied desire, new desires emerge; our only hope is detachment and withdrawal.

little salvation there is comes only from resisting the blind will to *live at all costs* and curtailing our desires.

Given his mental turmoil and deep dissatisfaction, Nietzsche responded enthusiastically to Schopenhauer. He craved some kind of meaning but was unable to find it in either pleasure or religion. At a precarious time in his life, Schopenhauer gave him something to hold on to:

> It seemed as if Schopenhauer were addressing me personally. I felt his enthusiasm, and seemed to see him before me. Every line cried aloud for renunciation, denial, resignation. Here I saw a mirror in which the world, life, my own mind were reflected in fearful grandeur. Here the wholly disinterested and heavenly eye of art looked at me; here I saw illness and salvation, banishment and refuge, hell and heaven.[10]

From Schopenhauer, Nietzsche concluded that life makes no objective, absolute sense. Life is not the result of divine plan, nor is nature orderly in any way that we can discern. Rather, life is the expression of *will*. Schopenhauer characterized the ultimate will as the will to live; Nietzsche disagreed. He insisted that life is governed by the **will to power**, a universal desire to control others and impose our values on them.

WILL TO POWER
Nietzsche's term for what he thought is a universal desire to control others and impose our values on them.

Beyond the Academy

Schopenhauer's pessimism, paradoxically, invigorated Nietzsche, and in 1868 Ritschl recommended him for a chair in classical philology. Ritschl was especially conservative, not given to excessive praise or hasty conclusions regarding the area of study to which he had devoted his life, so the recommendation he wrote for Nietzsche is all the more significant:

> However many young talents I have seen develop under my eyes for thirty-nine years . . . Nietzsche . . . is the first from whom I have ever accepted any contribution [to the philological journal *Museum*] at all while he was still a student. . . . He is the idol, and without wishing it, the leader of the whole younger generation of philologists here in Leipzig who—and they are rather numerous—cannot wait to hear him as a lecturer. You will say, I describe a phenomenon. Well, that is just what he is—and at the same time pleasant and modest. . . .
> . . . He will simply be able to do anything he wants to do.[11]

The Greek philosophers went through life feeling secretly that there were far more slaves than one might think—meaning that everybody who was not a philosopher was a slave. Their pride overflowed at the thought that even the most powerful men on earth belong among their slaves.
Friedrich Nietzsche

Though Nietzsche lacked his doctorate, his brilliance and Ritschl's strong advocacy combined to secure the position for him. "In *Germany*," Ritschl wrote, "that sort of thing happens absolutely never."

Nietzsche was only twenty-four when he was appointed professor. The university hurriedly conferred the doctorate on him—without requiring an

By the second half of the nineteenth century, art and literature,
as well as philosophy, began to reflect a romanticized vision of
Schopenhauer's pessimism. Caspar David Friedrich's painting *The
Polar Sea* depicts glaciers destroying a ship: a symbol of overcivi-
lized, industrialized man's inevitable defeat by the primal forces
of irrational nature.

examination—and Nietzsche plunged into a heavy academic routine. But
his heart and mind could not be confined to the limits of philology or philosophy—or any other academic area as then defined.

In spite of noble intentions, Nietzsche was not a particularly effective
professor. His lectures were often complex and difficult to follow, and fewer
and fewer students attended them. He did not socialize well, and found his
colleagues difficult. Academic routine drained him. His sole comforts came
from his own writing and a few close friends.

Tragic Optimism

In 1870, the Franco-Prussian War broke out. Nietzsche volunteered as a
medic and served for a short time before returning to Leipzig in poor health.
Germany humbled both Austria and France in the war. Under the powerful
vision of Otto von Bismarck (1815–1898), small German principalities were
unified into a single, powerful state dominated by Prussia. Nietzsche saw

Bismarck as an example of a "higher morality" based on strength, power, and the will to dominate. He was impressed that Bismarck ruled by "blood and iron."

About this time, Nietzsche became intrigued with Darwinism. Combining Bismarck's will to power and domination with Darwin's idea of evolution, Nietzsche transformed Schopenhauer's pessimism into his own utterly unique doctrine of overcoming. Schopenhauer was right, Nietzsche thought, in recognizing that life consists of continual struggle and hardship. But Schopenhauer's reaction—retreat and renunciation—struck Nietzsche as weak-willed and decadent. He concluded that Schopenhauer's pessimism was unhealthy and life-denying.

Yet because struggle is in fact the essence of life, optimism is a shallow, false response. Things do not always go well. There is no grand design in which everything turns out for the best at the end of the story: *no meaning is revealed.*

Nietzsche's solution was **tragic optimism**, the sense of joy and vitality that accompanies the superior individual's clear-sighted imposition of his own freely chosen values on a meaningless world. The superior person is the person who neither shrinks from struggle nor struggles blindly, controlled by a pessimistic instinct to survive at any cost. The superior person *wills* to live deliberately and consciously. The superior person *overcomes* pessimism without retreating into lies about ultimate meaning or purpose. In Nietzsche's view, Schopenhauer failed to recognize that the struggle to survive aims at the dominance of the strongest and the fittest. The tragic optimist imposes meaning on a meaningless universe and overcomes his or her own innate fears and weaknesses.

TRAGIC OPTIMISM
According to Nietzsche, the sense of joy and vitality that accompanies the superior individual's clear-sighted imposition of his own freely chosen values on a meaningless world.

Zarathustra Speaks

Citing ill health, Nietzsche resigned from the university in 1879, when he was thirty-four. He was granted a pension. Nietzsche knew he needed to break free from the confines of academic scholarship and carve out his own path. He came to see himself as the prophet of a higher, healthier morality, a morality so far beyond conventional values that it required the revaluation of all values. He took to referring to himself as an *immoralist* and an *iconoclast.* He spoke of "doing philosophy with a hammer"—tapping on the statues of great idols to see which are hollow and then smashing them to bits.

Freed from the demands of the university, Nietzsche polished and refined both his thinking and his writing. His greatest work was accomplished in the ten-year period following his retirement from teaching. For a time, he lost some of his ferocity, mellowed, perhaps, by the physical and cultural climates of Switzerland and Italy, where he spent most of his time.

His most "cheerful" books, *The Dawn of Day* (1881) and *The Gay Science* (1882), were written while he was friends with Lou Salome, a witty, appealing young Jewish intellectual. Nietzsche was quite taken with her. In their

Life is no argument. The conditions of life might include error.

Friedrich Nietzsche

walks and talks together he found a special kind of companionship. He seems to have found in her both a disciple and a lover. We do not know whether he ever proposed to her, as she later claimed. In any case, Lou Salome ultimately left Nietzsche for another man. (Years later, when Nietzsche was famous, Lou Salome capitalized on her relationship with him.)

Devastated by her abandonment, Nietzsche retreated to the Swiss Alps. In this agonizingly lonely, hurt, and bitter mood, he produced his most famous work, *Thus Spake Zarathustra* (1885). The title comes from the Sanskrit phrase *Iti vuttakam*, meaning "Thus spoke the Holy One."[12] Nietzsche used the name of the ancient Persian prophet Zoroaster, but created his own Zarathustra. *Zarathustra* was a call to rise above decadence and mediocrity. Nietzsche later described *Zarathustra* as a revelation:

> "One hears—one does not seek; one takes—one does not ask who gives; a thought suddenly flashes up like lightning, it comes with necessity, unhesitatingly—I have never had any choice in the matter."[13]

Nietzsche's Zarathustra is at once a great destroyer of false values and in the same instant a creator of new, higher, healthier values. Nietzsche said that Zarathustra "as a type . . . *overtook* me."[14] Zarathustra the destroyer-creator announces the arrival of the next evolutionary type, the *Übermensch*, or the overman.

Nietzsche followed *Zarathustra* with what many consider the two most coherent statements of his philosophy, *Beyond Good and Evil* (1886) and *The Genealogy of Morals* (1887). Consisting mostly of aphorisms and short essays, both books are essentially commentaries on the gospel of the overman espoused in *Zarathustra*. Nietzsche's purpose is clear: to destroy conventional morality and replace it with a higher "immoral" ideal. *Zarathustra* announces the death of God and of merely-human beings. It heralds the arrival of the next evolutionary step: overman.

The Last Philosopher

During this period of his life Nietzsche lived modestly, in rooming houses, refusing to succumb to pessimism. Writer Stefan Zweig's touching description of Nietzsche reminds us that there are many kinds of courage, many ways to be strong:

> Carefully the myopic man sits down to a table; carefully, the man with the sensitive stomach considers every item on the menu: whether the tea is not too strong, the food not spiced too much, for every mistake in his diet upsets his sensitive digestion, and every transgression in his nourishment wreaks havoc with his quivering nerves for days. No glass of wine, no

Both Nietzsche and Socrates are intensely personal thinkers, actively engaged in changing, in one way or another, the moral quality of the life of the people around them, though they pursue their goals in radically different ways. . . . Both desperately need their audience's attention.

Alexander Nehamas

[Nietzsche] never hesitated to change his attitudes according to the needs of life rather than those of mere logic.

Janko Lavrin

*For me, then nobility is syn-
onymous with a life of effort,
ever set on excelling oneself,
in passing beyond what one
is [at a given moment] to
what one sets up as a duty
and an obligation. In this
way the noble life stands opposed to the common or inert
life, which reclines statically
upon itself, condemned to
perpetual immobility, unless
external force compels it to
come out of itself.*

José Ortega y Gasset

beer, no alcohol, no coffee at his place, no cigar and no cigarette after his meal, nothing that stimulates, refreshes, or rests
him; only the short, meager meal and a little urbane, unpro-
found conversation in a soft voice with an occasional neighbor
(as a man speaks who for years has been unused to talking
and is afraid of being asked too much).

And upon entering again into the small, narrow, modest,
coldly furnished *chambre garnie*, where innumerable notes,
pages, writings, and proofs are piled up on the table, but no
flower, no decoration, scarcely a book and rarely a letter. Back
in a corner, a heavy and graceless wooden trunk, his only
possession, with the two shirts and the other worn suit. Otherwise only . . . manuscripts, and on a tray innumerable bottles
and jars and potions; against the migraines, which often render him all but senseless for hours, against his stomach cramps,
against spasmodic vomiting, against the slothful intestines, and
above all the dreadful sedatives against his insomnia, chloral
hydrate and Veronal. A frightful arsenal of poisons and drugs,
yet the only helpers in the empty silence of this strange room
in which he never rests except in brief artificially conquered
sleep. Wrapped in his overcoat and a woolen scarf (for the
wretched stove smokes and does not give warmth), his fin-
gers freezing, his double glasses pressed close to the paper,
his hurried hand writes for hours—words the dim eyes can
hardly decipher. For hours he sits like this and writes until his
eyes burn.[15]

Overwhelmed by disappointment and loneliness, disturbed by what he saw as
rampant mediocrity and hypocrisy, Nietzsche struggled on with his writing.

The last years of Nietzsche's life were tragic. His health deteriorated even
further, and he became increasingly, bitterly isolated and lonely.

I call myself the last philosopher because I am the last man.
Nobody talks to me but myself, and my voice comes to me like
that of a dying person. . . . Though I try to conceal my loneliness from myself—the terrible loneliness of the last philosopher!—and make my way into the multitude and into love by
lies, for my heart cannot bear the terror of the loneliest loneliness and compels me to talk as if I were two.[16]

As his disappointments mounted, Nietzsche quarreled with practically
everyone, his human contact reduced to innkeepers, shop clerks, and others with whom he had superficial interactions. To a friend he wrote, "For
the lonely one, even noise is a consolation. If I could give you an idea of my
feeling of loneliness! I have nobody among the living or among the dead, to
whom I feel related. This is indescribably horrible!"[17] In a bitingly poignant
letter, Nietzsche remarked that few of his friends cared enough to read the

copies of his books he sent them. For a soul with so much to say, this was the worst hurt of all.

In January 1889 in Turin, Italy, Nietzsche had another breakdown. His mother brought him home to Germany, and his life ended much as it had begun, in the care of his mother and sister. After their mother's death, Nietzsche's sister moved him to Weimar, where the prophet of struggle, of overcoming, spent the rest of his life half-paralyzed, slipping in and out of sanity. He died about midday, August 25, 1900.

I have always written my works with my whole body. I do not know what is meant by an intellectual problem.
Friedrich Nietzsche

GOD IS DEAD

Nietzsche's most famous single idea is probably his announcement that God is dead. What did he mean?

Nietzsche claimed he was the first to have "discovered" the death of God. In part, he meant that the *idea of God* had lost its full creative force, its full power. Science and technology were usurping God's place in people's lives. The full extent of the dethronement of God was not yet felt by the great masses, who still *believed that they believed* in God. Yet if we dig deep into our own psyches, Nietzsche prophesied, we will discover that we no longer have ultimate faith in God: our true faith is in scientific and technological progress.

Almost two thousand years, and no new god!
Friedrich Nietzsche

Moreover, Nietzsche thought there is no turning back; authentic faith in God is not possible in the modern world. God is dead and we have killed him, with "progress," with "optimism," with faith in this world. Yet so deeply ingrained is the language of God, the idea of God, that we are unaware of the great spiritual shift. The news of God's death has not reached us—that is, it has not penetrated to our very bones. We worship, but falsely. Our faith is empty at bottom, but though some of us may sense that the old religions are dead and dying, we are unable to face the consequences of life without God.

And terrible those consequences can be. If there is no God, Nietzsche said, then all values must be revalued. In one of the most famous passages in modern philosophy, Nietzsche, the prophet of the death of God, delivered his message in the form of a parable:

> *The madman.*—Have you not heard of the madman who lit a lantern in the bright morning hours, ran to the market place, and cried incessantly: "I seek God! I seek God!"—As many of those who did not believe in God were standing around just then, he provoked much laughter. Has he got lost? asked one. Did he lose his way like a child? asked another. Or is he hiding? Is he afraid of us? Has he gone on a voyage? emigrated?— Thus they yelled and laughed.
>
> The madman jumped into their midst and pierced them with his eyes. "Whither is God?" he cried; "I will tell you. *We have killed him*—you and I. All of us are his murderers. But how did we do this? How could we drink up the sea? Who

gave us the sponge to wipe away the entire horizon? What were we doing when we unchained the earth from its sun? Whither is it moving now? Whither are we moving? Away from all suns? Are we not plunging continually? Backward, sideward, forward, in all directions? Is there still any up or down? Are we not straying as through an infinite nothing? Do we not feel the breath of empty space? Has it not become colder? Is not night continually closing in on us? Do we not need to light lanterns in the morning? Do we hear nothing as yet of the noise of the gravediggers who are burying God? Do we smell nothing yet of the divine decomposition? Gods, too, decompose. God is dead. God remains dead. And we have killed him."[18]

This parable must be understood in light of Nietzsche's overall cultural critique, in which he predicted the decline of Christianity. That is, he saw the world as no longer innocent. Copernicus and Galileo had forever changed our sense of scale: the earth is a tiny, virtually invisible speck in a massive, purposeless universe. "What were we doing when we unchained the earth from its sun?" This new universe has no fixed center: "Is there still any up or down? Are we not straying as through an infinite nothing?" Darwin had forever altered our sense of ourselves as God's special creation. The new image of merely-human beings is ignoble: we are but one species among thousands struggling to survive, descendants of some primordial ooze.

What the masses think of as "progress" has come at a great price: the price of a way of life, the price of our vision of ourselves. It is difficult to comprehend the enormous scale of this change, this death of a worldview, Nietzsche insisted. Indeed, some of us may lack the intelligence, the courage, and the will to comprehend it.

How shall we comfort ourselves, the murderers of all murderers? What was holiest and mightiest of all that the world has yet owned has bled to death under our knives: who will wipe this blood off us? What water is there for us to clean ourselves? What festivals of atonement, what sacred games shall we have to invent? Is not the greatness of this deed too great for us? Must we not ourselves become gods simply to appear worthy of it? There has never been a greater deed; and whoever is born after us—for the sake of this deed he will belong to a higher history than all history hitherto.[19]

NIHILISM

According to Nietzsche, the death of God leads to nihilism. From the Latin word for "nothing," **nihilism** refers to the belief that the universe lacks meaning and purpose. Consequently, moral,

NIHILISM
From Latin for "nothing"; belief that the universe lacks meaning and purpose.

Nihilism as the wave of the future: The Nazis claimed Nietzsche as one of their philosophical fathers. While their doctrine of power and the master race often echoes Nietzschean language, no *mass* movement could ever reflect Nietzsche's philosophy of self-overcoming. How many supermen can you spot in this crowd?

social, and political values are *creative interpretations*; they reflect their subjective origins. Without God, there is no objective base for values.

According to Nietzsche, nihilism was the wave of the future (our present). He predicted that as more and more people perceive religious values to be empty and science as having no meaning or purpose to offer us, a sense of emptiness will initially prevail: "It all amounts to nothing. Life is a cosmic accident. There is no supernatural order; no divinely or rationally ordained goal." Without God, without *the* goal, what is left? Only many goals; only *this* momentary goal. Without God, we can turn only to ourselves.

Since there is no objective meaning, Zarathustra's new "law tablet" (which replaces the Ten Commandments of the dead God) rests on the will to power:

> For one should make no mistake about the meaning of the title that this gospel of the future wants to bear. "*The Will to Power*: Attempt at a Revaluation of All Values"—in this formulation a countermovement finds expression . . . a movement that in some future will take the place of this perfect nihilism . . . and certainly can come only after and out of it. For

We should be mindful of everything, for we can interpret everything.

Hermann Hesse

why has the advent of nihilism become *necessary*? Because the values we have had hitherto thus draw their final consequence; because nihilism represents the ultimate logical conclusion of our great values and ideals—because we must experience nihilism before we can find out what these "values" really had.—We require, sometime, *new values*.[20]

In a nihilistic universe, what determines what counts? What determines which physique is beautiful? What determines whether it is better to be meek or arrogant? According to Nietzsche, the answers are always found in the particular, subjective interests of individuals and groups. We *choose* value systems and philosophies based on our sense of power: which interpretation gives me and my kind advantage over others?

OVERMAN

The death of God signals both a great calamity and a great opportunity—depending on the individual. It is a calamity to those inferior types who cannot bear to stand on their own. It is a glorious opportunity for the fearless, the brave, the overman.

The **overman** is a new "higher type" that will emerge out of the weakness and hypocrisies of the common herd. He is more than a merely-human being. Zarathustra says the overman cannot emerge except through struggle and by abolishing the false idols of conventional morality and decadent religion.

OVERMAN
Nietzsche's "higher type," a more-than-human being that will emerge only by overcoming the false idols of conventional morality and religion; announced in *Thus Spake Zarathustra*.

> But my fervent will to create impels me ever again toward man; thus is the hammer impelled toward the stone, O men, in the stone there sleeps an image, the image of my images. Alas, that it must sleep in the hardest, the ugliest stone! Now my hammer rages cruelly against its prison. Pieces of rock rain from the stone; what is that to me? I want to perfect it; for a shadow came to me—the stillest and lightest of all things once came to me. The beauty of the overman came to me as a shadow. O my brothers, what are the gods to me now?
> Thus spoke Zarathustra.[21]

If we have our own why of life, we shall get along with almost any how.

Friedrich Nietzsche

Without God to limit us, to define us, to smother us, we can finally grow "beyond man." In Nietzsche's philosophy, "man," meaning the merely-human being, is defined in terms of God. We are created in "the image of God" and remain perpetual "children of God." When God dies, we are left without identity or purpose, in a vast universe that "just is." The same science that has given us so much has robbed us of purpose. The deeper science looks, the less it finds: molecules, atoms, electrons, quarks, energy . . . the abyss.

Nietzsche saw himself as the prophet of the next stage in human evolution. The next order is virtually a new species in terms of its psychological and spiritual differences from mere-man. Having no permanent, absolute, universal identity without God, we must create one. The overman is Nietzsche's answer to the pessimism and nihilism that follow in the wake of God's death:

> The greatest recent event—that "God is dead," that the belief in the Christian god has become unbelievable—is already beginning to cast its first shadows. . . . The event itself is far too great, too distant, too remote for the multitude's capacity for comprehension even for the tidings of it to be thought of as having *arrived* as yet. Much less may one suppose that many people know as yet *what* this event really means—and how much must collapse now that [the possibility of] faith has been undermined because it was built upon this faith [in God's existence], propped up by it, grown into it; for example, the whole of our . . . morality.[22]

Nietzsche never fully developed a picture of overman. Of course, given that the overman is further from mere-man than we are from an ape, no merely-human being can comprehend the overman. Nietzsche readily admitted that he is only the prophet of the higher type, adding, "But from time to time I may be granted a glance—only one glance—at something perfect, something that has attained its end, something happy, powerful, triumphant."[23]

SLAVE MORALITY

Though we may never fully grasp exactly what or who the overman is, we can perhaps glimpse its shadow indirectly by taking a look at the actions and beliefs of what amounts to its opposite: the slave or underman.

Underman, from the German *untermensch*, is one of the terms Nietzsche uses for the "merely human" type of person who cannot face being alone in a godless universe. Underman refuses to be an individual, does not even exist as an individual. Underman turns to the group or herd (Kierkegaard's "the crowd") for power, identity, and purpose. The inferior individual's awareness of his or her own inferiority produces envy and resentment of all "higher types" and "elitist" value systems.

In an effort to control their superiors, members of the herd create **slave morality**, a value system based on guilt, fear, and a distortion of the will to power in which the characteristics of the inferior type—humility, passivity, dependency—are praised as virtues, while the characteristics of the superior type—love of domination, delight in one's own talents, fearlessness—

I mistrust all systematizers and I avoid them. The will to a system is a lack of integrity.
Friedrich Nietzsche

UNDERMAN
Nietzsche's term for the type of person who cannot face being alone in a godless universe, an inferior individual seeking safety and identity in a group or from another; characterized by resentment and hypocrisy.

SLAVE MORALITY
In Nietzschean philosophy, a distortion of the will to power in which the characteristics of the inferior type (underman) are praised as virtues, and the characteristics of the superior type (overman) are condemned as arrogance and coldheartedness; a morality of inhibitions, equality, restrictive duties, and "bad conscience."

AN ICONOCLAST LOOKS AT EDUCATION

I have never tired of calling attention to the *despiritualizing* influence of our current science-industry. The hard [servitude] to which the tremendous range of the sciences condemns every scholar today is a main reason why those with a fuller, richer, *profounder* disposition no longer find a congenial education and congenial *educators*. There is nothing of which our culture suffers more than of the superabundance of pretentious jobbers and fragments of humanity; our universities are, *against* their will, the real hothouses for this kind of withering of the instincts of the spirit. And the whole of Europe already has some idea of this—power politics deceives nobody. . . .

To call the taming of an animal its "improvement" sounds almost like a joke to our ears. Whoever knows what goes on in menageries doubts that the beasts are "improved" there. They are weakened, they are made less harmful, and through the depressive effect of fear, through pain, through wounds, and through hunger they become sickly beasts. . . .

. . . What the "higher schools" . . . really achieve is a brutal training, designed to prepare huge numbers of young men, with as little loss of time as possible, to become usable, abusable. . . . "Higher education" and huge numbers—that is a contradiction to start with. All higher education belongs only

are condemned as arrogance and coldheartedness. Slave morality creates inhibitions, false ideals of equality, restrictive duties "owed" to our inferiors, and weakening of strong instincts by "bad conscience." The herd is always hostile to the individual.

In other words, slave morality tries to convince the powerful that they should protect the weak. According to Nietzsche, slave morality arose when rules conquered instincts in ancient Greece. Today, rationalistic Greek and Christian ethics are the two chief sources of slave morality in our culture. Fairness, equality, moderation, "stepping aside," refusing to claim the full rights accompanying superior ability and talent, and fear of confrontation are all characteristics of slave morality.

History up to the present is a record of the withering away of a noble *master morality*, as century by century the virtues of the herd weakened Western culture, Nietzsche says, until today, we resist even talk about higher types. We claim that all people are fundamentally equal. Zarathustra speaks:

> You higher men learn this from me: in the market place nobody believes in higher men. And if you want to speak there, very well! But the mob blinks: "We are all equal."
>
> "You higher men"—thus blinks the mob—"there are no higher men, we are all equal, man is man; before God we are all equal."

to the exception: one must be privileged to have the right to such a privilege. All great, all beautiful things can never be common property . . . What conditions the decline of German culture? That "higher education" is no longer a privilege. . . .

. . . No one is any longer free to give his children a noble education: our "higher schools" are all set up for the most ambiguous mediocrity, with their teachers, curricula, and teaching aims. And everywhere an indecent haste prevails, as if something would be lost if the young man of twenty-three were not yet "finished," or if he did not yet know the answer to the "main question": *which* calling? A higher kind of human being, if I may say so, does not like "callings," precisely because he knows himself to be called. He has time, he takes time, he does not even think of "finishing": at thirty one is, in the sense of high culture, a beginner, a child. Our overcrowded secondary schools, our overworked, stupefied secondary-school teachers, are a scandal: for one to defend such conditions . . . there may perhaps be *causes*—reasons there are none.

Friedrich Nietzsche
Twilight of the Idols, in *The Portable Nietzsche*, trans. Walter Kaufmann (New York: Penguin, 1968), pp. 508; 502; 510–11.

Before God! But now this God has died. And before the mob we do not want to be equal. You higher men, go away from the market place![24]

Ressentiment

Slave morality originates from a deep form of psychically polluting resentment that Nietzsche always referred to with the French word **ressentiment**. In the following passage from *Toward a Genealogy of Morals*, Nietzsche distinguishes between the slave morality of the underman and the master morality of the overman:

The slaves' revolt in morals begins with this, that *ressentiment* itself becomes creative and gives birth to values: the *ressentiment* of those who are denied the real reaction, that of the deed, and who compensate with an imaginary revenge. Whereas all noble morality begins out of a triumphant affirmation of oneself, slave morality immediately says No to what comes from outside, to what is different, to what is not oneself: and *this* No is its creative deed. This reversal of the value-positing glance—this *necessary* direction outward instead

RESSENTIMENT
French for "resentment"; term used in Nietzschean philosophy for a deep form of psychically polluting resentment that generates slave morality; the dominant emotion of the underman.

During a 1963 civil rights demonstration to protest segregation in
Atlanta, an angry mob abused the demonstrators with kicks,
punches, and burning cigarettes. This anonymous woman passerby
confronted the mob for its crude, herd-like behavior. According to
Nietzsche, "the herd" is always hostile to the genuine individual.

Another century of readers—
and the mind itself will stink.
Friedrich Nietzsche

of back to oneself—is of the nature of *ressentiment:* to come
into being, slave morality requires an outside world, a
counterworld; physiologically speaking, it requires external
stimuli in order to react at all: its action is always at bottom a
reaction.[25]

In other words, slave morality is alien to true individuality. It is so opposed to the authentic individual, that his or her own urges and impulses
are stifled in favor of "external stimuli" that function as guidelines from others and from the herd. Slave morality is inauthentic (phony and uncreative)
because it is "always a reaction," never an originating impulse. (See Chapter 18 for more on authenticity.) Slave morality settles for the "imaginary
revenge" of the afterlife: "God will punish the bad people since we are too
weak to do so."

That everyone can learn to
read will ruin in the long
run not only writing, but
thinking too.
Friedrich Nietzsche

The underman fears "the other" whether in the form of the authentic
individual or in the merely different. Thus, slave morality encourages conformity, national, racial, gender, and religious bigotry, and unthinking pa-

triotism: "slave morality immediately says No to what comes from outside, to what is different, to what is not oneself." The underman lacks the god-like confidence necessary for "the value-positing glance," the ability to impose one's own values without reference to "external stimuli" for guidance and security.

From a healthy aesthetic perspective, underman is repulsive, characterized by weakness, evasion, hypocrisy, and so forth. Slave morality is a morality of resignation, deferment, withdrawal from the full range of life, and prohibition. In reality, the underman does not reject the lusty, fateful, self-affirming, creative aspects of the human psyche because they are bad, but because the underman is too weak, sick, and corrupt to live up to them—and out of *ressentiment* wants to prevent others from living up to them, as well.

PHILOSOPHICAL QUERY

As you might expect, Nietzsche's characterization of slave morality was and remains controversial. Do you think it is dangerous? Is it unfair to expect people not to have some *ressentiment*? Is today's tendency to see many people as "victims" a reflection of slave morality? Discuss.

MASTER MORALITY

If there are two fundamentally different types of people (underman and overman), then there must be two radically different types of morality. One universal standard cannot apply equally to the "common herd" and the superior, perfected overman.

Although both types possess the *will to power*, they differ significantly in their approaches to power. For the overman, the will to power is expressed openly, honestly, and nobly through exuberant, life-affirming self-creation and self-imposition. That is, the overman creates a "new law tablet," a code of values that is the opposite of the weak underman's slave morality. Because the underman lacks courage and nobility, he or she must resort to appeals to a "father God," to neurotic guilt, and demands for pity (dressed up as an "obligation" to show compassion). In the herd, the will to power is perverted through manipulation, *ressentiment*, and indirection shaped by feelings of gross inadequacy—it is not expressed honestly and openly.

Master morality, in contrast to slave morality, is an *aesthetic-heroic* code of honor. That is, the overman looks only to him- or herself for value. And value is defined in aesthetic terms: noble–ignoble (shameful); glorious–degrading; honorable–dishonorable; refined–vulgar; and so on. In simple terms, for the overman, "good" equals "noble" and "evil" equals "vulgar."

According to Nietzsche:

> To be unable to take one's own enemies, accidents, and misdeeds seriously for long—that is the sign of strong and rich

If society consisted of highly valuable individuals, it would be worthwhile to adapt to it, but generally it is dominated by weak and stupid people and thus suffocates all higher individual values.

Marie-Louise von Franz

MASTER MORALITY
In Nietzschean philosophy, the *aesthetic* honor code of the overman; morality that looks only to the authentic individual (overman) for values that transcend the slave's good–evil dichotomy with: glorious–degrading; honorable–dishonorable; refined–vulgar, and so on; "good" equals "noble" and "evil" equals "vulgar."

NIETZSCHE AND THE NAZIS

Nietzsche's characterization of the overman in terms of a "master race" and "master morality" led to the misguided and unfortunate appropriation of his name by Adolf Hitler's Nazi party. Hitler was encouraged by Nietzsche's sister, Elisabeth Förster-Nietzsche. Like the Nazis, she and her husband, Bernard Förster, were indeed Aryan supremacist racists who failed to understand that by "master race" Nietzsche meant "psychological type," not biological, racial, ethnic, or national group. In her hunger for approval and resentful will to power, Nietzsche's sister destroyed much of his work and encour-

aged Hitler's public adoration of her brother as a philosophical support for Nazism.

Yet it is clear that no anti-Semite wrote the following, produced more than two generations before the Nazis even existed:

Incidentally, the whole problem of the *Jews* exists only in nation states, for here their energy and higher intelligence, their accumulated capital of spirit and will, gathered through a long school of suffering, must become so preponderant as to arouse mass envy and hatred. In almost all contemporary nations, therefore—in direct proportion to

natures. . . . Such a man simply shakes off with one shrug much vermin that would have buried itself deep in others; here alone is it also possible—assuming that is possible at all on earth—that there be real "*love* of one's enemies." How much respect has a noble person for his enemies! . . . Conversely, imagine "the enemy" as conceived by a man of *ressentiment*—and here precisely is his deed, his creation: he has conceived "the evil enemy," "*the evil one*"—and indeed as the fundamental concept from which he then derives, as an afterimage and counterinstance, a "good one"—himself.[26]

Since each morality originates as a reflection of those it serves, it is not surprising that slave morality reflects envy, *ressentiment*, authoritarian conformity, collectivism, and obligations to all others, who are defined as "equals." Master morality, in stark contrast, reflects the overman: proud, fierce, courageous, self-sufficient, glorious, bold, and so forth.

Whereas the overman's morality begins with her affirmation of her own beloved self, the underman's morality begins with the invention of the "evil other," the *evil one*. For the overman, "bad" is the after-image. For the underman, "good" is the after-image. Thus, master morality is positive in its orientation; slave morality is negative.

Whereas the overman shrugs off the "vermin" of guilt, regret, self-pity, envy, and *ressentiment*, the underman's entire moral code clings to them as safety checks on such "evil" impulses as self-love, joy in the midst of mistakes, and happiness here and now.

the degree to which they act up nationalistically—the literary obscenity is spreading of leading the Jews to slaughter as scapegoats of every conceivable public and internal misfortune. . . . I should like to know how much one must forgive a people in a total accounting when they have had the most painful history of all peoples, not without the fault of all of us, and when they have produced the noblest man (Christ), the purest sage (Spinoza), the most powerful book, and the most effective moral law in the world.*

The following selections from *Human, All-Too-Human* reflect Nietzsche's great, unwavering distaste for "true believers," "groupthink," and mass movements:

And to say it once more. Public opinions—private lazinesses.

Enemies of truth. Convictions are more dangerous enemies of truth than lies.

Not suitable as a party member. Whoever thinks much is not suitable as a party member: he soon thinks himself right through the party.**

*Friedrich Nietzsche
Human, All-Too-Human*, in *The Portable Nietzsche*, trans. Walter Kaufmann (New York: Penguin, 1968) section 475.
**Ibid., sections 482, 483, 579.

If Nietzsche is correct, we live in the twilight of a culture. The "horizon is free" because no new value system and vision have replaced the old dying one. Those who live through the twilight of the old beliefs will experience confusion, fear, a strong desire to hold on to idols; but they will also experience unlimited opportunities for growth. In the twilight of our idols, we are handed the opportunity to fashion our own way. It is up to us to define—to actually create—our very selves.

Zarathustra says:

"*I teach you the overman.* Man is something that shall be overcome. What have you done to overcome him?

"All beings so far have created something beyond themselves; and do you want to be the ebb of this great flood and even go back to the beasts rather than overcome man? What is the ape to man? A laughingstock or a painful embarrassment. And man shall be just that for the overman: a laughingstock or a painful embarrassment. You have made your way from worm to man, and much in you is still worm. Once you were apes, and even now, too, man is more ape than any ape. . . .

"Man is a rope, tied between beast and overman—a rope over an abyss. A dangerous across, a dangerous on-the-way, a dangerous looking-back, a dangerous shuddering and stopping. . . .

"I love all those who are as heavy drops, falling one by one out of the dark cloud that hangs over men; they herald the advent of lightning, and, as heralds, they perish.

No victor believes in chance.
Friedrich Nietzsche

"Behold, I am the herald of the lightning and a heavy drop from the cloud; but this lightning is called *overman*."[27]

COMMENTARY

Kierkegaard and Nietzsche are two of the very few philosophers sure to be found in virtually any popular bookstore. Other philosophers write as well or better. Other philosophers address important issues. But few speak to certain important problems of our time as pointedly or eloquently as they do. They understand the dangers of deferring choices to outsiders, to experts. Their strong attacks on traditional philosophy strike a chord with scholars and nonscholars alike.

Contemporary social science attests to the power of "the crowd," and we all experience the pressure caused by the massing of society. Despite our many freedoms, increased leisure, and psychological sophistication, authenticity seems rare. Kierkegaard's great virtue is his reclamation of the existing individual. It is easy to lose sight of the fact that individuals construct philosophies, individuals interpret revelations, individuals draw scientific conclusions. We run the risk of a kind of moral and intellectual psychosis if we fail to recognize the subjective element in all truth claims and decisions.

Yet Kierkegaard may swing too much in the direction of subjectivity and individuality. For all his insight and prophetic power, he was unable to overcome his own alienation from science and objectivity. Surely, not even the leap of faith can completely ignore objective reality. The problem here is to modify Kierkegaard without transforming his philosophy into just what he loathed: an abstract, rationalistic, objective "system."

Even though a lack of passion is deadly, the presence of passion is no guarantee of authenticity. Blind, uncontrollable passion can destroy individuality as surely as excessive abstraction. Anyone who has been "consumed" or "swept away" by passion knows that it is possible to lose ourselves in passion as well as in crowds.

On balance, Kierkegaard's critique of inauthentic faith, mass societies, and the dangers of sterile objectivity stands as a beacon in our perilous times. Our danger today seems to be not too much passion, but too little; not the leap of faith, but dogmatic mass-movement religion; not too much subjectivity, but too much self-centeredness. One might even say that in spite (or because?) of our knowledge of the human psyche, we still encounter few authentic individuals.

Nietzsche was nothing if not authentic. And as disturbing as much of his philosophy can be, there is no escaping its power to provoke a response—often a passionate response. His assertive denial of objective meaning has influenced a whole generation of scholars and literary critics (called new critics and deconstructionists). Nietzsche's influence on postmodern scholarship cannot be overestimated. Nietzschean influences on current critical theories are found in the rejection of the possibility of unbiased (objective)

I wonder how far Moses would have got if he'd taken a poll in Egypt? What would Jesus Christ have preached if he'd taken a poll in Israel?

Harry S. Truman

Nobody is normal, everybody is a little bit crazy or unbalanced, people's minds are running all the time. Their perceptions of the world are partial, incomplete. They are eaten alive by their egos. They think they see, but . . . all they do is project their madness upon the world. There is no clarity, no wisdom in that!

Taisen Deshimaru

interpretation, the view that all scholarship is autobiography, and unapologetic self-reference on the part of academic authors.

In the postmodern world, a world without objective value, without God, without "the truth," all that is left seems to be "my truth"—or more precisely, "my truths." Ironically, however, when nihilistic self-promotion becomes the trend and "being an individual" becomes a consciously contrived goal, Nietzschean originality and authenticity disappear. Being "a Nietzschean" is no more possible than following someone else's orders to be free! Nietzsche once said "Those who understand me, know that I can have no disciples." There is bitter (but not unexpected) irony in the notion of being "a Nietzschean."

Nietzsche's critique of contemporary culture is subtle and profound. On the whole, our culture seems to have lost faith in the very idea of a single true religion, a common value system. Education seems to have lost any central focus and seems increasingly reduced to training without purpose or to efforts by various groups (herds?) to enforce their individual points of view (today we call them agendas). Even the current national debate over school curricula has postmodern Nietzschean roots: If there is no objective meaning, then everything is a "point of view." If everything is a point of view, why should I have to accept your point of view or you mine? There is no true history; no true interpretation of literature; no clear hierarchy of values.

Though it is not currently politically correct to suggest that we are not all equal, that some of us are entitled to more than the rest, we do not seem to fully believe the doctrine of equality that we preach: each new wave of immigrants ("the evil other") generates hostility, fear, and resentment. We certainly seem to be a culture searching for something, some clear, unifying set of values.

So it is that for us, Nietzschean questions remain: Is God dead? If so, what next? If not, whence our widespread resentments, confusions, and fears? Are we all equal in any significant sense? If not, what then? Can we bear to ask these questions? Dare we not ask them?

> [Nietzsche] had more penetrating knowledge of himself than any other man who ever lived or ever was likely to live.
>
> Sigmund Freud

SUMMARY OF MAIN POINTS

Existentialism addresses fundamental questions of meaning and choice as they affect individuals. Existential themes include choice, freedom, identity, alienation, inauthenticity, despair, and awareness of our own mortality.

Søren Kierkegaard claimed that truth is subjectivity and the crowd is untruth. He rejected the view that science and objective truth could provide meaning for the individual. He criticized conformity

and the degradation that he claimed results when theories and systems are used to explain and define individuals.

For Kierkegaard, the most important issue facing any individual is how to relate to God. He criticized efforts to reduce that relationship to a performance contract and rejected as "false Christianity" all efforts to objectify faith or base belief on facts (science).

Kierkegaard criticized what he saw as the inflated reputations of Hegel and science. He was also deeply disturbed by the massing of society. He thought that "objective reason" and mass movements each contributed to an overall leveling effect that resulted in "a mathematical equality." The result is almost irresistible pressure to conform to types, with people becoming abstractions rather than authentic individuals.

Influenced by Schopenhauer's pessimism, Nietzsche concluded that life itself is an irrational, purposeless striving for a pointless existence. Nietzsche disagreed with Schopenhauer in a fundamental way, however, insisting that life is governed by the will to power, a universal desire to control others and impose our values on them. Nietzsche's response to pessimism was tragic optimism, the sense of joy and vitality that accompanies the superior individual's clear-sighted imposition of his own freely chosen values on a meaningless world.

Nietzsche claimed that he "discovered" the death of God: the idea of God had lost its full creative force, its full power, because science and technology have usurped God's place in people's lives. Nietzsche thought that authentic faith in God is no longer possible.

According to Nietzsche, the death of God leads to nihilism, the belief that the universe lacks meaning and purpose, and that moral, social, and political values are creative interpretations; they reflect their subjective origins, because without God, there is no objective base for values.

Slave morality is a distortion of the will to power in which the characteristics of the inferior type are praised as virtues, while the characteristics of the superior type are condemned as arrogance and coldheartedness. Slave morality creates inhibitions, false ideals of equality, restrictive duties "owed" to our inferiors, and weakening of strong instincts by "bad conscience."

Master morality is an aesthetic-heroic code of honor. The overman looks only to him- or herself for value defined in aesthetic terms: noble–ignoble (shameful); glorious–degrading; honorable–dishonorable; refined–vulgar; and so on; "good" equals "noble" and "evil" equals "vulgar."

According to Nietzsche, the death of God provides a glorious opportunity for the fearless, "perfect type" that is "more than human," the overman. The overman is a "higher type" that will emerge out of the weakness and hypocrisies of the common herd. The overman will abolish the false idols of conventional morality and decadent religion, replacing them with master morality.

STUDY QUESTIONS

1. Describe existentialism in your own words. How is it a "reaction" against previous philosophy? Explain in detail.

2. What was Kierkegaard's "universal formula"? How did it influence his thinking? What did he learn from the episode with Regina Olsen?

3. Sketch Kierkegaard's critique of "false Christianity." What is false Christianity?

4. Compare and contrast Kierkegaard's idea of faith with the more common conception of faith as belief.

5. Explain what Kierkegaard meant when he said that "truth is subjectivity." Is this the same as "truth is relative"? Explain.

6. Explain what Kierkegaard means by "passion," referring to his analysis of the "present age."

7. What is pessimism and how did it influence Nietzsche's philosophy?

8. What is tragic optimism? What is tragic about it? Optimistic? Why did Nietzsche reject ordinary optimism?

9. Who was Zarathustra? What is his relationship to the overman?

10. What did Nietzsche mean by the death of God?

11. What is nihilism and how is it related to the death of God?

12. What is the overman? How do the death of God and nihilism relate to the overman?

13. Characterize, contrast, and evaluate master and slave morality.

14. What is *ressentiment*, and what is its importance to Nietzsche's philsosophy?

CHAPTER SEVENTEEN

The Pragmatist:
William James

As a rule we disbelieve
all facts and theories for
which we have no use.

WILLIAM JAMES

William James

All our scientific and philosophic ideals are altars to unknown gods.
William James

PRAGMATISM
From the Greek for "deed"; belief that ideas have meaning or truth value to the extent that they produce practical results and effectively further our aims; empirically based philosophy that defines knowledge and truth in terms of practical consequences.

n Chapter 1 we saw that philosophy has a reputation for being dangerous and subversive, for destroying people's beliefs without replacing them. We also noted that it has the almost contradictory reputation of being irrelevant, of making no real difference in our lives. "Philosophy bakes no bread," it is said. We have seen very powerful minds disagree about the most fundamental things: Does the "mind" exist? Do we have free will? Do the consequences of our actions matter if the motives are good? What is knowledge? Is reason more reliable than experience, or is it the other way around? Is there only one reality? Is there a God? Is God good? Can we know anything? Is history a process? What is virtue?

What can a reasonable person, a person of genuine common sense, make of all this? It seems as if each of the great philosophers builds a whole system around one or two insights. These systems can appear farfetched and bizarre compared to life as most of us experience it; though intellectually stimulating and interesting, they hardly seem *useful*. Isn't life too short to waste on building grand philosophical systems full of abstract terms, which have no practical use except perhaps to provide philosophers with jobs?

The first truly great American philosopher demanded that philosophy answer these kinds of questions. **William James (1842–1910)** was the most original and influential advocate of **pragmatism**, an empirically based philosophy that defines knowledge and truth in terms of practical consequences. He believed philosophy must be more than a mere intellectual enterprise, that its true purpose is to help us live by showing us how to discover and adopt beliefs that fit our individual needs and temperaments. He thus shifted the focus of inquiry from the search for objectively true absolute beliefs to the search for *beliefs that work for us*. His philosophy is provocative, enthusiastic, optimistic, and vigorous; it speaks to the nearly universal need for ideas and truths that matter to individuals. Voicing the lament of the common person—"What difference does this or that philosophy make to my life?"—James offers an uncommonly rich answer.

AN AMERICAN ORIGINAL

William James was both a product and shaper of his time. The last half of the nineteenth century was a period of great confidence in science. People believed in continuous progress, influenced in part by a social interpretation of Darwin's theory of evolution that promised never-ending growth and improvement. This was also an age of bold action, as the Rockefellers and Carnegies and Vanderbilts carved up the land and established great industrial empires. People were impatient, wanting to move on, to get things done. In America, especially, it was an era of expansion, of strength. James captured this spirit so well and expressed him-

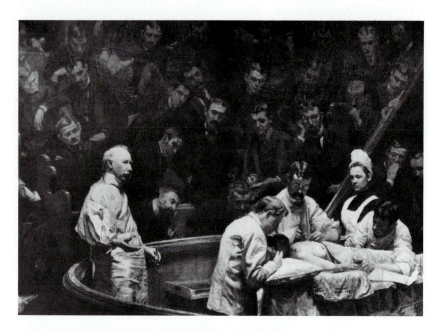

The late nineteenth century teetered between pessimistic despair and optimistic faith in scientific progress. Thomas Eakins's painting *The Agnew Clinic* depicts the kind of medical theater William James might have attended as a medical student.

self in such a clear, powerful, anti-intellectual way that he became the best-known, most popular, and most influential *American* philosopher so far.

The Education of a Philosopher

William James's father was a restless man, so William spent a considerable part of his childhood moving about. In 1855, when his father lost faith in American education, he moved the entire family to Europe. They left America in June; in August, James's father sent William and his younger brother Henry (the famous novelist) to school in Geneva; by October the entire family had moved to England. Later they moved to France. In Boulogne, sixteen-year-old William started college and for the first time managed to attend the same school for an entire year.

That spring, however, the Jameses moved to Rhode Island. William wanted to continue his college studies, but his father was unimpressed with American colleges and so prevented him. A year and a half later the family moved back to Switzerland. By this time, William's early interest in science was replaced by a desire to be an artist, but after a year of art study, he turned back to science.

There are some people, and I am one of them, who think that the most important and most practical thing about a man is still his view of the universe. We think that for a landlady considering a lodger it is important to know his income, but still more important to know his philosophy.
G. K. Chesterton

In 1861, William James entered Harvard as a chemistry major. His interests shifted to biology, anatomy, and ultimately physiology. James was so impressed by Jean Louis Agassiz, one of Harvard's most influential faculty members, that he accompanied him on an expedition to the Amazon. After eight months, James had had enough. He said, "When I get home I'm going to study philosophy all my days," but what he actually did was return to Harvard Medical School, where he had already taken some classes.

During his years as a student, James suffered mentally and physically. He described himself as being "on the continual verge of suicide." Unable to continue his medical studies because his hospital work put too much strain on his back, he went to Germany for the mineral baths. His letters home were funny and lighthearted, but elsewhere he noted that "thoughts of the pistol, the dagger and the bowl" were never far from him.[1] When he felt up to it, he returned to medical school and ultimately passed his licensing exam at age twenty-six. Later in the same year, though, he went into a severe depression, writing in his diary, "Nature & life have unfitted me for any affectionate relations with other individuals."[2] He was in a constant state of anxiety and dreaded being alone.

James was saved by an idea from the French philosopher Charles Renouvier, who had characterized free will as the ability to hold on to one idea among a number of possibilities. Willing himself to hold on to the idea of health and well-being, James effectively *decided* to get well: he *willed* himself well, by concentrating all his mental energy to produce "the self-governing resistance of the ego to the world."[3] James announced: "My first act of freedom will be to believe in free will." His depression lifted like a veil, and he was at last free to follow the restless intellect he had inherited from his father. As a result of his lingering sickness and unhappiness, he developed an interest in the relationship between mind and body. Speaking of James, a friend said:

> "Active tension," uncertainty, unpredictability, extemporized adaptation, risk, change, anarchy, unpretentiousness, naturalness—these are the qualities of life which James finds most palatable, and which give him the deepest sense of well-being. They are at the same time the qualities which he deems most authentic, the accents in which the existent world speaks to him most directly. . . .[4]

In 1872, James completed his education and took a job teaching physiology at Harvard. Within three years he was made assistant professor and remained affiliated with Harvard for nearly thirty-six years—the rest of his professional life.

In 1876, James's father announced to William, "I have met your future wife." And indeed he had. Alice Gibbens was a bright, vibrant, strikingly honest young woman. Though they fell in love, William declared himself unfit to marry her, and sent her a series of self-critical, suffering letters de-

My first act of freedom will be to believe in free will.
William James

signed to discourage any thoughts of marriage. Alice understood William well, and so went to Quebec, saying she did so "to remove temptation from his path." The distance apparently diminished James's fears, however, and made Alice even more appealing. His letters became ardent efforts at court-ship. Two years after his father's announcement, William and Alice were married.[5]

Though William James had found the support and care he needed to help steady his restless temperament and tendency to depression, for the rest of his life he struggled to remain healthy, using his particular good hu-mor, aggressive intellect, and psychological insights—but he gave credit for what success he achieved to his wife for saving him.

The Philosopher as Hero

James's interest in medicine and physiology developed into curiosity about psychology, and in 1878 the Henry Holt Company signed him to write a psy-chology textbook. It took him twelve years to finish *Principles of Psychology* (1890), but the wait was worth it, and the book's wide appeal established James as an important figure in the early history of modern psychology.

About this time, his focus began to shift once more. He became increas-ingly interested in philosophy, but because of his broad interests, his bouts with depression, and his experience in science, medicine, and psychology, he saw philosophy in a different light from most professional philosophers of his time. James regarded philosophy as a matter of personal involvement, as a function of the will, and as a means to overcome despair and futility. He developed the kind of philosophy *he needed* to cope with his life and pre-sented it in an appealing and powerful series of lectures that made it acces-sible to others.

Much of James's work is couched in heroic, often masculine terms, which were more fashionable and common then than they are now. But we would be doing a serious disservice to James if we reject his philosophy for that reason. Pragmatism is not a *male* philosophy but a philosophy that includes an element of heroic struggle; a philosophy of courage and action; a philos-ophy of vitality. A product of his times, James expressed these values in typ-ically masculine terms. James was trying to resist inertia, to resist giving in to self-pity and self-defeat—and he used a vocabulary of heroic action. He called on us to become consciously responsible for our lives by strenuous exertion of will. In our contemporary era, which seems so often to reduce us to the helpless products of environment and heredity, a philosophy like James's is a refreshing vote of confidence in the individual human spirit.

We are all ready to be savage in some cause. The difference between a good man and a bad one is the choice of the cause.
William James

PHILOSOPHICAL QUERY

Discuss the concept of "the hero." Identify heroic values and char-acter traits as you understand them. Do you think people today have a clear understanding of heroism?

PRAGMATIC STUDY HABITS

It is your relaxed and easy worker, who is in no hurry, and quite thoughtless most of the while of consequences, who is your efficient worker; and tension and anxiety, and present and future, all mixed up together in our mind at once, are the surest drags upon steady progress and hindrances to our success. . . .

My advice to students . . . would be somewhat similar. Just as a bicycle chain may be too tight, so may one's carefulness and conscientiousness be so tense as to hinder the running of one's mind. Take, for example, periods when there are many successive days of examination impending. One ounce of good nervous tone in an examination is worth many pounds of anx-

ious study for it in advance. If you really want to do your best in an examination, fling away the book the day before, say to yourself, "I won't waste another minute on this miserable thing, and I don't care one iota whether I succeed or not." Say this sincerely, and feel it; and go out and play, or go to bed and sleep, and I am sure the results next day will encourage you to use the method permanently.

William James
"The Gospel of Relaxation," in *Talks to Teachers of Psychology*, quoted in Lin Yutang, *The Wisdom of America* (New York: John Day, 1950), p. 243.

If we take the whole history of philosophy, the systems reduce themselves to a few main types which, under all the technical verbiage in which the ingenious intellect of man envelops them, are just so many visions, modes of feeling the whole push, and seeing the whole drift of life, forced on one by one's total character and experience, and on the whole preferred—there is no other truthful word—as one's best working attitude.

William James

James himself did not actually live the kind of life he described as ideal. But he wanted to. He recognized the dangers and limits of too much sentimentality, too much "tender-mindedness," and offered what he saw as a healthier, more useful alternative. He understood, from his own weaknesses, the frustration of being unable to stick to anything, the frustration of not knowing what we want, the frustration of trying to make up our minds and choose one important thing. James's own experiences convinced him that life was too important, too complex, too rich to reduce to any of the philosophical systems that had gone before. And so he refused to offer a system; instead, he offered a *method*, a way of marshaling the will. But his method was grounded in philosophy, as Guy W. Stroh points out in *American Philosophy from Edwards to Dewey*:

Here is where a philosophy is required that will see the *whole puzzle*, face it squarely, and not deny any of the concrete facts. Such a philosophy will certainly need to borrow from psychology, since the problem is based in part at least on the facts of man's actual experience. But such a philosophy will have to go beyond psychology and address itself to the moral, human, and even metaphysical side of the problem. Only a philosophy, according to James, takes in the full sweep of man's ultimate problems, since only a philosophy expresses one's basic orientation to the meaning of things. Philosophy has the patience

and courage to work continually at a problem when common sense and even science have long since set it aside or given it up.[6]

The Philosopher as Advocate

William James published his first philosophy book, *The Will to Believe and Other Essays in Popular Philosophy*, in 1896. In 1898, he was invited to give the Gifford Lectures in Edinburgh, Scotland, a truly rare honor for an American. These lectures were published in 1902 as *The Varieties of Religious Experience*. A classic of contemporary philosophy, this superb book still sells widely, its popularity extending far beyond academic circles.

After returning to Harvard, James delivered a series of lectures on pragmatism, and repeated these lectures at Columbia University to an audience of more than one thousand people. They were published as *Pragmatism* in 1907. *Pragmatism* also sold well and attracted the interest of both scholars and the general public. James was cheered up by its reception, to the point of announcing to his brother:

> I shouldn't be surprised if ten years hence it should be rated as "epoch-making," for of the definitive triumph of that general way of thinking I can entertain no doubt whatever—I believe it to be something quite like the protestant reformation.[7]

James's work became so influential that he effectively altered the shape of what has come to be known as American philosophy. He taught, among others, Supreme Court Justice Oliver Wendell Holmes, Teddy Roosevelt, and philosopher George Santayana. (Of all his students, he particularly disliked Roosevelt and Santayana.)

In 1907, the same year *Pragmatism* appeared, James retired from Harvard at the age of sixty-five. Responding at last to the criticism that he had failed to present a sustained, systematic explanation of his ideas, James resolved to craft a fuller expression of pragmatism in his remaining years. To his brother he wrote, "I live in apprehension lest the Avenger should cut me off before I get my message out. I hesitate to leave the volumes I have already published without their logical complement."[8]

James compiled a volume of essays, *The Meaning of Truth*, and one of lectures, *A Pluralistic Universe*. He hoped these books would be considered more "scholarly" and systematic than his others, but they were not the "logical complement" he sought. Alas, the Avenger did cut off the old rebel, the anti-intellectual champion of living philosophy, and these final books were published one year after his death, in 1911. Ironically, perhaps, William James remained truer to his philosophy than if he *had* written a more scholarly, systematic version of it, for then he would have been required to present an appeal to the abstract and logical "niceties" he had spent his whole life denouncing.

Materialism fails on the side of incompleteness. Idealism always presents a systematic totality, but it must always have some vagueness and this leads to error. . . . But if materialism without idealism is blind, idealism without materialism is void.

Charles Sanders Peirce

The very last words of James's very last essay reflect the spirit of pragmatism better than any scholarly system: "There is no conclusion. What has concluded that we might conclude regarding it? There are no fortunes to be told and there is no advice to be given. Farewell."[9]

CHARLES SANDERS PEIRCE

Charles Sanders Peirce

The first expression of pragmatism actually appears in the work of **Charles Sanders Peirce (1839–1914)**. The son of a Harvard mathematics professor, Peirce studied philosophy, science, and mathematics, receiving a master's degree in mathematics and chemistry from Harvard. After working at the Harvard astronomical observatory for three years, he went to work for the United States Coastal and Geodetic Survey, where he remained for thirty years. He also lectured briefly at Johns Hopkins University. A brilliant but eccentric man, Peirce was never able to secure a full-time university position. As a result, he had a difficult time publishing his work. The last years of his life were clouded by physical infirmity, poverty, and social isolation and rejection. Through it all, William James remained his friend, supporting him and presenting his ideas to a wide audience. After Peirce's death his writings were collected and published. Although massive and difficult, his works have achieved a measure of success and are experiencing renewed interest among philosophers.

Peirce's "Pragmaticism"

I regard Logic as the Ethics of the Intellect—that is, in the sense in which Ethics is the science of the methods of bringing Self-Control to bear to gain our Satisfactions.
Charles Sanders Peirce

Peirce first presented what he referred to as "pragmatism" in an 1878 article titled "How to Make Our Ideas Clear," written for a popular magazine. This essay was ignored by philosophers until James devoted a series of lectures to it. James had intended only to present Peirce's ideas to a wider audience, but Peirce so strenuously objected to James's version of pragmatism that he "gave" him the term and coined yet another one for himself, *pragmaticism*:

> [The] word "pragmatism" has gained general recognition in a generalized sense that seems to argue power of growth and vitality. The famed psychologist, James, first took it up. . . . So then, the writer, finding his bantling "pragmatism" so promoted, feels that it is time to kiss his child good-by and relinquish it to a higher destiny; while to serve the precise purpose of expressing the original definition, he begs to announce the birth of the word "pragmaticism," which is ugly enough to be safe from kidnappers.[10]

Peirce was not just being cranky in insisting on clear and precise use of his term. His philosophy rested on a new theory of meaning. He coined the term *pragmaticism* from the Greek word *pragma*, which means "an act" or "a consequence." He wanted to show that the meanings of words depend on some

kind of action. Peirce argued that ideas are meaningful only when they translate into actions and predict experiences associated with actions.

Pragmatic Theory of Meaning

Peirce argued that the only differences between the meanings of words such as *hard* and *soft* or *heavy* and *light* are how they *test out* in experience. He thus equated meaning with the effects related to words, saying, "Our idea of anything *is* our idea of its sensible effects." Meaningful statements must refer to predictable, observable, practical effects or consequences. "Consequently, the sum of experimental phenomena that a proposition implies makes up its entire bearing upon human conduct."[11] If a word cannot be tied to any observable practical results, it is meaningless, for its meaning is the sum total of its practical consequences:

> Now this sort of consideration, namely, that certain lines of conduct will entail certain kinds of inevitable experiences is what is called a "practical consideration." Hence is justified the maxim, belief in which constitutes [pragmaticism]; namely, *In order to ascertain the meaning of an intellectual conception one should consider what practical consequences might conceivably result by necessity from the truth of that conception; and the sum of these consequences will constitute the entire meaning of the conception.*[12]

Peirce's scientific background and interests influenced his strong dislike for the kind of vague, abstract rationalism found in Descartes and other "impractical" system spinners. Descartes had separated the mind and thinking from any necessary connection with experience. Peirce pointed out, however, that all thinking and all meaning are *context dependent*. Context includes material, social, and emotional components, as well as an intellectual one.

Agreeing with the empiricists, Peirce argued that meaning is based on experience and determined by experiment. He did not mean just formal, scientific experiment, but also the kind of informal testing we do every day, as when, say, we test a recently varnished tabletop to see whether it is hard yet. We "test" to see whether it is appropriate to apply the word *hard* to this surface, we "experiment" by looking to see whether it looks damp, by touching it lightly, and so on. Things are not just hard in some abstract, ideal, constant sense but in the real world of causal and material relationships.

> Let us illustrate this rule by examples; and, to begin with the simplest one possible, let us ask what we mean by calling a thing *hard*. Evidently that it will not be scratched by many other substances. The whole conception of this quality, as of every other, lies in its conceived effects. There is absolutely no difference between a hard thing and a soft thing so long as they are not brought to the test.[13]

The rational purport of a word or other expression lies exclusively in its conceivable bearing upon conduct; if one can define accurately all the conceivable experimental phenomena which the affirmation or denial of a concept implies, one will have therein a complete definition of the concept, and there is absolutely nothing more in it. . . .

Charles Sanders Peirce

If there is no way of testing the effects of words (and ideas), no way of verifying their public consequences, they are meaningless. *Meaningful ideas always make a practical difference.*

PRAGMATISM

Like Peirce, James yearned for a philosophy free of meaningless abstractions, a philosophy that stretched far beyond the merely technical and rationally coherent to embrace the whole of life. Building on Peirce's foundation, James advocated a new vision of a philosophical approach he claimed others had recognized before, but only in parts. In the process, James went beyond Peirce's intentions, and used pragmatism to present a moral theory and to make a case for religious belief. We might even say he made pragmatism into a kind of philosophical religion. That is, James attempted to present a philosophy that could provide values and ideals worth striving for, and that could satisfy our need to believe without appealing to metaphysical abstractions. Let us see how.

Pragmatic Method and Philosophy

Many of you are students of philosophy, and have already felt in your own persons the scepticism and unreality that too much grubbing in the abstract roots of things will breed This is, indeed, one of the regular fruits of the overstudious career. Too much questioning and too little active responsibility lead, almost as often as too much sensualism does, to the edge of the slope, at the bottom of which lie pessimism and the nightmare or suicidal view of life. But to the diseases which reflection breeds, still further reflection can oppose effective remedies.

William James

James reflected a growing trend among philosophers to resist the abstract, to demand relevance and immediacy, and to deal with the "living issues" that face us. As he put it, "The whole function of philosophy ought to be to find out what definite difference it will make to you and me, at definite instants of our life, if this world-formula or that world-formula be the true one." There is a strong moral tone implicit in this position: It is not enough for philosophers to tackle questions of consistency or spin out grand theories. People are struggling through their lives, suffering, rejoicing, searching, and dying. We have a right—indeed, an obligation—to ask: "What difference does the theory of forms make to me, *now*? How is my life different if a tree falling in the forest does or does not make a sound? What practical difference does it make to me if the mind and body are two different substances?"

James often talked about feeling "at home" in the universe. Pragmatism was meant to be a *method* for solving those problems that interfere with feeling at home. Thus James looked for the *cash value* of statements, the practical payoff, and he rejected any philosophy that lacked it. This includes virtually all metaphysics.

> The pragmatic method is primarily a method of settling metaphysical disputes that otherwise might be interminable. Is the world one or many?—fated or free?—material or spiritual?—here are notions either of which may or may not hold good of the world; and disputes over such notions are unending. The pragmatic method in such cases is to try to interpret each notion by tracing its respective practical consequences. What

difference would it practically make to anyone if this notion rather than that notion were true? If no practical difference whatever can be traced, then the alternatives mean practically the same thing, and all dispute is idle. Whenever a dispute is serious, we ought to be able to show some practical difference that must follow from one side or the other's being right. . . .

A pragmatist turns his back resolutely and once and for all upon a lot of inveterate habits dear to professional philosophers. He turns away from abstraction and insufficiency, from verbal solutions, from bad *a priori* reasons, from fixed principles, closed systems, and pretended absolutes and origins. He turns toward concreteness and adequacy, toward facts, toward action and toward power.[14]

James referred to theories as "only man-made language, a conceptual shorthand . . . in which we write our reports of nature; and languages, as is well known, tolerate much choice of expression and many dialects."[15]

If any theory with a practical payoff is true, does it not follow that one theory is as good as another to those who believe it? It would if James were advocating strict relativism, but for the most part, he did not see pragmatism that way. He saw it as a *method*, not a collection of beliefs. Thus he saw a use for various theories of verification and meaning so long as they are ultimately used to determine the "cash value" of beliefs. We may benefit from using both empirical and rational criteria, for instance.

> Pragmatism . . . asks its usual question, "Grant an idea or belief to be true," it says, "what concrete difference will its being true make in any one's actual life? How will the truth be realized? What experiences will be different from those which would obtain if the belief were false? What, in short, is the truth's cash-value in experiential terms?"
>
> The moment pragmatism asks this question, it sees the answer: *True ideas are those that we can assimilate, validate, corroborate and verify. False ideas are those that we cannot.* That is the practical difference it makes to us to have true ideas; that, therefore, is the meaning of truth, for it is all that truth is known as. . . .
>
> Our account of truth is an account of truths in the plural, of processes. . . . Truth for us is simply a collective name for verification-processes.[16]

From a strictly logical perspective, James's position seems to contradict itself, much as strict relativism contradicts itself: He asserts the truth of his theory, which in turn seems to deny the possibility of "a truth." If a theory is merely a "man-made language," then why should we speak James's language?

A possible answer is to view James as an *advocate*, whose chief purpose isn't to present a strict *argument* but rather to make a broad enough case to

We all, scientists and non-scientists, live on some inclined plane of credulity. The plane tips one way in one man, another way in another; and may he whose plane tips in no way be the first to cast a stone.
William James

convert and convince a wide audience. If we accept at face value James's insistence that he was offering us a *method* to live by, then we have to approach him differently than if he were offering philosophy as such. Indeed, James himself sometimes refers to pragmatism as a *creed*. A philosophical creed is a body of beliefs we can devote our lives to, whereas a philosophical *argument* is an attempt to make a rational case; the former appeals primarily to our hearts, the latter to our minds.

Pragmatism has been called "philosophically crude" because of its apparent indifference to theoretical precision and consistency. Yet it can be argued that precision and consistency *pay* in some areas—science and medicine, for instance—but *cost* in others—for example, when we demand rigor and precision that are inappropriate for the issue before us.

For James, our lives are shaped by our beliefs. And we *need to believe more than we can ever "prove" by overly strict, objective, neutral standards*, which he calls "agnostic rules for truth-seeking." He says, "If one should assume that pure reason is what settles our opinions, he would fly in the teeth of the facts." What does settle our opinions, then? James answers, *the will to believe*. And what we believe is a function of whether we are tough- or tender-minded.

The Temper of Belief

The philosophy which is so important in each of us is not a technical matter, it is our more or less dumb sense of what life honestly and deeply means.
William James

Because James was a brilliant, innovative, ground-breaking psychologist, he refused to confine philosophy to the intellectual realm. For him, the function of philosophy shifted from revealing "the truth" to learning how to live in the world. In psychological terms, pragmatic philosophy is meant to provide a way of becoming better adjusted to the world. This helps account for the inconsistency that troubles more traditional philosophers: Living "at home in the universe" does *not*, at least according to James, depend on knowing and believing what is true, but on believing things that suit *us*.

We can classify people, James thought, into two temperamental types.

> Now the particular difference of temperament that I have in mind in making these remarks is one that has counted in literature, art, government, and manners as well as in philosophy. In manners we find formalists and free-and-easy persons. In government, authoritarians and anarchists. In literature, purists or academicals, and realists. In art, classics and romantics. You recognize these contrasts as familiar; well, in philosophy we have a very similar contrast expressed in the pair of terms "rationalist" and "empiricist," "empiricist" meaning your lover of facts in all their crude variety, "rationalist" meaning your devotee to abstract and eternal principles. . . .
>
> I will write these traits down in two columns. I think you will practically recognize the two types of mental make-up that I mean if I head the columns by the titles "tender-minded" and "tough-minded" respectively.

THE TENDER-MINDED	THE TOUGH-MINDED
Rationalistic (going by "Principles"),	Empiricist (going by "facts"),
Intellectualistic,	Sensationalistic,
Idealistic,	Materialistic,
Optimistic,	Pessimistic,
Religious,	Irreligious,
Free-willist,	Fatalistic,
Monistic,	Pluralistic,
Dogmatical.	Sceptical.

Each of you probably knows some well-marked example of each type, and you know what each example thinks of the example on the other side of the line. They have a low opinion of each other. Their antagonism, whenever as individuals their temperaments have been intense, has formed in all ages a part of the philosophic atmosphere of the time. It forms a part of the philosophic atmosphere today. The tough think of the tender as sentimentalists and soft-heads. The tender feel the tough to be unrefined, callous, or brutal. Their mutual reaction is very much like that that takes place when Bostonian tourists mingle with a population like that of Cripple Creek. . . . [But] few of us are tender-footed Bostonians pure and simple, and few are typical Rocky Mountain toughs, in philosophy. Most of us have a hankering for the good things on both sides of the line.[17]

James thought philosophy had been dominated historically by extremists, so that most philosophies are unbalanced in either the tough or tender direction. The same might be said of contemporary philosophy. Today's tough-minded philosophies view scientific knowledge as the only secure kind; they include the strictest forms of behavioristic psychology and analytically oriented philosophies that apply such rigid standards of meaning that most basic, timeless questions are dismissed as meaningless. The extremes of tender-minded philosophy are anti-intellectual theology, pop psychologies, and "New Age metaphysics." Such extremism has rendered philosophy inappropriate for the vast majority of us, who are a mixture of tough and tender. But because we are easily persuaded, we end up trying to follow "fashion" or what James called the "most impressive philosopher in the neighborhood"—or the most impressive theologian, politician, or psychologist.

James believed that when we succumb to the "most impressive philosopher in the neighborhood," we do psychic violence to our unexpressed, preconscious sense of the world. We deny important parts of ourselves and exaggerate others. When we try to live according to beliefs that do not suit us, we become dissatisfied and unhappy. The issue, then, for James is how to find

Man is not to blame for what he is. He didn't make himself. He has no control over himself. All the control is vested in his temperament—which he did not create—and in the circumstances which hedge him round from the cradle to the grave and which he did not devise. . . . He is as purely a piece of automatic mechanism as is a watch. . . . He is a subject for pity, and not blame.
Mark Twain

a *cause*, how to find beliefs worth living for, worth fighting and dying for—how to find a philosophical religion.

PHILOSOPHICAL QUERY

If James is correct, those who criticize his free-floating style and apparently inconsistent views may be expressing their tough-minded temperaments. Do you agree with his distinction between tough- and tender-mindedness? Does it account for philosophical differences? Is it possible to evaluate this distinction without falling into one camp or the other? Which side are you on? Discuss the distinction.

My strongest moral and intellectual craving is for some stable reality to lean upon, and as a professed philosopher pledges himself publicly never to have done with doubt on these subjects, but every day to be ready to criticize afresh and call in question the grounds of his faith the day before, I fear the constant sense of instability generated by this attitude would be more than the voluntary faith I can keep going is sufficient to neutralize.

William James

The Will to Believe

We live according to beliefs that are products of our own temperaments and experience; they are not, according to James, the products of abstract reasoning; rather, we manage to find reasons to believe what we want and need to believe. And we have the right to do that, according to James, who once said he would have been better off titling his famous lecture *The Right to Believe* rather than *The Will to Believe*.

Because life *demands* a response, *demands* action, we have no choice but to believe *something*. Life presents us with what James calls *forced options*. We must make decisions whether we want to or not (even "not deciding" is a decision). We *cannot* remain detached and disinterested; life simply does not allow it. We are compelled to decide and to act, and reason is not a sufficient force for action. We do not act on what we understand, but on what we believe. The rationalist's and skeptic's demands for certainty cannot be met, yet we continue to live and act—without intellectual certainty.

I, therefore, for one cannot see my way to accept the agnostic rules for truth-seeking, or willfully agree to keep my willing nature out of the game. I cannot do so for the plain reason that *a rule of thinking which would absolutely prevent me from acknowledging certain kinds of truth if those kinds of truth were really there, would be an irrational rule. . . .* If we had an infallible intellect with its objective certitudes, we might feel ourselves disloyal to such a perfect organ of knowledge in not trusting to it exclusively. But if we are empiricists, if we believe that no bell in us tolls to let us know for certain when truth is in our grasp, then it seems a piece of idle fantasticality to preach so solemnly our duty of waiting for the bell. Indeed we *may* wait if we will—I hope you do not think I am denying that—(we ought, on the contrary, delicately and profoundly to respect one another's mental freedom) but if we do wait, we do so at our own peril as much as if we believed.[18]

William James stressed that life demands a response, demands action, whether we want to act or not. Even something as simple as waiting for a train requires a response: If we miss this train, do we wait for the next? Walk? Take a cab? Drive next time? Even doing "nothing" is a response.

The intellect does not discover the truths in which we believe; the will creates truth.

Truth Happens to an Idea

The rationalists' model of truth was taken from logic and mathematics. They said truth is universal, which amounts to saying it is *contextless*. The sum 2 + 2 = 4 is true at all times, in all languages, for all creeds, for all ages, races, and genders of people, in all conditions of health or sickness. Indeed, because it is true for all "rational entities," it is true throughout the universe.

James rejected this simplistic, universalist notion of truth. He said experience makes it clear that ideas *become* true. Elsewhere, he said "truth *happens* to an idea." We *decide* whether or not an idea is true by "testing" it, as Peirce pointed out. James extended Peirce's pragmaticist theory of truth:

> Any idea upon which we can ride, so to speak; any idea that
> will carry us prosperously from any one part of our experience

The truth happens to an idea: The issue of gays serving in the military achieved national prominence in the presidential election campaign of 1992 and consumed much of newly-elected President Bill Clinton's first months in office. The Clinton administration modified its original policy as it discovered that a major change had little "cash value" early in its tenure. Do controversies over issues like lesbian and gay priests, euthanasia, and abortion support the pragmatic theory of truth, since it seems as if ideas are rejected or modified when they stop "working"?

to any other part, linking things satisfactorily, working securely, simplifying, saving labor, is true for just so much, true in so far forth, true instrumentally.[19]

If James is correct, we accept ideas as true only after we test them against our past experiences. Though a common tendency may be to reject new ideas, the public, communitywide aspect of truth-seeking, which Peirce emphasized, forces us—or most of us—to test and reevaluate ideas, keeping some and discarding others as we and the world change.

We have all witnessed this process. It is especially clear in the areas of moral and religious belief (areas James thought vital to human happiness). For example, looking back over history, we see that ideas about vice have

Peirce and James thought that the process of testing and reevaluating ideas is vital to human happiness. As our beliefs change, our notions of what is desirable change. But these changes can be slow. For example, some people are still uncomfortable with the idea of a male teaching preschool. As more men do, however, our ideas on this matter will be reevaluated.

changed. Few contemporary Americans believe that it is wrong for women to appear in public with bare ankles, but many people used to. Churches regularly convene councils to modify basic articles of faith, and entirely new religions emerge when old ones no longer *pay*.

Individuals and groups may simply refuse to accept changes, but on the whole, our beliefs do change, and thus our notion of what is true about the world changes—though, as James observed, we try to hang on to as many of our old ideas as possible until

> The individual . . . meets a new experience that puts them to a strain. Somebody contradicts them; or in a reflective moment he discovers that they contradict each other; or he hears of facts with which they are incompatible; or desires arise in him which they cease to satisfy. The result is an inward trouble to which his mind till then had been a stranger, and from which he seeks to escape by modifying his previous mass of opinions. . . . until at last some new idea comes up which he can graft upon the ancient stock . . .

Individual action is a means and not our end. Individual pleasure is not our end; we are all putting our shoulders to the wheel for an end that none of us can catch more than a glimpse at—that which the generations are working out.

Charles Sanders Peirce

This new idea is then adopted as the true one. It preserves the older stock of truths with a minimum of modification, stretching them enough to make them admit the novelty, but conceiving them in ways as familiar as the case leaves possible. [A radical] explanation, violating all our preconceptions, would never pass as a true account. . . . We would scratch around industriously till we found something less eccentric. The most violent revolutions in an individual's beliefs leave most of his old order standing.[20]

Ideas are tested and accepted or rejected based on how well they work for us. Sometimes we see the virtue in a new idea; other times, we can no longer live with the stress and energy it takes to hold on to an old one.

So there is no such thing as disinterested truth. *Pragmatic truth is human truth.* "Purely objective truth," James asserts, "plays no role whatsoever, is nowhere to be found." He adds that the most absolute-seeming truths "also once were plastic. They were also called true for human reasons. They also mediate between still earlier truths and what in those days were novel observations."[21]

Useful, human truth is alive; rationalistic, abstract, dogmatic truth is "the dead heart of the living tree." Truth grows.

PHILOSOPHICAL QUERY

Can you think of recent examples supporting the claim that "truth happens to an idea"? Some Protestant churches, for example, have begun revising their policies regarding birth control, abortion, and gay marriages because older beliefs lack "cash value" for many of today's churchgoers. These churches usually experience a period of soul-searching turmoil, wrestling with the dilemma of holding on to old beliefs or losing touch with their congregations. Can you cite one or two recent examples of truth happening to an idea from current events or from your own situation?

This life is worth living, we can say, since it is what we make it, from the moral point of view; and we are determined to make it from that point of view so far as we have anything to do with it, a success.
William James

The Dilemma of Determinism

James agreed with most moral philosophers that free will is a necessary condition for moral responsibility. He offered a unique and intriguing argument for believing in free will in a famous essay titled "The Dilemma of Determinism." He begins with a novel admission: "I disclaim openly on the threshold all pretension to prove to you that freedom of the will is true. The most I hope is to induce some of you to follow my own example in assuming it true, and acting as if it were true." Having warned us not to expect an airtight argument, James goes on to present a compelling case nonetheless. Let's see how.

Determinism is the belief that everything that happens must happen exactly the way it does. Some materialistic philosophers and scientists say

DETERMINISM
Belief that everything that happens must happen exactly the way it does because all matter is governed by cause and effect and follows laws of nature.

determinism is inevitable since all matter is governed by cause and effect and follows laws of nature. James asks:

> What does determinism profess? It professes that those parts of the universe already laid down absolutely appoint and decree what the other parts shall be. . . . Indeterminism, on the contrary, says that the parts have a certain amount of loose play on one another, so that the laying down of one of them does not necessarily determine what the others shall be. It admits that possibilities may be in excess of actualities, and that things not yet revealed to our knowledge may really in themselves be ambiguous.[22]

Determinism asserts that possibilities are identical to actualities, that the future is already contained in the present. We cannot influence the future; it lacks ambiguity, having been sealed in the distant past. Clearly, this is a chilling, unsatisfying vision for most of us—at least James thought so.

Does determinism square with our actual feelings? James suggests that we answer this question by considering a newspaper article about the brutal murder of a woman by her husband. Ignoring his wife's screams for mercy, the husband chopped her to pieces. James asks whether any sane person can read such an account and not feel deep regret. But if the determinists are right, what is the point of regret? Determinists have no reasonable grounds for regretting anything.

> The judgment of regret calls the murder bad. Calling a thing bad means, if it means anything at all, that the thing ought not to be, that something else ought to be in its stead. Determinism, in denying that anything else can be in its stead, virtually defines the universe as a place in which what ought to be is impossible—in other words, as an organism whose constitution is afflicted with an incurable taint, an irremediable flaw. . . .
>
> It is absurd to regret the murder alone. It could not be different. . . . But how then about the judgments of regret themselves? If they are wrong, other judgments, judgments of approval, ought to be in their place. But as they are necessitated, nothing else could be in their place; and [for the determinist] the universe is just what it was before—namely, a place in which what ought to be appears impossible.[23]

Is it virtually impossible to think that such a murder "ought" to have occurred? Is it virtually impossible to be glad that it occurred? If James is correct, no sane person can help feeling some degree of sadness and regret when confronted by such horrors. Yet if the determinists are correct, such feelings are utterly pointless. *There is no rational ground for moral feelings, because ought can have no meaning.* If the determinists are correct, we are caused to have senseless, absurd, utterly false feelings and ideas.

The problem of human freedom is confused somewhat by the distinction between the self and the will. The will is only the self in its active side and freedom of the will really means freedom of the self. It is determination by the self.
Sarvepalli Radhakrishnan

The concept of responsibility offers little help. The issue is controllability. . . . What must be changed is not the responsibility of autonomous man but the conditions, environmental or genetic, of which a person's behavior is a function.
B. F. Skinner

James acknowledged that there is no scientific and objective way to refute such a possibility. But he insisted that our deep, unshakable moral sense of right and wrong, combined with our feelings of regret, make a *compelling* case for our need and right to believe in free will. We have to believe at least in the possibility, however remote, that some children will not be abused because some adults choose to help them; we have to believe that some bad will be avoided and some good done by our actions.

The Inner Sense of Freedom

James believed that change, surprise, and chance are regular parts of our experience.

> There is history. There are novelties, struggles, losses, gains . . . some things at least are decided here and now . . . the passing moment may contain some novelty, be an original starting-point of events, and not merely a push from elsewhere.[24]

I suppose life has made him like that, and he can't help it. None of us can help the things life has done to us. They're done before you realize it, and once they're done they make you do other things until at last everything comes between you and what you'd like to be.
Eugene O'Neill

James appealed directly do our *inner sense of freedom* to verify this, a sense shared by most people (the exceptions, perhaps, being the philosophical and psychological extremists). In fact, he thought most of us have a deep "spiritual need" to believe that we are active agents who exert control over significant aspects of our lives, that we affect events, that we make a difference. We *need* this belief for our spiritual and mental well-being, and we have a right to believe what we need to believe.

James was convinced that belief in determinism is incompatible with our spiritual need for freedom. He thought the prestige and influence of science make people try to believe in determinism, but he did not believe that the evidence supporting determinism is conclusive. Echoing Hume, he claimed that we need to believe in a "more rational shape" for nature than our individual experience reveals. Consequently, we *believe in* the uniformity of laws of nature. But this uniformity of nature cannot be conclusively proved true, as Hume showed. Belief in free will cannot be conclusively proved to be correct either, James noted, but this does not make it inferior to belief in determinism. The basic status of both beliefs is similar.

> All the magnificent achievements of mathematical and physical science—our doctrines of evolution, of uniformity to law, and the rest—proceed from our indomitable desire to cast the world into a more rational shape in our minds than the shape into which it is thrown there by the crude order of our experience. . . . I, for one, feel as free to try conceptions of moral as of mechanical or logical rationality. If a certain formula for expressing the nature of the world violates my moral demand, I shall feel as free to throw it overboard, or at least doubt it, as if it disappointed my demand for uniformity of sequence, for example; the one demand being, so far as I can see, quite

THE PROBLEM IS NOT A REAL ONE

It must be observed that those learned professors of philosophy or psychology who deny the existence of free will do so only in their professional moments and in their studies and lecture rooms. For when it comes to doing anything practical, even of the most trivial kind, they invariably behave as if they and others were free. They inquire from you at dinner whether you will choose this or that dish. They will ask a child why he told a lie, and will punish him for not having chosen the way of truthfulness. All of which is consistent with a belief in free will. This should cause us to suspect that the problem is not a real one; and this I believe is the case. The dispute is merely verbal, and is due to nothing but a confusion about the meanings of words.

W. T. Stace
Religion and the Modern Mind (New York: HarperCollins, 1952), p. 279.

as subjective and emotional as the other is. The principle of causality, for example—what is it but a postulate, an empty name covering simply a demand that the sequence of events shall one day manifest a deeper kind of belonging of one thing with another than the mere arbitrary juxtaposition which now phenomenally appears? It is as much an altar to an unknown god as the one Saint Paul found at Athens. All our scientific and philosophic ideals are altars to unknown gods. Uniformity is as much so as is free will.[25]

In the absence of conclusive proof, we must decide which belief better suits our needs. Believing as he did in the primacy of morality, James asserted that belief in free will better serves our need for "moral rationality." And since neither belief can be conclusively rejected, he argued that we have the right to test belief in free will against our regular experiences. If it "pays" more than believing that we have no control over our lives, then clearly it is the superior belief.

Perhaps the strongest "argument" against determinism is the fact that almost no one really believes absolutely everything he or she thinks, hopes, and does was determined from the first moments of the existence of the universe. Life presents us with inescapable moments of choice. How we respond is what matters most.

> Each man must act as he thinks best; and, if he is wrong, so much the worse for him. We stand on a mountain pass in the midst of whirling snow and blinding mist, through which we get glimpses now and then of paths which may be deceptive. If we stand still we shall be frozen to death. If we take the wrong road we shall be dashed to pieces. We do not certainly know whether there is any right one. What must we do? "Be

If . . . man's nature . . . makes him do what he does, how does his action differ from that of a stone or a tree? Have we not parted with any ground for responsibility? . . . Holding men to responsibility may make a decided difference in their future behavior; holding a stone or tree to responsibility is a meaningless performance.
John Dewey

strong and of a good courage." Act for the best, hope for the best, and take what comes.[26]

How can we know what is best? James says that we must discover the essence of the good.

PHILOSOPHICAL QUERY

Do you find it impossible to doubt that you possess free will—at least sometimes? Is belief in the possibility of free will necessary for your happiness?

Morality and the Good

James rejected metaphysical attempts to define the good. He argued that the only way to understand the good life was to study what people actually want and strive for. He surveyed and rejected strictly Aristotelian, hedonistic, Christian, Kantian, and utilitarian ethics, though he borrowed from each.

Please remember that optimism and pessimism are definitions of the world, and that your own reactions to the world, small as they are in bulk, are integral parts of the whole thing, and necessarily help to determine the definition.

William James

> Various essences of good have thus been . . . proposed as bases of the ethical system. . . .
>
> No one of the measures that have actually been proposed has, however, given general satisfaction. . . . The best, on the whole, of these marks and measures of goodness seems to be the capacity to bring happiness. But in order not to break down fatally, this test must be taken to cover innumerable acts and impulses that never *aim* at happiness; so that, after all, in seeking for a universal principle we inevitably are carried onward to the *most* universal principle—that *the essence of good is simply to satisfy demand*. The demand may be for anything under the sun. There is really no more ground for supposing that all our demands can be accounted for by one universal underlying kind of motive than there is ground for supposing that all physical phenomena are cases of a single law.[27]

We have a basic obligation to "maximize satisfactions" and minimize frustrations, not just for ourselves but for others, according to James. Such a course is most likely to lead to happiness and increase the world's stock of goodness. Yet this must remain a fundamental, general obligation. The sheer number of people, coupled with the sheer number of demands we each have, makes being more specific impossible. All we can do is try our best to increase the general level of satisfaction and goodness, while remaining aware of our fallibility.

James did not offer an ethical *theory* as such, though he suggested moral "guidelines." He proposed a form of altruistic utilitarianism based on an optimistic vision of social progress. He believed modern civilization is better than past eras—he cited examples of slavery and torture—because the constant give-and-take, the "push and pull," of history results in continual re-

CHOOSING A PHILOSOPHY IS A TEST OF CHARACTER

It is simply our total character and personal genius that are on trial; and if we invoke any so-called philosophy, our choice and use of that also are but revelations of our personal aptitude or incapacity for moral life. From this unsparing practical ordeal no professor's lectures and no array of books can save us. The solving word, for the learned and the unlearned man alike, lies in the last resort in the dumb willingnesses and unwillingnesses of their interior characters, and no-where else. It is not in heaven, neither is it beyond the sea; but the word is very nigh unto thee, in thy mouth and in thy heart, that thou mayst do it.

William James
"The Moral Philosopher and Moral Life," in *The Will to Believe and Other Essays in Popular Philosophy* (1897; reprinted in *Human Immortality*, New York: Dover, 1956), pp. 214–15.

finement of satisfactions. The radical's forward drive is compensated for by the conservative's inertia; the dreamer's whimsy balances and is balanced by the scientist's objective eye, and so on.

It is important not to lose sight of the fact that James was also a psychologist and scientist. He gave more credence to observation and experience than to systematic argument. Further, he did not believe in universal moral principles or in the possibility of any finite, closed expression of morality. Thus, from his perspective, the kind of argument and system that would satisfy most philosophers would also falsify the reality of moral experience.

The Heroic Life

William James believed that life without heroic struggle is dull, mediocre, and empty. He was thinking of two approaches to life. In one, we choose (will) safety, security, and compliance. We try to avoid risks, try to avoid "hassles." The other kind of life deliberately includes danger, courage, risk; it is based on a will to excitement and passion.

James was not advising us to take up hang gliding and shooting the rapids. He was talking about a "real fight" for something important, about the struggle between good and evil. He said evil is "out there," to be resisted and fought. We might find it in the form of discrimination or toxic dumping. When we do, we can ignore it, make a token effort at resisting it by voicing our objections, or actually do something. If we confront it, we may lose our jobs, money, time, or solid A grade-point average. We may fail. We may even be wrong: what we perceived as evil may not be evil. But at least we fought for or against something.

What sort of thing would life really be, with your qualities ready for a tussle with it, if it only brought fair weather and gave those higher faculties of yours no scope?
William James

> For my own part, I do not know what the sweat and blood of this life mean, if they mean anything short of this. If this life

be not a real fight, in which something is eternally gained for the universe by success, it is no better than a game of private theatricals from which we may withdraw at will. But it *feels* like a real fight—as if there were something really wild in the universe which we, with all our idealities and faithfulnesses, are needed to redeem: and first of all to redeem our own hearts from atheisms and fears. For such is a half-wild, half-saved universe adapted. The deepest thing in our nature is . . . this dumb region of the heart in which we dwell alone with our willingness and unwillingness, our faiths and fears.[28]

According to James, struggle and effort are vital elements of the good life. He believed that the "strenuous mood" is superior to sitting back and drifting along. Thus he did not think much of the Epicurean ideal of the retreat to the Garden or of Stoic detachment, when either meant reduced involvement in life and diminished passions (though he did admire the Stoic emphasis on strength of will).

James thought he had identified a natural fact of life: an active, strenuous approach is healthier and more satisfying than a passive, easygoing one.

When we reason about the liberty of the will, or about the free will, we do not ask if the man can do what he wills, but if there is enough independence in his will itself.

Gottfried Wilhelm Leibniz

The deepest difference, practically, in the moral life of man is the difference between the easy-going and the strenuous mood. When in the easy-going mood, the shrinking from present ill is our ruling consideration. The strenuous mood, on the contrary, makes us quite indifferent to present ill, if only the great ideal is to be attained. The capacity for the strenuous mood probably lies slumbering in every man, but it has more difficulty in some than in others in waking up. It needs wilder passions to arouse it, the big fears, loves, and indignations; or else the deeply penetrating appeal of some of the higher fidelities, like justice, truth, or freedom. Strong belief is a necessity of its vision; and a world where all the mountains are brought down and all the valleys are exalted is no congenial place for its habitation.[29]

PHILOSOPHICAL QUERY

Discuss your formal and informal education in terms of the preceding passage. Have you been encouraged to adopt a strenuous mood or an easygoing one? Give some specific examples. Do you think James is on the right track? Why or why not?

PRAGMATIC RELIGION

James had deep respect for a religion that enriches our lives, that has "cash value." He noted that people in all cultures turn to a god (or gods) who *gets things done*, an active God, a God of the "strenuous mood," not a passive, ineffective God. This led James to offer an intriguing suggestion: If people do not believe in God, it may be because God is not *doing anything* in their lives. In *The Varieties of Religious Experience*, he attempted to discover how God *works* in people's lives. Combining an empirical, psychological study of a number of cases with a keen philosophical analysis, *Varieties* is one of James's most influential, popular, and still widely read works.

James asserted that we judge the truth of religious ideas by what he calls their "immediate luminousness," adding, "in short, *philosophical reasonableness and moral helpfulness* are the only available criteria." He concluded that religious faith is important and meaningful on pragmatic grounds: Its presence or absence makes a clearly observable, practical, and concrete difference in our lives.

> The practical needs and experiences of religion seem to me sufficiently met by the belief that beyond man and in a fashion continuous with him there exists a larger power which is friendly to him and his ideals. All that the facts require is that the power shall be other and larger than our conscious selves.
>
> God is the natural appellation, for us Christians at least, for the supreme reality, so I will call this higher part of the universe by the name of God. We and God have business with each other; and in opening ourselves to his influence our deepest destiny is fulfilled.[30]

James thought that a religious orientation is more effective than a nonreligious one because it encompasses more. It addresses and derives from a wider range of experiences, including a wider, more expansive consciousness than a purely secular point of view. Besides the obvious psychological benefits of having God as a support and comfort, religious conversion can open us up and make us more responsive to all of life, according to James.

A Religious Dilemma

In his study of religious experience, James distinguished between two basic personalities, the "healthy-minded" and the "morbid-minded." Healthy-minded people "look on all things and see that they are good." Such people are vital, enthusiastic, and exuberant.

> In these states, the ordinary contrast of good and ill seems to be swallowed up in a higher denomination, an omnipotent excitement which engulfs the evil, and which the human being welcomes as the crowning experience of his life. This, he says, is truly to live, and I exult in the heroic opportunity and adventure. . . .[31]

In contrast, the attitude of the morbid-minded person is "based on the persuasion that the evil aspects of our life are its very essence, and that the

God is real since he produces real effects.
William James

world's meaning most comes home to us when we lay them most to heart."[32] In other words, morbid souls are negativistic and pessimistic. They see mostly (or only) evil, nastiness, untrustworthiness, and trouble.

> But there are others for whom evil is no mere relation of the subject to particular outer things, but something more radical and general, a wrongness or vice in his essential nature, which no alteration of the environment, or any superficial rearrangement of the inner self, can cure, and which requires a supernatural remedy.[33]

Interestingly, James the optimist says morbid-minded persons have a clearer, more realistic perspective than healthy-minded ones because they recognize a wider range of experience.

> It seems to me that we are bound to say that morbid-mindedness ranges over the wider scale of experience. . . . The method of averting one's attention from evil, and living simply in the light of good is splendid as long as it will work. It will work with many persons; it will work far more generally than most of us are ready to suppose; and within the sphere of its successful operation there is nothing to be said against it as a religious solution. But it breaks down impotently as soon as melancholy comes. . . .
>
> The normal process of life contains moments as bad as any of those which insane melancholy is filled with, moments in which radical evil gets its innings and takes its solid turn. The lunatic's visions of horror are all drawn from the material of daily fact. Our civilization is founded on the shambles, and every individual existence goes out in a lonely spasm of helpless agony. If you protest, my friend, wait till you arrive there yourself! . . . The completest religions would therefore seem to be those in which the pessimistic elements are best developed.[34]

The healthy-minded . . . need to be born only once . . . sick souls . . . must be born twice—born in order to be happy. The result is two different conceptions of the universe of our experience.
William James

To better grasp this point, think of what it means to be *always* joyful and enthusiastic in a world such as ours. This lopsided kind of "healthy-mindedness" might result from a lack of true empathy with the condition of other people. A shallow enough view of things can result in a childish (not childlike) view of life in which nothing is really bad. Or, if it is bad, it is not *that* bad. Or, if it is *that* bad, then it is somehow deserved.

In his analysis of healthy- and morbid-mindedness, James is interested in identifying the most practical spiritual balance. A soul that is blocked off from a major portion of experience, which, for want of a better word, we may refer to simply as evil, will be less effective, less "alive," than one that is not.

PHILOSOPHICAL QUERY

What do you think of James's claim that morbid-minded people have a fuller, more realistic view of things than healthy-minded ones? How would you classify yourself? Discuss some of the strengths and weaknesses of both orientations.

Ultramarginal Life

According to James, the experience of being *reborn* makes happiness possible in a complex world, without resorting to the limited perspective of the healthy-minded. *Rebirth* in James's sense refers to a profound alteration of consciousness, and though this change results in a "religious" outlook, it is not confined to religion as such. Rebirth offers a solution to the dilemma of achieving a morally decent measure of happiness while acknowledging the pervasive presence of evil in the world. Put another way: Are healthy-minded ignorance or despondent pessimism the only options? James says profound spiritual experience—a "third possibility"—can avoid the extremes of ignorance or pessimism.

James identified two kinds of conversion experience, "instantaneous" conversion and a slower, gradual process of conversion he labeled "natural." He claimed the fruits of both kinds are comparable: an expansion of ordinary consciousness. According to James, our "field of consciousness" is always in a state of flux, with a changing border he called the *margin of consciousness*. Arguing from a strictly psychological perspective, James concluded that religious experience evokes responses from an "ultramarginal life." In contemporary terms, genuine religious experience flows from and opens channels to otherwise inaccessible realms of experience.

> I cannot but think that the most important step forward that has occurred in psychology since I have been a student of that science is the discovery, first made in 1886, that, in certain subjects at least, there is not only the consciousness of the ordinary field, with its usual centre and margin, but an addition thereto in the shape of a set of memories, thoughts, and feelings which are extra-marginal and outside the primary consciousness altogether, but yet must be classed as conscious facts of some sort, able to reveal their presence by unmistakable signs.[35]

Saintliness and Mysticism

James divided the fruits of spiritual experience—the unmistakable signs of the ultramarginal life—into two areas, conduct and thinking. The fruit of reborn conduct is **saintliness**, a way of life devoted exclusively to a heightened religious consciousness; the fruit of reborn thinking is **mysticism**, a way of thinking that views everything in terms of a powerful religious experience.

James proposed to "test saintliness by common sense, to use human standards to help us decide how far the religious life commends itself as an ideal kind of human activity." He noted that some saints are fanatics and

Truth is made, just as health, wealth, and strength are made, in the course of experience.
William James

SAINTLINESS
According to James, a way of life devoted exclusively to a heightened religious consciousness; behavioral result of being reborn.

MYSTICISM (JAMESEAN)
According to James, a way of thinking that views everything in terms of a powerful religious experience; cognitive result of being reborn.

others are naive. The fanatics are "masterful and aggressive," whereas the naive saints are "a genuinely creative social force." He reminded us that "the fruits of religion are like all human products, liable to corruption by excess. Common sense must judge them."[36]

In this beautiful discussion of the naive saint, James is at his best.

There can be no final truth in ethics any more than in physics until the last man has had his experience and said his say.
William James

> If things are ever to move upward, someone must be ready to take the first step, and assume the risk of it. No one who is not willing to try charity, to try non-resistance as the saint is willing, can tell whether these methods will or will not succeed. When they do succeed, they are far more powerfully successful than force or worldly prudence. Force destroys enemies; and the best that can be said of prudence is that it keeps what we already have in safety. But non-resistance, when successful, turns enemies into friends; and charity regenerates its objects. These saintly methods are, as I said, creative energies; and genuine saints find in the elevated excitement with which their faith endows them an authority and impressiveness which makes them irresistible in situations where men of shallower nature cannot get on at all without the use of worldly prudence. This practical proof that worldly wisdom may be safely transcended is the saint's magic gift to mankind.[37]

Those of us who have not experienced the "ultramarginal life" have only our practical wisdom to guide us. No wonder we are afraid to help the dirty stranger at the door, afraid to let him into our house. He might hurt us, soil the carpet, steal something. Our fears are *prudent*. Despite the parable of the Good Samaritan, it is not prudent to stop and help stranded motorists—it is "smarter" to call for help. It is prudent to defend ourselves.

Mahatma Gandhi, Martin Luther King, and Mother Teresa were (and are) not prudent. Though they may not be saints, these three individuals reflect the saint's magic gift. Gandhi's passive resistance altered forever the plight of India's poor and untouchables. King's courageous passive resistance did more than inspire millions around the world: it triggered a long, difficult move toward social and civil equality in America (Chapter 19). Mother Teresa's work with the poor and sick brings comfort to them and inspiration to a beleaguered world.

Like the saint, the mystic has practical value, according to James.

> Looking back on my own experiences, they all converge towards a kind of insight to which I cannot help ascribing some metaphysical significance. The keynote of it is invariably reconciliation. It is as if the opposites of the world, whose contradictoriness and conflict make all our difficulties, were melted into unity. Not only do they, as contrasted species, belong to one and the same genus, but *one of the species*, the nobler and better one, *is itself the genus, and so soaks up and absorbs its op-*

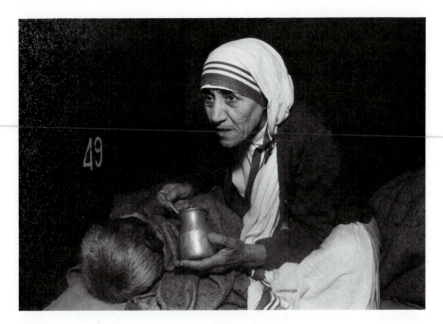

Mother Teresa is perhaps the best-known contemporary example of a holy person. Does she fit James's description of a saint or a mystic (or both)?

posite into itself. This is a dark saying, I know, when thus expressed in terms of common logic, but I cannot wholly escape from its authority. I feel as if it must mean something, something like what the Hegelian philosophy means, if one could only lay hold of it more clearly. Those who have ears to hear, let them hear; to me the living sense of its reality only comes in the artificial mystic state of the mind.[38]

The mystic state is not artificial in the sense of being phony or less real, but "unnatural" in the sense of being rare and short-lived: "Except in rare instances, half an hour, or at most an hour or two, seems to be the limit beyond which they fade in the light of common day," James said.

What shall we make of all this? Whatever we conclude, James reminds us, will *not* be based on "pure" objective criteria. We will bring to this analysis of religion what we bring to everything, our accumulation of memories, unique experiences, psychological temperament. Since there can never be conclusive, absolute proof that God does or does not exist, that mystical experience is or is not an insight into a higher wisdom, we each have a *right* to believe as we see fit. We have no *duty* to believe. We have no duty not to believe. We have no duty to accept the authority of another's religious experience, nor have we any duty to accept another's rejection of our own. But, clearly, William James believed in the healing, unifying, restorative power of belief.

COMMENTARY

The most significant weakness in James's pragmatism is so much a part of what he saw as his mission that we must consider it from two perspectives. By tying truth to "what works" *for us*, James cuts himself off from any possibility of objective verification. Yet most philosophers still hold that the truth must refer to something beyond and not entirely determined by the individual. James seems to blur the distinction between truth and how we discover it. While we do test ideas by acting on them and by comparing them with our more established beliefs, their *truth* is independent of this process. Penicillin remains an effective antibiotic whether or not I believe that it is, for example.

There are two different issues here. If we are looking at factual matters, this criticism of pragmatism is persuasive. But if we consider beliefs about moral and spiritual concerns, as well as some social and psychological beliefs, pragmatism has something important to say. We can become confused about James's position if we lump both general categories of belief statements together.

Consider, on James's behalf, the pattern that social scientists refer to as a **self-fulfilling prophecy**. This is a belief that so affects events, it causes itself to be true. For example, a man who believes his date will not like him may project a mood of surly defensiveness and hostility, or passive, defeatist self-pity. Either mood may alienate his companion, who otherwise would have found him quite pleasant. If so, his prophecy of "She won't like me" has fulfilled itself. Similarly, students who expect to do poorly in a given course may not retain information because they are frightened or depressed by their expectations of failure; they may unconsciously devote less energy to their studies than they would have if they had believed more in themselves. Conversely, students who expect to do well may be more open and pleasant in class, which can inspire the professor to be a better teacher; they may ask more questions, pay more attention, and so on, thereby fulfilling their own beliefs.

But this raises the basic **pragmatic paradox**: *Pragmatism works only if we believe our ideas are true according to nonpragmatic criteria.* For instance, can I really be "reborn" if I believe there is no more evidence for than against the existence of a benevolent God? Can I really just say to myself, "Well, belief in God makes people feel secure and gives their lives meaning. I would like to feel secure and find a purpose for my life. Therefore, I shall believe in God"? Does not such belief work only when I sincerely believe it to be true—really and factually true, not just true because I believe it is true? Paradoxically, it seems as if only by believing in a nonpragmatic view of truth can pragmatism work.

James's version of pragmatism, after its initial success, is rarely accepted by today's philosophers, who insist on standards of rigor that James labeled "extremist." Yet his influence cannot be overlooked. His insistence that philosophy return to its "original sense" and address the practical issues facing

SELF-FULFILLING PROPHECY A belief that affects events in such a way that it causes itself to be true; such as the student who does poorly on an exam because she expects to fail it.

PRAGMATIC PARADOX Pragmatism works only if we believe that our ideas are true according to nonpragmatic criteria.

us came at a time when the world was ready to listen. I am not sure how well "professional philosophers" have answered this vital challenge, but it lingers: branches of applied philosophy such as medical ethics, business ethics, computer ethics, the study of philosophers from other cultures, feminist and womanist analyses of modes of biased thinking share the pragmatic spirit of battling evil and fighting for the good.

Whether we wholeheartedly try to make philosophy "work" again or believe that practical social and moral reform are not the philosopher's concern, many professional philosophers are acutely aware of the challenge to do something that "matters" to a circle wider than that of their academic peers.

James's background in psychology led him to recognize how important belief and the will are to our basic sense of well-being. He demonstrated what other nineteenth-century philosophers and writers had begun to suspect, namely, that extreme rationalist and empiricist philosophies distort as much as (if not more than) they reveal. James was one of the great, early defenders of the individual, free will, and human complexity against the crushing forces of rationalistic abstraction and scientific determinism. He spoke eloquently for the person of "moderate" convictions and temperament; he spoke eloquently for the virtues of the active, vigorous struggle for good.

James offered a persuasive and unique defense of our right to believe. He showed that faith in a higher power cannot be dismissed as a form of psychological infantilism, and that its grounding in personal conviction is as solid as faith in science. Further, he showed that religious faith has restorative and unifying powers often missing from faith in science. James defended the "common sense" of the average person without pandering to it and called on us to test the higher life of the "strenuous mood." All in all, these are impressive accomplishments.

From his own early crisis and recurring periods of despair, William James fashioned a philosophy of salvation. He anticipated, because he felt, the deep despair that a cold, deterministic vision of life engenders. We shall see in the next chapter how much this pervasive view of life still affects all of us, how we pay for the comforts and cures of science with a picture of ourselves as puppets of cause and effect.

> Now I wish to make you feel, if I can . . . that we have a right to believe the physical order to be only a partial order; that we have a right to supplement it by an unseen spiritual order which we assume on trust, if only thereby life may seem to us better worth living again. But . . . such a trust will seem to some of you sadly mystical and execrably unscientific. . . . In this very University . . . I have heard more than one teacher say that all the fundamental conceptions of truth have already been found by science, and that the future has only the details of the picture to fill in. But the slightest reflection on the real conditions will suffice to show how barbaric such notions

These, then, are my last words to you: Be not afraid of life. Believe that life is worth living, and your belief will help create the fact. The "scientific proof" that you are right may not be clear before the day of judgment (or some stage of being which that expression may serve to symbolize) is reached. But the faithful fighters of this hour, or the beings that then and there will represent them, may then turn to the faint-hearted, who here decline to go on, with words like those with which Henry IV greeted tardy Crillon after a great victory had been gained: "Hang yourself, brave Crillon! we fought at Arques, and you were not there."

William James

are. . . . No! our science is but a drop, our ignorance a sea. Whatever else be certain, this at least is certain—that the world of our present natural knowledge is enveloped in a larger world of some sort of whose residual properties we at present can frame no positive idea.[39]

William James said "No!" to deterministic reductionism. If he answered with too much exuberance and subjectivity for some of today's philosophers, that does not diminish his genius or foresight. If his analysis of faith is too soft, too inconsistent for the philosophers and scientists, and too naturalistic, too philosophic for the preachers, it remains compelling nonetheless. Although I am not particularly fond of the expression "cash value," I wholeheartedly agree with James's insistence that philosophy—especially—must make a difference, must *pay*. Otherwise, the spirit of the old *sophos* will have faded from us forever.

SUMMARY OF MAIN POINTS

William James's pragmatism is based on Charles Sanders Peirce's pragmatic theory of meaning: Ideas are meaningful only when they translate into actions and predict experiences associated with actions.

James reflected a late-nineteenth-century trend among thinkers who resisted excessive abstraction and demanded relevance from philosophy. He argued that philosophy should make a "definite difference" in people's lives, and attempted to construct a philosophical religion that could provide beliefs worth living and dying for. Pragmatism was meant to be a method for helping us feel "at home" in the universe.

Pragmatism rejects any philosophy that lacks "cash value." James believed that virtually no metaphysical theory has any practical payoff (cash value). "True ideas," he said, "are those that we can assimilate, validate, corroborate and verify. False ideas are those we cannot." Pragmatic truth is human truth.

James expanded the realm of philosophy beyond "revealing the truth" to providing a way to become better adjusted to the world. Thus his interest was not so much rigorous philosophical argument as advocacy of pragmatic beliefs that could give life meaning and vitality.

James divided people into tough-minded or tender-minded types, claiming that historically philosophy has been dominated by extremists of one type or the other, and thus remained unbalanced. He advocated what he saw as a more useful combination of these two extremes.

Pragmatism holds that reason serves the will and we live according to our beliefs. James said because life demands an active response, we have no choice but to believe something. We face "forced options." The intellect does not discover the truths in which we believe; the will to believe creates truths.

The pragmatic life rejects determinism as incompatible with our immediate sense of freedom. According to James, determinism, the idea that everything must happen exactly the way it does, is incompatible with our spiritual need for freedom. Determinism has less cash value than belief in freedom, and since neither belief can be proved conclusively, the pragmatic thing to do is believe in what we need to be happy—freedom. Feelings of regret reflect our deep belief in free will.

Since we cannot escape choice, James advocated what he called the "heroic life," rejecting life without struggle as dull, mediocre, and empty.

The heroic life is characterized by a "real fight" for something important; it is about the struggle between good and evil.

James valued religion that has cash value because, in his view, belief in a God of "the strenuous mood" helps people get things done. Religious faith is important on pragmatic grounds: Its presence or absence makes an observable, practical difference in people's lives. James believed a religious orientation is more effective than a nonreligious one because it encompasses more.

James distinguished between two basic personalities: The healthy-minded personality looks at all things as good; healthy-minded people are exuberant, vital, and enthusiastic. The morbid-minded personality sees the very essence of life as evil, untrustworthy, and troublesome; morbid-minded people are negativistic and pessimistic. James thought the morbid view is the clearer and more realistic, because it recognizes a wider range of experience than does the healthy view.

Profound religious experience makes it possible to be both morally decent (without descending into the pessimism of morbid-mindedness) and happy (without resorting to the limited perspective of healthy-mindedness). James refers to the expansion of consciousness that results from religious experience as being reborn.

Rebirth (profound religious experience) evokes experiences from an "ultramarginal life," a state of awareness that flows from and opens channels to otherwise inaccessible realms of experience. Ultramarginal life is expressed in conduct as saintliness and in thinking as mysticism. According to James, saints and mystics have practical value because they challenge us to expand our own range of beliefs and consciousness.

STUDY QUESTIONS

1. Discuss how James's personal life influenced some of his major pragmatic beliefs.

2. What is the pragmatic theory of meaning? Illustrate with an example.

3. What is the pragmatic method? What is it used for?

4. Explain what pragmatists mean by the "cash value" of an idea.

5. Compare and contrast tough-mindedness with tender-mindedness. What is the significance of this distinction?

6. Discuss James's notion of the "will to believe." In what sense do "reasons serve the will" according to James? Do you agree with him? Why or why not?

7. Explain what it means to assert that "truth happens." Give an example, then evaluate.

8. What is the dilemma of determinism? How does James deal with it? What do you think of his approach?

9. Discuss the pragmatic conception of the good.

10. Explain what James meant by the "heroic life."

11. Explain what James meant when he claimed that a religious orientation is more effective than a nonreligious one. Do you agree? Why or why not?

12. State, then discuss, James's opinion of optimism.

13. What are the fruits of spiritual experience, according to James? What do they have to do with the "ultramarginal life"? What does James see as their "cash value"? Do you agree? Discuss.

CHAPTER EIGHTEEN

The Existentialist: Jean-Paul Sartre and Albert Camus

> But just as a scientific fact has its finality in the rest of knowledge, so the philosophy we would make our own has also its extrinsic object—it refers to our whole destiny, to our attitude in the face of life and the universe. And the tragic problem of philosophy is to reconcile intellectual necessities with the necessities of the heart and will.
>
> MIGUEL DE UNAMUNO

In this century, we have seen an entire generation of Europe's young men destroyed by the horrors of World War I. The marvels of technology were turned to mass destruction in the form of heavy artillery, airborne bombs, and chemical weapons (mustard gas, chiefly). Over the years, millions of people have been annihilated in revolutions, purges, and "ethnic cleansings" in Russia, Turkey, Poland, Czechoslovakia, Bosnia, Somalia, Iran, China, South Africa, Chile, and so on. World War II alone saw the systematic annihilation of anywhere from nine to twelve million people (including at least six million Jews, by the Nazis) and the first use of atomic weapons. The Korean War brought heightened techniques of mind control, and Vietnam ushered in napalm, Agent Orange, and "precision strikes."

The twentieth century is a century of worldwide smog, starvation on a mass scale, continued bigotry, environmental catastrophe, religious bickering, rapidly expanding population, widespread child abuse and substance abuse, a growing gap between the "haves" and the "have-nots." And through all of this, the apparent silence of God is deafening.

The timeless demand that philosphy should matter, that it should make a difference in a conflicted world, increased after World War I and really took off after the Holocaust of World War II became widely understood. This chapter is a brief look at the responses to these absurdities and horrors made by two of the most influential intellectuals of the contemporary era: Albert Camus and Jean-Paul Sartre.

Both Camus and Sartre lived through the German occupation of France. Both were involved with the Resistance movement. And both were profoundly altered by their wartime experiences. Both became famous as novelists, playwrights, and existentialists. They were friends for a while but ultimately became estranged. Both won Nobel Prizes in literature. Though utterly dissimilar personally—and though at one point Camus said that he was not an existentialist—Sartre and Camus each expressed a postmodern, atheistic philosophy that reflects in compelling terms the major existentialist themes identified in Chapter 16 (choice, freedom, identity, alienation, inauthenticity, despair, subjectivity, and awareness of our own mortality).

It is not an exaggeration to say that contemporary existentialism was the most widely influential philosophical orientation from 1945 until the emergence of feminism in the early 1970s. This is not to say that either existentialism or feminism is without rivals or critics. Rather, existentialism and feminism reflect major issues of the times, and their influence reaches beyond academic circles. Both existentialism and feminism challenged philosophy to make a difference. Both existentialism and feminism are advocated by powerful personalities and dynamic writers who address issues and speak in a language that nonscholars can understand. And lastly, both existentialism and feminism are controversial, exciting as much disfavor as favor—but in a way that irrevocably alters the philosophical and social landscape.

The instability, primitive anger, and irrational behavior that triggered the contemporary existential reaction in philosophy, art,
and literature continue today. What solace can more traditional
philosophers offer these children playing in ruins of the old
library in central Sarajevo? Is it possible to deny that life is absurd
after seeing so many scenes like this?

JEAN-PAUL SARTRE

Jean-Paul-Charles-Aymard Sartre (1905–1980) was born
in Paris. When his father died while Sartre was still an infant, his mother, Ann-Marie, moved in with her parents. Jean-Paul was
raised in the home of his grandfather, Charles Schweitzer, an uncle of Albert
Schweitzer, the famous Christian missionary doctor. In a passage from the
autobiographical *The Words*, Sartre suggested that his ultimate view of life
was shaped by "a deep childish revulsion against the sham façade of noble
rectitude behind which his [Sartre's grandfather's] bourgeois family hid
from itself, and from him, its real dereliction."[1] Sartre added that until the
age of ten he "remained alone between an old man and two women."[2]

Whatever Sartre the man thought of his grandfather, Charles Schweitzer
introduced Sartre the boy to the world of words and literature. Withdrawn

Jean-Paul Sartre

and isolated, disturbed by his mother's Catholicism and his grandparents' Lutheranism, young Sartre discovered the magical world of writing and ideas in his grandfather's impressive library. Before his tenth birthday he knew he would be a writer: "By writing, I was existing, I was escaping from grown-ups, but I existed only in order to write, and if I said 'I' that meant 'I who write.'"[3]

In 1929, Sartre graduated from the Ecole Normale Supérieure, which accepted only the finest students who had passed a series of competitive examinations. Sartre taught philosophy at various schools for the next ten years. During this time, he realized an enormous gap existed between his "living, breathing" life and the values he had learned in his grandfather's home and taught to others at school. Conventional, academic philosophy disappointed him; its abstractions and elaborate metaphysical systems bore little or no relevance to his actual existence. Life, Sartre noted, is made up of difficult decisions and concrete experiences, but traditional philosophy, on the whole, fails to address these living issues and choices.

Nausea

Sartre's philosophical disillusionment ended when he discovered the phenomenology of **Edmund Husserl (1859–1938)**. **Phenomenology** sees consciousness as the basis of reality and aims to provide a descriptive analysis of consciousness in all its forms. Stressing the concrete rather than the abstract, experienced facts rather than theory, phenomenology attempts to reveal the "essence" of human consciousness using purely descriptive statements. It aims at making no conceptual presuppositions, hoping to get beyond them to consciousness itself.

Sartre studied with Husserl in Berlin during the 1933–34 school year. Revitalized, he turned to writing as a way to discover who he was and to find a philosophical approach that worked. Much as Søren Kierkegaard studied himself, even "created himself," through reflexive (self-conscious) writing, Sartre began a series of projects aimed at helping him discover a way to live "alone, without God." Building on his newfound phenomenological approach, Sartre attempted to see and describe experience in its basic "uninterpreted" state. In his first novel, *Nausea*, he tried to get beyond words, theories, and assumptions in order to see life raw.

Unlike Descartes' methodical meditations, Sartre's phenomenological introspection yields no rational, permanent entity known as the self. Instead of order and permanence, Sartre found nausea—a pulsating, ever-flowing monstrous nothingness. The more Sartre contemplated existence, the less he found. Sitting in a garden, contemplating the roots of an old chestnut tree, Roquentin, the protagonist of *Nausea*, says:

> Never until these last few days have I understood the meaning of existence. . . . And then all of a sudden, there it was, clear as day: existence had suddenly unveiled itself. It had lost the harmless look of an abstract category: it was the very paste of things,

PHENOMENOLOGY
Philosophical method of analysis developed by Edmund Husserl; using purely descriptive statements, phenomenology tries to provide a "descriptive analysis" of consciousness in all its forms, stressing the concrete rather than the abstract and experienced facts rather than theory, in order to reveal the "essence" of human consciousness.

A man is involved in life, leaves his impress on it, outside of that there is nothing.
Jean-Paul Sartre

Calvin and Hobbes, © Watterson. Dist. by Universal Press Syndicate. Reprinted with permission. All rights reserved.

this root was kneaded into existence. Or rather the root, the park gates, the bench, the sparse grass, all that had vanished: the diversity of things, their individuality, were only an appearance, a veneer. This veneer had melted, leaving soft monstrous masses, all in disorder—naked, in a frightful, obscene nakedness.[4]

Existence Is Absurd

Having peered into himself and found nothing permanent; having peered beyond words and abstractions to glimpse the world as it is and found only "melted . . . soft monstrous masses, all in disorder—naked, in a frightful, obscene nakedness," Sartre concludes that existence is absurd:

> The word absurdity is coming to life under my pen; a little while ago . . . I couldn't find it, but neither was I looking for it, I didn't need it: I thought without words. . . . Without formulating anything clearly, I understood that I had found the key to Existence, the key to my Nausea, to my own life. In fact, all that I could grasp beyond that returns to this fundamental absurdity. Absurdity: another word; I struggle against words; down there I touched the thing.[5]

The world of explanations and reasons is not the world of existence.
Jean-Paul Sartre

Sartre's sense of the absurd was shaped by his experiences during World War II. He was drafted into the French army in 1939, and in 1940 was captured by the Germans. Sartre spent nine months as a prisoner of war before being released because of poor health. He returned to Paris and soon became an influential member of the French Resistance movement. During this time he met Albert Camus, his only near-rival in modern existential influence, and the brilliant **Simone de Beauvoir (1908–1986)**, who became Sartre's mistress and lifelong friend.

The German occupation of France drove home to Sartre the fact that evil is not a mere abstraction; it is real and concrete. He concluded that

OH, THE PURE INNOCENT CHILD!

Oh, tell me who was it first announced, who was it first proclaimed, that man only does nasty things because he does not know his own interests; and that if he were enlightened, if his eyes were opened to his real normal interests, man would at once cease to do nasty things, would at once become good and noble because, being enlightened and understanding his real advantage, he would see his own advantage in the good and nothing else, and we all know that not one man can, consciously, act against his own interests, consequently, so to say, through necessity, he would begin doing good? Oh, the babe! Oh, the pure innocent child!

Fyodor Dostoevsky
Notes from the Underground, trans. Constance Garnett, in *Existentialism from Dostoevsky to Sartre*, ed. Walter Kaufmann (New York: New American Library, 1975), p. 67.

The essential predicament of man has assumed a peculiar urgency in our time, living as we do in a civilization where factories were established in order to exterminate millions of men, women, and children; where soap was made of human flesh. What have we done to make such crimes possible? What are we doing to make such crimes impossible?

Abraham Joshua Heschel

civilization and order are a thin veneer: at any moment "the beast" can break loose and reveal "the absurd," which most of us try to deny through rationalizations in the form of abstractions and philosophical and religious beliefs. Failure to face the absurd is always accompanied by excessive denial, which prevents us from recognizing evil for what it is. Sartre wrote that during the occupation he had been taught "to take evil seriously."

> It is neither to our fault nor our merit if we lived in a time when torture was a daily fact. Chateaubriand, Oradour, the Rue des Saussaies, Dachau, and Auschwitz have all demonstrated to us that Evil is not an appearance, that knowing its cause does not dispel it, that it is not opposed to Good as a confused idea is to a clear one, that it is not the effect of passions that might be cured, of an ignorance that might be enlightened, that it can in no way be incorporated into idealistic humanism.[6]

After the horrors of the Holocaust and the terrors wrought by the Nazis' use of science and advanced technology, a whole generation shared a nauseating vision of the absurd. "It was the war," Sartre stated, "which made the obsolete frames of our thought explode, the war, occupation, resistance, the years that followed."[7]

The Celebrity Philosopher

After the war, Sartre devoted his life to reading, writing, and speaking out on various topics relating to social injustice and personal responsibility. Throughout this time, he maintained a rich and rewarding friendship with Simone de Beauvoir. She challenged and stimulated him as a man and as a thinker, greatly influencing both his ideas and their written expression, as he did hers.

Sartre's philosophy was shaped by the Holocaust, which made it difficult to simply dismiss the death of God and the Nietzschean abyss. Perhaps "forlornness" is too tame a term for the human condition following such atrocities. How could God let something like this happen? How could "decent, average" people let it happen?

Sartre and Beauvoir were a unique couple whose influence extended beyond their individual works to their lives, as they became role models for postwar intellectuals.

In 1960, Sartre published *The Critique of Dialectical Reason*, in which he advocated "existential Marxism." Recognizing that political Marxism had lost its original respect for the individual, Sartre nonetheless saw the contemporary era as the "age of Marx":

> There was the period of Descartes and Locke, then the period of Kant and Hegel, and since then there has been the period of Marx. Each of these three philosophies has been in turn the soil from which all individual ideas sprang and has formed the cultural horizon.[8]

Sartre accepted Marx's emphasis on economic and class-based determinism. He agreed that the individual is a product of his or her class. But Sartre thought Marxism lost sight of the individual in its emphasis on class struggle and economics. Marxian materialism objectifies the individual, Sartre argued, and consequently loses touch with his or her subjective consciousness. In other words, Marxism, like other nonexistential philosophies, abstracts the actual, living individual out of existence. Sartre's efforts to construct an existential Marxism were designed to place the existing individual once again at the focal point of Marxist criticism of bourgeois values.

Sartre and the Marxists were uneasy allies. Sartre's existentialism was not scientific enough, according to orthodox Marxism. Even more significant is the fact that Sartre's emphasis on the individual cannot be reconciled with Marxism's emphasis on classes, on the collective. Further, Sartre grew disillusioned with Soviet Communism. "The way I understand it," Sartre said, "I am a Communist, but I believe the USSR is destroying Communism."

Buoyed by the popularity of Sartre's and Camus's existential plays and novels, existentialism became the "in" philosophy of hipsters, beats, hippies, artists, students, and avant-garde thinkers. Sartre became a kind of philosophical godfather to radical French students and remained a well-known public figure throughout his life. He flirted with Maoism, a form of Communism practiced in China. In 1968, Sartre spoke out on behalf of a student revolt and two years later edited a Maoist newspaper called *The People's Cause*. During the Vietnam War, Sartre spoke out vehemently against American "war crimes."

Yet Sartre remained an enigma. He never joined the Communist party. Though he has been described as arrogant and snobbish, he also enjoyed the company of younger thinkers. His affair with Simone de Beauvoir grew into a complex friendship in which each party remained fiercely loyal to the other, while remaining free to have affairs with others. When he was awarded the 1964 Nobel Prize in Literature, Sartre refused it because he did not want to be "turned into an institution."

After years of failing health and eyesight, Jean-Paul Sartre died April 15, 1980.

FREEDOM AND ANGUISH

Sartre concluded that merely to *be* an authentic self is not possible. There is no fixed "essence" lingering behind the roles we play. We are whatever we do, the totality of our actions. Thus, *an authentic self exists as and through the choices it makes for itself, uncontrolled by the values of others*. Put another way, we do not *have* a given nature; we *become* a certain kind of person. We are existentially free. There is no fixed self we build on.

Authenticity is possible only when we realize the emptiness at the heart of the social self. So long as he tries to *think* himself into authenticity, Sartre remains nauseated, alienated, paralyzed. He must find a way to bridge the gap between merely observing life by acting out a social role (even the role of criminal or rebel), and full, passionate involvement in life. Sartre's term for this passionate involvement is *engagement*.

I was prepared at an early age to regard teaching as a priesthood and literature as a passion.

Jean-Paul Sartre

We are left alone, without excuse. That is what I mean when I say that man is condemned to be free.

Jean-Paul Sartre

Unlike those philosophers who seek to *understand* life, or to fit it into systems of thought governed by abstract principles, Sartre asked Kierkegaard's timeless question: "What am *I* to *do*?" Having seen beyond the facade of the social self to the reality of absolute freedom, Sartre had to decide what to do with such terrible freedom. The "social self" is an abstraction, a verbal portrait of what we *are* (our being), constructed from bits and pieces of past moments of self-consciousness. But at any given moment, through this or that choice, *we are whatever we do*. And no one can predict with anything approaching certainty what he or she will or will not do.

PHILOSOPHICAL QUERY

Describe yourself in terms of your mental concept of who you are (your social self), and give an objective description of what you do. Contrast how you live with how you think of yourself. Is there a difference? Why or why not?

Inauthenticity

For Sartre and countless others, living with the horror and irrationality of the Nazi occupation shattered any hope for an ordered universe governed by a wise, powerful, and loving God. Science provides no certainty; indeed, the Nazi concentration camps were "scientific" and "rationally ordered."

For Sartre, nature is only another bourgeois delusion, a mental construct designed to cover up the hideous absurdity of existence. By deceiving themselves into believing in either the certainty of science or the order of nature, individuals attempt to evade the awesomeness of choice. By pretending that facts dictate choices or that certain choices are "natural," we obscure our own responsibility. We are free to choose "the facts" or to reject them; free to "follow nature" or not, because we are free to define the facts and to define what is natural.

The characters in Sartre's most famous play, *No Exit*, are dead persons who never lived authentically, who identified themselves according to others' opinions of them. As a result, they became caricatures, mere sketches of living, real human beings. They meet in a hell fashioned by their own superficial choices. They have no exit from the consequences of their choices: they now *are* what they once only pretended to be: merely what others think of them. There is no real person behind the social mask.

In *No Exit* Sartre attacked the hypocrisy, inauthenticity, and cowardice of living for others rather than for oneself, of acting against one's "authentic self" to curry favor, to avoid rejection, and so on. While we do this, we never become authentic, *living individuals*; we remain mere "social types." Our duties—as social types—are defined by the group. In Kierkegaard's terms, we live through the crowd.

For instance, a young woman might try to live up to some currently faddish image of a successful type, say a businesswoman wearing stylish

By . . . getting in all sorts of worldly affairs, by becoming wise about how things go in this world, [the foolish] man forgets himself, forgets what his name is . . . does not dare to believe in himself, finds it too venturesome a thing to be himself, far easier and safer to be like the others, to become an imitation, a number, a cipher in the crowd.

Søren Kierkegaard

suits, driving a certain brand of car, and working for a Fortune 500 company. She might have constructed a plan for herself based on movies, magazine articles, and the popular image of this type. The qualities that make up this type are external to the individual, however. They are controlled by a social group. To succeed, the young woman will have to sacrifice until she becomes nothing more than a type of person. Her "success" will rest on other people's opinions of her. She may live under the delusion that she will be herself when she gets powerful enough or rich enough or when she retires. This delusion protects her from the truth: There is no real self waiting.

There is no exit from choice, no escape from freedom in a God-forsaken universe.

PHILOSOPHICAL QUERY

Identify some common social types from your own experience. What social type are you? Is it possible to be both a social type and an authentic self?

Forlornness

According to Sartre, since nothing limits our choices, we are not psychologically required to be this or that person. We are not chained to the past through heredity or environmental conditioning. Science and nature cannot tell us what to do, Sartre thought, and neither can God. God is truly dead: He does not answer us, but remains silent in the face of absurdity and horror. Thus we face life alone, without God, without certainty—we experience Sartrean **forlornness**—with only absolute freedom and the chilling responsibility that accompanies it.

FORLORNNESS
Jean-Paul Sartre's term for his belief that we face life alone, without God, without certainty, with only absolute freedom and the responsibility that accompanies it.

> When we speak of forlornness . . . we mean only that God does not exist and that we have to face all the consequences of this. The existentialist is strongly opposed to a certain kind of secular ethics which would like to abolish God with the least popular expense. . . .
>
> The existentialist, on the contrary, thinks it very distressing that God does not exist, because all possibility of finding values in a heaven of ideas disappears along with Him; there can no longer be an *a priori* Good, since there is no infinite and perfect consciousness to think it. Nowhere is it written that the Good exists, that we must be honest, that we must not lie; because the fact is we are on a plane where there are only men. Dostoievsky said, "If God didn't exist, everything would be possible." That is the very starting point of existentialism. Indeed, everything is permissible if God does not exist, and as a result man is forlorn, because neither within him nor without does he find anything to cling to. He can't start making excuses for himself.[9]

After World War II, existential themes were popular with poets, writers, painters, musicians, and "beatniks." Alberto Giacometti's 1960 sculpture *Walking Man* evokes a Sartrean sense of existential angst and lonely toughness.

Atheistic existentialism refuses to compensate for the silence of God by substituting a glib scientific or philosophic idol. Sartre denounced secular ethics that attempt to take ethical values seriously in such a way that "nothing will be changed if God does not exist." But if God does not exist, and if science cannot provide certainty, and if "nature" is a middle-class invention, *then everything has changed radically.*

Most significant, in Sartre's view, is that without God there is no fixed human nature, no "essence" that infuses us. *We* are not governed by fixed laws: we are free, not determined. First we exist; then we choose; then we act. We fashion our essence by how we actually live our lives—without God to guide and console us.

> If existence really does precede essence, there is no explaining things away by reference to a fixed and given human nature. In other words, there is no determinism, man is free, man is freedom. On the other hand, if God does not exist, we find no values or commands to turn to which legitimise our conduct. So, in the bright realm of values, we have no excuse behind us, nor justification before us. We are alone with no excuses.[10]

PHILOSOPHICAL QUERY

Given the horrors of our age—the threat of nuclear annihilation, chemical weapons, the Holocaust, child abuse, rampant pollution,

Let us labor under no illusions. There are no easy solutions for problems that are at the same time intensely personal and universal, urgent and eternal.

Abraham Joshua Heschel

AIDS and cancer, homelessness, and famine—which do you see as more horrible: the absence of God or the silence of God? Is God silent?

Condemned to Be Free

A strong case can be made that our age is indeed forlorn, at least psychologically. Though science continues to explain human conduct in biochemical terms and according to behavioristic models, we cannot fail to see signs of forlornness in desperate attempts to find guidelines, guarantees, certainty: We look to science to "cure" everything from warts to character defects. We seek to absolve ourselves with excuses: "I come from a disadvantaged background." "I couldn't help it." "I was drunk." "I was overcome by my emotions."

Sartre insisted that in one aspect we are indeed not free: *We are not free not to be free*. In his famous phrase, *we are condemned to be free*. No divine commandments, no prophecies or omens, limit or lead us; no powerful, "irresistible" feeling excuses us.

What a man actually needs is not the discharge of a tensionless state but rather the striving and struggling for some goal worthy of him. What he needs is not the discharge of tension at any cost, but the call of a potential meaning waiting to be fulfilled by him.

Viktor E. Frankl

This is the idea I shall try to convey when I say that man is condemned to be free. Condemned, because he did not create himself, yet, in other respects is free; because, once thrown into the world, he is responsible for everything he does. The existentialist does not believe in the power of passion. He will never agree that a sweeping passion is a ravaging torrent which fatally leads a man to certain acts and is therefore an excuse. He thinks that man is responsible for his passion.

The existentialist does not think that man is going to help himself by finding in the world some omen by which to orient himself. Because he thinks that man will interpret that omen to suit himself. Therefore, he thinks that man, with no support and no aid, is condemned every moment to invent man. . . . Whatever a man may be, there is a future to be forged, a virgin future before him. . . . But then we are forlorn.[11]

Sartre illustrated the freedom of forlornness with a story about one of his students. The young man's father had collaborated with the Nazis during the occupation of France, but his older brother had been killed fighting the Germans, and the young man wanted to avenge him. The boy and his mother lived alone, and the mother was upset by the father's betrayal of his country and dead son. Sartre's student was her sole consolation and reason for living. He faced the choice of leaving for England in order to fight, or staying in France to support his mother. What should the student do, and how could he know?

Who could help him choose? Christian doctrine? No. Christian doctrine says, "Be charitable, love your neighbor, take the more rugged path, etc., etc." But which is the more rugged path? Whom should he love as a brother? The fighting man or his mother? Which does the greater good, the vague act of fighting in a group or the concrete one of helping a particular human being to go on living? Who can decide *a priori*? Nobody. No book of ethics can tell him. The Kantian ethic says, "Never treat any person as a means, but as an end." Very well, if I stay with my mother, I'll treat her as an end and not as a means; but by virtue of this very fact, I'm running the risk of treating the people around me who are fighting, as means; and, conversely, if I go to join those who are fighting, I'll be treating them as an end, and, by doing that, I run the risk of treating my mother as a means.

If values are vague, and if they are always too broad for the concrete and specific case that we are considering, the only thing left is for us to trust our instincts. That's what this young man tried to do. . . .

But how is the value of a feeling determined? What gives his feeling for his mother value? Precisely the fact that he remained with her. I may say that I like so-and-so well enough to sacrifice a certain amount of money for him, but I may say so only if I've done it. I may say "I love my mother well enough to remain with her" if I have remained with her. The only way to determine the value of this affection is, precisely, to perform an act which confirms and defines it. But since I require this affection to justify my act, I am caught in a vicious circle.[12]

No system of ethics, no philosophy, could tell the student what choice to make, and if feelings "are formed by the act one performs," he could not seek the answer within himself. And so he turned to Sartre for advice.

But if you seek advice from a priest, for example, you have chosen this priest; you already knew, more or less, just about what advice he was going to give you. In other words, choosing your adviser is choosing yourself. . . . Which to choose? If the young man chooses a priest who is resisting or collaborating, he has already decided on the kind of advice he's going to get. Therefore, in coming to see me he knew the answer I was going to give: "You're free, choose, that is, invent." No general ethics can show you what is to be done; there are no omens in the world. The Catholics will reply, "But there are." Granted— but, in any case, I myself choose the meaning they have.

. . . Therefore, he is fully responsible for the interpretation. Forlornness implies that we ourselves choose our being.[13]

Man is always the same. The situation confronting him varies. Choice always remains choice in a situation. The problem has not changed.
Jean-Paul Sartre

PHILOSOPHICAL QUERY

If valuing depends on choosing, and not the other way around, what do you value? Assess your values with a Sartrean analysis of your actions. For instance, do you love your job more than school? To find out, see which receives most of your time, thoughts, and actions. Test other aspects of your life. What are the strengths and weaknesses of such a view of valuing and choosing?

The Self as Project

Sartre was concerned not with mere behavior, but with deliberate *action*. Action involves conscious choice. Unlike Mill, for Sartre it is not the consequences of our actions that matter but *whether or not we act at all*. By undertaking some freely and consciously chosen "project," we create the world in our own image. Acting cowardly, we create a craven world. Acting heroically, we create a heroic world. When we merely conform to social reality or attempt to live according to others' ideas and values, we "annihilate" our selves in order to maintain the world as we find it. Sartre called us to a more active, more heroic challenge: *Nihilate (re-create) the world as we find it in order to become an authentic self.*[14]

The question of the meaning of life is, as the Buddha taught, not edifying. One must immerse oneself in the river of life and let the question drift away.

Irvin D. Yalom

Sartre's call to a strenuous, courageous heroism is reminiscent of William James's—but with a tone of anguish and absurdity that was missing from James's more robust position. Sartre rejected the notion of a *given* world which forces one person to be cowardly, another lazy, a third an atheist. He insisted that we can "nihilate" the world that is given to us by taking action. Our actions, as opposed to our mere "behaviors," announce our intentions regarding "a result yet to be obtained." This "result yet to be obtained" is a *project*. We can overcome "the given" and thus nihilate it in the process of dedicating ourselves to a project.

> A first glance at human reality informs us that for it being is reduced to doing. . . . Thus we find no *given* in human reality in the sense that temperament, character, passions, principles of reason would be acquired or innate *data* existing in the manner of things. . . . Thus human reality does not exist first in order to act out later; but for human reality, to be is to act, and to cease to act is to cease to be. . . .
> . . . We shall never apprehend ourselves except as a choice in the making. But freedom is simply the fact that this choice is always unconditioned.[15]

For instance, in this view, a man is not born with the inescapable essence of "sufferer because of emotional abuse during childhood." He inherits that social self through the ideas and interpretations of others. That is his "given world." He can choose (intend) to overcome this interpretation by living a robust, heroic life; he can form his own "essence" by the way he acts.

This way of looking at things completely inverts the common understanding of human behavior. Instead of saying a man refuses to stand up to abuse because he is a coward, Sartre said that refusing to stand up to abuse makes him a coward. He lives in a coward's world. In Sartrean terms, a coward chooses to live in a particular world and that becomes his project. He could, according to Sartre, adopt a new project at any time.

A *free* project is not the same thing as an *easy* project. Lifelong habits, genetic disposition, social climate, and other factors may make it difficult for the coward to choose heroism, but they need not make it impossible.

Anguish

Sartre argued that even the most seemingly private and individual choices involve all people. By choosing to be this or that type of person, we create an image of the way others ought to be.

> If . . . existence precedes essence, and if we grant that we exist and fashion our image at one and the same time, the image is valid for everybody and for our whole age. Thus, our responsibility is much greater than we might have supposed because it involves all mankind. If I am a workingman and choose to join a Christian trade-union rather than be a communist . . . my action has involved all humanity. To take a more individual matter, if I want to marry, to have children; even if this marriage depends solely on my own passion or circumstances or wish, I am involving all humanity in monogamy and not merely myself. Therefore, I am responsible for myself and for everyone else. I am creating a certain image of man of my own choosing. In choosing myself, I choose man.[16]

Man is nothing else but what he makes of himself. Such is the first principle of existentialism.
Jean-Paul Sartre

Don't confuse Sartre's point with Kant's categorical imperative (Chapter 13). Kant attempted to prove that what is right (or wrong) is always right (or wrong). Sartre did not agree. Sartre thought, rather, that we are each free to choose and create our own world. Cowards choose and create a certain world, lovers create their own world, and so on. What is universal is not a specific act or kind of act, but the fact of human freedom. We cannot escape or evade freedom and, therefore, we cannot escape or evade responsibility. With awareness of freedom and responsibility comes **anguish**:

> The existentialists say at once that man is anguish. What that means is this: the man who involves himself and who realizes that he is not only the person he chooses to be, but also a lawmaker who is, at the same time, choosing all mankind as well as himself, cannot help escape the feeling of total and deep responsibility. Of course, there are many people who are not anxious, but we claim that they are hiding their anxiety, that they are fleeing from it. Certainly, many people believe that when they do something, they themselves are the only ones involved, and when someone says to them, "What if everyone acted that way?" they shrug their shoulders and answer,

ANGUISH
Term Sartre uses to describe the awareness that even our most seemingly private and individual choices involve all people; by choosing to be this or that type of person, we create an image of the way others ought to be; not to be confused with Kant's Categorical Imperative.

"Everyone doesn't act that way." But really, one should always ask himself, "What would happen if everybody looked at things that way?" There is no escaping this disturbing thought except by a kind of double dealing. A man who lies and makes excuses for himself by saying "not everybody does that," is someone with an uneasy conscience, because the act of lying implies that a universal value is conferred upon the lie.[17]

Here, Sartre is concerned both with motives, which he often refers to as intentions, and their consequences. Sartre's early phenomenological interests taught him the significance of consciousness as a component of temperament. We might sum up his point this way: *Consciousness has incalculable consequences.* Consider Sartre's example of the person who does something questionable and makes the excuse that not everybody does it. By attempting to become the exceptional case, such a person creates a sense of being apart from the rest of humanity. This alienated sense of being apart manifests itself as arrogance (being above others), inferiority (being below others), indifference (not identifying with others), or severe inwardness (not noticing others).

Perhaps more important than precisely what we choose deliberately and with anguish is that we choose with eyes open and with a full sense of our responsibility to choose in good faith. Kant was concerned chiefly with a rational ground for universal rules; Sartre is concerned with the character and choices of existing individuals, as they affect the individual and humanity. Among other things, existentialism is a philosophy of individuals, not of rules or problems of theoretical consistency.

The existentialist calls on us to conceal as little as possible, to see clearly and fully the horrible range of our freedom and the inescapable weight of our responsibility. There is no escape from having to choose for myself:

> Anguish is evident even when it conceals itself. This is the anguish Kierkegaard called the anguish of Abraham. You know the story: an angel has ordered Abraham to sacrifice his son; if it really were an angel who has come and said, "You are Abraham, you shall sacrifice your son," everything would be all right. But everyone might first wonder, "Is it really an angel, and am I really Abraham? What proof do I have?"
>
> There was a madwoman who had hallucinations; someone used to speak to her on the phone and give her orders. Her doctor asked her, "Who is it who talks to you?" She answered, "He says it's God." What proof did she really have that it was God? If an angel comes to me, what proof is there it's an angel? And if I hear voices, what proof is there that they come from heaven and not from hell, or from the subconscious, or a pathological condition? What proves that they are addressed to me? What proof is there that I have been appointed to impose my choice and my conception of man on humanity? I'll never

Be careful with your words, for someone will agree with them. Be careful with your conduct, for someone will imitate it.

Lie Zi

find any proof or sign to convince me of that. If a voice addresses me, it is always for me to decide that this is the angel's voice; if I consider that such an act is a good one, it is I who will choose to say it is good rather than bad.

Now, I'm not being singled out as an Abraham, and yet every moment I'm obliged to perform exemplary acts. For every man, everything happens as if all mankind has its eyes fixed on him and were guiding itself by what he does. And every man ought to say to himself, "Am I really the kind of man who has the right to act in such a way that humanity might guide itself by my actions?" And if he does not say that himself, he is masking his anguish.

. . . [The] kind of anguish . . . that existentialism describes is explained, in addition, by a direct responsibility to the other men whom it involves. It is not a curtain separating us from action, but is part of action itself.[18]

Because, during times of personal stress and cultural breakdown, people flock to the churches does not mean they are deriving genuine satisfaction from this religious activity . . . it is the therapist and not the priest who is looked to for the final word now.

René J. Muller

PHILOSOPHICAL QUERY

Parents contemplating divorce experience the anguish Sartre speaks of when they consider the incalculable consequences of their action. Staying married "for the sake of the children" implies one kind of world. Getting divorced because "everyone makes mistakes and there's no reason to pay for them forever" implies another kind. Analyze the different worlds "created" by these two interpretations. Are there other possible interpretations? What do you think of Sartre's claim that freedom involves responsibility and anguish?

Despair

If we adopt a rigorous Sartrean philosophy, then we must confine our planning and our efforts to what is under our immediate influence or control. We must stick to what falls under the domain of our will and ability. But this realistic, responsible approach, Sartre says, leads to **despair**. We are stripped of hoping that God, or society, or luck, or the general good will of others will come to our aid or rescue.

> As for despair, the term has a very simple meaning. It means that we shall confine ourselves to reckoning only with what depends upon our will, or on the ensemble of probabilities which make our action possible. . . . The moment the possibilities I am considering are not rigorously involved in my action, I ought to disengage myself from them, because no God, no scheme, can adapt the world and its possibilities to my will. When Descartes said, "Conquer yourself rather than the world," he meant essentially the same thing.

DESPAIR
Sartrean term referring to the refusal to base choices and actions on possibilities; the condition of confining ourselves to what directly falls under our present influence and control.

Man is but a foundling in the cosmos, abandoned by the forces that created him. Unparented, unassisted, and undirected by omniscient or benevolent authority, he must fend for himself, and with the aid of his own limited intelligence find his way about in an indifferent universe.

Carl Becker

. . . given that man is free and that there is no human nature for me to depend on, I cannot count on men whom I do not know by relying on human goodness or man's concern for the good of society. . . . I've got to limit myself to what I see.[19]

We must not confuse *possibilities* with *probabilities*. Many improbable things are possible. Someone might possibly walk up to you on the street and hand you a million dollars. But it would be foolish and irresponsible in the extreme for you to run up thousands of dollars on a credit card based on that possibility. It is possible that your philosophy final exam will be canceled and your professor will give you an A on it anyway. But . . .

When we consider only probabilities that are "rigorously involved" in our action, we not only live more authentically, we encounter despair. We are cut off from false optimism based on being saved from the outside. We can no longer "depend on the kindness of strangers" like Blanche DuBois in Tennessee Williams's play *A Streetcar Named Desire*. We must step forward and take what action we can. Sartre says:

> The doctrine I am presenting . . . declares, "There is no reality except in action." Moreover, it goes further, since it adds, "Man is nothing else than his plan; he exists only to the extent that he fulfills himself; he is therefore nothing else than the ensemble of his acts, nothing else than his life."
>
> According to this, we can understand why our doctrine horrifies certain people. Because often the only way they can bear their wretchedness is to think, "Circumstances have been against me. What I've been and done doesn't show my true worth. To be sure, I've had no great love, no great friendship, but that's because I haven't met a man or woman who was worthy. The books I've written haven't been very good because I haven't had the proper leisure. I haven't had children to devote myself to because I didn't find a man with whom I could have spent my life. So there remains within me, unused and quite viable, a host of propensities, inclinations, possibilities, that one wouldn't guess from the mere series of things I've done."[20]

PHILOSOPHICAL QUERY

Discuss this passage, especially the last part. Have you ever felt that circumstances are against you? To what extent do circumstances matter? To what extent do they excuse and explain our life? Our self? Our character?

Optimistic Toughness

For Sartre, value is expressed through action and choice. Thus "there is really no love other than one which manifests itself in a person's being in love. There is no genius other than one which is expressed in works of art."[21] In other words, there is no sense in excusing ourselves by talking about hidden, untapped genius or potential. Sartre's is a philosophy of the actual, not the potential.

Despair is a reminder of our limits and responsibilities. But by reminding us of our limits—probabilities "rigorously involved" in our action—Sartre also reminds us of our power. The other side of this coin is that once we stop waiting for God or others or fate to take action, we may be more inclined to begin to act for ourselves. From existential forlornness, anguish, and despair comes authentic optimism, based not on wishful thinking and vague possibilities, but on tough truths and clear vision.

To those who object to Sartre's apparently harsh doctrine, he replies that existentialism actually calls us to "optimistic toughness." Though it seeks to strip us of our dreams, hopes, and expectations, it does so for the purpose of turning our attention, and hence our lives, to the reality of here and now—not the fantasy of maybe there later.

> To be sure, this may seem a harsh thought to someone whose life hasn't been a success. But, on the other hand, it prompts people to understand that reality alone is what counts, that dreams, expectations, and hopes warrant no more than to define a man as a disappointed dream, as miscarried hopes, as vain expectations. In other words, to define him negatively and not positively. . . .
>
> When all is said and done, what we are accused of, at bottom, is not our pessimism, but an optimistic toughness. . . . When the existentialist writes about a coward, he says that this coward is responsible for his cowardice. He's not like that because he has a cowardly heart or lung or brain; he's not like that on account of his physiological make-up; but he's like that because he has made himself a coward by his acts. There is no such thing as a cowardly constitution; there are nervous constitutions; there is poor blood, as the common people say, or strong constitutions. But the man whose blood is poor is not a coward on that account, for what makes cowardice is the act of renouncing or yielding. A constitution is not an act; the coward is defined on the basis of the acts he performs. People feel, in a vague sort of way, that this coward we're talking about is guilty of being a coward, and the thought frightens them. What people would like is that a coward or a hero be born that way.
>
> . . . That's what people really want to think. If you're born cowardly, you may set your mind perfectly at rest; there's nothing you can do about it; you'll be cowardly all your life, whatever you may do. If you're born a hero, you may set your mind just as much at rest; you'll be a hero all your life; you'll drink

My matured conclusion has been that no system is to be trusted, not even that of science in any literal or pictorial sense; but all systems may be used and, up to a point, trusted as symbols.
George Santayana

A first glance at human reality informs us that for it being is reduced to doing.
Jean-Paul Sartre

like a hero and eat like a hero. What the existentialist says is that the coward makes himself cowardly, that the hero makes himself heroic. There's always a possibility for the coward not to be cowardly any more and for the hero to stop being heroic. What counts is total involvement; some one particular action or set of circumstances is not total involvement.[22]

Sartrean existentialism does not offer hope in the common understanding of that word. That is, it does not offer a comforting possibility that maybe someday the coward will cease being cowardly. It does, however, offer us a basic formula for transformation. In that, it is optimistic or hopeful, rather than pessimistic and negative.

Ironically, from a Sartrean perspective, excuses and explanations, though superficially comforting and compassionate, are ultimately pessimistic: they reduce us to the effects of uncontrollable forces (genes, childhood, culture). Our choices, if we believe such scientifically sophisticated explanations, are severely restricted. Our dignity is reduced to coping with the rough deal we've been dealt. "I've done pretty well considering the way I was treated as a child." "It's not my fault I went to inferior schools. I'm doing pretty well considering that my reading skills are weak."

We can understand how Sartre's position still "horrifies certain people." Determinism absolves us of complete responsibility. Perhaps the loss of free will is a small price to pay for being able to blame luck, heredity, and my past for the present condition of my life. Perhaps the comforts provided by wishes, dreams, and expectations are worth the price of losing sight of opportunities to act differently right now. Sartre, clearly, does not think so. For inevitably, with the loss of freedom comes the loss of human dignity:

> [Existentialism] defines man in terms of action; . . . there is no doctrine more optimistic, since man's destiny is within himself; . . . it tells him that his only hope is in his acting and that action is the only thing that enables a man to live. Consequently, we are dealing here with an ethics of action and involvement.
>
> . . . This theory is the only one which gives man dignity, the only one which does not reduce him to an object. The effect of materialism is to treat all men, including the one philosophizing, as objects, that is, as an ensemble of determined reactions in no way distinguished from the ensemble of qualities and phenomena which constitute a table or a chair or a stone.[23]

ALBERT CAMUS

Where can we find solace and wisdom amid the absurdities of the contemporary world? How can we fill an existential vacuum? Is there no better response than Sartrean forlornness, anguish, and despair?

Albert Camus (1913–1960) has a suggested strategy for us, a strategy derived from his personal experiences facing death (from disease and in war) and personal loss, and based on a firm conviction that there is no God to rescue us, no tradition to which we owe allegiance, and no objective solution to the existential vacuum.

Camus was born in Algeria on the North African coast. His father was killed early in World War I, and his Spanish mother supported Camus and his older brother. The family shared a small apartment in a poor section of Algiers with Camus's grandmother, who was dying of cancer, and a paralyzed uncle.

Remarkably, Camus did not resent his early life. It seems to have given him a clear sense of reality. Like Nietzsche and Kierkegaard, he remained forever distrustful of simplistic optimism and conventional values. Bathed in the brilliant North African sunlight, and loving the Mediterranean sea, Camus grew into a handsome, athletic young man.

In 1923, Camus was awarded a scholarship to the local *lycée*. He thoroughly enjoyed himself, attending movies, playing soccer, swimming in the Mediterranean, going dancing, and so forth. He seems to have read and taken some interest in Nietzsche and Schopenhauer, but was not a studious type.

When he was seventeen years old, Camus almost died from tuberculosis. This experience profoundly affected him, giving Camus a new seriousness. Between 1932 and 1936, Camus studied to become a teacher, joined and quickly left the Communist party. He wrote, acted in and directed plays. A recurrence of tuberculosis made Camus unfit for teaching, and he became a journalist.

Camus went to Paris at the beginning of World War II. During the Nazi occupation of Paris, he edited an underground newspaper for the Resistance. After the war, Camus became—along with Sartre—a most influential writer of essays, plays, and novels. He won the Nobel Prize in 1957. Camus was only forty-six when he died in an automobile accident in 1960.

Camus's works include *The Stranger* (1942), *The Myth of Sisyphus* (1942), *The Plague* (1947), and *The Fall* (1956).

Albert Camus

At this moment, when each of us must fit an arrow to his bow and enter the lists anew, to reconquer, within history and in spite of it, that which he owns already, the thin yields of his fields, the brief love of this earth, at this moment when at last man is born, it is time to forsake our age and its adolescent furies. The bow bends; the wood complains. At the moment of supreme tension, there will leap into flight an unswerving arrow, a shaft that is flexible and free.
Albert Camus

THE ABSURD

According to Camus, taken singly, neither the world nor human beings are absurd. But the relationship between them is. The **absurd** is Camus's term for the discord, friction, and "bad fit" between humans and the world.

What—exactly—is "absurd" about our relationship to the world? Consider your deepest desires, hopes, expectations. Do they include justice? honesty? love, real, lasting love? freedom? happiness? But "the world" is unfriendly and indifferent to these things. The world wears people out. Life is not fair (but we are convinced it ought to be, somehow). Young lovers—if they survive long enough—become indifferent, passionless companions. Many fresh-faced, idealistic political science majors become cynical, dishonest

THE ABSURD
Albert Camus's term to express the discord, friction, and "bad fit" between humans and the world.

politicians (yet that is not how they started out). More often than not, our youthful hopes and grand ideals get squeezed dry, tarnished by the constant discord that exists between us and the world.

Camus says:

> . . . [I]n a universe suddenly divested of illusions and lights, man feels an alien, a stranger. His exile is without remedy since he is deprived of the memory of a lost home or the hope of a promised land. This divorce between man and his life, the actor and his setting, is properly the feeling of absurdity.[24]

Our hopes are not—of themselves—absurd. And the world—by itself—is just the world, just "the way things are." There's nothing absurd about it. But, says Camus, together we and the world are a bad fit, a mismatch. Our relationship to the world will always be absurd. Reason itself, in the form of Descartes' reflexive consciousness, prevents us from being "at home" in the world.

> If I were a tree among trees, a cat among animals, this life would have meaning, or rather this problem would not arise, for I should belong to the world. I should *be* this world to which I am now opposed by my whole consciousness and my whole insistence upon familiarity. This ridiculous reason is what sets me in opposition to all creation. I cannot cross it out with a stroke of the pen. . . . And what constitutes the basis of that conflict, of the break between the world and my mind, but the awareness of it?[25]

According to Camus, our salvation, what there is of it, can come only when we first accept the absurd and then revolt against it so that we can live "existentially." Let's see what he has in mind.

PHILOSOPHICAL QUERY

Discuss the idea of being "of the world" in Camus's sense. Do you agree that humans cannot achieve such a state? What about "uncivilized" humans? Is Camus confusing consciousness with socialization? Compare this passage to Marx's notions of alienation and species-life discussed in Chapter 15.

Absurd Reasoning

According to Camus, everything boils down to one primal question: Why not commit suicide? And the shame of traditional philosophy and objectified science is that they cannot provide an adequate answer to such an important question:

> There is but one truly serious philosophical problem, and that is suicide. Judging whether life is or is not worth liv-

Technological progress creates more problems than it solves. Efficiency experts or social engineering will not redeem humanity. Important as their contributions may be, they do not reach the heart of the problem.

Abraham Joshua Heschel

ing amounts to answering the fundamental question of philosophy. All the rest . . . comes afterwards. These are games; one must first answer. And if it is true, as Nietzsche claims, that a philosopher, to deserve respect, must preach by example, you can appreciate the importance of that reply, for it will precede the definitive act. These are facts the heart can feel; yet they call for careful study before they become clear to the intellect. . . .

If I ask myself how to judge that this question is more urgent than that, I reply that one judges by the actions it entails. I have never seen anyone die for the ontological argument. Galileo, who held a scientific truth of great importance, abjured it with the greatest ease as soon as it endangered his life. In a certain sense he did right. . . . That truth was not worth the stake. Whether the earth or the sun revolves around the other is a matter of profound indifference. To tell the truth, it is a futile question. On the other hand, I see many people die because they judge that life is not worth living. I see others paradoxically getting killed for the ideas and illusions that give them a reason for living (what is called a reason for living is also an excellent reason for dying). I therefore conclude that the meaning of life is the most urgent of questions. . . .

. . . killing yourself amounts to confessing. It is confessing that life is too much for you or that you do not understand it. Let's not go too far in such analogies, however, but rather return to everyday words. It is merely confessing that "it is not worth the trouble."[26]

Man is never driven to moral behavior; in each instance he decides to behave morally. Man does not do so to satisfy a moral drive and to have a good conscience; he does so for the sake of a cause to which he commits himself, or for a person whom he loves, or for the sake of his God. If he actually did it for the sake of a good conscience, he would become a Pharisee and cease to be a truly moral person.
Viktor E. Frankl

Conscious Revolt

Camus thought that life could be lived all the better *because* it has no objective meaning. We have had it all backwards, thinking that life must have a meaning in order to be "worth the bother." Once consciousness recognizes the absurd, the only way to live robustly and authentically is to embrace the absurd through conscious "revolt."

Trying to convince ourselves that life really isn't absurd, that it somehow does make sense, is an evasion, a submission to the absurd rather than a revolt against it. For instance, I might hold on to my faith in God by clinging to "some doctrine that explains everything to me," and ignoring the widespread horrors and suffering of innocents, ignoring the nature of the world. I can also submit to the absurd by holding onto escapist romantic dreams or idealistic fantasies of some future "just world." Conversely, I might submit to the absurd by trying to accept the world as it is, and try to convince myself that I do not have the hopes and feelings that I really do have. I can try to "reason" myself out of living existentially by detaching myself from the world

MIGUEL DE UNAMUNO: A MAN OF FLESH AND BONE

Miguel de Unamuno (1864–1936) is one of the two greatest Spanish philosophers (George Santayana is the other). A powerful, mystical existentialist, de Unamuno saw philosophy's greatest task as the reconciliation of the demands of the intellect with the needs of the heart. He called awareness of the profound distance between the head and the heart the "tragic sense of life." *The Tragic Sense of Life* is also the name of his most famous book, which was written in 1913. Here's a taste of this magnificent work:

I am a man; no other man do I deem a stranger. . . . The man of flesh and bone; the man who is born, suffers, and dies— above all who dies; the man who eats and drinks and plays and sleeps and thinks and wills; the man who is seen and heard; the brother, the real brother. . . .

The man we have to do with is the man of flesh and bone—I, you, reader of mine . . . all of us who walk solidly upon the earth.

And this concrete man, this man of flesh and bone, is at once the subject and the supreme object of all philosophy, whether certain self-styled philosophers like it or not.

In most of the histories of philosophy that I know, philosophic systems are presented to us as if growing out of one another spontaneously, and their authors, the philosophers, appear as mere pretexts. The inner biography of the philosophers . . . occupies a secondary place. And yet it is precisely this inner biography that explains for us most things. . . .

Man is said to be a reasoning animal. I do not know why he has not been defined

like a Stoic or by retreating from it like a hermit or monk. In any case, I fail to live existentially, honestly, bravely whenever I deny the absurd.

Camus says:

> Living an experience, a particular fate, is living it fully. Now, no one will live this fate, knowing it to be absurd, unless he does everything to keep before him the absurd brought to light by consciousness. . . . To abolish conscious revolt is to evade the problem. The theme of permanent revolution is thus carried into individual experience. Living is keeping the absurd alive. Keeping it alive is, above all, contemplating it. . . . The revolt is the certainty of a crushing fate, without the resignation that ought to accompany it. . . .
>
> The revolt gives life its value. Spread out over the whole length of a life, it restores its majesty to that life. To a man devoid of blinders, there is no finer sight than that of the intelligence at grips with a reality that transcends it. The sight of human pride is unequaled. . . . To impoverish that reality whose inhumanity constitutes man's majesty is tantamount to impoverishing him himself. I understand then why the doctrines that explain everything to me also debilitate me at the

as an affective or feeling animal. Perhaps that which differentiates him from other animals is feeling rather than reason. More often I have seen a cat reason than laugh or weep. Perhaps it weeps or laughs inwardly—but then perhaps, also inwardly, the crab resolves equations of the second degree. . . .

. . . Contradiction? To be sure! The contradiction of my heart that says Yes and of my head that says No! Of course there is contradiction . . . Since we only live in and by contradictions, since life is tragedy and the tragedy is perpetual struggle, without victory or the hope of victory, life is contradiction.

The values we are discussing here are, as you see, the values of the heart, and against the values of the heart reasons do not avail. For reasons are only reasons— that is to say, they are not even truths. . . .

But just as a scientific fact has its finality in the rest of knowledge, so the philosophy we would make our own has also its extrinsic object—it refers to our whole destiny, to our attitude in the face of life and the universe. And the tragic problem of philosophy is to reconcile intellectual necessities with the necessities of the heart and will. For it is on this rock that every philosophy that pretends to resolve the eternal and tragic contradiction, the basis of our existence, breaks to pieces. . . . It is not enough to cure the plague: we must learn to weep for it.

Miguel de Unamuno
The Tragic Sense of Life, trans. J. E. Crawford Flitch (New York: Dover Books, 1954), pp. 1–17.

same time. They relieve me of the weight of my own life, and yet I must carry it alone.[27]

THE MYTH OF SISYPHUS

Among Camus's many popular writings, *The Myth of Sisyphus* is perhaps the most widely read and discussed, for it brilliantly distills his doctrine of "the absurd hero," the individual who "lives fully" his or her fate.

Sisyphus is a figure from Greek mythology. After offending the gods, Sisyphus was condemned to eternal drudgery. He was made immortal and assigned a useless, futile task: rolling an enormous boulder up a steep hill only to have the rock roll back again, and again, and again, throughout eternity. What a horrible punishment! Sisyphus knows that he cannot rest. He knows that no good comes from his labor. He knows that he cannot escape even in death.

Sisyphus's punishment is that he remains fully conscious of the absurdity of his task. As awful as his labor itself is, his consciousness of it is incalculably more horrible. We get the expression "Sisyphusean task" from this story. It refers to any futile, seemingly endless endeavor.

The universe was always insecure.
Herbert Butterfield

Camus was drawn to the tale of Sisyphus because it so elegantly captures the experience of "absurd consciousness," full, undistorted awareness of our objective condition. We are each like Sisyphus in our relationship to the world.

Reflecting on Sisyphus's condition, Camus discovered a strategy for transcending the absurdities of our lives. Here is an edited version of Camus's compelling version of the myth of Sisyphus. As you read it, notice how effectively Camus uses it to allude to such key atheistic existentialist themes as absurdity, godlessness, despair, consciousness, and the will:

> You have already grapsed that Sisyphus is the absurd hero. He *is*, as much through his passions as through his torture. His scorn of the gods, his hatred of death, and his passion for life won him that unspeakable penalty in which the whole being is exerted toward accomplishing nothing. This is the price that must be paid for the passions of this earth. . . . Myths are made for the imagination to breathe life into them. As for this myth, one sees merely the whole effort of a body straining to raise the huge stone, to roll it, to push it up a slope a hundred times over; one sees the face screwed up, the cheek tight against the stone, the shoulder bracing the clay-covered mass, the foot wedging it, the fresh start with arms outstretched, the wholly human security of two earth-clotted hands. At the very end of his long effort measured by skyless space and time without depth, the purpose is achieved. Then Sisyphus watches the stone rush down in a few moments toward that lower world whence he will have to push it up again toward the summit. He goes back down to the plain.
>
> It is during that return, that pause, that Sisyphus interests me. . . . I see that man going back down with a heavy yet measured step toward the torment of which he will never know the end. That hour like a breathing-space which returns as surely as his suffering, that is the hour of consciousness. At each of those moments when he leaves the heights and gradually sinks toward the lairs of the gods, he is superior to his fate. He is stronger than his rock.
>
> If this myth is tragic, that is because its hero is conscious. Where would his torture be, indeed, if at every step the hope of succeeding upheld him? The workman of today works every day in his life at the same tasks, and his fate is no less absurd. But it is tragic only at the rare moments when it becomes conscious. Sisyphus, proletarian of the gods, powerless and rebellious, knows the whole extent of his wretched condition: it is what he thinks of during his descent. The lucidity that was to constitute his torture at the same time crowns his victory. There is no fate that cannot be surmounted by scorn.

Knowledge for the sake of knowledge is, say what you will, nothing but a dismal begging of the question.

Miguel de Unamuno

If the descent is thus sometimes performed in sorrow, it can also take place in joy. This word is not too much. . . . crushing truths perish from being acknowledged. . . .

All Sisyphus's silent joy is contained [in this:] His fate belongs to him. His rock is his thing. Likewise, the absurd man, when he contemplates his torment, silences all the idols. . . . At that subtle moment when man glances backward over his life, Sisyphus returning toward his rock, in that slight pivoting he contemplates that series of unrelated actions which becomes his fate, created by him, combined under his memory's eye and soon sealed by his death. . . .

I leave Sisyphus at the foot of the mountain! One always finds one's burden again. But Sisyphus teaches the higher fidelity that negates the gods and raises rocks. He . . . concludes that all is well. This universe henceforth without a master seems to him neither sterile nor futile. Each atom of that stone, each mineral flake of that night-filled mountain, in itself forms a world. The struggle itself toward the heights is enough to fill a man's heart. One must imagine Sisyphus happy.[28]

PHILOSPHICAL QUERY

Why—exactly—*must* one imagine Sisyphus happy? Why not be realistic and imagine him depressed and miserable? Explain fully.

COMMENTARY

Sartre reminds us that with or without God, life remains the same: We must choose this or choose that. Not choosing is not an option. He reminds us of the dangers of excuse-making and fatalism. In a time when science threatens to explain and excuse away the individual, we need such reminders.

Since we do not know exactly where the line between freedom and determinism is, we cannot escape into excuses. We may be born with tendencies and limits, but as Sartre reminds us, we are not born cowards or heroes. We become what we do. Until science explains all facets of the human condition, freedom will remain for us to use wisely or to squander.

The Myth of Sisyphus captures a profound human experience: the full awareness of our smallness in the face of the universe, and the monumental nature of the "Sisyphusean task" of living consciously in the face of that awareness. Here is the bittersweet nature of the "examined life" that is reflected in all great poetry, drama, music, religious literature, and wisdom philosophy.

It is difficult not to glimpse the absurd today. We see around us a world of obscene inequality: Some nations cannot find places for their mountains of garbage, while others cannot feed their children. We possess enough nuclear weapons to destroy the world many times, yet research into chemical

To choose to be this or that is to affirm at the same time the value of what we choose, because we can never choose evil.

Jean-Paul Sartre

weapons continues. Many of us insist that life is sacred, yet older and "imperfect" children by the thousands await adoption. We have more laws than any nation in history—and more crime. Thirty years after the civil rights movement and twenty years after the beginning of the modern women's movement, racism and sexism seem to be on the rise. The more we try to fix things, the more convoluted and complex they appear to become.

It is easy to dismiss *The Myth of Sisyphus* as romanticized pessimism. We are tempted by the hope that knowledge will save us, that clearer thinking, better science, and social reform will make our world a better, decent place. Perhaps they will. But history suggests that although we make improvements, they always come at some price. Improving the lot of one group results in real or perceived losses for another group. As soon as one disease is cured, a newer, more complex one emerges. Each incremental increase in specialization makes it more difficult to communicate across and within disciplines, and we lose sight of the whole.

It is tempting to take solace in sophisticated explanations of why we are who we are, but reflection suggests that no one knows for sure. Modern science continues to discover knowledge of many things; systematic rationalistic philosophy continues to refine and clarify our understanding. But modern science and rationalistic philosophy leave us cold as we descend into the lower regions to shoulder our burdens for yet another ascent to the summit. Sisyphus's smile as he defeats his fate by claiming the stone as *his* stone speaks to needs that modern science, rationalistic philosophy, and social reform cannot touch.

I do not dismiss or turn my back on science, nonexistentialist philosophy, or social progress. It's just that if they achieved every one of their goals this minute, they would still have no answer to Camus's profound question: "Is living worth the bother?"

SUMMARY OF MAIN POINTS

Jean-Paul Sartre's experiences during World War II convinced him that the veneer of civilization barely and only temporarily obscures awareness of the absurdity of the human condition. Philosophical abstractions and metaphysical religious beliefs cannot account for such events as the Holocaust. "It was the war," Sartre said, "which made the obsolete frames of our thought explode." Sartre concluded that evil is real and concrete.

Sartre believed that existence precedes essence, that there is no fixed essence behind the roles we play. An authentic self exists only through the choices it makes, uncontrolled by the values of others. We create our essence by how we live. We are condemned to be free, since no essence determines our choices. Inauthenticity results from refusing to choose responsibly and courageously; it is a product of hiding behind abstractions in the form of social duties and roles defined by the group, not the individual.

Full awareness of our freedom to choose makes us anxious. God's silence as we face our choices makes us forlorn. Sartre's solution is that we create a heroic world by acting heroically. We refuse to deny our authentic self by conforming to social roles and re-create (or "nihilate") the world that is given to us by taking heroic action. The authentic self becomes a freely chosen project.

According to Sartre, even the most individual and seemingly private choices involve all people, because by choosing to be this or that type of person we create an image of how others ought to be. We cannot evade or escape the responsibility that accompanies all choice. Anguish accompanies all authentic choice because we can never calculate all the consequences of our actions—yet we cannot escape choosing.

Authentic choice must be confined to what is under our immediate influence or control. This limit strips us of relying on God, society, luck, or the good will of others. Sartre says that when we confine ourselves to considering only what depends on our will, we experience despair. Ultimately, though, passionate engagement and heroic action lead to optimistic toughness: life lived fully and authentically.

The *absurd* is Camus's term for the discord, friction, and "bad fit" between humans and the world. Salvation can come only when we first accept the absurd and then revolt against it so that we can live "existentially."

According to Camus, everything boils down to one primal question: Why not commit suicide? Traditional philosophy and objectified science cannot provide an adequate answer to this important question.

Camus says that life can be lived all the better *because* it has no objective meaning. The only way to really live is to embrace it through conscious "revolt." He denounces submitting to the absurd by trying to convince ourselves that life is really not absurd, that it somehow does make sense.

Camus's version of the myth of Sisyphus distills his doctrine of "the absurd hero," the individual who "lives fully" his or her fate. In the myth, Sisyphus is condemned to roll a large stone up a hill forever. When he reaches the summit, the stone rolls down again. Camus uses this story as a metaphor for the human condition. He says that we (like Sisyphus) can transcend our fate by fully embracing it, by consciously making it our own.

STUDY QUESTIONS

1. How did Sartre's experiences during World War II influence his philosophy?

2. What did Sartre mean by the phrase "existence precedes essence"? Why is the issue important to Sartre's philosophy? *Does* existence precede essence?

3. Distinguish between an authentic and an inauthentic self. What is the relationship between social roles and authenticity, according to Sartre?

4. What is forlornness and what causes it?

5. Explain what Sartre meant when he said we are condemned to be free. What kind of freedom did he have in mind?

6. What is a Sartrean project?

7. What does it mean to "nihilate the world as we find it"? Is it possible? Why does Sartre think we should try?

8. What is anguish? Can it be avoided? Explain.

9. What is despair? What is its relationship to probabilities?

10. Explain what Sartre meant by "optimistic toughness."

11. What is the absurd and what is its significance to Camus's view of the human condition?

12. According to Camus we cannot be "at home" in the world. Why not? What prevents us? Is he right? Explain.

13. Why is suicide so important, according to Camus?

14. What strategy does Camus propose for dealing with the absurd? Explain why he thinks this is the only salvation we can have.

15. What does Camus mean by submitting to the absurd? Explain by giving and analyzing two examples.

16. Tell the story of Sisyphus in your own words. Then explain its function in Camus's philosophy.

17. What did Camus mean when he said, "There is no fate that cannot be surmounted by scorn"? Is he correct? Explain.

The Prophet: Martin Luther King, Jr., and Malcolm X

Well, I don't know what will happen now. We've got some difficult days ahead. . . . I just want to do God's will. And He's allowed me to go up to the mountain. And I've looked over. And I've seen the promised land. I may not get there with you. But I want you to know . . . that we, as a people, will get to the promised land. And I'm happy.

MARTIN LUTHER KING, JR.
April 3, 1968, the eve of his assassination

Martin Luther King, Jr.

PROPHET
From the Greek roots *pro* (before) and *phanai* (to speak); originally a prophet was a person who spoke with divine guidance and who was said to be able to predict the course of events; prophets functioned as religious leaders and teachers, as advisers to rulers, and cried out for justice and mercy in the face of tyranny.

s we learned in Chapter 2, a **prophet** is a person who speaks with divine guidance, who functions as a religious leader and teacher, a person who cries out for justice and mercy in the face of tyranny.

Martin Luther King, Jr., (1929–1968) was a prophet on all these counts. Perhaps more than any other figure in recent American history, King brought important philosophical and moral concerns into the public arena. In the process, he became a figure of reverence and contempt, idolized and ridiculed during his life, analyzed and debated in death. King had the vision, intellect, and courage to take action against injustice without demonizing his oppressors—a most rare and beautiful and needful quality, indeed. King's powerful voice made him a model of prophetic philosophy in practice.

Martin Luther King, Jr., was the son of the Reverend Martin Luther King, Sr., and Alberta Williams King of Atlanta, Georgia. In 1947, while attending Morehouse College, the eighteen-year-old King was licensed to preach in his father's church, the Ebenezer Baptist Church of Atlanta. In 1948, King graduated from Morehouse with a bachelor's degree in sociology, and that fall he entered Crozer Theological Seminary in Chester, Pennsylvania. In 1951, he received a bachelor's degree in divinity, graduating in only three years and at the head of his class. He so impressed his professors at Crozer that they urged him to apply to the Boston University School of Theology doctoral program in systematic theology. King was accepted and received his Ph.D. in 1955.

During graduate school, King married Coretta Scott. In 1954, while still working on his dissertation, he became the pastor of the important Dexter Avenue Baptist Church of Montgomery, Alabama. King was barely settled into his role as an influential member of Montgomery's black community when a series of converging events changed America's view of itself forever and sparked the vision that transformed a Southern Baptist preacher into a national moral force.

LINDA BROWN AND ROSA PARKS

In the 1950s, public education for most black children meant attending black schools. Many school districts assigned children to schools based on race rather than on neighborhood. Although some educators and politicians argued that such policies provided "separate but equal education," the facts clearly showed otherwise. Black schools were notoriously inferior to white schools.

Linda Brown was a seven-year-old third grader in Topeka, Kansas, who was not allowed to enroll in a grade school only four blocks from her home. Instead, she was assigned to a black school almost two miles away. The National Association for the Advancement of Colored People (NAACP) sued

Rosa Parks is shown being booked into jail after her arrest for refusing to give up her bus seat to a white passenger and move to the back of the bus. Speaking of civil disobedience, Martin Luther King, Jr., said "this is not a method for cowards; it *does* resist."

the board of education on behalf of Linda Brown and twelve other black children. The suit was supported with "friend of the court" briefs from organized labor, Jewish organizations, and the U.S. government as represented by the Solicitor General. The case eventually reached the Supreme Court.

On May 17, 1954, in *Linda Brown et al. v. Board of Education of Topeka*, the U.S. Supreme Court ordered the desegregation of all public schools "with all deliberate speed." Chief Justice Earl Warren wrote the unanimous opinion that "in the field of public education the doctrine of 'separate but equal' has no place. Separate educational facilities are inherently unequal." The Court's ruling sent shock waves throughout the country, and white racist and separatist groups such as the Ku Klux Klan and White Citizens' Council initiated an escalating series of violent attacks on blacks. Shortly after the ruling, the black press in Mississippi recorded three cases of antiblack terrorism.

On December 1, 1955, Mrs. Rosa Parks, a forty-two-year-old black seamstress in Montgomery, Alabama, refused to yield her seat on a bus to a white man who disliked sitting next to black people. Rosa Parks was arrested, and the controversy that resulted marked the beginning of what has come to be known as the American civil rights movement.[1]

To be born in a free society and not be born free is to be born into a lie.
James Baldwin

Speaking of Rosa Parks, Martin Luther King, Jr., wrote:

> She was not "planted" there by the NAACP, or any other orga-
> nization; she was planted there by her personal sense of dig-
> nity and self-respect. She was anchored to that seat by the
> accumulated indignities of days gone by and the boundless
> aspirations of generations yet unborn. She was a victim of
> both the forces of history and the forces of destiny. She had
> been tracked down by the *Zeitgeist*—the spirit of the time.[2]

The reaction to the *Brown* case had divided the country. When Rosa Parks
refused to give up her seat on the bus almost a year and a half after the *Brown*
decision, the South erupted with murderous racial violence: the Reverend
George W. Lee was lynched in Belzoni, Mississippi, after he tried to register to
vote in Humphreys County; Lamar Smith was lynched in Brookhaven, Mississippi; fourteen-year-old Emmett Till was lynched in Money, Mississippi.[3]

THE BOYCOTT AGAINST INJUSTICE

Martin Luther King, Jr., acting as president of the Montgomery Improvement Association created to support Rosa
Parks, led a 381-day nonviolent boycott of the Montgomery public transportation system by blacks. The boycotters initially demanded that black bus
drivers be hired for buses serving mostly black areas. They also protested
the many insults and discourtesies blacks suffered. Ultimately, the boycotters
demanded an end to segregated seating. The Montgomery bus boycott was
the first of many nonviolent black demonstrations aimed at securing for blacks
those rights already enjoyed by whites.

During the boycott, four black churches were bombed, as well as the
homes of King and another protesting black pastor, the Reverend Ralph
Abernathy. Rosa Parks lost her job, as did other blacks. In spite of the lynchings, bombings, arson, and general intimidation, the push toward civil equality continued.

The Montgomery bus boycott marked a major turning point in King's
life. In addition to making Martin Luther King, Jr., an internationally recognized black leader and advocate of Christian nonviolent civil disobedience, the boycott crystallized King's vision for America. Referring to that time,
he said, "After prayerful consideration, I am convinced that the psychological moment has come when a concentrated drive against injustice can bring
great tangible gains."[4] In short, the bus boycott showed that King's nonviolent civil disobedience *worked*.

Seizing the momentum, King founded the Southern Christian Leadership
Conference (SCLC) in 1957. In 1960, he resigned from the Dexter Avenue
Baptist Church to become co-pastor of his father's Ebenezer Baptist Church
in Atlanta. This allowed him to devote virtually all of his time to the SCLC.

The Price of Courage

King's method of "nonviolent direct action" worked slowly and involved great struggle. It took seven years to desegregate Southern buses, for instance, and we've just noted the violence that followed Rosa Parks's refusal to give up her seat on the bus. The national fight over integrating schools took years, and remnants of that issue face us today in the form of questions, job quotas, and so forth.

In 1962, Mississippi state troopers and the nationalized Mississippi National Guard faced each other over the admission of the first black student, James Meredith, to the University of Mississippi. Many people were injured and two people killed during this particular conflict. In 1963, Alabama Gov. George Wallace literally stood in the schoolhouse door to prevent two blacks from entering the University of Alabama. Ultimately, President John F. Kennedy nationalized the Alabama National Guard and used them to guarantee that the students were admitted.

Clearly, attempts to overcome racism and gain equal rights took great stamina and courage. In this context, King's efforts to live out a philosophy of active, direct nonviolence are especially impressive. Risking his life, surviving scorn, ridicule, beatings, and jail, King expressed a powerful moral and social philosophy that led to social changes which affect all Americans. In 1964, King received the Nobel Peace Prize.

On April 4, 1968, Martin Luther King, Jr., was assassinated in Memphis, Tennessee.

Martin Luther King, Jr., belongs to a special class of activist philosophers whose philosophies and lives are inseparable. Because King's chief concerns were social progress and improvement of the human condition for all people, his philosophy of nonviolence is expressed in dialogical sermons and lectures aimed at stirring the soul and calling the mind and body to action—not in detailed philosophical analysis or rarefied theoretical disputations.

CIVIL DISOBEDIENCE

King was inspired by Henry David Thoreau's doctrine of civil disobedience and by Mohandas Gandhi's use of nonviolent passive resistance to bring an end to imperialistic British rule in India (see boxes on pages 578–579 and 582–583).

Though philosophers disagree over exactly what constitutes civil disobedience, in general, it differs from criminal disobedience in that its purpose is not individual gain, but social reform of an identified injustice. Civil disobedience differs from revolution, rebellion, and riot in that it takes deliberate care to respect the "legitimate social order" while publicly challenging specifically identified injustices on moral grounds. The goal of civil disobedience is civic (legal and social) change.

I'm for anybody who's for freedom. I'm for anybody who's for justice. I'm for anybody who's for equality. I'm not for anybody who tells me to sit around and wait for mine. I'm not for anybody who tells me to turn the other cheek when a cracker is busting up my jaw. I'm not for anybody who tells black people to be nonviolent while nobody is telling white people to be nonviolent.
Malcolm X

Gandhi not only spoke against the caste system but he acted against it. He took "untouchables" by the hand and led them into the temples from which they had been excluded. To equal that, President Eisenhower would have taken a Negro child by the hand and led her into Central High School in Little Rock.
Martin Luther King, Jr.

HENRY DAVID THOREAU (1817–1862)

Martin Luther King, Jr.'s philosophy was greatly influenced by Henry David Thoreau. Perhaps the most famous expression of civil disobedience in this country is a lecture Thoreau gave before the Concord, Massachusetts, Lyceum in January 1848.

At the heart of Thoreau's civil disobedience was the relationship between civil law and the so-called higher moral law, the relationship between individual conscience and statute law. Thoreau pointed out that majorities rule not because they are always right, but because they are strong. Here are some excerpts from the lecture that so greatly affected Martin Luther King, Jr.:

Can there not be a government in which majorities do not virtually decide right and wrong, but conscience? . . . Must the citizen ever for a moment, or in the least degree, resign his conscience to the legislator? Why has every man a conscience, then? I think that we should be men first, and subjects afterward. It is not desirable to cultivate respect for the law so much as for the right.

If I have unjustly wrested a plank from a drowning man, I must restore it to him though I drown myself. . . . This people must cease to hold slaves . . . though it cost them their existence as people. . . . .

. . . Practically speaking, the opponents to a reform in Massachusetts are not a hundred thousand politicians of the South, but a hundred thousand merchants and farmers here, who are more interested in commerce and agriculture than they are in humanity, and are not prepared to do justice to the slave. . . . There are thousands who are in opinion opposed to slavery . . . who yet in effect do nothing to put an end to [it]; who, esteeming themselves children of Washington and Franklin, sit down with their hands in their pockets, and say that they know not what to do, and do nothing; who even postpone the question of freedom to the question of free-trade, and quietly read the prices-current . . . What is the price-current of an honest man and patriot to-day? They hesitate, and they regret, and sometimes they petition; but they do nothing in

---

CIVIL DISOBEDIENCE
Public resistance to injustices in order that society be informed and educated, and thereby reformed; civil disobedience differs from revolution, rebellion, and riot in that it takes deliberate care to respect the "legitimate social order" while publicly challenging specifically identified injustices on moral grounds.

Civil disobedience is public resistance to injustices in order that society be informed and educated, and thereby re-formed. If the resistance is not public, then even though it may benefit an individual or a group, it produces no social or civic change. Some philosophers argue that civil dissenters must be willing to accept punishment for their actions, as a way of taking the moral high ground and calling attention to injustice. Many—though not all—advocates of civil disobedience strictly prohibit any use of force or violence to achieve their aims. They argue that by refusing to resist violence with violence, civil dissenters avoid perpetrating injustices themselves. This kind of *active but nonviolent resistance* sometimes accomplishes a great deal through moral force. For instance, as we saw in Chapter 5, Socrates' refusal to escape from his unjust sentence had a greater impact than anything he might later have said if he had escaped.

earnest and with effect. . . . There are nine hundred and ninety-nine patrons of virtue to one virtuous man.

All voting is a sort of gaming, like checkers or backgammon, with a slight moral tinge to it, a playing with right and wrong, with moral questions; and betting naturally accompanies it. The character of the voters is not staked. I cast my vote, perchance, as I think right; but I am not vitally concerned that the right should prevail. I am willing to leave it to the majority. Its obligation, therefore, never exceeds that of expediency. Even voting for the right is doing nothing for it. It is only expressing to men feebly your desire that it should prevail. A wise man will not leave the right to the mercy of chance.

If the injustice is part of the necessary friction of the machine of government, let it go, let it go . . . but if it is of such a nature that it requires you be the agent of injustice to another, then, I say, break the law. Let your life be a counter friction to stop the machine. What I have to do is to see, at any rate, that I do not lend myself to the wrong which I condemn.

As for adopting the ways which the State has provided for remedying the evil, I know not of such ways. They take too much time, and a man's life will be gone. . . .

. . . I know this well, that if one thousand, if one hundred, if ten men whom I could name—if ten honest men only—ay, if one HONEST man, in this State of Massachusetts, ceasing to hold slaves, were actually to withdraw from this copartnership [with the state], and be locked up in the county jail therefor, it would be the abolition of slavery in America. For it matters not how small the beginning may seem to be: what is once well done is done forever.

Henry David Thoreau, "On the Duty of Civil Disobedience," in *Walden; or Life in the Woods and On the Duty of Civil Disobedience* (New York: Holt, Rinehart and Winston, 1964), pp. 282; 285–86; 286–87; 290–91.

Like Thoreau and Gandhi, King believed that the moral law demands our allegiance even—or especially—when it conflicts with the law of the land. And though no one can say precisely what effect civil disobedience had on the civil rights movement, there can be no doubt that acts of civil disobedience played an important role in accelerating the pace of legislative reform.[5]

In his 1963 "Letter from Birmingham Jail," King expressed the basic structure of his philosophy of civil disobedience. It was founded on the following principles:

1. Resistance to injustice must be direct, clear, active, and nonviolent.

2. The sources of injustice must be confronted and attacked—not the individuals who perpetuate the injustice.

Many advocates of civil disobedience also advocate active but nonviolent resistance as the best method for making their case. They argue that by refusing to resort to violence, civil dissenters avoid perpetuating their own injustices, thereby strengthening the moral force of their claims.

A just law is a man-made law of God. An unjust law is a code that is out of harmony with the moral law.
Martin Luther King, Jr.

3. Opponents must be treated with dignity and respect and never humiliated, mistreated, or hated; whenever possible, they should be converted to friends and allies.

4. Resisters must suffer without fighting back.

5. Resisters should always act with the clear knowledge that the universe favors justice.

Moral Courage

King pointed out that nonviolence is not a method of cowardice or retreat. The nonviolent resister relies on *moral force* and *moral courage* (as well as physical courage in many cases):

> First, this is not a method for cowards; it *does* resist. The nonviolent resister is just as strongly opposed to the evil against which he protests as is the person who uses violence. His method is passive or nonaggressive in the sense that he is not physically aggressive toward his opponent. But his mind

and emotions are always active, constantly seeking to persuade the opponent that he is mistaken. This method is passive physically but strongly active spiritually; it is nonaggressive physically but dynamically aggressive spiritually.[6]

Active nonviolent resistance differs from passive acceptance of injustice in that nonviolent resistance *deliberately interferes* with whatever is being opposed. Refusing to move to the back of the bus, refusing to leave a segregated lunch counter, marching to protest discriminatory voter registration laws create tension by calling attention to injustice and trying to stop it.

Anyone who has seen newsreels of civil rights demonstrators being clubbed, dragged away, attacked by police dogs, or beaten back by powerful fire hoses realizes that such resistance also required considerable physical courage. Moreover, it produced a powerful effect on those who participated in it and on those who witnessed it—even in the safety and comfort of their living rooms.

Human history began with an act of disobedience, and it is not unlikely that it will be terminated by an act of obedience.
Erich Fromm

PHILOSOPHICAL QUERY

Contrast the effects of "active nonviolent resistance" with the effects of violent resistance in the form of riots or terrorism. Do you agree with King's policy? Do you think King's efforts helped make this a better society? You may need to do a little historical research before you respond. Ask people who lived through the 1950s and '60s how things now compare with then. Discuss.

The Virtue of Being "Maladjusted"

Just as Thoreau believed that in an unjust society a just man belongs in jail, King claimed that a good person will not be thought of as "well adjusted" in a "sick" society. How, he wondered, could a good and loving person be comfortable in a society that practices racism, that institutionalizes inequality, and that fails to care for its most disadvantaged and needful citizens, regardless of race?

Modern psychology has a word that is probably used more than any other word. It is the word "maladjusted." Now, we all should seek to live a well-adjusted life in order to avoid neurotic and schizophrenic personalities. But there are some things within our social order to which I am proud to be maladjusted and to which I call upon you to be maladjusted. I never intend to adjust myself to mob rule. I never intend to adjust myself to the tragic effects of the methods of physical violence and to tragic militarism. I call upon you to be as maladjusted as Amos, who in the midst of the injustices of his day cried out in words that echo across the generations, "Let judgment run down like waters and righteousness like a mighty

I still believe that standing up for the truth of God is the greatest thing in the world. This is the end of life. The end of life is not to be happy. The end of life is not to achieve pleasure and avoid pain. The end of life is to do the will of God, come what may.
Martin Luther King, Jr.

MOHANDAS KARAMCHAND GANDHI (1869–1948)

Mohandas Gandhi—known by the honorific term Mahatma for "great soul"—was the son of the chief minister of the Indian community of Porbanbar. His family was devoutly religious, practicing a combination of Hinduism and Jainism. After studying law in London, Gandhi went to South Africa when he was twenty-two. The racial discrimination he faced in South Africa altered his life. He became a tireless and ultimately powerful social reformer devoting himself to the abolition of all caste systems.

In 1919, Gandhi began a campaign of "passive resistance" to British rule of India. Against Gandhi's hopes, things turned violent, and Gandhi was arrested and sent to prison for two years. Gandhi led nonviolent protests in 1928 and 1940. In 1942 the British committed themselves to Indian "self-determination" at the end of World War II, and on July 17, 1948, India became an independent nation. Six months later, Gandhi was assassinated.

Gandhi was deeply impressed by the Jains' doctrine of *ahimsa* or noninjury to all living things. Among other things, Martin Luther King, Jr., was influenced by Gandhi's teaching that the means cannot be ethically isolated from the ends. The following passages are from *All Men Are Brothers*.

They say "means are after all means," I would say "means are after all everything." As the means so the end. There is no wall of separation between means and end. Indeed the Creator has given us control (and that too very limited) over means, none over the end. Realization of the goal is in exact proportion to that of the means. This is a proposition that admits of no exception. . . .

I am more concerned in preventing the brutalization of human nature than in

Hell is when you don't have justice!
Malcolm X

stream." As maladjusted as Abraham Lincoln, who had the vision to see that this nation could not exist half slave and half free. As maladjusted as Jefferson, who in the midst of an age amazingly adjusted to slavery could cry out, "All men are created equal and endowed by their Creator with certain inalienable rights and that among these are life, liberty and the pursuit of happiness." As maladjusted as Jesus of Nazareth, who dreamed a dream of the fatherhood of God and the brotherhood of man. God grant that we will be so maladjusted that we will be able to go out and change our world and our civilization. And then we will be able to move from the bleak and desolate midnight of man's inhumanity to man to the bright and glittering daybreak of freedom and justice.[7]

The Harmony of Means and Ends

King insisted that great care be taken to ensure the means used to achieve righteous goals did not tarnish those goals. The point of his nonviolent move-the prevention of the sufferings of my own people. I know that people who voluntarily undergo a course of suffering raise themselves and the whole of humanity; but I also know that people who become brutalized in their desperate efforts to get victory over their opponents or to exploit weaker nations or weaker men, not only drag down themselves but mankind also. And it cannot be a matter of pleasure to me or anyone else to see human nature dragged to the mire. If we are all . . . of the same God and partake of the same divine essence, we must partake of the sin of every person whether he belongs to us or to another race. You can understand how repugnant it must be to invoke the beast in any human being . . .

The method of passive resistance is the clearest and safest, because, if the cause is not true, it is the resisters, and they alone, who suffer.

Non-violence is the greatest force at our disposal. . . . It is mightier than the mightiest weapon of destruction . . . . Destruction is not the law of the humans. Man lives freely by his readiness to die, if need be, at the hands of his brother, never by killing him. Every murder or other injury, no matter for what cause, committed or inflicted on another is a crime against humanity. . . .

. . . I discovered in the earliest stages that pursuit of truth did not admit of violence being inflicted on one's opponent but that he must be weaned from error by patience and sympathy. For what appears to be truth to one . . . may appear to be error to another. And patience means self-suffering. So the doctrine came to mean vindication of truth, not by infliction of suffering on the opponent, but on one's self. . . .

Mahatma Gandhi,
All Men Are Brothers (New York: UNESCO and Columbia University Press, 1958), III.2, 3, and 8; IV.1, 9.

ment wasn't to achieve merely this or that specific law or right, but to create genuine social change. He knew that this required more than effective strategy—though effective strategy is also important. And he did not discount the vital importance of immediate change in the fundamental conditions of the poor of all races. The dilemma, then, was how to effect timely change without resorting to methods that violate someone else's basic rights. King insisted that no matter how reprehensible the wrong, the ends do not justify unjust means.

The movement is based on the philosophy that ends and means must cohere. Now, this has been one of the long struggles in history, the whole idea of means and ends. Great philosophers have grappled with it, and sometimes they have emerged with the idea, from Machiavelli on down, that the end justifies the means. . . .

. . . For in the long run, we must see that the end represents the means in process and the ideal in the making. In other words, we cannot believe, or we cannot go with the idea that the end justifies the means because the end is preexistent in

If we take care of the means, we are bound to reach the end sooner or later. When once we have grasped this point final victory is beyond question. . . .

Mohandas Gandhi

the means. So the idea of nonviolent resistance, the philosophy of nonviolent resistance, is the philosophy which says that means must be as pure as the end, that in the long run of history, immoral destructive means cannot bring about moral and constructive ends.[8]

PHILOSOPHICAL QUERY

Apply King's doctrine of the harmony of means and ends to such current controversies as the use of violence to stop abortions, forced "outing" of gays and lesbians by gay and lesbian activists, and so forth. At some colleges, women's groups have put up posters naming "potential date rapists." When it is objected that these men have not been officially judged guilty of any wrongdoing, the activists (who are not all women) justify the risk of condemning innocent individuals by appealing to the good that will result from ending violence against women. What do you think of such cases? Discuss them from both pro and con viewpoints.

Above All, Do No Harm

King insisted that civil disobedience must never resort to physical or emotional violence. He based his philosophy on both an ethics of justice and an ethics of caring, which he often simply referred to as love. By willingly suffering injustice for a truly good cause, civil dissenters could call attention to injustice and also reach out to what King called "the amazing potential goodness" in most people. Responding to violence with force—no matter how just the cause—deflects attention from the moral issues. Use of violence, for any reason, gives opponents fuel for criticism and risks harming others. The clearest moral statement, the greatest moral force, King argued, comes from active, courageous resistance, accompanied by a willingness to suffer when necessary:

The highest result of education is tolerance.
Helen Keller

> Those who adhere to or follow this philosophy must follow a consistent principle of noninjury. They must consistently refuse to inflict injury upon another. . . . Now this has an external aspect and it has an internal one. From the external point of view it means the individuals involved must avoid external physical violence. If they are hit in the process, they avoid external physical violence at every point. But it also means they avoid internal violence of the spirit. This is why the love ethic stands so high. . . .
>
> . . . There is something else: that one seeks to defeat the unjust system, rather than individuals who are caught in that system.[9]

During the Civil Rights Movement, the evening news on television regularly revealed the ugliness of racism and the moral
power of civil disobedience. Scenes of passive, nonviolent resis-
tors being hosed, beaten, and attacked by police dogs awakened
the conscience of the nation (at least for a time).

PHILOSOPHICAL QUERY

Rethink your response to the preceding Philosophical Query on
page 584 in light of this passage. Has your thinking changed? If
so, explain why.

The Danger of Self-Defense

King believed that the power of self-chosen, carefully directed sacrifice and
suffering could reform society by calling to the goodness that already exists
in most people. He believed that the general population would ultimately
respond to the abuses heaped on civil rights protesters, that—when clearly
exposed—the horrible and unjust sufferings of the protesters would capture
the public's attention. Once the public was paying attention, it could be educated and informed; once awakened, the public's sense of justice could be
turned from such immediate concerns as lynchings, bombings, hosings, and
beatings to other, deeper, historical patterns of injustice.

The importance of this cause, King reminded civil dissenters, required a
most scrupulous strategy. Opponents of civil rights reform could not be given
any opportunity to evade their responsibilities by citing demonstrators for
acts of violence or injustice. King realized that the civil rights movement
was always in danger of being misunderstood or dismissed as an irrational,

There's only one way to be
independent. There's only
one way to be free. It's not
something that someone gives
you. It's something that you
take. Nobody can give you
independence. Nobody can
give you freedom. Nobody can
give you equality or justice
or anything.
Malcolm X

irresponsible social disruption—thus his clear, strong stance regarding self-defense and willingness to suffer:

> In a nonviolent demonstration, self-defense must be approached from quite another perspective. One must remember that the cause of the demonstration is some exploitation or form of oppression that has made it necessary for men of courage and good will to demonstrate against the evil. For example, a demonstration against the evil of de facto school segregation is based on the awareness that a child's mind is crippled by inadequate educational opportunity. The demonstrator agrees that it is better for him to suffer publicly for a short time to end the crippling evil of school segregation than to have generation after generation of children suffer in ignorance.
>
> In such a demonstration the point is made that schools are inadequate. This is the evil to which one seeks to point; anything else detracts from that point and interferes with confrontation of the primary evil against which one demonstrates. Of course, no one wants to suffer and be hurt. But it is more important to get at the cause than to be safe. It is better to shed a little blood from a blow on the head or a rock thrown by an angry mob than to have children by the thousands grow up reading at a fifth- or sixth-grade level.
>
> It is always amusing to me when a Negro man says that he can't demonstrate with us because if someone hit him he would fight back. Here is a man whose children are being plagued by rats and roaches, whose wife is robbed daily at overpriced ghetto food stores, who himself is working for about two-thirds the pay of a white person doing a similar job and with similar skills, and in spite of all this daily suffering it takes someone spitting on him or calling him a nigger to make him want to fight.
>
> . . . When violence is tolerated even as a means of self-defense there is grave danger that in the fervor of emotion the main fight will be lost over the question of self-defense.
>
> When my home was bombed in 1955 in Montgomery, many men wanted to retaliate, to place an armed guard on my home. But the issue there was not my life, but whether Negroes would achieve first-class treatment on the city's buses. Had we become distracted by the question of my safety we would have lost the moral offensive and sunk to the level of our oppressors.
>
> I must continue by faith or it is too great a burden to bear and violence, even in self-defense, creates more problems than it solves. Only a refusal to hate or kill can put an end to the chain of violence in the world and lead us toward a community where men can live together without fear. Our goal is to create

We must never forget that everything Hitler did in Germany was "legal." . . . It was "illegal" to aid and comfort a Jew in Hitler's Germany. But I am sure that if I had lived in Germany during that time I would have aided and comforted my Jewish brothers even though it was illegal.
Martin Luther King, Jr.

They may have the gas ovens built before you realize that they're already hot.
Malcolm X

a beloved community and this will require a qualitative change in our souls as well as a quantitative change in our lives.[10]

PHILOSOPHICAL QUERY

Passive moral force may be as difficult as it is effective. The movie biography *Gandhi* effectively captures both aspects of nonviolent resistance, as do documentary films of civil rights demonstrations in the 1960s. Compare nonviolent resistance with riots and spontaneous violent outbursts such as those following the first Rodney King beating verdicts in 1992. Discuss the advantages and disadvantages of King's position. Is it realistic in the 1990s? Explain.

Birmingham Jail

In April 1963, Martin Luther King, Jr., was jailed for his participation in a civil rights demonstration in Birmingham, Alabama. In January of that year, eight prominent "liberal" white Alabama clergymen had published an open letter asking King to step back and allow the fight for civil rights and integration to move to the local and federal courts. The letter warned that King's nonviolent resistance movement was creating counterdisturbances and inciting anti-integrationists. It also complained that the protest movement was attracting civil rights activists from outside Alabama and the South.

King responded from his cell with one of his most famous works, the "Letter from Birmingham Jail," which begins by addressing the charge that his actions had resulted in outsiders coming in. After pointing out that the civil rights movement originated in the South and was built on Southern groups, he went to the moral heart of the matter:

> I am in Birmingham because injustice is here. Just as the eighth-century prophets left their little villages and carried their "thus saith the Lord" far beyond the boundaries of their hometowns; and just as the Apostle Paul left his little village of Tarsus and carried the gospel of Jesus Christ to practically every hamlet and city of the Greco-Roman world, I too am compelled to carry the gospel of freedom beyond my particular hometown. Like Paul, I must constantly respond to the Macedonian call for aid.
>
> Moreover, I am cognizant of the interrelatedness of all communities and states. I cannot sit idly by in Atlanta and not be concerned about what happens in Birmingham. Injustice anywhere is a threat to justice everywhere. We are caught in an inescapable network of mutuality, tied in a single garment of destiny. Whatever affects one directly affects all indirectly. Never again can we afford to live with the narrow, provincial "outside agitator" idea. Anyone who lives in the United States can never be considered an outsider anywhere in this country.[11]

Under a government which imprisons any unjustly, the true place for a just man is also in prison.

Henry David Thoreau

If ever America undergoes great revolutions, they will be brought about by the presence of the black race on the soil of the United States— that is to say, they will owe their origin, not to the equality, but to the inequality of conditions.

Alexis de Tocqueville

The Myth of Time

In their letter the clergymen had counseled patience, suggesting that conditions would improve if the protesters followed procedures, asked the courts for justice, spoke politely, and stated their case clearly. Their argument was that progress would come "in time," if we would only have patience. King argued that time is a luxury to a starving child, a luxury to any person denied basic rights, a luxury to an innocent person in jail, a luxury to a poor person in need of medical care, a luxury to the homeless.

They approach me in a half–hesitant sort of way, eye me curiously or compassionately, and then, instead of saying directly, How does it feel to be a problem? they say I know an excellent colored man in my town . . . or, Do not these Southern outrages make your blood boil? At these I smile, or am interested, or reduce the boiling to a simmer, as the question may require. To the real question, How does it feel to be a problem? I answer seldom a word.

W. E. B. Dubois

We know from experience that freedom is never voluntarily given by the oppressor; it must be demanded by the oppressed. Frankly, I have never engaged in a direct action movement that was "well-timed," according to the timetable of those who have not suffered unduly from the disease of segregation. For years now I have heard the word "Wait!" It rings in the ears of every Negro with a piercing familiarity. . . . I guess it is easy for those who have never felt the stinging darts of segregation to say, "Wait." But when you have seen vicious mobs lynch your mothers and fathers at will and drown your sisters and brothers at whim; when you have seen hate-filled policemen curse, kick, brutalize and even kill your black brothers and sisters with impunity; when you see the vast majority of your twenty million Negro brothers smothering in an airtight cage of poverty in the midst of an affluent society; when you suddenly find your tongue twisted and your speech stammering as you seek to explain to your six-year-old daughter why she can't go to the public amusement park that has just been advertised on television, and see tears welling up in her little eyes when she is told that Funtown is closed to colored children, and see the depressing clouds of inferiority begin to form in her little mental sky, and see her begin to distort her little personality by unconsciously developing a bitterness toward white people; when you have to concoct an answer for a five-year-old son asking in agonizing pathos: "Daddy, why do white people treat colored people so mean?"; when you take a cross-country drive and find it necessary to sleep night after night in the uncomfortable corners of your automobile because no motel will accept you; when you are humiliated day in and day out by nagging signs reading "white" and "colored"; when your first name becomes "nigger" and your middle name becomes "boy" (however old you are) and your last name becomes "John," and when your wife and mother are never given the respected title "Mrs."; when you are harried by day and haunted at night by the fact you are a Negro, living constantly at tiptoe stance never quite knowing what to expect next, and plagued with inner fears and outer resentments;

when you are forever fighting a degenerating sense of "no-bodiness": then you will understand why we find it difficult to wait. There comes a time when endurance runs over, and men are no longer willing to be plunged into an abyss of injustice where they experience the blackness of corroding despair. I hope, sirs, you can understand our legitimate and unavoidable impatience.[12]

Creative Moral Tension

To those who argued for negotiation rather than confrontation, King replied that negotiation was the very essence of civil disobedience. With time an indefensible luxury, with the law slow to act—sometimes the law was itself the source of injustice—with violence and self-defense ruled out as counter-productive and likely to create new abuses, the only course left for decent people was nonviolent direct action. Good people must be awakened from their moral slumber; the ability to live at peace in the midst of great injustice must be shattered. Complacency must be set aside, conscience must be aroused. But how? King's answer was to create moral tension:

> Nonviolent direct action seeks to create such a crisis and establish such creative tension that a community that has constantly refused to negotiate is forced to confront the issue. It seeks so to dramatize the issue that it can no longer be ignored. . . .
> This may sound rather shocking. But I must confess that I am not afraid of the word tension. I have earnestly worked and preached against violent tension, but there is a type of constructive nonviolent tension that is necessary for growth. Just as Socrates felt that it was necessary to create a tension in the mind so that individuals could rise from the bondage of myths and half-truths to the unfettered realm of creative analysis and objective appraisal, we must see the need of having nonviolent gadflies to create the kind of tension in society that will help men to rise from the dark depths of prejudice and racism to the majestic heights of understanding and brotherhood. So the purpose of direct action is to create a situation so crisis-packed that it will inevitably open the door to negotiation. We, therefore, concur with you in your call for negotiation. Too long has our beloved Southland been bogged down in the tragic attempt to live in monologue rather than dialogue.[13]

King said that moral tension is not *created* by nonviolent resisters; it is *exposed*:

> Actually, we who engage in nonviolent direct action are not the creators of tension. We merely bring to the surface the hidden tension that is already alive. We bring it out in the open where it can be seen and dealt with. Like a boil that can

Shallow understanding from people of good will is more frustrating than absolute misunderstanding from people of ill will. Lukewarm acceptance is much more bewildering than outright rejection.
Martin Luther King, Jr.

never be cured as long as it is covered up but must be opened with all its pus-flowing ugliness to the natural medicines of air and light, injustice must likewise be exposed, with all of the tension its exposing creates, to the light of human conscience and the air of national opinion before it can be cured.[14]

MALCOLM X

Malcolm X

I feel like a man who has been asleep somewhat and under someone else's control. I feel what I'm thinking and saying now is for myself.
Malcolm X

Malcolm X (1925–1965) spoke a different prophetic language than Martin Luther King, Jr. Malcolm X expressed the anger and power of a spiritual warrior who did not rule out the use of force in self-defense or the pursuit of justice. Whereas King's spiritual roots lay in Christian doctrine, Malcolm X found his voice in Islam.

Malcolm X was born Malcolm Little, the seventh son of a Baptist minister. In 1931 Malcolm X's father was brutally murdered, most likely by racists. His mother struggled to hold her family together, but circumstances eventually wore her down. As his mother's emotional condition deteriorated, state officials sent Malcolm to live with a friend's family. In 1927, his mother was sent to a mental hospital in Kalamazoo, where she remained for nearly 26 years.

Malcolm Little dropped out of school when he was 15 and was convicted of burglary when he was 21. While in prison, he converted to the Nation of Islam (the Black Muslims). In 1952 he left prison and adopted the name Malcolm X. For twelve years, Malcolm X was an effective supporter and activist in the Muslim cause. By 1964, Malcolm X was second only to Elijah Muhammed, the leader of the Nation of Islam, and tensions developed between the two men. Malcolm X had become the most powerful and brilliant voice of the black nationalist movement.

The *black nationalists* believed that blacks must resist all efforts to subordinate them and must learn to control their own destinies.[15] The impact of black nationalism on American culture should not be underestimated. Black psychologist William Cross credits black nationalist movements with creating a form of self-actualization that functions like a conversion experience. Cross called this *psychic conversion* the "Negro-to-Black" conversion experience.[16] As a result of this psychic conversion, Malcolm X underwent a radical transformation in his sense of himself. Qualities that were once looked upon with shame or discomfort by blacks trying to "go white"—black religious expression, African racial features, dress, food, and accent—became symbols of pride and a source of a strong, new identity not defined by whites.

Malcolm X left the Nation of Islam in 1964 and founded first the Muslim Mosque, Inc. and then the nonreligious Organization of Afro-American Unity. He made two trips to Africa and the Middle East in 1964, including a visit to Mecca.

At 2:30 a.m., February 14, 1965, someone threw Molotov cocktails at Malcolm X's house. The explosion was strong enough to cause extensive damage. Though terrified, Malcolm X's family was unharmed. One week later, during a February 21, 1965, meeting of the Organization of Afro-American Unity, Malcolm X—by then known as Malik El-Shabazz—was shot and killed in the Audubon Ballroom in Harlem.

At his death, Malcolm X was both a hero and a villain to blacks (and many whites) in America and around the world. In the nearly thirty years that have passed since his death, his reputation and stature have grown to nearly rival that of his fellow prophet, Martin Luther King, Jr.

Separation and Dignity

Malcolm X distinguished between *separation* and *segregation*. He insisted that segregation could not give blacks genuine equality because segregation is always understood in reference to some other group. Freedom for black people could only come through independence from white America—separatism:

> Segregation is when your life and liberty are controlled, regulated, by someone else. To segregate means to control. Segregation is that which is forced upon inferiors by superiors. But separation is that which is done voluntarily, by two equals—for the good of both![17]

Malcolm X's views often clashed with King's, and some members of the civil rights movement thought that his speeches and personal style only fueled bigotry and increased the potential for violence. Malcolm insisted that equality and full citizenship could not be "granted" by the very same people who created and sustained conditions of immoral inequality:

> In the past the civil rights groups in America have been foolishly attempting to obtain constitutional rights from the same Government that has conspired against us to deny our people these rights.[18]

Malcolm X repeatedly insisted that he was a separatist, not a racist. His role was that of a prophet and diagnostician, a gadfly like Socrates, trying to show America the consequences of racism. He felt that this could not be done without first recognizing the breadth and depth of racism's influence on society.

In an article written six months before his death, Malcolm X called racism a "cancer" and warned white America that the time for change was at hand:

> . . . I can state in all sincerity that I wish nothing but freedom, justice, and equality, life, liberty, and the pursuit of happiness for all people.
>
> However, the first law of nature is self-preservation, so my first concern is with the oppressed group of people to which I belong, the 22 million Afro-Americans, for we, more than any other people on earth today, are deprived of these inalienable *human rights.*

His profound commitment to affirm black humanity at any cost and his tremendous courage to accent the hypocrisy of American society made Malcolm X the prophet of black rage—then and now.

Cornel West

A thing not originally stolen
must nonetheless be classified
as stolen property, if one pos-
sesses it without needing it.
Mohandas Gandhi

But time is running out for America. . . . The universal law of justice is sufficient to bring judgment upon the American whites who are guilty of racism. The same law will also punish those who have benefitted from the racist practices of their forefathers and have done nothing to atone for the "sins of their fathers." Just look around on this earth today and see the increasing troubles this generation of American whites is having. . . .

But it is not necessary to look for their victim—the Afro-American—to seek revenge. The very conditions the American whites created are already plaguing them into insanity and death. . . .

A real honest effort to remove the just grievances of the 22 million Afro-Americans must be made immediately or in a short time it will be too late.[19]

PHILOSOPHICAL QUERY

Compare the preceding passage to Martin Luther King's comments on "the myth of time" on page 588. You might consider to what extent Malcolm X and Martin Luther King are—or are not— saying the same thing. Do events of the almost thirty years that have passed since they died strengthen or weaken their warnings? Explain.

The Voice of Righteous Anger

Malcolm X was greatly influenced by his trips to Africa and the Middle East. When he returned to America, he was more convinced than ever that anger was a more effective path to freedom for oppressed people than love or polite resistance:

If each retained possession
only of what he needed, no
one would be in want, and
all would live in content-
ment. As it is, the rich are
discontented no less than
the poor.
Mohandas Gandhi

When I was in Africa . . . I noticed that in the areas where independence had been gotten, someone got angry. And in the areas where independence had not been achieved yet, no one was angry. . . .

But when [people] get angry, they bring about a change. When they get angry, they aren't interested in logic, they aren't interested in odds, they aren't interested in consequences. When they get angry, they realize the condition that they're in—that their suffering is unjust, immoral, illegal, and that anything they do to correct it or eliminate it, they're justified. When you develop that type of anger and speak in that voice, then we'll get some kind of respect and recognition, and some changes from these people who have been promising us falsely for far too long.[20]

PHILOSOPHICAL QUERY

Compare Malcolm X's statement "When they get angry, they realize the condition that they're in—that their suffering is unjust, immoral, illegal, and that anything they do to correct it or eliminate it, they're justified" in the passage above with King's comments regarding the harmony of means and ends. Discuss the strengths and weaknesses of each perspective. Which do you favor? Why?

It is crucial to remember that even in the fifties, Malcolm X's vision and practice were international in scope . . . King never confined himself to being solely the leader of black America . . .

Cornel West

Malcolm X And Nonviolence

Malcolm X disagreed with King's faith in the power of love and creative moral tension. He was convinced that it is futile to speak the language of morality, love, and reason to racists:

> So you have to speak their language . . . the language of brutality. . . . the language of a brute, the language of someone who has no sense of morality, who absolutely ignores law—when you and I learn how to speak [this] language, then we can communicate. But we will never communicate . . . while you and I are running around with this little chicken-picking type of language. . .
>
> Let's learn [the racist's] language. If his language is with a shotgun, get a shotgun. Yes, I said if he only understands the language of a rifle, get a rifle. If he only understands the language of a rope, get a rope. But don't waste time talking the wrong language to a man if you really want to communicate with him. Speak his language—there's nothing wrong with that. If something was wrong with that language, the federal government would have stopped the cracker from speaking it to you and me.[21]

I don't think that any black person can speak of Malcolm and Martin without wishing they were here. . . . Our children need them, which is, indeed, the reason that they are not here: and now we, the blacks, must make certain our children never forget them.

James Baldwin

Malcolm X did not believe the methods of nonviolent resistance were working, or if they were working, they were not working fast enough. Thus, another strategy was called for:

> Everywhere you look, people get their freedom faster than we do. They get more respect and recognition faster than we do. We get promises, but we never get the real thing. And primarily because we have yet to learn the proper tactic or strategy or method to bring freedom to existence.[22]

In a December 31, 1964, speech made to thirty-seven McComb, Mississippi, teenagers who were very active in their community's fight for civil rights, Malcolm X discussed nonviolence as a strategy for achieving full, equal civil rights. He pointed out that although many black people discussed nonviolence, blacks were not nonviolent and loving and forgiving with each other: "Usually when they say they're nonviolent, they mean they're nonviolent

This 1989 photograph of Nazi skinheads marching through Pulaski, Tennessee, during an anti-Martin Luther King Day parade is a graphic example of the kind of hate that Malcolm X referred to when he spoke against "the language of the brute, the language of someone who has no sense of morality . . ."

with somebody else. . . . with the enemy." Malcolm X continued, stressing what he saw as a fundamental inconsistency:

Violence ends by defeating itself. It creates bitterness in the survivors and brutality in the destroyers.
Martin Luther King, Jr.

I myself would go for nonviolence if it was consistent, if everybody was going to be nonviolent all the time. I'd say, okay, let's get with it, we all will be nonviolent. But I don't go along with any kind of nonviolence unless everybody's going to be nonviolent. If they make the Ku Klux Klan nonviolent, I'll be nonviolent. If they make the White Citizen's Council nonviolent, I'll be nonviolent. But as long as you've got somebody else not being nonviolent, I don't want anybody coming to me talking any nonviolent talk. I don't think it is fair to tell our people to be nonviolent unless there is somebody out there making the Klan and the Citizens Council and these groups also be nonviolent.

Now I'm not criticizing those here who are nonviolent. I think everybody should do it the way they feel best, and I congratulate anybody who can be nonviolent in the face of all that kind of action in that part of the world. I don't think that in 1965 you will find the upcoming generation of our people, especially those who have been doing some thinking, who will go along with any form of nonviolence unless nonviolence is going to be practiced all the way around. . . .

You get freedom by letting your enemy know that you'll do anything to get your freedom; then you'll get it. It's the only way you'll get it. . . .[23]

PHILOSOPHICAL QUERY

Compare the preceding passage to Martin Luther King, Jr.'s comments on the dangers of self-defense, the harmony of means and ends, and the power of creative moral tension. Can the teachings of Malcolm X and Martin Luther King, Jr. be combined in a reasonable, effective way? Are they necessarily opposed? Do they, perhaps, each address different stages of the struggle for full civil rights for blacks? for nonblacks? There's a lot here to consider.

Cornel West's Prophetic Framework

Where are we today? Though some of what Malcolm X and Martin Luther King, Jr., hoped for is now reality, the great struggle for full civil rights and opportunity for all Americans continues. As growing numbers of immigrants come to the "promised land" of America, new strains of the old disease of racism flourish. Increasing numbers of groups choose to identify themselves as minorities in respect to ethnic background, color, religious practices, gender, sexual orientation, age, size, income, and so on. Colleges and universities struggle to redefine a basic educational core—or to reject the possibility of any consensus, as different groups assert what they perceive as their rights.

Cornel West, formerly professor of religion and director of Afro-American Studies at Princeton University and now teaching philosophy and religion at Harvard, considers himself "a religious and intellectual freedom fighter . . . who regards philosophy as a weapon that should be used in the arena of social action—to clarify issues and to help build progressive alliances across racial lines."[24]

West argues that the old framework of "racial reasoning" needs to be dismantled; in its place he calls for a *prophetic* framework:

> This new framework should be a *prophetic* one of moral reasoning . . . a prophetic viewpoint bases mature black self-love on the moral quality of black responses to undeniable racist degradation in the American past and present. . . .
>
> Instead of a closing-ranks mentality, a prophetic framework encourages a coalition strategy that solicits genuine solidarity with those deeply committed to antiracist struggle. . . .

The undermining and dismantling of the framework of racial reasoning . . . should be a prophetic *one of moral reasoning. . . . Instead of a closing-ranks mentality, a prophetic framework encourages a coalition strategy that solicits genuine solidarity with those deeply committed to antiracist struggle.*
Cornel West

Such coalitions are important precisely because they not only enhance the plight of black people but also because they enrich the quality of life in America. . . . Where there is no vision, the people perish; where there is no framework of moral reasoning, the people close ranks in a war of all against all.[25]

So where are we today—all of us, every age, gender, color, size, and shape of us? Can the voice of wisdom be heard over the din of anger, confusion, materialistic seduction, economic fear, nearly tribal identification with some particular feature of ourselves?

Of course no one knows for sure; but whether or not wisdom can be heard by the masses, we have heard its call, and we can pursue it in our own ways and in our own lives. There is wisdom, for example, in Cornel West's efforts to take philosophy out of the academy and into the streets. Listen to the voice of *sophia* as West talks about building on—not denying—the rage expressed by Malcolm X:

> If we are to build on the best of Malcolm X, we must preserve and expand his notion of psychic conversion that cements networks and groups . . . [Our] visions, analyses, and strategies never lose sight of black rage, yet they focus this rage where it belongs: on any form of racism, sexism, homophobia, or economic injustice that impedes the opportunities of "everyday people" . . . to live lives of dignity and decency. For example, poverty can be as much a target of rage as degraded identity.
>
> . . . This kind of critical and democratic sensibility flies in the face of any policing of borders and boundaries of "blackness," "maleness," "femaleness," or "whiteness."[26]

The first condition of nonviolence is justice all round in every department of life.
Mohandas Gandhi

COMMENTARY

Interest in Malcolm X has been increasing in the last few years, along with growing ambivalence about King's philosophy of nonviolence. Fueled by the persistence of racism and an apparently widening gap between the haves and the have nots, critics of King's approach argue that a more direct assault on institutionalized racism is called for—perhaps even a violent assault.

The major difficulty with this view is that it overlooks a significant point: King's assassination, coupled with sweeping civil rights legislation, all but stopped widespread use of nonviolent resistance to injustice. Ironically, isolated improvements in education, employment, and social opportunities for many blacks (and others) may have actually slowed racial progress because a decline in the most obvious forms of racism (racially segregated drinking fountains and waiting rooms, lynchings, and such) led many Americans to conclude that all major racial problems had been solved. Events of recent years show otherwise.

Malcolm X understood the rage of the black community and realized that such rage would grow as long as blacks were denied dignity and opportunities to exercise self-respect. He realized that many people need to express their righteous rage before they can be expected to shoulder the burdens of social reform. The expression of justified rage need not be violent, however.

West's suggestion that we can all benefit by actively resisting any form of injustice that "impedes the opportunities of everyday people" strikes at the taproot of most types of prejudice, social insecurity, and divisiveness. He reminds us that "poverty can be as much a target of rage as degraded identity." From Malcolm X, Cornel West, and others, we learn that the real danger lies not in being angry at gross injustice; the real danger lies in being too comfortable while others suffer unnecessarily. Maybe we need righteous anger to call us to action.

But rage, no matter how righteous, is not enough. We must not forget that King's program was cut down before it really flowered. We have yet to experience widespread, genuine, significant, nonviolent resistance to all forms of injustice. For that, we need the vision of a prophet, vision to see that all forms of prejudice, homelessness, poverty, lack of opportunity, inferior education, and social decay are wrong in and of themselves—not because they affect this or that class of people, but because they affect human beings. We need to remember that King's great dream included everybody.

"I Have a Dream," Martin Luther King, Jr.'s most famous speech, was delivered in front of the Lincoln Memorial in Washington, D.C., on August 28, 1963. Officially the keynote address for the great civil rights march on Washington, his talk transcended its official function. The thousands of people present, and the millions watching on television, witnessed an epiphany. King seemed to speak for thousands of dead slaves, for millions of oppressed black people in America, and, ultimately, for *all* oppressed and powerless people everywhere. With the power of a prophet, Martin Luther King, Jr., speaks across time to the goodness and wisdom in most of us:

> I have a dream that one day on the red hills of Georgia, sons of former slaves and sons of former slave-owners will be able to sit down together at the table of brotherhood. . . .
>
> I have a dream my four little children will one day live in a nation where they will not be judged by the color of their skin but by the content of their character. I have a dream today!
>
> I have a dream that one day . . . little black boys and little black girls will be able to join hands with little white boys and little white girls as sisters and brothers. I have a dream today!
>
> I have a dream that one day every valley shall be exalted, every hill and mountain shall be made low, the rough places shall be made plain, and the crooked places shall be made straight and the glory of the Lord will be revealed and all flesh shall see it together.

No individual can live alone, no nation can live alone, and anyone who feels that he can live alone is sleeping through a revolution. The world in which we live is geographically one. The challenge we face today is to make it one in terms of brotherhood.
Martin Luther King, Jr.

What both Martin and Malcolm began to see was that the nature of the American hoax had to be revealed—not only to save black people but in order to change the world in which everyone, after all, has a right to live.
James Baldwin

. . . With this faith we will be able to work together, to pray together, to struggle together, to go to jail together, to stand up for freedom together, knowing that we will be free one day. This will be the day when all of God's children will be able to sing with new meaning—"my country 'tis of thee; sweet land of liberty; of thee I sing; land where my fathers died, land of the pilgrim's pride; from every mountain side, let freedom ring"—and if America is to become a great nation, this must become true. . . .

And when we allow freedom to ring, when we let it ring from every village and hamlet, from every state and city, we will be able to speed up that day when all of God's children— black men and white men, Jews and Gentiles, Catholics and Protestants—will be able to join hands and to sing in the words of the old Negro spiritual, "Free at last, free at last; thank God almighty, we are free at last."[27]

SUMMARY OF MAIN POINTS

In 1956 Martin Luther King, Jr., rose to national prominence as a leader of the Montgomery bus boycott organized to protest racial discrimination. King practiced a form of "nonviolent direct action" which he based on Thoreau's doctrine of civil disobedience and Gandhi's nonviolent passive resistance.

Civil disobedience is public resistance to injustices in order that society be informed and educated, and thereby re-formed. If the resistance is not public, then it produces no social or civic change. Civil disobedience differs from revolution, rebellion, and riot in that it takes deliberate care to respect the "legitimate social order" while publicly challenging specifically identified injustices on moral grounds.

In his 1963 "Letter from Birmingham Jail," King expressed the basic structure of his philosophy of civil disobedience. It was founded on the following principles: (1) Resistance to injustice must be direct and nonviolent. (2) The sources of injustice must be confronted and attacked—not the individuals who perpetuate the injustice. (3) Opponents must be treated with dignity and respect, and, whenever possible, converted to friends and allies. (4) Resisters must suffer without fighting back. (5) Resisters should always act with the clear knowledge that the universe favors justice.

Active nonviolent resistance differs from passive acceptance of injustice in that nonviolent resistance *deliberately interferes* with whatever is being opposed.

King claimed that a good person will not be "well adjusted" in a "sick" society because a good and loving person will not be comfortable in a society that practices racism, that institutionalizes inequality, and that fails to care for its most disadvantaged and needful citizens, regardless of race.

King based his philosophy on both the ethics of justice and the ethics of caring, which he often simply referred to as love. He believed that the power of self-chosen, carefully directed sacrifice and suffering could reform society by calling to the goodness that exists in most people. King thought that most people would ultimately respond to the abuses heaped on civil rights protesters and that the horrible and unjust sufferings of the protesters would capture the public's attention.

King argued that time is a luxury to a starving child, a luxury to any person denied basic rights, a luxury to an innocent person in jail, a luxury to a poor person in need of medical care, a luxury to the homeless. The only course left for decent people was nonviolent direct action. The ability to live at peace in the midst of great injustice must be shattered. King taught that conscience could be aroused by the "creative moral tension" generated by civil disobedience.

By the time of his death, Malcolm X had become the most powerful and brilliant voice of the black nationalist movement. The black nationalists believed that blacks must resist all efforts to subordinate them and must learn to control their own destinies.

Black psychologist William Cross credits black nationalist movements with creating a form of self-actualization that functions like a *psychic conversion* experience. The result of this conversion is a radical transformation in the individual. Qualities that were once looked upon with shame or discomfort by blacks trying to "go white"—black religious expression, African racial features, dress, food, and accent—become symbols of pride and a source of a strong, new identity not defined by whites.

Malcolm X distinguished between separation and segregation. He insisted that segregation could not give blacks genuine equality because segregation is always understood in reference to some other group. He believed that freedom for black people could only come through independence from white America.

Malcolm X's views often clashed with Martin Luther King, Jr.'s, and some members of the civil rights movement thought that his speeches and personal style only fueled bigotry and increased the potential for violence. Malcolm X did not believe the methods of nonviolent resistance were working, or if they were working, they were not working fast enough.

Cornel West is a Harvard professor who argues that the old framework of racial reasoning needs to be dismantled. In its place he calls for a *prophetic* framework that, he says, "flies in the face of any policing of borders and boundaries of 'blackness,' 'maleness,' 'femaleness,' or 'whiteness.'"

STUDY QUESTIONS

1. Who are Linda Brown and Rosa Parks, and what is their significance to the American civil rights movement?

2. What was the Montgomery bus boycott? What role did Martin Luther King, Jr., play in it?

3. What is civil disobedience? How does it differ from riot, rebellion, and so forth?

4. What is "active nonviolent resistance"? What is "creative moral tension"? How are they related?

5. What did King mean when he claimed that being maladjusted is a virtue?

6. What was King's position regarding means and ends? Why was the issue so important to him?

7. Discuss King's views on self-defense during protest activities.

8. What is "the myth of time"?

9. Who was Henry David Thoreau? What was his relationship with Martin Luther King, Jr.?

10. Who was Mohandas (Mahatma) Gandhi? What was his relationship with Martin Luther King, Jr.?

11. What is "psychic conversion," and what role did it play in the philosophy of Malcolm X?

12. What was Malcolm X's view of nonviolence as a civil rights strategy? Compare his view with King's.

13. What did Malcolm X mean by separatism and why did he advocate it?

14. Explain what Cornel West means by "new prophetic framework."

15. How does West build on Malcolm X's rage?

CHAPTER TWENTY

The Feminist: Susan Moller Okin and Carol Gilligan

As we have listened for centuries to the voices of men and the theories that their experience informs, so we have come more recently to notice not only the silence of women but the difficulty in hearing what they say when they speak. Yet in the different voice of women lies the truth of an ethic of care, the tie between relationship and responsibility, and the origins of aggression in the failure of connection.

CAROL GILLIGAN

As we noted in Chapter 1—and have seen during our survey of philosophy—the history of philosophy has been male dominated. And even though women are now entering the ranks of professional philosophers in increasing numbers, men still outnumber women in the field. According to the U.S. Department of Education, of the 406 people who received doctoral degrees in philosophy and religion between 1987 and 1988, only 99 were women.[1]

Because the history of Western philosophy has been so dominated by an emphasis on logical reasoning and written argument, other components of wisdom have sometimes been given little attention. As the early Greeks developed and refined rational skills, they increasingly valued personal detachment and the suppression of traits that today we associate with maternal and caring qualities. Objectivity and emotional detachment, traits traditionally associated with masculinity, were considered essential aspects of knowledge, while subjectivity and emotional involvement were considered hindrances.

When the sophos first emerged from the mists of prehistory, knowledge and wisdom were not neatly divided. But as their civilization became more refined and sophisticated, the ancient Greeks dissociated themselves from *Gaea*, Mother Earth (who symbolized care), and turned toward Zeus (representing impersonal justice). As noted in Chapter 3, ancient Greek philosophy developed in a series of increasingly abstract steps, until growing concern with logical consistency and rules of thinking led to theories which, though logically consistent, did not match observed facts.[2] One result was a form of alienation from a major part of life.

Historian of philosophy Amaury De Riencourt says, "The absolute predominance of the dissociating, analytical masculine principle in Greek thought is obvious—hence its strength and its weakness."[3] That is, detached, unemotional knowing dominated responsive, intuitive knowing. But it could not destroy it, as the work of contemporary philosophers and historians reassessing the history of ideas makes clear. These scholars are discovering ancient women philosophers whose work has been ignored or misclassified. In Chapter 3, we read a recently recovered passage from the Pythagorean philosopher Aesara of Lucania. Let's take a look at another example of an ancient wise woman to underscore the tragedy of what's been lost to philosophers for so long.

Now perhaps you may think it not fitting for a woman to philosophize, just as it is not fitting for her to ride horses or speak in public. But I think that some things are peculiar to a man, some to a woman, some are common to both. . . . I say that courage and justice and wisdom are common to both.

Phintys of Sparta

PERICTIONE THE HARMONIOUS WOMAN

In *On the Harmony of Women*, **Perictione (c. 450–350 B.C.)** calls women to philosophy in terms reminiscent of Socrates, whom we have seen in Chapter 5, and Epicurus and Epictetus, whom we met in Chapters 8 and 9, respectively. Perictione is believed to have been

Plato's mother, and we hear in her work echoes of Socrates' disdain for vanity, his ideal of self-control, and his affirmation of the superiority of inner or essential beauty over mere physical attractiveness. We must wonder about the influence Perictione had on her son, as well as about the influence other forgotten and overlooked women philosophers may have had on their more famous peers. Here, Perictione argues that wisdom and self-control produce other virtues, which lead to ultimate harmony and happiness:

> One must deem the harmonious woman to be full of wisdom and self-control; a soul must be exceedingly conscious of goodness to be just and courageous and wise, embellished with self-sufficiency and hating empty opinion. Worthwhile things come to a woman from these—for herself, her husband, her children, her household, perhaps even for a city. . . .
>
> But one must also train the body to natural measures concerning nourishment and clothing, baths and anointings, the arrangement of the hair, and ornaments of gold and precious stone. Women who eat and drink every costly thing, who dress extravagantly and wear the things that women wear, are ready for the sin of every vice both with respect to the marriage bed and the rest of wrongdoing. It is necessary merely to appease hunger and thirst, even if this be done by frugal means; in the case of cold, even a goat-skin or rough garment would suffice. . . . So the harmonious woman will not wrap herself in gold or precious stone from India or anywhere else, nor will she braid her hair with artful skills or anoint herself with infusions of Arabian scent, nor will she paint her face, whitening or rouging it, darkening her eye-brows and lashes and treating her gray hair with dye; nor will she be forever bathing. The woman who seeks these things seeks an admirer for feminine weakness. It is the beauty that comes from wisdom, not from these, that gratifies women who are well-born. . . .
>
> But I think a woman is harmonious in the following way: if she becomes full of wisdom and self-control. For this benefits not only her husband, but also the children, relatives, slaves; the whole house, including possessions and friends, both fellow-citizens and foreign guest friends. Artlessly, she will keep their house, speaking and hearing fair things, and obeying her husband in the unanimity of their common life, attending upon the relatives and friends whom he extolls, and thinking the same things sweet and bitter as he—lest she be out of tune in relation to the whole.[4]

May the gods grant you all things which your heart desires . . . , and may they give you a home with gracious concord, for there is nothing greater and better than this—when a husband and wife keep a household in oneness of mind, a great woe to their enemies and joy to their friends, and win high renown.

Homer

PHILOSOPHICAL QUERY

What do you think of the last paragraph in the preceding passage? Is Perictione putting too much pressure to conform on the

SHE FEELS SHE HAS BEEN SWINDLED

Simone de Beauvoir (1908–1986) studied philosophy at the Sorbonne and taught school from 1931 until 1943, when she became a full-time writer. De Beauvoir challenged and stimulated Sartre, greatly influencing both his ideas and their written expression. Friends for most of their lives, Sartre and de Beauvoir were a unique couple whose influence extended beyond their individual works as they became role models for postwar intellectuals.

Her book *The Second Sex* is one of the most important works of contemporary feminist philosophy. In it she argues that "women are not born but are made" to see themselves as inferior—second—to men,

that the lives of women are "not dictated to woman by her hormones nor predetermined by the structure of the female brain: they are shaped . . . by her situation." De Beauvoir was a superb existential feminist writer, as the following excerpt from *The Second Sex* shows:

Many of the faults for which women are reproached—mediocrity, laziness, frivolity, servility—simply express the fact that their horizon is closed . . . [woman] has been shut up in it . . . she considers little things important for lack of any access to great things, and, furthermore, the futilities that fill her days are often of the most serious practical concern to her. . . . the occupa-

---

harmonious woman? Does the "harmonious man" have equal obligations to "think the same things bitter and sweet as his wife"? Is there, perhaps, merit in having one spouse fulfill the harmonious role—if we do not force that role on anyone, but allow each couple to "harmonize" their own unique relationship? Discuss.

WISDOM AS APPLIED ETHICS

How grossly do they insult us who thus advise us only to render ourselves gentle, domestic brutes!

Mary Wollstonecraft

Determining the line between subservience and a realistic acceptance of conditions beyond our control has plagued philosophers since before the time of Socrates. That line is difficult to find in our own lives, making it imperative that we be cautious before accusing others of failing to find it—especially when they inhabited a world radically different from our own.

Unfortunately, some scholars have dismissed the writings of ancient women philosophers as "just writing about home economics." Indeed, the fragments and letters of these ancient women philosophers often address such matters as raising children, woman's role in society, and a variety of domestic concerns. But closer scrutiny of their work suggests that these philosophers were both analyzing and applying philosophical ideas to their own

tions available to her are as empty as the pure passage of time. . . .

But no existent can be satisfied with an inessential role, for that immediately makes means into ends—as may be observed, for example in politicians—and the value of the means comes to be seen as an absolute value. . . . Woman is shut up in a kitchen or in a boudoir, and astonishment is expressed that her horizon is limited. Her wings are clipped and it is found deplorable that she cannot fly. Let but the future be opened to her, and she will no longer be compelled to live in the present. . . .

A free individual blames only himself for his failures, he assumes responsibility for them; but everything happens to women through the agency of others, and therefore these others are responsible for her woes. . . . She holds the entire world responsible because it has been made without her, and against her; she has been protesting against her condition since her adolescence, ever since her childhood. She has been promised compensations, she has been assured that if she would place her fortune in man's hands, it would be returned a hundredfold—and she feels she has been swindled. She puts the whole masculine universe under indictment. Resentment is the reverse side of dependence: when one gives all, one never receives enough in return.

Simone de Beauvoir, *The Second Sex*, trans. H. M. Parshley (New York: Alfred A. Knopf, 1952), Part 5, Chap. 21.

lives, to the nature of society, to politics, and to the structure and nature of the family viewed as a microcosm of the state.[5] Dismissing these women as "just writing about home economics" is as misleading as dismissing Socrates because he "just wandered around and talked."

The wise women of ancient Greece were interested in the same things as the wise men: justice, the nature of the state, the relationship of the individual to the whole, the cosmos, and virtue, but they were also responsible for caring in ways that men were not. Understandably, they chose illustrative examples from their own lives. In a sense, they anticipated what is known today as applied ethics, the study of ethical concerns related to actual circumstances. If their emphasis is sometimes more practical than theoretical, that is no more a weakness for a woman philosopher than it is for any *sophos*. Both theory and practice are part of wisdom.

By its very nature, wisdom is applied knowledge. Thus the ancient wise women rightly understood that wisdom encompasses domestic concerns. They understood the importance of early education to the formation of adult character. They understood the connections between the nature of the family and the nature of the state, between the head and the heart. They recognized the significance of relationships, and they understood the need for genuine dialogue. It is a tragedy of philosophy that so many philosophers lost sight of the responsive, affective function of wisdom for so long.

Human nature seems to me to provide a standard of law and justice both for the home and for the city.
Aesara of Lucania

Wisdom is applied knowledge, as ancient women philosophers knew. They recognized the need for relationship and dialogue. It is a tragedy of philosophy that so many philosophers lost sight of the responsive, affective function of wisdom for so long. Fortunately, contemporary women and men philosophers are expanding the range of philosophy to include the kind of applied ethics that cannot be confined to arguments and textbooks.

PHILOSOPHICAL QUERY

Think carefully about the criticism that the ancient wise women were "just writing about home economics." Don't most of our lives center on domestic and everyday issues at least as much, if not more, than complex, technical philosophical issues? Could a wise woman reverse the criticism and ask traditional philosophers: "How can you ignore home economics and family concerns and justice between wife and husband or parent and child?" Discuss.

CONTEMPORARY FEMINISM

FEMINIST
A person who believes in the fundamental equality of women and men, and who actively contributes to the struggle to achieve such equality.

A **feminist** is a person who believes in the fundamental equality of women and men and actively contributes to the struggle to achieve such equality. Some female feminists insist that only women can be feminists. They sometimes refer to men who otherwise satisfy their criteria for being a feminist as "profeminists." For reasons that will become clear as this chapter progresses, I prefer a gender-neutral feminism that accepts men and women.

THE PROBLEM WITH NO NAME

The problem lay buried, unspoken, for many years in the minds of American women. It was a strange stirring, a sense of dissatisfaction, a yearning that women suffered in the middle of the twentieth century in the United States. Each suburban wife struggled with it alone. As she made beds, shopped for groceries, matched slipcover material, ate peanut butter sandwiches with her children, chauffeured Cub Scouts and Brownies, lay beside her husband at night—she was afraid to ask even of herself the silent question—"Is this all?"

. . . Gradually I came to realize that the problem that has no name was shared by countless women in America. As a magazine writer I often interviewed women about problems with their children, or their marriages, or their houses, or their communities. But after a while I began to recognize the telltale signs of this other problem. I saw the same signs in suburban ranch houses and split levels on Long Island, in New Jersey, and Westchester County; in colonial houses in a small Massachusetts town; on patios in Memphis; in suburban and city apartments; in living rooms in the Midwest. Sometimes I sensed the problem, not as a reporter, but as a suburban housewife, for during this time I was also bringing up three children . . . I heard echoes of the problem in college dormitories and semi-private maternity wards . . .

Just what was this problem that has no name? What were the words women used when they tried to express it? Sometimes a woman would say, "I feel empty somehow . . . incomplete." Or she would say, "I feel as if I don't exist."

Betty Friedan
The Feminine Mystique (New York: W. W. Norton, 1963), quoted in Michael E. Adelstein and Jean G. Pival, eds., *Women's Liberation*, Perspectives Series (New York: St. Martin's Press, 1972), pp. 3–7.

Often, the term feminist is used to characterize any woman who studies women's issues or advocates any radical change in the statuses of women and men. Feminists themselves—like philosophers in general—debate the issue of who is or is not a true feminist. Conservative feminists, for example, accuse more radical feminists of being antifamily. Some feminists seek to abolish all biological sex differences, looking forward to a time when technology will make it possible for women to reproduce without men—or for men to give birth. Other feminists seek to clarify the differences between men and women.

One of the most interesting and important current feminist discussions centers on whether or not men and women approach moral issues differently. If they do, are these differences inevitable or the product of social conditioning? If there are significant differences, is one way superior to the other? If there are significant differences, are they tied to gender or temperament?

In philosophy, woman is always on the side of passivity.
Hélène Cixous

Let's take a look at some issues related to these concerns, keeping in mind that this is only the tip of a complex and controversial iceberg.

A THEORY OF JUSTICE

In 1971, Harvard professor **John Rawls** published *A Theory of Justice*, which became one of the most significant philosophical books of our time. Rawls's attempt to refine Kant's moral philosophy greatly influenced political scientists, economists, and moral philosophers. First, we'll take a look at one of the key concepts Rawls used to identify fundamental principles of "justice as fairness," then, we will look at a feminist's intriguing response to Rawls's work.

According to Rawls, the fundamental principles of justice are those principles to which "free and rational" persons would agree if they were in an "original position" of equality. Of course, Rawls continued, we are not in and cannot create a position of perfect equality. How, then, he asked, can we ever determine what justice is, since any inquiry into justice will be influenced by our actual—and unequal—circumstances?

One way to deal with the limits imposed by our actual circumstances is known as a thought experiment. A **thought experiment** is a way of using our imaginations to test a hypothesis that cannot be tested in fact. As the name suggests, we "think" rather than field-test the hypothesis, using reasoned imagination to provide the necessary conditions for the experiment, and then carefully reason out the most likely consequences according to our hypothesis.

In Chapter 13 we learned that Kant had already tried to overcome the limits of personal circumstances and bias with the Categorial Imperative, which is supposed to overlook all merely personal considerations and inclinations. (You might want to review Kant's moral philosophy in Chapter 13.) Rawls used a thought experiment in an attempt to improve upon Kant's efforts to overcome the limits of personal concerns in ethical deliberations.

The **original position** of equality is Rawls's term for an imaginary setting in which we can identify the fundamental principles of justice from an objective, impartial perspective—as "rational agents," rather than as "interested parties."

But why bother with an imaginary circumstance in the first place? Rawls has an answer:

> I have emphasized that this original position is purely hypo-
> thetical. It is natural to ask why, if this agreement is never
> actually entered into, we should take any interest in these
> principles, moral or otherwise [that might be based on it]. The
> answer is that the conditions embodied in the description of
> the original position are ones that we do in fact accept. Or if
> we do not, then perhaps we can be persuaded to do so by phi-

THOUGHT EXPERIMENT
A way of using our imaginations to test a hypothesis; we "think" rather than field test a hypothesis, using reasoned imagination to provide the necessary conditions for the "experiment," and carefully reasoning out the most likely consequences according to our hypothesis.

ORIGINAL POSITION
John Rawls's imaginary setting in which we can identify the fundamental principles of justice from an objective, impartial perspective, as rational agents, rather than as "interested parties"; similar to the "state of nature" in the social contract theories of Thomas Hobbes, Jean-Jacques Rousseau, and John Locke.

losophical reflection. . . . Thus what we shall do is to collect together into one conception a number of conditions on principles that we are ready upon due consideration to recognize as reasonable.[6]

The original position can help us clarify both *what* principles we accept and *why* they are rational and just.

The Veil of Ignorance

We "enter into the original position" by imaginatively placing ourselves behind a "veil of ignorance." As Rawls conceived it, the **veil of ignorance** is a problem-solving device that prevents us from knowing our social status, what property we own, what we like and don't like, how intelligent we are, what our talents and strengths are, "and the like." In the following passage, Rawls introduces the veil of ignorance and the original position:

> The original position is not, of course, thought of as an actual historical state of affairs, much less as a primitive condition of culture. It is understood as a purely hypothetical situation characterized so as to lead to a certain conception of justice. . . . Among the essential features of this situation is that no one knows his place in society, his class position or social status, nor does any one know his fortune in the distribution of natural assets and abilities, his intelligence, strength, and the like. I shall even assume that the parties do not know their conceptions of the good or their special psychological propensities. The principles of justice are chosen behind a veil of ignorance. This assures that no one is advantaged or disadvantaged in the choices of principles by the outcome of natural chance or the contingency of social circumstances.[7]

PHILOSOPHICAL QUERY

Conduct your own thought experiment by using the concept of a veil of ignorance to write a code of conduct for college courses. Imagine that you do not know if you are a pupil or professor, or any other personal factors. Does the veil of ignorance aid in such tasks, or is something overlooked? Discuss.

Justice as Fairness

According to Rawls, principles arrived at behind the veil of ignorance will result in a "fair agreement or bargain." Rawls says that "our social situation is just if it is such that by this sequence of hypothetical agreements we would have contracted into the general system of rules which defines it."[8]

VEIL OF IGNORANCE
John Rawls's mechanism for imaginatively entering into the original position by avoiding all personal considerations in the process of determining principles of justice; the veil of ignorance is a problem solving device that prevents us from knowing our social status, what property we own, what we like and don't like, how intelligent we are, what our talents and strengths are, and so on.

*All social primary goods—
liberty and opportunity, income and wealth, and the
bases of self-respect—are to
be distributed equally unless
an unequal distribution of
any or all of these goods is
to the advantage of the least
favored.*

John Rawls

Rawls advocates a type of *contractarian* or *social contract theory*, a political philosophy based on the idea that our social and political obligations constitute a kind of contract in which we all agree to the basic principles which govern how we live together in a society. The nature of this contract varies among contract theorists according to their conceptions of life outside the contract (usually referred to as the "state of nature").

In *A Theory of Justice*, Rawls argues that persons in the original position would all agree—being rational and mutually disinterested—to principles of equal political liberty and opportunity. That is, as rational agents looking out for our own self-interest, we would all agree to two basic principles: (1) everyone has an equal right to "the most extensive basic liberty compatible with a similar liberty for others," and (2) any social and economic inequalities must be such that "they are both (a) reasonably expected to be to everyone's advantage and (b) attached to positions and offices open to all."[9] When the two principles conflict, reason directs us to defer to the first.

According to Rawls, "whenever social institutions satisfy these principles those engaged in them can say to one another that they are cooperating on terms to which they would agree if they were free and equal persons whose relations with respect to one another were fair."[10]

PHILOSOPHICAL QUERY

Have you agreed—in spirit—to the social contract? Do things like voting, accepting police protection, calling 911, attending college on financial aid, and so forth, commit a person to abiding by the social contract? Are there other ways of agreeing to the contract? Can a person refuse to participate in the social contract? How? Discuss.

JUSTICE AND GENDER

In her insightful book *Justice, Gender, and the Family*, Stanford University professor **Susan Moller Okin** analyzes Rawls's theory of justice, with special attention to issues of gender and the family. In her powerful introduction, Okin reminds us that:

Susan Moller Okin

We as a society pride ourselves on our democratic values. We don't believe people should be constrained by innate differences from being able to achieve desired positions of influence or to improve their well-being; equality of opportunity is our professed aim. The Preamble to our Constitution stresses the importance of justice, as well as the general welfare and the blessings of liberty. The Pledge of Allegiance asserts that our republic preserves "liberty and justice for all."

Yet substantial inequities between the sexes still exist in our society. In economic terms, full-time working women (after

**That's an excellent suggestion, Miss Triggs.
Perhaps one of the men here would like to
make it.**

some very recent improvement) earn on average 71 percent of
the earnings of full-time working men. One-half of poor and
three-fifths of chronically poor households with dependent
children are maintained by a single female parent. The poverty
rate for elderly women is nearly twice that for elderly men.[11]

Okin goes on to point out the disproportionate number of women in Congress, on the Supreme Court, and so forth. She points out that women still
do most of the child rearing in this country. Even when both parents work,
the woman commonly does more of the child rearing and housekeeping
than the man.

Okin also points out that no adequate theory of justice can fail to include
an analysis of justice within the family, since the family—in whatever form—
is still the primary shaper of basic personality, as well as basic attitudes of
self-respect (self-esteem), gender, and race. In sum, justice cannot be separated from family experience. This includes justice for each member of the
family.

Clearly, in our present society, wealth, equality, and liberty are not
evenly or justly apportioned. Okin continues:

> Yet, remarkably, major contemporary theorists of justice have
> almost without exception ignored the situation I have just de-
> scribed [the status of women and all family members]. They
> have displayed little interest in or knowledge of the findings of
> feminism. They have largely bypassed the fact that the society

*Family justice must be
of central importance for
social justice.*
Susan Moller Okin

*A moral theory (or family
of moral theories) that made
trust its central problem
could do better justice to
men's and women's moral
intuitions than do the going
men's theories.*
Annette C. Baier

WHAT MUST BE THE EFFECT OF THIS LESSON?

All the selfish propensities, the self-worship, the unjust self-preference, which exist among mankind, have their source and root in, and derive their principal nourishment from, the present constitution of the relation between men and women. Think what it is to a boy, to grow up to manhood in the belief that without any merit or exertion of his own, though he may be the most frivolous and empty or the most ignorant and stolid of mankind, by the mere fact of being born a male he is by right the superior of all and every one of an entire half of the human race; including probably some whose real superiority to himself he has daily or hourly occasion to feel; . . . if he is a fool, he thinks that of course she is not, and cannot be, equal in ability and judgment to himself; and if he is not a fool, he does worse—he sees that she is superior to him, and believes that, notwithstanding her superiority, he is entitled to command and she is bound to obey. What must be the effect of this lesson?

John Stuart Mill
The Subjection of Women (London: D. Appleton, 1869), Chapter 4.

Women live on the side-lines of this world; they have contact with it only through their private lives, through men, in a mediated rather than an immediate way; they have a lot more free time than men do . . . to observe, to criticize; they are used to being spectators. . . .

Simone de Beauvoir

to which their theories are supposed to pertain is heavily and deeply affected by gender, and faces difficult issues of justice stemming from its gendered past and present assumptions. Since theories of justice are centrally concerned with whether, how, or why persons should be treated differently from one another, this neglect seems inexplicable. . . . [*Justice, Gender, and the Family*] is about this remarkable case of neglect. It is also an attempt to . . . point the way toward a more fully humanist theory of justice by confronting the question, "How just is gender?"[12]

Okin argues that Rawls's analysis of justice is "ambiguous" regarding gender because, she says, he rarely indicates "how deeply and pervasively gender-structured" this society is.

Okin notes that Rawls uses "supposedly generic male terms of reference" throughout his writing: "*Men, mankind, he,* and *his* are interspersed with gender-neutral terms of reference such as *individual* and *moral person*. Examples of intergenerational concern are worded in terms of 'fathers' and 'sons' . . ." (emphasis is Okin's).[13] Further, Okin points out that Rawls fails to mention that Kant did not intend for his moral theory to apply to women. Okin asserts that in his discussion of Sigmund Freud's theory of the formulation of the male superego, Rawls ignores the fact that Freud thought that women's moral development was "psychologically deficient." "Thus," Okin concludes, "there is a blindness to the sexism of the tradition in which Rawls is a participant, which tends to render his terms of reference more ambiguous than they might otherwise be. A feminist reader finds it difficult not to keep asking, Does this theory apply to women?"[14]

According to Okin, Rawls's work is "ambiguous" rather than flatly sexist because he does acknowledge that sex is one of the morally relevant contingencies that are to be hidden behind the veil of ignorance. But reconsider Rawls's language regarding these contingencies in light of Okin's observations: "Among the essential features of this situation is that no one knows *his* place in society, *his* class position or social status, nor does any one know *his* fortune in the distribution of natural assets and abilities, *his* intelligence, strength, and the like" (emphasis added).[15]

Okin says that "one might think that whether or not they knew their sex might matter enough to be mentioned." "Perhaps," she suggests, "Rawls meant to cover it by his phrase 'and the like,' but it is also possible that he did not consider it significant."[16]

A Second Look at the Veil of Ignorance

Rawls hoped that the veil of ignorance could be used to "correct for" the "arbitrariness of the world" by putting people in a position to reason independently of "morally relevant contingencies" such as actual social status, talent, race, and the like. As "pure rational agents," they would think from an identical standpoint. Each one's perspective would be the perspective of all.

Okin rightly observes that the veil of ignorance has been pierced if we retain knowledge of our gender. She thinks that:

> The significance of Rawls's central, brilliant idea, the original position, is that it forces one to question and consider traditions, customs, and institutions from all points of view, and ensures that the principles of justice will be acceptable to everyone, regardless of what position "he" ends up in. . . . The theory, in principle, avoids both the problem of domination that is inherent in theories of justice based on traditions or shared understandings and the partiality of libertarian theory to those who are talented or fortunate. For feminist readers, however, the problem of the theory as stated by Rawls himself is encapsulated in the ambiguous "he." . . . If, however, we read Rawls in such a way as to take seriously both the notion that those behind the veil of ignorance do not know what sex they are and the requirement that the family and gender system, as basic social institutions, are to be subject to scrutiny, constructive feminist criticism of these contemporary institutions follows. . . .
>
> Finally . . . if those in the original position did not know whether they were to be men or women, they would surely be concerned to establish a thoroughgoing social and economic equality between the sexes that would protect either sex from

Our ultimate goal should be a non-gendered, non-dichotomized, moral framework in which all moral concerns could be expressed. We might, with intentional irony, call this project, "de-moralizing the genders."
Marilyn Friedman

A sword that repelled a huge army in days past is no longer useful. Similarly, some of the dictums of the people of old may no longer be applicable in today's world.
Lie Zi

Plato's argument . . . is not valid . . . , it is irrelevant to facts about women's desires, and it is irrelevant to the injustice of sexual equality.

Julia Annas

the need to pander to or servilely provide for the pleasure of the other. They would emphasize the importance of girls and boys growing up with an equal sense of respect for themselves and equal expectations of self-definition and development. . . . In general, they would be unlikely to tolerate basic social institutions that asymmetrically either forced or gave strong incentives to members of one sex to serve as sex objects for the other.

. . . I reach the conclusions not only that our current gender structure is incompatible with the attainment of social justice, but also that the disappearance of gender is a prerequisite for the *complete* development of a nonsexist, fully human theory of justice.[17]

PHILOSOPHICAL QUERY

Reevaluate your response to the Philosophical Query on page 609 in light of Okin's modification of the veil of ignorance. Would ignorance of your gender alter the course syllabus? Does it add new issues? Does it change any wording? Explain.

Also consider Okin's suggestion that "the disappearance of gender" is a prerequisite for a just society? Or is that what she said? Can a gender-based society be just? Discuss.

WHOSE RATIONALITY ARE WE TALKING ABOUT?

Although they speak in considerably diluted tones, there are still those who would claim that women's reason is less reliable than men's, or that it occurs in a different—perhaps even in an intuitive—manner.

Carolyn W. Korsmeyer

Building on Kant's foundation, Rawls hoped that the veil of ignorance would result in an impersonal perspective "common to all" rational agents. Okin expanded Rawls's conception of the original position to include "the perspective of *everybody*, in the sense of *each in turn.*" Each in turn includes all members of families—children as well as adults—both sexes, and all *genders*. Gender and biological sex are not the same, by the way. Gender refers to sexual orientation and includes masculine, feminine, bisexual, homosexual, lesbian, and androgynous.

Any discussion of gender is controversial in today's social climate. Some philosophers argue that any assertion of fixed gender differences contributes to divisiveness and sexism, whether it is promale or profemale, promasculine or profeminine. Then, too, there are disagreements over the extent to which gender is biological or social. That is, to what extent are gender differences and preferences socially conditioned or biologically inevitable?

Especially important to philosophers are recent discussions concerning rationality and other sources of knowledge in light of gender. Recently published work poses a series of interrelated questions that call into doubt the exclusive status of the traditional model of rationality as detached, objective knowing: Is there only one way of reasoning? Is objective reasoning the only or best way of knowing? To what extent, if any, are personal detachment and objectivity possible? Perhaps most important, when—if ever—are personal detachment and objectivity desirable? Perhaps we do not want a veil of ignorance at all, but should base our decisions on who we really are and our actual social place.

Some feminist philosophers applaud what they see as the long-overdue acknowledgment of women's ways of knowing and welcome a reevaluation of traditional notions of reasonableness and rationality. Other feminist philosophers object to what they see as stigmatizing women by characterizing a special "woman's way of knowing."

Philosophy and psychology overlap when questions of knowledge and rationality involve factual issues that require both philosophical analysis and scientific scrutiny. Further, if, as some researchers suggest, men and women (as they are currently socialized) somehow experience the world differently, then their ideas about such things as moral values, human virtues, and justice may reflect these differences. The answers to these questions are too important for us to rely on untested assumptions. They require psychological and philosophical research.

Harvard psychologist **Carol Gilligan**, whose groundbreaking 1982 book *In a Different Voice: Psychological Theory and Women's Development* has prompted a necessary reassessment of moral reasoning, reminds us of the importance and delicacy of psychological research into this area:

> A word, finally, about the politics and the controversy of this research. The stark fact of the all-male research sample, accepted for years as representative by psychologists studying human development, in one sense speaks for itself. That such samples were not seen long ago as problematic by women or men points to different blindnesses on the part of each sex. The fact that these samples passed the scrutiny of peer review boards, that studies of . . . moral development . . . using all-male samples were repeatedly funded and widely published in professional journals indicates that the psychological research community needs to reexamine its claims to objectivity and dispassion. If the omission of half the human population was not seen, or not seen as significant, or not spoken about as a problem (by women or men), what other omissions are not being seen? The contribution of women's thinking . . . is a different voice, a different way of speaking about relationships and about the experience of the self. The inclusion of this voice changes the map of the moral domain. Listening to girls and women, we have come to listen differently to boys and men. And we have come to think differently about human nature

Carol Gilligan

The blind willingness to sacrifice people to truth, however, has always been the danger of an ethics abstracted from life. . . . It is the ethics of an adulthood that has become principled at the expense of care.
Carol Gilligan

and the human condition, and in turn, about . . . disciplines devoted to improving human life.[18]

Susan Moller Okin's reassessment of John Rawls's theory of justice reflects the "different voice" Gilligan refers to above. Okin's emphasis on the need to include the family in any theory of justice is an improvement on Rawls, based as it is on a fuller sense of what matters. Although Rawls does recognize the importance of childhood moral development and the need for a just family, Okin criticizes him for failing to follow up on this important observation. Although Rawls says that the first assumption is that "given family institutions are just," he does not explain the basis for this assumption.[19] (Rawls does, however, recognize the importance of feelings, saying, for example, that "the sense of justice is continuous with the love of mankind."[20])

Okin points out that Rawls's discussion is "expressed in terms of mutual disinterest and rationality"—what some feminist philosophers call the "masculine voice." And indeed, such criticism can be (and has been) leveled at many philosophers, both women and men. Not all criticism of the masculine voice is from feminists, by the way. The existentialists and sages, for instance, reject relying exclusively on an objectivistic rational ideal as distorting, inaccurate, and destructive. But some of the most consistent, compelling recent criticisms of this "masculine" perspective are being developed by feminist philosophers and psychologists.

PHILOSOPHICAL QUERY

Which—if any—of the philosophers you have studied this term speak in a "different voice" from the traditional "masculine voice"? Do they have anything in common? What? Do any of the philosophers speak in a "blended voice"? Who? Explain.

A MORE INCLUSIVE WAY OF KNOWING

In a 1986 study, psychologists Mary Field Belenky, Blythe McVicker Clinchy, Nancy Rule Goldberger, and Jill Mattuck Tarule reported that men and women develop knowledge in significantly different ways.[21] Specifically, their research seems to suggest that as a general rule, women develop into mature thinkers by including intuition and emotional response in the process of determining truth and making value judgments, whereas men are discouraged from doing so. Yet, historically, both women and men have been encouraged to develop into mature thinkers by detaching their thinking from their personal responses and emotions. Individuals who could not or would not do this were often labeled immature, emotional, perhaps even irrational.

The inclusive model of thinking does not reject objectivity and detached rationality. Rather, it holds that at the highest level of knowing, logical reasoning and objectivity must be balanced by subjective response and empathy.

**The association of rationality with masculinity is being challenged
by contemporary women (and men) philosophers, reaffirming
some of the earliest, most compelling archetypal representations
of woman as a symbol of both wisdom (Athena, right) and love
(Aphrodite, left). Many of these contemporary philosophers also
challenge the association of femininity with emotions, pointing
out that both men and women can be wise.**

Rather than simply rejecting the traditional model of knowing, the inclusive model proposes to enrich it. Adding intuition and empathy to logic and objectivity provides a much broader base of information and experience from which to draw conclusions and make decisions.

The questions current psychological research raises about exclusively male-based theories of knowledge are echoed by contemporary women philosophers. In particular, the work of **Alison Jaggar** challenges the fundamental assumptions of traditional Western theories of knowledge. Jaggar argues that emotions are vital aspects of anyone's picture of reality. They influence thinking as they help determine what we notice or ignore. Emotions impart degrees of interest and importance to experience. According to Jaggar, emotions select, direct, and help define observations and experiences. Yet, Jaggar notes, traditional Western philosophy has viewed emotion as inferior to reason and even viewed emotions as subversive hindrances to

Alison Jaggar

knowledge. In "Love and Knowledge: Emotion in Feminist Epistemology," she writes:

> From Plato until the present, with a few notable exceptions, reason rather than emotion has been regarded as the indispensable faculty for acquiring knowledge. . . . [Objective] testability became accepted as the hallmark of natural science; this, in turn, was viewed as the paradigm of genuine knowledge. . . . Because values and emotions had been identified as variable and idiosyncratic, [the objective standard] stipulated that trustworthy knowledge could be established only by methods that neutralized the values and emotions of individual [thinkers].[22]

Jaggar denies that a gap exists between emotion and knowledge: far from being hindrances to the construction of knowledge, she says, "emotions may be helpful and even necessary."

PHILOSOPHICAL QUERY

Do you believe that women and men think in different ways? Do people of different ethnic backgrounds think differently? Do men from different ethnic backgrounds all think alike *as men*? Do rich people think differently from poor people? Discuss these issues based on your own present beliefs, and then do some research to see what different scientists and philosophers think.

THE DIFFERENT VOICE

Carol Gilligan's study of possible differences in the moral development of men and women distinguishes between a masculine-oriented ethics of justice, such as Rawls's and Kant's, and a feminine-oriented ethics of care. In general terms, an **ethic of justice** stresses rules and rights and an **ethic of care** stresses responsibilities and relationships. The ethic of justice is based on an expression of the traditional model of knowing that Gilligan calls *justice reasoning*. *Care reasoning*, by contrast, depends on a sense of connectedness, sometimes referred to as relationship, that is the opposite of objective detachment. Okin's position incorporates both justice and care; we might describe such a position as "caring justice."

Gilligan, among others, was initially troubled by the work of **Lawrence Kohlberg (1927–1987)**, which received widespread attention in education as well as in philosophical and psychological circles. Kohlberg, a prominent psychologist, identified six distinct "stages of moral development," based on years of research with male subjects. They can be summarized as:

1. Goodness is power.
2. Goodness satisfies my needs.

One race there is of men, one of gods, but from one mother we both draw our breath.
Pindar

ETHIC OF JUSTICE
Carol Gilligan's term for ethical theories that stress rules over responsibilities and relationships, and that are based on an expression of the traditional impersonal, rationalistic, objective, detached model of knowing.

ETHIC OF CARE
Carol Gilligan's term for ethical theories that stress responsibilities and relationships over rules, and that are based on "care reasoning," which depends on a sense of connectedness, or "relationship," and that is the opposite of objective detachment.

3. Goodness comes from pleasing and helping others.

4. Goodness is doing our duty to ensure law and order.

5. Goodness is a matter of fairness according to a social contract like the Constitution.

6. Goodness is based on universal principles of justice and equality—the ethic of justice.

In Kohlberg's scheme, reasoning at the lower levels is particularly characteristic of children, and relatively few people attain the sixth stage, even as adults.

Gilligan noted that most women remained at the three lowest levels in Kohlberg's classification. Kohlberg himself thought that, as a rule, women were excluded from the highest stages of moral development. Thus, if Kohlberg's theory is sound, then women are morally inferior to men (as Kant and Freud thought). But what if Kohlberg's theory is not sound?

As noted above, philosophy for the most part has spoken in the same masculine voice that dominates moral discourse in this culture, and until very recently, women's voices have been largely absent from the mainstream of Western philosophy. Yet the idea that women are morally inferior to men is not only intellectually repugnant, it flies in the face of actual experience. Worse yet, the issue goes beyond gender because many men do not fit the model Kohlberg described.

Traditionally, women and men whose ways of knowing do not conform to the objective model have been devalued and regularly consigned to such nonphilosophical roles as poet or religious figure. Even when this culture acknowledges that such individuals express moral insight or wisdom, their explanations and accounts are sometimes dismissed as "anecdotal" or "merely personal" by academic philosophers and social scientists. If they cannot or do not wish to speak in the voice of "objective" scientific evidence and logical argument, they may not be heard at all.

In the introduction to *In a Different Voice*, Gilligan writes:

> Over the past ten years I have been listening to people talking about morality and about themselves. Halfway through that time, I began to hear a distinction in these voices, two ways of speaking about moral problems, two modes of describing the relationship between other and self. . . .
>
> The different voice I describe is characterized not by gender but by theme. Its association with women is an empirical observation, and it is primarily through women's voices that I trace its development. But this association is not absolute, and the contrasts between male and female voices . . . highlight a distinction between two modes of thought and . . . focus [on] a problem of interpretation rather than represent a generalization about either sex.[23]

I conclude then that, even granting the assumptions that natural psychological differences and therefore role differences, between the sexes are inevitable, it does not follow that there must be sanctions enforcing correlations between roles and sex. Indeed, if individual freedom is valued, those who vary from the statistical norm should not be required to conform to it.

Joyce Trebilcot

Gilligan suggests that because they idealized objective, logical, impersonal knowledge, philosophers have progressively developed an interest in the ethic of justice—at the expense of the ethic of care.[24] Interest in justice, she argues, has increasingly dominated Western values by restricting most moral and political discussion to issues of rights and duties. But the ethic of care is about actual relationships and intimate concerns, which cannot be confined to a set of rules and list of duties.

Gilligan points out, "The blind willingness to sacrifice people to truth, however, has always been the danger of an ethics abstracted from life. . . . It is the ethics of an adulthood that has become principled at the expense of care."[25]

The Need for Caring Justice

In Western culture, the ethic of care is often associated with religious figures who transcend or ignore objective knowledge and with a feminine-nurturing-maternal orientation toward other people. Yet, with notable exceptions, philosophers have dismissed and distrusted subjective emotional responses to moral problems, seeing only the dangers inherent in impulsive subjectivity. Okin, Gilligan, Jaggar, and others point out, however, that objectivity and detachment are as susceptible to abuse as overreliance on emotions or indiscriminate personal response.

Justice reasoning can be blind to its own biases and influences, resulting in a form of egocentrism that views a particular standard of what is reasonable as if it is the only standard. For example, when being fully human is taken to mean being rational, being fully human is characterized as deferring to a single objective, impersonal way of knowing. The responsible person is thus defined as one who has reached "the age of reason" and exhibits the capacity to think in an objective, impersonal, unemotional way. Yet we all probably know "reasonable" people who lack moral wisdom and character.

Gilligan notes that fallacious justice reasoning results in too little justice by excluding those oriented toward care from full participation in philosophy, science, law, higher education—and by denying access to the full range of knowledge necessary for wise choices.

Classical Christian spirituality viewed man as a "rational spirit." The male alone was said to fully possess this "human nature" in its essence. The male alone was made in the "image of God," modeled in his inward being after the intellectual Logos. . . . Woman was thereby modeled after the rejected part of the psyche.
Rosemary Radford Ruether

When we confine our standard of reasoning to the traditional model, we fail to recognize wisdom as it is expressed in some Eastern, Native American, African, and Hispanic philosophies that are not built on the objective, rationalistic model. The result is that nontraditional philosophies tend to be classified as religions or mythologies rather than philosophies. The model of knowing in such wisdom philosophies is based on relationship (with clan, tribe, others, God, nature) and demands personal involvement and intuitive understanding rather than objective detachment and logical conformity.

It is a mistake, however, to equate justice reasoning with bias and care reasoning with wisdom. Fallacious care reasoning can obscure the fact that the caregiver has rights and a separate point of view. One danger is that the caregiver succumbs to a delusional view of reality by failing to achieve any distance from others' needs and values. This results in caregivers who become so identified with taking care of others that they sacrifice themselves in ineffective, inappropriate ways. Gilligan discovered, for example, that many women find it easier to care for and help others than to apply the same standards of care and compassion to themselves. (Men can do this, too.)

Fallacious care reasoning can also result in a variant of the character disorder known as the "borderline personality." The name comes from the fact that such individuals are unable to separate themselves from others. They lack a clearly identified borderline between themselves and other people. As a consequence, individuals suffering from borderline personality disorder define themselves in terms of significant others; they are unable to achieve significant objectivity or detachment in their thinking.

Gilligan characterizes the fundamental weaknesses of justice reasoning and care reasoning as follows:

> The potential error in justice reasoning lies in its latent egocentrism, the tendency to confuse one's perspective with an objective standpoint or truth, the temptation to define others in one's own terms by putting oneself in their place. The potential error in care reasoning lies in the tendency to forget that one has terms, creating a tendency to enter into another's perspective and see oneself as "selfless" by defining oneself in others' terms. The two types of error underlie two common equations that signify distortions or deformations of justice and care: the equation of human with male, unjust in its omission of women; and the equation of care with self-sacrifice, uncaring in its failure to represent the activity and agency of care.[26]

Almost everyone will agree that there have been more geniuses for being human among women than there have been among men.
Ashley Montagu

Efforts to make the world better are often motivated by great love (care motivation) or a powerful sense of outrage (justice motivation). Care-motivated social reform results in injustice and abuse when love for the beloved group blinds us to the human qualities of their perceived oppressors. When that happens, the "other" (whether bigot, spouse abuser, or sexist) becomes demonized and thereby excluded from the realm of love. This encourages a shift of injustices, rather than a more just society.

Justice-motivated social reform results in a kind of "passive cruelty" when excessive concern for regulations, mathematically precise equality, and technical procedure blinds us to inherent disadvantages and human needs of presently oppressed groups. When justice loses touch with care, the legitimate demands of the oppressed become demonized as they are trivialized in "us-them" language that reveals contempt for their suffering by automatically characterizing their demands as "whining" or "special pleading."

De-Moralizing Gender

Feminist philosopher **Marilyn Friedman** thinks that neither justice nor care are adequate bases for moral considerations. Friedman points out that the most caring personal relationships also recognize rights and responsibilities "in which fairness can be reflected in ongoing interpersonal mutuality."

Friedman notes that impersonal theories of justice, such as Rawls's, are fine for identifying duties owed to all people, but are incapable of uncovering "*special* duties of justice which arise in close personal relationships the foundation of which is affection or kinship, rather than contract." The veil of ignorance, Friedman says, blinds us "to the role of justice among mutually interested and/or intimate parties."[27]

Friedman thinks that even though Gilligan recognizes the possibility of fallacious care reasoning, her efforts at blending care and justice reasoning fail to protect caregivers from succumbing to self-sacrifice because they do not adequately stress justice and rights. Friedman says:

> The trust and intimacy which characterize special relationships create special vulnerabilities to harm. Commonly recognized harms, such as physical injury and sexual assault, become more feasible; and special relationships, in corrupt, abusive, or degenerate forms, make possible certain uncommon emotional harms not even possible in impersonal relationships. When someone is harmed in a personal relationship, she is owed a rectification of some sort, a righting of the wrong which has been done her. The notion of justice emerges, once again, as a relevant moral notion. . . .[28]

According to Friedman "the justice perspective . . . arises from a more complex, and more realistic, estimate of the nature of human interrelationship" than Gilligan provides. Friedman suggests that

it seems wise both to reconsider the seeming dichotomy of care and justice, and to question the moral adequacy of either orientation dissociated from the other. Our aim would be to advance "beyond caring," that is, beyond *mere* caring dissociated from a concern for justice. In addition, we would do well to progress beyond gender stereotypes which assign distinct and different moral roles to women and men. Our ultimate goal should be a non-gendered, non-dichotomized, moral framework in which all moral concerns could be expressed. We might, with intentional irony, call this project, "de-moralizing the genders."[29]

PHILOSOPHICAL QUERY

Do you agree with Friedman that it is wrong to distinguish between an ethics of justice and one of care? Are they truly inseparable? Or are they distinct but equally important? Discuss.

The question is, after all, not what women and men naturally are, but what kind of society is morally justifiable. In order to answer this question, we must appeal to the notions of justice, equality, and liberty. It is these moral concepts, not the empirical issue of sex differences, which should have pride of place in the philosophical discussion of sex roles.

Joyce Trebilcot

In its more noble manifestation, care in the public realm would show itself, perhaps, in foreign aid, welfare programs, famine or disaster relief, or other social programs designed to relieve suffering and attend to human needs.

Marilyn Friedman

COMMENTARY

So long as impersonal, objective knowing is considered the highest type of knowledge, emotional, intuitive, personal ways of knowing and responding to life's demands will be seen as inadequate, if not dangerous. Yet care reasoning is not inferior to justice reasoning. As Marilyn Friedman points out, *mere* caring is not an adequate basis for the best life, nor can justice reasoning alone provide either sufficient justice or adequate care. Consider how so many of the major problems facing us today involve both care and justice: health care, homelessness, hunger, poverty, unadopted children.

Although our society has one of the most complicated sets of laws defining rights ever devised, we are discovering that emphasis on rights without equal emphasis on real caring creates a legalistic atmosphere of petty resentments and continually increasing demands for more rights. All around us we see the need for a dialogue between the voice of justice and the voice of care. Yet public emotional responses are still seen as immature or childishly out of place by many people in politics, education, science, and philosophy. We see signs of the tension between "emotions and reason," considerations of both justice and care throughout society.

In recent years, the public conversation about gender (and race) and too many other social and political issues has taken on a harsh, divisive tone as we struggle over how to redress deeply institutionalized patterns of unjust discrimination without creating newer patterns of unjust discrimination, and so forth. To cite just a few examples: Ellie Nessler's 1993 trial and conviction for shooting to death the man accused of sexually molesting her son was seen by some as a referendum on women's (mothers') issues and by others as a matter of "justice" for child molesters. A few years earlier, the William Kennedy Smith and Mike Tyson "date rape" trials generated contentious discussions of gender and race issues: Are rape victims denied justice when they are subjected to detailed cross-examination about their sex lives? Are black men given the same justice as white men? Do the rich and famous receive "more justice" than the poor and unknown? The 1994 Lorena Bobbitt trial, and its controversial "not guilty by reason of insanity" verdict, raised similar issues over whether Bobbitt's Hispanic heritage and gender would affect her chances for justice. News reports of the hung jury in Lyle Menendez's 1993–1994 trial centered on claims made by female jurors of harassment and ridicule from the male jurors, suggesting to some that gender, not legal evidence, swayed both groups.

Yet what too frequently seems to be missing from the public scene is genuine *dialogue:* clear, mutually respectful conversation designed to inform and enrich all parties. In place of dialogue, we too often find belligerence, sloganeering, appeals to group loyalty at all costs, a them-and-us mindset that hinders the possibility of what the philosopher **Martin Buber (1878–1965)** called "meeting," a recognition that the other person is also a *you*, not merely an *it*.

It is the age of Socrates again: our moral life is threatened, and our intellectual life is quickened and enlarged by the disintegration of ancient customs and beliefs. Everything is new and experimental in our ideas and our actions; nothing is established or certain any more. The rate, complexity, and variety of change in our time are without precedent . . . all forms about us are altered, from the tools that complicate our toil, to the wheels that whirl us restlessly about the earth, to the innovations in our sexual relationships, and to the hard disillusionment of our souls. . . .

Will Durant

According to Buber, human beings are "manifold" beings because we approach life from many perspectives. In his most famous book, *I and Thou*, Buber discussed what he characterized as the two "basic words" that determine whether we experience life objectively and from a distance or engage in it fully. According to Buber, "One basic word is the word pair *I-You* . . . The other basic word is the word pair *I-It*." The I-It is generally characterized as a detached intellectual attitude toward life, in contrast with I-You, which is characterized as personal engagement and passionate involvement. I-It prevents genuine dialogue because it does not recognize "persons," it cannot see or respond to an "other." I-It is personally unresponsive to experience. We might say that I-It is the language of the exclusive-justice orientation and I-You is the language of the inclusive-care orientation.

You probably know what Buber meant by unresponsiveness if you have ever felt that you were "being treated like an object." In such an experience, we realize that the other person does not see us as an equal, as a subject, a person. We are invisible, seen only as an object, as "the patient" or "the student" or the "white male" or "babe." Perhaps the other person is so wrapped up in his or her beliefs or emotions that everything is subordinated to them—including us. Such encounters are frustrating when the stakes are trivial and infuriating when they are not. We rightly feel that we have been disrespected in the most fundamental way possible: we are not recognized as genuine human beings; instead we are labeled, stereotyped, used, seduced, objectified, looked *through* not *at*. In Kantian terms, our dignity has been assaulted because we have been used as means only (see Chapter 13).

Dialogical philosophy addresses fundamental human concerns in a universal voice that transcends the particularities of our lives without trivializing them. Dialogical philosophy is responsive and engaging in that it speaks from and to both the heart and mind. Socrates (Chapter 5), Kierkegaard and Nietzsche (Chapter 16), and Martin Luther King, Jr., and Malcolm X (Chapter 19) are examples of dialogical thinkers.

In recent years, many feminist philosophers have been among the most effective and incisive dialogical philosophers. Risking the wrath and contempt of the "philosophical establishment," the dialogical feminists are bringing philosophy back to life. By insisting that philosophy tackle the everyday concerns of women and men—issues of family, fair employment, body image, education, justice, knowledge, and such—these feminists are performing the functions of the sophos. In their refusal to objectify either themselves or their subjects, feminists are helping heal the artificial and ultimately destructive split between reason and emotion, between abstract and concrete, and between philosophy and "real life."

Western history makes it clear that ignoring or trivializing subjective and emotional ways of knowing will not make them go away. Rather, it will confine care reasoning to the unofficial, relatively powerless, personal domain—with the result that what should be public moral dialogue becomes a monologue about rights and duties. Excessive emphasis on objective think-

DIALOGICAL PHILOSOPHY Philosophy that addresses fundamental human concerns in a universal voice that transcends the particularities of our lives without trivializing them; speaks from and to both the heart and mind.

ing and justice reasoning may actually increase the kind of impulsively destructive emotional reactions traditional Western philosophers have so often feared, because only the most intense personal responses can cut through centuries of reliance on one way of knowing. So long as philosophers are rewarded for impersonal thinking only, and ignored or trivialized when they express other forms of knowledge, they will fail in the pursuit of wisdom.

Certainly we have benefitted from scientific, objective knowledge and the ethic of justice. The noblest products of justice reasoning include the doctrine of inalienable rights and efforts to ensure civil rights, women's rights, and equal rights for all segments of our society. But as we have discovered throughout our search for wisdom, there is more to happiness and goodness than justice and rights can provide. It is impossible to calculate what women and men have lost by the exclusion of women and more inclusive ways of knowing from the "official" history of philosophy.

Just as women are capable of justice reasoning, men are capable of care reasoning. The sophos's wisdom was a responsive, dialogical product of both. And we must never forget that wisdom is about loving. Philosophy as the *love* of wisdom is inclusive and open to all seekers of the truly good life, when "the good life" is understood in its richest sense.

I have written this book as my way of inviting *you* to join my philosophical friends and me in the ongoing search for wisdom and all that wisdom entails.

SUMMARY OF MAIN POINTS

Perictione (c. 450–350 B.C.) was an ancient wise woman who argued that wisdom and self-control produce other virtues, which lead to ultimate harmony and happiness.

The wise women of ancient Greece were interested in the same things as the wise men: justice, the nature of the state, the relationship of the individual to the whole, the cosmos, and virtue, but they were also responsible for caring for their households in ways that men were not. They anticipated what is known today as applied ethics, the study of ethical concerns related to actual circumstances.

A feminist is a person who believes in the fundamental equality of women and men, and who actively insists that they be treated equally.

John Rawls attempted to refine Kant's moral philosophy by expanding upon Kant's conception of "the rational agent." He introduced the veil of ig-

norance, a powerful thought experiment designed to improve upon Kant's efforts to overcome the limits of personal concerns in ethical deliberations. The veil of ignorance prevents us from knowing our social status, what property we own, what we like and don't like, how intelligent we are, what our talents and strengths are, "and the like."

The "original position" of equality is Rawls's term for the imaginary setting in which we can identify the fundamental principles of justice from an objective, impartial perspective, rather than as "interested parties." Rawls argues that, being rational and mutually disinterested, persons in the original position would all agree to principles of equal political liberty and opportunity.

Susan Moller Okin analyzes Rawls's theory of justice, with special attention to issues of gender and the family. She argues that Rawls's analysis of justice is "ambiguous" regarding gender because he rarely indicates "how deeply and pervasively gender-structured" this society is. Okin notes that Rawls uses "supposedly generic male terms of reference" such as "men," "mankind," "he," and "his" throughout his writing.

Alison Jaggar challenges the fundamental assumptions of traditional Western theories of knowledge, arguing that emotions are vital aspects of anyone's picture of reality because they help determine what we notice or ignore. According to Jaggar, emotions, select, direct, and help define observations and experiences. Her more inclusive model of thinking suggests that at the highest level of knowing, logical reasoning and objectivity must be balanced by subjective response and empathy.

Troubled by the work of Lawrence Kohlberg, Carol Gilligan's research into moral development led her to distinguish between a masculine-oriented ethic of justice, such as Rawls's, and a feminine-oriented ethic of care. Kohlberg identified six distinct "stages of moral development." Gilligan noted that most women remained at the three lowest levels in Kohlberg's classification.

Gilligan suggests that interest in justice dominates Western values by restricting most moral and political discussion to issues of rights and duties. The ethic of care, in contrast, is about actual relationships and intimate concerns, which cannot be confined to a set of rules and list of duties.

Fallacious justice reasoning results in too little justice by excluding those oriented toward care from full participation in philosophy, science, law, and higher education—and by denying access to the full range of knowledge necessary for wise choices. Fallacious care reasoning can obscure the fact that the caregiver has rights and a point of view, too; this results in caregivers who become so identified with taking care of others that they sacrifice themselves in ineffective, inappropriate ways.

Marilyn Friedman thinks that neither justice nor care are adequate bases for moral considerations. She does not think that Gilligan's efforts to incorporate considerations of justice and rights into care reasoning adequately protect caregivers from succumbing to self-sacrifice.

Friedman advocates progressing beyond gender stereotypes which assign distinct and different moral roles to women and men to a nongendered, nondichotomized, moral framework in which all moral concerns could be expressed. She refers to this as "de-moralizing the genders."

Genuine dialogue is mutually respectful conversation designed to inform and enrich all parties. Dialogical philosophy addresses fundamental human concerns in a universal voice that transcends the particularities of our lives without trivializing them. Dialogical philosophy is responsive and engaging in that it speaks from and to both the heart and mind.

STUDY QUESTIONS

1. What is the connection between harmony and wisdom, according to Perictione?

2. What is feminism? Can men be feminists?

3. What is a thought experiment? Give an example of one and explain how it works.

4. What is the original position?

5. What is the veil of ignorance?

6. What is the relationship between the original position and the veil of ignorance?

7. In what sense is John Rawls's *A Theory of Justice* an elaboration on Kant's moral philosophy?

8. What are the two justice principles Rawls thought all rational persons would accept? Which one is primary?

9. Why does Susan Moller Okin say that Rawls's theory of justice is ambiguous?

10. What is Okin's chief criticism of Rawls?

11. In your words, give the recent criticisms of rationality discussed in this chapter.

12. What is meant by "the inclusive way of knowing"? What other way(s) is(are) there?

13. What is Alison Jaggar's theory of knowledge?

14. What is the "different voice" Carol Gilligan refers to? What is its significance?

15. Compare and contrast the ethic of justice with the ethic of care.

16. What was Lawrence Kohlberg's theory of moral development? What was Gilligan's criticism of it?

17. Describe fallacious justice reasoning.

18. Describe fallacious care reasoning.

19. What does Marilyn Friedman mean by "demoralizing the genders?"

20. What is Marilyn Friedman's chief criticism of Carol Gilligan? Is she right? Explain.

21. What is dialogical philosophy?

22. Distinguish between the *I-You* attitude and the *I-It*.

POSTSCRIPT

Say not, "When I have leisure I will study." Perhaps you will have no leisure.

HILLEL

I find myself returning again and again to a select few philosophical master-pieces. In them I find consolation, encouragement, and wisdom. One of my favorites is Epictetus's *Enchiridion* or *Handbook*. You will recall that the handbook was originally compiled for Roman soldiers to carry on long, difficult military campaigns. We might also think of it as a handbook to carry and consult in our daily campaign against the confusions, deceptions, and distractions of modern life.

The Stoic *sophos* speaks across time and cultures as he invites you to join the philosophical journey from confusion toward wisdom:

> How long do you put off thinking yourself worthy of the best things, and [worthy of] never going against the definitive capacity of reason? You have received the philosophical propositions that you ought to agree to and you have agreed to them. Then what sort of teacher are you still waiting for, that you put off improving yourself until he comes? You are not a [child] anymore, but already . . . full grown. . . . If you now neglect things and are lazy and are always making delay after delay and set one day after another as the day for paying attention to yourself, then without realizing it you will make no progress but will end up a non-philosopher all through life and death. So decide now that you are worthy of living as a full-grown [human being] who is making progress, and make everything that seems best be a law you cannot go against. And if you meet with any hardship or anything pleasant or reputable or disreputable, then remember that the contest is *now* and the Olympic games are *now* and you cannot put things off any more and that your progress is made or destroyed by a single day and a single action. Socrates became fully perfect in this way. . . . You, even if you are not yet Socrates, ought to live as one wanting to be [like] Socrates.[1]

NOTES

CHAPTER 1 PHILOSOPHY AND WISDOM

1. Mary Ellen Waithe, ed., *Introduction to the Series, A History of Women Philosophers*, vol. 1, 600 B.C.– A.D. 500 (Dordrecht: Martinus Nijhoff Publishers, 1987), pp. ix–x.

2. "Newsmakers," *Los Angeles Times*, December 29, 1989.

3. Albert Hakim, *A Historical Introduction to Philosophy* (New York: Macmillan, 1987), pp. vi ff.

4. Will Durant, *The Mansions of Philosophy: A Survey of Human Life and Destiny* (New York: Simon & Schuster, 1929), pp. vii, viii, x ff.

CHAPTER 2 THE SAGE: BUDDHA AND LAO-TZU

1. Mircea Eliade, *Shamanism* (Princeton, N.J.: Princeton University Press, 1964), pp. 3–13. See also Denise L. Carmody and John T. Carmody, *Eastern Ways to the Center: An Introduction to Religions of the West* (Belmont, Calif.: Wadsworth Publishing, 1981), pp. 9–11.

2. Carmody and Carmody, *Eastern Ways to the Center*, pp. 9–11.

3. See Denise L. Carmody and John T. Carmody, *Western Ways to the Center: An Introduction to Religions of the West* (Belmont, Calif.: Wadsworth Publishing, 1981), pp. 210–13.

4. Carmody and Carmody, *Eastern Ways to the Center*, p. 200.

5. The brief sketch that follows is based on Nancy Wilson Ross, *Buddhism: A Way of Life and Thought* (New York: Vintage, 1981); see also Edward Conze, *Buddhism: Its Essence and Development* (New York: Harper Torchbooks, 1965), *Stories of the Buddha: Being Selections from the Jataka*, trans. and ed. Caroline A. F. Rhys Davids (New York: Dover Publications, 1989), and Richard H. Robinson and Willard L. Johnson, *The Buddhist Religion* (Encino, Calif.: Dickenson, 1977).

6. Ross, *Buddhism*, p. 6.

7. Ibid., p. 10.

8. Ibid., p. 18.

9. Ibid.

10. Ibid., p. 33.

11. The Buddha, "The Discourse on Universal Love," in Ross, *Buddhism*, p. 32.

12. Ross, *Buddhism*, pp. 23ff.

13. Modified from Ross, *Buddhism*, p. 24.

14. See Ross, *Buddhism*, pp. 24ff.

15. Ibid., p. 35.

16. Ibid., p. 26.

17. Ibid.

18. Ibid., p. 26f.

19. Ibid., p. 27

20. Ibid., p. 37.

21. E. A. Burtt, ed., *The Teachings of the Compassionate Buddha* (New York: Mentor, 1982), pp. 202ff.

22. Ibid., pp. 34ff, 36.

23. Holmes Welch, *Taoism: The Parting of the Way* (Boston: Beacon Press, 1965), p. 2.

24. Lao-tzu, *The Wisdom of Laotse*, trans. and ed. Lin Yutang (New York: Modern Library, 1976), p. 41.

25. Lao-tzu, *Tao Te Ching: A New English Version*, trans. Stephen Mitchell (New York: Harper & Row, 1988), p. 1.

26. Lao-tzu, *Te-Tao Ching: A New Translation Based on the Recently Discovered Mawang-tui Texts*, trans. with introduction and commentary by Robert G. Henricks (New York: Ballantine Books, 1989), p. 53.

27. Lao-tzu, *Tao Te Ching* Wing-Tsit Chan, trans. and comp., *A Source Book in Chinese Philosophy* (Princeton, N.J.: Princeton University Press, 1963), p. 146.

28. Ibid., p. 140.

29. Ibid., p. 136.

30. Ibid., pp. 162–63.

31. Ibid., p. 140.

32. Ibid., pp. 169–67.

33. Chuang-tzu, in Yutang, p. 287.

34. Chuang-tzu, *The Chuang-Tzu*, in Chan, *A Source Book in Chinese Philosophy*, p. 206.

35. Carmody and Carmody, *Eastern Ways to the Center*, pp. 201–3.

CHAPTER 3 THE SOPHOS: HERACLITUS AND PARMENIDES

1. W. T. Jones, *The Classical Mind: A History of Western Philosophy*, 2nd ed. (New York: Harcourt Brace Jovanovich, 1970), p. 2.

2. Plato, *Theatetus*, 174A, trans. F. M. Cornford in *The Collected Dialogues of Plato: Including the Letters*, ed. Edith Hamilton and Huntington Cairns (New York: Pantheon Books, 1961), p. 879.

3. Herodotus mentions this in his *History*.

4. Aristotle, *Metaphysics*. M'Mahon translation, i,3.

5. Giovanni Reale, *A History of Ancient Philosophy vol. 1, From the Origins to Socrates*, trans. John R. Catan (Albany: State University of New York Press, 1987), p. 35.

6. Will Durant, *The Story of Civilization, vol. 2: The Life of Greece* (New York: Simon & Schuster, 1966), p. 137.

7. Ibid., pp. 138–39.

8. Heraclitus, Frg. 28, *Herakleitos and Diogenes*, trans. Guy Davenport (San Francisco: Grey Fox Press, 1979), p. 16.

9. Charles H. Kahn, *The Art and Thought of Heraclitus* (Cambridge: Cambridge University Press, 1979), pp. 1–3.

10. Heraclitus, Frg. 72, *Herakleitos and Diogenes*, p. 23.

11. Heraclitus, Frg. 23, *Herakleitos and Diogenes*, p. 15.

12. Fragments 20, 21, 29, 36, 110, and 113 in *Herakleitos and Diogenes*.

13. Jones, p. 16.

14. Fragments 1, 17, 57, and 116 in the Davenport translation.

15. Frg. 117, Davenport, p. 31.

16. Jones, *The Classical Mind*, p. 16.

17. Fragments 25, 26, 27, 98, and 99 in *Herakleitos and Diogenes*.

18. Kahn, *The Art and Thought of Heraclitus*, p. 21; Reale, *A History of Ancient Philosophy*, p. 53.

19. Reale, *A History of Ancient Philosophy*, p. 53.

20. Fragments 1, 64, 73, 106, 118, and 121 in *Herakleitos and Diogenes*.

21. Reale, *A History of Ancient Philosophy*, p. 53.

22. G. S. Kirk and J. E. Raven, *The Presocratic Philosophers* (Cambridge: Cambridge University Press, 1957), pp. 217–21; Reale, *A History of Ancient Philosophy*, pp. 60–61.

23. Reale, *A History of Ancient Philosophy*, p. 61ff.

24. Ibid., p. 65.

25. Plato, *Parmenides*, trans. F. M. Cornford, *The Collected Dialogues of Plato*, p. 921.

26. *On Nature*, Frg. 2, Freeman translation in Reale, *A History of Ancient Philosophy*, pp. 83–84.

27. Parmenides, Frg. 3, Freeman translation, Reale, *A History of Ancient Philosophy*, p. 84.

28. Reale, *A History of Ancient Philosophy*, p. 87.

29. Frg. 8, modified by Zeller-Reale; Reale, *A History of Ancient Philosophy*, p. 85.

30. Jones, *The Classical Mind*, pp. 21–22.

31. Theophrastus, quoted in Kirk and Raven, *The Presocratic Philosophers*, p. 344.

32. Kirk and Raven, *The Presocratic Philosophers*, p. 345.

33. Aristotle, *De Caelo*, 300B30, and Aelian, Frg. 61, *Nat. Anim.*, XVI, 29; both in Kirk and Raven, *The Presocratic Philosophers*, pp. 336–37.

34. Jones, *The Classical Mind*, p. 27.

35. Anaxagoras, Frg. 10, Kirk and Raven, *The Presocratic Philosophers*, p. 378.

36. Anaxagoras, Frg. 11; J. Burnet, *Early Greek Philosophy*, 4th ed. (London, 1930).

37. Anaxagoras, Frg. 21; Jones, *The Classical Mind*, p. 29.

38. Jones, *The Classical Mind*, p. 29; Peter Angeles, *Dictionary of Philosophy* (New York: Barnes & Noble Books, 1981), p. 191.

39. Anaxagoras, Frg. 12, Burnet, p. 260.

40. Reale, *A History of Ancient Philosophy*, p. 114.

41. Anaxagoras, Frg. 12, Reale, *A History of Ancient Philosophy*, p. 114.

42. Amaury de Riencourt, *Sex and Power in History* (New York: David McKay, 1974), pp. 97ff.

43. Ibid., p. 99.

CHAPTER 4 THE SOPHIST: PROTAGORAS

1. Plato, *The Republic*, trans. H. D. P. Lee (London: Penguin, 1955), bk. 7, sec. 6.

2. See W. K. C. Guthrie, *The Sophists* (Cambridge: Cambridge University Press, 1971); Giovanni Reale, *A History of Ancient Philosophy*; Will Durant, *The Story of Civilization*, vol. 2, *The Life of Greece* (New York: Simon & Schuster, 1939); Frederick Copleston, S. J., *A History of Philosophy, vol. 1, Greece and Rome* (New York: Image, 1985).

3. Will Durant, *The Life of Greece* (New York: Simon & Schuster, 1939), p. 358.

4. Guthrie, *The Sophists*, p. 35.

5. Plato, *The Sophist*, 231D-E, in Reale, *A History of Ancient Philosophy*, p. 149.

6. Xenophon, *Memorabilia*, trans. E. C. Marchant, in *Xenophon, Memorabilia and Oeconomics* (London and Cambridge, Mass.: Loeb Classical Library, 1959), bk. 1, sec. 6, line 13.

7. Plato, *Theaetetus*, trans. F. M. Cornford, 151E–152A, in Reale, *A History of Ancient Philosophy*, p. 157.

8. Gregory Vlastos, *Protagoras* (Indianapolis: Bobbs-Merrill, Library of Liberal Arts edition, 1956), pp. xii–xvi, xviii–xix.

9. Plato, *Theaetetus*, 166D, in Reale, *A History of Ancient Philosophy*, pp. 160ff.

10. Robert J. Ringer, *Winning Through Intimidation* (New York: Fawcett Crest, 1974), p. 33.

11. Plato, *The Republic*, bk. 1, lines 338ff.

12. Plato, *Gorgias*, trans. W. C. Helmbold (Indianapolis: Bobbs-Merrill, Library of Liberal Arts edition, 1952), 482–86.

13. Ibid., 457B.

CHAPTER 5 THE WISE MAN: SOCRATES

1. W. K. C. Guthrie, *Socrates* (Cambridge: Cambridge University Press, 1971), p. 6.

2. Plato, *Phaedo*, 60C-D, trans. Benjamin Jowett, in *The Dialogues of Plato*, 3rd ed. (Oxford: Clarendon Press, 1892).

3. Guthrie, *Socrates*, p. 4.

4. Ibid.

5. Xenophon, *Symposium*, trans. E. C. Marchant (London and Cambridge, Mass.: Loeb Classical Library, 1959), ch. 2, line 18.

6. Plato, *Gorgias*, 470E, in Reale, *A History of Ancient Philosophy*, p. 219.

7. Xenophon, *Symposium*, ch. 5, in Guthrie, *Socrates*, p. 68.

8. Xenophon, *Memorabilia*, bk. 1, sec. 6, line 10, in Reale, *A History of Ancient Philosophy*, p. 216. Reprinted by permission of the publishers and the Loeb Classical Library, Harvard University Press.

9. Xenophon, *Memorabilia*, bk. 4, sec. 5, lines 9ff., in Reale, *A History of Ancient Philosophy*, p. 218. Reprinted by permission of the publishers and the Loeb Classical Library, Harvard University Press.

10. Plato, *Apology*, 34D, trans. Benjamin Jowett, in *The Dialogues of Plato; Phaedo*, 60A.

11. Durant, *Life of Greece*, p. 367.

12. Karl Jaspers, *Socrates, Buddha, Confucius, Jesus: The Paradigmatic Individuals*, trans. Ralph Manheim, ed. Hannah Arendt (New York: Harcourt Brace Jovanovich, Harvest paperback, 1962), p. 87.

13. Ibid., pp. 90, 92.

14. Plato, *Apology*, 40A.

15. Plato, *Phaedo*, 115Dff.

16. Ibid., 117Bff.

17. Plato, *Apology*, 17A.

18. Reale, *A History of Ancient Philosophy*, p. 202.

19. Plato, *Apology*, 21B-E.

20. Plato, *Apology*, 20C.

21. Ibid., 22D, 23A.

22. Plato, *Apology*, pp. 29D–30B.

23. Plato, *Gorgias*, 468b-c.

24. Plato, *Protagoras*, Benjamin Jowett translation, Martin Ostwald revision, 345e (Indianapolis: Bobbs-Merrill, 1956), p. 49.

25. Plato, *Meno*, Benjamin Jowett translation, 87–89, in *Plato's Meno: Text and Criticism*, eds. Alexander Sesonski and Noel Fleming (Belmont, Calif.: Wadsworth Publishing, 1965), pp. 24–26.

26. Plato, *Meno*, Jowett translation, 77b–78b, pp. 12–13.

CHAPTER 6
THE PHILOSOPHER-KING: PLATO

1. Diogenes Läertius, *Life of Plato*, in *Lives of Eminent Philosophers*, trans. R. H. Hicks (Cambridge, Mass.: Harvard University Press, 1925).

2. Plato, *Letter: VII*, 324E, trans. L. A. Post, in *Plato: The Collected Dialogues*, p. 1575.

3. See A. W. Levi, "Ancient Philosophy: The Age of the Aristocrat," Chapter 2 in *Philosophy as Social Expression* (Chicago: University of Chicago Press, 1974), for full discussion of the influence of social class on Plato.

4. Ibid., p. 66.

5. Plato, *Letter: VII*, 325D–326B, p. 1575F.

6. A. E. Taylor, *Plato: The Man and His Work* (London: Methuen & Co., 1966), pp. 6ff.

7. Plato, *Timaeus*, 27D–28A, trans. Benjamin Jowett, in *The Dialogues of Plato*, 3rd ed. (Oxford: The Clarendon Press, 1892).

8. Plato, *The Republic*, trans. H. D. P. Lee (Baltimore: Penguin Books, 1967), 506, pp. 269–70.

9. Ibid., p. 275.

10. Ibid., 510–11, pp. 276–77.

11. Ibid., 505–9, pp. 268–73.

12. Ibid., 511, p. 278.

13. Ibid., bk. VII–516, pp. 278–81.

14. Ibid., 516–17, pp. 281–82.

15. Ibid., bk. 1, Prelude, 327–28, p. 51F.

16. H. D. P. Lee, introduction to Plato, *The Republic*, p. 87.

17. B. A. G. Fuller, *History of Greek Philosophy*, vol. 2 (New York: Henry Holt & Company, 1931), p. 214.

18. Plato, *The Republic*, bk. 2, 363, pp. 94ff.

19. A. E. Taylor, *Plato: The Man and His Works* (London: Methuen & Co., 1966), p. 270.

20. Plato, *The Republic*, bk. 4, 442E–43A, p. 194.

21. Ibid., bk. 8, sec. 6, p. 327.

22. Ibid.

23. Ibid., 557, pp. 329ff.

24. Ibid.

25. Ibid., p. 331.

26. Ibid., 561, p. 334.

27. Ibid., 563, pp. 336ff.

28. Ibid., bk. 9, 573–74, pp. 346ff.

CHAPTER 7
THE NATURALIST: ARISTOTLE

1. In the 1970s, psychologists Daniel Levinson and G. E. Vailant identified something called a *mid-life crisis* which, they claimed, prompted major disruptions in men's lives. Since then, other psychologists, like Carol Gilligan (see Chapter 20), have pointed out that in mid-life both men and

women try to establish better balance in their lives. Phillip G. Zimbardo, *Psychology and Life*, 12th ed. (Glenview, Ill.: Scott, Foresman, 1988), pp. 98–99.

2. Durant, *Life of Greece*, p. 526.

3. Diogenes Laërtius, *Life of Plato*, sec. 25.

4. Samuel Enoch Stumpf, *Philosophy: History and Problems*, 4th ed. (New York: McGraw-Hill, 1989), bk. 1, p. 83.

5. Durant, *Life of Greece*, p. 525.

6. Aristotle, *Physics*, bk. 2, ch. 8, sec. 199b, line 15, in trans. Phillip Wheelwright, *Aristotle* (New York: Odyssey, 1951).

7. Sir David Ross, *Aristotle* (London: Methuen, 1966), p. 129.

8. Aristotle, *Nicomachean Ethics*, bk. 1, 1094A, trans. J. C. Welldon, in *Philosophers Speak for Themselves*, ed. T. V. Smith (Chicago: University of Chicago Press, 1934).

9. Ibid., 1094B.

10. Ibid., 1095A.

11. Ibid., 1095B.

12. Ibid., 1096A.

13. Ibid., 1095B.

14. This treatment of *eudaimonia* is based in part on material found in Burton F. Porter, *Reasons for Living: A Basic Ethics* (New York: Macmillan, 1988), pp. 204–7.

15. Aristotle, *Nicomachean Ethics*, bk. 1, 1095Bff, trans. J. C. Welldon, in *Philosophers Speak for Themselves*.

16. Aristotle, *Nicomachean Ethics*, 1103B30, trans. Martin Ostwald (Indianapolis: Library of Liberal Arts, 1962).

17. Ibid., 1104A13.

18. Ibid., 1104Aff.

19. Aristotle, *Nicomachean Ethics*, 1103A17ff, trans. W. D. Ross, in *Basic Works of Aristotle*, p. 952.

20. Aristotle, *Nicomachean Ethics*, trans. Martin Ostwald, 1143B22.

21. Ibid., 1144A6.

22. Ibid., 1106B15.

23. I am indebted to Porter's *Reasons for Living* for excellent examples of recent trends in self-realization.

24. Abraham Maslow, *Motivation and Personality* (New York: Harper & Row, 1970), p. 279.

25. Carol Rogers, *On Becoming a Person* (Boston: Houghton Mifflin, 1961), pp. 187ff.

26. Ibid., p. 195.

27. Thomas Merton, *New Seeds of Contemplation* (New York: New Directions, 1961), p. 98.

CHAPTER 8
THE EPICUREAN: EPICURUS

1. *Newsweek*, January 15, 1990.

2. Lin Yutang, *The Importance of Living* (New York: John Day, 1937), p. 127.

3. Walter Pater, *Marius the Epicurean* (1883; reprint, New York: Everyman's Library, 1960), p. 79.

4. From the transcript of Wilde's first trial, quoted by Philip Rieff in "The Impossible Culture: Wilde as a Modern Prophet," in *The Soul of Man Under Socialism and Other Essays* (New York: Harper Colophon Books, 1970), p. vii.

5. Christopher Lasch, *The Culture of Narcissism: American Life in an Age of Diminishing Expectations* (New York: W. W. Norton, 1979), quoted in Christina Sommers and Fred Sommers, *Vice and Virtue in Everyday Life* (San Diego: Harcourt Brace Jovanovich, 1989), pp. 664–65.

6. Xenophon, *Memorabilia*, bk. 2, sec. 1, line 11, trans. E. C. Marchant, *Xenophon, Memorabilia*.

7. Epicurus, Fragment 221, in Giovanni Reale, *A History of Ancient Philosophy, vol. 3, The Systems of the Hellenistic Age*, ed. and trans. John R. Catan (Albany: State University of New York Press, 1985), p. 111.

8. Reale, *Systems of the Hellenistic Age*, p. 113.

9. Ibid.

10. Durant, *Life of Greece*, p. 645.

11. Robert F. Davidson, *Philosophies Men Live By* (New York: Holt, Rinehart and Winston, 1974), p. 36.

12. Stobaeus, *Anthology*, bk. 3, sec. 17, line 33, in Reale, *Systems of the Hellenistic Age*, p. 170.

13. Epicurus, Fragment 138, trans. G. Murray, in *History of Greek Religion* (Oxford: Oxford University Press, 1930), p. 141.

14. Diogenes Läertius, *Epicurus*, sec. 10, in Hicks, *Lives of Eminent Philosophers*.

15. Epicurus, *Letter to Herodotus 38*, in Reale, *Systems of the Hellenistic Age*, p. 134.

16. Epicurus, *Letter to Herodotus 67*, in Reale, *Systems of the Hellenistic Age*, p. 151.

17. Lin Yutang, *The Importance of Living* (New York: Capricorn Books, 1974), pp. 25ff.

18. Epicurus, *Letter to Menoceceus*, trans. George D. Strodach, quoted in *Hellenistic Philosophy*, ed. Herman Shapiro and Edwin M. Curley (New York: The Modern Library, 1965), p. 5.

19. Epicurus, *Leading Doctrine*, trans. George K. Strodach, in *Hellenistic Philosophy*, p. 10.

20. Epicurus, *Letter to Menoceceus*, p. 6.

21. Ibid., pp. 7ff.

22. Ibid., p. 8.

23. Reale, *Systems of the Hellenistic Age*, p. 178.

24. Ibid.

25. Epicurus, *Sententiae Vaticanae 78*, trans. W. Y. Oates, in Reale, *Systems of the Hellenistic Age*, p. 179.

26. Epicurus, *Principal Doctrines 23*, quoted in Reale, *Systems of the Hellenistic Age*, p. 179.

27. Epicurus, *Principal Doctrines 39*, p. 179.

28. Epicurus, *Sententiae Vaticanae*, p. 179.

29. Epicurus, *Letter to Menoceceus*, p. 8.

30. Pater, *Marius the Epicurean*, pp. 149, 151.

CHAPTER 9 THE STOIC: EPICTETUS AND MARCUS AURELIUS

1. Epicurus, *Principal Doctrines 4*.

2. Epictetus, *Discourses*, trans. P. E. Matheson (Oxford: Clarendon Press, 1916), in William Sahakian and Mabel Lewis Sahakian, *Realms of Philosophy* (Cambridge, Mass.: Schenkman, 1965), p. 133.

3. Epictetus, *Handbook of Epictetus*, trans. Nicholas P. White (Indianapolis: Hackett, 1983), p. 13.

4. This sketch of Epictetus's life is based on Philip Hallie's entry on Epictetus in *The Encyclopedia of Philosophy*, vol. 3, ed. Paul Edwards et al. (New York: Macmillan and the Free Press, 1967), p. 1.

5. Marcus Aurelius, *Meditations*, bk. 7, sec. 54, trans. George Long, in *Plato, Epictetus, Marcus Aurelius* (Harvard Classics edition) (New York: P. Collier & Son, 1937).

6. Ibid., bk. 6, sec. 2.

7. Ibid., bk. 7, sec. 58, 59.

8. From Maxwell Staniforth's entry in *Encyclopedia of Philosophy*, vol. 5, p. 156.

9. Seneca, "On Tranquility," in *The Stoic Philosophy of Seneca*, trans. Moses Hadas (New York: W. W. Norton, 1958), p. 93.

10. Epictetus, *Enchiridion*, sec. 27, trans. George Long, in *The Discourses of Epictetus with the Encheiridion and Fragments* (New York: A. L. Burt Company, 1929).

11. Seneca, *Letter 41*, in *Stoic Philosophy of Seneca*, p. 188.

12. Ibid.

13. Marcus Aurelius, *Meditations*, bk. 7, sec. 22, 23, 25, trans. Maxwell Staniforth (Middlesex: Penguin Books, 1970).

14. Ibid.

15. Seneca, "On Self-Control," trans. Gunmere, in *Philosophers Speak for Themselves*, pp. 623ff.

16. Epictetus, *Enchiridion*, sec. 1.

17. Ibid., sec. 4.

18. Ibid., sec. 1.

19. Ibid.

20. Ibid., sec. 30.

21. Ibid., sec. 25.

22. Seneca, "On Providence," in *Stoic Philosophy of Seneca*, p. 37.

23. Ibid., pp. 38–39.

24. William Glasser, *Positive Addiction* (New York: Harper & Row, 1976), p. 1.

25. Albert Ellis, *Humanistic Psychotherapy*, ed. Edward Sagarin (New York: McGraw-Hill, 1973), p. 32.

26. Ibid., p. 32.

27. Albert Ellis and Robert A. Harper, *A New Guide to Rational Living* (North Hollywood: Wilshire Book Co., 1978), p. 5.

28. Ibid., pp. 178–79.

29. Viktor E. Frankl, *Man's Search for Meaning: An Introduction to Logotherapy* (New York: Pocket Books, 1963), p. 178.

30. Ibid., p. 179.

31. Viktor E. Frankl, "Logotherapy and the Challenge of Suffering," in *Psychotherapy and Existentialism: Selected Papers by Viktor E. Frankl* (New York: Simon & Schuster, 1967), p. 90.

32. Frankl, *Man's Search for Meaning*, p. 183.

33. James Bond Stockdale, "The World of Epictetus," *Atlantic Monthly*, April 1978, reprinted in Sommers and Sommers, *Vice and Virtue in Everyday Life*, pp. 592–93.

34. James Bond Stockdale, *Epictetus' Enchiridion*, in *Text and Teaching: The Search for Human Excellence*, ed. Michael J. Collins and Frances J. Ambosio (Washington, D.C.: Georgetown University Press, 1991), pp. 39–42.

CHAPTER 10
THE SCHOLAR:
THOMAS AQUINAS

1. W. T. Jones, *A History of Western Philosophy: The Medieval Mind*, 2nd ed. (New York: Harcourt Brace Jovanovich, 1969), p. 2.

2. Vernon J. Bourke, in *Aquinas' Search for Wisdom* (Milwaukee: The Bruce Publishing Company, 1965), identifies discrepancies in many biographical sketches of Thomas Aquinas, since most are based on William of Tocco. Bourke points out that all we know for sure is Thomas was born between 1220 and 1227. The commonly cited date of 1225 originated with Tocco and cannot be verified.

3. Bourke, *Aquinas' Search for Wisdom*, p. 18.

4. Levi, *Philosophy as Social Expression*, p. 106.

5. William of Tocco in Bourke, *Aquinas' Search for Wisdom*, p. 37.

6. See "The Age of the Saint" in Levi, *Philosophy as Social Expression*.

7. Ibid.

8. Martin Grabmann, *Die Geschichte der scholastichen Methode* (1957), trans. A. W. Levi, quoted in *Philosophy as Social Expression*, p. 125.

9. Based on Pater A. Angeles, *Dictionary of Philosophy* (New York: Barnes & Noble Books, 1981), p. 250.

10. Levi, *Philosophy as Social Expression*, pp. 122ff.

11. Ibid., p. 124.

12. From Thomas Aquinas's commentary on Aristotle's *Metaphysics*, quoted in Levi, *Philosophy as Social Expression*, p. 102.

13. "More Turning to Prayer to Handle Life: Spiritual Path Often Leads Outside Church," *Sacramento Bee*, March 11, 1990.

14. The Five Ways are found in *Summa Theologica*, trans. the Dominican Fathers, *Basic Writings of Saint Thomas Aquinas*, ed. A. C. Pegis (New York: Random House, 1945), part 1, ques. 2, art. 3.

15. Ibid.

16. Ibid.

17. Ibid.

18. Ibid.

19. Jones, *The Medieval Mind*, pp. 220ff.

20. Thomas Aquinas, *Summa contra Gentiles*, trans. English Dominican Fathers (London: Bunns Oates, 1924), part 3, ques. 25.

CHAPTER 11
THE RATIONALIST:
RENÉ DESCARTES

1. Martin Luther, *A Treatise on Christian Liberty*, trans. W. A. Lambert, in *Works of Martin Luther*, vol. 2 (Philadelphia: A. J. Holman, 1915), p. 318.

2. Quoted in William K. Hartmann, *Astronomy: The Cosmic Journey* (Belmont, Calif.: Wadsworth Publishing, 1991), p. 64.

3. *The Philosophical Works of Descartes*, vol. 1, trans. Elizabeth Haldane and G. R. T. Ross (Cambridge: Cambridge University Press, 1931; reprint, New York: Dover, 1931), p. 87.

4. Quoted in Levi, *Philosophy as Social Expression*, p. 185.

5. René Descartes, *Discourse on Method*, in *Philosophical Works*, vol. 1, p. 83.

6. Descartes, *Rules for the Direction of the Mind*, in *Philosophical Works*, vol. 1, p. 6.

7. Ibid., p. 9, 14ff.

8. Descartes, *Discourse on Method*, p. 88.

9. Ibid., pp. 81ff.

10. Descartes, *Meditation I*, in *Philosophical Works*, vol. 1, pp. 144–45.

11. Ibid., pp. 145–146.

12. Ibid., p. 148.

13. Descartes, *Meditation II*, in *Philosophical Works*, vol. 1, p. 150.

14. Ibid., pp. 151–53.

15. Descartes, *Meditation III*, in *Philosophical Works*, vol. 1, p. 159.

16. Ibid., p. 165.

17. Ibid., p. 166.

18. Ibid., p. 169.

19. Ibid., p. 170.

20. Ibid., pp. 170–71.

21. Descartes, *Meditation VI*, in *Philosophical Works*, vol. 1, p. 185.

22. Ibid., p. 191.

23. Ibid., p. 195.

24. Gilbert Ryle, *The Concept of Mind* (New York: Harper & Row, 1941), p. 11.

25. Descartes, *Meditation VI*, in *Philosophical Works*, vol. 1, p. 192.

26. Robert Paul Wolff, *About Philosophy*, 4th ed. (Englewood Cliffs, N.J.: Prentice-Hall, 1989), pp. 330ff.

CHAPTER 12 THE SKEPTIC: DAVID HUME

1. H. R. Fox Bourne, *The Life of John Locke*, vol. 1 (New York: Harper, 1876), pp. 200–1.

2. John Locke, "Epistle to the Reader," in *An Essay Concerning Human Understanding*, ed. A. C. Fraser (Oxford: Clarendon Press, 1894), p. 9.

3. Locke, *An Essay Concerning Human Understanding*, bk. 2, ch. 1, sec. 2.

4. Ibid., ch. 23, sec. 29.

5. George Berkeley, *Three Dialogues Between Hylas and Philonous*, in *Selections*, ed. Mary W. Calkins (New York: Scribner's, 1957), pp. 268–69.

6. Ibid., pp. 238–39.

7. George Berkeley, *A Treatise Concerning the Principles of Human Knowledge*, in *The Works of George Berkeley*, vol. 1, ed. A. C. Fraser (Oxford: Clarendon Press, 1901), pt. 1, sec. 3.

8. Ernest C. Mossner, *Life of David Hume* (1954; reprint, Oxford: Clarendon Press, 1970), p. 51.

9. Thomas H. Huxley, *Hume* (New York, 1901), p. 3.

10. Mossner, *Life of David Hume*, p. 94.

11. Richard Watson, *The Philosopher's Diet: How to Lose Weight and Change the World* (Boston: Atlantic Monthly Press, 1985), p. 97.

12. Mossner, *Life of David Hume*, p. 111.

13. Ibid., p. 213.

14. Ibid., pp. 223, 318.

15. David Hume, "My Own Life," in *Dialogues Concerning Natural Religion*, ed. Henry D. Aiken (New York: Hafner, 1948), p. 239.

16. Mossner, *Life of David Hume*, p. 568.

17. Hume, "My Own Life," p. 239.

18. Ibid., p. 244.

19. Mossner, *Life of David Hume*, pp. 598–600.

20. David Hume, *An Enquiry Concerning Human Understanding*, ed. L. A. Selby-Bigge (Oxford: Clarendon Press, 1894), sec. 2.

21. Ibid.

22. I owe using the idea of God to illustrate the empirical criterion of meaning to Robert Paul Wolff's *About Philosophy*.

23. David Hume, *A Treatise of Human Nature*, ed. L. A. Selby-Bigge (Oxford: Clarendon Press, 1896), bk. 1, pt. 4, sec. 6.

24. Ibid.

25. Ibid.

26. Hume, *Enquiry Concerning Human Understanding*, bk. 12, pt. 1.

27. Hume, *Treatise*, bk. 1, pt. 4, sec. 2.

28. Ibid.

29. Hume, *Enquiry Concerning Human Understanding*, sec. 7, pt. 1, 2.

30. Hume, *Dialogues Concerning Human Religion*, ed. Norman Kemp-Smith (Edinburgh: Nelson, 1947), pt. 2.

31. Ibid., pt. 11, and *Enquiry Concerning Human Understanding*, sec. 1.

32. *Dialogues*, pt. 10, 11.

33. Ibid., pt. 7.

34. Ibid.

35. *Treatise*, Bk. II, § III.

36. David Hume, *An Enquiry Concerning the Principles of Morals*, ed. L. A. Selby-Bigge (Oxford: The Clarendon Press, 1894), *Appendix I.*

37. Ibid., § I.

38. Hume, *Treatise*, bk. 2, pt. 3, sec. 3.

39. Hume, *Treatise*, bk. 3, pt. 1, sec. 1.

40. Hume, *An Enquiry Concerning the Principles of Morals*, § I.

41. Hume, *Treatise*, bk. 3, pt. 1, sec. 2.

42. Hume, *An Enquiry Concerning the Principles of Morals, Appendix II.*

43. Ibid.

44. Ibid.

45. Hume, *Dialogues*, pt. 10, 1.

46. Hume, *Treatise*, bk. 1, pt. 4, sec. 7.

47. Hume, *Enquiry Concerning Human Understanding*, pt. 1.

CHAPTER 13
THE FORMALIST:
IMMANUEL KANT

1. In A. D. Lindsay, *Kant* (London: Oxford University Press, 1934), p. 2.

2. Henry Thomas and Dana Lee Thomas, *Living Biographies of Great Philosophers* (Garden City, N.Y.: Blue Ribbon Books, 1941), p. 191.

3. Ben-Ami Scharfstein, *The Philosophers: Their Lives and the Nature of Their Thought* (New York: Oxford University Press, 1980), p. 230.

4. Thomas and Thomas, *Living Biographies*, p. 193.

5. In Josiah Royce, *The Spirit of Modern Philosophy* (Boston: Houghton Mifflin, 1892), p. 108.

6. Scharfstein, *The Philosophers*, pp. 210–30.

7. R. B. Jachmann, in *Immanuel Kant: Sein Leben in Darstellungen von Zietgenossen*, ed. Felix Gross (Berlin: DeutscheBibliothek, 1912), trans. Ben-Ami Scharfstein, 9th letter, pp. 171–73.

8. A. C. Wasianski, in *Immanuel Kant: Sein Leben*, p. 232.

9. Scharfstein, *The Philosophers*, pp. 214–15ff.

10. Thomas and Thomas, *Living Biographies*, p. 198.

11. Immanuel Kant, *Religion Within the Limits of Reason Alone*, trans. T. H. Greene and H. H. Hudson (Chicago: Open Court, 1934), p. xxxiv.

12. Quoted in Will Durant, *The Story of Civilization, vol. 10, Rousseau and Revolution* (New York: Simon & Schuster, 1967), p. 547.

13. Norman Kemp Smith, *Commentary to Kant's "Critique of Pure Reason"* (London: Macmillan, 1923), p. xix.

14. Immanuel Kant, preface to first edition of *Critique of Pure Reason*, trans. Norman Kemp Smith (London: Macmillan, 1929), p. 13.

15. Thomas and Thomas, *Living Biographies*, p. 196.

16. Friedrich Schiller, *Poems in Works* (London, 1901).

17. Crane Brinton, *The Portable Age of Reason Reader* (New York: Viking, 1956), p. 1.

18. W. T. Jones, *A History of Western Philosophy: Kant and the Nineteenth Century*, 2nd ed. rev. (New York: Harcourt Brace Jovanovich, 1975), p. 1.

19. Immanuel Kant, *What Is Enlightenment?*, trans. W. T. Jones, in *Immanuel Kant Werke*, vol. 4, ed. E. Cassirer (Berlin: E. Cassirer, 1922), pp. 169ff.

20. Quoted by Robert Paul Wolff in *About Philosophy*, p. 358.

21. Immanuel Kant, *Prolegomena to Any Future Metaphysics*, trans. Lewis White Beck (Indianapolis: Liberal Arts Press, 1950), introduction, pp. 5–6.

22. See Jones, *Kant and the Nineteenth Century*, pp. 19ff.

23. Immanuel Kant, *Critique of Pure Reason*, 2nd ed., trans. Norman Kemp Smith, unabridged edition (New York: St. Martin's Press, 1929), pp. 41–42.

24. See Immanuel Kant, *Critique of Practical Reason and Other Essays*, trans. Lewis White Beck (Chicago: University of Chicago Press, 1949), p. 8, B, ix.

25. S. Körner, *Kant* (Baltimore: Penguin, 1955), pp. 129ff.

26. Immanuel Kant, *Fundamental Principles of the Metaphysics of Morals*, trans. T. K. Abbott (London: Longmans, Green, 1927), sec. 1, p. 10.

27. Ibid., p. 16.

28. Ibid., p. 17.

29. Ibid., sec. 2, p. 36.

30. Ibid., sec. 1, p. 18.

31. Mary Corey, "Cheating Common for Many," *Redding (Calif.) Record-Searchlight*, May 25, 1990.

32. Kant, *Metaphysics of Morals*, sec. 2, pp. 46–47.

33. H. J. Paton, trans., *Kant's Groundwork of the Metaphysics of Morals*, 3rd ed. (New York: Harper & Row Torchbook, 1964), p. 96.

CHAPTER 14
THE UTILITARIAN:
JOHN STUART MILL

1. Jones, *Kant and the Nineteenth Century*, p. 162.

2. Thomas Malthus, *An Essay on the Principle of Population as It Affects the Future Improvement of Society* (London, 1798), p. 4.

3. John Stuart Mill, "Bentham," 1838, in *On Bentham and Coleridge* (New York: Harper & Row Torchbook, 1962), p. 41.

4. Jeremy Bentham, *An Introduction to Principles of Morals and Legislation* (Oxford: Oxford University Press, 1823 ed.), ch. 1, sec. 1.

5. Ibid., sec. 3.

6. Ibid., sec. 6.

7. Ibid., ch. 4, sec. 5.

8. A. Bain, *John Stuart Mill* (1882; reprint, New York: Augustus M. Kelley, 1966), p. 334.

9. B. Mazlish, *James and John Stuart Mill* (New York: Basic Books, 1975), p. 66.

10. John Stuart Mill, *Autobiography*, ed. J. D. Stillinger (London: Oxford University Press, 1971), pp. 6, 9.

11. John Stuart Mill, *Autobiography* (New York: Columbia University Press, 1924), pp. 21–22.

12. Mill, *Autobiography*, ed. J. D. Stillinger, p. 20.

13. Ibid., p. 33, note 3.

14. Mazlish, *James and John Stuart Mill*, pp. 201–2, and M. St. John Packe, *The Life of John Stuart Mill* (London: Stecker & Warburg, 1954), pp. 66–68.

15. Mill, *Autobiography*, ed. J. D. Stillinger, pp. 32, 33, note 3.

16. Mill, *Autobiography* (Columbia), pp. 97–98.

17. Mill, *Autobiography*, ed. J. D. Stillinger, pp. 83–84.

18. Ibid., p. 85.

19. Mill, *Autobiography* (Columbia), p. 122.

20. John Stuart Mill, "Bentham," in *The Philosophy of John Stuart Mill*, ed. M. Cohen (New York: Random House, Modern Library, 1961), pp. 24–26.

21. Lewis S. Feuer, "John Stuart Mill as a Sociologist: The Unwritten Ethology," in John Stuart Mill, *On Socialism* (1879; reprint, Buffalo, N.Y.: Prometheus Books, 1987), p. 10.

22. Mill, *Autobiography* (Columbia), pp. 180–81.

23. Jeremy Bentham, *The Rationale of Reward*, in *The Works of Jeremy Bentham* (Edinburgh: Tait, 1838–43), pt. 2, sec. 1, p. 253.

24. John Stuart Mill, *Utilitarianism*, Chapter 2, "What Utilitarianism Is," in *The Utilitarians* (Garden City, N.Y.: Dolphin Books, 1961), p. 407.

25. Ibid., pp. 408–9.

26. Ibid., p. 409.

27. Ibid., pp. 410–11.

28. Ibid., p. 418.

29. Ibid., pp. 412–13.

30. Ibid., pp. 414–15.

31. Ibid., p. 415.

32. Ibid., pp. 415ff.

33. Ibid., p. 416.

34. Mill, *Utilitarianism*, chapter 3, p. 437.

35. Mill, *Autobiography* (Columbia), p. 100.

CHAPTER 15
THE MATERIALIST:
KARL MARX

1. Quoted in Isaiah Berlin, *Karl Marx* (New York: Oxford University Press, 1939), p. 73.

2. Condensed from "Karl Marx's Funeral," in Robert Payne, *Marx* (New York: Simon & Schuster, 1968), pp. 500–2.

3. Karl Marx, *Critique of Political Economy*, trans. N. I. Stone, in *Marx and Engels: Selected Works*, vol. 1 (Moscow: Foreign Languages Publishing House, 1955), pp. 362–64.

4. In Sidney Hook, *Towards the Understanding of Karl Marx* (New York: John Day, 1932), pp. 80–81, and "Theses on Feuerbach, III," in *Karl Marx and Friedrich Engels on Religion*, ed. Reinhold Niebuhr (New York: Schocken Books, 1964), p. 70.

5. Karl Marx, *Economic and Philosophic Manuscripts*, trans. T. B. Bottomore, in Erich Fromm, *Marx's Concept of Man* (New York: Ungar, 1961), p. 181.

6. Karl Marx, *Critique of Political Economy*, trans. N. I. Stone (Chicago: C. H. Kerr, 1911), p. 11.

7. Karl Marx and Friedrich Engels, *Manifesto of the Communist Party*, 1888 edition, reprinted in Avrum Stroll and Richard H. Popkin, *Introductory Readings in Philosophy* (New York: Holt, Rinehart and Winston, 1972), p. 412.

8. Ibid., p. 413.

9. Ibid., p. 415.

10. Ibid.,

11. Ibid., pp. 415ff.

12. Ibid., p. 416.

13. Ibid., pp. 416–17.

14. Ibid., p. 418.

15. Karl Marx, *Economic and Philosophic Manuscripts* (1844), in *Writings of the Young Marx on Philosophy and Society*, ed. and trans. Loyd D. Easton and Kurt H. Guddat (Garden City, N.Y.: Anchor Doubleday, 1967), p. 290.

16. Ibid., p. 292.

17. Ibid., p. 294.

18. Herbert Marcuse, *One-Dimensional Man: Studies in the Ideology of Advanced Industrial Society* (Boston: Beacon Press, 1964), pp. x, xiv.

19. Erich Fromm, *The Art of Loving* (1956; reprint, New York: Perennial Library, 1974), pp. 70–71, 72–73, 89.

CHAPTER 16
THE INDIVIDUALIST:
SØREN KIERKEGAARD AND
FRIEDRICH NIETZSCHE

1. Samuel Enoch Stumpf, *Philosophy: History and Problems*, 4th ed., (New York: McGraw-Hill, 1989), bk. 1, p. 475.

2. Søren Kierkegaard, *The Journals of Søren Kierkegaard*, trans. Alexander Dru (New York: Oxford University Press, 1938), p. 94.

3. Søren Kierkegaard, *The Point of View for My Work as an Author*, conclusion (abridged), trans. Walter K. Lowrie, in *A Kierkegaard Anthology*, ed. Robert Bretall (New York: Modern Library, 1946), pp. 337, 339.

4. Kierkegaard, *Journals*, p. 4.

5. Kierkegaard's *Concluding Unscientific Postscript*, trans. D. F. Swenson, L. M. Swenson, and W. K. Lowrie, 1846 edition, in *A Kierkegaard Anthology*, p. 276, and *The Journals of Kierkegaard*, trans. and ed. Alexander Dru (London: Collins, 1958), p. 46.

6. Søren Kierkegaard, *Either/Or, vol. 1, Diaspsalmata*, trans. David F. Swenson, Lillian Marvin Swenson, and Walter Lowrie, in *A Kierkegaard Anthology*, p. 33.

7. William Barrett, *Irrational Man, A Study in Existential Philosophy* (Garden City, N.Y.: Doubleday Anchor, 1958), p. 173.

8. Søren Kierkegaard, "The Individual and the Public," in *The Present Age*, trans. Alexander Dru, in *A Kierkegaard Anthology*, pp. 260–61.

9. Ibid., p. 263.

10. Friedrich Nietzsche, *The Birth of Tragedy*, trans. W. A. Haussmann (New York: Russell & Russell, 1964), p. xvii.

11. In *The Portable Nietzsche*, trans. Walter Kaufmann (New York: Penguin, 1968), pp. 8–9.

12. R. J. Hollingdale, introduction to his translation of *Thus Spake Zarathustra* (Baltimore: Penguin, 1967), p. 26.

13. Friedrich Nietzsche, *Ecce Homo*, quoted in *Thus Spake Zarathustra*, trans. Thomas Cotton (New York: Modern Library, 1967), pp. 18–19.

14. Nietzsche, *Ecce Homo*, in *The Portable Nietzsche*, p. 298.

15. Stefan Zweig, quoted in *The Portable Nietzsche*, p. 104.

16. Quoted in Karl Jaspers, *Nietzsche: An Introduction to the Understanding of His Philosophical Activity* (Tucson: University of Arizona Press, 1965), p. 56.

17. Nietzsche, letter to Franz Overbeck, quoted in Jaspers, *Nietzsche*, p. 87.

18. Friedrich Nietzsche, *The Gay Science*, trans. Walter Kaufmann (New York: Vintage Books, 1974), p. 181.

19. Ibid.

20. Friedrich Nietzsche, *The Will to Power*, trans. Walter Kaufmann and R. J. Hollingdale, ed. Walter Kaufmann (New York: Vintage Books, 1967), pp. 3–4.

21. Nietzsche, *Thus Spoke Zarathustra*, in *The Portable Nietzsche*, pp. 199–200.

22. Nietzsche, *The Gay Science*, p. 279.

23. Quoted in Jaspers, *Nietzsche*, p. 162.

24. Nietzsche, *Thus Spoke Zarathustra*, in *The Portable Nietzsche*, p. 398.

25. Nietzsche, *Toward a Genealogy of Morals*, Kaufmann translation, "Good and Evil Versus Good and Bad," section 10, in *The Portable Nietzsche*, pp. 451–52.

26. Ibid.

27. Nietzsche, *Thus Spoke Zarathustra*, in *The Portable Nietzsche*, pp. 124–28.

CHAPTER 17
THE PRAGMATIST:
WILLIAM JAMES

1. G. W. Allen, *William James: A Biography* (New York: Viking, 1967), p. 134.

2. Ibid., p. 163.

3. Ibid., pp. 168–69.

4. Ralph Barton Perry, *The Thought and Character of William James* (Cambridge, Mass.: Harvard University Press, 1948), p. 386.

5. Allen, *William James*, pp. 214–20.

6. Guy W. Stroh, *American Philosophy from Edwards to Dewey: An Introduction* (Princeton, N.J.: Van Nostrand, 1968), p. 123.

7. Perry, *The Thought and Character of William James*, p. 300.

8. Ibid.

9. Quoted in Robert F. Davidson, *Philosophies Men Live By*, p. 296.

10. Charles Sanders Peirce, *Collected Papers of Charles Sanders Peirce, vol. 5*, ed. Charles Hartshorne and Paul Weiss (Cambridge, Mass.: Harvard University Press, 1931–35), pp. 276ff.

11. Ibid., pp. 284ff.

12. Ibid., p. 6.

13. Ibid., pp. 272–73, 259–62.

14. William James, *The Will to Believe and Other Essays in Popular Philosophy* (1897; reprinted in *Human Immortality: Two Supposed Objections to the Doctrine*, New York: Dover, 1956), pp. 146–47.

15. Ibid., p. 177.

16. William James, *Pragmatism*, 1907 text, in *William James: Writings 1902–1910* (New York: Library of America, 1987), pp. 573ff.

17. Ibid., pp. 489, 490, 491.

18. James, *The Will to Believe*, pp. 28, 30.

19. William James, *Pragmatism* (New York: Longmans, Green, 1907), p. 58.

20. Ibid., pp. 59–64.

21. Ibid., p. 64.

22. William James, "The Dilemma of Determinism," in *The Will to Believe*, p. 150.

23. Ibid., pp. 161–63.

24. William James, "Some Problems in Philosophy," in *The Moral Equivalent of War and Other Essays*, ed. John K. Roth (New York: Harper & Row, 1971), p. 164.

25. William James, "The Dilemma of Determinism," in *The Will to Believe*, pp. 146–47.

26. James, *The Will to Believe*, p. 31.

27. Ibid., pp. 200–1.

28. William James, "Is Life Worth Living?", an address to the Harvard Young Men's Christian Association, published in the *International Journal of Ethics*, October 1895, and in Robert F. Davidson, ed., *The Search for Meaning in Life: Readings in Philosophy* (New York: Holt, Rinehart and Winston, 1962), p. 61.

29. William James, "The Moral Philosopher and Moral Life," in *The Will to Believe*, pp. 211ff.

30. William James, *The Varieties of Religious Experience* (New York: Longmans, Green, 1902), pp. 516–17, 525.

31. James, *The Varieties of Religious Experience*, in *William James: Writings*, 1902–1910, p. 88.

32. Ibid., p. 124.

33. Ibid., p. 127.

34. Ibid., p. 152.

35. Ibid., pp. 213–15.

36. Ibid., p. 310.

37. Ibid., pp. 325ff.

38. Ibid., pp. 349–50.

39. James, "Is Life Worth Living?", p. 53.

CHAPTER 18
THE EXISTENTIALIST: JEAN-PAUL SARTRE AND ALBERT CAMUS

1. Cited in Albert Camus and Jean-Paul Sartre, *Camus and Sartre* (New York: Dell, 1972), p. 71.

2. Jean-Paul Sartre, *The Words*, trans. Bernard Frechtman (New York: Fawcett World Library, 1966), p. 52.

3. Ibid., p. 25.

4. Jean-Paul Sartre, *Nausea*, trans. L. Alexander (New York: New Directions, 1959), p. 171.

5. Ibid., p. 173.

6. Jean-Paul Sartre, *What Is Literature?*, trans. Bernard Frechtman (New York: Philosophical Library, 1949), p. 217.

7. Jean-Paul Sartre, *Critique of Dialectical Reason*, trans. H. E. Barnes (New York: Vintage, 1960), p. 24.

8. Ibid., p. 25.

9. Jean-Paul Sartre, *Existentialism Is a Humanism*, trans. Bernard Frechtman, 1957, in *The Fabric of Existentialism: Philosophical and Literary Sources*, ed. Richard Gill and Ernest Sherman (Englewood Cliffs, N.J.: Prentice-Hall, 1973), p. 523.

10. Ibid., pp. 523–24.

11. Ibid., p. 524.

12. Ibid., pp. 524–25.

13. Ibid., p. 525.

14. See W. T. Jones, *A History of Western Philosophy: The Twentieth Century to Wittgenstein and Sartre*, vol. 5, 2nd ed., rev. (San Diego: Harcourt Brace Jovanovich, 1975), p. 356.

15. Jean-Paul Sartre, *Being and Nothingness*, trans. H. E. Barnes (New York: Philosophical Library, 1956), pp. 476–79.

16. Sartre, *Existentialism Is a Humanism*, p. 522.

17. Ibid.

18. Ibid., pp. 522–23.

19. Ibid., pp. 525–26.

20. Ibid., pp. 526–27.

21. Ibid., p. 527.

22. Ibid.

23. Ibid., p. 528.

24. Albert Camus, *An Absurd Reasoning*, in *The Myth of Sisyphus & Other Essays*, trans. Justin O'Brien (New York: Vintage Books, 1955), p. 5.

25. Ibid., p. 38.

26. Ibid., pp. 3–5.

27. Ibid., pp. 40–41.

28. Camus, *The Myth of Sisyphus*, pp. 89–91.

CHAPTER 19 THE PROPHET: MARTIN LUTHER KING, JR., AND MALCOLM X

1. James M. Washington, ed., *A Testament of Hope: The Essential Writings of Martin Luther*

King, Jr. (San Francisco: Harper & Row, 1986), pp. xviii–xix.

2. Martin Luther King, Jr., *Stride Toward Freedom: The Montgomery Story* (New York: Harper & Row, 1958), p. 29.

3. Washington, *Testament of Hope*, p. xix.

4. Quoted in Sydney E. Ahlstrom, "The Radical Turn in Theology and Ethics: Why It Occurred in the 1960s," *Annals of the American Academy of Political and Social Science 387* (January 1970), p. 10.

5. Lewis F. Powell, Jr., "A Lawyer Looks at Civil Disobedience," *Washington & Lee Law Review 23* (1966), cf. p. 216.

6. Martin Luther King, Jr., *Christian Century 74*, February 6, 1957, p. 166.

7. Martin Luther King, Jr., address to the YMCA and YWCA at UC Berkeley, June 4, 1957, in Washington, *Testament of Hope*, pp. 14–15.

8. Martin Luther King, Jr., "Love, Law and Civil Disobedience," address before the Fellowship of the Concerned, November 16, 1961, in Washington, *Testament of Hope*, p. 45.

9. Ibid., pp. 46–47.

10. Martin Luther King, Jr., "Nonviolence: The Only Road to Freedom," in Washington, *Testament of Hope*, pp. 57–58.

11. Martin Luther King, Jr., "Letter from Birmingham Jail," in Washington, *Testament of Hope*, p. 290.

12. Ibid., pp. 292–93.

13. Ibid., pp. 291–92.

14. Ibid., pp. 295–96.

15. Richard T. Schaefer, *Racial and Ethnic Groups*, 5th ed. (New York: HarperCollins College Publishers), 1993, pp. 210–12.

16. Ibid., p. 210.

17. Malcolm X, *The Autobiography of Malcolm X* (New York: Grove Press, 1964), p. 246.

18. Malcolm X, "Racism: The Cancer That Is Destroying America," written for the *Egyptian Gazette*, August 25, 1964, in *Malcolm X: The Man and His Times*, ed. John Henrik Clarke (New York: The Macmillan Company, 1969), pp. 302–6.

19. Ibid.

20. Malcolm X, "With Mrs. Fannie Lou Hamer" in *Malcolm X Speaks: Selected Speeches and Statements*, ed. George Breitman (New York: Grove Weidenfeld, 1965), pp. 107–8.

21. Ibid., p. 108.

22. Malcolm X, "At The Audubon" in *Malcolm X Speaks*, p. 116.

23. Malcolm X, "To Mississippi Youth" in *Malcolm X Speaks*, pp. 138–39 and 146.

24. Jervis Anderson, "The Public Intellectual," *The New Yorker*, January 17, 1994, p. 40.

25. Cornel West, *Race Matters* (Boston: Beacon Press, 1993), pp. 28–29, 31.

26. Ibid., pp. 104–5.

27. Martin Luther King, Jr., "I Have a Dream," in Washington, *Testament of Hope*, pp. 219–20.

CHAPTER 20 THE FEMINIST: SUSAN MOLLER OKIN AND CAROL GILLIGAN

1. U.S. Department of Education, Center for Education Statistics, Completions in Institutions of Higher Education 1987–1988.

2. Amaury de Riencourt, *Sex and Power in History* (New York: David McKay, 1974), pp. 97ff.

3. Ibid., p. 99.

4. Perictione, *On the Harmony of Women*, Fragment 1, trans. Vicki Lynn Harper in *A History of Women Philosophers*, vol. 1, 600 B.C.–500 A.D., ed. Mary Ellen Waithe (Dordrecht: Martinus Nijhoff Publishers, 1987), pp. 32–34.

5. Mary Ellen Waithe, introduction to the series *A History of Women Philosophers*, vol. 1, p. xi.

6. John Rawls, *A Theory of Justice* (Cambridge, Mass.: Harvard University Press, 1971), p. 21.

7. Ibid., p. 12.

8. Ibid., p. 13.

9. Ibid., pp. 60–61.

10. Ibid., p. 13.

11. Susan Moller Okin, *Justice, Gender, and the Family* (New York: Basic Books, 1989), p. 3.

12. Ibid., p. 8.

13. Ibid., p. 90.

14. Ibid., p. 91.

15. Rawls, *A Theory of Justice*, p. 12.

16. Okin, *Justice, Gender, and the Family*, p. 91.

17. Ibid., pp. 101, and 104–5.

18. Carol Gilligan, *Mapping the Moral Domain: A Contribution of Women's Thinking to Psychological Theory and Education*, ed. Carol Gilligan, Janie Victoria Ward, Jill McLean Taylor, with Betty Baridge (Cambridge, Mass.: Center for the Study of Gender Education and Human Development, distributed by Harvard University Press, 1988), p. v.

19. Rawls, *A Theory of Justice*, p. 490.

20. Ibid., p. 476.

21. See Mary Field Belenky, Blythe McVicker Clinchy, Nancy Rule Goldberger, and Jill Mattuck Tarule, *Women's Ways of Knowing: The Development of Self, Voice, and Mind* (New York: Basic Books, 1986); and Thomas I. White, "Psychology, Gender, and Thinking," Chapter 14 in *Discovering Philosophy* (Englewood Cliffs, N.J.: Prentice-Hall, 1991).

22. Alison M. Jaggar, "Love and Knowledge: Emotion in Feminist Epistemology," in *Women, Knowledge, and Reality: Explorations in Feminist Philosophy*, ed. Ann Garry and Marilyn Pearsall (Boston: Unwin Hyman, 1988), pp. 123ff.

23. Carol Gilligan, *In a Different Voice: Psychological Theory and Women's Development* (Cambridge, Mass.: Harvard University Press, 1982), pp. 1–2.

24. See Carol Gilligan's preface to *Mapping the Moral Domain*.

25. Gilligan, *In a Different Voice*, pp. 104–5.

26. Carol Gilligan, "Moral Orientation and Moral Development," in *Women and Moral Theory*, ed. Eva Feder Kittay and Diane T. Mayers (Totowa, N.J.: Rowman and Littlefield, 1987), pp. 19–33.

27. Marilyn Friedman, "Beyond Caring: The De-Moralization of Gender," in *Science, Morality, and Feminist Theory*, eds. M. Haner and K. Nielsen, *Canadian Journal of Philosophy, Supp. Vol. 13*, 1987, pp. 87–105.

28. Ibid.

29. Ibid.

POSTSCRIPT

1. Epictetus, *Handbook of Epictetus*, trans. Nicholas P. White, pp. 28ff.

GLOSSARY

This Glossary contains all of the terms defined in the margins of the text. The chapter in which the term is defined is indicated in parentheses.

A priori ideas Truths that are not derived from observation or experiment, characterized as being certain, deductive, universally true, and independent of all experience. (See also Innate ideas.) (Ch. 11)

Absolute idealism, see idealism (absolute or Hegelian)

Absurd (the) Albert Camus's term to express the discord, friction, and "bad fit" between humans and the world. (Ch. 18)

Aesthetes Individuals who live according to the doctrines of aestheticism. (Ch. 8)

Aestheticism Amoral form of the pursuit of pleasure that focuses on the worship of beauty and beautiful objects. (Ch. 8)

Aesthetics Branch of philosophy that studies all forms of art. (Ch. 1)

Alienated life Unconscious, unspontaneous, and unfulfilled life; deprived of fundamental conditions necessary for self-actualization. (Ch. 15)

Alienation According to Marx, condition of workers separated from the products of their labor; primarily an objective state, but can also refer to not feeling "at one" with the product of labor. (Ch. 15)

Altruism From Latin for other, the capacity to promote the welfare of others; opposed to egoism. (Ch. 14)

Amoral, see Nonmoral

Anguish Term Sartre uses to describe the awareness that even our most seemingly private and individual choices involve all people; by choosing to be this or that type of person, we create an image of the way others ought to be; not to be confused with Kant's categorical imperative. (Ch. 18)

Apeiron According to Anaximander, the first principle from which all existing things develop, a vast "Indefinite-Infinite"; the aperion is an infinite mass of forces with no specific qualities. (Ch. 3)

Archetypal individual (or paradigmatic individual) A special class of teachers, philosophers, and religious figures whose nature becomes a standard by which a culture judges the "ideal" human being; a rare human being whose very nature represents something elemental about the human condition. (Ch. 5)

Archetype Basic image that represents our conception of the essence of a certain type of person; according to psychologist C. G. Jung, some of these images have been shared by the whole human race from the earliest times. (Ch. 1)

Archetype (philosophical) A philosopher who represents an original or influential point of view in a way that significantly affects philosophers and non-

philosophers: cynic, saint, pessimist, optimist, atheist, rationalist, idealist, and such. (Ch. 1)

Argument from gradation Argument for the existence of God based on the idea that being progresses from inanimate objects to increasingly complex animated creatures, culminating in a qualitatively unique God; Aristotelian argument that forms the basis for the fourth of Aquinas's Five Ways. (Ch. 10)

Argument from motion Attempt to prove the existence of God based on the reasoning that in order to avoid an infinite regress, there must be an Unmoved Mover capable of imparting motion to all other things; Aristotelian argument that forms the basis for the first of Aquinas's Five Ways. (Ch. 10)

Argument from necessity Argument for the existence of God based on the idea that if nothing had ever existed, nothing would always exist; therefore, there is something whose existence is necessary (an eternal something); Aristotelian argument that forms the basis for the third of Aquinas's Five Ways. (Ch. 10)

Ascetic Individual who turns away from pleasure and severely limits all sensual appetites in order to achieve salvation or peace of mind. (Ch. 2)

Atomism Early Greek philosophy developed by Leucippus and Democritus and later refined by Epicurus and Lucretius; materialistic view that the universe consists entirely of empty space and ultimately simple entities that combine to form objects. (Ch. 3)

Atoms From the Greek *atomos*, meaning indivisible, having no parts, or uncuttable; minute material particles; the ultimate material constituents of all things. Atoms have such properties as size, shape, position, arrangement (combination), and motion, but lack qualities like color, taste, temperature, or smell. (Ch. 3)

Authenticity Subjective condition of an individual living honestly and courageously in the moment, refusing to make excuses, and not relying on groups or institutions for meaning and purpose. (Ch. 16)

Axiology Branch of philosophy that studies values in general. (Ch. 1)

Barbarian From a rude "bar-bar" noise used to mock dialects considered crude by the ancient Athenians; originally referred to other cultures considered "less than human" or uncivilized. (Ch. 4)

Belief Conviction or trust that a claim is true; an individual's subjective mental state; distinct from knowledge. (Ch. 1)

Belief (mere) A conviction that something is true for which the only evidence is the sincerity of the believer. (Ch. 1)

Bodhisattva An enlightened being who voluntarily postpones his own nirvana in order to help all other conscious life forms find "supreme release"; not a savior. (Ch. 2)

Bourgeoisie All those who do not produce anything yet who own and control the means of production. (Ch. 15)

Bundle theory of the self Humean theory that there is no fixed "self," but that the self is merely a "bundle of perceptions"; a self is merely an habitual way of discussing certain perceptions. (Ch. 12)

Capitalism Economic system in which the means of production and distribution are all (or mostly) privately owned and operated for profit under fully competitive conditions; tends to be accompanied by concentration of wealth and growth of great corporations. (Ch. 15)

Categorical imperative According to Kant, a command that is universally binding on all rational creatures; the ultimate foundation of all moral law: "Act as if the maxim of thy action were to become a universal law of nature."

Character From the Greek *charakter*, a word derived from *charassein*, "to make sharp" or "to engrave," character refers to the sum total of a person's traits, including behavior, habits, likes and dislikes, capacities, potentials, and so on; a key element of Aristotelian ethics and psychology, meaning the overall (generally fixed) nature or tone of a person's habits. (Ch. 7)

Civil disobedience Public resistance to injustices in order that society be informed and educated, and thereby re-formed; civil disobedience differs from revolution, rebellion, and riot in that it takes deliberate care to respect the "legitimate social order" while publicly challenging specifically identified injustices on moral grounds. (Ch. 19)

Co-opted In Marxian social analysis, workers are co-opted when they identify with the economic system that oppresses them by confusing the remote possibility of accumulating wealth with their actual living and working conditions; being co-opted also refers to anyone who is somehow convinced to further interests that are to her or his ultimate disadvantage. (Ch. 15)

Cogito, ergo sum Latin version of Descartes' famous sentence "I think, therefore I am." (Ch. 11)

Coherence theory of truth Truth test in which new or unclear ideas are evaluated in terms of rational or logical consistency and in relation to already established truths. (Ch. 11)

Correspondence theory of truth Truth test that holds that an idea (or belief or thought) is true if whatever it refers to actually exists (corresponds to a fact). (Ch. 12)

Cosmological argument From the Greek work *kosmos* meaning world, universe, or orderly structure, argument for the existence of God that since it is impossible for any natural thing to be the complete and sufficient source of its own existence, there must be an Uncaused Cause capable of imparting existence to all other things; Aristotelian argument that forms the basis for the second of Aquinas's Five Ways. (Ch. 10)

Cosmology In philosophy, the study of the universe as a rationally ordered system or cosmos; sometimes used to refer to metaphysics in general; in science, the study of the nature and physical origins of the universe itself, astronomy. (Ch. 3)

Cosmos Greek term for *ordered whole*; first used by the Pythagoreans to characterize the universe as an ordered whole consisting of harmonies of contrasting elements. (Ch. 3)

Critical philosophy Kant's term for his effort to assess the nature and limits of "pure reason" unadulterated by experience in order to identify the actual relationship of the mind to knowledge. (Ch. 13)

Cynic Individual who lives an austere, unconventional life based on Cynic doctrine. (Ch. 9)

Cynicism Philosophy based on the belief that the very essence of civilization is corrupt and that civilization destroys individuals by making them soft and subject to the whims of fortune. (Ch. 9)

Despair Sartrean term referring to the refusal to base choices and actions on possibilities; the condition of confining ourselves to what directly falls under our present influence and control. (Ch. 18)

Determinism Belief that everything that happens must happen exactly the way it does because all matter is governed by cause and effect and follows laws of nature. (Ch. 17)

Dialectic (Hegelian) According to Hegel, a three-step pattern in which an original idea, known as a thesis, struggles with a contrary idea, known as the antithesis, to produce a new synthesis that combines elements of both. (Ch. 15)

Dialectic (Socratic), see Socratic method

Dialectical process (Hegelian) Internally governed evolutionary cycle in which progress occurs as the result of a struggle between two opposing conditions. (Ch. 15)

Dialogical philosophy Philosophy that addresses fundamental human concerns in a universal voice that transcends the particularities of our lives without trivializing them; speaks from and to both the heart and mind. (Ch. 20)

Dualism Any philosophical position that divides existence into two completely distinct, independent, unique substances. (Ch. 3; see also Ch. 11)

Dualism (epistemological) The view that knowing consists of two distinct aspects: the knower and the known. (Ch. 12)

Economic (as used by Marx) Term Marx used to refer to the complete array of social relationships and arrangements that constitute a particular social order. (Ch. 15)

Egocentric predicament Problem generated by epistemological dualism: If all knowledge comes in the form of my own ideas, how can I verify the existence of anything external to them? (Ch. 12)

Egoism (Socratic) Socratic belief that human beings always seek what they perceive to be their own welfare and cannot deliberately do otherwise (psychological egoism), and that they ought to seek only their own welfare (ethical egoism); for Socrates, the welfare in question was always the welfare of the soul. (Ch. 5)

Eightfold path Buddha's prescription for rooting out suffering: (1) right understanding; (2) right purpose; (3) right speech; (4) right conduct; (5) right livelihood; (6) right effort; (7) right mindfulness; (8) right meditation. (Ch. 2)

Empirical criterion of meaning Meaningful ideas are those that can be traced back to sense experience (impressions); beliefs that cannot be reduced to sense experience are not ideas at all, but meaningless utterances. (Ch. 12)

Empiricism Belief that all knowledge is ultimately derived from the senses (experience) and that all ideas can be traced to sense data. (Ch. 12)

Entelechy From the Greek for "having its end within itself": according to Aristotle, an inner urge that drives all things to blossom into their own unique selves; inner order or design which governs all natural processes. (Ch. 7)

Epicurean fallacy Error of confusing the active pursuit of specialized pleasures with Epicurus's philosophy of disciplined moderation and restraint. (Ch. 8)

Esse est percipi Latin for Berkeley's belief that "to be is to be perceived." (Ch. 12)

Ethic of care Carol Gilligan's term for ethical theories that stress responsibilities and relationships over rules, and that are based on "care reasoning," which depends on a sense of connectedness or relationship, and that is the opposite of objective detachment. (Ch. 20)

Ethic of justice Carol Gilligan's term for ethical theories that stress rules over responsibilities and relationships, and that are based on an expression of the traditional impersonal, rationalistic, objective, detached model of knowing. (Ch. 20)

Ethnocentrism From Greek roots meaning "the race is the center"; belief that the customs and beliefs of one's own culture are inherently superior to all others. (Ch. 4)

Eudaimonia Often translated as happiness; term Aristotle used to refer to fully realized existence; state of being fully aware, vital, alert. (Ch. 7)

Existentialism Term used to refer to any philosophy that emphasizes fundamental questions of meaning and choice as they affect existing individuals; existential themes include choice, freedom, identity, alienation, inauthenticity, despair, and awareness of our own mortality. (Ch. 16)

False authority (fallacy of) The error in reasoning that results from accepting the word of experts who are speaking outside their proper fields or uncritically relying on the testimony of others without checking it against our own experiences and reason. (Ch. 11)

Feminist A person who believes in the fundamental equality of women and men and actively contributes to the struggle to achieve such equality.

Forces of production In philosophical Marxism, the forces of production are factories, equipment, technology, knowledge, and skill; a part of the substructure of society. (Ch. 15)

Forlornness Jean-Paul Sartre's term for his belief that we face life alone, without God, without certainty, with only absolute freedom and the responsibility that accompanies it. (Ch. 18)

Forms, see platonic forms

Four noble truths Foundation of Buddha's teachings: (1) to exist is to suffer; (2) self-centeredness is the chief cause of human suffering; (3) the cause of suffering can be understood and rooted out; (4) suffering can be alleviated by following the Eightfold Path. (Ch. 2)

Functionalist theory of morality Moral position that right and wrong can be understood only in terms of their effect on anything's natural function; each kind of thing has a natural purpose or function. (Ch. 6)

Hedonism From the Greek root for pleasure, the general term for any philosophy that says pleasure = good and pain = evil. (Ch. 8)

Hedonism (Cyrenaic) Philosophy that advocates the unreflective pursuit of intense, immediate pleasure; makes no qualitative distinctions among pleasures. (Ch. 8)

Hedonism (ethical) The belief that though it is possible to deliberately avoid pleasure or choose pain, it is morally wrong to do so. (Ch. 8)

Hedonism (psychological) The belief that all decisions are based on considerations of pleasure and pain because it is psychologically impossible for human beings to do otherwise. (Ch. 8)

Hedonistic paradox The harder we try to be happy, the harder it is to be happy. (Ch. 8)

Hedonistic utility Principle of maximizing pleasure and minimizing pain. (Ch. 8)

Hypothetical imperatives Propositions that tell us what to do under specific, variable conditions. (Ch. 13)

Idealism (absolute or Hegelian) Term used to identify Hegel's particular form of German Idealism; a monistic philosophy which is based on an all-encompassing Absolute Spirit that is self-actualizing into perfection; Reality (Absolute Mind or Absolute Spirit) is independent of any individual's mind; not to be confused with Berkeleian idealism (immaterialism), in which objective reality is said to exist in the individual's mind. (Ch. 15)

Idealism (immaterialism) Belief that only ideas (mental states) exist; the material world is a fiction, it does not exist. (Ch. 12)

Immoral Morally wrong, bad, or not right; a moral value judgment or prescriptive claim. (Ch. 13)

Inauthenticity Condition that results when the nature and needs of the individual are ignored, denied, and obscured, or sacrificed for institutions, abstractions, or groups. (Ch. 16)

Inductive reasoning Reasoning pattern that proceeds from the particular to the general or from some to all and results in generalized rules or principles established with degrees of probability. (Ch. 12)

Innate ideas Ideas present in the mind at birth. (Ch. 11)

Instrumental theory of morality Moral position that right and wrong must be determined by the consequences of acts; right and wrong viewed as means (instruments) for getting something else. (Ch. 6)

Intellectualism Term used to refer to the claim that behavior is always controlled by beliefs about what is good and the means to that good. (Ch. 5)

Irony Communication on at least two levels, a literal or obvious level and a hidden or real level; favored by Socrates as a technique for keeping his listeners alert and involved. (Ch. 5)

Justice (Platonic) Excellence of function for the whole; in a just society, individuals perform their natural functions according to class; in a just individual, reason rules the spirit and the appetites. (Ch. 6)

Kantian formalism (also known as Kantian idealism and transcendental idealism) Theory that knowledge is the result of the interaction between the mind and sensation, structured by regulative ideas called categories. (Ch. 13)

Knowledge Justified true belief. (Ch. 1)

Knowledge (a posteriori) Empirical knowledge derived from sense experience and not regarded as universal because the conditions under which it is acquired change, perceivers vary, and factual relationships change. (Ch. 11)

Knowledge (a priori) Derived from reason without reference to sense experience. Examples include: "All triangles contain 180 degrees" and "Every event has a cause." (Ch. 11)

Knowledge (practical) Consists of skills needed to do things like play the piano, use a bandsaw, remove a tumor, or bake a cake. (Ch. 1)

Knowledge (theoretical) The accurate compilation and assessment of factual and systematic relationships. (Ch. 1)

Law of contradiction (sometimes known as the law of noncontradiction) Rule of inference that says no statement can be both true and false at the same time and under the same conditions. (Ch. 10)

Law of noncontradiction, see Law of contradiction

Logos One of the richest and most complex terms in ancient philosophy, associated meanings include: intelligence, speech, discourse, thought, reason, word, meaning; the root of *log* (record), *logo, logic*, and the *ology* suffix found in terms like sociology and physiology; according to Heraclitus, the rule according to which all things are accomplished and the law which is found in all things; according to the Stoics, World Reason, also referred to as Cosmic Mind, God, Zeus, Nature, Fate: the force that governs the world. (Ch. 3; see also Ch. 9)

Logos (Stoic) According to Stoic doctrine, World Reason, also referred to as Cosmic Mind, God, Zeus, Nature, Providence, Cosmic Meaning, and Fate; force that governs the universe. (Ch. 9; see also Ch 3)

Master morality In Nietzschean philosophy, the *aesthetic* honor code of the overman; morality that looks only to the authentic individual (overman) for values that transcend the slave's good-evil dichotomy with: glorious-degrading; honorable-dishonorable; refined-vulgar, and so on; "good" equals "noble" and "evil" equals "vulgar." (Ch. 16)

Materialism (also known as behaviorism, mechanism, or reductionism): belief that everything is composed of matter (and energy), and can be explained by physical laws, that all human activity can be understood as the natural behavior of matter according to mechanical laws, and that thinking is merely a complex form of behaving: the body is a fleshy machine. (Ch. 11)

Materialism (Marxian) Form of social determinism based on a reciprocal relationship between individuals and their environment; distinguished from strict materialism and hard determinism. (Ch. 15)

Mean From the Latin *medius*, the midpoint between two other points; for Aristotle, moral virtue was characterized as a mean between too little (deficiency) and too much (excess). (Ch. 7)

Means of production In philosophical Marxism, the means of production include natural resources such as water, coal, land, and so forth; a part of the substructure of society. (Ch. 15)

Mere belief, see Belief (mere)

Methodic doubt Cartesian strategy of deliberately doubting everything it is possible to doubt in the least degree so that what remains will be known with absolute certainty. (Ch. 11)

Monism General name for the belief that everything consists of only one, ultimate, unique substance such as matter or spirit. (Ch. 3; see also Ch. 11)

Moral From the Latin moralis, meaning "custom," "manner," or "conduct," refers to what people consider good or bad, right or wrong; used descriptively as a contrast to amoral or nonmoral and prescriptively as a contrast to immoral. (Ch. 13)

Mysticism From the Greek root mystes, meaning "initiate of the secret mysteries of life and the higher realities," belief that ordinary levels of understanding and ordinary language cannot grasp the "ultimate something" variously referred to as the One, Logos, Nature, God, Tao, the Way, the Great Spirit, and so forth. (Ch. 2; see also Ch. 17)

Mysticism (Jamesean) According to James, a way of thinking that views everything in terms of a powerful religious experience; cognitive result of being reborn. (Ch. 17; see also Ch. 2)

Mystification Use of cloudy abstractions to create elaborate metaphysical systems that distract us from concrete material reality. (Ch. 15)

Naturalism Belief that reality consists of the natural world; denial of the existence of a separate supernatural order of reality; belief that nature follows orderly, discoverable laws. (Ch. 7)

Nihilism From Latin for nothing; belief that the universe lacks meaning and purpose. (Ch. 16)

Nirvana Annihilation of the ego; a state of emptiness or "no-thing-ness"; "pure consciousness" that leads to release from suffering while remaining conscious. (Ch. 2)

Nonmoral (amoral) Not pertaining to moral, a value-neutral descriptive claim or classification. (Ch. 13)

Noumenal reality Kant's term for reality as it is, independent of our perceptions; what is commonly called "objective reality." (Ch. 13)

Nous From the Greek for mind; according to Anaxagoras, "the all-pervading Mind which imposes (brings about) an intelligible pattern in an otherwise unintelligible universe"; a material being that affects all things without being in them. (Ch. 3)

Ontological argument An attempt to prove the existence of God either by referring to the meaning of the word *God* when it is understood a certain way or by referring to the purportedly unique quality of the concept of God. (Ch. 11)

Ontology From the Greek root *onta* meaning "the really existing things" or "true reality"; the study of "being" itself as opposed to the study of particular existing things; branch of philosophy which deals with the order and structure of reality in the broadest possible sense. (Ch. 3)

Original position John Rawls's imaginary setting in which we can identify the fundamental principles of justice from an objective, impartial perspective, as rational agents, rather than as "interested parties"; similar to the "state of nature" in the social contract theories of Thomas Hobbes, Jean-Jacques Rousseau, and John Locke. (Ch. 20)

Overman Nietzsche's "higher type," a more-than-human being that will emerge only by overcoming the false idols of conventional morality and religion; announced in *Thus Spake Zarathustra*. (Ch. 16)

Paradigmatic individual, see Archetypal individual

Pessimism Schopenhauer's theory that life is disappointing and that for every satisfied desire, new desires emerge; our only hope is detachment and withdrawal. (Ch. 16)

Phenomenal reality Kant's term for the world as we experience it. (Ch. 13)

Phenomenology Philosophical method of analysis developed by Edmund Husserl; using purely descriptive statements, phenomenology tries to provide a "descriptive analysis" of consciousness in all its forms, stressing the concrete rather than the abstract and experienced facts rather than theory, in order to reveal the essence of human consciousness. (Ch. 18)

Philosophical archetype, see Archetype (philosophical)

Philosophy From Greek roots meaning "the love of wisdom." (Ch. 1)

Philosophy (political) Branch of philosophy concerned with the state and issues of sovereignty. (Ch. 1)

Philosophy (social) Branch of philosophy concerned with social institutions and relations. (Ch. 1)

Platonic forms Independently existing, nonspatial, nontemporal "somethings" known only through thought and that cannot be known through the senses; independently existing objects of thought; that which makes a particular thing uniquely and essentially what it is. (Ch. 6)

Platonic virtue, see Virtue (Platonic)

Pluralism The belief that there exist many realities or substances. (Ch. 3; see also Ch. 11)

Pneuma According to Anaximenes, the ultimate, pervasive spirit that holds the world together; all things are produced by either "rarefaction" of the *pneuma*, which creates fire, or condensation of the *pneuma*, which creates in order of density wind, cloud, water, earth, and stone. (Ch. 3)

Practical imperative (or principle of dignity) Kant's formulation of the Categorical Imperative based on the concept of dignity: "Act in such a way that you always treat humanity, whether in your own person or in the person of another, never simply as a means but always at the same time as an end."

Practical knowledge, see Knowledge (practical)

Pragmatic paradox Pragmatism works only if we believe that our ideas are true according to nonpragmatic criteria. (Ch. 17)

Pragmatism From the Greek for deed; ideas have meaning or truth value to the extent that they produce practical results and effectively further our aims; empirically based philosophy that defines knowledge and truth in terms of practical consequences. (Ch. 17; see also Ch. 4)

Principle of utility, see Utility (principle of)

Principles of reason (or rules of inference) Principles such as the law of contradiction that define the limits of rationality by their very structure and that cannot be rationally refuted since we rely on them in order to reason. (Ch. 10)

Problem of evil If God can prevent the suffering of the innocent, yet chooses not to, He is not good. If God chooses to prevent the suffering, but cannot, He is not omnipotent. If God cannot recognize the suffering of the innocent, He is not wise. (Ch. 10; see also Ch. 12)

Proletariat All those whose labor produces goods and provides essential services, yet who do not own the means of production. (Ch. 15)

Prophet From the Greek roots *pro* (before) and *phanai* (to speak), originally a prophet was a person who spoke with divine guidance and who was said to be able to predict the course of events; prophets functioned as religious leaders and teachers, as advisers to rulers, and cried out for justice and mercy in the face of tyranny. (Ch. 2; see also Ch. 19)

Psyche Greek for soul; in today's terms, combination of mind and soul, including capacity for reflective thinking. (Ch. 5)

Rational discourse The interplay of carefully argued ideas; the use of reason to order, clarify, and identify reality and truth according to agreed upon standards of verification. (Ch. 3)

Reason (practical) According to Kant, moral function of reason that produces religious feelings and intuitions based on knowledge of moral conduct. (Ch. 13)

Reason (theoretical) According to Kant, a function of reason confined to the empirical, phenomenal world. (Ch. 13)

Reductio ad absurdum From the Latin for "reduce to absurdity"; form of argument that refutes an opponent's position by showing that accepting it leads to absurd, unacceptable, or contradictory conclusions because: (1) accepting it leads to a logical contradiction, or (2) it leads to a logical conclusion that is somehow obviously ridiculous because it offends either our reason or common sense. (Ch. 3; for examples see Zeno's Paradoxes in Ch. 3 and Hume's critique of religion in Ch. 12.)

Relationships of production In philosophical Marxism, relationships of production consist of who does what, who owns what, and how this affects members of both groups; a part of the substructure of society (Ch. 15)

Relativism Belief that knowledge is determined by specific qualities of the observer including age, race, gender, cultural conditioning. (Ch. 4)

Ressentiment French for resentment: term used in Nietzschean philosophy for a deep form of psychically polluting resentment that generates slave morality; the dominant emotion of the underman. (Ch. 16)

Rules of inference, see Principles of reason

Sage Derived from the Latin *sapiens*, meaning wise; in Asian traditions, an archetypal figure who combines religious inspiration with a love of wisdom; gurus, *yogis*, and Zen *roshis* are examples of sages; in Western traditions, the *sophos* and Hasidic *rebbe* fulfill the role of sage. (Ch. 2)

Saintliness According to James, a way of life devoted exclusively to a heightened religious consciousness; behavioral result of being reborn. (Ch. 17)

Scholasticism Christian philosophy that dominated medieval Europe from about a.d. 1000 to 1300, stressing logical and linguistic analysis of texts and arguments in order to produce a systematic statement and defense of Christian beliefs. (Ch. 10)

Self-fulfilling prophecy A belief that affects events in such a way that it causes itself to be true; such as the student who does poorly on an exam because she expects to fail it. (Ch. 17)

Shaman A specialist in techniques for making contact with the sacred forces that govern the world by going "outside of" him- or herself; in tribal cultures the shaman usually receives wisdom through a public initiation ceremony that involves "ritualized suffering" and ecstatic trance, though in some cultures the gods come to the shaman. (Ch. 2)

Skeptic From the Greek *skeptesthai*, "to consider or examine," a person who demands clear, observable, undoubtable evidence before accepting any knowledge claim as true.

Slave morality In Nietzschean philosophy, a distortion of the will to power in which the characteristics of the inferior type (underman) are praised as virtues, while the characteristics of the superior type (overman) are condemned as arrogance and coldheartedness; a morality of inhibitions, equality, restrictive duties, and "bad conscience." (Ch. 16)

Socratic egoism, see Egoism, Socratic

Socratic method (or socratic dialectic) Question-and-answer technique perfected by Socrates to draw truth out of his pupils. (Ch. 5)

Sophistry The teachings and practices of the original Sophists; modern usage refers to subtle, plausible, but fallacious reasoning used to persuade rather than discover truth. (Ch. 4)

Sophists Fifth-century b.c. paid teachers of rhetoric; relativists who taught that might makes right, truth is a matter of appearance and convention, and power is the ultimate value. (Ch. 4)

Sophos Sage or wise man; term applied to the first philosophers; from the Greek word for wise. (Ch. 3)

Sophrosyne Wisdom as moderation; hitting the mark; quality of finding the mean between excess and deficiency. (Ch. 7)

Species-life Fully human life lived productively and consciously; not alienated. (Ch. 15)

Stoic Individual who attempts to live according to Stoic doctrine. (Ch. 9)

Stoicism Philosophy that counsels self-control, detachment, and acceptance of one's fate as identified by the objective use of reason. (Ch. 9)

Subjectivism Belief that we can know only our own sensations, not their objective causes. (Ch. 8)

Substructure of society In philosophical Marxism, the material substructure or base of society determines the nature of all social relationships, as well as religions, art, philosophies, literature, science, and government. (Ch. 15)

Superstructure of society According to philosophical Marxism, the superstructure of a culture consists of the ideas and institutions (religious beliefs, educational systems, philosophies, the arts, and such) compatible with and produced by the material substructure of the society. (Ch. 15)

Surplus value Term Marx used to refer to the capital accumulated by owners; the result of keeping prices higher than the costs of production at the expense of workers. (Ch. 15)

Tabula rasa Latin expression for a "clean slate," used by John Locke to challenge the possibility of innate ideas by characterizing the mind at birth as a blank tablet or clean slate. (Ch. 12)

Tao Literally *way* or *path* in the sense of "the way to go," fundamental principle of the universe according to Taoist philosophy; sometimes referred to as Mother, Father, Nature, One, the Nameless. (Ch. 2)

Techne From the Greek for art, skill, craft, technique, trade, system, or method of doing something; root of English words such as *technique*, *technical*, and *technology*;

term Socrates used when he asserted that virtue (*arete*) is knowledge or wisdom (*techne*). (Ch. 5)

Teleological argument Also called the argument from design, this widely known argument for the existence of God claims that the universe manifests order and purpose that can only be the result of a conscious intelligence (God); Aristotelian argument that forms the basis for the fifth of Aquinas's Five Ways and the basis of William Paley's watchmaker argument. (Ch. 10)

Teleological thinking Way of explaining things in terms of their ultimate goals; understanding things functionally in terms of the relationship of the parts to the whole. (Ch. 7)

Theology From the Greek *theos* (God) and *logos* (study of), talking about God or the study or science of God. (Ch. 10)

Thought experiment A way of using our imaginations to test a hypothesis; we "think" rather than field-test a hypothesis, using reasoned imagination to provide the necessary conditions for the experiment, and carefully reasoning out the most likely consequences according to our hypothesis. (Ch. 20)

Timeless questions Questions concerning ultimate values, general principles, and the very nature of reality, knowledge, justice, happiness, truth, God, beauty, and morality; asked in virtually every culture. (Ch. 1)

Timely questions Questions involving issues that are important to a particular time or place. (Ch. 1)

Tragic optimism According to Nietzsche, the sense of joy and vitality that accompanies the superior individual's clear-sighted imposition of his own freely chosen values on a meaningless world. (Ch. 16)

Tyranny Form of government in which all power rests in a single individual, known as the tyrant. (Ch. 6)

Ultimate ends Goals that are valued for their own sake, not as means to something else. (Ch. 1)

Underman Term Nietzsche used for the type of person who cannot face being alone in a Godless universe, an inferior individual seeking safety and identity in a group or from another; characterized by resentment and hypocrisy. (Ch. 16)

Utility (principle of) Always act to promote the greatest happiness for the greatest number. (Ch. 14)

Utopia Term for a perfect or ideal society derived from Sir Thomas More's 1516 novel of the same name; the word was created from the Greek root meaning nowhere. (Ch. 6)

Veil of ignorance John Rawls's mechanism for imaginatively entering into the original position by avoiding all personal considerations in the process of determining principles of justice; the veil of ignorance is a problem-solving device that prevents us from knowing our social status, what property we own, what we like and don't like, how intelligent we are, what our talents and strengths are, and so on. (Ch. 20)

Virtue From the Greek *arete*, meaning "that at which something excels," or "excellence of function." (Ch. 5)

Virtue (Platonic) Excellence of function. (Ch. 6)

Void (the) Democritus's term for no-thing (no-bodies); empty space in Atomist theory. (Ch. 3)

Will to power Nietzsche's term for what he thought is a universal desire to control others and impose our values on them. (Ch. 16)

Willed ignorance An attitude of indifference to the possibility of error or enlightenment that holds on to beliefs regardless of the facts. (Ch. 1)

Wisdom General knowledge of what does and does not produce human happiness, including the difference between right and wrong combined with the desire and ability to act in basic accord with that knowledge. (Ch. 1)

Wu wei Taoist principle of "inaction," a warning against "unnatural" or "demanding" action which runs counter to Tao and so produces disharmony or violence. (Ch. 2)

Yang One of two inseparable but opposing forces whose continual interaction imbues all of nature, according to Taoist thought: active, strong, positive, light, and constructive. (Ch. 2)

Yin One of two inseparable but opposing forces whose continual interaction imbues all of nature, according to Taoist thought: passive, weak, negative, dark, and destructive. (Ch. 2)

BIBLIOGRAPHY OF INTERESTING SOURCES

This list highlights some especially well-written, interesting, and important books that supplement the material covered in *Archetypes of Wisdom*, second edition. Not only are they philosophically valuable, most of them are "good reads." As a general rule, this list does not duplicate the main philosophical sources cited in the text, since these are fully annotated in the Notes section. Regardless of their publication dates, the vast majority of works listed below are available in many large bookstores and college libraries. If your college library does not own a particular book, it can probably get it for you through an interlibrary loan arrangement.

GENERAL SOURCES

Angeles, Peter A. *Dictionary of Philosophy*. New York: Barnes & Noble Books, 1981. A clear, readable, and comprehensive dictionary useful for instructors and students.

Copleston, Frederick, S. J. *A History of Philosophy*. New York: Doubleday, Image edition, 1985. Copleston's strength is his ability to summarize and explain other philosophers' ideas without intruding. His own editorial comments are always clearly identified. An excellent history, now available in a cumbersome, but affordable, three-book edition. The individual nine-volume series is still available in most large bookstores; these smaller books are much easier to handle.

The Encyclopedia of Philosophy. Paul Edwards, editor in chief. New York: Macmillan & The Free Press, 1967. Two versions of this indispensable source are available, the regular edition of eight separate volumes and a four-volume "student edition" that contains exactly the same material. Though some of the articles in the *Encyclopedia* can be difficult for novice philosophers, this is an excellent source of general information regarding philosophers and philosophical issues and arguments. For those interested in building a personal library, the Book-of-the-Month Club occasionally offers the student edition as a premium for new members for about thirty dollars plus shipping—a true bargain (if you use your membership wisely).

Jones, W. T. *A History of Western Philosophy*. 2nd ed. New York: Harcourt Brace Jovanovich, 1970. This four-volume series is narrower in scope than Copleston's but more detailed in its treatment of philosophical issues. Sophisticated but valuable resource for the serious student.

Scharfstein, Ben-Ami. *The Philosophers: Their Lives and the Nature of Their Thought*. Oxford: Oxford University Press, 1989. Fascinating blend of philosophy, history, and psychology.

Stumpf, Samuel Enoch. *Philosophy: History & Problems*. 4th ed. New York: McGraw-Hill, 1989. This is really two books in one volume. The first is Stumpf's comprehensive history of philosophy, the second is an excellent anthology of original sources. Another good resource.

CHAPTER 1 PHILOSOPHY AND WISDOM

Berry, Wendell. *What Are People For?* Berkeley, Calif: North Point Press, 1990. Elegant, powerful essays reflecting rare moral power. The opening essay on damage reminds me of some of the finest Taoist literature.

Kaplan, Abraham. *In Pursuit of Wisdom*. Beverly Hills, Calif.: Glencoe Press, 1977. Reprint. Lanham, Md.: University Press of America, 1988. The first chapter on philosophy and last section on wisdom reflect the mind of a true lover of wisdom. Kaplan blends fine writing and a comprehensive vision of philosophy in the original sense that appeals equally to head and heart.

Klagsbrun, Francine. *Voices of Wisdom: Jewish Ideals and Ethics for Everyday Living*. New York: Pantheon, 1980. Fascinating collection of sayings, anecdotes, and legends of universal appeal. A browser's delight.

Needleman, Jacob. *The Heart of Philosophy*. New York: Knopf, 1982. Needleman's adventures teaching philosophy through dialogue to high school students and their parents produced intriguing ideas about education, society, and the need for philosophy.

Rand, Ayn. *Philosophy: Who Needs It*. The Ayn Rand Library, vol. 1. New York: Signet, 1982. Rand ranks as one of the few best-selling philosophical writers of recent years. In this collection of essays she argues for her own objectivist philosophy. Even when her argument is weak, her confrontational style raises questions about the value of philosophy rarely asked in popular literature.

The following available books present entertaining, often funny, thought-provoking portraits and anecdotes of gurus, sages, wise people:

Black Elk, *The Sacred Pipe: Black Elk's Account of the Seven Rites of Ogala Sioux*. Edited by Joseph E. Brown. New York: Penguin, 1988.

Black Elk, Wallace, and William S. Lyon. *Black Elk: The Sacred Ways of a Lakota*. San Francisco: Harper & Row, 1990.

Boyd, Doug, *Rolling Thunder*. New York: Dell, 1974.

——— *Swami*. New York: Paragon House, 1990.

Campbell, Joseph, with Bill Moyers. *The Power of Myth*. New York: Doubleday, 1988.

Capra, Fritjof. *Uncommon Wisdom*. New York: Simon & Schuster, 1988.

Nisker, Wes "Scoop." *Crazy Wisdom*. Berkeley, Calif.: Ten Speed Press, 1990.

Shah, Idries. *The Exploits of the Incomparable Mulla Nasrudin*. New York: Dutton, 1966.

CHAPTER 2 THE SAGE: BUDDHA AND LAO-TZU

Bankei. *The Unborn*. Translated by Norman Waddell. San Francisco: North Point Press, 1984. Delightful collections of talks and sermons by a seventeenth-century Japanese sage. Bankei's wisdom is funny, profound, and relevant. An excellent introduction to Buddhism without technical language.

Benares, Camden. *Zen Without Zen Masters*. Berkeley, Calif.: And/Or Press, 1977. Bizarre collection of Buddhist-like tales, most with punch lines. A kind of stand-up comedy approach to philosophy.

Buddha. *The Teachings of the Buddha*. Rev. ed. Tokyo: Bukkyo Deudo Kyokai, 1976. Good, standard collection.

Chan, Wing-Tsit, trans. and comp. *A Source Book in Chinese Philosophy*. Princeton, N.J.: Princeton University Press. A bargain in more ways than one. Chan's collection and commentaries are among the best introductions to Chinese philosophy. Modestly priced, worth having.

Hesse, Hermann. *Siddhartha*. Translated by Hilda Rosner. Toronto: Bantam, 1951. An easy-to-read fictionalized account of the Buddha's life by a gifted storyteller.

Hoff, Benjamin. *The Tao of Pooh*. New York: Penguin, 1982. Delightful use of Winnie-the-Pooh as an introduction to Taoism. A joy to read.

Huxley, Aldous. *Perennial Philosophy*. New York: Harper Colophon Books, 1945. Huxley's attempt to demonstrate the principles of a universal (perennial) spiritual philosophy yields a rich source of offbeat quotes from a wide range of traditions. Heavy on Hinduism and transcendentalism.

Lao-tzu. *Tao Te Ching: A New English Version*. Translated by Stephen Mitchell. New York: Harper & Row, 1988. Interesting transliteration of the Taoist classic containing contemporary terms and use of feminine imagery for the Tao. Nicely produced, attractively designed.

———*Te-Tao Ching: A New Translation Based on the Recently Discovered Ma-wang-tui Texts*. Translated with introduction and commentary by Robert G. Henricks. New York: Ballantine Books, 1989. This one's a treasure. It's scholarly, accessible, and pleasing to the eye.

——— *The Wisdom of Laotse*. Translated and edited by Lin Yutang. New York: Modern Library, 1948. This is one of my favorite books. It's a modestly priced little hardback containing excellent translations of both Lao-tzu and Chuang-tzu. Wise and witty.

Maugham, W. Somerset. *The Razor's Edge*. New York: Penguin, 1979. A classic of spiritual discovery.

Merton, Thomas. *The Way of Chuang Tzu*. New York: New Directions, 1965. Merton's personalized versions of passages from Chuang-tzu remain true to the spirit of the original.

Payne, David. *Confessions of a Taoist on Wall Street: A Chinese American Romance*. New York: Ballantine Books, 1984. This novel about a man's odyssey from a Taoist monastery to Wall Street is a refreshing change of pace.

Pirsig, Robert. *Zen and the Art of Motorcycle Maintenance: An Inquiry into Values*. New York: Morrow, 1974. A remarkably moving book that works on many levels. It's about motorcycles, parenthood, traveling, mental breakdowns, values, Plato, Buddhism, courage, loneliness, and wisdom.

Richie, Donald. *Zen Inklings*. New York: Weatherhill, 1982. The playful title tips us off to a treat. The "inklings" are both notions and elusive ideas, and ink drawings. Richie presents classic Buddhist tales in modern form.

Suzuki, D. T. *An Introduction to Zen Buddhism*. New York: Grove Press, 1964. This short collection of essays is a good introduction to Buddhism for the curious general reader. If it piques your interest, then you will want to turn to Suzuki's longer works.

Tendzin, Ösel. *Buddha in the Palm of Your Hand*. Boulder, Colo.: Shambala, 1982. More sophisticated style than Nancy Wilson Ross's *Buddhism: A Way of Life and Thought*, and less comprehensive, this makes a good next-level introduction to Buddhist thinking.

Tenzin Gyatso, His Holiness the Fourteenth Dali Lama. *Kindness, Clarity and Insight*. Translated and edited by Jeffrey Hopkins. Co-edited by Elizabeth Napper. Ithaca, N.Y.: Snow Lion Publications, 1984. This warm, witty, and profound collection is an interesting example of Buddhism in practice today.

CHAPTER 3 THE SOPHOS: HERACLITUS AND PARMENIDES

Grant, Michael. *The Classical Greeks*. New York: Scribner's, 1989. This nicely written history of classical Greece often reads like a novel. Good index, useful for selective research.

Kirk, G. S., J. E. Raven, and M. Schofield. *The Presocratic Philosophers*. Cambridge University Press, 1983. Perhaps the best single volume of commentary and original sources in this area.

CHAPTER 4 THE SOPHIST: PROTAGORAS

Guthrie, W. K. C. *The Sophists*. Cambridge: Cambridge University Press, 1971. Thorough, major source of general information. Best read in conjunction with a general history of the period.

Henry, Jules. *Culture Against Man*. New York: Vintage Books, 1963. The section on advertising as a philosophical system, though dated in its examples, is a stinging indictment of modern sophistry.

Plato. *The Collected Dialogues*. Edited by Edith Hamilton and Huntington Cairns. New York: Pantheon Books, Bollingen Series LXXI. 1966. See especially the *Gorgias, Protagoras, Republic*, and *Sophist*. Good, basic collection of Plato's dialogues, including the Letters.

CHAPTER 5 THE WISE MAN: SOCRATES

Guthrie, W. K. C. *Socrates*. Cambridge: Cambridge University Press, 1971. Comprehensive survey of Socrates' life and philosophy. Sophisticated reading level, but valuable source for research papers.

Jaspers, Karl. *Socrates, Buddha, Confucius, Jesus: The Paradigmatic Individuals*. Edited by Hannah Arendt. Translated by Ralph Manheim. New York: Harcourt Brace Jovanovich, 1962. This excerpt from Jaspers's history of philosophy presents his fascinating notion of the paradigmatic individual. Worth tracking down for those interested in wise people.

Plato. *Five Dialogues (Euthyphro, Apology, Crito, Meno, Phaedo)*. Translated by G. M. A. Grube. Indianapolis: Hackett, 1981. Excellent translation at an affordable price.

Stone, I. F. *The Trial of Socrates*. Toronto: Little, Brown, 1988. Valuable as an alternative view of Socrates and as an example of a first-rate mind driven by wonder. Working outside the academic establishment, Stone, like Joseph Campbell, reminds us of the virtues of curiosity and independence.

CHAPTER 6 THE PHILOSOPHER-KING: PLATO

Levi, A. W. *Philosophy as Social Expression*. Chicago: University of Chicago Press, 1974. See Chapter 2, "Ancient Philosophy: The Age of the Aristocrat," for a full discussion of the influence of social class on Plato.

Taylor, A. E. *Plato: The Man and His Work*. London: Methuen, 1966. Scholarly and sometimes difficult, but useful for research papers.

CHAPTER 7 THE NATURALIST: ARISTOTLE

Andrews, Lewis M. *To Thine Own Self Be True: The Rebirth of Values in the New Ethical Theory*. New York: Doubleday/Anchor Press, 1987. Intriguing blend of philosophy and psychology. Lewis's ethical therapy is based on universal moral principles derived from Plato and Aristotle.

Horney, Karen. *Neurosis and Human Growth: The Struggle Toward Self-Realization*. New York: W. W. Norton, 1950. Norton has recently reissued a comprehensive collection of Horney's work in inexpensive paperback editions. *Neurosis and Human Growth* is her clear, penetrating discussion of self-realization in contemporary terms. One of the best.

MacIntyre, Alasdair. *After Virtue*. Notre Dame, Ind.: University of Notre Dame Press, 1981. MacIntyre argues that virtues are necessary for society and human development. An impressive assessment of excellence and community.

Maslow, Abraham H. *Toward a Psychology of Being*. New York: D. Van Nostrand, 1968. Though aptly criticized for lacking precise, scientific criteria, Maslow's theory of the ever-developing self has a certain intuitive appeal.

Merton, Thomas. *New Seeds of Contemplation*. New York: New Directions, 1961. This is one of Merton's best, a rare combination of literature, philosophy, psychology, and Catholic theology. This book is a little gem.

Shaef, Anne Wilson. *When Society Becomes an Addict*. San Francisco: Harper & Row, 1987. The unfortunate title is misleading. Though the focus of Shaef's work is addiction and codependency, her assessment of the relationship between society and self-realization is penetrating and thought-provoking.

CHAPTER 8 THE EPICUREAN: EPICURUS

Lasch, Christopher. *The Culture of Narcissism: American Life in an Age of Diminishing Expectations*. New York: W. W. Norton, 1979. Interesting, troubling analysis of contemporary culture by a social historian.

Lin Yutang. *The Importance of Living*. New York: Capricorn Books, 1974. A genuinely delightful book that raises questions about what's important and what's not. Some dated

passages, but much of this is elegant, pleasant, everything a hedonist looks for.

Watts, Alan. *Does It Matter?* New York: Vintage Books, 1970. Effective example of "popular philosophy," this overlooked collection of essays raises philosophical issues that may be obscured by Watts's playful, polished style.

CHAPTER 9 THE STOIC: EPICTETUS AND MARCUS AURELIUS

Buber, Martin. *Tales of the Hasidim*. 2 vols. New York: Schocken Books, 1948. Rich, powerful tales, often expressing a blend of Stoicism and compassion. Some of them are difficult to follow for readers unfamiliar with Hasidism, but just keep reading. There are enough gems among this collection to make it clearly worth the effort. Volume 2 seems to be the more accessible for the general reader.

Ellis, Albert, and Robert A. Harper. *A New Guide to Rational Living*. North Hollywood, Calif.: Wilshire Book Company, 1978. Presents basic principles of Ellis's influential rational-emotive therapy. Contains fascinating glimpses into the interaction between therapist and client reminiscent of descriptions of teacher-disciple encounters expressed in philosophical and religious anecdotes.

Epictetus. *Handbook of Epictetus*. Translated by Nicholas P. White. Indianapolis: Hackett, 1983. First-rate translation, inexpensive edition.

Frankl, Viktor E. *Man's Search for Meaning: An Introduction to Logotherapy*. New York: Pocket Books, 1963. A modern classic. Frankl's account of his concentration camp experiences is harrowing, and the conversion of those experiences into a form of philosophical therapy is inspiring. Almost qualifies as required reading.

Lippmann, Walter. *A Preface to Morals*. 1929. Reprint. New Brunswick, N.J.: Transaction Books, 1982. Though dated, the opening and closing chapters present a stirring Stoic analysis of American culture.

Marcus Aurelius. *The Meditations*. Translated by G. M. A. Grube. Indianapolis: Hackett, 1983. Good, contemporary translation of one of the finest works of philosophy in the Western tradition. A number of editions of George Long's elegant Victorian translation are widely available as well. Truly timeless.

Peck, M. Scott. *The Road Less Traveled: A New Psychology of Love, Traditional Values and Spiritual Growth*. New York: Touchstone Books, 1978. Phenomenally popular book advocating the virtues of discipline and suffering. Though it is written from a Christian perspective, one need not be a believer to find this a worthwhile psychological study of virtue.

Seneca. *The Stoic Philosophy of Seneca*. Translated by Moses Hadas. New York: W. W. Norton, 1958. This excellent translation is still available as a paperback reprint. Seneca's letters remain edifying.

Wiesel, Elie. *Somewhere a Master: Further Hasidic Portraits and Legends*. New York: Summit Books, 1982. Modern renderings of Hasidic tales, on a par with Buber's more comprehensive collection. Wiesel's commentaries are superbly moving. A text of great moral authority.

CHAPTER 10 THE SCHOLAR: THOMAS AQUINAS

Augustine. *Confessions*. Translated by R. S. Pine-Coffin. Middlesex, England: Penguin Books, 1961. The first "autobiography" as such. You'll be surprised how contemporary Augustine sounds in this honest, introspective blend of philosophy and journal writing.

Cloud of Unknowing and Other Works. Translated by Clifton Wolters. New York: Penguin, 1982. This mystical classic stands in stark contrast to Aquinas's Scholasticism.

Hick, John. *Philosophy of Religion*. 3rd ed. Englewood Cliffs, N.J.: Prentice-Hall, 1983. Introduction to philosophical questions raised by religion.

Kaufmann, Walter. *The Faith of a Heretic*. New York: New American Library, 1978. Stimulating, powerful analysis and attack on theology.

Küng, Hans. *Does God Exist? An Answer for Today*. Translated by Edward Quinn. New York: Vintage Books, 1981. Intriguing, comprehensive effort by a major theologian to prove that God exists. Individual chapters are excellent summaries of important ideas and philosophers.

Lewis, C. S. *Mere Christianty*. New York: Macmillan, 1976. One of the most popular examples of contemporary apologetics. Lewis attempts to construct a rational argument for Christianity. Quite interesting.

Russell, Bertrand. *Why I Am Not a Christian, and Other Essays on Religion and Related Subjects*. New York: Simon & Schuster, 1957. Russell's tightly argued but clear account of his objections to Christianity. Intelligent atheism at its best.

Thomas à Kempis. *The Imitation of Christ*. Translated by E. M. Blaiklock. Nashville: Thomas Nelson Publishers, 1979. Readable translation of the fifteenth-century mystical classic aimed at what today is called "personal transformation." Not strictly philosophical, but an important work in the Christian mystical tradition.

CHAPTER 11 THE RATIONALIST: RENÉ DESCARTES

Churchland, Paul M. *Matter and Consciousness: A Contemporary Introduction to the Philosophy of Mind*. Cambridge, Mass.: MIT Press, 1988. Sophisticated survey of the philosophy of mind. Good resource for dedicated students, which should be especially appealing to science and psychology majors.

Descartes, René. *Objections and Replies* to Descartes' *Meditations*, in *The Philosophical Works of Descartes*, vol. 2. Translated by Elizabeth S. Haldane and G. R. T. Ross. Cambridge: Cambridge University Press, 1968. This witty exchange of letters between Descartes and Hobbes (and others) is philosophically important and has the added virtue of showing us philosophy in action.

Frankfurt, Harry G. *Demons, Dreamers, and Madmen: The Defense of Reason in Descartes's Meditations*. Indianapolis: Bobbs-Merrill, 1970. Detailed, tightly reasoned assessment of Descartes' method of doubt.

Ryle, Gilbert. *The Concept of Mind*. New York: Barnes & Noble Books, 1949. Important work in the analytic tradition. Quite readable introduction to early analytic method.

Sesonske, Alexander, and Noel Fleming, eds. *Meta-Meditations: Studies in Descartes*. Belmont, Calif.: Wadsworth, 1965. Variety of articles concerning the evil genius, dreaming, and other Cartesian themes, many accessible to uninitiated readers.

CHAPTER 12 THE SKEPTIC: DAVID HUME

Annas, Julia, and Jonathan Barnes. *The Modes of Scepticism: Ancient Texts and Modern Interpretations*. Cambridge: Cambridge University Press, 1985. First-rate contemporary look at skepticism.

Hallie, Phillip P. "Classical Scepticism—A Polemical Introduction." In Sextus Empiricus, *Selections from the Major Writings on Scepticism, Man, & God,* edited by Phillip P. Hallie, translated by Sanford G. Etheridge. Indianapolis: Hackett, 1985. Lucid commentary on classical skepticism.

Naess, Arne. *Scepticism*. London: George Allen & Unwin, 1968. Supportive analysis of classical skepticism.

Russell, Bertrand. *Human Knowledge: Its Scope and Limits*. London: George Allen & Unwin, 1948. Challenging, direct assault on metaphysical confusion geared to a general audience.

———— *Our Knowledge of the External World*. Chicago: Open Court, 1915. First-rate assessment of some fundamental epistemological problems.

Santayana, George. *Scepticism and Animal Faith*. 1923. Reprint. New York: Dover, 1955. Santayana's challenge to skepticism is an excellent example of precise thinking presented in nontechnical terms. Very well written.

Watson, Richard. *The Philosopher's Diet: How to Lose Weight and Change the World*. Boston: Atlantic Monthly Press, 1985. Watson talks about diets, exercise, philosophy, and David Hume in a powerful, witty, surprisingly effective manner. This is a delightful book you'll want to reread. A refreshing change of pace.

CHAPTER 13 THE FORMALIST: IMMANUEL KANT

Kant, Immanuel. *Kant Selections*. Edited by Lewis White Beck. New York: Scribner's/Macmillan, 1988. Excellent set of readings and editorial introductions.

Körner, S. *Kant*. Baltimore: Penguin, 1955. Basic study of Kant, good as a resource.

Paton, H. J. *The Categorical Imperative*. London: Hutchinson, 1946. Helpful commentaries on Kantian ethics.

Wellman, Carl. *Morals and Ethics*. Englewood Cliffs, N.J.: Prentice-Hall, 1988. Good introduction to moral philosophy.

CHAPTER 14 THE UTILITARIAN: JOHN STUART MILL

Mazlish, B. *James and John Stuart Mill*. New York: Basic Books, 1975. Interesting look at the remarkable education of a remarkable man, and its consequences.

Mill, John Stuart. *Autobiography*. New York: Columbia University Press, 1924. A classic autobiography.

Nagel, Thomas. *The Possibility of Altruism*. Oxford: Clarendon Press, 1970. Sophisticated analysis of egoism.

Narveson, Jan. *Morality and Utility*. Baltimore: Johns Hopkins Press, 1967. Sophisticated defense of basic utilitarianism. Chapters 1 and 3 are quite good.

Rawls, John. *A Theory of Justice*. Cambridge, Mass.: Harvard University Press, 1971. Important, exceptionally clear attempt to discover the fundamental conditions necessary for a just society. I recommend reading it together with Okin's *Justice, Gender, and the Family*, cited below.

CHAPTER 15 THE MATERIALIST: KARL MARX

Fromm, Erich. *Marx's Concept of Man*. New York: Ungar, 1961. Psychological and sociological interpretation of Marx.

———— *The Art of Loving*. 1956. Reprint. New York: Perennial Library, 1974. Another good book with a potentially misleading title. This is not a self-help book; it's much more. The chapter on the disintegration of love is a superb humanistic analysis of modern capitalism.

Marcuse, Herbert. *One-Dimensional Man: Studies in the Ideology of Advanced Industrial Society*. Boston: Beacon Press, 1964. Powerful critique of modern capitalism.

Marx, Karl. *Marx Selections*. Edited by Allen Wood. New York: Scribner's/Macmillan. Fine selection of material accompanied by editorial comments.

CHAPTER 16 THE INDIVIDUAL: SØREN KIERKEGAARD AND FRIEDRICH NIETZSCHE

Barrett, William. *Irrational Man: A Study in Existential Philosophy*. Garden City, N.Y.: Doubleday/Anchor Books, 1962. Impressive analysis of the contemporary intellectual and social scene.

Gilman, Sander L., and David J. Parent. *Conversations with Nietzsche: A Life in the Words of His Contemporaries*. Oxford University Press, 1987. Eighty-seven memoirs, anecdotes, and recollections from famous and ordinary people provide glimpses of Nietzsche the philosopher and human being. Entertaining mix of scholarly information and gossip.

Kaufmann, Walter. *Without Guilt and Justice: From Decidophobia to Autonomy*. New York: Delta Books, 1973. Kaufmann's attempt to construct a Nietzschean ethic is easy to read and guaranteed to get you thinking about contemporary values. His assessment of the various strategies of "decidophobia" (fear of making decisions) is especially effective.

Nietzsche, Friedrich. *The Portable Nietzsche*. Edited and translated by Walter Kaufmann. New York: Penguin, 1968. A "best buy," this handy collection includes Kaufmann's helpful comments.

Slater, Phillip. *The Pursuit of Loneliness*. Boston: Beacon Press, 1970. Influential and readable assessment of the relationship between self-chosen reliance on technology and quality of life. Disturbing and moving.

CHAPTER 17 THE PRAGMATIST: WILLIAM JAMES

James, William. *William James: Writings 1902–1910*. New York: Literary Classics of the United States, Library of America–volume 38, 1987. Excellent edition, though both Collier and Dover have inexpensive paperback editions of *The Will to Believe* and *Varieties of Religious Experience* available.

Stroh, Guy W. *American Philosophy from Edwards to Dewey: An Introduction*. Princeton, N.J.: D. Van Nostrand, 1968. Short but thorough survey of the highlights of American philosophy.

CHAPTER 18 THE EXISTENTIALIST: JEAN-PAUL SARTRE AND ALBERT CAMUS

Gill, Richard, and Ernest Sherman, eds. *The Fabric of Existentialism: Philosophical and Literary Sources*. Englewood Cliffs, N.J.: Prentice-Hall, 1973. Comprehensive selection of readings.

Kaufmann, Walter, ed. *Existentialism from Dostoevsky to Sartre*. New York: New American Library, 1975. Excellent anthology with a first-rate introduction.

Unamuno, Miguel de. *The Tragic Sense of Life in Men and in Peoples*. 1913. Reprint. New York: Dover, 1954. Spanish philosopher's compelling plea for passion over rationalism, heart over head. Sophisticated but worth the effort, especially the first chapter.

Weil, Simone. *The Need for Roots*. Translated by Arthur Wills. New York: Harper/Colophon, 1971. Brilliant analysis of modern culture and the need for charity by a remarkable woman, noted for both her brilliance and her sanctity.

Wilson, Colin. *The Outsider*. New York: Delta Books, 1956. This modern classic of alienation is still widely available. Of special interest to literature majors.

CHAPTER 19 THE PROPHET: MARTIN LUTHER KING, JR., AND MALCOLM X

Baldwin, James. *Nobody Knows My Name: More Notes of a Native Son*. New York: Dial Press, 1961. Collection of essays by the brilliant social observer, touching and frightening.

Chapman, Abraham, ed. *Black Voices: An Anthology of Afro-American Literature*. New York: New American Library, Mentor edition, 1968. Good collection of sources.

Ellison, Ralph. *Invisible Man*. New York: Random House, 1952. Powerful novel about being socially, politically, and economically "invisible" in a racist culture.

King, Martin Luther, Jr. *A Testament of Hope: The Essential Writings of Martin Luther King, Jr*. Edited by James M. Washington. New York: Harper and Row, 1986. All of King's important speeches, essays, and books are included. An impressive collection.

Malcolm X. *Autobiography*. New York: Grove Press, 1965. Stunning work by an activist who challenged both blacks and whites.

CHAPTER 20 THE FEMINIST: SUSAN MOLLER OKIN AND CAROL GILLIGAN

Anderson, Bonnie S., and Judith P. Zinsser. *A History of Their Own: Women in Europe from Prehistory to the Present*, vol. 1. New York: Harper & Row, 1988.

Belenky, Mary Field, Blythe McVicker Clinchy, Nancy Rule Goldberger, and Jill Mattuck Tarule. *Women's Ways of Knowing: The Development of Self, Voice, and Mind*. New York: Basic Books, 1986.

Freeman, Jo. *A Feminist Perspective*. 4th ed. Palo Alto, Calif.: Mayfield, 1989. Anthology of feminist philosophy.

Friedan, Betty. *The Feminine Mystique*. New York: W. W. Norton, 1963. Friedan's moving description of "the problem with no name" awakened America to what became the contemporary women's movement.

Garry, Ann, and Marilyn Pearsall, eds. *Women, Knowledge, and Reality: Explorations in Feminist Philosophy*. Boston: Unwin Hyman, 1988. Another good anthology, though some selections are difficult for novice philosophers.

Jaggar, Alison M., and Susan R. Bordo, eds. *Gender/Body/Knowledge: Feminist Reconstructions of Being and Knowing*. New Brunswick, N.J.: Rutgers University Press, 1989. Sophisticated anthology of current feminist analyses of epistemological and metaphysical issues.

Kohlberg, Lawrence. *Psychology of Moral Development: The Nature and Validity of Moral Stages*. New York: Harper & Row, 1984. Expression of the theory of moral stages that has attracted so much attention. Should be read in conjunction with Carol Gilligan's *In a Different Voice*.

Noddings, Nell. *Caring: A Feminine Approach to Ethics and Moral Education*. Berkeley: University of California Press, 1984. Second only to Gilligan as an introduction to the literature of care. Should be of interest to anyone concerned with moral education.

——— *Women and Evil*. Berkeley: University of California Press, 1989. Important addition to the growing contemporary literature about evil.

Okin, Susan Moller. *Justice, Gender, and the Family*. New York: Basic Books, 1989. Disturbing (in a valuable way) challenge to John Rawls's influential theory of justice, and the possibility of gender-free rationality. Excellent discussion of "original position" reasoning.

Osborne, Martha Lee, ed. *Woman in Western Thought*. New York: Random House, 1979. Good collection of shorter pieces showing the variety of attitudes toward women throughout history—many of them negative.

Perry, William B., Jr. *Forms of Intellectual and Ethical Development in College Years*. New York: Holt, Rinehart and Winston, 1968. Significant male-based theory of psychological development that prompted the work of Belenky et al. (cited above). Comparison of Perry and Belenky provides a helpful background to current debate over ways of knowing.

Trebilcot, Joyce, ed. *Mothering: Essays in Feminist Theory*. Totowa, N.J.: Rowan & Allanheld, 1984. First-rate collection of essays offering a range of positions, some of which should challenge most readers.

INDEX OF MARGIN QUOTES

INDEX

CREDITS

QUOTATIONS

The numbers in parentheses before each entry are the page numbers on which the material appears.

Chapter 2: (32–39) From *Buddhism: A Way of Life and Thought* by Nancy Wilson Ross. Copyright ©1980 Nancy Wilson Ross. Used by permission of Alfred A. Knopf, Inc. (40) From *The Teachings of the Compassionate Buddha* by E. A. Burtt, Mentor Edition, 1982. Used by permission of the Estate of E. A. Burtt. (45–46) From *The Way of Lao Tzu: Tao-te Ching* translated by Wing-tsit Chan. Copyright ©1963 Macmillan Publishing Company, Inc. Used by permission. (46–7; 50) From *A Source Book in Chinese Philosophy* translated by Wing-tsit Chan, Princeton University Press, 1963. Used by permission. (93) From *A History of Women Philosophers* by Mary Ellen Waithe, Martinus Nijhoff, 1987. Used by permission of Kluwer Academic Publishers. **Chapter 4:** (93–95) From *Protagoras* by Plato, Benjamin Jowett, translator; revised translation by Martin Ostwald. Copyright ©1956 by Macmillan Publishing Company; copyright © renewed 1984. Used by permission. (101–102) From *The Republic* by Plato, translated by Desmond Lee, Penguin Classics, 1955. Copyright ©1973, 1974, 1987 H. D. P. Lee. Used by permission. **Chapter 5:** (115–117) From *Xenophon: Memorabilia and Oeconomics* translated by E. C. Marchant, Harvard University Press, 1923. Used by permission. **Chapter 6:** (154; 155–156; 158–164) From *The Republic* by Plato, translated by Desmond Lee, Penguin Classics, 1955. Copyright ©1973, 1974, 1987 H. D. P. Lee. Used by permission. **Chapter 8**: (212–213) From *Translations from the Chinese* by Arthur Waley. Copyright 1919 and renewed 1947 by Arthur Waley. Used by permission of Alfred A. Knopf, Inc.

and Unwin Hyman, HarperCollins Publishers Limited. (216) From *The Importance of Living* by Lin Yutang. Copyright ©1965 by Lin Yutang. Used by permission of H. J. Lin (226–230) From "Letter to Menoceceus" by Epicurus, *Readings in Hellenistic Philosophy* Shapiro and Curley, eds., Northwestern University Press, 1963. Used by permission. (232–233) From *Does It Matter?* by Alan Watts. Copyright ©1968, 1969, 1970 by Alan Watts. Used by permission of Pantheon Books, a division of Random House, Inc. **Chapter 9:** (240) From *Herakleitos and Diogenes* by Guy Davenport, Grey Fox Press, 1979. Used by permission of the author. (260–261) From *A New Guide to Rational Living* by Albert Ellis and Robert A. Harper, Wilshire Book Company, 1978. Used by permission of Albert Ellis. (262) From *Man's Search for Meaning* by Viktor E. Frankl, Pocket Books, 1963. Used by permission of Beacon Press. (263–265) From "The World of Epictetus" by James B. Stockdale, *Atlantic Monthly* April, 1978. Used by permission of the author. (266–267) From *Epictetus' Enchiridion* ©1991 by James Bond Stockdale. Reprinted by permission of the author. **Chapter 11:** (308–329) From *Discourse on Method Meditations* and *Rules for the Direction of the Mind* by René Descartes, translated by Haldane and Ross, Cambridge University Press, 1931. Used by permission. **Chapter 12:** (360–361) From *Dialogues Concerning Natural Religion* by David Hume, edited by Norman Kemp-Smith, Bobbs-Merrill, 1947. Used by permission of Thomas Nelson & Sons Limited. **Chapter 15:** (461–463) From *Economic and Philosophic Manuscripts* by Karl Marx in *Writings of the Young Marx on Philosophy and Society* edited and translated by Loyd D. Easton and Kurt H. G. Guddat, Anchor Doubleday Edition, 1967. Used by permission of Loyd D. Easton and Mrs. Kurt H. Guddat. (466–468) From *The Art of Loving* by

Erich Fromm. Copyright ©1956 Erich Fromm. Used by permission of HarperCollins Publishers, Inc. (480–486) From *A Kierkegaard Anthology* edited by Robert Bretall, The Modern Library, 1946. Used by permission of Princeton University Press. **Chapter 16:** (488, 491, 492, 496, 498–499, 503–504) From *The Portable Nietzsche* by Walter Kaufman. Copyright 1954 The Viking Press, renewed ©1982 Viking Penguin Inc. Used by permission of Viking Penguin, a division of Penguin Books USA Inc. (493, 498) From *The Gay Science* by Friedrich Nietzsche, translated by Walter Kaufman. Copyright ©1974 Random House, Inc. Used by permission. **Chapter 18:** (547) From *Nausea* by Jean-Paul Sartre. Copyright ©1964 New Directions Publishing Corporation. Reprinted by permission of the publisher. (552, 554) From Jean-Paul Sartre, *Existentialism Is a Humanism* trans. Bernard Frechtman; copyright 1957 Philosophical Library Inc. Used by permission of Philosophical Library, Inc. (568–569) From *The Myth of Sisyphus and Other Essays* by Albert Camus, trans., J. O'Brien. ©1955 by Alfred A. Knopf, Inc. Reprinted by permission of the publisher. **Chapter 19:** (580–581, 581–582, 583–584, 586–587) From *A Testament of Hope: The Essential Readings of Martin Luther King Jr.*, edited by James M. Washington. Copyright ©1986 by Coretta Scott King. Reprinted by arrangement with The Heirs to the Estate of Martin Luther King, Jr., c/o Joan Daves Agency as agent for the proprietor. (587–590) From "Letter from Birmingham Jail" in *Why We Can't Wait* by Martin Luther King, Jr. Copyright ©1963, 1964 by Martin Luther King, Jr. Reprinted by arrangement with The Heirs to the Estate of Martin Luther King, Jr., c/o Joan Daves Agency as agent for the proprietor. (597–598) From "I Have a Dream" by Martin Luther King, Jr. in *A Testament of Hope* Harper & Row Publishers, 1986. Copyright 1963 Martin Luther King, Jr. Reprinted by arrangement with The Heirs to the Estate of Martin Luther King, Jr., c/o Joan Daves Agency as agent for the proprietor. **Chapter 20:** (610–614) From *Justice, Gender and the Family* by Susan Moller Okin. ©1989 by Basic Books, Inc. Reprinted by permission of BasicBooks, a division of HarperCollins Publishers, Inc. **Postscript:** (628) From *The Handbook of Epictetus* translated by Nicholas P. White, Hackett Publishing Company, 1983. Used by permission.

PICTURES

The title page image and all chapter opener images are details of original art works. Title page: Raphael, *School of Athens*. Vatican Museums, Vatican State. Alinari/Art Resource, NY. Chapter openers: Chapter 1: Hermensz van Rijn Rembrandt, *Two Philosophers Disputing*, National Gallery of Victoria, Melbourne/Bridgeman Art Library, London. Chapter 2: *Buddha*. Berlin Ethnological Museum/The Bettmann Archive. Chapter 3: Greek Cup. The Louvre Museum. Alinari/Art Resource, NY. Chapter 4: *Oedipus and the Sphinx*. Vatican Museum/Archiv für Kunst und Geschichte, Berlin. Chapter 5: Louvre Museum, Paris. Eric Lessing/Archiv für Kunst und Geschichte, Berlin. Chapter 6: Brygos painter, Attic Cup, 5th BCE. Vatican Museums, Vatican State. Alinari/Art Resource, NY. Chapter 7: Attic Public Fountain, 6th BCE. Vatican Museums, Vatican State. Alinari/Art Resource, NY. Chapter 8: Attic Hydra, 6th BCE. Museo Giulia, Rome. Alinari/Art Resource, NY. Chapter 9: *Jupiter and Juno*. Museo Archeologico Nazionale, Naples. Alinari/Art Resource, NY. Chapter 10: *Canterbury Psalter* c. 1148. MS. R. 17, fol. 23 or. Masters and Fellows, Trinity College, Cambridge. Chapter 11: Georges de la Tour, *The Dream of St. Joseph.* Musee des Beaux-Arts, Nantes. Giraudon/Art Resource, NY. Chapter 12: Thomas Gainsborough, *Self-Portrait*; National Portrait Gallery, London/Superstock. Chapter 13: Philipp Otto Runge, *The Artist's Parents*, 1806–07. Kunsthalle, Hamburg. Foto Margburg/Art Resource, NY. Chapter 14: Rosetti, *Sybilla Palmifera*, The Trustees of The Lady Lever Art Gallery, Port Sunlight. Chapter 15: Wilhelm Leibl, *Three Women in a Church*, 1878–1881; Kunsthalle, Hamburg. Foto Marburg/Art Resource, NY. Chapter 16: Ernst Ludwig Kirchner, *Dr. Bauer*, Superstock. Chapter 17: Henri Rousseau, *The Muse Inspiring the Poet*, 1909. Kunstmuseum, Basel Giraudon/Art Resource, NY. Chapter 18: Mark Tobey, *E Pluribus Unum*, 1942; Gift of Mrs. Thomas D. Stimson, Seattle Art Museum. Chapter 19: Allan Rohan Crite, *Shadow and Sunlight*, 1941, National Museum of American Art, Washington D.C./Art Resource, NY. Chapter 20: Henri Matisse, *Reader*, Coll. Girardin, Paris. Giraudon/Art Resource, NY. ©1994 Succession H. Matisse, Paris/ARS, NY.

p. 6: Agence France-Presse; p. 12: *(left)* Scala/Art Resource, NY; *(right)* Leonard Freed/Magnum; p. 27: Alex Milovsky, from *Natural History*; p. 33: The Bettmann Archive; p. 35: David M. Grossman/Photo Researchers, Inc; p. 43: The Granger Collection; p. 47: The National Palace Museum, Taiwan; p. 49: Allan Clear/Impact Visuals; p. 61: The Bettmann Archive; p. 62: Archiv für Kunst und Geschichte, Berlin; p. 70: Anglo-Australian Telescope Board, courtesy David Malin; p. 80: Blair Seitz/Photo Researchers, Inc; p. 93: Gilles Peress/Magnum; p. 96: Eli Reed/Magnum; p. 97: Keystone/The Image Works; p. 100: Ted Soqui/Impact Visuals; p. 114: The Granger Collection; p. 125: The Metropolitan Museum of Art, New York. Wolfe Fund, 1931; p. 132: UPI/Bettmann; p. 133: Reuters/Bettmann; p. 150: Scala/Art Resource, NY; p. 160: Dick Cole & Associates; p. 168: Paul Fortin/Stock, Boston; p. 174: Joe Munroe/Photo Researchers; p. 185: Archiv für Kunst und Geschichte, Berlin; p. 195: Virginia Blaisdell/Stock, Boston; p. 197: Mel Rosenthal/The Image Works; p. 214: UPI/Bettmann; p. 215: The Bettmann Archive; p. 226: Magnum Photos; p. 231: Jack Spratt/The Image Works; p. 251: Alan

Fold here

CUT PAGE OUT

Fold here

BUSINESS REPLY MAIL

FIRST CLASS   PERMIT NO.34   BELMONT, CA

Postage will be paid by addressee

Douglas Soccio
Wadsworth Publishing Company
10 Davis Drive
Belmont, CA 94002

To the owner of this book

I hope that you have enjoyed *Archetypes of Wisdom,* second edition, as much as I enjoyed writing it. I would like to know as much about your experience as you would care to offer. Only through your comments and those of others can I learn how to make this a better text for future readers.

School _____ Your instructor's name _____

1. What did you like most about *Archetypes of Wisdom*? _____

_____

_____

_____

2. Do you have any recommendations for ways to improve the next edition of this text? _____

_____

_____

_____

3. In the space below or in a separate letter, please write any other comments you have about the book. (For example, were any chapters or concepts particularly difficult?) I'd be delighted to hear from you! _____

_____

_____

_____

_____

_____

_____

_____

_____

_____

_____

_____

_____

_____

Optional:

Your name/address: _____ Date _____

May Wadsworth quote you, either in promotion for *Archetypes of Wisdom* or in future publishing ventures?

Yes ☐   No ☐

Thank you!

MAJOR FIGURES		EVENTS AND PUBLICATIONS	
		Critique of Pure Reason (Kant)	1781
		Foundations of the Metaphysics of Morals (Kant)	1785
Arthur Schopenhauer	1788–1860	French Revolution	1789–1791
		Introduction to the Principles of Morals and Legislation (Bentham)	1789
		Reign of Terror and Defeat of Reason	1793–1794
		Essay on the Principles of Population (Malthus)	1798
Ludwig Feuerbach	1804–1872	Age of Reform	c. 1800–1900
John Stuart Mill	1806–1873		
Charles Darwin	1809–1882	*The Phenomenology of Mind (or Spirit)* (Hegel)	1807
Søren Kierkegaard	1813–1855		
Otto Von Bismarck	1815–1898		
Henry David Thoreau	1817–1862		
Karl Marx	1818–1883		
Friedrich Engels	1820–1895		
Leo Tolstoy	1828–1910	Industrial Revolution ends	c. 1835
Charles Sanders Pierce	1839–1914		
Walter Pater	1839–1894		
William James	1842–1910	*Either/Or: A Fragment of a Life; Fear and Trembling;* and *Repetition: An Essay in Experimental Psychology* (Kierkegaard)	1843
Friedrich Nietzsche	1844–1900	*The Present Age* (Kierkegaard)	1846
		Communist Manifesto (Marx & Engels)	1848
		Thoreau expresses doctrine of civil disobedience	1848
		The Sickness Unto Death (Kierkegaard)	1849
		Training in Christianity (Kierkegaard)	1850
Oscar Wilde	1854–1900	*Attack Upon "Christendom"* (Kierkegaard)	1854
Sigmund Freud	1856–1939		
Edmund Husserl	1859–1938	Abraham Lincoln issues Emancipation Proclamation	1863
Miguel de Unamuno	1864–1936	*Utilitarianism* (Mill)	1863
		Volume One of *Das Kapital* (Marx)	1867
Mahatma Gandhi	1869–1948		
Bertrand Russell	1872–1970		
C.G. Jung	1875–1961	Pragmaticism appears in "How to Make Our Ideas Clear" (Peirce)	1878
Martin Buber	1878–1965	*The Gay Science* (Nietzsche)	1882
		"God is dead!"—*Thus Spake Zarathustra* (Nietzsche)	1883–1892
		Beyond Good and Evil (Nietzsche)	1886
		Principles of Psychology (James)	1890